AF763130

COLLECTED WORKS OF JOHN STUART MILL

VOLUME II

By Courtesy of the National Portrait Gallery, London

Principles of Political Economy

with Some of Their Applications to Social Philosophy

by JOHN STUART MILL

*

BOOKS I–II

Introduction by

V. W. BLADEN

Dean of Arts and Professor of Political Economy,
University of Toronto

Textual Editor

J. M. ROBSON

Associate Professor of English,
Victoria College, University of Toronto

ROUTLEDGE

First published in Great Britain in 1965
by Routledge

Reprinted in 1996
by Routledge
2 Park Square, Milton Park, Abingdon, Oxon, OX14 4RN

Transferred to Digital Printing 2009

© 1965 Routledge

All rights reserved. No part of this book may be reprinted or reproduced or utilized in any form or by any electronic, mechanical, or other means, now known or hereafter invented, including photocopying and recording, or in any information storage or retrieval system, without permission in writing from the publishers.

British Library Cataloguing in Publication Data
A catalogue record for this book is available from the British Library

ISBN 0–415–14535–X (set of 33 volumes)

ISBN10: 0–415–14537–6 (hbk)
ISBN10: 0–415–48749–8 (pbk)

ISBN13: 978–0–415–14537–4 (hbk)
ISBN13: 978–0–415–48749–8 (pbk)

Publisher's Note
The publisher has gone to great lengths to ensure the quality of this reprint but points out that some imperfections in the original may be apparent.

Contents

*

[1]In this Table of Contents the only variants indicated are those involving major alterations in sections.

[a]48 [*in addition*] § 5. The institution of property requires, not subversion, but improvement] 49 [*in addition*] § 5. Examination of Fourierism § 6. [*as* § 5. *in* 48]
[b-b]+52, 57, 62, 65, 71
[c-c]+49, 52, 57, 62, 65, 71
[d-d]48 § 6.

[e–e]48, 49 § 1. Mode of disposing of a cottier population, the vital question for Ireland § 2. To convert them into hired labourers not desirable nor practicable § 3. Limitation of rent, by law or custom, indispensable § 4. Fixity of Tenure considered § 5. Tenant Right § 6. Location of peasant proprietors on the waste lands § 7. Resources supplementary to the waste lands § 8. Probable consequences of the measures recommended] 52, 57 § 1. [*as* 48] § 2. Means of effecting this object § 3. [*as* § 8. *in* 48, 49]] 62 § 1. [*as* 48] § 2. Inapplicability of this advice to present circumstances [f-f]+57, 62, 65, 71 [g-g]48, 49, 52 § 5. [h-h]48, 49, 52 § 6.

**

BOOK III: EXCHANGE

[i-i]+57, 62, 65, 71
[j-j]48, 49, 52 § 7.
[k-k]49, 52, 57 § 4. Examination of the doctrine that a convertible currency does not expand with the increase of wealth
[l-l]49, 52, 57 § 5.
[m-m]49, 52, 57 § 6.
[n-n]49, 52, 57 § 7.

[o-o]+52, 57, 62, 65, 71
[p-p]48, 49 § 6.

[q-q]48, 49, 52, 57, 62 not really connected with the value of money, but often confounded with it

[r-r]48, 49 the labourers in the profits of industrial undertakings
[s-s]48, 49 Probable future developement of this principle
[t-t]+52, 57, 62, 65, 71

BOOK V: ON THE INFLUENCE OF GOVERNMENT

APPENDICES

[u]57 [*in addition*] APPENDIX Latest Information on the French Industrial Associations [*see* Appendix E]

FACSIMILES

Introduction

V. W. BLADEN

I. THE APPROACH

THE TEXTUAL PRECISION and inclusiveness of this edition of the *Principles of Political Economy* are due entirely to the intelligence and industry of the textual editor, Professor Robson, and it is only proper that he has written the second introduction, which is concerned with the successive changes in thought and exposition recorded in this edition, and which lays down the principles of textual criticism and procedure followed in preparing the text. It is my privilege to contribute an economist's introduction to the *Principles* as a single complete work, rather than to deal with variations of text. I fully recognize the importance of the work of the textual editor and the value of this edition, but I must explain how different is my own approach. I welcomed an edition which would make the *Principles* in its final form readily available and easy to read because I believe that it is a living book which has present value and significance. The members of the editorial committee have emphasized always the importance of providing easy reading of the main text of the *Works* for those who want to ignore changes over successive editions, and I was glad to have this 7th edition of the *Principles* in such a form. I have always set a high value on the Ashley edition, and was anxious that its virtues should be retained in this edition. Ashley's was not a fully collated edition: it did not meet the needs of the scholar trying to reconstruct the successive editions after 1848; but as a working edition for the modern economist it was superb. It indicated nearly all the textual changes of importance to the modern economist. I am proud that it was the work of the first professor of economics in this University and it is with some sentiment of filial piety that I, one of his successors in the Department of Political Economy, write this introduction.

I have said that this book has present value and significance, and this I must defend. I know that in many universities economists are trained without reading any economics written before World War I. I know that in most universities the history of economic thought, if included in the curriculum, is, nevertheless, considered of no real importance, though possibly of some antiquarian interest. Even where the classical literature is seriously studied the attitude is often that stated by Professor Frank Knight in his brilliant article on the "Ricardian Theory of Production and Distribution":[1] he there said that our "primary interest in the 'ancients' in such a field as economics is to learn from their mistakes," and the primary theme of his article was "the contrast between the 'classical' system and 'correct' views." By contrast, I am not interested in examining the inadequacies of the "founders" but rather in discovering what we can still learn from them. From my own experience, and from observation of the development of my students, I would argue that the study of the classical economists, and in particular of Adam Smith and John Stuart Mill, is important in the development of the modern economist, in the development of insight if not in the development of analytical skill.

The advance of our science has not been even on all fronts: while we now answer with greater precision and certainty some of the questions the classical economists asked, there are many other questions that we have ceased to ask because we have seen no better way of answering and have been dissatisfied with the apparent lack of a sound basis for the answers given. Some of these questions are, I suggest, as important as, or more important than, the ones we now answer. One of the values of the classical literature is to remind us to ask these questions and to seek anew ways of answering them. The student of this book will not improve his technical analytical skill, but he may come to recognize more fully how much more he needs than technical equipment. There is, as Professor Redfield reminded us, an element of art in science.[2] Alfred Marshall had this in mind when he said: "The economist needs the three great intellectual faculties, perception, imagination and reason: and most of all he needs imagination."[3] More recently, Professor Boulding has said: "Insight (judgment) and logic (mathematics) are strictly complementary goods."[4] We know a good deal about training in the techniques of science, we know incredibly little about the development of imagination or judgment. Indeed I am sometimes worried lest we kill off imagination in the process of such training. I cannot prove that a study of the great classics will

[1]Frank Knight, "The Ricardian Theory of Production and Distribution," *Canadian Journal of Economics and Political Science*, I (1935), 3.

[2]R. Redfield, "The Art of Social Science," *American Journal of Sociology*, LIV (1948), 181–90.

[3]Alfred Marshall, *Principles of Economics*, Variorum Edition, ed. C. W. Guillebaud (London, 1961), 43.

[4]K. E. Boulding, "Samuelson's *Foundations of Economic Analysis*: The Role of Mathematics in Economics," *Journal of Political Economy*, LVI (1948), 190.

develop those scarce qualities of imagination and judgment; but I assert that it will develop those qualities in some of us.

This is a lonely position, and I therefore take great comfort in the support of the late Professor Schumpeter and of Lord Robbins. Said Schumpeter in his *History of Economic Analysis*:[5]

> Teachers or students who attempt to act upon the theory that the most recent treatise is all they need will soon discover that they are making things unnecessarily difficult for themselves. . . . Any treatise that attempts to render "the present state of science" really renders methods, problems, and results that are historically conditioned and are meaningful only with reference to the historical background from which they spring. . . . The state of any science at any given time implies its past history and cannot be satisfactorily conveyed without making this implicit history explicit.

And Schumpeter went on to a further justification of the study of the classical literature with which I am particularly sympathetic. "Our minds," he said, "are apt to derive new inspiration from the study of the history of science. Some do so more than others, but there are probably few that do not derive from it any benefit at all. A man's mind must be indeed sluggish if, standing back from the work of his time and beholding the wide mountain ranges of past thought, he does not experience a widening of his own horizon." Lord Robbins, in his *Theory of Economic Policy*,[6] gives similar support: "I suspect," he there said, "that damage has been done, not merely to historical and speculative culture, but also to our practical insight, by this indifference to our intellectual past—this provincialism in time—which has been so characteristic of our particular branch of social studies." Lord Robbins went on to a further comment of great importance: "It is no exaggeration to say that it is impossible to understand the evolution and meaning of Western liberal civilization without some understanding of Classical Political Economy." The contribution of the classical political economists to this cultural heritage may well have been as important as their contribution to the development of the science of economics. Modern economists have some responsibility for conserving and interpreting this part of our cultural and intellectual heritage.

I have said that there is an element of "art" in the science of economics; I need hardly add that economic policy making is an "art". It involves much more than prescribing on the basis of scientific analysis a particular action with a view to achieving a stated end. In this it is like medicine: in both political economy and medicine when practitioners diagnose and prescribe, judgment is involved. There must be a readiness to act in spite

[5]J. A. Schumpeter, *History of Economic Analysis* (New York, 1954), 4–5.
[6]Lord Robbins, *Theory of Economic Policy* (London, 1952), 1 and 4.

of incomplete knowledge which makes the result of the action uncertain. For economists the problem is frequently complicated by the desire of the public to promote two, or more, ends without recognition of their conflict; to make such conflict clear so that the public may be faced with the necessity of choice is an important function of the economist. But perhaps a more important function of the political economist is to make explicit the implicit but unrecognized values of the community of which he is a member, values which he is likely to share. This function John Stuart Mill performed more fully than most: study of his work may lead more of us to recognize the values implicit in our policy statements, and to attempt to develop similar recognition on the part of the public. Political Economy in the classical tradition comprehended more than economic analysis; some of its inadequacies in analysis may be forgiven when we consider the total contribution it made.

Some of its supposed inadequacies I shall later argue are the product of misinterpretation of the literature, the inadequacy being in the modern reader rather than in the classical writer. Most frequently the source of misinterpretation lies in the failure to identify the question which the writer was trying to answer. Too often we assume that the ancients asked the same questions that we ask; their answers seem stupid in relation to our questions, but may be very intelligent in relation to those they asked. This habit of ours is sometimes a barrier to understanding in current discussion between modern economists; it is a formidable one in understanding the classics. The habit of mind developed in the sympathetic study of the classics may well contribute to more effective communication between modern economists.

It is over fifty years since W. J. Ashley wrote his introduction to his edition of the *Principles*,[7] but what he said of it then is not inappropriate at this later date:

> . . . Mill's *Principles* will long continue to be read and will deserve to be read. It represents an interesting phase in the intellectual history of the nineteenth century. But its merit is more than historical. It is still one of the most stimulating books that can be put into the hands of students, if they are cautioned at the outset against regarding it as necessarily final in all its parts. On some topics there is still, in my opinion, nothing better in the English language; on others Mill's treatment is still the best point of departure for further enquiry. Whatever its faults, few or many, it is a great treatise, conceived and executed on a lofty plane, and breathing a noble spirit. Mill—especially when we penetrate beneath the magisterial flow of his final text, as we are now enabled to do by the record in this edition of his varying moods—is a very human personality. The reader of to-day is not likely to come to him in too receptive a spirit; and for a long time there will be much that even those who most differ from him will still be able to learn from his pages.

[7]John Stuart Mill, *Principles of Political Economy*, ed. W. J. Ashley (London, 1909), xxiv.

II. METHOD: SCIENCE AND VALUES

THOUGH MILL HAD BEEN RAISED in the Ricardian tradition, the *Principles* is in the tradition of Adam Smith (and Malthus) rather than of Ricardo. Its title suggests this: *Principles of Political Economy with Some of Their Applications to Social Philosophy*. His Preface to the 1st edition elaborates the point made in the title. Of Adam Smith's work Mill says:

> The most characteristic quality . . . is that it invariably associates the principles with their applications. This of itself implies a much wider range of ideas and of topics, than are included in Political Economy, considered as a branch of abstract speculation. For practical purposes, Political Economy is inseparably intertwined with many other branches of social philosophy. Except on matters of mere detail, there are perhaps no practical questions, even among those which approach nearest to the character of purely economical questions, which admit of being decided on economical premises alone. And it is because Adam Smith never loses sight of this truth; because, in his applications of Political Economy, he perpetually appeals to other and often far larger considerations than pure Political Economy affords—that he gives that well-grounded feeling of command over the principles of the subject for purposes of practice. . . . (I.xci.19—xcii.3.)[8]

But Mill felt that advances in "Political Economy, properly so called," and in "the philosophy of society" had rendered the *Wealth of Nations* "in many parts obsolete" (I.xcii. 11–3). So he decided to attempt to "combine his practical mode of treating his subject with the increased knowledge since acquired of its theory" and to "exhibit the economical phenomena of society in the relation in which they stand to the best social ideas of the present time" (I.xcii.17–20). But while he wanted to make his treatise "more than a mere exposition of the abstract doctrines of Political Economy" he intended that "such an exposition should be found in it" (I.xcii. 28–30). The *Principles* is, then, the product of a Ricardian economist who was also, in the judgment of F. Y. Edgeworth,[9] "pre-eminent in general philosophy," in which respect he, and he alone, was "comparable to Adam Smith."

A full understanding of Mill's view of the scope and method of Political Economy involves some semantic difficulty. The term "political economy" as distinguished from "economics" has come to refer to a study of the functioning of the economy in which historical, political, sociological, customary, and non-logical aspects are treated, and in which "values" are examined and policies are discussed not only with reference to the probability of the expected results being achieved, but with reference to the acceptability of the results in the light of values of the individual political

[8]Page references to the present edition are given in parentheses in the text.

[9]F. Y. Edgeworth, "John Stuart Mill," *Dictionary of Political Economy*, ed. R. H. I. Palgrave (London, 1910), II, 763.

economist or of the society of which he is a member. Since most policies have indirect as well as direct effects, it is the business of the political economist to determine as carefully and as fully as he can these indirect effects. The problem of values then becomes not simply that of the choice of the end directly sought, but of the net advantage of achieving the chosen direct end plus the advantages and minus the disadvantages of the indirect results of pursuing the given policy. A simple prescription of policy is only possible when there is certainty as to its direct and indirect effects, and when there is no doubt, or disagreement, as to the net advantages, that is, when there is complete agreement as to the "values" involved. The art of political economy requires, along with the best scientific estimate of probable effects of action (or inaction), a readiness to act (or to recommend action) even though the results are uncertain, and even though the results, if achieved, will not be universally recognized as good. How far the political economist should be honest in indicating the degree of probability of the result, and in identifying the value system which leads him to consider the net advantages of the policy to be positive (and greater than the net advantages of alternative policies which might have been adopted) may be disputed. My own use of the word "honest" indicates my bias. The science of political economy is related to the art of government in much the same way that the science of medicine is related to the art of medicine: there is the same necessity to decide what to do (if anything) in spite of the uncertainty as to the effect of that action (or of inaction): in relation to the art of medicine, the choice of values might seem to be absent, since health is an agreed end, but of course the conflict of values must still enter in since "health" is not simple and indivisible. Even Bentham's formula, "minimize pain," may prove an inadequate guide.

Now what has all this to do with John Stuart Mill? Political Economy meant to him something different from the modern conception, and the difference is not just a matter of words. Political Economy he seems to have used as the name for what we would now call Economic Theory; prescription of policy required, in his view, a consideration of many factors excluded from the abstract analysis of political economy, the effects of which factors could not be as adequately determined as could those of the factors which formed the basis of the analytic part of the study; but if the knowledge and understanding of the economy and of the society were adequate, then Mill would, I think, claim that a "scientific" decision on policy was possible. The problem of values and the conflict of values as something beyond science does not seem to have arisen. I have sometimes argued that the absence of the discussion of values in the classical literature of political economy is explicable in terms of the common acceptance of an implicit scheme of values which, being taken for granted, did not need to be made explicit. But this is hard to maintain in the face of the vigorous criticism in Mill's *Principles* of many of the "bourgeois" ideals, some examples of which will be noted later in this introduction.

I must try to justify these general remarks by some specific examination of Mill's writings, and this takes me back to his early essay on method. In his essay "On the Definition of Political Economy; and on the Method of Investigation Proper to It,"[10] Mill restricted the term "political economy" to the narrow sphere that we would now call "economic theory." He ruled out not only the "art" but even much of the science on which the art must depend:

What is now commonly understood by the term "Political Economy" is not the science of speculative politics, but a branch of that science. It does not treat of the whole of man's nature as modified by the social state, nor of the whole conduct of man in society. It is concerned with him solely as a being who desires to possess wealth, and who is capable of judging of the comparative efficacy of means for obtaining that end. It predicts only such of the phenomena of the social state as take place in consequence of the pursuit of wealth. It makes entire abstraction of every other human passion or motive; except those which may be regarded as *perpetually antagonizing principles to the desire of wealth, namely, aversion to labour, and desire of the present enjoyment of costly indulgences*. . . . [The actions it studies], though many of them are really the result of a plurality of motives, are considered by Political Economy as flowing solely from the desire of wealth. The science then proceeds to investigate the laws which govern these several operations, under the supposition that man is a being who is determined, by the necessity of his nature, to prefer a greater portion of wealth to a smaller in all cases, without any other exception *than that constituted by the two counter-motives already specified*. Not that any political economist was ever so absurd as to suppose that mankind are really thus constituted, but because this is the mode in which science must necessarily proceed. . . . With respect to those parts of human conduct of which wealth is not even the principal object, to these Political Economy does not pretend that its conclusions are applicable. But there are also certain departments of human affairs, in which the acquisition of wealth is the main and acknowledged end. It is only of these that Political Economy takes notice. . . . [It treats] the main and acknowledged end as if it were the sole end. . . . The political economist inquires, what are the actions which would be produced by this desire, if . . . it were unimpeded by any other. In this way a nearer approximation is obtained than would otherwise be practicable. . . . This approximation is then to be corrected by making proper allowance for the effects of any impulses of a different description. . . .

[10]J. S. Mill, "On the Definition of Political Economy; and on the Method of Investigation Proper to It," Essay V in *Essays on Some Unsettled Questions of Political Economy* (London, 1844). Reprinted as number 7 in the *Series of Scarce Works on Political Economy*, by the London School of Economics and Political Science (London, 1948), 137–40. My italics.

Given this definition of the nature of the science as "abstract," the "method of investigation proper to it" is obviously *a priori*. "It reasons, and, as we contend, must necessarily reason, from assumptions, not from facts. . . . Geometry presupposes an arbitrary definition of a line. . . . Just in the same manner does Political Economy presuppose an arbitrary definition of a man, as a being who invariably does that by which he may obtain the greatest amount of necessaries, conveniences, and luxuries, with the smallest quantity of labour and physical self-denial with which they can be obtained in the existing state of knowledge." Mill regretted that this "definition of man is not formally prefixed to any work on Political Economy," for if it were, "it would be less in danger of being forgotten." He warned the economist to be "on his guard not to ascribe to conclusions which are grounded upon an hypothesis a different kind of certainty from that which really belongs to them. They would be true without qualification, only in a case which is purely imaginary."[11]

All of this is very sound comment on the character and limitation of what we would now call "pure theory," what Mill refers to in the preface to the *Principles* as "pure political economy." But Mill asserted that the *a priori* method was not only a legitimate method but was the only legitimate method for the study of economics and social phenomena:[12] "it is vain," he said, "to hope that truth can be arrived at, either in Political Economy or in any other department of the social science, while we look at the facts in the concrete, clothed in all the complexity with which nature has surrounded them, and endeavour to elicit a general law by a process of induction. . . ."[13] Yet he urged the political economist to study the facts. "Although . . . a philosopher be convinced that no general truths can be attained in the affairs of nations by the *à posteriori* road, it does not the less behove [*sic*] him . . . to sift and scrutinize the details of every specific experiment. Without this, he may be an excellent professor of abstract science," but "he must rest contented to take no share in practical politics; to have no opinion, or to hold it with extreme modesty, on the applications which should be made of his doctrines to existing circumstances."[14]

Before writing the *Principles*, Mill wrote his *Logic*; he again discussed the problem of method, but this time he was concerned with the social sciences in general rather than with political economy in particular. The approach remained substantially the same: "The conclusions of theory cannot be trusted, unless confirmed by observation; nor those of observation,

[11]Mill, "On the Definition of Political Economy," 144–5.
[12]*Ibid.*, 146.
[13]*Ibid.*, 148–9.
[14]*Ibid.*, 155.

unless they can be affiliated to theory. . . ."[15] This indicates some further recognition of the value of "observation," due probably to the influence of Comte. It was, however, for "ethology" and particularly for the "general science of society" that the "inverse deductive or historical method"[16] was suggested. This general science of society was concerned with the laws of the development of social institutions. This, he saw, required historical study, not only for verification, but for suggestion of hypotheses:

> while it is an imperative rule never to introduce any generalization from history into the social science unless sufficient grounds can be pointed out for it in human nature, I do think any one will contend that it would have been possible, setting out from the principles of human nature and from the general circumstances of the position of our species, to determine *à priori* the order in which human development must take place, and to predict, consequently, the general facts of history. . . .[17]

But for political economy the method remained deductive, "reasoning from . . . one law of human nature, and from the principal outward circumstances (whether universal or confined to particular states of society)."[18]

One should not take too seriously what people say about method; what they do is often very different. In the *Principles* Mill decided to follow the example of Adam Smith in associating "the principles with their applications" (I.xci.22). This, he recognized, "implies a much wider range of ideas and of topics, than are included in Political Economy, considered as a branch of abstract speculation," for there are, perhaps, no practical questions "which admit of being decided on economical premises alone" (I.xci.23–9). That Mill was wise in choosing to go beyond the bounds of the abstract science can scarcely be doubted. He should, perhaps, have been readier to distinguish those propositions which were precise but limited in application by the nature of the assumptions from which they were deduced, from those propositions which were less precise but were relevant to the real society, not the unreal model. He should also have been more confident, and more venturesome, in his study of the actual. He recognized that in society "custom" was a determinant of income distribution along with "competition." But he had not yet perceived the possibility of the "scientific" study of custom: "only through the principle of competition," he said, "has political economy any pretension to the character of a science" (I.239.13–4). Recognition of the modifying influence of custom was essential: "To escape error, we ought, in applying the

[15]J. S. Mill, *A System of Logic, Ratiocinative and Inductive*, 8th ed. (London, 1872), II, 463.
[16]*Ibid.*, II, 508ff.
[17]*Ibid.*, II, 513.
[18]*Ibid.*, II, 495.

conclusions of political economy to the actual affairs of life, to consider not only what will happen supposing the maximum of competition, but how far the result will be affected if competition falls short of the maximum" (I.244.22–6). But he gave no estimate of how far short of the maximum competition did fall and no estimate of how much the result was affected. Nor did he see that pure political economy might be able to deal with problems of monopoly and of limited competition. But he did anticipate the results of such modern theory when he argued with reference to retail trade that "when competition does exist, it often, instead of lowering prices, merely divides the gains of the high price among a greater number of dealers" (I.243.7–9).

Curiously enough Mill said little about another source of divergence between "the laws of the science and the facts of life" arising from the unreality of the concept of the economic man. Professor Edgeworth questioned, in his article in Palgrave's *Dictionary of Political Economy*, whether Mill could consistently retain his view of the deductive character of the science as he began to "doubt the universality of the principle of self-interest." This doubt was reflected in the chapter on communism, where Mill said: "Mankind are capable of a far greater amount of public spirit than the present age is accustomed to suppose possible" (I.205.16–8). But his eulogy of peasant proprietorship, and for that matter of co-operative factories, was based on the expectation of increased productivity from more direct pecuniary incentive to produce, as it would become the interest of the workers "to do the utmost, instead of the least possible, in exchange for their remuneration" (II.792.4–5). The principle of self-interest might not be universal, but it was recognized to be very powerful. Like Alfred Marshall, Mill seems to have been ready to take advantage of the strongest rather than the highest motives in order to get things done.

In spite of the insistence on the *a priori* character of the science of economics, the complementary insistence on observation of concrete facts opened the way to a more general attack on problems of society through historical and statistical studies; and indeed Mill did not restrict himself to explanations that could be derived *a priori*. Though he was not prepared to consider his broader inquiries as "scientific," he appears to have been quite confident in the reliability of his explanations, predictions, and judgments in the broader field. What I find missing is a recognition of the dependence of many of his prescriptions on the choice of ends. There is, in the last pages of the *Logic*, a brief discussion of the "Logic of Practice or Art; including Morality and Policy." He here stated very properly: "A scientific observer or reasoner, merely as such, is not an adviser for practice. His part is only to show that certain consequences follow from certain causes, and that to obtain certain ends, certain means are the most effectual. Whether the ends themselves are such as ought to be pursued . . . it is no part of his business as a cultivator of science to decide, and science alone will never qualify him for the decision."[19] If we combine this statement on teleology with his statements on the nature of the science one might suppose that Mill would specify the end before prescribing policy. Much of the best writing in the *Principles* is relevant to the choice of ends, yet there appears to be no recognition of the dependence of his policy prescriptions on the choice of ends. Curiously enough this failure to discuss the choice of ends is explained by the definition of the "science," and some of the inadequacy of the "abstract science" for purposes of explanation and prediction is related to the neglect of the problems of the choice of ends by the people who are being studied. I propose to elaborate this proposition because I believe it to have contemporary significance.

The definition of "political economy" quoted above specified the end: "the pursuit of wealth." But two "perpetually antagonizing principles . . . namely aversion to labour and desire of the present enjoyment of costly indulgences" were noted. Here we have a problem of competing ends: more wealth or more leisure, more wealth or more current income. Some passages in the *Principles* are relevant. "In England, it is not the desire of wealth that needs to be taught, but the use of wealth, and appreciation of the objects of desire which wealth cannot purchase. . . . Every real improvement in the character of the English, whether it consist in giving them higher aspirations, or only a juster estimate of the value of their present objects of desire, must necessarily moderate the ardour of their devotion to the pursuit of wealth" (I.105.4–10). The first two editions had put this even more strongly, referring to "the all engrossing torment of their industrialism." "The desirable medium," he went on to argue, "is one which mankind have not often known how to hit: when they labour, to do it with all their might, and especially with all their mind; but to devote to labour, for mere pecuniary gain, fewer hours in the day, fewer days in the year, and fewer years of life" (I.105.14—106.3). This is good preaching of values; and is highly relevant to the "art" of political economy, but it also illustrates the need to determine what values are held in order to predict, that is, for the purpose of the science. To treat the problem as one of defining the supply function of labour does not change it from a problem of values.

What Mill thought of as the purely scientific part of economics had only predictive value as long as the specified end was in fact the choice of the people studied. If the chosen end is other than that specified not only is the prescription necessarily different, but this other end enters into

[19] *A System of Logic*, II, 553–4.

the making of the prediction as to the effect of proposed action on which the prescription is based. This relation between the science and the art can be illustrated by a homely example: John Doe is in Toronto one morning and wants to be in Montreal by evening. He has chosen his end; knowledge of the timetables for air and railway travel, of the state of the weather and of the roads, enables him to select the means of getting to Montreal: such knowledge constitutes his science. But suppose the problem really to be that of the scientist in predicting where John Doe (or a thousand like him) will be on a particular night. Knowledge of the timetables (the science relevant to the simpler question) is not enough: the scientist must know what end John Doe has chosen, to stay in Toronto, to go to Montreal, or to go to Windsor.

Consider next the other "antagonizing" principle, "desire of the present enjoyment of costly indulgences." My first comment is that this involves confusion between "wealth" and "income." Surely the motive assumed for the abstract science is not the maximum accumulation of wealth with consumption limited to "productive consumption," so that even the few luxuries of the poor come under scrutiny as doubtfully proper. ". . . [C]onsumption even of productive labourers is not all of it productive consumption. . . . What they consume in keeping up or improving their health, strength, and capacities of work, or in rearing other productive labourers to succeed them, is productive consumption. But consumption on pleasures or luxuries, whether by the idle or by the industrious . . . must be reckoned unproductive: with a reservation perhaps of a certain quantum of enjoyment which may be classed among necessaries, since anything short of it would not be consistent with the greatest efficiency of labour" (I.52.24–33). If consumption were assumed to be so limited the abstract science would be easier, but Mill does not pretend that it either is, or ought to be, so limited. "It would be a great error to regret the large proportion of the annual produce, which in an opulent country goes to supply unproductive consumption. It would be to lament that the community has so much to spare from its necessities, for its pleasures and for all higher uses. This portion of the produce is the fund from which all the wants of the community, other than that of mere living, are provided for. . . . That so great a surplus should be available for such purposes . . . can only be a subject of congratulation" (I.54.29–30).

What then of the antagonizing principle? Mill the preacher is offended by the "costly indulgences": what is to be regretted is not the size of the surplus available for unproductive consumption but the "prodigious inequality with which this surplus is distributed, the little worth of the objects to which the greater part of it is devoted, and the large share which falls to the lot of persons who render no equivalent service in return" (I.54.32–5). For the abstract science the problem is to establish a supply function for savings which emerges from these values, the choices, of the people. For the art a conflict of ends has emerged: is the wealth pursued worth pursuing, would it be worth pursuing if that wealth were more equally divided? Mill returns to this theme in the chapter on the "Stationary State":

> those who do not accept the present very early stage of human improvement as its ultimate type, may be excused for being comparatively indifferent to the kind of economical progress which excites the congratulations of ordinary politicians; the mere increase of production and accumulation. . . . I know not why it should be a matter of congratulation that persons who are already richer than any one needs to be, should have doubled their means of consuming things which give little or no pleasure except as representative of wealth. . . . It is only in the backward countries of the world that increased production is still an important object. . . . (II.754.29—755.13.)

(This J. K. Galbraith has elaborated in his *The Affluent Society*.[20])

The unkind reference to the Americans in the 1st edition was a dramatic condemnation of the motive "assumed" for the science and of the Malthusian sin of the people. "They have the six points of Chartism, and they have no poverty: and all that these advantages do for them is that the life of the whole of one sex is devoted to dollar-hunting, and of the other to breeding dollar-hunters" (II.754[a–a]). This is preaching, but success in preaching a different set of values would change the data of the science. The scientific study of the values of the community is, therefore, I reiterate, a major part of political economy in the wide sense as distinct from political economy conceived as an abstract science; assessment of values is relevant to the determination of means, as well as to the choice of ends. The choice of means requires prediction of the effect of any proposed action (prediction that requires a knowledge of the values held by the community); the choice of ends requires an assessment of cost (what is foregone) of any proposed action. Knowledge of values is required for the science; skill in the science is required for realization of the values.

A very important element remains to be noticed: the means may become partially ends in themselves. Of modern writers, Professor Frank Knight has dealt most effectively with this problem:

> When we consider that productive activity takes up the larger part of the waking lives of the great mass of mankind, it is surely not to be assumed without investigation or inquiry that production is a means only, a necessary evil, a sacrifice made for the sake of some good entirely outside the production process. We are impelled to look for ends in the economic process itself, other

[20] J. K. Galbraith, *The Affluent Society* (Boston, 1958).

than the mere consumption of the produce, and to give thoughtful consideration to the possibilities of participation in economic activity as a sphere of self expression and creative achievement.[21] . . . Economists and publicists are coming to realize how largely the efficiency of business and industry is the result of this appeal to intrinsic interest in action; how feeble, in spite of the old economics, is the motivation of mere appetite or cupidity; and how much the driving power of our economic life depends on making and keeping the game interesting. A rapidly growing literature on "incentive" is a witness to this awakening.[22]

That Mill was not unaware of this interplay of means and ends is shown in the chapter on the "Stationary State" where he argues that increased production is a matter of minor importance because it means consuming more things that give little or no pleasure, but also argues: "That the energies of mankind should be kept in employment by the struggle for riches, as they were formerly by the struggle of war, until the better minds succeed in educating the others into better things, is undoubtedly more desirable than that they should rust and stagnate" (II.754.24–7).

Some of the elements of this problem have been exposed (or possibly hidden) in modern discussion of the "net advantages" of particular occupations; but here it is only differential advantages of particular occupations that are considered, not the net advantages of the process of production as a whole. In the calculation of these "net advantages" one needs to consider what the process of production to satisfy the wants of the people does to the character of the people. The means most effective in the supply of their existing wants may mould people into more or less desirable patterns. To Ruskin it appeared that there was a premium on the less desirable characteristics, for success in the business world seemed to depend on these. "In a community regulated by the law of demand and supply but protected from open violence," Ruskin said, "the persons who become rich are, generally speaking, industrious, resolute, proud, covetous, prompt, methodical, sensible, unimaginative, insensitive and ignorant. The persons who remain poor are the entirely foolish, the entirely wise, the idle, the reckless, the humble, the thoughtful, the dull, the imaginative, the sensitive, the well-informed, the improvident, the irregularly and impulsively wicked, the clumsy knave, the open thief, the entirely merciful, just, and godly person."[23] One may not accept this condemnation, but one must recognize that the effect of the process on the people is relevant to the choice of the kind of process.

Mill's discussion of communism raises another aspect of this when he asks whether communism or competitive capitalism is "consistent with the greatest amount of human liberty and spontaneity" (I.208.34–5). The

[21]F. H. Knight, *The Ethics of Competition* (London, 1935), 59.
[22]*Ibid.*, 60–1.
[23]Quoted in *ibid.*, 66.

fluctuation in his assessment of the desirability of communism involves conflict of ends and uncertainty as to the efficacy of means. "After the means of subsistence are assured," he said, "the next in strength of the personal wants of human beings is liberty . . ." (I.208.35–7). But the schemes which he discussed seemed to involve renouncing "liberty for the sake of equality" (I.209.3–4); and there was reason to fear that equality might weaken the motivation for production. He recognized that the "restraints of Communism would be freedom in comparison with the present condition of the majority of the human race" (I.209.14–5) and he urged his readers to "compare Communism at its best, with the régime of individual property, not as it is but as it might be made" (I.207.23–5). It was not enough for communism to promise "greater personal and mental freedom than is now enjoyed by those who have not enough of either to deserve the name" (I.209.24–6); nor was it acceptable to denounce the restriction on freedom under socialism while accepting the restrictions on freedom of the existing society. "The generality of labourers . . . ," said Mill, "have as little choice of occupation or freedom of locomotion, are practically as dependent on fixed rules and on the will of others, as they could be on any system short of actual slavery . . ." (I.209.15–9). With this should be read those splendid pages at the beginning of his chapter on the "Probable Futurity of the Labouring Classes" (IV.vii), where he discussed "the two conflicting theories respecting the social position desirable for manual labourers," the "theory of dependence and protection," and the "theory of self dependence." Liberty implies independence. There were those who were arguing for a paternal relationship between the rich and the poor, "affectionate tutelage on the one side, respectful and grateful deference on the other" (II.759.25–6) ("spaniel-like servility" was the phrase William Thomas Thornton used). To them Mill pointed out that "All privileged and powerful classes, as such, have used their power in the interest of their own selfishness, and have indulged their self-importance in despising, and not in lovingly caring for, those who were, in their estimation, degraded, by being under the necessity of working for their benefit" (II.760.8–12). He made it clear that even if the "superior classes could be sufficiently improved to govern in the tutelary manner supposed, the inferior classes would be too much improved to be so governed" (II.760.17–9). "Of the working men, at least in the more advanced countries of Europe, it may be pronounced certain, that the patriarchal or paternal system of government is one to which they will not again be subject" (II.761.28—762.2).

Liberty, spontaneity, equality, productivity, all must be considered and to them we now add the preservation of natural beauty. His plea in the chapter on the "Stationary State" is still worthy of consideration: "solitude in the presence of natural beauty and grandeur, is the cradle of thoughts and aspirations which are not only good for the individual, but which society could ill do without" (II.756.11–4). There is little satisfaction in contemplating a world "with nothing left to the spontaneous activity of nature; . . . [with] every flowery waste or natural pasture ploughed up, all quadrupeds or birds which are not domesticated for man's use exterminated as his rivals for food . . . , and scarcely a place left where a wild shrub or flower could grow without being eradicated as a weed in the name of improved agriculture" (II.756.15–21). He feared that the earth might lose that "great portion of its pleasantness which it owes to things that the unlimited increase of wealth and population would extirpate from it" (II.756.22–4). This became the theme of George Gissing's novel *Demos*.[24] At the opening of the novel, Stanbury Hill, "remote but two hours' walk from a region blasted with mine and factory and furnace, shelters with its western slope a fair green valley, a land of meadows and orchard, untouched by poisonous breath."[25] In Chapter vii, John Eldon looks out on a different scene: "building of various kinds was in progress in the heart of the vale; a great massive chimney was rising to completion, and about it stood a number of sheds. Beyond was to be seen the commencement of a street of small houses, promising infinite ugliness in a little space . . . in truth, the benighted valley was waking up and donning the true nineteenth-century livery."[26] But a turn of fortune puts Eldon back in the position of owner and all is changed. "It is springtime, and the valley of Wanley is bursting into green and flowery life, peacefully glad as if the foot of Demos had never come that way. Incredible that the fumes of furnaces ever desecrated that fleece-sown sky of tenderest blue, that hammers clanged and engines roared where now the thrush utters his song so joyously. Hubert Eldon has been as good as his word. In all the valley no trace is left of what was called New Wanley."[27] Whether we consider this a case of competing ends, wealth or beauty, or whether we consider beauty part of the wealth which is to be maximized, the problems raised are still relevant. Professor Joseph Spengler has, for instance, turned to this theme in his address as President of the Population Association of America, "The Aesthetics of Population."[28] "Every year 1.1 million acres reportedly are taken permanently out of crop use by urban and suburban development, together with the expansion of industry, airports, military establishments,

[24]Published 1886. Quotations are from the edition in the Wayfarers Library (London, n.d.).

[25]*Ibid.*, 1.

[26]*Ibid.*, 62.

[27]*Ibid.*, 428.

[28]Joseph Spengler, "The Aesthetics of Population," *Population Bulletin*, XIII (1957), 61–75.

and new highways; and another 700,000 acres are lost annually through soil erosion, tree planting, water-logging, salt deposits, and other contamination."[29] There is a "continuing replacement of Arcadian beauty by car-dominated, bill-boarded, neon-signed shabbiness."[30] Or again: "these uses chew up and uglify the countryside."[31] All of which is not to say that all beauty must be preserved at any cost: but that growth in the gross national product is not the sole object of the community without reference to the consequent destruction of natural beauty.

III. THE *PRINCIPLES OF POLITICAL ECONOMY*

WHILE MILL THE PREACHER might doubt the importance of increasing production except in "the backward countries," Mill the political economist was more realistic and put the problem of production, the causes of productivity and of increasing productivity, at the forefront of his study. Perhaps this was related to his expectation of continued population increase: increasing accumulation and increasing productivity would be necessary even if no further improvement in standards of living were desired; and whatever improvement in the condition of the poor might be achieved by redistribution with a stationary population, the existing standard could not be maintained with increasing population without such increase in productivity. The preacher was contemplating the Stationary State, the political economist was concerned with the practical problems of contemporary society. Increase in the productivity of labour, and accumulation of capital were recognized as urgent necessities. They remain urgently necessary, and modern economists in developing countries, backward or advanced, particularly in countries where population is once again increasing rapidly, do well to reconsider Mill's treatment if only to stimulate them to develop a modern theory of production.

INVESTMENT IN HUMAN BEINGS

One important element in Mill's treatment is his emphasis on investment in human beings. After a century of neglect this has come to the fore as a result of the immense investment in education required in backward and advanced countries alike. In discussing "Labour as an Agent of Production" (I, ii) he devotes one section (§7) to "labour of which the subject is human beings" (I.40.35). Much of this labour is "incurred from other motives than to obtain such ultimate return, and, for most purposes of political economy, need not be taken into account as expenses of pro-

[29]*Ibid.*, 70. [30]*Ibid.*, 71. [31]*Ibid.*, 72.

duction" (I.41.6–8). But "technical or industrial education" is generally "undergone for the sake of the greater or more valuable produce thereby attained" and should therefore be treated as "part of what the produce costs to society" (I.41.8–19). Similarly "the labour employed in keeping up productive powers; in preventing them from being destroyed or weakened by accident or disease," though not generally employed by the individual patients from "economical motives," must be considered "as part of the advance by which society effects its productive operations" (I.41.19–37). There follows a section on the labour of the inventor and the savant. Again there is the difference between the individual and the social aspect: "these material fruits, though the result, are seldom the direct purpose of the pursuits of savants . . . . But when (as in political economy one should always be prepared to do) we shift our point of view, and consider not individual acts, and the motives by which they are determined, but national and universal results, intellectual speculation must be looked upon as a most influential part of the productive labour of society . . ." (I.43.4–16).

Mill recurs to this theme in the chapter on "Unproductive Labour" (I, iii) where he discusses "utilities fixed and embodied in human beings." He would have preferred, he says, to "regard all labour as productive which is employed in creating permanent utilities, whether embodied in human beings, or in any other animate or inanimate objects" (I.48.21–3). But he accepted the usage which limited the term to labour which produces "utilities embodied in material objects" (I.49.23). He then broke through this limitation to include as productive, "labour expended in the acquisition of manufacturing skill . . . not in virtue of the skill itself, but of the manufactured products created by the skill" (I.49.28–30). The emphasis is on the "investment" aspect of some part of education: if the labour of the teacher is classed as "unproductive" this is not "derogatory," but in classing it as "productive" its contribution to increasing future productivity is established. That part of education expense is essentially part of the "accumulation" which is so urgently required. Finally one notes the chapter on the degrees of productiveness (I, vii). "Successful production . . . depends more on the qualities of the human agents, than on the circumstances in which they work . . ." (I.103.13–5). So he discussed as the second of the causes of superior productiveness "the greater energy of labour" (I.103.27). Here the preacher comes back into the picture (the sermon varying somewhat between the editions but remaining essentially the same). In the first edition the essential problem is stated: "An Englishman, of almost every class, is the most efficient of all labourers, because, to use a common phrase, his heart is in his work. But it is surely quite possible to put heart into his work without being incapable of putting it

The insistence on qualitative assessment means more than a mere rejection of Bentham's famous remark about push-pin and poetry. It involves primarily a rejection of the reductionist Helvetian psychology, which tended to analyse *all* pleasure ultimately down to simple sensual pleasure, in favour of the Hartleian, which recognizes that the process of association actually gives rise to a qualitative hierarchy of pleasures, ending with those of theopathy and the moral sense. Hartley thus offers an escape from the genetic reductionism which says, in effect, since all feelings, including the loftiest, originate in simple pleasure-pain reactions of sensation, they are ultimately nothing but these simple reactions. It is the reductionist psychology implicit in the calculus which lays Utilitarianism open to the charge of being simple hedonism. Moreover, it is the Hartleian, rather than the Helvetian psychology, which allows the possibility of Mill's doctrine of progress, which allows him to assert that "it is better to be a human being dissatisfied than a pig satisfied; better to be Socrates dissatisfied than a fool satisfied."

Since the term "pleasure" is so strongly associated with simple hedonism, Mill not only follows Bentham in substituting for it the broader term "happiness," but moves from it to the still broader one, "satisfaction." He thus broadens the whole base of the theory. In escaping from the narrow circle of the reductionist psychology, he may seem to be building his own circular argument. When he says, for example, that it is an "unquestionable fact" that "those who are equally acquainted with, and equally capable of appreciating and enjoying, both, do give a most marked preference to the manner of existence which employs their higher faculties" (211), the "fact" is unquestionable because those who do not so choose are *ipso facto* judged not "equally acquainted" or "equally capable." And when he asserts that "no person of feeling and conscience would be selfish and base" (211), it is clear that selfishness and baseness denote a person of no feeling and conscience. But what Mill is actually doing is calling attention to a range of motives qualitatively different from simple pleasure, and confirmed by observation as operative in human nature. The establishing of an ideal of higher conduct, of pursuits suitable to a "being of higher faculties," and the refusal to sink into a low category, may be motivated by pride, by the love of liberty and personal independence, by the love of power, the love of excitement, but it is most properly described as proceeding from "a sense of dignity." And this in fact, says Mill, leads to the greatest happiness. It is a necessary part of his doctrine of progress that men, unless rendered incapable "not only by hostile influences, but by mere want of sustenance," will voluntarily choose the higher pleasures (213).

Beccaria and Bentham had avoided qualitative assessments in the belief that the quantitative is more certain and more readily determined. Mill rapidly dismisses the calculus of pleasure and pain. Quantity of pleasure and pain is no more readily measured than quality. In either case, the only test is in "the feelings and judgment of the experienced" (213).

And finally, the Utilitarian standard is not "the agent's own greatest happiness, but the greatest amount of happiness altogether." Utilitarianism could, therefore, only attain its end "by the general cultivation of nobleness of character" (213–14). By this line of argument, Mill has brought the doctrine round to an apparent total conformity with orthodoxy, to the view that virtue is the sole source of happiness. The doctrine of utility becomes "the rules and precepts for human conduct, by the observance of which an existence such as has been described might be, to the greatest extent possible, secured to all mankind; and . . . to the whole sentient creation." The two great obstacles are selfishness and want of mental cultivation, which both make life "unsatisfactory." The "highest virtue which can be found in man," as long as the world is in its present imperfect state, is the readiness to make an absolute sacrifice of one's own happiness. "The utilitarian morality does recognise in human beings the power of sacrificing their own greatest good for the good of others." And, paradoxically, "the conscious ability to do without happiness gives the best prospect of realizing such happiness as is attainable" (214–18). By this point, the simple original statement of doctrine, "that pleasure, and freedom from pain, are the only things desirable as ends," might seem to have been transformed out of existence. The transformation is no doubt partly tactical, at least in its mode of presentation, to show the compatibility of the doctrine with orthodox morality, but for the most part it is an elaboration of Mill's genuine view of the doctrine, as more briefly suggested in his earlier attacks on Bentham. If there is a special tactical intention in his assertion that "in the golden rule of Jesus of Nazareth, we read the complete spirit of the ethics of utility," it is still a profound part of Mill's interpretation of the doctrine, that "as between his own happiness and that of others, utilitarianism requires" the agent to be "as strictly impartial as a disinterested and benevolent spectator," and that the doctrine of utility is as connected as any other ethical system with "beautiful or more exalted developments of human nature" and with varied "springs of action" (218–19).

This is the major re-statement of the essay. Mill easily disposes of some of the common charges against the doctrine, once he has established his own definition. Like William Godwin, he distinguishes between the morality of an action and the moral worth of an agent, and acknowledges that most actions will have a view to the good of a small circle of immediate family and friends, rather than the whole of society. Like Godwin, too, he dismisses the notion that every act must proceed from a detailed and deliberate calculation of consequences. Many of these points, like the defence against the charge that the doctrine is one of mere expediency, had been dealt with in the "Whewell" essay.

In the third chapter, on the ultimate sanction of the principle of utility, he turns to the accusation that Utilitarianism provides no basis for obligation. In what might be termed the prototype of the doctrine, as presented by Helvetius, this accusation is well grounded. The psychology of Helvetius is so firmly fixed in egoistic hedonism that the impartial and disinterested spectator Mill posits is an impossibility, as is any motive which could lead to a preference for the general pleasure over the personal. But as we have seen, Mill's radically different view of human nature, including a relatively orthodox view of moral character, creates for him no such problem. The aim of the Utilitarian philosophy is, as he defines it, to create through the improvement of education a "feeling of unity with our fellow-creatures" and to root it deeply in our character (227). When he links this aim with Christ's intention, he is again asserting the compatibility of his doctrine with Christian ethical orthodoxy, and at the same time intimating that the source of obligation, in Christian and Utilitarian alike, must lie in moral disposition. Both ethics must rely on the formation of moral character, on the sentiments of the "ordinarily well brought up young person" (227).

The external sanctions of reward and punishment, whether physical or moral, whether from God or from our fellow men, along with disinterested devotion to God or to one's fellow men, can be just as operative for any ethical system. So too with the internal sanction of the sense of duty. The pain attendant on the violation of duty is the essence of Conscience. Granted, says Mill, that Conscience is a highly complex feeling, "encrusted over with collateral associations," but its binding force is constituted by it *qua* feeling —"a mass of feeling which must be broken through in order to do what violates our standard of right." The ultimate internal sanction of all morality, then, is "a subjective feeling in our own minds." Where the feeling does not exist, nor does the sanction. The belief in God, as an internal sanction, apart from expectation of reward or punishment (the external sanction), "only operates on conduct through, and in proportion to, the subjective religious feeling." It will be noted that Mill by-passes the hotly argued question of the nature of Conscience: "Whatever theory we have of the nature or origin of conscience," he says, "this is what essentially constitutes it"—a feeling (228–9). He thus sweeps aside the whole tradition, represented by the Cambridge Platonists and their successors, of Conscience as rational and cognitive in essence. This is again a reflection of his own views and at the same time a tactical move. It is not unorthodox to define Conscience as a feeling, and he has already argued that Utilitarianism is directed towards, and is capable of, producing such a feeling. The true Utilitarian will develop a Christian Conscience.

If the Christian objects that the Utilitarian Conscience is "implanted," whereas the Christian is innate, Mill has an answer. Those who prefer the innate may consider the "regard to the pleasures and pains of others" as the innate feeling which is the essence of Conscience. And this indeed would be orthodox Utilitarianism as well. But acquired moral feelings are just as natural as innate ones. Echoing Burke's "Art is man's nature" (and behind Burke, Aristotle) Mill asserts, "It is natural to man to speak, to reason, to build cities, to cultivate the ground, though these are acquired faculties"; the "moral faculty, if not a part of our nature, is a natural outgrowth from it. . ." (230). Indeed, the Utilitarian philosophy is based upon the naturalness of the social feelings of mankind. If social sentiments were artificial associations, they "might be analysed away" (231). Ultimately, then, the source of the feeling of the obligation is in the Conscience, which is itself a development and cultivation of the natural social feelings. And once again, apart from the elimination of the supernatural, Mill has suggested the compatibility of Utilitarianism and orthodox Christianity. He has also, of course, developed in detail an area of human behaviour and an area of Utilitarian theory neglected by Bentham.

The fourth chapter, "Of what sort of proof the principle of utility is susceptible," has been prepared for in the first chapter. The logic of the argument of this chapter, like that of the previous chapters, is rigorously examined in Professor Dryer's essay (lxxiiiff below). What is important in the context of my argument is the discussion of virtue, which again has the effect of radically modifying the original doctrine, despite Mill's assertion to the contrary. The doctrine, says Mill, maintains "not only that virtue is to be desired, but that it is to be desired disinterestedly, for itself." The Utilitarians "not only place virtue at the very head of the things which are good as means to the ultimate end, but they also recognise as a psychological fact the possibility of its being, to the individual, a good in itself. . . ; and hold, that the mind is not in a right state, . . . not in the state most conducive to the general happiness, unless it does love virtue in this manner..." (235).

This is a very clever, and very carefully composed statement. It gives the appearance of putting Utilitarianism even more on the side of orthodoxy, of recognizing virtue as an end in itself, along with happiness. It would be easy for the orthodox to miss the qualifications. "Actions and dispositions are only virtuous because they promote another end than virtue"—that is, happiness. Once Utilitarians have decided "what *is* virtuous," they then "place virtue at the very head" (235). Would their decisions concerning what is virtuous coincide with the decisions of the orthodox? Is the "virtue" to be desired by the Utilitarians identical with the "virtue" to be pursued by the orthodox Christian? And is there not a difference between accepting virtue as an end in itself, and accepting "as a psychological fact" that it may become "to individuals" an end in itself? In fact, the modifications of Utilitarian doctrine are here more apparent than real. The associationist explanation of how minds come to think of what were originally means to an end as part of the end itself does not affect the real category of virtue. It does, however, by implication, perhaps remind the orthodox that in their own ethical system, virtue was originally a means to salvation, not an end in itself.

The psychological emphasis in this statement about utility and virtue might at first sight seem a digression from the subject of the chapter. It is instead a necessary preparation, for the only "proof" of which the principle of utility is susceptible is psychological. It can be determined only by "practised self-consciousness and self-observation, assisted by observation of others" (237). Examination of the psychological evidence leads Mill to an account, in terms of Hartleian associationism, of the relations of will, desire, and habit. The will to virtue must start by desire and become habitual through education. "Will is the child of desire, and passes out of the dominion of its parent only to come under that of habit" (239). Habit alone imparts certainty in establishing a stable state of the will. The state of the will is a means to good, not intrinsically a good. Hence nothing is a good that is not pleasurable or a means to pleasure or to avoiding pain, and "the principle of utility is proved." Whether the proof induces assent or not, Mill leaves to "the consideration of the thoughtful reader" (239). The kind of thoughtful reader he hoped for is undoubtedly someone like Professor Dryer, whose patient and careful analysis below ought to be read with care. The ordinary reader, less patient and less expert, might well be brought up short by Mill's last paragraphs. After so much movement away from the original pleasure-pain formula, after pleasure had given way to happiness, then to satisfaction, then apparently to the pursuit of virtue, he has suddenly, in the space of one long paragraph, been whirled rapidly through a lecture on the psychology of volition to a Q.E.D. of the original premisses. The performance is a *tour de force* that must have had for many readers the baffling fascination of a magician's trick. What is significant for the argument I have been conducting, however, is that in thus coming back full circle Mill is completing his tactical manoeuvre. He is not discarding Bentham and the original statement of the creed; he is giving the old creed its proper interpretation. He began with the formal (and narrow) statement, he elucidated, elaborated, corrected, and defended—now he brings the whole *corpus* of his exposition back to its starting point in the formal enunciation of the doctrine.

The fifth chapter of the essay is, in a sense, an appendix. In choosing "Justice and Utility" as its subject, Mill is able once again to argue that the principle of utility is not a principle of mere expediency. And since the concept of justice is associated with ideas of natural law, of absolute standards, and of the general ethical position implied in the title of Cudworth's treatise, *The Eternal and Immutable Morality*, its discussion permits Mill to argue in detail, as he has argued generally elsewhere, that it is possible to derive from the principle of utility moral standards and rules as satisfactory as those of the intuitionist school. He consequently starts by attacking first the philosophy of innate ideas, and then that of moral sense. First he insists that "intellectual instincts" are no more infallible in judgment than animal instincts are in action (240). Then, turning to the second school, he inquires whether we have a sense of justice, peculiar and immediate like our senses of colour or taste. This inquiry he disposes of by an inductive appeal to the evidence, listing six varied notions of what is just or unjust.

He then proceeds to an analysis of the *feeling* which accompanies the idea of justice, examining on the way concepts of duty, rights, doctrines of punishment, doctrines of just wage, just taxation. The only sure criterion in all these matters is social utility. And justice is "a name for certain classes of moral rules, which concern the essentials of human well-being more nearly, and are therefore of more absolute obligation, than any other rules for the guidance of life. . ."; it is "a name for certain moral requirements, which, regarded collectively, stand higher in the scale of social utility, and are therefore of more paramount obligation, than any others. . ." (255, 259). Justice "is involved in the very meaning of Utility, or the Greatest-Happiness Principle." "Bentham's dictum, 'everybody to count for one, nobody for more than one,' might be written under the principle of utility as an explanatory commentary." (257.)

Two things are significant about the conclusion. One is that Mill repeats the definition of justice three times, with little substantial variation, as if to drive home again and again the two claims, that justice is not only *not* explained away and reduced to expediency by the principle of utility, but that it retains something like absolute status, and that the traditional concept of justice as fair play for all stands at the very heart of the doctrine. The other significant thing is the introduction of Bentham's name and his dictum, so that the pattern of affirming the unity of old creed and new exegesis noted at the end of chapter four is repeated at the end of the whole essay. Bentham is gathered in by name into the fold of the new church.

AUGUSTE COMTE AND POSITIVISM

It is perhaps not too fanciful to see an analogy between Mill's attitude towards Comte and his later attitude towards Bentham, and to see this essay as a further practice of what I have called Mill's new tactics. Indeed the parallel is suggested by his comment at the opening of the essay, that the time has come to express a judgment on Positivism, now that Comte has "displayed a quantity and quality of mental power, and achieved an amount of success, which have not only won but retained the high admiration of thinkers as radically and strenuously opposed as it is possible to be, to nearly the whole of his later tendencies, and to many of his earlier opinions."[21] That Mill himself is one of the thinkers so described the rest of the essay makes evident. "It would have been a mistake," he continues, "had such thinkers busied themselves in the first instance with drawing attention to what they regarded as errors in his great work. Until it had taken the place in the world of thought which belonged to it, the important matter was not to criticise it, but to help in making it known." (264.) These sentences parallel exactly the terms in which he had defined his reasons for adopting the new tactics in dealing with Bentham. And the parallel suggests further that Mill, in seeing the need for the same tactics, sees at least something of the same relationship between Comte and Positivism as he had seen between Bentham and Utilitarianism: namely, a valid and important doctrine harmed in its definition and interpretation by the limitations of its proponent. And since Mill is not likely to extend these protective tactics to doctrines opposed to Utilitarianism, it also appears that he sees in Utilitarianism and Positivism a common cause.

This he soon makes fully explicit. He defines the "fundamental doctrine" of Positivism in very broad terms: "We have no knowledge of anything but Phaenomena; and our knowledge of phaenomena is relative, not absolute. We know not the essence, nor the real mode of production, of any fact, but only its relations to other facts in the way of succession or of similitude. These relations are constant. . . . The constant resemblances . . . and the constant sequences . . . are termed their laws. The laws of phaenomena are all we know respecting them." (265.) Only through these laws can we predict, and in some cases, control effects. This general statement of empiricism Mill easily identifies with the scientific mode of philosophy, imperfectly but partly grasped by Bacon and Descartes, fully by Newton, Hume, and Thomas Brown; and "the same great truth formed the groundwork of all the speculative philosophy of Bentham, and pre-eminently of James Mill. . . ." "The philosophy called Positive is not a recent invention of M. Comte, but a simple adherence to the traditions of all the great scientific minds whose discoveries have made the human race what it is." (267.)

Comte thus joins Bentham (and James Mill) as an apostle of the true philosophy, and an opponent of the Theological and Metaphysical—or, as Mill prefers to put it, a supporter of the Phaenomenal and Experiential philosophy against the "Personal, or Volitional explanation of facts" and the "Abstractional or Ontological" (267). Comte "has taken his place in a fight long since engaged, and on the side already in the main victorious." He is on the side of the Nominalists against the Realists, of the Rationalists against the Voluntarists, the latter conflict being here defined in secular

[21]*Auguste Comte and Positivism*, 263 below. Subsequent references are to the present edition, and are given in parentheses.

terms. Like Montesquieu, "even Macchiavelli," Adam Smith "and the political economists universally," Bentham "and all thinkers initiated by him," Comte believes that "social phaenomena conform to invariable laws," as do the phaenomena of Nature. He rejects "the whole system of ideas connected with supernatural agency," and like Mill, sees the doctrine of Voluntarism as stemming from ignorance. "No one, probably," Mill scoffingly remarks, "ever believed that the will of a god kept parallel lines from meeting, or made two and two equal to four; or ever prayed to the gods to make the square of the hypothenuse equal to more or less than the sum of the squares of the sides." "In the case of phaenomena which science has not yet taught us either to foresee or to control, the theological mode of thought [that is, the Voluntarist] has not ceased to operate: men still pray for rain, or for success in war, or to avert a shipwreck or a pestilence, but not to put back the stars in their courses, . . . or to arrest the tides." (288.) Like Bentham, Comte rejects the whole philosophy of law based on "the imaginary law of the imaginary being Nature," along with divine rights and Natural Rights (299). In brief, Comte is, insofar as he expresses the fundamental principle of Positivism, a good Utilitarian, and conversely, Utilitarians are good Positivists. "All theories in which the ultimate standard of institutions and rules of action was the happiness of mankind, and observation and experience the guides . . . are entitled to the name Positive, whatever, in other respects, their imperfections may be" (299). As we have seen, they are also entitled, with the same qualification, to the name Utilitarian.

Granted this move towards identifying the two doctrines in their fundamental principles, it is with no surprise that we discover that "M. Comte has got hold of half the truth. . ." (313). But by this time, the other half is not in the possession of Coleridgians or Kantians. Whatever weight Mill may have given in 1838 and 1840 to the notion of a synthesis of doctrinal thesis and antithesis, that notion has now been superseded by the progressive hierarchy of Comte.[22] Theological thought yields to Metaphysical, Metaphysical to Positive. The whole tradition of Germano-Coleridgian thought is now relegated to the Metaphysical. The half of truth M. Comte has not got is to be found, not there, but in "the so-called liberal or revolutionary school." As in the earlier case of Bentham and Coleridge, and of the two traditions they represent, "each sees what the other does not see, and seeing it exclusively, draws consequences from it which to the other appear mischievously absurd" (313). The near-identity of phrasing makes more emphatic the radical change of reference. The two halves of truth now belong both within the same fundamental philosophic tradition.

To the extent to which Comte is an enemy of "the whole *a priori* philosophy, in morals, jurisprudence, psychology, logic," and on the side of "obser-

[22]Cf. xx–xxi, xxix above.

vation and experiment" (300), he is, if not thoroughly Utilitarian, at least a valuable ally. In some respects (but only some), he is a sounder ally than Herbert Spencer or G. H. Lewes, both of whom fall back on *a priori* logic for their "ultimate test of truth" in "the inconceivability of its negative" (301). It is the total and radical nature of Comte's rejection of "the metaphysical mode of thought" that seems to constitute his main claim to Mill's praise (301). When the rigorous principle is applied, for example, to Bentham's conception of social science, it leads Comte to the same conclusions as Mill had been led to earlier: that to start from "universal laws of human nature" and draw deductions from them is fallacious, because "as society proceeds in its development, its phaenomena are determined, more and more, not by the simple tendencies of universal human nature, but by the accumulated influence of past generations over the present. The human beings themselves, on the laws of whose nature the facts of history depend, are not abstract or universal but historical human beings, already shaped, and made what they are, by human society. This being the case, no powers of deduction could enable any one, starting from the mere conception of the Being Man, placed in a world such as the earth may have been before the commencement of human agency, to predict and calculate the phaenomena of his development. . . ." Facts of history must be "empirically considered" (307).[23]

Comte is, indeed, superior to Bentham in the greater rigour of his insistence on the empirical and inductive. "All political truth he deems strictly relative, implying as its correlative a given state or situation of society" (323). In thus emphasizing the importance of history as the body of social phaenomena from which the social scientist draws his conclusions by induction, Comte makes his greatest contribution. He is at his most striking in his long survey of universal history. This survey is concerned with "the main stream of human progress, looking only at the races and nations that led the van. . . . His object is to characterize truly, though generally, the successive states of society through which the advanced guard of our species has passed, and the filiation of these states on one another—how each grew out of the preceding and was the parent of the following state." (318.) As Mill's phrases, "led the van" and "advanced guard," indicate, his approval of Comte as historian attaches to his philosophy of history as a doctrine of progress, his rôle as a new and more thorough Condorcet, more than to any really scientific quality in his historiography. Since Mill's own Utilitarianism is strongly progressive, he welcomes the presentation of a mass of historical evidence, admittedly selective rather than truly "universal," which offers inductive and empirical support for the "fact" of progress.

There is no doubt that Mill finds Comte's analysis, in general terms,

[23]Probably Mill is here recalling not only Coleridge's influence on him, but also Macaulay's criticism of James Mill's *Essay on Government*.

sound. He also praises the nice balance Comte observes between treating history (as Carlyle does) in terms of the influence of individuals, and treating it in terms solely of general causes. He is not unjust to the past, seeing (as Condorcet and Godwin had before him, though Mill does not note this) "in all past modes of thought and forms of society . . . a useful, in many a necessary, office, in carrying mankind through one stage of improvement into a higher." He avoids the error of regarding the intellectual "as the only progressive element in man, and the moral as too much the same at all times to affect even the annual average of crime" (322–3). He links, in short, intellectual to moral progress. Nor does Comte think of moral progress as dependent solely on intellectual improvement. "He not only personally appreciates, but rates high in moral value, the creations of poets and artists in all departments, deeming them, by their mixed appeal to the sentiments and the understanding, admirably fitted to educate the feelings of abstract thinkers, and enlarge the intellectual horizon of people of the world" (324). Once again we hear unvoiced echoes of Mill's view of Bentham and his limitations, from some of which at least Comte is free.

But at the same time, the balance must not be allowed to tip too far in reaction. Comte is not so far from Bentham as to hand over progress to the poets and artists. He does indeed, like Bentham, insist that "the main agent in the progress of mankind is their intellectual development," and while it is true that the passions are "a more energetic power than a mere intellectual conviction," the passions "tend to divide, not to unite, mankind." "It is only by a common belief that passions are brought to work together, and become a collective force. . . ." The passions are the gale, but Reason must be the compass. "All human society," as Godwin had argued, "is grounded on a system of fundamental opinions, which only the speculative faculty can provide," and which only improvement of the speculative faculty can improve (316). Herbert Spencer is wrong in asserting that "ideas do not govern and overthrow the world; the world is governed or overthrown by feelings, to which ideas serve only as guides." That is, he is wrong if he thinks this a refutation of Comte. The sentiments "are only a social force at all, through the definite direction given to them by . . . some . . . intellectual conviction," and the sentiments do not of themselves "spontaneously throw up" convictions (317). "To say that men's intellectual beliefs do not determine their conduct, is like saying that the ship is moved by the steam and not by the steersman" (317).

In many respects, then, Comte can be praised as another apostle of the true faith, a true Utilitarian in his fundamental principles, and free of some of the limitations of personality and of intellectual equipment which so narrowed Bentham. But his own limitations are more disastrous than Bentham's.

Even in the earlier work with which the first part of Mill's essay deals, the *Cours de Philosophie Positive*, there is much that arouses Mill's strong disapproval. In the first place, Comte's psychology is inadequate. He gives psychology as a science no place in his classification, and "always speaks of it with contempt." He reduces it, in fact, to a branch of physiology, totally rejecting introspection, or "psychological observation properly so called . . . internal consciousness." As Mill dryly observes, "How we are to observe other people's mental operations, or how interpret the signs of them without having learnt what the signs mean by knowledge of ourselves, he does not state" (296). Comte relies, as "Organon for the study of 'the moral and intellectual functions' " on Phrenology, which, says Mill, is in process of becoming discredited as a science. Moreover, it tends to be entirely meaningless unless related to a psychology of association. Comte shows no knowledge, and makes no use, of the work of Hartley, Brown, and James Mill. The real scientific development of psychology has been made by Bain and Herbert Spencer. Comte's failure to take psychology seriously as a mental science is not a "mere hiatus" in his system, but "the parent of serious errors in his attempt to create a Social Science" (298).

Probably even more culpable, from Mill's point of view, are some of Comte's political attitudes, his reliance on authority, his eagerness to commit power to single persons or small groups, his rejection, not only of popular sovereignty, but of any principle of responsibility. It is not only that Comte runs foul of most of Mill's fundamental political principles, and those of the Utilitarians generally, but also of the ethical attitudes underlying them. "No one to count as more than one" is an axiom at the heart of the Utilitarian ethic. Further, Mill is clearly shocked to find that Comte relegates to the "metaphysical," and hence to oblivion, "the first of all the articles of the liberal creed, 'the absolute right of free examination, or the dogma of unlimited liberty of conscience.' " Comte accepts the *legal* right, but "resolutely denies" the *moral* right (301). On a strict Utilitarian basis, of course, Comte is quite correct, and Mill himself would found an absolute right not on natural rights but on permanent utility. But he is pushed here, as in *On Liberty*, away from Utilitarian relativism into something like "metaphysical" absolutism, for fear, as he says, of the use to be made of the contrary doctrine. And although Comte by no means wishes "intellectual dominion to be exercised over an ignorant people," and is as strong an advocate of popular education as any Utilitarian, viewing the possibilities of such education with a "startling" optimism, his scheme to have a "salutary ascendency over opinion" exercised by an *organized* body of "the most eminent thinkers" makes Mill decidedly nervous (314). So does Comte's dismissal of the whole revolutionary and liberal set of ideas as "metaphysical" and merely negative, and consequently as a serious impediment to the reorganization of society (301). Mill himself had insisted on the negative nature of eighteenth-century revolutionary thought, and the aberration of Rousseau in trying to found a positive philosophy of government on negation, but again he senses the presence of dangerous conclusions and applications. Though there is truth in what Comte says, Mill feels like the man "who being asked whether he admitted that six and five make eleven, refused to give an answer until he knew what use was to be made of it" (302).

Underlying his misgivings about the use Comte wishes to make of these ideas is his lively distrust of the whole programme for the future of society Comte seems to envisage. On the "statical" side of social phænomena, the laws of social existence "considered abstractedly from progress," Comte is relatively satisfactory. On the "dynamical" side, that of social progress, the laws of the evolution of the social state, he is at his weakest, trite and often invalid (309). For Mill, of course, the "statical" is important as a preliminary to the "dynamical"; his real concern is with the means of ensuring the progress of society and of man in society. Comte's means seem to him totally wrong.

Apart from the ideas we have been examining, there is much in the first part of the essay on Comte with which we need not concern ourselves here. The very interesting sections in which Mill discusses and criticizes Comte's classification of the sciences, his philosophy of science, the Organon of Discovery and the Organon of Proof, the difference between Laws and Causes, and so on, are important in other contexts. Our concern has been with the ethical, and with the political insofar as it touches the ethical.

In part two of the essay, as Mill turns to Comte's later writings, the balance of praise and blame shifts radically. None the less, the Religion of Humanity can be made to coincide in its essentials, as Mill sees them, with the essential ethical basis of Utilitarianism, and Comte can remain in some sense a high priest of the true creed. "The power which may be acquired over the mind by the idea of the general interest of the human race, both as a source of emotion and as a motive to conduct, many have perceived; but we know not if anyone, before M. Comte, realized so fully as he has done, all the majesty of which that idea is susceptible." "We, therefore, not only hold that M. Comte was justified in the attempt to develop his philosophy into a religion, and had realized the essential conditions of one, but that all other religions are made better in proportion as, in their practical result, they are brought to coincide with that which he aimed at constructing." (334–5.)

But if Comte is right in general principle, he is often wrong in interpretation and application. He falls into the error often charged against the Utilitarian moralists, in requiring "that the test of conduct should also be the exclusive motive to it" (335). And in his enthusiasm for loving one's neighbour, he insists on conscious suppression of all self-regarding actions. If he merely meant "that egoism is bound, and should be taught, always to give way to the well-understood interests of enlarged altruism," no one could object, least of all Mill. But his naïve phrenology, combined with a biological theory of organic growth or atrophy through use or disuse, leads him to something like the old ascetic mortification of the flesh (335).

Mill sees in this tendency a symptom of a general trend in Comte's thought which underlies many of his errors, a tendency to accept as axiomatic "that all perfection consists in unity." "Why is it necessary," asks Mill, "that all human life should point but to one object, and be cultivated into a system of means to a single end? May it not be the fact that mankind, who after all are made up of single human beings, obtain a greater sum of happiness when each pursues his own, under the rules and conditions required by the good of the rest, than when each makes the good of the rest his only subject. . . ?" (337.) Comte's passion for "unity" and "systematization" leads not only to a denial of the value Mill places upon variety, but to a system of compulsion towards uniformity. In Halévy's terms, Comte plans the "artificial identification of interests," while Mill believes in the "natural identification of interests," as his words above indicate.

The "mania for regulation" by which Comte seems obsessed appears in full development in the *cultus* of the Religion of Humanity. The elaborate provision of ceremony, ritual, and doctrine strikes Mill, of course, as an unseemly imitation of Roman Catholicism. Earlier in the essay, in discussing Comte's treatment of history, Mill had remarked that Comte had no understanding of Protestantism (321). It is equally evident that Mill has no understanding of Catholicism. It is interesting to recall how many writers, in the period from the French Revolution on into the nineteenth century, either from a conviction that Christianity ought to be destroyed, or from a belief that the Enlightenment had in fact virtually destroyed it, urge the creation of a new religion to supply the social need once filled by Christianity. And it is important to note how their conceptions differ as to what religion is, how it functions in society, and particularly how it serves as a social bond. The English Protestants define religion in terms of feeling, and of ethical attitudes. Arnold can thus express the hope that poetry can take over the task formerly performed by religion.[24] Their emphasis is wholly on the individual, and the inner sentiments; they do not think at all in terms of any need of a corporate church, of corporate worship, of external ritual or sacraments. The Continental Catholics, on the contrary, think mainly in these terms, of

[24]Cf. John M. Robson, *The Improvement of Mankind: The Social and Political Thought of John Stuart Mill* (Toronto: University of Toronto Press, 1968), 122n: "Bain reports, without noticeable sympathy, that Mill 'seemed to look upon Poetry as a Religion, or rather as Religion and Philosophy in one.' "

religion as a corporate public act, of communal participation in ritual, of public symbols and festivals. The whole contrast is pointed up by Mill's rather astonished comment that Comte proposes prayers and devotional practices, not because the individual's "feelings require them, but for the premeditated purpose of getting his feelings up" (343). If Mill understands, as he undoubtedly does, some aspects of human psychology much better than Comte, it is also true that Comte understands others better than Mill.

The contrast is not simply that of Protestant and Catholic views of religion, however. There is also a contrast in their views of the primary need religion must fulfil for society. Just as Mill and Arnold differ in their diagnoses of English society, Mill fearing an excessive unity and uniformity, Arnold fearing an excess of individuality leading to moral and social anarchy, so Mill and Comte differ. Comte observes that in the pre-Positivist stage of society "the free development of our forces of all kinds was the important matter." Now, "the principal need is to regulate them." From this doctrine, Mill expresses his "entire dissent." He sees in Comte's scheme "an elaborate system for the total suppression of all independent thought." It seems obvious that Comte is concerned about the instability of the French society, about what he sees as the continuing effects of the negative and destructive forces of the Revolution. He sees the intellectuals as "desiring only to prolong the existing scepticism and intellectual anarchy," and as "rootedly hostile to the construction of the new" religious and social order (351–2). He has no faith in popular rule: "Election of superiors by inferiors, except as a revolutionary expedient, is an abomination in his sight." He has only "detestation and contempt" for "parliamentary or representative institutions in any form," and for a system in which the executive is responsible to an elected body (344). But Mill turns no attention to the national and historical context of Comte's project. And for this he has a double justification. Comte himself is presenting his system not in historical and relativist, but in absolute terms, taking the French situation as universal for the Positive period of history.[25] Moreover, for Mill there is no historical situation in any country in the mid-nineteenth century for which Comte's system would be valid.

There is no need here, nor would it be appropriate, to discuss all the interesting ideas in the essay. Mill's comments on the rôle of women, on Comte's views of the family and of marriage, on proper wages for workmen, on the idle rich, on "useful" knowledge, on Comte's system of education, on his limitation of books, provide links to a wide range of his writings. One curious note is that where Comte puts forward ideas which are "Positivist" in a twentieth-century sense, Mill sometimes disagrees. When Comte says,

[25]Here one recalls Mill's criticism of Bentham's propensity to legislate for all mankind, regardless of the implications of the title of his *Influence of Time and Place in Matters of Legislation*.

for example, that the scientist's concern with "complete proof," and a "perfect rationalization of scientific processes" is mere pedantry, and it "ought to be enough that the doctrines afford an explanation of phaenomena, consistent with itself and with known facts, and that the processes are justified by their fruits" (356). Mill disapproves, although he praises the comment "that the infinitesimal calculus is a conception analogous to the corpuscular hypothesis in physics; which last M. Comte has always considered as a logical artifice; not an opinion respecting matters of fact" (365).

The essay closes, in conformity with Mill's tactics, after so much devastating criticism, with high praise. Comte, like Descartes and Leibniz, whom he most resembles, has an "extraordinary power of concatenation and co-ordination," and has "enriched human knowledge with great truths and great conceptions of method." He is, in fact, greater than his predecessors, "not intrinsically, yet by the exertion of equal intellectual power in a more advanced state of human preparation" (368). His absurdities appear more ridiculous than theirs because our age is less tolerant of palpable absurdities.

The "concatenation and co-ordination" clearly refer to the sweeping view of history as a record of human progress. The "great truths and great conceptions of method" must apply, not to the "systematization, systematization, systematization," but to the fundamental Positivist principles, so closely identified with the Utilitarian, and to the scientific method, the use of history in search of generalizations and "laws" of human behaviour which Mill himself advocates.[26] Comte emerges finally, then, as a high priest of Utilitarianism and of the Religion of Humanity, misled into becoming High Priest and Pontiff of his absurd *cultus*.

THREE ESSAYS ON RELIGION

The essays which Helen Taylor published after Mill's death as *Three Essays on Religion*, present, as she points out in her Introductory Notice, his "deliberate and exhaustive treatment of the topics under consideration." She also notes that although the first two, on Nature and on the Utility of Religion, were written between 1850 and 1858, while the third, on Theism, was not written until between 1868 and 1870, Mill certainly "considered the opinions expressed in these different Essays, as fundamentally consistent," and "his manner of thinking had undergone no substantial change."[27] Indeed, the various allusions to religious thought in his earliest ethical writings, the treatment of religious ideas in *On Liberty*, and in *Auguste Comte and Positivism*,

[26]See especially Mill's *Logic*, Book VI, Chap. x, "Of the Inverse Deductive, or Historical Method."

[27]*Three Essays on Religion*, 371–2 below. Subsequent references are to the present edition, and are given in parentheses.

all suggest that Mill's opinions on what his orthodox contemporaries meant by religion, both revealed and natural, stayed virtually constant throughout his mature career. All that changed was the openness and explicitness of his attack.

The fundamentals of his position have already been made clear. His thinking is firmly rooted in empiricism; his whole concept of truth is strongly defined by the "canons of induction"—truth is what can be proved by induction from empirical experience. His concept of a true religion is consequently of a religion of naturalism, as opposed to one of supernaturalism, a religion of the this-worldly as opposed to one of the other-worldly. The sort of religion he can approve of he finds in Comte's Religion of Humanity. The ethical system dependent on this religion is the Utilitarian. And finally, he sees this religion as an instrument of progress, of an emergent ethical evolution. These simple attitudes, which underlie all his comments on religion, provide the basic points of reference for the more elaborate treatment in the three essays.

The essay "The Utility of Religion" is directed towards persuading the reader that all the needs, both of society and of the individual, commonly thought of as satisfied by orthodox religion, can be fully satisfied without it, and that in fact the effects ascribed to religion have been due, not to religion itself, but to the force of opinion. Religious authority, by being in control of opinion and of education, has received credit for the support of the virtues, and for the instilling of them in the young, but Mill insists that the results of control by religious authority in no way differ from the results obtainable by essentially secular control: "early religious teaching has owed its power over mankind rather to its being early than to its being religious" (410). As to the sanctions religion lends to morality through its system of eternal rewards and punishments, morality needs no supernatural sanctions: moral truths are strong enough in their own evidence to retain the belief of mankind when once they have acquired it. Moreover, an application of Bentham's calculus reinforces the impressions gained by observation that even infinite rewards and punishments postponed to the after life and never witnessed have little effect on ordinary minds. The real sanctions come from public opinion and the passions affected by it: "the love of glory; the love of praise; the love of admiration; the love of respect and deference; even the love of sympathy. . . ." "The fear of shame, the dread of ill repute or of being disliked or hated, are the direct and simple forms of its deterring power." "Belief, then, in the supernatural . . . cannot be considered to be any longer required, either for enabling us to know what is right and wrong in social morality, or for supplying us with motives to do right and to abstain from wrong." (417.) Cannot an ethical system for both society and the individual, then, be purely secular? Cannot the public and private morality be imposed merely by the power of education and public opinion, in the tradition of Utilitarianism? What need is there of a substitute Religion of Humanity to replace the old supernatural religion?

Once again, as Mill proceeds to answer these questions (which he does not explicitly ask) our thoughts revert to the *Autobiography* and the description of the crisis of his youth. "Religion and poetry," he now writes, "address themselves, at least in one of their aspects, to the same part of the human constitution: they both supply the same want, that of ideal conceptions grander and more beautiful than we see realized in the prose of human life. Religion, as distinguished from poetry, is the product of the craving to know whether these imaginative conceptions have realities answering to them in some other world than ours." Religion adds to "the poetry of the supernatural" a positive belief which unpoetical minds can share with the poetical. It satisfies the craving for "the better which is suggested" by the good partially seen and known on earth, the craving for "higher things." The question for Mill is not whether this "poetry of the supernatural" is valuable: he readily acknowledges that it meets an important psychological need—but whether it has to be connected with the supernatural. Is it necessary, he asks, "to travel beyond the boundaries of the world which we inhabit" to obtain this good, or is "the idealization of our earthly life, the cultivation of a high conception of what *it* may be made . . . not capable of supplying a poetry, and, in the best sense of the word, a religion, equally fitted to exalt the feelings, and (with the same aid from education) still better calculated to ennoble the conduct, than any belief respecting the unseen powers" (420).

Such a religion can even offer, in terms of the human species, the aspirations appropriate to immortality and, in conjunction with a faith in progress, an earthly Paradise: "if individual life is short, the life of the human species is not short; its indefinite duration is practically equivalent to endlessness; and being combined with indefinite capability of improvement, it offers to the imagination and sympathies a large enough object to satisfy any reasonable demand for grandeur of aspiration" (420). Once man has abandoned the "baseless fancies" of supernatural immortality, his mind will expand into new dimensions at thoughts of the Grand Etre and its limitless future. When it has expanded from love of country to love of the world, as it can be made to expand by proper training, the universal morality will be the Utilitarian:

> A morality grounded on large and wise views of the good of the whole, neither sacrificing the individual to the aggregate nor the aggregate to the individual, but giving to duty on the one hand and to freedom and spontaneity on the other their proper province, would derive its power in the superior natures from sympathy and benevolence and the passion for ideal excellence: in the inferior, from the same feelings cultivated up to the measure of their capacity, with the superadded force of shame. . . . A support in moments of weakness would not be a problematical future existence, but the approbation . . . of those whom we respect, and

ideally of all those, dead or living, whom we admire or venerate. . . . To call these sentiments by the name morality . . . is claiming too little for them. They are a real religion. . . . (422.)

Here is undoubtedly Mill's lasting confession of faith. The Religion of Humanity fulfils all the conditions he demands: "The essence of religion is the strong and earnest direction of the emotions and desires towards an ideal object, recognized as of the highest excellence, and as rightfully paramount over all selfish objects of desire" (422). It fulfils them for him much more satisfactorily than orthodox (or unorthodox) Christianity.

Given an understanding of Mill's religious position, and of the principles on which it is based, the long essay on Theism offers the reader no surprises. There can in fact be few works of Mill's which show so little originality. Any reader familiar with nineteenth-century writings on religion will find himself constantly recalling other expressions of the same views. Much of the essay could as readily have been written by Huxley. The elaborate attack on *a priori* and *a posteriori* "proofs" of the Being and Attributes of God, carrying one's mind back to Samuel Clarke and the eighteenth century, seems quaintly old-fashioned, especially when the *a priori* is so easily dismissed as "unscientific" (434). The most entertaining passages are those which exhibit the full savagery of Mill's combative style, such as the one in Part II on man's God-given potentialities for development: "It is to suppose that God could not, in the first instance, create anything better than a Bosjeman or an Andaman islander, or something still lower; and yet was able to endow the Bosjeman or the Andaman islander with the power of raising himself into a Newton or a Fénelon. We certainly do not know the nature of the barriers which limit the divine omnipotence; but it is a very odd notion of them that they enable the Deity to confer on an almost bestial creature the power of producing by a succession of efforts what God himself had no other means of creating." (459.) Or again, in Part III, on God's being either unable or unwilling to grant our desires: "Many a man would like to be a Croesus or an Augustus Caesar, but has his wishes gratified only to the moderate extent of a pound a week or the Secretaryship of his Trades Union" (466). The writing is often as lively as Mill's best, even where the ideas are commonplace.

The criticism of Hume's essay on miracles in Part IV (471), the remarks on brain and mind and the warning against "giving *à priori* validity to the conclusions of an *à posteriori* philosophy" in Part III (461) are of interest as examples either of Mill's wish to be fair, or of his insistence on precise argument. But perhaps the most interesting part for its content is the final one, in which, like Tennyson and Browning, Mill asserts the value of imaginative aspirations, of hope, and of "cleaving to the sunnier side of doubt," as Tennyson puts it. One senses again here that other side of Mill, responding in something like poetic terms to the realities of the human situation and of human psychology. "To me it seems that human life, small and confined as it is, and as, considered merely in the present, it is likely to remain even when the progress of material and moral improvement may have freed it from the greater part of its present calamities, stands greatly in need of any wider range and greater height of aspiration for itself and its destination, which the exercise of imagination can yield to it without running counter to the evidence of fact . . ." (483). Or, as Arnold put it, "men have such need of joy! But joy whose grounds are true. . . ."[28]

Again, when Mill praises "the tendency, either from constitution or habit, to dwell chiefly on the brighter side both of the present and of the future," noting that "a hopeful disposition gives a spur to the faculties and keeps all the active energies in good working order," or when he observes that it is not necessary "for keeping up our conviction that we must die, that we should be always brooding over death," that we should not "think perpetually of death, but . . . of our duties, and of the rule of life" (484), we seem to be listening to Tennyson's Ancient Sage. When "the reason is strongly cultivated, the imagination may safely follow its own end, and do its best to make life pleasant and lovely inside the castle, in reliance on the fortifications raised and maintained by Reason round the outward bounds." The "indulgence of hope with regard to the government of the universe and the destiny of man after death . . . is legitimate and philosophically defensible." Such a hope "makes life and human nature a far greater thing to the feelings, and gives greater strength as well as greater solemnity to all the sentiments which are awakened in us by our fellow-creatures and by mankind at large" (485). Throughout this last section, Mill emphasizes the importance of the imagination, not to supplant reason, but to supplement it. Ultimately it is this addition of imagination to reason, of poetry to fact, which constitutes religion, especially "that real, though purely human religion, which sometimes calls itself the Religion of Humanity and sometimes that of Duty" (488).

Although there are clear connections between the essay "Nature" and the other two essays on religion, it does not fit simply into the pattern I have been tracing, nor are the issues it discusses all related simply or exclusively to Mill's religious thought. For some classes of reader, it will be by far the most interesting of the three essays. For students of literature concerned with the development of Romanticism, for example, it will be an important document.

It is easy to recognize in the essay a number of distinct, though related, themes. The words "nature" and "natural" have become a source, says Mill, of "false taste, false philosophy, false morality, and even bad law" (373).

[28]Matthew Arnold, "Obermann Once More," ll.237–8.

The last term, recalling Bentham's attacks on the concept of Natural Law, points up the first theme: an attack on "the great *à priori* fallacies," which are to be exposed here, as the list suggests, in aesthetic theory, in philosophy, and in moral philosophy (383). The attack involves the rejection of Nature as an aesthetic norm, and of Nature as an ethical norm, and the repudiation generally of the injunction to "follow Nature." Since these "*à priori* fallacies," including the establishing of Nature as a norm, are based upon what Mill sees as a false metaphysical view of Nature, the first step is to correct this view. The "Nature" of a thing is simply "its entire capacity of exhibiting phenomena." "Nature in the abstract is the aggregate of the powers and properties of all things. Nature means the sum of all phenomena, together with the causes which produce them. . . ." (374.) There is no justification for opposing Nature and Art, "Art is as much Nature as anything else . . . ; Art is but the employment of the powers of Nature for an end" (375). In this purely empirical sense, everything is Nature, and everything must conform to Nature, Nature being simply what *is*.

But there is another sense in which Nature means phaenomena not caused by man, and in this sense a distinction can be made between Nature and Art. In this case, says Mill, the artificial is an improvement; man controls Nature to improve it. "If the artificial is not better than the natural, to what end are all the arts of life?" "All praise of Civilization, or Art, or Contrivance, is so much dispraise of Nature. . . ." (381.) So also in the ethical sphere. Cruelty is as natural as benevolence, and "the most criminal actions are to a being like man, not more unnatural than most of the virtues." "There is hardly a bad action ever perpetrated which is not perfectly natural, and the motives to which are not perfectly natural feelings." (401.) The moral man is, like the carefully tilled garden, a work of Art, not of Nature. "This artificially created or at least artificially perfected nature of the best and noblest human beings, is the only nature which it is ever commendable to follow" (396–7).

The setting up of Civilization in opposition to Nature, and the allusion to the "artificially perfected nature" of the best human beings point up the exact object of Mill's attack. In the conflict between the competing Romantic doctrines of primitivism and progress, Mill is on the side of progress. He is particularly antagonistic towards the sentimental Romantic primitivism which exalts the natural instincts. "Savages are always liars," he remarks (395). The sentiment of justice is wholly artificial in origin. No virtues are natural to man, merely a capacity for acquiring them (and also for acquiring vices). It is the duty of man to amend nature, including his own.

The notion of Nature as a norm is not, however, solely associated with or derived from primitivism. It is also part of Deist optimism, of the natural theology Mill attacks in the essay "Theism." For the astro- and physicotheologians, Nature exhibited not merely a physical order, but an ethical one. But, asks Mill, "how stands the fact? That next to the greatness of these cosmic forces, the quality which most forcibly strikes every one who does not avert his eyes from it is their perfect and absolute recklessness." Nature is totally amoral. "All which people are accustomed to deprecate as 'disorder' and its consequences, is precisely a counterpart of Nature's ways." "If imitation of the Creator's will as revealed in nature, were applied as a rule of action . . . ; the most atrocious enormities of the worst men would be more than justified by the apparent intention of Providence that throughout all animated nature the strong should prey upon the weak." Since Nature has no right or wrong, "Conformity to nature, has no connection whatever with right and wrong" (400).

The attack on the natural theologians links this essay with the essay on Theism, and the doctrine put forward in that essay, that the state of the natural world is compatible with a theory of a wise and benevolent, but not an omnipotent Creator, is put forward here, with an interesting reference to Leibniz. Much of the argument on the evidence offered by Nature for *a posteriori* discovery of the divine attributes parallels the more formal argument of the later essay on Theism. But there is much more looking backward to the eighteenth century and its controversies here; the essay on Theism, although it glances back occasionally, is solidly fixed in the world of Darwin and of the Higher Criticism.

Finally, it is possible to see in the essay on Nature a further significance. From the time of Helvetius and the early French Utilitarians, the taint of "naturalism" had clung to the doctrine. In its most narrowly rigorous form, it insisted that the sole absolute good was pleasure, the sole absolute evil, pain. It reduced motivation to the natural instinct to seek pleasure and avoid pain. In referring everything in ethics and in politics to these irreducible natural elements, and explaining everything in terms of primary natural instincts, it was not indeed setting up the natural as a norm, as the pattern of what ought to be. But it was setting up the natural as the pattern of what has to be, of what is and is inescapable. Moreover, in finding the origins of normative ideas, of ideals of value, in the purely natural, it attacked the validity usually ascribed to them. Those opponents who saw in the Helvetian doctrine a system of hedonist, egoist naturalism had some good reasons for their judgment. And it is a short step from proclaiming the inevitability of the natural to accepting it as the norm. If it is inevitably natural for dogs to bark and bite, then let them delight to do so. The natural becomes the right.

The "naturalistic" fallacy can then, and historically does, become part not only of the metaphysical views of Nature associated with Shaftesburian deists, neo-classical literary critics and pre-Romantic primitivism, but also of narrowly empirical Utilitarians. And since the Utilitarians tend to be "naturalistic" in the other sense of rejecting the supernatural and the "metaphysical," the "naturalism" ascribed to them is seen as of the most opprobrious sort. As we have seen, Mill is constantly aware of the need to break the association of Utilitarianism with the tradition of Helvetius' pattern. The essay on Nature, in defining precisely his attitude towards Nature and the natural, and the relation of the natural to the ethical norms of Utilitarianism, is Mill's main reply to those who still think of Utilitarianism in the old terms of the "naturalistic" fallacy.

University of Toronto

F.E.L.P.

Mill's Utilitarianism

THE MAJORITY of serious students of ethics today are utilitarians, and those who are not see utilitarianism as the chief position in need of amendment. John Stuart Mill's writings on ethics, and especially on utilitarianism, are thus of vital contemporary interest and importance. More than any other thinker, Mill is responsible for laying down the principal directions ethics has taken since his day. He did not, however, embody his full views in any single volume or one set of writings, and the main lines in ethics which he sketched were worked out in detail only after his death by Henry Sidgwick. A generation later, G. E. Moore sought to refine upon Sidgwick's results, and subsequent ethical theory has taken Moore's work as its starting point.

The most complete guide to undertaking a detailed examination of Mill's ethical views is his *Utilitarianism*, and so I have used it as the basis of this introductory essay. His other essays on ethics are valuable as supplements to the opinions he puts forward in this work, and they are referred to where appropriate. Five main topics have been selected for detailed treatment in the discussion that follows. The first section sorts out some of Mill's more important principles. Section II examines his dictum that the sole evidence that anything is desirable is that people desire it. In the third, consideration is given to what Mill holds that this evidence discloses. Section IV deals with Mill's analysis of moral concepts. The discussion concludes with an examination of his views on the use of the principle of utility.

I. THE PRINCIPLE OF UTILITY

Mill writes, "happiness is the sole end of human action, and the promotion of it the test by which to judge of all human conduct. . . ."[1] He also makes it clear that the test is its promotion of happiness "to the greatest extent possible" (214). By such conduct Mill does not mean that which would promote happiness to the greatest extent conceivable, but that which would promote it to a greater extent than would any alternative. Mill also makes it

[1] *Utilitarianism*, 237. Subsequent references are to the present edition of *Utilitarianism*, and are given in parenthesis.

clear that when he speaks of the promotion of happiness as "the test by which to judge of all human conduct," the aspect of conduct of which he means that it is a test is whether it should be done.[2] He thus holds that the test of whether something should be done is whether it would promote more happiness than would any alternative to it. Mill implies that if an action would satisfy this test, it should be done, and that if it would not, it is not one that should be done. Accordingly, the main principle which Mill maintains is that something should be done if and only if it would cause more happiness than would any alternative, and that something should not be done if and only if it would fail to cause as much happiness as would some alternative.

The chief support Mill offers for this principle is that "happiness is desirable, and the only thing desirable, as an end. . ." (234). He distinguishes things desirable as a means and things desirable for their own sake. What is desirable for its own sake he speaks of as desirable as an end. He argues that it is because happiness is the only thing desirable for its own sake that the test of conduct generally is its promotion of happiness. The principle he employs in taking this step is that if there is one sort of thing which is alone desirable for its own sake, then the promotion of it is the test of all human conduct. By test of human conduct he means test of what should be done. An action is then one that should be done if and only if it satisfies this test. Mill thus takes it for granted that something should be done if and only if its consequences would be more desirable than would those of any alternative to it.

From his main principle in turn Mill draws a conclusion about what it would be right to do and what it would be wrong to do. The question of whether it would be right or wrong to do a certain action is a question about its morality. Mill writes, "the morality of an individual action is . . . a question . . . of the application of a law to an individual case" (206). He thus holds that it would be wrong to do a certain action only if it would be at variance with a certain rule. If we ask what sort of rule he is referring to, Mill makes it clear that he means a rule that should generally be observed. By his main principle Mill has already given a general answer as to what should be done. In accordance with it he holds that a certain rule is one that should generally be observed if and only if its general observance would cause more happiness than would any alternative to its general observance.[3]

[2] *A System of Logic*, 8th ed. (London: Longmans, Green, Reader, and Dyer, 1872), II, 552–4 (VI, xii, 6).

[3] "[H]appiness is the sole end of human action, and the promotion of it the test by which to judge of all human conduct; from whence it necessarily follows that it must be the criterion of morality, since a part is included in the whole." Morality consists of "the rules . . . by the observance of which . . . [happiness] might be, to the greatest extent possible, secured. . . ." (*Utilitarianism*, 237, 214.)

Mill thus maintains that it would be wrong to do a certain action only if it would be at variance with such a rule.[4]

Some prolixity is required to clarify what Mill understands by an action that would cause more happiness than any alternative to it.[5] The only respect in which an action is thereby compared to its alternatives is its consequences, and the only consequences by which it is compared are those consisting of happiness and unhappiness. Mill writes, "By happiness is intended pleasure, and the absence of pain; by unhappiness, pain, and the privation of pleasure" (210). He states: "Of . . . philosophers who have taught that happiness is the end of life . . . [the] happiness which they meant was not a life of rapture; but moments of such, in an existence made up of few and transitory pains, many and various pleasures. . ." (215). Hence the only consequences of an action that are relevant are pleasures and pains. All the pleasures and pains among the consequences of an action are relevant, whether remote or near, whether experienced by humans or by other sentient creatures.[6]

If Mill held that the only relevant difference among pleasures and pains was whether one was greater than another, there would be only six possibilities for the total effects of an action. They would contain (1) an excess of pleasure over pain, (2) an excess of pain over pleasure, (3) an excess of neither, (4) pleasure and no pain, (5) pain and no pleasure, (6) neither pleasure nor pain. Mill argues, however, that pleasures and pains differ in a further respect which is relevant—some are more desirable than others.[7] Accordingly, eight possibilities may be distinguished with regard to the total effects of an action:

(1) They contain some pleasures and no pains.

(2) They contain both pleasures and pains, and regardless of whether there is an excess of pleasure over pain, the pleasures are on the whole more desirable than the pains are undesirable.

(3) They contain both pleasures and pains; neither the pleasures nor pains are of sorts such that the pleasures on the whole are more desirable than the pains are undesirable or such that the pains on the whole are more undesirable than the pleasures are desirable; but there is an excess of pleasure over pain.

(4) They contain some pains and no pleasures.

(5) They contain both pleasures and pains, and regardless of whether

[4]"[A]ctions are right in proportion as they tend to promote happiness, wrong as they tend to produce the reverse of happiness" (*ibid.*, 210).

[5]Cf. G. E. Moore, *Ethics* (London: Oxford University Press, 1911), Chapter 1.

[6]See *Utilitarianism*, 214; "Sedgwick," 69.

[7]"According to the Greatest Happiness Principle . . . the ultimate end . . . is an existence exempt as far as possible from pain, and as rich as possible in enjoyments, both in point of quantity and quality . . ." (*Utilitarianism*, 214).

there is an excess of pain over pleasure, the pains are on the whole more undesirable than the pleasures are desirable.

(6) They contain both pleasures and pains; neither the pleasures nor pains are of sorts such that the pleasures on the whole are more desirable than the pains are undesirable or such that the pains on the whole are more undesirable than the pleasures are desirable; but there is an excess of pain over pleasure.

(7) They contain no pleasures or pains.

(8) They contain both pleasures and pains, and regardless of whether there is an excess of pleasure over pain, of pain over pleasure, or an excess of neither, the pleasures and pains they contain are of sorts such that the pleasures on the whole are not more desirable than the pains are undesirable and such that the pains on the whole are not more undesirable than the pleasures are desirable.

If (1) or (2) or (3) holds of a certain action, Mill would classify it as one that would cause an excess of happiness over unhappiness. If (4) or (5) or (6) holds, he would classify it as one that would cause an excess of unhappiness over happiness. If one of the other alternatives holds, he would classify an action as one that would cause an excess of neither.

Having distinguished the possibilities for any action, taken by itself, we may notice how any two actions taken at random may stand to one another in these respects. Since there are three possibilities for each, there are nine possible combinations. Call one action A and the other B. (1) Both A and B would cause an excess of happiness. (2) A would cause an excess of happiness but B would cause an excess of neither. (3) A would cause an excess of happiness but B would cause an excess of unhappiness. (4) A would cause an excess of neither but B would cause an excess of happiness. (5) Both would cause an excess of neither. (6) A would cause an excess of neither but B would cause an excess of unhappiness. (7) A would cause an excess of unhappiness but B would cause an excess of happiness. (8) A would cause an excess of unhappiness but B would cause an excess of neither. (9) Both would cause an excess of unhappiness. Within (9) three possibilities are to be distinguished: (9.1) B would cause a greater excess of unhappiness. (9.2) Neither would cause a greater excess of unhappiness. (9.3) A would cause a greater excess of unhappiness. Also, within (1), that is, where both A and B would cause an excess of happiness, three possibilities are to be distinguished: (1.1) A would cause a greater excess of happiness. (1.2) Neither would cause a greater excess of happiness. (1.3) B would cause a greater excess of happiness. There are thus thirteen ways in which any two actions may stand to one another. These thirteen ways may be grouped into three. If (1.1), (2), (3), (6) or (9.1) obtains, Mill would say that A would cause more happiness than B or that B would cause less than A. If (1.3), (4), (7), (8) or (9.3) obtains, he would say that B would cause more happiness than A or that A would cause less than B. If any of the three remaining combinations obtains, he would say that either would cause as much happiness as the other.

We have noticed three ways in which Mill would hold that any two actions taken at random could stand to one another. If any set of two or more actions is considered, we may notice three ways in which one of the actions of the set might stand to the others: (1) it would cause more happiness than any of the others, (2) it would cause less happiness than some of the others, (3) it would cause as much happiness as any of the others. The only sort of set of two or more actions to which Mill directs attention is that made up of a certain action and of the alternatives to it. This set includes whatever an agent would succeed in doing upon a given occasion if he tried hard enough, and excludes whatever he would not succeed in doing no matter how hard he tried. Accordingly, Mill would distinguish three ways in which an action may stand to the alternatives to it: (1) it would cause more happiness than any alternative, (2) it would cause less happiness than some alternative, (3) it would cause as much happiness as any alternative.

So far attention has been paid to one set of features of which Mill's main principle makes mention, apart from their role in it. There is a second set of features of actions which this principle mentions—whether it is one that should be done or one that should not. What Mill's main principle asserts is a relation between features of the first set and features of the second. It asserts that something should be done if and only if it would cause more happiness than any alternative; that something should not be done if and only if it would cause less happiness than some alternative; and that a certain action is not one that should not be done if and only if it would cause as much happiness as any alternative.

By his main principle Mill thus declares that a certain feature is a universal and peculiar feature of actions that should be done, and that a certain other feature is a universal and peculiar feature of actions that should not be done. It implies that whenever anyone judges that a certain action should be done, this is a condition that must be fulfilled for the judgment to be true. This is the case whether the judgment is about a past or future action, an actual or possible action, something done by oneself or another, or something done by an individual, a nation, or any group. Mill's principle does not, however, imply that the only way by which anyone can know whether a certain action should be done is by seeking to make out whether it would cause more happiness than any alternative. Although Mill speaks of it as the "sole criterion," his principle is quite compatible with using many other tests. It is compatible with using now one test and now another. Nor does Mill's principle imply that it affords the only universal test by which to judge what should be done. All that it does imply is that whatever other test be used, it must yield results compatible with this principle. Mill's principle does not supply the only test; it only lays down a condition to which any test must comply.

Although Mill's principle sets forth a universal and peculiar feature of actions that should be done, there is nothing about it which implies that this is the only universal and peculiar feature of such actions. It would be compatible with it to maintain, for instance, that something should be done if and only if it is commanded by God. Mill's principle provides nothing that rules this out. Indeed, it is conceivable that there are ten thousand other universal and peculiar features of actions that should be done. One consequence which Mill draws from his principle is that it would be wrong to do a certain action only if it would violate a rule the general observance of which would cause more happiness. Many would agree with Mill in this. They would agree that whenever anyone does what is wrong, he is violating a rule the general observance of which would in fact cause more happiness. But they would not hold that this is the reason it would be wrong to do it. They would hold that the reason it is wrong to do any action is that it violates God's law. They would urge that God wants his creatures to be happy and that because of this whoever disobeys God's laws violates a law the general observance of which would cause more happiness. They would agree with Mill that by doing what is wrong someone violates a rule the general observance of which would cause more happiness. But they would say that it is not because of this that someone is doing wrong; it is rather because he breaks a rule laid down by God.

There is nothing in this view incompatible with what we have so far seen of Mill's main principle. When we notice how Mill deals with such a view, we find that he takes a further step. He holds not merely that someone does what is wrong only if he breaks a rule the general observance of which would cause more happiness, but also that what he does is wrong because it violates such a rule. Mill maintains not merely that those rules which should generally be observed would in fact cause more happiness, but also that it is because their general observance would cause more happiness that they should be observed. He does not thereby deny that by violating rules that should generally be observed, someone is disobeying God's will. But he holds that the reason why a rule should be generally observed is not because it is prescribed by God but because its observance would cause more happiness.[8]

There is a further implication differentiating Mill from the view we have been considering. Those who maintain that the reason why a certain action is wrong is that it violates a rule laid down by God are committed to holding that if God should will something other than the happiness of his creatures, then an action would be wrong even though it would not violate a rule whose

[8]See "Sedgwick," 53; "Blakey," 27; *Utilitarianism*, 222.

general observance would cause more happiness. Anyone who holds that an action is wrong because it violates a rule laid down by God is committed to holding that if there is no god or if he lays down no rules for men, then there is nothing which it would be wrong to do or wrong not to do. Mill not only holds that an action is wrong if it violates a rule the general observance of which would cause more happiness, he also contends that it is because it violates such a rule that an action is wrong. He thereby implies that even if God should will something other than the happiness of his creatures, or even if there is no god, an action would be wrong if it were to violate a rule the general observance of which would cause more happiness.[9] In the first step, Mill asserts that a certain feature is a universal and peculiar feature of actions that should be done. In the second step, he states that it is because they have this feature that actions should be done.

There is nothing incompatible between Mill's principle and the view that something should be done if and only if it would bring about a greater realization of men's capacities than would any alternative. But his principle is incompatible with the view that something should be done because it would have this result. Similarly, Mill's principle is not incompatible with the view that something should be done if and only if it would bring about a greater fulfilment of human wants than would any alternative. But it is incompatible with the view that something should be done because it would have this result. One alternative to Mill's principle is the view that something should be done because it would maximize human happiness. Another alternative to it is that something should be done because it would maximize the agent's happiness. The former is the humanistic variant to Mill's principle; the latter the egoistic variant to it. In contrast to both, Mill's principle is the universalistic variant. Many other alternatives to Mill's principle are conceivable. One view already noted is that which maintains that something should be done because it would maximize fulfilment of human wants. The universalistic variant to this view is that something should be done because it would maximize fulfilment of wants generally. The egoistic variant is that something should be done because it would maximize fulfilment of the agent's wants. The theistic variant to this is that something should be done because it would maximize fulfilment of God's wants. Still another alternative is the view that something should be done because it would maximize the fulfilment of human capacities. Two further conceivable views are the egoistic and universalistic variants of this.

All such views differ from Mill's principle in but one respect. They all agree that there is some feature which not only holds of every action that should be done and only of such, but which also constitutes the reason why it should be done. They all agree that this feature consists in a respect in

[9]See "The Utility of Religion," 417.

which an action compares with its alternatives. They are also all agreed that this feature consists in how an action's consequences would compare with those of its alternatives. These several views differ from each other and from Mill's principle only in the sorts of consequences which they specify and the sorts of beings to whom they accrue.

The chief support that Mill offers for his main principle, to vindicate it against such other views, is that happiness is the only thing desirable for its own sake. From this contention it does indeed follow that an action would have more desirable consequences than any alternative if and only if it would cause more happiness. But this contention does not by itself support his main principle. It does so only if a further premise is added, namely, that something should be done if and only if it would have more desirable consequences than any alternative. Mill does not explicitly avow this further premise. Yet, since he holds that the contention which he offers in support of his main principle does in fact support it, he may be presumed to take this premise for granted as not requiring any attention or defence. It then looks as if Mill contends that something should be done because it would cause more happiness, but that it is not only because of this that it should be done; that the reason in turn why what would cause more happiness should be done is that happiness is the only thing desirable for its own sake.

One can at most speculate as to how Mill would meet this challenge. He might retort that the fact that an action would have more desirable consequences than any alternative could not be the ultimate reason why it should be done, since the ultimate reason why something should be done must consist in some other fact about it than the fact that it should be done, but in saying that an action would have more desirable consequences than any alternative, nothing more nor less is then said than that it should be done. Although it is not transparently evident that these are but two ways of saying the same thing, it is far from implausible to urge that by analysis they amount to the same. Two steps are involved in the analysis: (1) something should be done if and only if it would on the whole be more desirable for it to be done than any alternative; (2) it would on the whole be more desirable for something to be done than any alternative to it if and only if what would come of its being done would be more desirable than what would come of any alternative to it. If each of these is analytically true, nothing further is required.

In behalf of the first step, the following may be urged. Whenever it is said that something should be done it is implied that it is capable of being done. It is also implied that it is capable of not being done, that is, that some alternatives are capable of being done in its stead. When it is said that something should be done, it is not only implied that it is one of a number of alternatives; it is also implied that it stands in a certain relation to the others. When it is said that something should be done, it is not implied that it would be more desirable for some alternative to it to be done; nor is it implied that it would be as desirable for some alternative to be done in its stead. What is rather implied is the denial of both these implications. When it is said that something should be done, it is thus implied that it would on the whole be more desirable for it rather than any alternative to be done.[10] In behalf of the second step the following may be urged. It cannot be denied that an action may have consequences, and that whether it would be desirable for it to be done is affected by what would come of its being done. Nor can it be denied that the desirability of some alternative being done is affected by the desirability of what would come of it. It is then more desirable on the whole that one alternative rather than another be done if and only if what would come of the first would be more desirable than what would come of the other. Hence it would on the whole be more desirable for something to be done rather than any alternative if and only if what would come of it would be more desirable than what would come of any alternative.

The chief premise that Mill offers in support of his main principle is that happiness is the only thing desirable for its own sake. This premise affords support only in conjunction with the added premise, that something should be done if and only if it would have more desirable consequences than any alternative. Consequently, Mill's contention that happiness is the only thing desirable for its own sake cannot support his main principle against any sort of ethical theory which rejects the second premise. Against any such theory he seeks to vindicate his main principle by clearing up the relation of the conception of a wrong action and of an action which there is an obligation not to do to that of an action that should not be done.[11] On the other hand, any sort of ethical theory that rejects Mill's main principle but which holds that whether something should be done turns on how its consequences would compare with those of any alternative to it need not be incompatible with the second premise. To vindicate his main principle against any theory of that sort, it is sufficient for Mill to make good his contention that happiness is the only thing desirable for its own sake.[12]

Before we go on to examine how Mill seeks to make good this contention, certain implications of it may be noted. It implies that if A are the consequences of one action, X, and B the consequences of another action, Y, A would be more desirable for their own sake than B if and only if they would contain more happiness. It implies that if A should be the consequences of some other action than X, they would still be more desirable for

[10] Mill comes closest to this when he writes: "The hygienic and medical arts assume, the one that the preservation of health, the other that the cure of disease, are fitting and desirable ends. These . . . propositions . . . do not assert that anything is, but enjoin or recommend that something should be. They are . . . expressed by the words *ought* or *should be*. . . ." (*Logic*, II, 552–3; VI, xii, 6.)

[11] See §§ IV and V, xcv–cxiii below.

[12] See §§ II and III, lxxiii–xcv below.

their own sake than B. It thus implies that whether the consequences of an action are more desirable for their own sake than those of another does not depend on what action they are the consequences of. Mill's contention also implies that if A are the consequences of a natural occurrence and B the consequences of another natural occurrence, A would still be more desirable for their own sake than B. This thus means that whether one set of consequences is more desirable for its own sake than another does not depend on what caused them. It does not depend on A or B being a set of consequences. Mill's contention that happiness is the only thing desirable for its own sake has therefore a wider scope than his main principle. It implies that any state of affairs is more desirable for its own sake than another if and only if it contains more happiness than the other.

When Mill is described as speaking of one state of affairs as "containing more happiness" than another, it must be borne in mind that this expression is used in the same sense as that in which he understands the consequences of one action as related to those of another when he regards one action as "causing more happiness" than the other. Accordingly, Mill's contention that happiness is the only thing desirable for its own sake may be stated more fully as signifying that something is desirable for its own sake if and only if it is a state of affairs of one of three sorts: (1) a state containing some pleasure and no pain; (2) a state containing both pleasure and pain, but in which, whether or not there is an excess of pleasure over pain, the pleasures on the whole are more desirable than the pains are undesirable; (3) a state containing both pleasure and pain, and in which, although neither the pleasures nor pains are of sorts such that the pleasures on the whole are more desirable than the pains are undesirable or such that the pains on the whole are more undesirable than the pleasures are desirable, there is an excess of pleasure over pain. Mill likewise holds that something is undesirable for its own sake if and only if it is a state of affairs the opposite of one of these three.

Mill's contention implies that no inanimate thing or state of affairs made up only of inanimate things is desirable or undesirable for its own sake. It implies that no human being or human disposition is desirable or undesirable for its own sake. According to it, the only sort of matter that is desirable or undesirable for its own sake is a state of affairs comprising sentient beings. It implies that neither justice nor liberty nor peace is desirable for its own sake. It implies, moreover, that there is nothing desirable for its own sake save where there is life; and that there is nothing undesirable for its own sake save where there is life. Although Mill's contention affirms a certain universal and peculiar feature of whatever is desirable for its own sake, it does not also state any such feature of whatever is desirable. While it implies that an inanimate thing, a human being, or justice or liberty or peace or life is

The alterations caused by time are easily accounted for: most of them are simple changes of tense, or of adjectives of time (I.159^{p-p} reads "forty years"; in 1852 and 1857 it read "thirty years"; in MS, 1848, and 1849, "sixteen years"). Slightly different are those like that at I.148^{k-k}, where "as until lately in Ireland" read "as hitherto in Ireland" in 1857, and "as in Ireland" in MS, 1848, 1849, and 1852. Such changes as the inclusion of the note to I.37 in 1849, quoting a review of the 1st edition, are not infrequent, and there are a few like that at I.65^{b-b}, where in 1862 the words "(now called Western Australia)" were added after "the Swan River settlement".

The changes which are most characteristic of Mill are those which I have described as alterations which qualify, emphasize, or give technical clarity. Professional interest and personal taste will determine one's attitude towards these, and they spread (whatever one's interests and tastes) from the territory of stylistics to that of factual interpretation. An extreme example of Mill's worry over apparently small matters is found in his revisions of the following sentence (I.42^{c-c}): "The stupidest hodman, who repeats from day to day the mechanical act of climbing a ladder, performs a function partly intellectual; so much so, indeed, that the most intelligent dog or elephant could not, probably, be taught to do it." In the MS, the sentence ends, "could not be taught to do it"; in 1848 and 1849, "probably could not be taught to do it"; in 1852 and 1857, "could not, perhaps, be taught to do it"; the final reading appeared in 1862. More typical is the introduction in 1852 of the qualifying "in some degree" at I.52^{o-o}, or the alteration on the next page, $^{g-g}$ and $^{h-h}$, of "no labour really tends to the enrichment of society, which . . ." to "no labour tends to the permanent enrichment of society, which . . ." in 1865. Small changes presumably in the interest of technical clarity may be illustrated by the substitution in 1857 of "productive reinvestment" for "productive employment" at I.57^{g-g}. An alteration in 1865 which would interest few (and which may even be accidental), but which I would argue reveals Mill's adherence to part of his father's training, is the reversing, in a persuasive context, of "stronger and clearer" to read "clearer and stronger" (I.59^{a-a}). Another change, and a typical one, appears to me indicative of his movement away from his father's modes of thought: at I.79^{e-e}, the final reading, "This theorem, that to purchase produce is not to employ labour . . . ", replaced in 1852 the original, "This truth, that purchasing produce is not employing labour . . . ." The following case is, I suppose, a factual correction, but of a very minor kind: at I.101^{b-b}, when Mill is listing agricultural products found as one moves to the south and east in Europe, the final reading of part of the list, "silk, figs, olives", appeared only in 1871, as a correction of "figs, olives, silk". Another kind of change could be the result of altered opinion or simply of a desire for precision: these are typified at I.109^{g-g} where in the sentence, "As soon as any idea of equality enters the mind of an uneducated English working man, his head is turned by it", the reading until 1865 was "ordinary English working man".[25]

The most important changes, those which I have described as alterations in opinion or fact, including major amplifications and corrections of information, occur mainly in the chapters mentioned by Mill in his prefaces, and should be studied in close detail. But the grossest changes can be briefly described. In II, i, the first major change occurs in §2 ("Statement of the Question") in the 2nd edition. The 1st edition here contained a short account of St. Simonism, which was deleted in the 2nd, and replaced by a longer and more favourable account of all kinds of socialism; this account remained throughout all editions (with minor changes). The long preceding sentence which argued that attacks on property will necessarily increase until laws of property are made just, was cut down in the 3rd edition to a clause of no special weight. In §3 ("Examination of Communism") only a few sentences from the 1st and 2nd editions correspond to those in later versions; parts of the section are roughly equivalent but in different order, and some parts of §6 in the edition of 1849 are here incorporated in later editions. The general tone in 1852 is more favourable to socialism, but the change is less dramatic than might be thought. In both early and late versions the emphasis is on liberty. An interesting change in 1849 is the deletion of one long and one short passage emphasizing the comparative advantages of a competitive economy. In 1852 the account of Fourierism which was added in 1849 as §5 was combined with the account of St. Simonism in §4, and a long introductory paragraph was added to point out more clearly the differences between St. Simonism and Fourierism on the one hand, and strict and theoretical Communism on the other. Also in 1852 Mill deleted his recommendation of St. Simonism as a probable stimulant to social diversity. Finally, the concluding paragraph of §4 (the last section) in 1852 replaced the end of §5 in the version of 1849, and all of §6 in the versions of 1848 and 1849.

In II, x, the eight sections of 1848 and 1849 were reduced in 1852 to three, and in 1862 to two. In 1852, §1 is a rewriting of §§1–3 in the earlier versions; in 1862, §1 is a further rewriting of §§1–7 in the 1848 and 1849 versions (§§1–2 of 1852 and 1857); the final §2 (which was further rewritten in 1865) replaces §8 of 1848 and 1849 (§3 of 1852

[25]That this was less than a change of opinion is probable, for in 1852 the passage containing this sentence replaced the concluding part of a quotation from Escher, in which a contrary opinion is affirmed of the "educated English workmen."

and 1857). This final section contained in its early versions a long footnote which was incorporated in II, vii from 1862 on.

Book III contains many alterations in sections, mostly additions to the early text. In III, xii, for example, §7 ("Are bank notes money?") was added in 1857. In III, xviii, §6 ("The preceding theory not complete"), §7 ("International values depend not solely on the quantities demanded, but also on the means of production available in each country for the supply of foreign markets"), and §8 ("The practical result little affected by this additional element") were added in 1852. In III, xxiii, most of §4 ("The rate of interest, how far, and in what sense connected with the value of money") was rewritten in 1865; it was formerly entitled: "The rate of interest not really connected with the value of money, but often confounded with it." The other chapter in Book III to which Mill calls attention, xxiv, was not altered in its sections, the rewriting being mostly of paragraphs in §§3, 4, and 6 (most of which took place in 1857, as Mill indicates, but §3 was as much altered again in 1865).

Finally, in Book IV, Chapter vii, the main changes are in the final sections: §5 ("Examples of the association of labourers with capitalists"), §6 ("Examples of the association of labourers among themselves"), and §7 ("Competition not pernicious, but useful and indispensable"); these replaced in 1852 §5 ("Examples of the association of the labourers in the profits of industrial undertakings") and §6 ("Probable future developement of this principle").

Other gross changes, involving new or greatly altered sections, but not mentioned by Mill in his prefaces, are in II, vi (§6 added in 1849), II, xv (§5 added in 1857), and III, xiii (§4 added in 1849 and deleted in 1862).

A few remarks should be made about changes in spelling and punctuation. The changes in spelling seem to indicate indecision rather than careless proofreading. Such changes as "recognise" (7th edition) for "recognize" occur in the 3rd, 5th, and 6th editions, the earlier form remaining in isolated places until these editions. The earlier "shews," "shewed," etc., are altered in the 2nd, 3rd, 4th, and 5th editions. And "artisan(s)" is replaced by "artizan(s)" sixteen times, with the reverse change occurring once in the 2nd edition. The only other frequent change is the substitution of initial "e" for initial "i" in such words as "enclosure" and "encumbrance," and the reverse change in such words as "inquiry" and "insure" (fifty-five words in all are altered). There is also (especially in the later editions) an increase in initial capitalization and in hyphenation. A common change, especially in the 6th edition, is from the simple adjectival or singular possessive forms to the plural possessive in such words as "days.' "

Concerning punctuation little need be said, and again little can be inferred, because the printers may be responsible for most of the changes. There is an increase in the number of commas (especially in the 2nd edition) until the 5th, and a decrease in the last two editions (which were published, it will be recalled, by Longmans rather than Parker). There is a tendency throughout to substitute semi-colons for colons and (less frequently) for commas. After the first two editions, the one showing most revision is the 5th; and the 7th, apart from a few comma changes, is almost free from alteration.

About one hundred sources are quoted by Mill, some of them at considerable length. The notes to these quotations are typical of nineteenth-century practice, in being often too slender for accurate identification, and not infrequently wrong in page reference. The quotations themselves are fairly accurate by nineteenth-century standards; that is, there is considerable variation in punctuation and paragraphing, occasional words are wrongly transcribed, passages are sometimes summarized or rearranged within quotation marks, and words and sentences and even paragraphs are omitted without indication. (See Appendix I below.) A few of the word errors show once more the printers' difficulty in reading Mill's hand; in other cases the printer has simply made an error not justified by such difficulty; in others the error is Mill's.[26] Summary and rearrangement within quotation marks, without indication, which are not common, are both found in one passage, I.168.13–4, where the interpolation "(who seems . . . all classes,)" is a summary of the note which occurs a page further on in the original (John Rae, *Statement of Some New Principles . . . of Political Economy*).

Omission of words, sentences, and notes is quite common, and longer omissions are not rare. For example, at I.382.19–20, after "employment," he omits two of Adam Smith's paragraphs, and at II.780.n2–3, he omits one of Cherbuliez's. These omissions suggest again carelessness and also a desire for brevity, rather than suppression or distortion.[27] Some but by no means all of the longer omissions actually are indicated in the MS by two or more dots which the printer ignored (e.g., I.129^{i}, where six sentences are omitted). But occasionally an omission, or the point at which a quotation ends, suggests that bias is involved. For example, his

[26]Examples of the first kind: I.263.19, "heavy" should read "hung"; I.264^{f-f}, "when" should read "where"—in both cases, in my opinion, the MS gives the correct reading, but certainly in the second case the other is possible. An example of the second kind: I.263^{b-b}, "among" should read "amongst". An example of the third kind: I.257.6, "two, or three" is an incorrect transcription of "two and four".

[27]In quoting from his own *Essays on Some Unsettled Questions of Political Economy*, he—or the printer, as the MS is not known—three times, at II.633.n14, II.634.n6, and II.851.15, omits a sentence; in each case the omitted sentence ends with the same word as the previous sentence, an easily explained confusion.

attitude towards religion is surely evident when, in quoting (II.770) from Samuel Laing, Mill ends the praise of the Cornish miners with the word "miners", whereas the original, after a semi-colon and quotation marks, continues:

and, finally, they are, as a class, "a religious people, leading habitually excellent and religious lives, and giving conclusive evidence of the real influence of the great doctrines of revelation on their hearts, by their equanimity under suffering and privation, and in calmness and resignation when death is known to be inevitable." This is, by many degrees, the brightest picture we have ever met with of the condition of any considerable portion of the labouring class in England at the present day.

To this, Laing appends a note (which, of course, is also omitted by Mill), beginning: "The reasons assigned for the high moral standard among a large proportion of the Cornish Miners are 'the ministration of the Church of England, exercised by an able and excellent body of clergy, and the persevering zeal of the Wesleyan methodists. . . .' "[28]

The omission of one long note by Mill is as indicative of his tastes (and his sense of relevance) as the note is of its author's: in quoting the passage from de Quincey's *Logic of Political Economy* about musical snuff-boxes (II.463), Mill omits a long note concerning de Quincey's personal acquaintance with snuff-boxes and their owners.[29]

One final matter merits mention: the text of the People's edition, which has some peculiarities.[30] Its Preface, after the paragraphs common to all the prefaces, reads:

The present edition is an exact transcript from the sixth, except that all extracts and most phrases in foreign languages have been translated into English, and a very small number of quotations, or parts of quotations, which appeared superfluous, have been struck out. A reprint of an old controversy with the "Quarterly Review" on the condition of landed property in France, which had been subjoined as an Appendix, has been dispensed with.

As indicated in the discussion of Ashley's edition, this description is partly accurate: the People's edition does translate passages from foreign languages (usually including book titles), and omits the Appendix to Volume I. A few, but only a few, quotations or parts of quotations are deleted (e.g., I.123n—People's, 76n—where only the identification of the

[28]In these quotations I omit two referential footnotes. Laing is quoting from the *Appendix to the Report of the Children's Employment Commission in Mines and Collieries.*

[29]It might also be noted that occasionally in the Library editions Mill translates from the French without indication (in one of these cases, I.285n, the MS note says "Translated from the").

[30]The following remarks are based on partial comparison, not on complete collation.

source remains). Many titles are italicized, as they are not in the Library editions, and the English equivalents of French measures are usually given in square brackets following the French (Ashley adopts this practice). The foreign phrases and tags in the text are occasionally translated, but Mill is erratic.[31] The main point of interest, however, is that—admitting the exceptions—the description of the text as "an exact transcript from the sixth" edition is not accurate. A paragraph added (I.9^{w-w}) in 1865 is, as Miss Ellis notes, interchanged with the following one (People's, 5–6), and in three of the four other places where the paragraphing differs from that in the 6th edition, the relevant passage was added in or rewritten for the 6th edition. In two other cases, the paragraphing of Mill's translations in the People's edition differs from that of his rendering of the original in the Library editions. These differences suggest that others exist, and a check of those places in Book I where the 5th and 6th editions differ shows that the People's edition follows the 5th rather than the 6th in fourteen of eighty-four cases.[32] The destruction of Longmans' records during the London Blitz makes explanation uncertain, but it is clear at least that the People's edition is properly seen as intermediate between the 5th and 6th rather than as an altered version of the 6th. Certainly the People's and the 6th editions cannot have used the same proof.

It can safely be concluded, from all the evidence above, that second versions were second nature to Mill. He could not, of course, remember the vast number of minor changes which he made as successive editions passed through his hands. New knowledge and new opponents led to important changes (though not so many as in his *Logic*), as did a few second and third thoughts; and these will provide the main interest in the collated text. But the rewriting as a whole should be seen as rhetorical—and that, of course, not in a pejorative sense. Isolation of analytical, descriptive, and normative approaches in social science is possible, and the twentieth century has seen a plethora of works in which persuasion towards a 'better' point of view is expressly excluded, although often the exclusion

[31]For example, "*cæteris paribus*" is rendered at I.148.31 as "other things being the same" (People's, 93), and at II.807.6 as "on the average" (People's, 484), but elsewhere is not translated. Similarly, "*inter vivos*" (II.811.26) rendered as "during life" (People's, 487), is not translated at II.895.15 (People's, 541).

[32]Two cases might be mentioned: at I.49^{c-c}, the reading is, "as most conducive to the ends of classification; and I am still of that opinion." In 1862 the reading was, "as the most conducive to the ends of classification, though not strictly conformable to the customs of language." The People's edition follows the 5th in retaining "the" after "as", but follows the 6th in the clause following "classification". And at I.195.4, the People's edition follows the 6th in rejecting one sentence and its footnote (a reference to another part of the *Principles*), but incorporates the footnote of the 6th in its text.

is specious or founded on a naive attitude towards structural analysis and statistics. But Mill in his Preface states his determination to go beyond the "theory of the subject" and "abstract speculation" in order to challenge and indeed surpass Adam Smith on his own grounds, by associating the applications of the theory with the principles. And his reference to the "improved ideas of the present age" and "the best social ideas of the present time" surely suggests that he hopes his book will be 'better' than Adam Smith's not simply in an economic way. In fact, his determination to subordinate such special sciences as economics to sociology, and further to subordinate sociology to ethics, makes it impossible for him to keep theoretical, actual, and ideal models separate, and while he aims at honesty (a more valid goal than objectivity) in his account of economic phenomena, he is deeply concerned with the furthering of social justice. His attempt to be honest prevents him, for the most part, from ignoring facts and tendencies which he dislikes, but not from presenting those which he likes in the most persuasive form.

His dedication of the *Principles* to Harriet Taylor (quoted in full in Appendix G below) again indicates, both in tone and implication, his purpose. He praises her for her ability "to originate" and "to appreciate speculations on social improvement," and says the *Principles* is an "attempt to explain and diffuse ideas many of which were first learned from herself. . . ." The implications here[33] are made explicit in the Preface, where Mill states that his intention has been to write a "practical" and "popular" work, without sacrificing "strict scientific reasoning." The *Principles of Political Economy* is not simply a textbook; it is also a measured polemic. As such, it was open to endless revision, always in the direction of clarity and effective persuasion, and also in response to the changing climate of opinion. The successive revisions show this, as they show in their relative density in certain parts of the work just what Mill felt most deeply about. The cumulative effects of nearly 3500 changes over a period of twenty-four years cannot be precisely assessed, but the *Principles* was, in its final form, undeniably a more satisfactory work. He would not, and I cannot, consider that the revisions were wasted effort.

II. THE PRESENT TEXT

THERE WILL ALWAYS BE arguments about the "best" text of any work, centring on two main issues: which text represents the author at his best; and which most accurately reproduces what the author wrote. When a book has gone through as many authorial revisions as the *Principles* has, a consensus of opinion on the first of these issues is hard to achieve. For the

[33]Cf. Dean Bladen's argument in the first two sections of his Introduction above.

reasons stated above and below, and because Mill was not senile when the 7th edition was prepared, I believe it shows him at his best.

With the intention of producing texts which most closely approximate accuracy, literary scholars now, following the lead of Sir Walter Greg and Professor Fredson Bowers, commonly use as a basic text the manuscript or (if it is not known, or in conjunction with it) the earliest edition known to have been supervised by the author. The virtues of this approach need not be presented here, but it should be made clear why it has not been adopted. The method was devised to deal with Elizabethan and other early texts in which, because of printing-house and publishing practices, there is demonstrable evidence of corruption. Seldom did an author see his work through the press for edition after edition, and reprinting almost always took the text further away from the author's intention.

A different approach is valid for nineteenth-century works such as the *Principles*. Each edition was revised by Mill himself, who read and altered the proofs carefully; there is no question of substantial corruption in the editions published during his lifetime. The manuscript and 1st edition have validity primarily as a starting point, as an indication of the state of economic thought in 1848, and of Mill's knowledge of, and attitude towards, economic phenomena and theory at that time. There can surely be few who believe in plenary economic inspiration. Each successive edition reveals more information, as well as changed attitudes, and therefore, considered primarily as a textbook of economics, the 7th edition best represents Mill's considered judgment, and is, because of the constant re-readings, more reliable than any previous edition. For him, and for the student of political economy from 1871 to the present, this is the best text, and it has been adopted in this edition.

The *Principles,* however, must now appear in a light different from that of the years immediately following its publication. Both in evidence and analysis, the science of economics has advanced beyond Mill, and its primacy as a textbook cannot be asserted, although, as Dean Bladen argues in his Introduction above, its value purely as an economic text has been under-exploited.

Its importance in other areas, however, has steadily increased. It served as an economic text to several generations of policy framers and law makers, even into the twentieth century, and its influence on them must be recognized. If one is to study the effect of political and economic thought on events, the changes in such thought are of obvious importance. Each edition of the *Principles* takes on separate value then, as do the changes from edition to edition. Similarly, the way in which events alter theory is shown by a comparison of the various editions. One might examine, for example, the changes in Mill's expressed opinions about socialism after the French Revolution of 1848, or the effect of Irish experience on his views concerning land tenure. Again, any study in the history of economic and social ideas can benefit from a close study of the changing attitudes revealed by a comparison of the various editions. Here one might look at Mill's remarks on slavery in the years before and during the American Civil War. And most obviously, the development of Mill's own thought is demonstrated by such a comparison. For example, his increased attention to co-operative experiments is evident in the revisions of IV, vii.

We have, therefore, while accepting the 7th edition as the best in both senses, incorporated the textual changes found in a complete collation of the seven Library editions of the *Principles*. Of all editorial practices, the recording of variants is most obviously a matter of diminishing returns. Furthermore, the returns, defying all quantification, do not accrue to one person or group, and are certainly not monetary. There is no clear distinction between the significant and the insignificant, between stylistic orchestration and mere fiddling. Given the exigencies of printing and the frailty of editors, which make it impossible to record all changes, and the justifiable impatience of readers who cannot follow the text through jungles of textual apparatus, some compromise is necessary. The one adopted for this edition is intended to meet the needs of all potential readers, and does not represent a licentious acceptance of particular views (including those of the editors).

In simple statement, the following pages contain all substantive variants amongst the various editions. "Substantive" here means all changes of text except spelling, capitalization, hyphenation, punctuation, demonstrable typographical errors, such necessary alterations as changed footnote references to the *Principles* itself, and such printing-house concerns as type size, etc. (There are two exceptions—to prove the rule—Mill's frequent changes between "though" and "although" and between "on" and "upon" are not recorded.)

A glance at any of the heavily revised pages in this edition will reveal the difficulties involved in providing variant readings without at the same time making the text difficult if not impossible to follow. The method adopted, after considerable trial, has these objectives: a text as little interrupted by editorial apparatus as possible; variant readings which allow reconstruction of the earlier texts without separate instructions for each variant; the minimum number of levels of text on each page consistent with accuracy and with the above objectives. The method is, I believe, harder to describe than to apply, and I beg the reader's indulgence in the following account.

On a typical page, there will be three levels of text: the text of the 7th edition; in slightly smaller type, Mill's own notes; in smaller type again, notes containing the variant readings. In the text itself, the usual indicators (*, †, etc.) call attention to Mill's notes, while small italic superscript letters, in alphabetical sequence (beginning anew in each section) call attention to variant readings. These variants are of three kinds: addition of a word or words, substitution of a word or words, deletion of a word or words. Examples to illustrate these three kinds will be drawn from the "Preliminary Remarks."

Addition of a word or words: see I.7^{p-p}. In the text, the word "power" appears as "^{p}power^{p}"; the variant note reads "$^{p-p}$+65, 71". Here the plus sign indicates that the word "power" was added; the following numbers (65, 71) indicate the editions in which it appears. The editions are always indicated by the last two numbers of the year of publication, as follows: 48 = 1848 (1st edition), 49 = 1849 (2nd edition), 52 = 1852 (3rd edition), 57 = 1857 (4th edition), 62 = 1862 (5th edition), 65 = 1865 (6th edition), 71 = 1871 (7th edition). The manuscript is indicated by MS. (This indicator does not appear in variants after Book III, Chapter vi, where the manuscript ends.) If the variant occurs within a quotation, and the earlier version (i.e., that in the variant note) is the reading of the source from which Mill is quoting, the word "Source" precedes the manuscript and edition indicators in the variant note. If the reading in the text, as opposed to that in the variant note, is the same as that of the source, no indicator is needed. If the text varies from the source, but not amongst editions, there is no variant note; the variant will, however, appear in Appendix I.

Placing the example above (I.7^{p-p}) in context, then, the interpretation is that from the manuscript through the 5th edition, the reading is "grinding by water instead of by hand"; in the 6th edition (65) this is altered to "grinding by water power instead of by hand", and the reading of the 6th edition is retained (as is clear in the text) in the 7th edition (71).

Before going on to the second kind of variant, it should be noted that in all cases, any added editorial information, except "Source," "MS," the edition indicators, and page references, is in italics. Also, in the case of long added or substituted passages, the second enclosing superscript may be found on the next page, or even several pages, after the first; when necessary, the superscript notation in the footnote will give the page number on which the variant passage concludes (see, e.g., I.81^{l-l84}).

Substitution of a word or words: see I.5^{e-e}. In the text the word "promoting" appears as "^{e}promoting^{e}"; the variant note reads "$^{e-e}$MS, 48, 49, 52, 57, 62 favouring". Here the word following the edition indicators is that for which "promoting" was substituted; again applying the same rules and putting the variant in context, the interpretation is that from the manuscript through the 5th edition the reading is "concurred in favouring it"; in the 6th edition this was altered to "concurred in promoting it", and the reading of the 6th edition was retained (as is clear in the text) in the 7th edition.

Deletion of a word or words: see I.5[f]. In the text, a *single* superscript [f] appears *centred* between "absurdity" and "seemed"; the variant note reads "[f]MS, 48, 49 must have". Here the words following the edition indicators are those deleted; applying the same rules and putting the variant in context, the interpretation is that the manuscript (MS), 1st edition (48), and 2nd edition (49) read "absurdity must have seemed"; the words "must have" were deleted in the 3rd edition and the reading of the 3rd edition was retained through all subsequent editions.

Variants within variants: see I.10[a–a]. Often, of course, Mill altered a passage more than once. In this case the text reads "[a]among most savages[a]"; the variant note reads "[a–a]MS even in the most savage state] 48, 49 in most savage states". The different readings are given in chronological order, with a square bracket separating them, and the interpretation is that in the manuscript the reading is "exists even in the most savage state"; in the 1st and 2nd editions the reading is "exists in most savage states"; and the final reading is found in all editions from the 3rd through the 7th. In longer variants of this sort, it seems unnecessary to repeat the whole passage, and so such variant notes as those at I.7[n–n] and I.21[m–m] appear. In the first of these the note reads "[n–n]MS want, answers no purpose whatsoever:] 48, 49 *as* MS . . . purpose:"—the interpretation is that the 1st and 2nd editions have the same reading as the manuscript up to and including the word "purpose" and end in the same way (i.e., with a colon); in other words, "whatsoever" is found in the manuscript but not in the 1st and 2nd editions. At I.21[m–m] the variant note reads "[m–m]MS determined by laws as rigid, & as independent of human control, as those of Production itself] 48, 49 *as* MS . . . rigid as those . . . *as* MS"—the interpretation is, similarly, that the passage ", & as independent of human control," which appears in the manuscript, is not in the 1st and 2nd editions.

Variants in Mill's footnotes. To avoid four levels of text on the page, a different method has been used to indicate changes in the notes supplied by Mill. An example will be seen at I.37[n], where the footnote reads in part ". . . According to these definitions [49 this distinction], the . . . ." Here a simple substitution of "these definitions" for "this distinction" took place in the 3rd edition. Often, to allow for accurate placing of the variant, the words before and/or after the altered passage are given (see the other variants in the same note).

Dates of footnotes. Here the practice (borrowed from Ashley's edition, but applied more rigorously) is to place immediately after the footnote indicator, in square brackets, the figure indicating the edition in which the note first appeared. In the last cited example, for instance, the beginning of the note reads "*[49] The . . .", indicating that the note was added in the 2nd edition. If no such figure appears, the note is in the first version (manuscript or 1st edition) and in all subsequent editions. If a note was deleted, it will appear in the variant notes at the bottom of the page, with suitable indication (see, for example, I.27[b]). If a note was lengthened in a subsequent edition, the appropriate date is given, again in square brackets, before the added passage (see, for example, I.174n, where the original MS note was added to in the 1st edition).

Punctuation and spelling. In general, changes in punctuation and spelling (including capitalization and hyphenation) are ignored. Those changes which occur as part of a substantive variant are included in that variant, and the superscript letters in the text are placed exactly with reference to punctuation. Changes *within* variants are ignored, however, so that if a reference is, say, to MS, 48, 49 the punctuation and spelling derive from the 2nd edition, the last cited. In a few cases changes in capitalization and punctuation (especially terminal punctuation) reveal at least a change in emphasis, and these are noted as normal variants. Changes from or to italic type are noted.

Prefaces. After the Preface to the 1st edition, the additional prefatory passages have been added in chronological order (as in Ashley's edition).

Other textual liberties. The typographical errors in the 7th edition have been silently corrected.[34] Mill's section titles in the Table of Contents

[34]Typographical errors in earlier editions are ignored. It should be noted that no correction has been made in such matters as French accents unless there is authority in the earlier editions or the MS. The errors which have been corrected are (with the reading of the 7th edition first, followed by the corrected reading in square brackets):

VOLUME I

43.13 individnal [individual]
146.n5 côte [côté]
147.n1 recemment [récemment]
157.35 concientious [conscientious]
165.31 St [St.]
284.11 , [.]
387.2 farmers' [farmer's]
300.n14 opére [opère]
301.34 : [:"]
307.n14 epoux [époux]
308.21 pour [par]
308.25 diner [dîner]
378.5 he [be]
445.19 opuleut [opulent]
446.n10 , fr.; et [fr.; et]
447.n2 corréspond [correspond]
449.35 farms [farms.]

VOLUME II

461.4 often [oftener]
475.2 people [people;]
540.32 obstruction [obstructions]
543.4 latter [later]
640.17 due, [due;]
660.7 alterations [alternations]
777.6 resterènt [restèrent]
777.22 plias [plais]
781.n28 *total omitted* [66,752]
794.n10 order. [order."]
866.25 dlrect [direct]
944.24 Unhapily [Unhappily]

have been introduced, in square brackets and italics, after each section number. (The wording has been slightly altered in a few cases for the sake of brevity and clarity.) The volumes are divided between Books II and III, instead of between Chapters vi and vii of Book III, and the Appendix to Volume I has been moved to the end of Book II, to which it has reference. Mill occasionally uses square brackets in his footnotes; these have been altered to round brackets to avoid confusion with editorial information. Mill's footnotes referring to sources have been completed and corrected, with all added information being placed in square brackets. Also in Mill's footnotes, the page references to other parts of the *Principles* have been altered to apply to the present edition. A few alterations in printing style have been made: for example, small capitals for proper names have been replaced by lower case in a few places; the form of tables has been altered; and periods have been removed after section titles. The running heads and the style of chapter headings, etc., have been altered when necessary or desirable.

III. APPENDICES

Appendices A to D. Further to avoid difficulty in reading and reconstruction, those sections most heavily revised by Mill have been printed separately as appendices. *Appendix A* contains Book II, Chapter i, §§3–6 in the 2nd edition, with variant notes giving the readings of the manuscript and 1st edition. *Appendix B* contains Book II, Chapter x, §§1–7 in the 2nd edition, again with variants from the manuscript and 1st edition. *Appendix C* contains (from the same heavily revised chapter) Book II, Chapter x, §3 in the 4th edition, with variants from the manuscript, 1st, 2nd, and 3rd editions. *Appendix D* contains Book IV, Chapter vii, §§5–6 in the 2nd edition, with variants from the 1st edition. For all these passages, then, the text itself (as is indicated at the appropriate places) does not indicate variants from editions earlier than that reproduced in the appendices; that is, variants in Book II, Chapter i, §3, for example, will be found in the text proper only for the 3rd and later editions—the earlier variants will be found only in Appendix A. To facilitate comparison of the appendices with the text, square brackets have been placed around those passages which are retained into the 7th edition, with referential notes. Again, the rule is more complicated than its application, and it will easily be seen that to include these long and complicated variants in the notes would make normal reading impossible.

Appendix E. In an appendix to Volume II of the 4th edition, Mill included information he had lately gathered from Villiaumé, which he incorporated into Book IV, Chapter vii in the 5th and subsequent editions.

This appendix is here reproduced in its original form, with square brackets in the text indicating those passages which were later used in IV, vii.

Appendix F. In this appendix the press-copy manuscript of the *Principles* is described and discussed, and examples of cancelled readings are given.

Appendix G. Little is known about the specific role played by Harriet Taylor in the writing and revision of the *Principles*, but the epistolary evidence (mostly quoted by Professor Hayek in his *John Stuart Mill and Harriet Taylor*) is best understood in close conjunction with the text, and so has been here included.

Appendix H. In the Preface to the 6th edition, as mentioned above, Mill pays warm tribute to John E. Cairnes for his helpful suggestions concerning revision. The extent of his debt is revealed only when one sees the lengthy and detailed letters and notes which Cairnes sent to Mill late in 1864 and early in 1865, when the revision for the 6th edition was taking place. The relevant parts of their correspondence and of Cairnes' notes are here reproduced, with added references indicating which passages were being criticized, and which were altered as a result of the criticism.

Appendix I. One's admiration for the speed with which Mill wrote the *Principles* is perhaps slightly lessened when one becomes aware of the extent of his quotations. A list of the sources from which he drew material or opinions is in itself a guide to nineteenth-century economic literature, and this appendix was devised to provide such a list. At the same time, the slight disservice which the inaccuracy of the quotations does to their sources and to readers is compensated by the inclusion of substantive variants between the sources and the *Principles*. Because this appendix includes all references to authors and books, it is in effect also an index of names and titles, which are therefore omitted in the Index proper.

Index. As will be seen by reference to II.1090–1 below, Cairnes' need rather than Mill's scepticism has been recognized in the provision of an index of topics, which has been prepared by Julian Patrick.

ACKNOWLEDGEMENTS

FOR PERMISSION to publish manuscript material, we are indebted to the National Provincial Bank (literary executors and residual legatees of Mary Taylor, Mill's step-grand-daughter), to the Pierpont Morgan Library and Herbert Cahoon (the manuscript of the *Principles*), to the British Library of Political and Economic Science and C. G. Allen (the Mill—Cairnes correspondence and "Notes on the Principles"), to the National Library of Ireland and Alf Mac Lochlainn (Cairnes' "Notes on

Ireland"), to Dr. C. K. Mill (for the heirs of J. E. Cairnes), to the Yale University Library (the Mill—Harriet Taylor letters), to the Huntington Library (the letter to Furnivall), and to the University of Illinois Library (the letter to Villiaumé). I should also like to thank the library staff of the British Museum Reading Room and of the British Library of Political and Economic Science for patience, help, and guidance. To Dean Bladen and Professor Priestley, and the other members of the Editorial Committee of the *Collected Works*, to the staff of the University of Toronto Press, and especially to the Editor, Miss Francess Halpenny, and our copy-editor, Dr. Ron Schoeffel, my grateful thanks are overdue. Without invidious intent, I shall mention only a few of the individuals whose labours have lessened mine and made them a pleasure: Bernard J. Harrison, William H. Hughes, Peter M. Jackson, Dennis B. Lee, Miss Pamela Millar, Professor Francis E. Mineka, Professor Jack Stillinger, Dr. Adelaide Weinberg, and John Willoughby. Also, and not merely for Millian or conventional reasons, I am deeply grateful to my wife, who was involved from the beginning of my textual work up to the beginning of this sentence.

J.M.R.

Victoria College

PREFACES

Preface

[To all editions]

THE APPEARANCE OF A TREATISE like the present, on a subject on which so many works of merit already exist, may be thought to require some explanation.

It might, perhaps, be sufficient to say, that no existing treatise on Political Economy contains the latest improvements which have been made in the theory of the subject. Many new ideas, and new applications of ideas, have been elicited by the discussions of the last few years, especially those on Currency, on Foreign Trade, and on the important topics connected more or less intimately with Colonization: and there seems reason that the field of Political Economy should be re-surveyed in its whole extent, if only for the purpose of incorporating the results of these speculations, and bringing them into harmony with the principles previously laid down by the best thinkers on the subject.

To supply, however, these deficiencies in former treatises bearing a similar title, is not the sole, or even the principal object which the author has in view. The design of the book is different from that of any treatise on Political Economy which has been produced in England since the work of Adam Smith.

The most characteristic quality of that work, and the one in which it most differs from some others which have equalled [a]and[a] even surpassed it as mere expositions of the general principles of the subject, is that it invariably associates the principles with their applications. This of itself implies a much wider range of ideas and of topics, than are included in Political Economy, considered as a branch of abstract speculation. For practical purposes, Political Economy is inseparably intertwined with many other branches of social philosophy. Except on matters of mere detail, there are perhaps no practical questions, even among those which approach nearest to the character of purely economical questions, which admit of being decided on economical premises alone. And it is because Adam Smith never loses sight of this truth; because, in his applications of Political Economy, he perpetually appeals to other and often far larger considera-

[a-a]48, 49, 52, 57, 62 or

tions than pure Political Economy affords—that he gives that well-grounded feeling of command over the principles of the subject for purposes of practice, owing to which the "Wealth of Nations," alone among treatises on Political Economy, has not only been popular with general readers, but has impressed itself strongly on the minds of men of the world and of legislators.

It appears to the present writer, that a work similar in its object and general conception to that of Adam Smith, but adapted to the more extended knowledge and improved ideas of the present age, is the kind of contribution which Political Economy at present requires. The "Wealth of Nations" is in many parts obsolete, and in all, imperfect. Political Economy, properly so called, has grown up almost from infancy since the time of Adam Smith; and the philosophy of society, from which practically that eminent thinker never separated his more peculiar theme, though still in a very early stage of its progress, has advanced many steps beyond the point at which he left it. No attempt, however, has yet been made to combine his practical mode of treating his subject with the increased knowledge since acquired of its theory, or to exhibit the economical phenomena of society in the relation in which they stand to the best social ideas of the present time, as he did, with such admirable success, in reference to the philosophy of his [b]century[b].

Such is the idea which the writer of the present work has kept before him. To succeed even partially in realizing it, would be a sufficiently useful achievement, to induce him to incur willingly all the chances of failure. It is requisite, however, to add, that although his object is practical, and, as far as the nature of the subject admits, popular, he has not attempted to purchase either of those advantages by the sacrifice of strict scientific reasoning. Though he desires that his treatise should be more than a mere exposition of the abstract doctrines of Political Economy, he is also desirous that such an exposition should be found in it.

[Concluding paragraph in the 2nd edition (1849)]

The additions and alterations in the present edition are generally of little moment; but the increased importance which the Socialist controversy has assumed since this work was written, has made it desirable to enlarge the chapter which treats of it; the more so, as the objections therein stated to the specific schemes propounded by some Socialists, have been erroneously understood as a general condemnation of all that is commonly included under that name. A full appreciation of Socialism, and of the questions which it raises, can only be advantageously attempted in a separate work.

[b-b]49 country

[Additional Preface in the 3rd edition (1852) only]

The present edition has been revised throughout, and several chapters either materially added to or entirely re-cast. Among these may be mentioned that on the "Means of abolishing Cottier Tenantry," the suggestions contained in which, had reference exclusively to Ireland, and to Ireland in a condition which has been much modified by subsequent events. An addition has been made to the theory of International Values laid down in the eighteenth chapter of the Third Book.

The chapter on Property has been almost entirely re-written. I was far from intending that the statement which it contained, of the objections to the best known Socialist schemes, should be understood as a condemnation of Socialism, regarded as an ultimate result of human progress. The only objection to which any great importance will be found to be attached in the present edition, is the unprepared state of mankind in general, and of the labouring classes in particular; their extreme unfitness at present for any order of things, which would make any considerable demand on either their intellect or their virtue. It appears to me that the great end of social improvement should be to fit mankind by cultivation, for a state of society combining the greatest personal freedom with that just distribution of the fruits of labour, which the present laws of property do not profess to aim at. Whether, when this state of mental and moral cultivation shall be attained, individual property in some form (though a form very remote from the present) or community of ownership in the instruments of production and a regulated division of the produce, will afford the circumstances most favourable to happiness, and best calculated to bring human nature to its greatest perfection, is a question which must be left, as it safely may, to the people of that time to decide. Those of the present are not competent to decide it.

The chapter on the "Futurity of the Labouring Classes" has been enriched with the results of the experience afforded since this work was first published, by the co-operative associations in France. That important experience shows that the time is ripe for a larger and more rapid extension of association among labourers, than could have been successfully attempted before the calumniated democratic movements in Europe, which though for the present put down by the pressure of brute force, have scattered widely the seeds of future improvement. I have endeavoured to designate more clearly the tendency of the social transformation, of which these associations are the initial step; and at the same time to disconnect the co-operative cause from the exaggerated or altogether mistaken declamations against competition, so largely indulged in by its supporters.

July, 1852.

[Concluding paragraph in the 4th edition (1857)]

The present edition (the fourth) has been revised throughout, and some additional explanations inserted where they appeared to be necessary. The chapters to which most has been added are those on the Influence of Credit on Prices, and on the Regulation of a Convertible Paper Currency.

[Concluding paragraph in the 5th edition (1862)]

The present fifth edition has been revised throughout, and the facts, on several subjects, brought down to a later date than in the former editions. Additional arguments and illustrations have been inserted where they seemed necessary, but not in general at any considerable length.

[Concluding paragraph in the 6th edition (1865)]

The present, like all previous editions, has been revised throughout, and additional explanations, or answers to new objections, have been inserted where they seemed necessary; but not, in general, at any considerable length. The chapter in which the greatest addition has been made is that on the Rate of Interest; and for most of the new matter there introduced, as well as for many minor improvements, I am indebted to the suggestions and criticisms of my friend Professor Cairnes, one of the most scientific of living political economists.

[Concluding paragraph in the 7th edition (1871)]

The present edition, with the exception of a few verbal corrections, corresponds exactly with the last Library Edition and with the People's Edition. Since the publication of these, there has been some instructive discussion on the theory of Demand and Supply, and on the influence of Strikes and Trades Unions on wages, by which additional light has been thrown on these subjects; but the results, in the author's opinion, are not yet ripe for incorporation in a general treatise on Political Economy.* For an analogous reason, all notice, of the alteration made in the Land Laws of Ireland by the recent Act, is deferred until experience shall have had time to pronounce on the operation of that well-meant attempt to deal with the greatest practical evil in the economic institutions of that country.

*The present state of the discussion may be learnt from a review (by the author) of Mr. Thornton's work "On Labour," in the "Fortnightly Review" of May and June, 1869 [n.s. V, 505–18, 680–700], and from Mr. Thornton's reply to that review in the second edition of his very instructive book.

PRINCIPLES OF POLITICAL ECONOMY

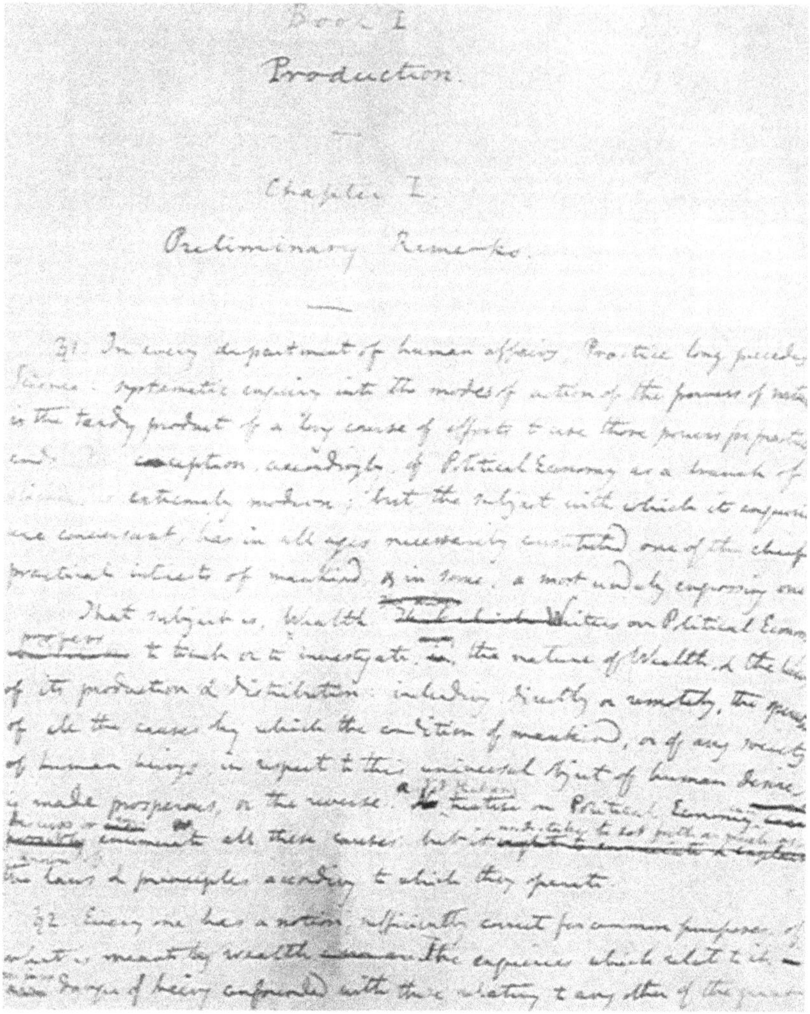

Book I

Production.

Chapter I.

Preliminary Remarks.

§1. In every department of human affairs, Practice long precedes Science: systematic enquiry into the modes of action of the powers of nature is the tardy product of a long course of efforts to use those powers for practical ends. The conception, accordingly, of Political Economy as a branch of Science is extremely modern; but the subject with which its enquiries are conversant has in all ages necessarily constituted one of the chief practical interests of mankind, & in some, a most unduly engrossing one.

That subject is, Wealth. Writers on Political Economy profess to teach or to investigate the nature of Wealth, & the laws of its production & distribution: including, directly or remotely, the operation of all the causes by which the condition of mankind, or of any society of human beings, in respect to this universal object of human desire, is made prosperous, or the reverse. Not that any treatise on Political Economy can discuss or even enumerate all these causes; but it undertakes to set forth as much as is known of the laws & principles according to which they operate.

§2. Every one has a notion, sufficiently correct for common purposes, of what is meant by wealth. The enquiries which relate to it are in no danger of being confounded with those relating to any other of the great

The first folio of the text, from the MS in the Pierpont Morgan Library

Preliminary Remarks

[a] In every department of human affairs, Practice long precedes Science: systematic enquiry into the modes of action of the powers of nature, is the tardy product of a long course of efforts to use those powers for practical ends. The conception, accordingly, of Political Economy as a branch of science is extremely modern; but the subject with which its enquiries are conversant has in all ages necessarily constituted one of the chief practical interests of mankind, and, in some, a most unduly engrossing one.

That subject is Wealth. Writers on Political Economy profess to teach, or to investigate, the nature of Wealth, and the laws of its production and distribution: including, directly or remotely, the operation of all the causes by which the condition of mankind, or of any society of human beings, in respect to this universal object of human desire, is made prosperous or the reverse. Not that any treatise on Political Economy can discuss or even enumerate all these causes; but it undertakes to set forth as much as is known of the laws and principles according to which they operate.

[b] Every one has a notion, sufficiently correct for common purposes, of what is meant by wealth. The enquiries which relate to it are in no danger of being confounded with those relating to any other of the great human interests. All know that it is one thing to be rich, another thing to be enlightened, brave, or humane; that the questions how a nation is made wealthy, and how it is made free, or virtuous, or eminent in literature, in the fine arts, in arms, or in polity, are totally distinct enquiries. [c]Those[c] things, indeed, are all indirectly connected, and react upon one another. A people has sometimes become free, because it had first grown wealthy; or wealthy, because it had first become free. The creed and laws of a people act powerfully upon their economical condition; and this again, by its influence on their mental development and social relations, reacts upon their creed and laws. But though the subjects are in very close contact, they are essentially different, and have never been supposed to be otherwise.

It is no part of the design of this treatise to aim at metaphysical nicety of definition, where the ideas suggested by a term are already as determinate as practical purposes require. But, little as it might be expected that any

[a]MS § 1. [b]MS § 2. [c-c]MS, 48 These

mischievous confusion of ideas could take place on a subject so simple as the question, what is to be considered as wealth, it is matter of history, that such confusion of ideas has existed—that theorists and practical politicians have been equally and at one period universally, infected by it, and that for many generations it gave a thoroughly false direction to the policy of Europe. I refer to the set of doctrines designated, since the time of Adam Smith, by the appellation of the Mercantile System.

While this system prevailed, it was assumed, either expressly or tacitly, in the whole policy of nations, that wealth consisted solely of money; or of the precious metals, which, when not already in the state of money, are capable of being directly converted into it. According to the doctrines then prevalent, whatever tended to heap up money or bullion in a country added to its wealth. Whatever sent the precious metals out of a country impoverished it. If a country possessed no gold or silver mines, the only industry by which it could be enriched was foreign trade, being the only one which could bring in money. Any branch of trade which was supposed to send out more money than it brought in, however ample and valuable might be the returns in another shape, was looked upon as a losing trade. Exportation of goods was favoured and encouraged (even by means extremely onerous to the real resources of the country), because, the exported goods being stipulated to be paid for in money, it was hoped that the returns would actually be made in gold and silver. Importation of anything, other than the precious metals, was regarded as a loss to the nation of the whole price of the things imported; unless they were brought in to be re-exported at a profit, or unless, being the materials or instruments of some industry practised in the country itself, they gave the power of producing exportable articles at smaller cost, and thereby effecting a larger exportation. The commerce of the world was looked upon as a struggle among nations, which could draw to itself the largest share of the gold and silver in existence; and in this competition no nation could gain anything, except by making others lose as much, or, at the least, preventing them from gaining it.

It often happens that the universal belief of one age of mankind—a belief from which no one *was*, nor without an extraordinary effort of genius and courage, *could* at that time be free—becomes to a subsequent age so palpable an absurdity, that the only difficulty then is to imagine how such a thing can ever have appeared credible. It has so happened with the doctrine that money is synonymous with wealth. The conceit seems too preposterous to be thought of as a serious opinion. It looks like one of the crude fancies of childhood, instantly corrected by a word from any grown person. But let no one feel confident that he [d]would[d] have escaped the delusion if he had lived at the time when it prevailed. All the associations

[d–d]MS, 48, 49, 52, 57, 62 should

engendered by common life, and by the ordinary course of business, concurred in [e]promoting[e] it. So long as those associations were the only medium through which the subject was looked at, what we now think so gross an absurdity [f] seemed a truism. Once questioned, indeed, it was doomed; but no one was likely to think of questioning it whose mind had not become familiar with certain modes of stating and of contemplating economical phenomena, which have only found their way into the general understanding through the influence of Adam Smith and of his expositors.

In common [g]discourse[g], wealth is always expressed in money. If you ask how rich a person is, you are answered that he has so many thousand pounds. All income and expenditure, all gains and losses, everything by which one becomes richer or poorer, are reckoned as the coming in or going out of so much money. It is true that in the inventory of a person's fortune are included, not only the money in his actual possession, or due to him, but all other articles of value. These, however, enter, not in their own character, but in virtue of the sums of money which they would sell for; and if they would sell for less, their owner is reputed less rich, though the things themselves are precisely the same. It is true, also, that people do not grow rich by keeping their money unused, and that they must be willing to spend in order to gain. Those who enrich themselves by commerce, do so by giving money for goods as well as goods for money; and the first is as necessary a part of the process as the last. But [h]a person[h] who buys goods for purposes of gain, does so to sell them again for money, and in the expectation of receiving more money than he laid out: to get money, therefore, seems even to the person himself the ultimate end of the whole. It often happens that he is not paid in money, but in something else; having bought goods to a value equivalent, which are set off against those he sold. But he accepted these at a money valuation, and in the belief that they would bring in more money eventually than the price at which they were made over to him. A dealer doing a large amount of business, and turning over his capital rapidly, has but a small portion of it in ready money at any one time. But he only feels it valuable to him as it is convertible into money: he considers no transaction closed until the net result is either paid or credited in money: when he retires from business it is into money that he converts the whole, and not until then does he deem himself to have [i]realized[i] his gains: just as if money were the only wealth, and money's worth were only the means of attaining it. If [j]it be now asked[j] for what end money is desirable, unless to supply the wants or pleasures of [k]oneself[k] or

[e-e]MS, 48, 49, 52, 57, 62 favouring
[f]MS, 48, 49 must have
[g-g]MS parlance
[h-h]MS, 48, 49 he
[i-i]MS *realized*
[j-j]MS, 48, 49 you now ask
[k-k]MS, 48, 49 yourself

others, the champion of the system would not be at all embarrassed by the question. True, he would say, these are the uses of wealth, and very laudable uses while confined to domestic commodities, because in that case, by exactly the amount which you expend, you enrich others of your countrymen. Spend your wealth, if you please, in whatever indulgences you have a taste for; but your wealth is not the indulgences, it is the sum of money, or the annual money income, with which you purchase them.

While there were so many things to render the assumption which is the basis of the mercantile system plausible, there is also some small foundation in reason, though a very insufficient one, for the distinction which that system so emphatically draws between money and every other kind of valuable possession. We really, and justly, look upon a person as possessing the advantages of wealth, not in proportion to the useful and agreeable things of which he is in the actual enjoyment, but to his command over the general fund of things useful and agreeable; the power he possesses of providing for any exigency, or obtaining any object of desire. Now, money is itself that power; while all other things, in a civilized state, seem to confer it only by their capacity of being exchanged for money. To possess any other article of wealth, is to possess that particular thing, and nothing else: if you wish for another thing instead of it, you have first to sell it, or to submit to the inconvenience and delay (if not the impossibility) of finding some one who has what you want, and is willing to barter it for what you have. But with money you are at once able to buy whatever things are for sale: and [l]one[l] whose fortune is in money, or in things rapidly convertible into it, seems both to himself and others to possess not any one thing, but all the things which the money places it at his option to purchase. The greatest part of the utility of wealth, beyond a very moderate quantity, is not the indulgences it procures, but the reserved power which its possessor holds in his hands of attaining purposes generally; and this power no other kind of wealth confers so immediately or so certainly as money. It is the only form of wealth which is not merely applicable to some one use, but can be turned at once to any use. And this distinction was the more likely to make an impression upon governments, as it is one of considerable importance to them. A civilized government derives comparatively little advantage from taxes unless it can collect them in money: and if it has large or sudden payments to make, especially payments in foreign countries for wars or subsidies, either for the sake of conquering or of not being conquered (the two chief objects of national policy until a late period), scarcely any medium of payment except money will serve the purpose. All these causes conspire to make both individuals and governments, in estimating their means, attach almost exclusive importance to money, either *in esse*

[l-l]MS, 48, 49 he

or *in posse*, and look upon all other things (when viewed as part of their resources) scarcely otherwise than as the remote [m]means[m] of obtaining that which alone, when obtained, affords the indefinite, and at the same time instantaneous, command over objects of desire, which best answers to the idea of wealth.

An absurdity, however, does not cease to be an absurdity when we have discovered what were the appearances which made it plausible; and the Mercantile Theory could not fail to be seen in its true character when men began, even in an imperfect manner, to explore into the foundations of things, and seek their premises from elementary facts, and not from the forms and phrases of common discourse. So soon as they asked themselves what is really meant by money—what it is in its essential characters, and the precise nature of the functions it performs—they reflected that money, like other things, is only a desirable possession on account of its uses; and that these, instead of being, as they delusively appear, indefinite, are of a strictly defined and limited description, namely, to facilitate the distribution of the produce of industry according to the convenience of those among whom it is shared. Further consideration showed that the uses of money are in no respect promoted by increasing the quantity which exists and circulates in a country; the service which it performs being as well rendered by a small as by a large aggregate amount. Two million quarters of corn will not feed so many persons as four millions; but two millions of pounds sterling will carry on as much traffic, will buy and sell as many commodities, as four millions, though at lower nominal prices. Money, as money, satisfies no [n]want;[n] its worth to any one, consists in its being a convenient shape in which to receive his incomings of all sorts, which incomings he afterwards, at the times which suit him best, converts into the forms in which they can be useful to him. [o]Great as the difference would be between a country with money, and a country altogether without it, it[o] would be only one of convenience; a saving of time and trouble, like grinding by water [p]power[p] instead of by hand, or (to use Adam Smith's illustration) like the benefit derived from roads; and to mistake money for wealth, is the same sort of error as to mistake the highway which may be the easiest way of getting to your house or lands, for the house and lands themselves.

[q] Money, being the instrument of an important public and private purpose, is rightly regarded as wealth; but everything else which serves any human purpose, and which nature does not afford gratuitously, is wealth also. To be wealthy is to have a large stock of useful articles, or the means of

[m–m]MS, 48, 49, 52, 57 medium
[n–n]MS want, answers no purpose whatsoever:] 48, 49 *as* MS . . . purpose:
[o–o]MS, 48, 49, 52, 57, 62 The difference between a country with money, and a country altogether without it,
[p–p]+65, 71 [q]MS § 3.

purchasing them. Everything forms therefore a part of wealth, which has a power of purchasing; for which anything useful or agreeable would be given in exchange. Things for which nothing could be obtained in exchange, however useful or necessary they may be, are not wealth in the sense in which the term is used in Political Economy. Air, for example, though the most absolute of necessaries, bears no price in the market, because it can be obtained gratuitously: to accumulate a stock of it would yield no profit or advantage to any one; and the laws of its production and distribution are the subject of a very different study from Political Economy. But though air is not wealth, mankind are much richer by obtaining it gratis, since the time and labour which would otherwise be required for supplying the most pressing of all wants, can be devoted to other purposes. It is possible to imagine circumstances in which air would be a part of wealth. If it became customary to sojourn long in places where the air does not naturally penetrate, as in diving-bells sunk in the sea, a supply of air artificially furnished would, like water conveyed into houses, bear a price: and if from any revolution in nature the atmosphere became too scanty for the consumption, or could be monopolized, air might acquire a very high marketable value. In such a case, the possession of it, beyond his own wants, would be, to its owner, wealth; and the general wealth of mankind might at first sight appear to be increased, by what [r]would be[r] so great a calamity to them. [s]The error would lie in not [t]considering[t], that[s] however rich the possessor of air might become at the expense of the rest of the community, all persons else would be poorer by all that they were compelled to pay for what they had before obtained without payment.

[u] This leads to an important distinction in the meaning of the word wealth, as applied to the possessions of an individual, and to those of a nation, or of mankind. In the wealth of mankind, nothing is included which does not of itself answer some purpose of utility or pleasure. To an individual anything is wealth, which, though useless in itself, enables him to claim from others a part of their stock of things useful or pleasant. Take, for instance, a mortgage of a thousand pounds on a landed estate. This is wealth to the person to whom it brings in a revenue, and who could perhaps sell it in the market for the full amount of the debt. But it is not wealth to the country; if the engagement were annulled, the country would be neither poorer nor richer. The mortgagee would have lost a thousand pounds, and the owner of the land would have gained it. Speaking nationally, the mortgage was not itself wealth, but merely gave A a claim to a portion of the wealth of B. It was wealth to A, and wealth which he could transfer to a third person; but what he so transferred was in fact a joint ownership, to the extent of a

[r-r]MS is
[s-s]MS, 48, 49 But this would be an error; for
[t-t]52, 57 perceiving
[u]MS § 4.

thousand pounds, in the land of which B was nominally the sole proprietor. The position of fundholders, or owners of the public debt of a country, is similar. They are mortgagees on the general wealth of the country. The cancelling of the debt would be no destruction of wealth, but a transfer of it: a wrongful abstraction of wealth from certain members of the community, for the profit of the government, or of the tax-payers. Funded property therefore cannot be counted as part of the national wealth. This is not always borne in mind by the dealers in statistical calculations. For example, in estimates of the gross income of the country, founded on the proceeds of the income-tax, incomes derived from the funds are not always excluded: though the tax-payers are assessed on their whole nominal income, without being permitted to deduct from it the portion levied from them in taxation to form the income of the fundholder. In this calculation, therefore, one portion of the general income of the country is counted twice over, and the aggregate amount made to appear greater than it is by [v]almost[v] thirty millions. A country, however, may include in its wealth all stock held by its citizens in the funds of foreign countries, and other debts due to them from abroad. But even this is only wealth to them by being a part ownership in wealth held by others. It forms no part of the collective wealth of the human race. It is an element in the distribution, but not in the composition, of the general wealth.

[w]Another example of a possession which is wealth to the person holding it, but not wealth to the nation, or to mankind, is slaves. It is by a strange confusion of ideas that slave property (as it is termed) is counted, at so much per head, in an estimate of the wealth, or of the capital, of the country which tolerates the existence of such property. If a human being, considered as an object possessing productive powers, is part of the national wealth when his powers are owned by another man, he cannot be less a part of it when they are owned by himself. Whatever he is worth to his master is so much property abstracted from himself, and its abstraction cannot augment the possessions of the two together, or of the country to which they both belong. In propriety of classification, however, the people of a country are not to be counted in its wealth. They are that for the sake of which its wealth exists. The term wealth is wanted to denote the desirable objects which they possess, not inclusive of, but in contradistinction to, their own persons. They are not wealth to themselves, though they are means of acquiring it.[w]

It has been proposed to define wealth as signifying "instruments:" meaning not tools and machinery alone, but the whole accumulation possessed by individuals or communities, of means for the attainment of their ends.

[v-v]MS, 48, 49, 52, 57 about
[w-w]+65, 71

Thus, a field is an instrument, because it is a means to the attainment of corn. Corn is an instrument, being a means to the attainment of flour. Flour is an instrument, being a means to the attainment of bread. Bread is an instrument, as a means to the satisfaction of hunger and to the support of life. Here we at last arrive at things which are not instruments, being desired on their own account, and not as mere means to something beyond. This view of the subject is philosophically correct; or rather, this mode of expression may be usefully employed along with others, not as conveying a different view of the subject from the common one, but as giving more distinctness and reality to the common view. It departs, however, too widely from the custom of language, to be likely to obtain general [x]acceptance[x], or to be of use for any other purpose than that of occasional illustration.

Wealth, then, may be defined, all useful or agreeable things which possess exchangeable value; or, in other words, all useful or agreeable things except those which can be obtained, in the quantity desired, without labour or sacrifice. To this definition, the only objection seems to be, that it leaves in uncertainty a question which has been much debated—whether what are called immaterial products are to be considered as wealth: whether, for example, the skill of a workman, or any other natural or acquired power of body or mind, shall be called wealth, or not: a question, not of very great importance, and which, so far as requiring discussion, will be more conveniently considered in [y]another place[y].*

[z] These things having been premised respecting wealth, we shall next turn our attention to the extraordinary differences in respect to it, which exist between nation and nation, and between different ages of the world; differences both in the quantity of wealth, and in the kind of it; as well as in the manner in which the wealth existing in the community is shared among its members.

There is, perhaps, no people or community, now existing, which subsists entirely on the spontaneous produce of vegetation. But many tribes still live exclusively, or almost exclusively, on wild animals, the produce of hunting or fishing. Their clothing is skins; their habitations, huts rudely formed of logs or boughs of trees, and abandoned at an hour's notice. The food they use being little susceptible of storing up, they have no accumulation of it, and are often exposed to great privations. The wealth of such a community consists solely of the skins they wear; a few ornaments, the taste for which exists [a]among most savages[a]; some rude utensils; the

*[48] Infra, book i. chap. iii. [Vol. I, pp. 45–54.]

[x-x]MS, 48, 49, 52 acceptation
[y-y]MS a future chapter
[z]MS § 5.
[a-a]MS even in the most savage state] 48, 49 in most savage states

weapons with which they kill their game, or fight [b]against[b] hostile competitors for the means of subsistence; canoes for crossing rivers and lakes, or fishing in the sea; and perhaps some furs or other productions of the wilderness, collected to be exchanged with civilized people for blankets, brandy, and tobacco; of which foreign produce also there may be some unconsumed portion in store. To this scanty inventory of material wealth, ought to be added their land; an instrument of production of which they make slender use, compared with more settled communities, but which is still the source of their subsistence, and which has a marketable value if there be any agricultural community in the neighbourhood requiring more land than it possesses. This is the state of greatest poverty in which any entire community of human beings is known to exist; though there are much richer communities in which portions of the inhabitants are in a condition, as to subsistence and comfort, [c] as little enviable as that of the savage.

The first great advance beyond this state consists in the domestication of the more useful animals; giving rise to the pastoral or nomad state, in which mankind do not live on the produce of hunting, but on milk and its products, and on the annual increase of flocks and herds. This condition is not only more desirable in itself, but more conducive to further progress: and a much more considerable amount of wealth is accumulated under it. So long as the vast natural pastures of the earth are not yet so fully occupied as to be consumed more rapidly than they are spontaneously reproduced, a large and constantly increasing stock of subsistence may be collected and preserved, with little other labour than that of guarding the cattle from the attacks of wild beasts, and from the force or wiles of predatory men. Large flocks and herds, therefore, are in time possessed, by active and thrifty individuals through their own exertions, and by the heads of families and tribes through the exertions of those who are connected with them by allegiance. There thus arises, in the shepherd state, inequality of possessions; a thing which scarcely exists in the savage state, where no one has much more than absolute necessaries, and in case of deficiency must share even those with his tribe. In the nomad state, some have an abundance of cattle, sufficient for the food of a multitude, while others have not contrived to appropriate and retain any superfluity, or perhaps any cattle at all. But subsistence has ceased to be precarious, since the more successful have no other use which they can make of their surplus than to feed the less fortunate, while every increase in the number of persons connected with them is an increase both of security and of power: and thus they are enabled to divest themselves of all labour except that of government and superintendence, and acquire dependents to fight for them in war and to serve them in peace. One of the features of this state of society is, that a

[b-b]MS, 48, 49 with [c]MS, 48, 49 probably

part of the community, and in some degree even the whole of it, possess leisure. Only a portion of time is required for procuring food, and the remainder is not engrossed by anxious thought for the morrow, or necessary repose from muscular activity. Such a life is highly favourable to the growth of new wants, and opens a possibility of their gratification. A desire arises for better clothing, utensils, and implements, than the savage state contents itself with; and the surplus food renders it practicable to devote to these purposes the exertions of a part of the tribe. In all or most nomad communities we find domestic manufactures of a coarse, and in some, of a fine kind. There is ample evidence that while those parts of the world which have been the cradle of modern civilization were still generally in the nomad state, considerable skill had been attained in spinning, weaving, and dyeing woollen garments, in the preparation of leather, and in what appears a still more difficult invention, that of working in metals. Even speculative science took its first beginnings from the leisure characteristic of this stage of social progress. The earliest astronomical observations are attributed, by a tradition which has much appearance of truth, to the shepherds of Chaldea.

[d] From this state of society to the agricultural the transition is not indeed easy (for no great change in the habits of mankind is otherwise than difficult, and in general either painful or very slow), but it lies in what may be called the spontaneous course of events. The growth of the population of men and cattle began in time to press upon the earth's capabilities of yielding natural pasture: and this cause doubtless produced the first tilling of the ground, just as at a later period the same cause made the superfluous hordes of the nations which had remained nomad precipitate themselves upon those which had already become agricultural; until, these having become sufficiently powerful to repel such inroads, the invading nations, deprived of this outlet, were [e]obliged also[e] to become agricultural communities.

But after this great step had been completed, the subsequent progress of mankind seems by no means to have been so rapid (certain rare combinations of circumstances excepted) as might perhaps have been anticipated. The quantity of human food which the earth is capable of returning even to the most wretched system of agriculture, so much exceeds what could be obtained in the purely pastoral state, that a great increase of population is invariably the result. But this additional food is only obtained by a great additional amount of labour; so that not only an agricultural has much less leisure than a pastoral population, but, with the imperfect tools and unskilful processes which are for a long time employed (and which over the greater part of the earth have not even yet been abandoned), agriculturists do not, unless in unusually advantageous circumstances of climate

[d]MS § 6.   [e–e]MS, 48, 49 also obliged

and soil, produce so great a surplus of food, beyond their necessary consumption, as to support any large class of labourers engaged in other departments of industry. The surplus, too, whether small or great, is usually torn from the producers, either by the government to which they are subject, or by individuals, who by superior force, or by availing themselves of religious or traditional feelings of subordination, have established themselves as lords of the soil.

The first of these modes of appropriation, by the government, is characteristic of the extensive monarchies which from a time beyond historical record have occupied the plains of Asia. The government, in those countries, though varying in its qualities according to the accidents of personal character, seldom leaves much to the cultivators beyond mere necessaries, and often strips them so bare even of these, that it finds itself obliged, after taking all they have, to lend part of it back to those from whom it has been taken, in order to provide them with seed, and enable them to support life until another harvest. Under the régime in question, though the bulk of the population are ill provided for, the government, by collecting small [f]contributions[f] from great numbers, is enabled, with any tolerable management, to make a show of riches quite out of proportion to the general condition of the society; and hence the inveterate impression, of which Europeans have only at a late period been disabused, concerning the great opulence of Oriental nations. In this wealth, without reckoning the large portion which adheres to the hands employed in collecting it, many persons of course participate, besides the immediate household of the sovereign. A large part is distributed among the various functionaries of government, and among the objects of the sovereign's favour or caprice. A part is occasionally employed in works of public utility. The tanks, wells, and canals for irrigation, without which in [g]many[g] tropical climates cultivation could hardly be carried on; the embankments which confine the rivers, the bazars for dealers, and the seraees for travellers, none of which could have been made by the scanty means in the possession of those using them, owe their existence to the liberality and enlightened self-interest of the better order of princes, or to the benevolence or ostentation of here and there a rich individual, whose fortune, if traced to its source, is always found to have been drawn immediately or remotely from the public revenue, most frequently by a direct grant of a portion of it from the sovereign.

The ruler of a society of this description, after providing largely for his own support, and that of all persons in whom he feels an interest, and after maintaining as many soldiers as he thinks needful for his security or his state, has a disposable residue, which he is glad to exchange for articles of luxury suitable to his disposition: as have also the class of persons who

[f-f]MS, 48, 49, 52, 57, 62 sums [g-g]MS, 48, 49 most

have been enriched by his favour, or by handling the public revenues. A demand thus arises for elaborate and costly manufactured articles, adapted to a narrow but a wealthy market. This demand is often supplied almost exclusively by the merchants of more advanced communities, but often also raises up in the country itself a class of artificers, by whom certain fabrics are carried to as high excellence as can be given by patience[h], quickness of perception and observation,[h] and manual dexterity, without any considerable knowledge of the properties of objects: such as some of the cotton fabrics of India. These artificers are fed by the surplus food which has been taken by the government and its agents as their share of the produce. So literally is this the case, that in some countries the workman, instead of taking his work home, and being paid for it after it is finished, proceeds with his tools to his customer's house, and is there subsisted until the work is complete. The insecurity, however, of all possessions in this state of society, induces even the richest purchasers to give a preference to such articles as, being of an imperishable nature, and containing great value in small bulk, are adapted for being concealed or carried off. Gold and jewels, therefore, constitute a large proportion of the wealth of these nations, and many a rich Asiatic carries nearly his whole fortune on his person, or on those of the women of his harem. No one, except the monarch, thinks of investing his wealth in a manner not susceptible of removal. He, indeed, if he feels safe on his throne, and reasonably secure of transmitting it to his descendants, sometimes indulges a taste for durable edifices, and produces the Pyramids, or the Taj Mehal and the Mausoleum at Sekundra. The rude manufactures destined for the wants of the cultivators are worked up by village artisans, who are remunerated by land given to them rent-free to cultivate, or by fees paid to them in kind from such share of the crop as is left to the villagers by the government. [i]This[i] state of society, however, is not destitute of a mercantile class; composed of two divisions, grain dealers and money dealers. The grain dealers do not usually buy grain from the producers, but from the agents of government, who, receiving the revenue in kind, are glad to devolve upon others the business of conveying it to the places where the prince, his chief civil and military officers, the bulk of his troops, and the artisans who supply the wants of these various persons, are assembled. The money dealers lend to the unfortunate cultivators, when ruined by bad seasons or fiscal exactions, the means of supporting life and continuing their cultivation, and are repaid with enormous interest at the next harvest; or, on a larger scale, they lend to the government, or to those to whom it has granted a portion of the revenue, and are indemnified by assignments on the revenue collectors, or by having certain districts put into their possession, that they may pay themselves from the revenues; to enable

[h-h]+52, 57, 62, 65, 71 [i-i]57 The

them to do which, a great portion of the powers of government are usually made over simultaneously, to be exercised by them until either the districts are redeemed, or their receipts have liquidated the debt. Thus, the commercial operations of both these classes of dealers take place principally upon that part of the produce of the country which forms the revenue of the government. From that revenue their capital is periodically replaced with a profit, and that is also the source from which their original funds have almost always been derived. Such, in its general features, is the economical condition of most of the countries of Asia, as it has been from beyond the commencement of authentic history, and is still, wherever not disturbed by foreign influences.

[j] In the agricultural communities of ancient Europe whose early condition is best known to us, the course of things was different. These, at their origin, were mostly small town-communities, at the first plantation of which, in an unoccupied country, or in one from which the former inhabitants had been expelled, the land which was taken possession of was [k]regularly[k] divided, in equal or [l]in graduated[l] allotments, among the families composing the community. In some cases, instead of a town there was a confederation of towns, occupied by people of the same reputed race, and who were supposed to have settled in the country about the same time. Each family produced its own food and the materials of its clothing, which were worked up within itself, usually by the women of the family, into the coarse fabrics with which the age was contented. Taxes there were none, as there were either no paid officers of government, or if there were, their payment had been provided for by a reserved portion of land, cultivated by slaves on account of the state; and the army consisted of the body of citizens. The whole produce of the soil, therefore, belonged, without deduction, to the family which cultivated it. So long as the progress of events permitted this disposition of property to last, the state of society was, for the majority of the free cultivators, probably not an undesirable one; and under it, in some cases, the advance of mankind in intellectual culture was extraordinarily rapid and brilliant. This more especially happened where, along with [m]advantageous[m] circumstances of race and climate, and no doubt with many favourable accidents of which all trace is now lost, was combined the advantage of a position on the [n]shores[n] of a great inland sea, the other coasts of which were already occupied by settled communities. The knowledge which in such a position was acquired of foreign productions, and the easy access of foreign ideas and inventions, made the chain of

[j]MS § 7.
[k-k]MS, 48, 49 systematically
[l-l]MS, 48, 49, 52, 57 nearly equal
[m-m]MS favourable
[n-n]MS, 48 shore

routine, usually so strong in a rude people, hang loosely on these communities. To speak only of their industrial development; they early acquired variety of wants and desires, which stimulated them to extract from their own soil the utmost which they knew how to make it yield; and when their soil was sterile, or after they had [o]reached the limit[o] of its capacity, they often became traders, and bought up the productions of foreign countries, to sell them in other countries with a profit.

The duration, however, of this state of things was from the first precarious. These little communities lived in a state of almost perpetual war. For this there were many causes. In the ruder and purely agricultural communities a frequent cause was the mere pressure of their increasing population upon their limited land, aggravated as that pressure so often was by deficient harvests, in the rude state of their agriculture, and depending as they did for food upon a very small extent of country. On these occasions, the community often emigrated *en masse*, or sent forth a swarm of its youth, to seek, sword in hand, for some less warlike people, who could be expelled from their land, or detained to cultivate it as slaves for the benefit of their despoilers. What the less advanced tribes did from necessity, the more prosperous did from ambition and the military spirit: and after a time the whole of these city-communities were either conquerors or conquered. In some cases, the conquering state contented itself with imposing a tribute on the vanquished: who being, in consideration of that burden, freed from the expense and trouble of their own military and naval protection, might enjoy under it a considerable share of economical prosperity, while the ascendant community obtained a surplus of wealth, available for purposes of collective luxury or magnificence. From such a surplus the Parthenon and the Propylæa were built, the sculptures of Pheidias paid for, and the festivals celebrated, for which Æschylus, Sophocles, Euripides, and Aristophanes composed their dramas. But this state of political relations, most useful, while it lasted, to the progress and ultimate interest of mankind, had not the elements of durability. A small conquering community which does not incorporate its conquests, always ends by being conquered. Universal dominion, therefore, at last rested with the people who practised this art—with the Romans; who, whatever were their other devices, always either began or ended by taking a great part of the land to enrich their own leading citizens, and by adopting into the governing body the principal possessors of the remainder. It is unnecessary to dwell on the melancholy economical history of the Roman empire. When inequality of wealth once commences, in a community not constantly engaged in repairing by industry the injuries of fortune, its advances are gigantic; the great masses of wealth swallow up the smaller. The Roman empire ultimately became covered with

[o-o]MS, 48, 49, 52, 57 come to the end

the vast landed possessions of a comparatively few families, for whose luxury, and still more for whose ostentation, the most costly products were raised, while the cultivators of the soil were slaves, or small tenants in a nearly servile condition. From this time the wealth of the empire progressively declined. In the beginning, the public revenues, and the resources of rich individuals, sufficed at least to cover Italy with splendid edifices, public and private; but at length so dwindled under the enervating influences of misgovernment, that what remained was not even sufficient to keep those edifices from decay. The strength and riches of the civilized world became inadequate to make head against the nomad population which skirted its northern frontier; they overran the empire, and a different order of things succeeded.

[p] In the new frame in which European society was now cast, the population of each country may be considered as composed, in unequal proportions, of two distinct nations or races, the conquerors and the conquered: the first the proprietors of the land, the latter the tillers of it. These tillers were allowed to occupy the land on conditions which, being the product of force, were always onerous, but seldom to the extent of absolute slavery. Already, in the later times of the Roman empire, predial slavery had extensively transformed itself into a kind of serfdom: the *coloni* of the Romans were rather villeins than actual slaves; and the incapacity and distaste of the barbarian conquerors for personally superintending industrial occupations, left no alternative but to allow to the cultivators, as an incentive to exertion, some real interest in the soil. If, for example, they were compelled to labour, three days in the week, for their superior, the produce of the remaining days was their own. If they were required to supply the provisions of various sorts, ordinarily [q]needed[q] for the consumption of the castle, and were often subject to requisitions in excess, yet after supplying these demands they were suffered to dispose at their will of whatever additional produce they could raise. Under this system during the Middle Ages it was not impossible, no more than in [r]modern Russia (where, up to the recent measure of emancipation, the same system still essentially prevailed),[r] for serfs to acquire property; and in fact, their accumulations are the primitive source of the wealth of modern Europe.

In that age of violence and disorder, the first use made by a serf of any small provision which he had been able to accumulate, was to buy his freedom and withdraw himself to some town or fortified village, which had remained undestroyed from the time of the Roman dominion; or, without

[p]MS § 8.
[q-q]MS, 48, 49 required
[r-r]MS, 48, 49, 52, 57, 62 Russia at present (where the same system still essentially prevails)

buying his freedom, to abscond thither. In that place of refuge, surrounded by others of his own class, he attempted to live, secured in some measure from the outrages and exactions of the warrior caste, by his own prowess and that of his fellows. These emancipated serfs mostly became artificers; and lived by exchanging the produce of their industry for the surplus food and material which the soil yielded to its feudal proprietors. This gave rise to a sort of European counterpart of the economical condition of Asiatic countries; except that, in lieu of a single monarch and a fluctuating body of favourites and employés, there was a numerous and in a considerable degree fixed class of great landholders; exhibiting far less splendour, because individually disposing of a much smaller surplus produce, and for a long time expending the chief part of it in maintaining the body of retainers whom the warlike habits of society, and the little protection afforded by government, rendered indispensable to their safety. The greater stability, the fixity of personal position, which this state of society afforded, in comparison with the Asiatic polity to which it economically corresponded, was [s] one main reason why it was also found more favourable to improvement. From this time the economical advancement of society has not been further interrupted. Security of person and property grew slowly, but steadily; the arts of life made constant progress; plunder ceased to be the [t]principal[t] source of accumulation; and feudal Europe ripened into commercial and manufacturing Europe. In the latter part of the Middle Ages, the towns of Italy and Flanders, the free cities of Germany, and some towns of France and England, contained a large and energetic population of artisans, and many rich burghers, whose wealth had been acquired by manufacturing industry, or by trading in the produce of such industry. The Commons of England, the Tiers-Etat of France, the bourgeoisie of the Continent generally, are the descendants of this class. As these were a saving class, while the posterity of the feudal aristocracy were a squandering class, the former by degrees substituted themselves for the latter as the owners of a great proportion of the land. This natural tendency was in some cases retarded by laws contrived for the purpose of detaining the land in the families of its [u]existing[u] possessors, in other cases accelerated by political revolutions. Gradually, though more slowly, the immediate cultivators of the soil, in all the more civilized countries, ceased to be in a servile or semi-servile state: though the legal position, as well as the economical condition attained by them, vary extremely in the different nations of Europe, and in the great communities which have been founded beyond the Atlantic by the descendants of Europeans.

[v] The world now contains several extensive regions, provided with the

[s]MS, 48, 49, 52, 57 probably
[t-t]MS, 48, 49 only
[u-u]+62, 65, 71
[v]MS § 9.

various ingredients of wealth in a degree of abundance of which former ages had not even the idea. Without compulsory labour, an enormous mass of food is annually extracted from the soil, and maintains, besides the actual producers, an equal, sometimes a greater number of labourers, occupied in producing conveniences and luxuries of innumerable kinds, or in transporting them from place to place; also a multitude of persons employed in directing and superintending these various labours; and over and above all these, a class more numerous than in the most luxurious ancient societies, of persons whose occupations are of a kind not directly productive, and of persons who have no occupation at all. The food thus raised supports a far larger population than had ever existed (at least in the same regions) on an equal space of ground; and supports them with certainty, exempt from those periodically recurring famines so abundant in the early history of Europe, and in Oriental countries even now not unfrequent. Besides this great increase in the quantity of food, it has greatly improved in quality and variety; while conveniences and luxuries, other than food, are no longer limited to a small and opulent class, but descend, in great abundance, through many widening strata in society [w] . The collective resources of one of these communities, when it chooses to put them forth for any unexpected purpose; its ability to maintain fleets and armies, to execute public works, either useful or ornamental, to perform national acts of beneficence like the ransom of the West India slaves; to found colonies, to have its people taught, to do anything in short which requires expense, and to do it with no sacrifice of the necessaries or even the substantial comforts of its inhabitants, are such as the world never saw before.

But in all these particulars, characteristic of the modern industrial communities, those communities differ widely from one another. Though abounding in wealth as compared with former ages, they do so in very different degrees. Even of the countries which are justly accounted the richest, some have made a more complete use of their productive resources, and have obtained, relatively to their territorial extent, a much larger produce, than others; nor do they differ only in amount of wealth, but also in the rapidity of its increase. The diversities in the distribution of wealth are still greater than in the production. There are great differences in the condition of the poorest class in different countries; and in the proportional numbers and opulence of the classes which are above the poorest. The very nature and designation of the classes who originally share among them the produce of the soil, vary not a little in different places. In some, the landowners are a class in themselves, almost entirely separate from the classes engaged in industry: in others, the proprietor of the land is

[w]MS, 48, 49 , whatever doubt may exist as to the amount of improvement effected in the condition of the lowest of all

almost universally its cultivator, owning the plough, [x]and often[x] himself holding it. Where the proprietor himself does not cultivate, there is sometimes, between him and the labourer, an intermediate agency, that of the farmer, who advances the subsistence of the labourers, supplies the [y]instruments[y] of production, and receives, after paying a rent to the landowner, all the produce: in other cases, the landlord, his paid agents, and the labourers, are the only sharers. Manufactures, again, are sometimes carried on by scattered individuals, who own or hire the tools or machinery they require, and employ little labour besides that of their own family; in other cases, by large numbers working together in one building, with expensive and complex machinery owned by rich manufacturers. The same difference exists in the operations of trade. The wholesale operations indeed are everywhere carried on by large capitals, where such exist; but the retail dealings, which collectively occupy a [z]very great[z] amount of capital, are sometimes conducted in small shops, chiefly by the personal exertions of the dealers themselves, with their families, and perhaps an apprentice or two; and sometimes in large establishments, of which the funds are supplied by a wealthy individual or association, and the agency is that of numerous salaried shopmen or shopwomen. Besides these differences in the economical phenomena presented by different parts of what is usually called the civilized world, all those earlier states which we previously passed in review, have continued in some part or other of the world, down to our own time. Hunting communities still exist in America, nomadic in Arabia and the steppes of Northern Asia; Oriental society is in essentials what it has always been; [a]the great empire of Russia is[a] even now, in many respects, the scarcely modified image of feudal Europe. Every one of the great types of human society, down to that of the Esquimaux or Patagonians, is still extant.

[b] These remarkable differences in the state of different portions of the human race, with regard to the production and distribution of wealth, must, like all other phenomena, depend on causes. And it is not a sufficient explanation to ascribe them exclusively to the degrees of knowledge possessed at different times and places, of the laws of nature and the physical arts of life. Many other causes co-operate; and that very progress and unequal distribution of physical knowledge are partly the effects, as well as partly the causes, of the state of the production and distribution of wealth.

In so far as the economical condition of nations turns upon the state of physical knowledge, it is a subject for the physical sciences, and the arts founded on them. But in so far as the causes are moral or psychological,

[x-x]MS, 48, 49, 52, 57 if not
[y-y]MS, 48 implements
[z-z]MS much greater
[a-a]MS, 48 Russia and Hungary are
[b]MS § 10.

dependent on institutions and social relations, or on the principles of human nature, their investigation belongs not to physical, but to moral and social science, and is the object of what is called Political Economy.

The production of wealth; the extraction of the instruments of human subsistence and enjoyment from the materials of the globe, is evidently not an arbitrary thing. It has its necessary conditions. Of these, some are physical, depending on the properties of matter[c], [d]and[d] on the amount of knowledge of those properties possessed at the particular place and time[c]. These Political Economy does not investigate, but assumes; referring for [e]the grounds[e], to physical science or common experience. Combining with these facts of outward nature other truths [f]relating to[f] human nature, it attempts to trace the secondary or derivative laws, by which the production of wealth is determined; [g] in which must lie the explanation of the diversities of riches and poverty in the present and past, and the ground of whatever [h]increase[h] in wealth is reserved for the future.

Unlike the laws of Production, those of Distribution are partly of human institution: since the manner in which wealth is distributed in any given society, depends on the statutes or usages therein [i]obtaining[i]. But though governments or nations [j]have the power of deciding[j] what institutions shall [k]exist[k], they cannot arbitrarily determine how those institutions shall work. The conditions on which the power they possess over the distribution of wealth is dependent, and the manner in which the distribution is [l]effected[l] by the various modes of conduct which society may think fit to adopt, are [m]as much a subject for scientific enquiry as any of the physical laws of nature[m].

The laws of Production and Distribution, and some of the practical consequences deducible from them, are the subject of the following treatise.

[c-c]+52, 57, 62, 65, 71
[d-d]52, 57, 62 or rather
[e-e]MS, 48, 49 proof
[f-f]MS, 48, 49 which are laws of
[g]MS, 48, 49 and
[h-h]MS, 48, 49 progress
[i-i]MS, 48, 49, 52, 57 prevalent
[j-j]MS, 48, 49 can in some measure determine
[k-k]MS, 48, 49 be established
[l-l]MS, 48, 49, 52, 57 affected
[m-m]MS determined by laws as rigid, & as independent of human control, as those of Production itself] 48, 49 *as* MS . . . rigid as those . . . *as* MS

BOOK I

PRODUCTION

CHAPTER I

Of the Requisites of Production

§ 1. [*Requisites of production, what*] The requisites of production are two: labour, and appropriate natural objects.

Labour is either bodily or mental; or, to express the distinction more comprehensively, either muscular or nervous; and it is necessary to include in the idea, not solely the exertion itself, but all feelings of a disagreeable kind, all bodily inconvenience or mental annoyance, connected with the employment of one's thoughts, or muscles, or both, in a particular occupation. Of the other requisite—appropriate natural objects—it is to be remarked, that some objects exist or grow up spontaneously, of a kind suited to the supply of human wants. There are caves and hollow trees capable of affording shelter; fruit, roots, wild honey, and other natural products, on which human life can be supported; but even here a considerable quantity of labour is generally required, not for the purpose of creating, but of finding and appropriating them. In all but these few and (except in the very commencement of human society) unimportant cases, the objects supplied by nature are only instrumental to human wants, after having undergone some degree of transformation by human exertion. Even the wild animals of the forest and of the sea, from which the hunting and fishing tribes derive their sustenance—though the labour of which they are the subject is chiefly that required for appropriating them—must yet, before they are used as food, be killed, divided into fragments, and subjected in almost all cases to some [a]culinary process[a], which are operations requiring a certain degree of human labour. The amount of transformation which natural substances undergo before being brought into the shape in which they are directly applied to human use, varies from this or a still less degree of alteration in the nature and appearance of the object, to a change so total that no trace is perceptible of the original shape and structure. There is little resemblance between a piece of a mineral substance found in the earth, and a plough, an axe, or a saw. There is less resemblance between porcelain and the decomposing granite of which it is made, or between sand mixed with sea-weed, and glass. The difference is greater still between the fleece of a sheep, or a handful of cotton seeds, and a web

[a-a]MS, 48, 49, 52, 57 process of cookery

of muslin or broad cloth; and the sheep and seeds themselves are not spontaneous growths, but results of previous labour and care. In these several cases the ultimate product is so extremely dissimilar to the substance supplied by nature, that in the custom of language nature is represented as only furnishing materials.

Nature, however, does more than supply materials; she also supplies powers. The matter of the globe is not an inert recipient of forms and properties impressed by human hands; it has active energies by which it co-operates with, and may even be used as a substitute for, labour. In the early ages [b]people[b] converted their corn into flour by pounding it between two stones; they next hit on a contrivance which enabled them, by turning a handle, to make one of the stones revolve upon the other; and this process, a little improved, is still the common practice of the East. The muscular exertion, however, which it required, was very severe and exhausting, insomuch that it was often selected as a punishment for slaves who had offended their masters. When the time came at which the labour and sufferings of slaves were thought worth economizing, the greater part of this bodily exertion was rendered unnecessary, by contriving that the upper [c]stone[c] should be made to revolve upon the lower, not by human strength, but by the force of the wind or of falling water. In this case, natural agents, the wind or the gravitation of the water, are made to do a portion of the work previously done by labour.

§ 2. [*The function of labour defined*] Cases like this, in which a certain amount of labour has been dispensed with, its work being devolved upon some natural agent, are apt to suggest an erroneous notion of the comparative functions of labour and natural powers; as if the co-operation of those powers with human industry were limited to the cases in which they are made to perform what would otherwise be done by labour; as if, in the case of things made (as the phrase is) by hand, nature only furnished passive materials. This is an illusion. The powers of nature are as actively operative in the one case as in the other. A workman takes a stalk of the flax or hemp plant, splits it into separate fibres, twines together several of these fibres with his fingers, aided by a simple instrument called a spindle; having thus formed a thread, he lays many such threads side by side, and places other similar threads directly across them, so that each passes alternately over and under those which are at right angles to it; this part of the process being facilitated by an instrument called a shuttle. He has now produced a web of cloth, either linen or sackcloth, according to the material. He is said to have done this by hand, no natural force being supposed to have acted in concert with him. But by what force is each step of

[b-b]MS, 48, 49 men [c-c]MS millstone

this operation rendered possible, and the web, when produced, held together? [a]By the tenacity, or force of cohesion, of the fibres:[a] which is one of the forces in nature, and which we can measure exactly against other mechanical forces, and ascertain how much of any of them it suffices to neutralize or counterbalance.

If we examine any other case of what is called the action of man upon nature, we shall find in like manner that the powers of nature, or in other words the properties of matter, do all the work, when once objects are put into the right position. This one operation, of putting things into fit places for being acted upon by their own internal forces, and by those residing in other natural objects, is all that man does, or can do, with matter [b] . He only moves one thing to or from another. He moves a seed into the ground; and the natural forces of vegetation produce in succession a root, a stem, leaves, flowers, and fruit. He moves an axe through a tree, and it falls by the natural force of gravitation; he moves a saw through it, in a particular manner, and the physical properties by which a softer substance gives way before a harder, make it separate into planks, which he arranges in certain positions, with [c]nails driven through them, or[c] adhesive matter between them, and produces a table, or a house. He moves a spark to fuel, and it [d]ignites[d], and by the force [e]generated in[e] combustion it cooks the food, melts or softens the iron, converts into beer or sugar the malt or cane-juice, which he has previously moved to the spot. He has no other means of acting on matter than by moving it. Motion, and resistance to motion, are the only things which his muscles are constructed for. By muscular contraction he can create a pressure on an outward object, which, if sufficiently powerful, will set it in motion, or if it be already moving, will check or modify or altogether arrest its motion, and he can do no more. But this is enough to have given [f] all the command which mankind have acquired over natural forces immeasurably more powerful than themselves; a command which, great as it is already, is without doubt destined to become indefinitely greater. He [g]exerts[g] this power either by availing himself of natural forces in existence, or by arranging objects in those mixtures and combinations by which natural forces are generated; as when by putting a lighted match to fuel, and water into a boiler over it, he

[a–a]MS, 48, 49 Is it not by the tenacity, or force of cohesion, of the fibres?

[b]MS [*footnote:*] *Note.* See the first chapter of Mill's Elements of Political Economy. [Mill, James. *Elements of Political Economy.* London: Baldwin, Cradock, and Joy, 1821. Chapter i: "Production," pp. 6–7. JSM later quotes from the 3rd ed., 1826, in which the passage occurs on pp. 5–6.]

[c–c]MS, 48, 49 some

[d–d]MS takes fire

[e–e]MS, 48, 49, 52, 57 of

[f]MS, 48, 49 him

[g–g]MS exercises

generates the expansive force of steam, a power which has been made so largely available for the attainment of human purposes.*

Labour, then, in the physical world, is always and solely employed in putting objects in motion; the properties of matter, the laws of nature, do the rest. The skill and ingenuity of human beings [h]are[h] chiefly exercised in discovering movements, practicable by their powers, and capable of bringing about the effects which they desire. But, while movement is the only effect which man can immediately and directly produce by his muscles, it is not necessary that he should produce directly by them all the movements which he requires. The first and most obvious substitute is the muscular action of cattle: by degrees [i]the powers of inanimate nature are made to aid[i] in this too, as by making the wind, or water, things already in motion, communicate a part of their motion to the [j]wheels[j], which before that invention [k]were made to[k] revolve by muscular force. [l]This service is extorted[l] from the powers of wind and water by a set of actions, consisting like the former in moving certain objects into certain positions in which they constitute what is termed a [m]machine[m]; but the muscular action necessary for this is not constantly renewed, but performed once for all, and there is on the whole a great economy of labour.

§ 3. [*Does nature contribute more to the efficacy of labour in some occupations than in others?*] Some writers have raised the question, whether nature gives more assistance to labour in one kind of industry or in another; and have said that in some occupations labour does most, in others nature most. In this, however, there seems much confusion of ideas. The part which nature has in any work of man, is indefinite and incommensurable. It is impossible to decide that in any one thing nature does more than in any other. One cannot even say that labour does less. [a]Less labour may be[a] required; but if that which is required is absolutely indispensable, the result is just as much the product of labour, as of nature. When two conditions are equally necessary for producing the effect at all, it is [b]unmeaning[b] to say that so much of it is produced by one and so much by the other; it is like

*[62] This essential and primary law of man's power over nature was, I believe, first illustrated and made prominent as a fundamental principle of Political Economy, in the first chapter of Mr. Mill's *Elements*. [*See* Vol. I, p. 27[b], *where the same passage is referred to.*]

[h-h]MS, 48 is
[i-i]MS, 48, 49 he makes the powers of inanimate nature aid him
[j-j]MS millstones
[k-k]MS, 48, 49 he made
[l-l]MS, 48, 49 He extorts this service
[m-m]MS windmill or watermill
[a-a]MS, 48, 49 One may say, that less labour is
[b-b]MS, 48, 49, 52, 57 useless

attempting to decide which half of a pair of scissors has most to do in the act of cutting; or which of the factors, five and six, contributes most to the production of thirty. The form which this conceit usually assumes, is that of supposing that nature lends more assistance to human endeavours in agriculture, than in manufactures. This notion, held by the French Economistes, and from which Adam Smith was not free, arose from a misconception of the nature of rent. The rent of land being a price paid for a natural agency, and no such price being paid in manufactures, these writers imagined that since a price was paid, it was because there was a greater amount of service to be paid for: whereas a better consideration of the subject would have shown [c] that the reason why the use of land bears a price is simply the limitation of its quantity, and that if air, heat, electricity, chemical agencies, and the other powers of nature employed by manufacturers, were sparingly supplied, and could, like land, be engrossed and appropriated, a rent could be exacted for them also.

§ 4. [*Some natural agents limited, others practically unlimited, in quantity*] This leads to a distinction which we shall find to be of primary importance. Of natural powers, some are unlimited, others limited in quantity. By an unlimited quantity is of course [a]not meant[a] literally, but practically unlimited: a quantity beyond [b]the use which can in any, or at least[b] in present circumstances, be made of it. Land is, in some newly settled countries, practically unlimited in quantity: there is more than can be used by the existing population of the country, or by any accession likely to be made to it for [c]generations[c] to come. But even there, land favourably situated with regard to markets or means of carriage, is generally limited in quantity: there is not so much of it as persons would gladly occupy and cultivate, or otherwise turn to use. In all old countries, land capable of cultivation, land at least of any tolerable fertility, must be ranked among agents limited in quantity. Water, for ordinary purposes, on the banks of rivers or lakes, may be regarded as of unlimited abundance; but if required for irrigation, it may even there be insufficient to supply all wants, while in places which depend for their consumption on cisterns or tanks, or on wells which are not copious, or are liable to fail, water takes its place among things the quantity of which is most strictly limited. Where water itself is plentiful, yet waterpower, *i.e.* a fall of water applicable by its mechanical force to the service of industry, may be exceedingly limited, compared with the use which would be made of it if it were more abundant. Coal, metallic

[c]MS them
[a-a]MS meant not
[b-b]MS any use which can ever, or at least which can
[c-c]MS a century

ores, and other useful substances found in the earth, are still more limited than land. They are not only strictly local but exhaustible; though, at a given place and time, they may exist in much greater abundance than would be applied to present use even if they could be obtained gratis. Fisheries, in the sea, are in most cases a gift of nature practically unlimited in amount; but the Arctic whale fisheries have long been insufficient for the demand which exists even at the very considerable price necessary to defray the cost of appropriation: and the immense extension which the Southern fisheries have in consequence assumed, is tending to exhaust them likewise. River fisheries are a natural resource of a very limited character, and would be rapidly exhausted, if allowed to be used by every one without restraint. Air, even that state of it which we term wind, may, in most situations, be obtained in a quantity sufficient for every possible use; and so likewise, on the sea coast or on large rivers, may water carriage: though the wharfage or harbour-room applicable to the service of that mode of transport is in many situations far short of what would be used if easily attainable.

It will be seen hereafter how much of the economy of society depends on the limited quantity in which some of the most important natural agents exist, and more particularly land. For the present I shall only remark that so long as the quantity of a natural agent is practically unlimited, it cannot, unless susceptible of artificial monopoly, bear any value in the market, since no one will give anything for what can be obtained gratis. But as soon as a limitation becomes practically operative; as soon as there is not so much of the thing to be had, as would be appropriated and used if it could be obtained for asking; the ownership or use of the natural agent acquires an exchangeable value. When more [d]water power is[d] wanted in a particular district, than there are falls of water to supply [e]it[e], persons will give an equivalent for the use of a fall of water. When there is more land wanted for cultivation than a place possesses, or than it possesses of a certain quality and certain advantages of situation, land of that quality and situation may be sold for a price, or let for an annual rent. This subject will hereafter be discussed at length; but it is often useful to anticipate, by a brief suggestion, principles and deductions which we have not yet reached the place for exhibiting and illustrating fully.

[d-d]MS watermills are
[e-e]MS them

CHAPTER II

Of Labour as an Agent of Production

§ 1. [*Labour employed either directly about the thing produced, or in operations preparatory to its production*] The labour which terminates in the production of an article fitted for some human use, is either employed directly about the thing, or in previous operations destined to facilitate, perhaps essential to the possibility of, the subsequent ones. In making bread, for example, the labour employed about the thing itself is that of the baker; but the labour of the miller, though employed directly in the production not of bread but of flour, is equally part of the aggregate sum of labour by which the bread is produced; as is also the labour of the sower and of the reaper. Some may think that all these persons ought to be considered as employing their labour directly about the thing; the corn, the flour, and the bread being one substance in three different states. Without disputing about this question of mere language, there is still the ploughman, who prepared the ground for the seed, and whose labour never came in contact with the substance in any of its states; and the plough-maker, whose share in the result was still more remote. All these persons ultimately derive the remuneration of their labour from the bread, or its price: the plough-maker as much as the rest; for since ploughs are of no use except for tilling the soil, no one would make or use ploughs for any other reason than because the increased returns, thereby obtained from the ground, afforded a source from which an adequate equivalent could be assigned for the labour of the plough-maker. If the produce is to be used or consumed in the form of bread, it is from the bread that this equivalent must come. The bread must suffice to remunerate all these labourers, and several others; [a]such as[a] the carpenters and bricklayers who erected the farm-buildings; the hedgers and ditchers who made the fences necessary for the protection of the crop; the [b]miners and smelters[b] who extracted or prepared the iron of which the plough and other [c]instruments[c] were made. These, however, and the plough-

[a-a]MS the millwright who built the mill;
[b-b]MS, 48, 49, 52, 57 miner and smelter
[c-c]MS, 48, 49, 52, 57, 62 implements

maker, do not depend for their remuneration upon the bread made from the produce of a single harvest, but upon that made from the produce of all the harvests which are successively gathered until the plough, or the [d] buildings and fences, are worn out. We must add yet another kind of labour; that of transporting the produce from the place of its production to the place of its destined use: the labour of carrying the corn to market, and from market to the miller's, the flour from the miller's to the baker's, and the bread from the baker's to the place of its final consumption. This labour is sometimes very considerable: flour is transported to England from beyond the Atlantic, corn from the heart of Russia; and in addition to the labourers immediately employed, the waggoners and sailors, there are also costly instruments, such as ships, in the construction of which much labour has been expended: that labour, however, not depending for its whole remuneration upon the bread, but for a part only; ships being usually, during the course of their existence, employed in the transport of many different kinds of commodities.

To estimate, therefore, the labour of which any given commodity is the result, is far from a simple operation. The items in the calculation are very numerous—as it may seem to some persons, infinitely so; for if, as a part of the labour employed in making bread, we count the labour of the blacksmith who made the plough, why not also (it may be asked) the labour of making the tools used by the blacksmith, and the tools used in making those tools, and so back to the origin of things? But after mounting one or two steps in this ascending scale, we come into a region of fractions too minute for calculation. Suppose, for instance, that the same plough will last, before being worn out, a dozen years. Only one-twelfth of the labour of making the plough must be placed to the account of each year's harvest. A twelfth part of the labour of making a plough is an appreciable quantity. But the same set of tools, perhaps, suffice to the plough-maker for forging a hundred ploughs, which serve during the twelve years of their existence to prepare the soil of [e]as many[e] different farms. A twelve-hundredth part of the labour of making [f]his[f] tools, is as much, therefore, as has been expended in procuring one year's harvest of a single farm: and when this fraction comes to be further apportioned among the various sacks of corn and loaves of bread, it is seen at once that such quantities are not worth taking into the account for any practical purpose connected with the commodity. It is true that if the tool-maker had not laboured, the corn and bread never would have been produced; but they will not [g]be sold[g] a tenth part of a farthing dearer in consideration of his labour.

[d]MS farm
[e-e]MS, 48, 49, 52, 57 a hundred
[f-f]MS, 48, 49, 52, 57, 62 the
[g-g]MS, 48 sell

§ 2. [*Labour employed in producing subsistence for subsequent labour*] Another of the modes in which labour is indirectly or remotely instrumental to the production of a thing, requires particular notice: namely, when it is employed in producing subsistence, to maintain the labourers while they are engaged in the production. This previous employment of labour is an indispensable condition to every productive operation, on any other than the very smallest scale. Except the labour of the hunter and fisher, there is scarcely any kind of labour to which the returns are immediate. Productive operations require to be continued a certain time, before their fruits are obtained. Unless the labourer, before commencing his work, possesses a store of food, or can obtain access to the stores of some one else, in sufficient quantity to maintain him until the production is completed, he can undertake no labour but such as can be carried on at odd intervals, concurrently with the pursuit of his subsistence. He cannot obtain food itself in any abundance; for every mode of so obtaining it, requires that there be already food in store. Agriculture only brings forth food after the lapse of months; and though the labours of the agriculturist are not necessarily continuous during the whole period, they must occupy a considerable part of it. Not only is agriculture impossible without food produced in advance, but there must be a very great quantity in advance to enable any considerable community to support itself wholly by agriculture. A country like England or France is only able to carry on the agriculture of the present year, because that of past years has provided, in those countries or somewhere else, sufficient food to support their agricultural population until the next harvest. They are only enabled to produce so many other things besides food, because the food which was in store at the close of the last harvest suffices to maintain not only the agricultural labourers, but a large industrious population besides.

The labour employed in producing this stock of subsistence, forms a great and important part of the past labour which has been necessary to enable present labour to be carried on. But there is a difference, requiring particular notice, between this and the other kinds of previous or preparatory labour. The miller, the reaper, the ploughman, the plough-maker, the waggoner and waggon-maker, even the sailor and ship-builder when employed, derive their remuneration from the ultimate product—the bread made from the corn on which they have severally operated, or supplied the instruments for operating. The labour that produced the food which fed all these labourers, is as necessary to the ultimate result, the bread of the present harvest, as any of those other portions of labour; but is not, like them, remunerated from it. That previous labour has received its remuneration from the previous food. In order to raise any product, there are needed labour, tools, and materials, and food to feed the labourers. But the tools and materials are of no use except for obtaining the product, or at least are to be applied to no other use, and the labour of their construction can be remunerated only from the product when obtained. The food, on the contrary, is intrinsically useful, and is applied to [a]the direct use[a] of feeding human beings. The labour expended in producing the food, and recompensed by it, needs not be remunerated over again from the produce of the subsequent labour which it has fed. If we suppose that the same body of labourers carried on a manufacture, and grew food to sustain themselves while doing it, they have had for their trouble the food and the manufactured article; but if they also grew the material and made the tools, they have had nothing for that trouble but the manufactured article alone.

The claim to remuneration founded on the possession of food, available for the maintenance of labourers, is of another kind; remuneration for abstinence, not for labour. If a person has a store of food, he [b]has it in his power to[b] consume it himself in idleness, or in feeding others to attend on him, or to fight for him, or to sing or dance for him. If, instead of these things, he gives it to productive labourers to support them during their work, he can, and naturally will, claim a remuneration from the produce. He will not be content with simple repayment; if he receives merely that, he is only in the same situation as at first, and has derived no advantage from delaying to apply his savings to his own benefit or pleasure. He will look for some equivalent for this forbearance: he will expect his advance of food to come back to him with an increase, called in the language of business, a profit; and the hope of this profit will generally have been a part of the inducement which made him accumulate a stock, by economizing in his own consumption; or, at any rate, which made him forego the application of it, when accumulated, to his personal ease or satisfaction. The food also which maintained other workmen while producing the tools or materials, must have been provided in advance by some one, and he, too, must have his profit from the ultimate product; but there is this difference, that here the ultimate product has to supply not only the profit, but also the remuneration of the labour. The tool-maker (say, for instance, the plough-maker) does not indeed usually wait for his payment until the harvest is reaped; the farmer advances it to him, and steps into his place by becoming the owner of the plough. Nevertheless, it is from the harvest that the payment is to come; since the farmer would not undertake this outlay unless he expected that the harvest would repay him, and with a profit too on this fresh advance; that is, unless the harvest would yield, besides the remuneration of the farm labourers (and a profit for advancing it), a sufficient residue to remunerate the plough-maker's labourers, give the plough-maker a profit, and a profit to the farmer on both.

[a-a]MS, 48, 49 its direct use, that [b-b]MS may

§ 3. [*Labour employed in producing materials*] From these considerations it appears, that in an enumeration and classification of the kinds of industry which are intended for the indirect or remote furtherance of other productive labour, we need not include the labour of producing subsistence or other necessaries of life to be consumed by productive labourers; for the main end and purpose of [a]this[a] labour is the subsistence itself; and though the possession of a store of it enables other work to be done, this is but an incidental consequence. The remaining modes in which labour is indirectly instrumental to production, may be arranged under five heads.

First: Labour employed in producing materials, on which industry is to be afterwards employed. This is, in many cases, a labour of mere appropriation; *extractive* industry, as [b]it has been aptly named by M. Dunoyer[b]. The labour of the miner, for example, consists of operations for digging out of the earth substances convertible by industry into various articles fitted for human use. Extractive industry, however, is not confined to the extraction of materials. Coal, for instance, is employed, not only in the [c]process[c] of industry, but in directly warming human beings. When so used, it is not a material [d]of production[d], but is itself the ultimate product. So, also, in the case of a mine of precious stones. These are to some small extent employed in the productive arts, as diamonds by the glass-cutter, emery and corundum for polishing, but their principal destination, that of ornament, is a direct use; though they commonly require, before being so used, some process of manufacture, which may perhaps warrant our regarding them as materials. Metallic ores of all sorts are materials merely.

Under the head, production of materials, we must include the industry of the wood-cutter, when employed in cutting and preparing timber for building, or wood for the purposes of the carpenter's or any other art. In the forests of America, Norway, Germany, the Pyrenees and Alps, this sort of labour is largely employed on trees of spontaneous growth. In other cases, we must add to the labour of the wood-cutter that of the planter and cultivator.

[e]Under the same head are also comprised[e] the labours of the agriculturist in growing flax, hemp, cotton, feeding silkworms, raising food for cattle, producing bark, dye-stuffs, [f]some[f] oleaginous plants, and many other things only useful because required in other departments of industry. So, too, the labour of the hunter, as far as his object is furs or feathers; of the shepherd and the cattle-breeder, in respect of wool, hides, horn, bristles, horse-hair,

[a-a]62 his
[b-b]MS M. Dunoyer terms it] 48, 49, 52, 57 it has been called
[c-c]MS, 48, 49, 52, 57, 62 processes
[d-d]+62, 65, 71
[e-e]MS The same head also comprises
[f-f]+62, 65, 71

and the like. The things used as materials in some process or other of manufacture are of a most miscellaneous character, drawn from almost every quarter of the animal, vegetable, and mineral kingdoms. And besides this, the finished products of many branches of industry are the materials of others. The thread produced by the spinner is applied to hardly any use except as material for the weaver. Even the product of the loom is chiefly used as material for the fabricators of articles of dress or furniture, or of further instruments of productive industry, as in the case of the sailmaker. The currier and tanner find their whole occupation in converting raw material into what may be termed prepared material. In strictness of speech, almost all food, as it comes from the hands of the agriculturist, is nothing more than material for the occupation of the baker or the cook.

§ 4. [*Labour employed in producing implements*] The second kind of indirect labour is that employed in making tools or implements for the assistance of labour. I use these terms in their most comprehensive sense, embracing all permanent instruments or helps to production, from a flint and [a] steel for striking a light, to a steam ship, or the most complex apparatus of manufacturing machinery. There may be some hesitation where to draw the line between implements and materials; and some things used in production (such as fuel) would scarcely in common language be called by either name, popular phraseology being shaped out by a different class of necessities from those of scientific exposition. To avoid a multiplication of classes and denominations answering to distinctions of no scientific importance, political economists generally include all things which are used as *immediate* means of production (the means which are not immediate will be considered presently) either in the class of implements or in that of materials. Perhaps the line is most usually and most conveniently drawn, by considering as a material every instrument of production which can only be used once, being destroyed (at least as an instrument for the purpose in hand) by a single employment. Thus fuel, once burnt, cannot be again used as fuel; what can be so used is only any portion which has remained unburnt the first time. And not only it cannot be used without being consumed, but it is only useful by being consumed; for if no part of the fuel were destroyed, no heat would be generated. A fleece, again, is destroyed as a fleece by being spun into thread; and the thread cannot be used as thread when woven into cloth. But an axe is not destroyed as an axe by cutting down a tree: it may be used afterwards to cut down a hundred or a thousand more; and though deteriorated in some small degree by each use, it does not do its work by being deteriorated, as the coal and the fleece do theirs by being destroyed; on the contrary, it is the better instrument the better it

[a]MS, 48, 49 a piece of

resists deterioration. There are some things, rightly classed as materials, which may be used as such a second and a third time, but not while the product to which they at first contributed remains in existence. The iron which formed a tank or a set of pipes may be melted [b] to form a plough or a steam-engine; the stones with which a house was built may be used after it is pulled down, to build another. But this cannot be done while the original product subsists; their function as materials is suspended, until the exhaustion of the first use. Not so with the things classed as implements; they may be used repeatedly [c]for[c] fresh work, until the time, sometimes very distant, at which they are worn out, while the work already done by them may subsist unimpaired, and when it perishes, does so by its own laws, or by casualties of its own.*

The only practical difference of much importance arising from the distinction between materials and implements, is one which has attracted our attention in another case. Since materials are destroyed as such by being once used, the whole of the labour required for their production, as well as the abstinence of the person who supplied the means for carrying it on, must be remunerated from the fruits of that single use. Implements, on the contrary, being susceptible of repeated employment, the whole of the products which they are instrumental in bringing into existence are a fund which can be drawn upon to remunerate the labour of their construction, and the abstinence of those by whose accumulations that labour was supported. It is enough if each product contributes a fraction, commonly an insignificant one, towards the remuneration of that labour and abstinence, or towards indemnifying the immediate producer for advancing that remuneration to the person who produced the tools.

§ 5. [*Labour employed in the protection of labour*] Thirdly: Besides materials for industry to employ itself on, and implements to aid it, pro-

*[49] The able and friendly reviewer [49, 52, 57 The reviewer] of this treatise in the Edinburgh Review (October 1848) conceives [49, 52, 57, 62 states] the distinction between materials and implements rather differently: proposing to consider as materials "all the things which, after having undergone the change implied in production, are themselves matter of exchange," and as implements (or instruments) "the things which are employed in producing that change, but do not themselves become part of the exchangeable result." According to these definitions [49 this distinction], the fuel consumed in a manufactory would be considered, not as a material, but as an instrument. This use of the terms accords better than that proposed in the text, with the primitive physical meaning of the word "material;" but the distinction on which it is grounded is one almost irrelevant to political economy [49 instrument. The question is of little importance]. [*Edinburgh Review*, LXXXVIII (Oct., 1848), 314. The review is by Nassau Senior.]

[b]MS, 48, 49 down   [c-c]MS in

vision must be made to prevent its operations from being disturbed, and its products injured, either by the destroying agencies of nature, or by the violence or rapacity of men. This gives rise to another mode in which labour not employed directly about the product itself, is instrumental to its production; namely, when employed for the *protection* of industry. Such is the object of all buildings for industrial purposes; all manufactories, warehouses, docks, granaries, barns, farm-buildings devoted to cattle, or to the operations of agricultural labour. I exclude those in which the labourers live, or which are destined for their personal accommodation: these, like their food, supply actual wants, and must be counted in the remuneration of their labour. There are many modes in which labour is still more directly applied to the protection of productive operations. The herdsman has little other occupation than to protect the cattle from harm: the positive agencies concerned in the realization of the product, go on nearly of themselves. I have already mentioned the labour of the hedger and ditcher, of the builder of walls or dykes. To these must be added that of the soldier, the policeman, and the judge. These functionaries are not indeed employed exclusively in the protection of industry, nor does their payment constitute, to the individual producer, a part of the expenses of production. But they are paid from the taxes, which are derived from the produce of industry; and in any tolerably governed country they render to its operations a service far more than equivalent to the cost. To society at large they are therefore part of the expenses of production; and if the returns to production were not sufficient to maintain these labourers in addition to all the others required, production, at least in that form and manner, could not take place. Besides, if the protection which the government affords to the operations of industry were not afforded, the producers would be under a necessity of either withdrawing a large share of their time and labour from production, to employ it in defence, or of engaging armed men to defend them; all which labour, in that case, must be directly remunerated from the produce; and things which [a]could[a] not pay for this additional labour, would not be produced. Under the present arrangements, the product pays its quota towards the same protection, and notwithstanding the waste and prodigality incident to government expenditure, obtains it of better quality at a much smaller cost.

§ 6. [*Labour employed in the transport and distribution of the produce*] Fourthly: There is a very great amount of labour employed, not in bringing the product into existence, but in rendering it, when in existence, accessible to those for whose use it is intended. Many important classes of labourers find their sole employment in some function of this kind. There is first the

[a–a]MS, 48, 49, 52, 57 would

whole class of carriers, by land or water: muleteers, waggoners, bargemen, sailors, wharfmen, coalheavers, porters, railway establishments, and the like. Next, there are the constructors of all the implements of transport; ships, barges, carts, locomotives, &c., to which must be added roads, canals, and railways. Roads are sometimes made by the government, and opened gratuitously to the public; but the labour of making them is not the less paid for from the produce. Each producer, in paying his quota of the taxes levied generally for the construction of roads, pays for the use of those which conduce to his convenience; and if made with any tolerable judgment, they increase the returns to his industry by far more than an equivalent amount.

Another numerous class of labourers employed in rendering the things produced accessible to their intended consumers, is the class of dealers and traders, or, as they may be termed, distributors. There would be a great waste of time and trouble, and an inconvenience often amounting to impracticability, if consumers could only obtain the articles they want by treating directly with the producers. Both producers and consumers are too much scattered, and the latter often at too great a distance from the former. To diminish this loss of time and labour, the contrivance of fairs and markets was early had recourse to, where consumers and producers might periodically meet, without any intermediate agency; and this plan answers tolerably well for many articles, especially agricultural produce, agriculturists having at some seasons a certain quantity of spare time on their hands. But even in this case, attendance is often very troublesome and inconvenient to buyers who have other occupations, and do not live in the immediate vicinity; while, for all articles the production of which requires continuous attention from the producers, these periodical markets must be held at such considerable intervals, and the wants of the consumers must either be provided for so long beforehand, or must remain so long unsupplied, that even before the resources of society [a]admitted of[a] the establishment of shops, the supply of these wants fell universally into the hands of itinerant dealers: the pedlar, who might appear once a month, being preferred to the fair, which only returned once [b]or twice[b] a year. In country districts, remote from towns or large villages, the industry of the pedlar is not yet wholly superseded. But a dealer who has a fixed abode and fixed customers is so much more to be depended on, that consumers prefer resorting to him if he is conveniently accessible; and dealers therefore find their advantage in establishing themselves in every locality where there are sufficient consumers near at hand to afford them a remuneration.

In many cases the producers and dealers are the same persons, at least

[a-a]MS, 48, 49 permitted
[b-b]+52, 57, 62, 65, 71

as to the ownership of the funds and [c]the[c] control of the operations. The tailor, the shoemaker, the baker, and many other tradesmen, are the producers of the articles they deal in, so far as regards the last stage in the production. This union, however, of the functions of manufacturer and retailer is only expedient when the article [d]can[d] advantageously be made at or near the place convenient for retailing it, and is, besides, manufactured and sold in small parcels. When things have to be brought from a distance, the same person cannot effectually superintend both the making and the retailing of them; when they are best and most cheaply made on a large scale, a single manufactory requires so many [e]local channels[e] to carry off its supply, that the retailing [f]is most conveniently[f] delegated to other agency; and even shoes and coats, when they are to be furnished in large quantities at once, as for the supply of [g]a regiment[g] or of a workhouse, are usually obtained not directly from the producers, but from intermediate dealers, who make it their business to ascertain from what producers they can be obtained best [h]and[h] cheapest. Even when things are destined to be at last sold by retail, convenience soon creates a class of wholesale dealers. When products and transactions have multiplied beyond a certain point; when one manufactory supplies many shops, and one shop has often to obtain goods from many different manufactories, the loss of time and trouble both to the manufacturers and to the retailers by treating directly with one another makes it more convenient to them to treat with a smaller number of great dealers or merchants, who only buy to sell again, collecting goods from the various producers and distributing them to the retailers, to be by them further distributed among the consumers. Of these various elements is composed the [i] Distributing Class, whose agency is supplementary to that of the Producing Class: and the produce so distributed, or its price, is the source from which the distributors are remunerated for their [j] exertions, and for the abstinence which enabled them to advance the funds needful for the business of distribution.

§ 7. [*Labour which relates to human beings*] We have now completed the enumeration of the modes in which labour employed on external nature is subservient to production. But there is yet another mode of employing labour, which conduces equally, though still more remotely, to that end: this is, labour of which the subject is human beings. Every human being has been brought up from infancy at the expense of much labour to some person or persons, and if this labour, or part of it, had not been bestowed, the

[c-c]+48, 49, 52, 57, 62, 65, 71
[d-d]MS may
[e-e]MS shops
[f-f]MS must necessarily be
[g-g]MS an army,
[h-h]52, 57 or
[i]MS great
[j]MS, 48, 49 personal

child would never have attained the age and strength which enable him to become a labourer in his turn. To the community at large, the labour and expense of rearing its infant population [a]form[a] a part of the outlay which is a condition of production, and [b]which[b] is to be replaced with increase from the future produce of their labour. By the [c]individuals[c], this labour and expense are usually incurred from other motives than to obtain such ultimate return, and, for most purposes of political economy, need not be taken into account as expenses of production. But the technical or industrial education of the community; the labour employed in learning and in teaching the arts of production, in acquiring and communicating skill in those arts; this labour is really, and in general solely, undergone for the sake of the greater or more valuable produce thereby attained, and in order that a remuneration, equivalent or more than equivalent, may be reaped by the learner, besides an adequate remuneration for the labour of the teacher, when a teacher has been employed.

As the labour which confers productive powers, whether of hand or of head, may be looked upon as part of the labour by which society accomplishes its productive operations, or in other words, as part of what the produce costs to society, so too may the labour employed in keeping up productive powers; in preventing them from being destroyed or weakened by accident or disease. The labour of a physician or surgeon, when made use of by persons engaged in industry, must be regarded in the economy of society as a sacrifice incurred, to preserve from perishing by death or infirmity that portion of the productive resources of society which is fixed in the lives and bodily or mental powers of its productive members. To the individuals, indeed, this forms but a part, sometimes an imperceptible part, of the motives that induce them to submit to medical treatment: it is not principally from economical motives that persons have a limb amputated, or endeavour to be cured of a fever, though when they do so, there is generally sufficient inducement for it even on that score alone. This is, therefore, one of the cases of labour and outlay which, though conducive to production, yet not being incurred for that end, or for the sake of the returns arising from it, are out of the sphere of most of the general propositions which political economy has occasion to assert respecting productive labour: though, when society and not the individuals are considered, this labour and outlay must be regarded as part of the advance by which society effects its productive operations, and for which it is indemnified by the produce.

§ 8. [*Labour of invention and discovery*] Another kind of labour, usually classed as mental, but conducing to the ultimate product as directly,

[a-a]MS, 48, 49 forms [b-b]+49, 52, 57, 62, 65, 71 [c-c]MS, 48, 49 individual

though not so immediately, as manual labour itself, is the labour of the inventors of industrial processes. I say, usually classed as mental, because in reality it is not exclusively so. All human exertion is compounded of some mental and some bodily elements. The stupidest hodman, who repeats from day to day the mechanical act of climbing a ladder, performs a function [a]partly[a] intellectual; [b]so much so, indeed, that[b] the most intelligent dog or elephant [c]could not, probably,[c] be taught to do it. The dullest human being, instructed beforehand, is capable of turning a mill; but a horse cannot turn it without somebody to [d]drive[d] and watch him. On the other hand, there is some bodily ingredient in the labour most purely mental, when it generates any external result. Newton could not have produced the Principia without the bodily exertion either of penmanship or of dictation; and [e]he must have drawn many diagrams, and written out many calculations and demonstrations,[e] while he was preparing it in his mind. Inventors, besides the labour of their brains, generally go through much labour with their hands, in the models which they construct and the experiments they have to make before their idea can realize itself successfully in act. Whether mental, however, or bodily, their labour is a part of that by which the production is brought about. The labour of Watt in contriving the steam-engine was as essential a part of production as that of the mechanics who build or the engineers who work the instrument; and was undergone, no less than theirs, in the prospect of a remuneration from the produce. The labour of invention is often estimated and paid on the very same plan as that of execution. Many manufacturers of ornamental goods have inventors in their employment, who receive wages or salaries for designing patterns, exactly as others do for copying them. All this is strictly part of the labour of production; as the labour of the author of a book is equally a part of its production with that of the printer and binder.

In a national, or universal point of view, the labour of the savant, or speculative thinker, is as much a part of production in the very narrowest sense, as that of the inventor of a practical art; many such inventions having been the direct consequences of theoretic discoveries, and every extension of knowledge of the powers of nature being fruitful of applications to the purposes of outward life. The electromagnetic telegraph was the wonderful and most unexpected consequence of the experiments of Œrsted and the mathematical investigations of Ampère: and the modern art of navigation is an unforeseen emanation from the purely speculative and apparently merely

[a-a]MS essentially
[b-b]+65, 71
[c-c]MS could not] 48, 49 probably could not] 52, 57 could not, perhaps,
[d-d]MS, 48, 49 guide
[e-e]MS many a figure must he have drawn & calculation or demonstration written out] 48, 49, 52, 57, 62 *as* 71 . . . drawn many figures . . . *as* 71

curious enquiry, by the mathematicians of Alexandria, into the properties of three curves formed by the intersection of a plane surface and a cone. No limit can be set to the importance, even in a purely productive and material point of view, of mere thought. Inasmuch, however, as these material fruits, though the result, are seldom the direct purpose of the pursuits of savants, nor is their remuneration in general derived from the increased production which may be caused incidentally, and mostly after a long interval, by their discoveries; this ultimate influence does not, for most of the purposes of political economy, require to be taken into consideration; and speculative thinkers are generally classed as the producers only of the books, or other useable or saleable articles, which directly emanate from them. But when (as in political economy one should always be prepared to do) we shift our point of view, and consider not individual acts, and the motives by which they are determined, but national and universal results, intellectual speculation must be looked upon as a most influential part of the productive labour of society, and the portion of its resources employed in carrying on and in remunerating such labour, as a highly productive part of its expenditure.

§ 9. [*Labour agricultural, manufacturing, and commercial*] In the foregoing survey of the modes of employing labour in furtherance of production, I have made little use of the popular distinction of industry into agricultural, manufacturing, and commercial. For, in truth, this division fulfils very badly the purposes of a classification. Many great branches of productive industry find no place in it, or not without much straining; for example (not to speak of hunters or fishers) the miner, the road-maker, and the sailor. The limit, too, between agricultural and manufacturing industry cannot be precisely drawn. The miller, for instance, and the baker—are they to be reckoned among agriculturists, or among manufacturers? Their occupation is in its nature manufacturing; the food has finally parted company with the soil before it is handed over to them: this, however, might be said with equal truth of the thresher, the winnower, the makers of butter and cheese; operations always counted as agricultural, probably because it is the custom for them to be performed by persons resident on the farm, and under the same superintendence as tillage. For many purposes all these persons, the miller and baker inclusive, must be placed in the same class with ploughmen and reapers. They are all concerned in producing food, and depend for their remuneration on the food produced; [a]when[a] the one class abounds and flourishes, the others do so too; they form collectively the "agricultural interest;" they render but one service to the community by their united labours, and are paid from one common

[a-a]MS, 48, 49 where

source. Even the tillers of the soil, again, when the produce is not food, but the materials of what are commonly termed manufactures, belong in many respects to the same division in the economy of society as manufacturers. The cotton-planter of Carolina, and the wool-grower of Australia, have more interests in common with the spinner and weaver than with the corn-grower. But, on the other hand, the industry which operates immediately upon the soil has, as we shall see hereafter, some properties on which many important consequences depend, and which distinguish it from all the subsequent stages of production, whether carried on by the same [b]person[b] or not; from the industry of the thresher and winnower, as much as from that of the cotton-spinner. When I speak, therefore, of agricultural labour, I shall generally mean this, and this exclusively, unless the contrary is either stated or implied in the context. The term manufacturing is too vague to be of much use when precision is required, and when I employ it, I wish to be understood as intending to speak popularly rather than scientifically.

[b-b]MS persons

CHAPTER III

Of Unproductive Labour

§ 1. [*Labour does not produce objects, but utilities*] Labour is indispensable to production, but has not always production for its effect. There is much labour, and of a high order of usefulness, of which production is not the object. Labour has accordingly been distinguished into Productive and Unproductive. There has been not a little controversy among political economists on the question, what kinds of labour should be reputed to be unproductive; and they have not always perceived, that there was in reality no matter of fact in dispute between them.

Many writers have been unwilling to class any labour as productive, unless its result is palpable in some material object, capable of being transferred from one person to another. There are others (among whom are Mr. M'Culloch and M. Say) who looking upon the word unproductive as a term of disparagement, remonstrate against imposing it upon any labour which is regarded as useful—which produces a benefit or a pleasure worth the cost. The labour of officers of government, of the army and navy, of physicians, lawyers, teachers, musicians, dancers, actors, domestic servants, &c., when they really accomplish what they are paid for, and are not more numerous than is required for its performance, ought not, say these writers, to be "stigmatized" as unproductive, an expression which they appear to regard as synonymous with wasteful or worthless. But this seems to [a]be[a] a misunderstanding of the matter in dispute. Production not being the sole end of human existence, the term unproductive does not necessarily imply any stigma; nor was ever intended to do so in the present case. The question is one of mere language and classification. Differences of language, however, are by no means unimportant, even when not grounded on differences of opinion; for though either of two expressions may be consistent with the whole truth, they generally tend to fix attention upon different parts of it. We must therefore enter a little into the consideration of the various meanings which may attach to the words productive and unproductive when applied to labour.

In the first place, even in what is called the production of material objects, it must be remembered that what is produced is not the matter

[a–a]MS, 48, 49, 52, 57, 62 me

composing them. All the labour of all the human beings in the world could not produce one particle of matter. To weave broadcloth is but to re-arrange, in a peculiar manner, the particles of wool; to grow corn is only to put a portion of matter called a seed, into a situation where it can draw [b]together particles of matter from the earth and air, to form[b] the new combination called a plant. Though we cannot create matter, we can cause it to assume properties, by which, from having been useless to us, it becomes useful. What we produce, or desire to produce, is always, as M. Say rightly terms it, an utility. [c]Labour[c] is not creative of objects, but of utilities. Neither, again, do we consume and destroy the objects themselves; the matter of which they were composed remains, more or less altered in form: what has really been consumed is only [d]the qualities by which they were fitted for the purpose they have been applied to[d]. It is, therefore, pertinently asked by M. Say and others—since, when we are said to produce objects, we only produce utility, why should not all labour which produces utility be accounted productive? Why refuse that title to the [e]surgeon who sets a limb[e], the judge or legislator who confers security, and give it to the lapidary who cuts and polishes a diamond? Why deny it to the teacher from whom I learn an art by which I can gain my bread, and accord it to the confectioner who makes bonbons for the momentary pleasure of a sense of taste?

It is quite true that all these kinds of labour are productive of utility; and the question which now occupies us could not have been a question at all, if the production of utility were enough to satisfy the notion which mankind have usually formed of productive labour. Production, and productive, are of course elliptical expressions, involving the idea of a something produced; but this something, in common apprehension, I conceive to be, not utility, but Wealth. Productive labour means labour productive of wealth. We are recalled, therefore, to the question touched upon in our first chapter, what Wealth is, and whether only material products, or all useful products, are to be included in it.

§ 2. [*These utilities are of three kinds*] Now the utilities produced by labour are of three kinds. They are,

First, utilities fixed and embodied in outward objects; by labour employed in [a]investing[a] external material things with properties which render them serviceable to human beings. This is the common case, and requires no illustration.

[b-b]MS to itself other particles of matter from the earth & air, forming
[c-c]MS Our labour
[d-d]MS their useful qualities
[e-e]MS physician who restores health
[a-a]MS impressing

Secondly, utilities fixed and embodied in human beings; the labour being in this case employed in conferring on human beings, qualities which render them serviceable to themselves and others. To this class belongs the labour of all concerned in education; not only schoolmasters, tutors, and professors, but [b] governments, so far as they aim successfully at the improvement of the people; moralists, and clergymen, as far as productive of [c] benefit; the labour of physicians, as far as instrumental in preserving life and physical or mental efficiency; of the teachers of bodily exercises, and of the various trades, sciences, and arts, together with the labour of the learners in acquiring them; and all labour bestowed by any persons, throughout life, in improving the knowledge or cultivating the bodily or mental faculties of themselves or others.

Thirdly and lastly, utilities not fixed or embodied in any object, but consisting in a mere service rendered; a pleasure given, an inconvenience or a pain averted, during a longer or a shorter time, but without leaving a permanent acquisition in the improved qualities of any person or thing; the labour being employed in producing an utility directly, not (as in the two former cases) in fitting some other thing to afford an utility. Such, for example, is the labour of the musical performer, the actor, the public declaimer or reciter, and the showman. Some good may no doubt be produced, [d]and much [e]more[e] might be produced,[d] beyond the moment, upon the feelings and disposition, or general state of enjoyment of the spectators; or instead of good there may be harm; but neither the one nor the other is the effect intended, is the result for which the exhibitor works and the spectator pays; nothing but the immediate pleasure. Such, again, is the labour of the army and navy; they, at the best, prevent a country from being conquered, or from being injured [f]or[f] insulted, which is a service, but in all other respects leave the country neither improved nor deteriorated. Such, too, is the labour of the legislator, the judge, the officer of justice, and all other agents of government, in their ordinary functions, apart from any influence they may exert on the improvement of the national mind. The service which they render, is to maintain peace and security; these compose the utility which they produce. It may appear to some, that carriers, and merchants or dealers, should be placed in this same class, since their labour does not add any properties to objects: but I reply that it does: it adds the property of being in the place where they are wanted, instead of being in some other place: which is a very useful property, and the utility it confers is embodied in the things themselves, which now

[b]MS parents, so far as they concern themselves in the education of their children;
[c]MS any
[d-d]+52, 57, 62, 65, 71
[e-e]+62, 65, 71
[f-f]MS, 48, 49 and

actually are in the place where they are required for use, and in consequence of that increased utility could be sold at an increased price, proportioned to the labour expended in conferring it. This labour, therefore, does not belong to the third class, but to the first.

§ 3. [*Productive labour is that which produces utilities fixed and embodied in material objects*] We have now to consider which of these three classes of labour should be accounted productive of wealth, since that is what the term productive, when used by itself, must be understood to import. Utilities of the third class, consisting in pleasures which only exist while being enjoyed, and services which only exist while being performed, cannot be spoken of as wealth, except by an acknowledged metaphor. It is essential to the idea of wealth to be susceptible of accumulation: things which cannot, after being produced, be kept for some time before being used, are never, I think, regarded as wealth, since however much of them may be produced and enjoyed, the person benefited by them is no richer, is nowise improved in circumstances. But there is not so distinct and positive a violation of usage in considering as wealth any product which is both useful and susceptible of accumulation. The skill, and the energy and perseverance, of the artisans of a country, are reckoned part of its wealth, no less than their tools and machinery.* According to this definition, we should regard all labour as productive which is employed in creating permanent utilities, whether embodied in human beings, or in any other animate or inanimate objects. [a]This[a] nomenclature I have, in a former

*[65] Some authorities look upon it as an essential element in the idea of wealth, that it should be capable not solely of being accumulated but of being transferred; and inasmuch as the valuable qualities, and even the productive capacities, of a human being, cannot be detached from him and passed to some one else, they deny to these the appellation of wealth, and to the labour expended in acquiring them the name of productive labour. It seems to me, however, that the skill of an artisan (for instance) being both a desirable possession, and one of a certain durability (not to say productive even of national wealth), there is no better reason for refusing to it the title of wealth because it is attached to a man, than to a coalpit or manufactory because they are attached to a place. Besides, if the skill itself cannot be parted with to a purchaser, the use of it may; if it cannot be sold, it can be hired; and it may be, and is, sold outright in all countries whose laws permit that the man himself should be sold along with it. Its defect of transferability does not result from a natural but from a legal and moral obstacle. The human being himself (as formerly observed) I do not class as wealth. He is the purpose for which wealth exists. But his acquired capacities, which exist only as means, and have been called into existence by labour, fall rightly, as it seems to me, within that designation.

[a-a]MS, 48, 49, 52, 57, 62 And this

publication,* recommended, as [b]most conducive to[b] the ends of classification[c]; and I am still of that opinion[c].

But in applying the term wealth to the industrial capacities of human beings, there seems always, in popular apprehension, to be a tacit reference to material products. The skill of an artisan is accounted wealth, only as being the means of acquiring wealth in a material sense; and any qualities not tending visibly to that object are scarcely so regarded at all. A country would hardly be said to be richer, except by a metaphor, however precious a possession it might have in the genius, the virtues, or the accomplishments of its inhabitants; unless indeed these were looked upon as marketable articles, by which it could attract the material wealth of other countries, as the Greeks of old, and several modern nations have done. While, therefore, I should prefer, were I constructing a new technical language, to make the distinction turn upon the permanence rather than upon the materiality of the product, yet when employing terms which common usage has taken complete possession of, it seems advisable so to employ them as to do the least possible violence to [d] usage; since any improvement in terminology obtained by straining the received meaning of a popular phrase, is generally purchased beyond its value, by the obscurity arising from the conflict between new and old associations.

I shall, therefore, in this treatise, when speaking of wealth, understand by it only what is called material wealth, and by productive labour only those kinds of exertion which produce utilities embodied in material objects. But in limiting myself to this sense of the word, I mean to avail myself of the full extent of that restricted acceptation, and I shall not refuse the appellation productive, to labour which yields no material product as its direct result, provided that an increase of material products is its ultimate consequence. Thus, labour expended in the acquisition of manufacturing skill, I class as productive, not in virtue of the skill itself, but of the manufactured products created by the skill, and to the creation of which the labour of learning the trade is essentially conducive. The labour of officers of government in affording the protection which, afforded in some manner or other, is indispensable to the prosperity of industry, must be classed as productive even of material wealth, because without it, material wealth, in anything like its present abundance, could not exist. Such labour may

**Essays on some Unsettled Questions of Political Economy* [London: Parker, 1844]. Essay III. On the words Productive and Unproductive [pp. 75–89].

[b-b]MS a kind of compromise between] 48, 49 the most conformable to] 52, 57, 62 the most conducive to

[c-c]MS and the existing customs of language] 48, 49, 52, 57, 62 , though not strictly conformable to the customs of language

[d]MS, 48, 49 that

be said to be productive indirectly or mediately, in opposition to the labour of the ploughman and the cotton-spinner, which are productive immediately. They are all alike in this, that they leave the community richer in material products than they found it; they increase, or tend to increase, material wealth.

§ 4. [*All other labour, however useful, is classed as unproductive*] By Unproductive Labour, on the contrary, will be understood labour which does not terminate in the creation of material wealth; which, however largely or successfully practised, does not render the community, and the world at large, richer in material products, but poorer by all that is consumed by the labourers while so employed.

All labour is[a], in the language of political economy,[a] unproductive, which ends in immediate enjoyment, without any increase of the accumulated stock of permanent means of enjoyment. And [b]all[b] labour, according to our present definition, must be classed as unproductive, which terminates in a permanent benefit, however important, provided that an increase of material products forms no part of that benefit. The labour of saving a friend's life is not productive, unless the friend is a productive labourer, and produces more than he consumes. To a religious person the saving of a soul must appear a far more important service than the saving of a life; but he will not therefore call a missionary or a clergyman productive labourers, unless they teach, as the South Sea Missionaries have in some cases done, the arts of civilization in addition to the doctrines of [c]their[c] religion. It is, on the contrary, evident that the greater number of missionaries or clergymen a nation maintains, the less it has to expend on other things; while the more it expends judiciously in keeping agriculturists and manufacturers at work, the more it will have for every other purpose. By the former it diminishes, *cæteris paribus*, its stock of material products; by the latter, it increases them.

Unproductive may be as useful as productive labour; it may be more useful, even in point of permanent advantage; or its use may consist only in pleasurable sensation, which when gone leaves no trace; or it may not afford even this, but may be absolute waste. In any case society or mankind grow no richer by it, but poorer. All material products consumed by any one while he produces nothing, are so much subtracted, for the time, from the material products which society would otherwise have possessed. But though society grows no richer by unproductive labour, the individual may. An unproductive labourer may receive for his labour, from those

[a-a]+48, 49, 52, 57, 62, 65, 71
[b-b]+48, 49, 52, 57, 62, 65, 71
[c-c]+52, 57, 62, 65, 71

who derive pleasure or benefit from it, a remuneration which may be to him a considerable source of wealth; but his gain is balanced by their loss; they may have received a full equivalent for their expenditure, but they are so much poorer by it. When a tailor makes a coat and sells it, there is a transfer of the price from the customer to the tailor, and a coat besides which did not previously exist; but what is gained by an actor is a mere transfer from the spectator's funds to his, leaving no article of wealth for the spectator's indemnification. Thus the community collectively gains nothing by the actor's labour; and it loses, of his receipts, all that portion which he consumes, retaining only that which he lays by. A community, however, may add to its wealth by unproductive labour, at the expense of other communities, as an individual may at the expense of other individuals. The gains of Italian opera singers, [d]German[d] governesses, French ballet dancers, &c., are a source of wealth, as far as they go, to their respective countries[e], if they return thither[e]. The petty states of Greece, especially the ruder and more backward of those states, were nurseries of soldiers, who hired themselves to the princes and satraps of the East to carry on useless and destructive wars, and returned with their savings to pass their declining years in their own country: these were unproductive labourers, and the pay they received, together with the plunder they took, was an outlay without return to the countries which furnished it; but, though no gain to the world, it was a gain to Greece. At a later period the same country and its colonies supplied the Roman empire with another class of adventurers, who, under the name of philosophers or of rhetoricians, taught to the youth of the higher classes what were esteemed the most valuable accomplishments: these were mainly unproductive labourers, but their ample recompense was a source of wealth to their own country. In none of these cases was there any accession of wealth to the world. The services of the labourers, if useful, were obtained at a sacrifice to the world of a portion of material wealth; if useless, all that these labourers consumed was [f]to the world[f] waste.

To be wasted, however, is a liability not confined to unproductive labour. Productive labour may equally be [g]wasted[g], if more of it is expended than really conduces to production. If defect of skill in labourers, or of judgment in those who direct them, causes a misapplication of productive industry; if a farmer [h]persists[h] in ploughing with three horses and two men, when experience has shown that two horses and one man are sufficient, the surplus labour, though employed for purposes of production, is wasted. If a new process is adopted which proves no better, or not so good as those

[d-d]MS Swiss
[e-e]+48, 49, 52, 57, 62, 65, 71
[f-f]+65, 71
[g-g]MS, 48, 49, 52, 57, 62 waste
[h-h]MS, 48, 49 perseveres

before in use, the labour expended in perfecting the invention and in carrying it into practice, though [i]employed for a productive purpose[i], is wasted. Productive labour may render a nation poorer, if the wealth it produces, that is, the increase it makes in the stock of useful or agreeable things, be of a kind not immediately wanted: as when a commodity is unsaleable, because produced in a quantity beyond the present demand; or when speculators build docks and warehouses before there is any trade. [j]Some of the[j] States of North America, [k]by making[k] premature railways and canals, [l]are thought to[l] have made this kind of mistake; and it [m]was for some time doubtful[m] whether England, in the disproportionate development of railway enterprise, [n]had[n] not[o], in some degree,[o] followed the example. Labour sunk in expectation of a distant return, when the great exigencies or limited resources of the community require that the return be rapid, may leave the country not only poorer in the meanwhile, by all which those labourers consume, but less rich even ultimately than if immediate returns had been sought in the first instance, and enterprises for distant profit postponed.

§ 5. [*Productive and Unproductive Consumption*] The distinction of Productive and Unproductive is applicable to consumption as well as to labour. All the members of the community are not labourers, but all are consumers, and consume either unproductively or productively. Whoever contributes nothing directly or indirectly to production, is an unproductive consumer. The only productive consumers are productive labourers; the labour of direction being of course included, as well as that of execution. But the consumption even of productive labourers is not all of it productive consumption. There is unproductive consumption by productive consumers. What they consume in keeping up or improving their health, strength, and capacities of work, or in [a]rearing[a] other productive labourers to succeed them, is productive consumption. But consumption on pleasures or luxuries, whether by the idle or by the industrious, since production is neither its object nor is in any way advanced by it, must be reckoned unproductive: with a reservation perhaps of a certain quantum of enjoyment which may be classed among necessaries, since anything short of it would not be consistent with the greatest efficiency of labour. That alone is productive consumption, which goes to maintain and increase the productive powers

[i-i]MS productive
[j-j]MS, 48, 49, 52, 57, 62, 65 The bankrupt
[k-k]MS, 48, 49, 52, 57, 62, 65 with their
[l-l]+71
[m-m]MS, 48, 49, 52, 57 remains to be shown
[n-n]MS, 48, 49, 52, 57 has
[o-o]+52, 57, 62, 65, 71
[a-a]MS, 48, 49 raising

of the community; either those residing in its soil, in its materials, in the number and efficiency of its instruments of production, or in its people.

There are numerous products which [b]may be said not to[b] admit of being consumed otherwise than unproductively. The annual consumption of gold lace, pine apples, or champagne, [c]must be reckoned[c] unproductive, since these things [d]give no assistance to production, nor any support to life or strength, but what would equally be given by things much less costly[d]. Hence it might be supposed that the labour employed in producing [e]them[e] ought not to be regarded as productive, [f]in the sense in which the term is understood by political economists[f]. I grant that no labour [g] tends to the [h]permanent[h] enrichment of society, which is employed in producing things for the use of unproductive consumers. The tailor who makes a coat for a man who produces nothing, is a productive labourer; but in a few weeks or months the coat is worn out, while the wearer has not produced anything to replace it, and the community is then no richer by the labour of the tailor, than if the same sum had been paid for a [i]stall[i] at the opera. Nevertheless, society has been richer by the labour while the coat lasted, that is, until society, through one of its unproductive members, chose to consume the produce of the labour unproductively. The case of the gold lace or the pine apple is no further different, than that [j]they are still further removed than the coat from the character of necessaries[j]. These things also are wealth until they have been consumed.

§ 6. [*Labour for the supply of Productive Consumption, and labour for the supply of Unproductive Consumption*] We see, however, by this, that there is a distinction, more important to the wealth of a community than even that between productive and unproductive labour; the distinction, namely, between labour for the supply of productive, and for the supply of unproductive, consumption; between labour employed in keeping up or in adding to the productive resources of the country, and that which is employed otherwise. Of the produce of the country, a part only is destined to be consumed productively; the remainder supplies the unproductive consumption of producers, and the entire consumption of the unproductive

[b-b]MS do not
[c-c]MS is all
[d-d]MS supply no natural want, support neither life nor strength nor give any assistance to production] 62 *as* 71 . . . production, or . . . *as* 71
[e-e]MS such things
[f-f]MS since the temporary addition which it makes to the wealth of the community, unavoidably perishes in the very next stage
[g]MS, 48, 49, 52, 57, 62 really
[h-h]+65, 71
[i-i]MS box
[j-j]MS society in this case had not the option of consuming them productively

classes. Suppose that the proportion of the annual produce applied to the first purpose amounts to half; then one-half the productive labourers of the country are all that are employed in the operations on which the permanent wealth of the country depends. The other half are occupied from year to year and from generation to generation in producing things which are consumed and disappear without return; and whatever this half consume is as completely lost, as to any permanent effect on the national resources, as if it were consumed unproductively. Suppose that this second half of the labouring population ceased to work, and that the government or their parishes maintained them in idleness for a whole year: the first half would suffice to produce, as they had done before, their own necessaries and the necessaries of the second half, and to keep the stock of materials and implements undiminished: the unproductive classes, indeed, would be either starved or obliged to produce their own subsistence, and the whole community would be reduced during a year to bare necessaries; but the sources of production would be unimpaired, and the next year there would not necessarily be a smaller produce than if no such interval of inactivity had occurred; while if the case had been reversed, if the first half of the labourers had suspended their accustomed occupations, and the second half had continued theirs, the country at the end of the twelvemonth would have been entirely impoverished.

It would be a great error to regret the large proportion of the annual produce, which in an opulent country goes to supply unproductive consumption. It would be to lament that the community has so much to spare from its necessities, for its pleasures and for all higher uses. This portion of the produce is the fund from which all the wants of the community, other than that of mere living, are provided for; the measure of its means of enjoyment, and of its power of accomplishing all purposes not productive. That so great a surplus should be available for such purposes, and that it should be applied to them, [a]can only be a subject[a] of congratulation. The things to be regretted, and [b]which are not incapable of being[b] remedied, are the prodigious inequality with which this surplus is distributed, [c]the little worth of the objects to which the greater part of it is devoted,[c] and the large share which falls to the lot of persons who render no equivalent service in return [d] .

[a-a]MS, 48, 49 is a subject only
[b-b]MS , as far as may be, to be] 48, 49, 52, 57 to be
[c-c]+52, 57, 62, 65, 71
[d]MS, 48, 49 ; topics of the greatest importance, but for the discussion of which, the proper place is in another division of our inquiry

CHAPTER IV

Of Capital

§ 1. [*Capital is wealth appropriated to reproductive employment*] It has been seen in the preceding chapters that besides the primary and universal requisites of production, labour and natural agents, there is another requisite without which no productive operations, beyond the rude and scanty beginnings of primitive industry, are possible: namely, a stock, previously accumulated, of the products of former labour. This accumulated stock of the produce of labour is termed Capital. The function of Capital in production, it is of the utmost importance thoroughly to understand, since a number of the erroneous notions with which our subject is infested, originate in an imperfect and confused apprehension of this point.

Capital, by persons wholly unused to reflect on the subject, is supposed to be synonymous with money. To expose this misapprehension, would be to repeat what has been said in the introductory chapter. Money is no more synonymous with capital than it is with wealth. Money cannot in itself perform any part of the office of capital, since it can afford no assistance to production. To do this, it must be exchanged for other things; and anything, which is susceptible of being exchanged for other things, is capable of contributing to production in the same degree. What capital does for production, is to afford the shelter, protection, tools and materials which the work requires, and to feed and otherwise maintain the labourers during the process. These are the services which present labour requires from past, and from the produce of past, labour. Whatever things are destined for this use—destined to supply productive labour with these various prerequisites—are Capital.

To familiarize ourselves with the conception, let us consider what is done with the capital invested in any of the branches of business which compose the productive industry of a country. A manufacturer, for example, has one part of his capital in the form of buildings, fitted and destined for carrying on [a]his[a] branch of manufacture. Another part he has in the form of machinery. A third consists, if he be a spinner, of raw cotton, flax, or wool; if a weaver, of flaxen, woollen, silk, or cotton, thread; and the like, according to the nature of the manufacture. Food and clothing for his

[a-a]62 this

operatives, it is not the custom of the present age that he should directly provide; and few capitalists, except the producers of food or clothing, have any portion worth mentioning of their capital in that shape. Instead of this, each capitalist has money, which he pays to his workpeople, and so enables them to supply themselves: he has also finished goods in his warehouses, by the sale of which he obtains more money, to employ in the same manner, as well as to replenish his stock of materials, [b]to keep his buildings and machinery in repair, and to replace them[b] when worn out. His money and finished goods, however, are not wholly capital, for he does not wholly devote them to these purposes: he employs a part of the one, and of the proceeds of the other, in supplying his personal consumption and that of his family, or in hiring grooms and valets, or maintaining hunters and hounds, or in educating his children, or in paying taxes, or in charity. What then is his capital? Precisely that part of his possessions, whatever it be, which [c]is to constitute his fund for[c] carrying on fresh production. It is of no consequence that a part, or even the whole of it, is in a form in which it cannot directly supply the wants of labourers.

Suppose, for instance, that [d]the[d] capitalist is a hardware manufacturer, and that his stock in trade, over and above his machinery, consists at present wholly in iron goods. Iron goods cannot feed labourers. Nevertheless, by a mere change of the destination of these iron goods, he can cause labourers to be fed. Suppose that with a portion of the proceeds he intended to maintain a pack of hounds, or an establishment of servants; and that he changes his intention, and employs it in his business, paying it in wages to additional workpeople. These workpeople are enabled to buy and consume the food which would otherwise have been consumed by the hounds or by the servants; and thus without the employer's having seen or touched one particle of the food, his conduct has determined that so much more of the food existing in the country has been devoted to the use of productive labourers, and so much less consumed in a manner wholly unproductive. Now vary the hypothesis, and suppose that what is thus paid in wages would otherwise have been laid out not in feeding servants or [e]hounds[e], but in buying plate and jewels; and in order to render the effect perceptible, let us suppose that the change takes place on a considerable scale, and that a large sum is diverted from buying plate and jewels to employing productive labourers, whom we shall suppose to have been previously, like the Irish peasantry, only half employed and half fed. The labourers, on receiving their increased wages, will not lay them out in plate

[b-b]MS, 48, 49 and to replace his buildings and machinery
[c-c]MS, 48, 49, 52, 57, 62 he designs to employ in
[d-d]MS, 48, 49 our
[e-e]MS animals

and [f]jewels,[f] but in food. There is not, however, additional food in the country; nor any unproductive labourers or animals, as in the former case, whose food is set free for productive purposes. Food will therefore be imported if possible; if not possible, the labourers will remain for a season on their short allowance: but the consequences of this change in the demand for commodities, occasioned by the change in the expenditure of capitalists from unproductive to productive, is that next year more food will be produced, and less plate and jewellery. So that again, without having had anything to do with the food of the labourers directly, the conversion by individuals of a portion of their property, no matter of what sort, from an unproductive destination to a productive, has had the effect of causing more food to be appropriated to the consumption of productive labourers. The distinction, then, between Capital and Not-capital, does not lie in the kind of commodities, but in the mind of the capitalist—in his will to employ them for one purpose rather than another; and all property, however ill adapted in itself for the use of labourers, is a part of capital, so soon as it, or the value to be received from it, is set apart for productive [g]reinvestment[g]. The sum of all the values so destined by their respective possessors, composes the capital of the country. Whether all those values are in a shape directly applicable to productive uses, makes no difference. [h]Their shape, whatever it may be, is a temporary accident: but once destined for production[h], they do not fail to find a way of transforming themselves into things [i]capable of being[i] applied to it.

§ 2. [*More capital devoted to production than actually employed in it*] As whatever of the produce of the country is devoted to production is capital, so, conversely, the whole of the capital of the country is devoted to production. This second proposition, however, must be taken with some limitations and explanations. A fund may be seeking for productive employment, and find none, adapted to the inclinations of its possessor: it then is capital still, but unemployed capital. Or the stock may consist of unsold goods, not susceptible of direct application to productive uses, and not, at the moment, marketable: these, until sold, are in the condition of unemployed capital. Again, artificial or accidental circumstances may render it necessary to possess a larger stock in advance, that is, a larger capital before entering on production, than is required by the nature of things. Suppose that the government lays a tax on the production in one of its earlier stages, as for instance by taxing the material. The manufacturer

[f-f]MS jewellery
[g-g]MS, 48, 49, 52 employment
[h-h]MS, 48, 49, 52, 57, 62 Once appropriated to that end
[i-i]MS, 48, 49, 52, 57, 62 fitted to be

has to advance the tax, before commencing the manufacture, and is therefore under a necessity of having a larger accumulated [a]fund[a] than is required for, or is actually employed in, the production which he carries on. He must have a larger capital, to maintain the same quantity of productive labour; or (what is equivalent) with a given capital he maintains less labour. This mode of levying taxes, therefore, limits unnecessarily the industry of the country: a portion of the fund destined by its owners for production being diverted from its purpose, and kept in a constant state of advance to the government.

For another example: a farmer may enter on his farm at such a time of the year, that he may be required to pay one, two, or even three quarters' rent before obtaining any return from the produce. This, therefore, [b]must be paid[b] out of his capital. Now rent, when paid for the land itself, and not for improvements made in it by labour, is not a productive expenditure. It is not an outlay for the support of labour, or for the provision of implements or materials the produce of labour. It is the price paid for the use of an appropriated natural agent. [c]This[c] natural agent is indeed as indispensable (and even more so) as any implement: but the having to pay a price for it, is not. In the case of the implement (a thing produced by labour) a price of some sort is the necessary condition of its existence: but the land exists by nature. The payment for it, therefore, is not one of the expenses of production; and the necessity of making [d]the[d] payment out of capital, makes it requisite that there should be a greater capital, a greater antecedent accumulation of the produce of past labour, than is naturally necessary, or than is needed where land is occupied on a different system. This extra capital, though intended by its owners for production, is in reality employed unproductively, and annually replaced, not from any produce of its own, but from the produce of the labour supported by the remainder of the farmer's capital.

Finally, that large portion of the productive capital of a country which is employed in paying the wages and salaries of labourers, evidently is not, all of it, strictly and indispensably necessary for production. As much of it as exceeds the actual necessaries of life and health (an excess which in the case of skilled labourers is usually considerable) is not expended in supporting labour, but in remunerating it, and the labourers could wait for this part of their remuneration until the production is completed; it needs not necessarily pre-exist as capital: and if they unfortunately had to forego it altogether, the same amount of production might take place. In order

[a-a]MS, 48, 49, 52, 57 stock
[b-b]MS, 48, 49 he is compelled to pay
[c-c]MS, 48, 49, 52 That
[d-d]MS, 48, 49 that

that the whole remuneration of the labourers should be advanced to them in daily or weekly payments, there must exist in advance, and be appropriated to productive use, a greater stock, or capital, than would suffice to carry on the existing extent of production: greater, by whatever amount of remuneration the labourers receive, beyond what the self-interest of a prudent slave-master would assign to [e]his[e] slaves. In truth, it is only after an abundant capital had already been accumulated, that the practice of paying in advance any remuneration of labour beyond a bare subsistence, could possibly have arisen: since whatever is so paid, is not really applied to production, but to the unproductive consumption of productive labourers, indicating a fund for production sufficiently ample to admit of habitually diverting a part of it to a mere convenience.

It will be observed that I have assumed, that the labourers are always subsisted from capital: and this is obviously the fact, though the capital needs not necessarily be furnished by a person called a capitalist. When the labourer maintains himself by funds of his own, as when a peasant-farmer or proprietor lives on the produce of his land, or an artisan works on his own account, they are still supported by capital, that is, by funds provided in advance. The peasant does not subsist this year on the produce of this year's harvest, but on that of the last. The artisan is not living on the proceeds of the work he has in hand, but on those of work previously executed and disposed of. Each is supported by a small capital of his own, which he periodically replaces from the produce of his labour. The large capitalist is, in like manner, maintained from funds provided in advance. If he personally conducts his operations, as much of his [f]personal or household expenditure[f] as does not exceed a fair remuneration of his labour at the market price, must be considered [g] a part of his capital, expended, like any other capital, for production: and his personal consumption, so far as it consists of necessaries, is productive consumption.

§ 3. [*Examination of some cases illustrative of the idea of Capital*] At the risk of being tedious, I must add a few more illustrations, to bring out into a still [a]clearer and stronger[a] light the idea of Capital. As M. Say truly remarks, it is on the very elements of our subject that illustration is most usefully bestowed, since the greatest errors which prevail in it may be traced to the want of a thorough mastery over the elementary ideas. Nor is this surprising: a branch may be diseased and all the rest healthy, but unsoundness at the root diffuses unhealthiness through the whole tree.

[e-e]52, 57 the
[f-f]MS, 48, 49 expenditure on himself and family
[g]MS, 48, 49 as
[a-a]MS, 48, 49, 52, 57, 62 stronger and clearer

Let us therefore consider whether, and in what cases, the property of those who live on the interest of what they possess, without being personally engaged in production, can be regarded as capital. It is so called in common language, and, with reference to the individual, not improperly. All funds from which the possessor derives an income, which income he can use without sinking and dissipating the fund itself, are to him equivalent to capital. But to transfer hastily and inconsiderately to the general point of view, propositions which are true of the individual, has been a source of innumerable errors in political economy. In the present instance, that which is virtually capital to the individual, is or is not capital to the nation, according as the fund which by the supposition he has not dissipated, has or has not been dissipated by somebody else.

For example, let property of the value of ten thousand pounds belonging to A, be lent to B, a farmer or manufacturer, and employed profitably in B's occupation. It is as much capital as if it belonged to B. A is really a farmer or manufacturer, not personally, but in respect of his property. [b]Capital worth[b] ten thousand pounds is employed in production—in maintaining labourers and providing tools and materials; which capital belongs to A, while B takes the trouble of employing it, and receives for his remuneration the difference between the profit which it yields and the interest he pays to A. This [c]is the simplest case[c].

Suppose next that A's ten thousand pounds, instead of being lent to B, are lent on mortgage to C, a landed proprietor, [d]by whom they are[d] employed in improving the productive powers of his estate, by fencing, draining, road-making, or permanent manures. This is productive employment. The ten thousand pounds are sunk, but not dissipated. They yield a permanent return; the land now affords an increase of produce, sufficient, in a few years, if the outlay has been judicious, to replace the amount, and in time to multiply it manifold. Here, then, is a value of ten thousand pounds, employed in increasing the produce of the country. This constitutes a capital, for which C, if he lets his land, receives the returns in the nominal form of increased rent; and the mortgage entitles A to receive from these returns, in the shape of interest, such annual sum as has been agreed [e]on[e]. We will now vary the circumstances, and suppose that C does not employ the loan in improving his land, but in paying off a former [f] mortgage, or in making a provision for children. Whether the ten thousand pounds thus employed are capital or [g]not[g], will depend on what is done with the amount

[b-b]MS A capital of
[c-c]MS, 48, 49 case is the simplest of all
[d-d]MS, 48, 49 and by him
[e-e]MS, 48, 49, 52 upon between them
[f]MS, 48, 49 and more onerous
[g-g]MS no

by the ultimate receiver. If the children invest their fortunes in a productive employment, or the mortgagee on being paid off lends the amount to another [h]landholder[h] to improve his land, or to a manufacturer to extend his business, it is still capital, because productively employed.

Suppose, however, that C, the borrowing landlord, is a spendthrift, who burdens his land not to increase his fortune but to squander it, expending the amount in equipages and entertainments. In a year or two it is dissipated, and without return. A is as rich as before; he has no longer his ten thousand pounds, but he has a lien on the land, which he could still sell for that amount. C, however, is 10,000*l*. poorer than formerly; and nobody is richer. It may be said that those are richer who have made profit out of the money while it was being spent. No doubt if C lost it by gaming, or was cheated of it by his servants, that is a mere transfer, not a destruction, and those who have gained the amount may employ it productively. But if C has received the fair value for his expenditure in articles of subsistence or luxury, which he has consumed on himself, or by means of his servants or guests, these articles have ceased to exist, and nothing has been produced to replace them: while if the same sum had been employed in farming or manufacturing, the consumption which would have taken place would have been more than balanced at the end of the year by new products, created by the [i]labour[i] of those who would in that case have been the consumers. By C's prodigality, that which would have been consumed with a return, is consumed without return. C's tradesmen may have made a profit during the process; but if the capital had been expended productively, an equivalent profit would have been made by builders, fencers, tool-makers, and the tradespeople who supply the consumption of the labouring classes; while at the expiration of the time (to say nothing of any increase), C would have had the ten thousand pounds or its value replaced to him, which now he has not. There is, therefore, on the general result, a difference to the disadvantage of the community, of at least ten thousand pounds, being the amount of C's unproductive expenditure. To A, the difference is not material, since his income is secured to him, and while the security is good, and the market rate of interest the same, he can always sell the mortgage at its original value. To A, therefore, the lien of ten thousand pounds on C's estate, is virtually a capital of that amount; but is it so in reference to the community? It is not. A had a capital of ten thousand pounds, but this has been extinguished—dissipated and destroyed by C's prodigality. A now receives his income, not from the produce of his capital, but from some other source of income belonging to C, probably from the rent of his land, that is, from payments made to him by farmers

[h-h]MS landowner
[i-i]MS, 48, 49 hands

out of the produce of *their* capital. The national capital is diminished by ten thousand pounds, and the national income by all which those ten thousand pounds, employed as capital, would have produced. The loss does not fall on the owner of the destroyed capital, since the destroyer has agreed to indemnify him for it. But his loss is only a small portion of that sustained by the community, since what was devoted to the use and consumption of the proprietor was only the interest; the capital itself was, or would have been, employed in the perpetual maintenance of an equivalent number of labourers, regularly reproducing what they consumed: and of this maintenance they are deprived without compensation.

Let us now vary the hypothesis still further, and suppose that the money is borrowed, not by a landlord, but by the State. A lends his capital to Government to carry on a war: he buys from the State what are called government securities; that is, obligations [j]on[j] the government to pay a certain annual income. If the government employed the money in making a railroad, this might be a productive employment, and A's property would still be used as capital; but since it is employed in war, that is, in the pay of officers and soldiers who produce nothing, and in destroying a quantity of gunpowder and bullets without return, the government is in the situation of C, the spendthrift landlord, and A's ten thousand pounds are so much national capital which once existed, but exists no longer: virtually thrown into the sea, as far as wealth or production is concerned; though for other reasons the employment of it may have been justifiable. A's subsequent income is derived, not from the produce of his own capital, but from taxes drawn from the produce of the remaining capital of the community; to whom his capital is not yielding any return, to indemnify them for the payment; it is lost and gone, and what he now possesses is a claim on the returns to other people's capital and industry. This claim he can sell, and get back the equivalent of his capital, which he may afterwards employ productively. True; but he does not get back his own capital, or anything which it has produced; that, and all its possible returns, are extinguished: what he gets is the capital of some other person, which that person is willing to exchange for his lien on the taxes. Another capitalist substitutes himself for A as a mortgagee of the public, and A substitutes himself for the other capitalist as the possessor of a fund employed in production, or available for it. By this exchange the productive powers of the community are neither increased nor diminished. The breach in the capital of the country was made when the government [k]spent[k] A's money: whereby a value of ten thousand pounds was withdrawn or withheld from productive employment, placed in the fund for unproductive consumption, and destroyed without equivalent.

[j-j]MS, 48, 49, 52, 57 by
[k-k]MS, 48, 49, 52, 57 took

CHAPTER V

Fundamental Propositions Respecting Capital

§ 1. [*Industry is limited by Capital*] If the preceding explanations have answered their purpose, they have given not only a sufficiently complete possession of the idea of Capital according to its definition, but a sufficient familiarity with it in the concrete, and amidst the obscurity with which the complication of individual circumstances surrounds it, to have prepared even the unpractised reader for certain elementary propositions or theorems respecting capital, the full comprehension of which is already a considerable step out of darkness into light.

The first of these propositions is, That industry is limited by capital. This is so obvious as to be taken for granted in many common forms of speech; but to see a truth occasionally is one thing, to recognise it habitually, and admit no propositions inconsistent with it, is another. The axiom was until lately almost universally disregarded by legislators and political writers; and doctrines irreconcileable with it are still very commonly professed and inculcated.

The following are common expressions, implying its truth. The act of directing industry to a particular employment is described by the phrase "applying capital" to the employment. To employ industry on the land is to apply capital to the land. To employ labour in a manufacture is to invest capital in the manufacture. This implies that industry cannot be employed to any greater extent than there is capital to invest. The proposition, indeed, must be assented to as soon as it is distinctly apprehended. The expression "applying capital" is of course metaphorical: what is really applied is labour; capital being an indispensable condition. Again, we often speak of the "productive powers of capital." This expression is not literally correct. The only productive powers are those of labour and natural agents; or if any portion of capital can by a stretch of language be said to have a productive power of its own, it is only tools and machinery, which, like wind or water, may be said to co-operate with labour. The food of labourers and the materials of production have no productive power; but labour cannot exert its productive power unless provided with them. There can be no more industry than is supplied with materials to work up and food to eat. Self-evident as the thing is, it is often forgotten that the people of a country are maintained and have their wants supplied, not by the produce of present labour, but of past. They consume what has been produced, not what is about to be produced. Now, of what has been produced, a part only is allotted to the support of productive labour; and there will not and cannot be more of that labour than the portion so allotted (which is the capital of the country) can feed, and provide with the materials and instruments of production.

Yet, in disregard of a fact so evident, it long continued to be believed that laws and governments, without creating capital, could create industry. Not by making the people more laborious, or increasing the efficiency of their labour; these are objects to which the government can, in some degree, [a]indirectly[a] contribute. But [b]without [c] any increase in the skill or energy of the labourers, and without causing any persons to labour who had previously been maintained in idleness[b], it was still thought that the government, without providing additional funds, could create additional employment. A government would, by prohibitory laws, put a stop to the importation of some commodity; and when by this it had caused the commodity to be produced at home, it would plume itself upon having enriched the country with a new branch of industry, would parade in statistical tables the amount of produce yielded and labour employed in the production, and take credit for the whole of this as a gain to the country, obtained through the prohibitory law. Although this sort of political arithmetic has fallen a little into discredit in England, it still flourishes in the nations of Continental Europe. Had legislators been aware that industry is limited by capital, they would have seen that, the aggregate capital of the country not having been increased, any portion of it which they by their laws had caused to be embarked in the newly-acquired branch of industry must have been withdrawn or withheld from some other; in which it gave, or would have given, employment to probably about the same quantity of labour which it employs in its new occupation.*

*An exception must be admitted when the industry created or upheld by the restrictive law belongs to the class of what are called domestic manufactures. These being carried on by persons already fed—by labouring families [MS, 48, 49 by the labourer, or his wife or children], in the intervals of other employment—no transfer of capital to the occupation is necessary to its being undertaken, beyond the value of the materials and tools, which is often [MS, 48, 49 often quite] inconsiderable. If, therefore, a protecting duty causes this occupa-

[a-a]+57, 62, 65, 71
[b-b]MS, 48, 49 when the people already worked as hard and as skilfully as they could be made to do
[c]52, 57 supposing

§ 2. [*Industry is limited by Capital, but does not always come up to that limit*] Because industry is limited by capital, we are not however to infer that it always reaches that limit. [a]Capital may be temporarily unemployed, as in the case of unsold goods, or funds that have not yet found an investment: during this interval it does not set in motion any industry. Or there[a] may not be as many labourers obtainable, as the capital would maintain and employ. This has been known to occur in new colonies, where capital has sometimes perished uselessly for want of labour: the Swan River settlement [b](now called Western Australia)[b], in the first years after its foundation, was an instance. There are many persons maintained from existing capital, who produce nothing, or who might produce much more than they do. If the labourers were reduced to lower wages, or induced to work more hours for the same wages, or if their families, who are already maintained from capital, were employed to a greater extent than they now are in adding to the produce, a given capital would afford employment to more industry. The unproductive consumption of productive labourers, the whole of which is now supplied [c]by[c] capital, might cease, or be postponed until the produce came in; and additional productive labourers might be maintained with the amount. By such means society might obtain from its existing resources a greater quantity of produce: and to such means it has been driven, when the sudden destruction of some large portion of its capital rendered the employment of the remainder with the greatest possible effect, a matter of paramount consideration for the time.

[d]When[d] industry has not come up to the limit imposed by capital, governments may, in various ways, for example by importing additional labourers, bring it nearer to that limit: as [e]by[e] the importation of Coolies

---

tion to be carried on, when it otherwise would not, there is in this case a real increase of the production of the country.

In order to render our theoretical proposition [MS propositions] invulnerable, this peculiar case must be allowed for; but it does not touch the practical doctrine of free trade. Domestic manufactures cannot, from the very nature of things, require protection, since the subsistence of the labourers being provided from other sources, the price of the product, however much it may be reduced, is nearly all clear gain. If, therefore, the domestic producers retire from the competition, it is never from necessity, but because the product is not worth the labour it costs, in the opinion of the best judges, those who enjoy the one and undergo the other. They prefer the sacrifice of buying their clothing to the labour of making it. They will not continue their labour unless society will give them more for it, than in their own opinion its product is worth.

[a-a]MS, 48, 49, 52, 57, 62 There
[b-b]+62, 65, 71
[c-c]MS, 48, 49, 52, 57 from
[d-d]MS, 48, 49, 52, 57, 62 Where
[e-e]MS, 48, 49 in

and free Negroes into [f]the West Indies[f]. There is another way in which governments can create additional industry. They can create capital. They may lay on taxes, and employ the amount productively. They may do what is nearly equivalent; they may lay taxes on income or expenditure, and apply the proceeds towards paying off the public debts. The fundholder, when paid off, would still desire to draw an income from his property, most of which therefore would find its way into productive employment, while a great part of it would have been drawn from the fund for unproductive expenditure, since people do not [g]wholly[g] pay their taxes from what they would have saved, but partly, if not chiefly, from what they would have spent. It may be added, that any increase in the productive power of capital (or, more properly speaking, of labour) by improvement in the arts of life, or otherwise, tends to increase the employment for labour; since, when there is a greater produce altogether, it is always probable that some portion of the increase will be saved and converted into capital; especially when the increased returns to productive industry hold out an additional temptation to the conversion of funds from an unproductive destination to a productive.

§ 3. [*Increase of capital gives increased employment to labour, without assignable bounds*] While, on the one hand, industry is limited by capital, so on the other, every increase of capital gives, or is capable of giving, additional employment to industry; and this without assignable limit. I do not mean to deny that the capital, or part of it, may be so employed as not to support labourers, being fixed in machinery, buildings, improvement of land, and the like. In any large increase of capital a considerable portion will generally be thus employed, and will only co-operate with labourers, not maintain them. What I do intend to assert is, that the portion which is destined to their maintenance, may (supposing no alteration in anything else) be indefinitely increased, without creating an impossibility of finding them employment: in other words, that if there are human beings capable of work, and food to feed them, they may always be employed in producing something. This proposition requires to be somewhat dwelt upon, being one of those which it is exceedingly easy to assent to when presented in general terms, but somewhat difficult to keep fast hold of, in the crowd and confusion of the actual facts of society. It is also very much opposed to common doctrines. There is not an opinion more general among mankind than this, that the unproductive expenditure of the rich is necessary to the employment of the poor. Before Adam Smith, the doctrine had hardly been questioned; and even since his time, authors of the highest name and of

[f-f]MS, 48, 49 our sugar colonies
[g-g]MS, 48, 49, 52 usually

great merit* have contended, that if consumers were to save and convert into capital more than a limited portion of their income, and were not to devote to unproductive consumption an amount of means bearing a certain ratio to the capital of the country, the extra accumulation would be merely so much waste, since there would be no market for the commodities which the capital so created would produce. I conceive this to be one of the many errors arising in political economy, from the practice of not beginning with the examination of simple cases, but rushing [a]at once into the complexity of concrete phenomena[a].

Every one can see that if a benevolent government possessed all the food, and all the implements and materials, of the community, it could exact productive labour from all [b]capable of it,[b] to whom it allowed a share in the food, and could be in no danger of wanting a field for the employment of this productive labour, since as long as there was a single want unsaturated (which material objects could supply), of any one individual, the labour of the community could be turned to the production of something capable of satisfying that want. Now, the individual possessors of capital, when they add to it by fresh accumulations, are doing precisely the same thing which we suppose to be done by [c]a[c] benevolent government. As it is allowable to put any case by way of hypothesis, let us imagine the most extreme case conceivable. Suppose that every capitalist came to be of opinion that not being more meritorious than a well-conducted labourer, he ought not to fare better; and accordingly laid by, from conscientious motives, the surplus of his profits; or [d] suppose this abstinence not spontaneous, but imposed by law or opinion upon all capitalists, and upon landowners likewise. Unproductive expenditure is now reduced to its lowest limit: and it is asked, how is the increased capital to find employment? Who is to buy the goods which it will produce? There are no longer customers even for those which were produced before. The goods, therefore, [e](it is said)[e] will remain unsold; they will perish in the warehouses; until capital is brought down to what it was originally, or rather to as much less, as the demand of the consumers has lessened. But this is seeing only one-half of the matter. In the case supposed, there would no longer be any demand for luxuries, on the part of capitalists and landowners. But when these classes turn their income into capital, they do not thereby annihilate their power of consumption; they do but transfer it from themselves to the labourers to whom they

*For example, Mr. Malthus, Dr. Chalmers, M. de Sismondi.

[a-a]MS into the complexity of concrete phenomena, without first obtaining a clue to disentangle it
[b-b]+62, 65, 71
[c-c]MS, 48, 49 our
[d]MS (to abate a little from the extravagance of the supposition)
[e-e]+52, 57, 62, 65, 71

give employment. Now, there are two possible suppositions in regard to the labourers; either there is, or there is not, an increase of their numbers, proportional to the increase of capital. If there is, the case offers no difficulty. The production of necessaries for the new population, takes the place of the production of luxuries for a portion of the old, and supplies exactly the amount of employment which has been lost. But suppose that there is no increase of population. The whole of what was previously expended in luxuries, by capitalists and landlords, is distributed among the existing labourers, in the form of additional wages. We will assume them to be already sufficiently supplied with necessaries. What follows? That the labourers become consumers of luxuries; and the capital previously employed in the production of luxuries, is still able to employ itself in the same manner: the difference being, that the luxuries are shared among the community generally, instead of being confined to a few. The increased accumulation and increased production, might, rigorously speaking, continue, until every labourer had every indulgence of wealth, consistent with continuing to work; [f]supposing that the power of their labour were[f] physically sufficient to produce all this amount of indulgences for their whole number. Thus the limit of wealth is never deficiency of consumers, but of producers and productive power. Every addition to capital gives to labour either additional employment, or additional remuneration; enriches either the country, or the labouring class. If it finds additional hands to set to work, it increases the aggregate produce: if only the same hands, it gives them a larger share of it; and perhaps even in this case, by stimulating them to greater exertion, augments the produce itself.

§ 4. [*Capital is the result of saving*] A second fundamental theorem respecting Capital, relates to the source from which it is derived. It is the result of saving. The evidence of this lies abundantly in what has been already said on the subject. But the proposition needs some further illustration.

If all persons were to expend in personal indulgences all that they produce, and all the income they receive from what is produced by others, capital could not increase. All capital, with a trifling exception, was originally the result of saving. I say, with a trifling exception; because a person who labours on his own account, may spend on his own account all he produces, without becoming destitute; and the provision of necessaries on which he subsists until he has reaped his harvest, or sold his commodity, though a real capital, cannot be said to have been saved, since it is all used for the supply of his own wants, and [a]perhaps as speedily as if it had been

[f-f]MS were it not that the power of their labour would not be
[a-a]MS, 48, 49 no abstinence has been practised

consumed in idleness[a]. We may imagine a number of individuals or families settled on as many separate pieces of land, each living on what their own labour produces, and consuming the whole produce. But even these must save (that is, spare from their personal consumption) as much as is necessary for seed. Some saving, therefore, there must have been, even in this simplest of all states of economical relations; people must have produced more than they used, or used less than they produced. Still more must they do so before they can employ other [b]labourers[b], or increase their production beyond what can be accomplished by the work of their own hands. All that any one employs in supporting and carrying on any other labour than his own, must have been originally brought together by saving; somebody must have produced it and forborne to consume it. We may say, therefore, without material inaccuracy, that all capital, and especially all addition to capital, are the result of saving.

In a rude and violent state of society, it continually happens that the person who has capital is not the very person who has saved it, but some one who, being stronger, or belonging to a more powerful community, has possessed himself of it by plunder. And even in a state of things [c]in which property was protected[c], the increase of capital has usually been[d], for a long time, mainly[d] derived from privations which, though essentially the same with saving, are not generally called by that name, because not voluntary. The actual producers have been slaves, compelled to produce as much as force could extort from them, and to consume as little as the self-interest or the usually very slender humanity of their [e]taskmasters[e] would permit. This kind of compulsory saving, however, would not have caused any increase of capital, unless a part of the amount had been saved over again, voluntarily, by the master. If all that he made his slaves produce and forbear to consume, had been consumed by him on personal indulgences, he would not have increased his capital, nor been enabled to maintain an increasing number of slaves. To maintain any slaves at all, implied a previous saving; a stock, at least of food, provided in advance. This saving may not, however, have been made by any self-imposed privation of the master; but more probably by that of the slaves themselves while free; the rapine or war, which deprived them of their personal liberty, having transferred also their accumulations to the conqueror.

There are other cases in which the term saving, with the associations usually belonging to it, does not exactly fit the operation by which capital is increased. If it were said, for instance, that the only way to accelerate the

[b-b]MS labour
[c-c]MS, 48, 49 several degrees more advanced
[d-d]MS, 48, 49 in a great measure
[e-e]MS taskmaster

increase of capital is by increase of saving, the idea would probably be suggested of greater abstinence, and increased privation. But it is obvious that whatever increases the productive power of labour, creates an additional fund to make savings from, and enables capital to be enlarged not only without additional privation, but concurrently with an increase of personal consumption. Nevertheless, there is here an increase of saving, in the scientific sense. Though there is more consumed, there is also more spared. There is a greater excess of production over consumption. It is consistent with correctness to call this a greater saving. Though the term is not unobjectionable, there is no other which is not liable to as great objections. To consume less than is produced, is saving; and that is the process by which capital is increased; not necessarily by consuming less, absolutely. We must not allow ourselves to be so much the slaves of words, as to be unable to use the word saving in this sense, without being in danger of forgetting that to increase capital there is another way besides consuming less, namely, to produce more.

§ 5. [*All capital is consumed*] A third fundamental theorem respecting Capital, closely connected with the one last discussed, is, that although saved, and the result of saving, it is nevertheless consumed. The word saving does not imply that what is saved is not consumed, [a]nor even necessarily that its consumption is deferred; but only that, if consumed immediately,[a] it is not consumed by the person who saves it. If merely laid by for future use, it is said to be hoarded; and while hoarded, is not consumed at all. But if employed as capital, it is all consumed; [b]though not[b] by the capitalist [c]. Part is exchanged for tools or machinery, which are worn out by use; part for seed or materials, which are destroyed as such by being sown or wrought up, and destroyed altogether by the consumption of the ultimate product. The remainder is paid in wages to productive labourers, who consume it for their daily wants; or if they in their turn save any part, this also is not, generally speaking, hoarded, but (through savings banks, benefit clubs, or some other channel) re-employed as capital, and consumed.

The principle now stated is a strong example of the necessity of attention to the most elementary truths of our subject: for it is one of the most elementary of them all, and yet no one who has not bestowed some thought on the matter is habitually aware of it, and most are not even willing to admit it when first stated. To the vulgar, it is not at all apparent that what is saved is consumed. To them, every one who saves, appears in the light

[a-a]MS, 48, 49 but only that
[b-b]MS, 48, 49 not indeed
[c]MS, 48, 49 , but by his workpeople

of a person who hoards: they may think such conduct permissible, or even laudable, when it is to provide for a family, and the like; but they have no conception of it as doing good to other people: saving is to them another word for keeping a thing to oneself; while spending appears to them to be distributing it among others. The person who expends his fortune in unproductive consumption, is looked upon as diffusing benefits all around; and is an object of so much favour, that some portion of the same popularity attaches even to him who spends what does not belong to him; who not only destroys his own capital, if he ever had any, but under pretence of borrowing, and on promise of repayment, possesses himself of capital belonging to others, and destroys that likewise.

This popular error comes from attending to a small portion only of the consequences that flow from the saving or the spending; all [d]the effects of either which are[d] out of sight, being out of mind. The eye follows what is saved, into an imaginary strong-box, and there loses sight of it; what is spent, it follows into the hands of [e]tradespeople[e] and dependents; but without reaching the ultimate destination in either case. Saving (for productive investment), and spending, coincide very closely in the first stage of their operations. The effects of both begin with consumption; with the destruction of a certain portion of wealth; only the things consumed, and the persons consuming, are different. There is, in the one case, a wearing out of tools, a destruction of material, and a quantity of food and clothing supplied to labourers, which they destroy by use: in the other case, there is a consumption, that is to say, a destruction, of wines, equipages, and furniture. Thus far, the consequence to the national wealth has been much the same; an equivalent quantity of it has been destroyed in both cases. But in the spending, this first stage is also the final stage; that particular amount of the produce of labour has disappeared, and there is nothing left; while, on the contrary, the saving person, during the whole time that the destruction was going on, has had labourers at work repairing it; who are ultimately found to have replaced, with an increase, the equivalent of what has been consumed. And as this operation admits of being repeated indefinitely without any fresh act of saving, a saving once made becomes a fund to maintain a corresponding number of labourers in perpetuity, reproducing annually their own maintenance with a profit.

It is the intervention of money which obscures, to an unpractised apprehension, the true character of these phenomena. Almost all expenditure being carried on by means of money, the money comes to be looked upon as the main feature in the transaction; and since that does not perish, but only changes hands, people overlook the destruction which takes place in

[d-d]MS, 48, 49 that part of the effects of either which is
[e-e]MS, 48, 49 tradesmen

the case of unproductive expenditure. The money being merely transferred, they think the wealth also has only been handed over from the spendthrift to other people. But this is simply confounding money with wealth. The wealth which has been destroyed was not the money, but the wines, equipages, and furniture which the money purchased; and these having been destroyed without return, society collectively is poorer by the amount. It may be said, perhaps, that wines, equipages, and furniture, are not subsistence, tools, and materials, and could not in any case have been applied to the support of labour; that they are adapted for no other than unproductive consumption, and that the detriment to the wealth of the community was when they were produced, not when they were consumed. I am willing to allow this, as far as is necessary for the argument, and the remark would be very pertinent if these expensive luxuries were drawn from an existing stock, never to be replenished. But since, on the contrary, they continue to be produced as long as there are consumers for them, and are produced in increased quantity to meet an increased demand; the choice made by a consumer to expend five thousand a year in luxuries, keeps a corresponding number of labourers employed from year to year in producing things which can be of no use to production; their services being lost so far as regards the increase of the national wealth, and the tools, materials, and food which they annually consume being so much subtracted from the general stock of the community applicable to productive purposes. In proportion as any class is improvident or luxurious, the industry of the country takes the direction of producing luxuries for their use; while not only the employment for productive labourers is diminished, but the subsistence and instruments which are the means of such employment do actually exist in smaller quantity.

Saving, in short, enriches, and spending impoverishes, the community along with the individual; which is but saying in other words, that society at large is richer by what it expends in maintaining and aiding productive labour, but poorer by what it consumes in its enjoyments.*

*It is worth [MS, 48, 49, 52, 57, 62 is perhaps worth] while to direct attention to several circumstances which to a certain extent diminish the detriment [MS the mischief] caused to the general wealth by the prodigality of individuals, or raise up a compensation, more or less ample, as a consequence of the detriment itself. One of these is, that spendthrifts do not usually [MS, 48, 49, 52, 57 not really] succeed in consuming all they spend. Their habitual carelessness as to expenditure causes them to be cheated and robbed on all quarters, often by persons of frugal habits. Large accumulations are continually made by the agents, stewards, and even domestic servants, of improvident persons of fortune; and they pay much higher prices for all purchases than people of careful habits, which accounts for their being popular as customers. They are, therefore, actually not able to get into their possession and destroy a quantity of

§ 6. [*Capital is kept up, not by preservation, but by perpetual reproduction*] To return to our fundamental theorem. Everything which is produced is consumed: both what is saved and what is said to be spent; and the former quite as rapidly as the latter. All the ordinary forms of language tend to disguise this. When [a]people[a] talk of the ancient wealth of a country, of riches inherited from ancestors, and similar expressions, the idea suggested is, that the riches so transmitted were produced long ago, at the time when they are said to have been first acquired, and that no portion of the capital of the country was produced this year, except as much as may have been this year added to the total amount. The fact is far otherwise. The greater part, in value, of the wealth now existing in England has been produced by human hands within the last twelve months. A very small proportion indeed of that large aggregate was in existence ten years ago;—

---

wealth by any means equivalent to the fortune which they dissipate. Much of it is merely transferred to others, by whom a part may be saved. Another thing to be observed is, that the prodigality of some may reduce others to a forced economy. Suppose a sudden demand for some article of luxury, caused by the caprice of a prodigal, which not having been calculated on beforehand, there has been no increase of the usual supply. The price will rise; and may rise beyond the means or the inclinations of some of the habitual consumers, who may in consequence forego their accustomed indulgence, and save the amount. If they do not, but continue to expend as great a value as before on the commodity, the dealers in it obtain, for only the same quantity of the article, a return increased by the whole of what the spendthrift has paid; and thus the amount which he loses is transferred bodily to them, and may be added to their capital: his increased personal consumption being made up by the privations of the other purchasers, who have obtained less than usual of their accustomed gratification for the same equivalent. On the other hand, a counter-process must be going on somewhere, since the prodigal must have diminished his purchases in some other quarter to balance the augmentation in this; he has perhaps called in funds employed in sustaining productive labour, and the dealers in subsistence and in the instruments of production have had commodities left on their hands, or have received, for the usual amount of commodities, a less than usual return. But such losses of income or capital, by industrious persons, except when of extraordinary [MS when extreme in] amount, are generally made up by increased pinching and privation; so that the capital of the community may not be, on the whole, impaired, and the prodigal may have had his self-indulgence at the expense not of the permanent resources, but of the temporary pleasures and comforts of others. For in every case the community are poorer by what any one spends, unless others are in consequence led to curtail their spending. There are yet other and more recondite ways in which the profusion of some may bring about its compensation in the extra savings of others; but these can only be considered in [MS, 48, 49, 52, 57 these cannot be considered until] that part of the Fourth Book, which treats of the limiting principle to the accumulation of capital. [IV, v; *see* Vol. II, pp. 747–51 *below*.]

[a-a]MS, 48, 49 men

of the present productive capital of the country scarcely any part, except farm-houses and [b]manufactories[b], and a few ships and machines; and even these would not in most cases have survived so long, if fresh labour had not been employed within that period in putting them into repair. The land subsists, and the land is almost the only thing that subsists. Everything which is produced perishes, and most things very quickly. Most kinds of capital are not fitted by their nature to be long preserved. There are a few, and but a few productions, capable of a very prolonged existence. Westminster Abbey has lasted many centuries, with occasional repairs; some [c]Grecian[c] sculptures have existed above two thousand years; the Pyramids perhaps double or treble that time. But these were objects devoted to unproductive use. If we except bridges and aqueducts (to which may [d]in some countries[d] be added tanks and embankments), there are few instances of any edifice applied to industrial purposes which has been of great duration; such buildings do not hold out against wear and tear, nor is it good economy to construct them of the solidity necessary for permanency. Capital is kept in existence from age to age not by preservation, but by perpetual reproduction: every part of it is used and destroyed, generally very soon after it is produced, but those who consume it are employed meanwhile in producing more. The growth of capital is similar to the growth of population. Every individual who is born, dies, but in each year the number born exceeds the number who die: the population, therefore, always increases, though not one person of those composing it was alive until a very recent date.

§ 7. [*Why countries recover rapidly from a state of devastation*] This perpetual consumption and reproduction of capital affords the explanation of what has so often excited wonder, the great rapidity with which countries recover from a state of devastation; the disappearance, in a short time, of all traces of the mischiefs done by earthquakes, floods, hurricanes, and the ravages of war. An enemy lays waste a country by fire and sword, and destroys or carries away nearly all the moveable wealth existing in it: all the inhabitants are ruined, and yet in a few years after, everything is much as it was before. This *vis medicatrix naturæ* has been a subject of sterile astonishment, or has been cited to exemplify the wonderful strength of the principle of saving, which can repair such enormous losses in so brief an interval. There is nothing at all wonderful in the matter. What the enemy have destroyed, would have been destroyed in a little time by the inhabitants themselves: the wealth which they so rapidly reproduce, would have needed

[b-b]MS, 48, 49, 52, 57 factories
[c-c]MS, 48, 49 ancient
[d-d]MS, 48, 49, 52, 57 sometimes

to be reproduced and would have been reproduced in any case, and probably in as short [a]a time[a]. Nothing is changed, except that during the reproduction they have not now the advantage of consuming what had been produced previously. The possibility of a rapid repair of their disasters, mainly depends on whether the country has been depopulated. If its effective population have not been extirpated at the time, and are not starved afterwards; then, with the same skill and knowledge which they had before, with their land and its permanent improvements undestroyed, and the more durable buildings probably unimpaired, or only partially injured, they have nearly all the requisites for their former amount of production. If there is as much of food left to them, or of valuables to buy food, as enables them by any amount of privation to remain alive and in working condition, they will in a short time have raised as great a produce, and acquired collectively as great wealth and as great a capital, as before; by the mere continuance of that ordinary amount of exertion which they are accustomed to employ in their occupations. Nor does this evince any strength in the principle of saving, in the popular sense of the term, since what takes place is not intentional abstinence, but involuntary privation.

Yet so fatal is the habit of thinking through the medium of only one set of technical phrases, and so little reason have studious men to value themselves on being exempt from the very same mental infirmities which beset the vulgar, that this simple explanation was never given (so far as I am aware) by any political economist before Dr. Chalmers; a writer many of whose opinions I think erroneous, but who has always the merit of studying phenomena at first hand, and expressing them in a language of his own, which often uncovers aspects of the truth that the received phraseologies only tend to hide.

§ 8. [*Effects of defraying government expenditure by loans*] The same author carries out this train of thought to some important conclusions on another closely connected subject, that of government loans for war purposes or other unproductive expenditure. These loans, being drawn from capital (in lieu of taxes, which would generally have been paid from income, and made up in part or altogether by increased economy) must, according to the principles we have laid down, tend to impoverish the country: yet the years in which expenditure of this sort has been on the greatest scale, have often been years of great apparent prosperity: the wealth and resources of the country, instead of diminishing, have given every sign of rapid increase during the process, and of greatly expanded dimensions after its close. This was confessedly the case with Great

[a-a]MS, 48, 49, 52, 57 an interval

Britain during the last [a]long[a] Continental war; and it would take some space to enumerate all the unfounded theories in political economy, to which that fact gave rise, and to which it secured temporary credence; almost all tending to exalt unproductive expenditure, at the expense of productive. Without entering into all the causes which operated, and which commonly do operate, to prevent these extraordinary drafts on the productive resources of a country from being so much felt as it might seem reasonable to expect, we will suppose the most unfavourable case possible: that the whole amount borrowed and destroyed by the government, was abstracted by the lender from a productive employment in which it had actually been invested. The capital, therefore, of the country, is this year diminished by so much. But unless the amount abstracted is something enormous, there is no reason in the nature of the case why next year the national capital should not be as great as ever. The loan cannot have been taken from that portion of the capital of the country which consists of tools, machinery, and buildings. It must have been wholly drawn from the portion employed in paying labourers: and the labourers will suffer accordingly. But if none of them are starved; if their wages can bear such an amount of reduction, or if charity interposes between them and absolute destitution, there is no reason that their labour should produce less in the next year than in the year before. If they produce as much as usual, having been paid less by so many millions sterling, [b]these[b] millions are gained by their employers. The breach made in the capital of the country is thus instantly repaired, but repaired by the privations and often the real misery of the labouring class. Here is ample reason why such periods, even in the most unfavourable circumstances, may easily be times of great gain to those whose prosperity usually passes, in the estimation of society, for national prosperity. [c] *

* [57] On the other hand, it must be remembered that war abstracts from productive employment not only capital, but likewise labourers; that the funds withdrawn from the remuneration of productive labourers are partly employed in paying the same or other individuals for unproductive labour; and that by this portion of its effects, war expenditure acts in precisely the opposite manner to that which Dr. Chalmers points out, and, so far as it goes, directly counteracts the effects described in the text. So far as labourers are taken from production, to man the army and navy, the labouring classes are *not* damaged, the capitalists are *not* benefited, and the general produce of the country *is* diminished, by war expenditure. Accordingly, Dr. Chalmers's doctrine, though true of this country, is wholly inapplicable to countries differently circumstanced; to France, for example, during the Napoleon wars. At that period the draught on the labouring population of France, for a long series of years, was enormous,

[a–a]+57, 62, 65, 71
[b–b]MS, 48, 49, 52, 57 those
[c]MS To see the hideous wrong side of the picture, we must look below.] 48, 49 *as* MS . . . look beneath.

This leads to the vexed question to which Dr. Chalmers has very particularly adverted; whether the funds required by a government for extraordinary unproductive expenditure, are best raised by loans, the interest only being provided by taxes, or whether taxes should be at once laid on to the whole amount; which is called in the financial vocabulary, raising the whole of the supplies within the year. Dr. Chalmers is strongly for the latter method. He says, the common notion is that in calling for the whole amount in one year, you require what is either impossible, or very inconvenient; that the people cannot, without great hardship, pay the whole at once out of their yearly income; and that it is much better to require of them a small payment every year in the shape of interest, than so great a sacrifice once for all. To which his answer is, that the sacrifice is made equally in either case. Whatever is spent, cannot but be drawn from yearly income. The whole and every part of the wealth [d]produced[d] in the country, forms, or helps to form, the yearly income of somebody. The privation which it is supposed must result from taking the amount in the shape of taxes is not avoided by taking it in a loan. The suffering is not averted, but only thrown upon the labouring classes, the least able, and who least ought, to bear it: while all the inconveniences, physical, moral, and political, produced by maintaining taxes for the perpetual payment of the interest, are incurred in pure loss. Whenever capital is withdrawn from production, or from the fund destined for production, to be lent to the State, and expended unproductively, that whole sum is withheld from the labouring classes: the loan, therefore, is in truth paid off the same year; the whole of the sacrifice necessary for paying it off is actually made: only it is paid to the wrong persons, and therefore does not extinguish the claim; and paid by the very worst of taxes, a tax exclusively on the labouring class. And after having, in this most painful and unjust [e]way[e], gone through the whole effort necessary for extinguishing the debt, the country remains charged with it, and with the payment of its interest in perpetuity.

---

while the funds which supported the war were mostly supplied by contributions levied on the countries overrun by the French arms, a very small proportion alone consisting of French capital. In France, accordingly, the wages of labour did not fall, but rose; the employers of labour were not benefited, but injured; while the wealth of the country was impaired by the suspension or total loss of so vast an amount of its productive labour. In England all this was reversed. England employed comparatively few additional soldiers and sailors of her own, while she diverted hundreds of millions of capital from productive employment, to supply munitions of war and support armies for her Continental allies. Consequently, as shown in the text, her labourers suffered, her capitalists prospered, and her permanent productive resources did not fall off.

[d-d]MS, 48 existing
[e-e]MS, 48, 49, 52, 57, 62 of ways

These views appear to me strictly just, in so far as the value absorbed in loans would otherwise have been employed in productive industry within the country. The practical state of the case, however, seldom exactly corresponds with this supposition. The loans of the less wealthy countries are made chiefly with foreign capital, which would not, perhaps, have been brought in to be invested on any less security than that of the government: while those of rich and prosperous countries are generally made, not with funds withdrawn from productive employment, but with the new accumulations constantly making from income, and often with a part of them which, if not so taken, would have migrated to colonies, or sought other investments abroad. In these cases (which will be more particularly examined hereafter*), the sum wanted may be obtained [f]by loan[f] without detriment to the labourers, or derangement of the national industry, and even perhaps with [g] advantage to both, in comparison with raising the amount by taxation, since taxes, especially when heavy, are almost always partly paid at the expense of what would otherwise have been saved and added to capital. [h]Besides[h], in a country which makes so great yearly additions to its wealth that a part can be taken and expended unproductively without diminishing capital, or even preventing a considerable increase, it is evident that even if the whole of what is so taken would have become capital, and obtained employment in the country, the effect on the labouring classes is far less prejudicial, and the case against the loan system much less strong, than in the case first supposed. This brief anticipation of a discussion which will find its proper place elsewhere, appeared necessary to prevent false inferences from the premises previously laid down.

§ 9. [*Demand for commodities is not demand for labour*] We now pass to a fourth fundamental theorem respecting Capital, which is, perhaps, oftener overlooked or misconceived than even any of the foregoing. What supports and employs productive labour, is the capital expended in setting it to work, and not the demand of purchasers for the produce of the labour when completed. Demand for commodities is not demand for labour. The demand for commodities determines in what particular branch [a]of production the[a] labour and capital shall be employed; it determines the *direction* of the labour; but not the more or less of the labour itself, or of the maintenance or payment of the labour. [b]These depend[b] on the amount of the capital, or other funds directly devoted to the sustenance and remuneration of labour.

* Infra, book iv. chaps. iv. v. [Vol. II, pp. 733–51.]

[f-f]+57, 62, 65, 71
[g]MS, 48, 49, 52, 57, 62 an
[h-h]MS, 48, 49 Moreover
[a-a]62 the production of [*printer's error?*]
[b-b]MS, 48, 49, 52, 57, 62 That depends

Suppose, for instance, that there is a demand for velvet; a fund ready to be laid out in buying velvet, but no capital to establish the manufacture. It is of no consequence how great the demand may be; unless capital is attracted into the occupation, there will be no velvet made, and consequently none bought; unless, indeed, the desire of the intending purchaser for it is so strong, that he employs part of the price he would have paid for it, in making advances to work-people, that they may employ themselves in making velvet; that is, unless he converts part of his income into capital, and invests that capital in the manufacture. Let us now reverse the hypothesis, and suppose that there is plenty of capital ready for making velvet, but no demand. Velvet will not be made; but there is no particular preference on the part of capital for making velvet. Manufacturers and their labourers do not produce for the pleasure of their customers, but for the supply of their own wants, and having still the capital and the labour which are the essentials of production, they can either produce something else which is in demand, or if there be no other demand, they themselves have one, and can produce the things which they want for their own consumption. So that the [c]employment afforded to labour does not depend on the purchasers, but on the capital.[c] I am, of course, not taking into consideration the effects of a sudden change. If the demand ceases unexpectedly, after the commodity to supply it is already produced, [d]this introduces a different element into the question[d]: the capital has actually been consumed in producing something which nobody wants or uses, and it has therefore perished, and the employment which it gave to labour is at an end, not because there is no longer a demand, but because there is no longer a capital. This case therefore does not test the principle. The proper test is, to suppose that the change is gradual and foreseen, and is attended with no waste of capital, the manufacture being discontinued by merely not replacing the machinery as it wears out, and not reinvesting the money as it comes in from the sale of the produce. The capital is thus ready for a new employment, in which it will maintain as much labour as before. The manufacturer and his work-people lose the benefit of the skill and knowledge which they had acquired in the particular business, and which can only be partially of use to them in any other; and that is the amount of loss to the community by the change. But the labourers can still work, and the capital which previously employed them will, either in the same hands, or by being lent to others, employ either those labourers or an equivalent number in some other occupation.

This [e]theorem, that to purchase produce is not to employ[e] labour; that

[c–c]MS, 48, 49 capital cannot be dispensed with—the purchasers can.
[d–d]MS then is a different element introduced
[e–e]MS, 48, 49 truth, that purchasing produce is not employing

the demand for labour is constituted by the wages which precede the production, and not by the demand which may exist for the commodities resulting from the production; is a proposition which greatly needs all the illustration it can receive. It is, to common apprehension, a paradox; and even among political economists of reputation, I can hardly point to any, except Mr. Ricardo and M. Say, who have kept it constantly and steadily in view. Almost all others occasionally express themselves as if a person who buys commodities, the produce of labour, was an employer of labour, and created a demand for it as really, and in the same sense, as if he bought the labour itself directly, by the payment of wages. It is no wonder that political economy advances slowly, when such a question as this still remains open at its very threshold. [f]I apprehend, that if by demand for labour be meant the demand by which wages are raised, or the number of labourers in employment increased, demand for commodities does not constitute demand for labour. I conceive that a person who buys commodities and consumes them himself, does no good to the labouring classes; and that it is only by what he abstains from consuming, and expends in direct payments to labourers in exchange for labour, that he benefits the labouring classes, or adds anything to the amount of their employment.[f]

For the better illustration of [g]the[g] principle, let us put the following case. A consumer may expend his income either in buying services, or commodities[h]. He[h] may employ part of it in hiring journeymen bricklayers to build a house, or excavators to dig artificial lakes, or labourers to make plantations and lay out pleasure grounds; or, instead of this, he may expend the same value in buying velvet and lace. The question is, whether the difference between these two modes of expending his income affects the interest of the labouring classes. It is plain that in the first of the two cases he employs labourers, who will be out of employment, or at least out of that employment, in the opposite case. But those from whom I differ say that this is of no consequence, because in buying velvet and lace he equally employs labourers, namely, those who make the velvet and lace. [i]I contend, however, that in this last case he does not employ labourers; but merely decides in what kind of work some other person shall employ them[i]. The consumer does not with his own funds pay to the weavers and

[f-f]MS I think it most important to impress on the reader that a demand for commodities does not in any manner constitute a demand for labour, but only determines into a particular channel a portion, more or less considerable, of the demand already existing. It determines that a part of the labour and capital of the community shall be employed in producing certain things instead of other things. The demand for labour is constituted solely by the funds directly set apart for the use of labourers.] 48, 49 I am desirous of impressing on . . . *as* MS

[g-g]MS, 48, 49 our

[h-h]MS, 48, 49, 52, 57 ; he

[i-i]MS, 48, 49 This, according to the principle we laid down, is an error, and I proceed to shew still more clearly that it is so

lacemakers their day's wages. He buys the finished commodity, which has been produced by labour and capital, the labour not being paid nor the capital furnished by him, but [j]by the manufacturer[j]. Suppose that he had been in the habit of expending this portion of his income in hiring journeymen bricklayers, who laid out the amount of their wages in food and clothing, which were also produced by labour and capital. He, however, determines to prefer velvet, for which he thus creates an extra demand. This demand cannot be satisfied without an extra supply, nor can the supply be produced without an extra capital: where, then, is the capital to come from? There is nothing in the consumer's change of purpose which makes the capital of the country greater than it otherwise was. It appears, then, that the increased demand for velvet could not for the present be supplied, were it not that the very circumstance which gave rise to it has set at liberty a capital of the exact amount required. The very sum which the consumer now employs in buying velvet, formerly passed into the hands of journeymen bricklayers, who expended it in food and necessaries, which they now either go without, or squeeze by their competition, from the shares of other labourers. The labour and capital, therefore, which formerly produced necessaries for the use of these bricklayers, are deprived of their market, and must look out for other employment; and they find it in making velvet for the new demand. I do not mean that the very same labour and capital which produced the necessaries turn themselves to producing the velvet; but, in some one or other of a hundred modes, they take the place of that which does. There was capital in existence to do one of two things—to make the velvet, or to produce necessaries for the journeymen bricklayers; but not to do both. It was at the option of the consumer which of the two should happen; [k]and[k] if he chooses the velvet, they go without the necessaries.

[l]For further illustration, let us suppose the same case reversed. The consumer has been accustomed to buy velvet, but resolves to discontinue that expense, and to employ the same annual sum in hiring bricklayers. If the

[j-j]MS, 48, 49 pre-existing
[k-k]+48, 49, 52, 57, 62, 65, 71
[l-l84]MS, 48 It must not be inferred from this, that it is, or that I am bound to think it, advantageous to the labouring class, that consumers should expend their income in services, rather than in commodities. The difference does not lie there, but in their employing it or not in the direct payment or maintenance of labour, without the intervention of another capital. The detriment to the labourers would have been the same if the consumer had persisted in building a house, but instead of engaging labourers himself and paying them, had given an order to a builder, and settled the account after the work was finished. For in this manner of proceeding, the consumer no longer himself maintains the labour, but attracts the capital of another person from some other place or occupation to do it, and therefore does not open a new employment for labour, but merely changes the course of an existing employment.]
49 *as* MS . . . finished, keeping the money in the meanwhile unemployed. For . . . *as* MS

common opinion be correct, this change in the mode of his expenditure gives no additional employment to labour, but only transfers employment from velvet-makers to bricklayers. On closer inspection, however, it will be seen that there is an increase of the total sum applied to the remuneration of labour. The velvet manufacturer, supposing him aware of the diminished demand for his commodity, diminishes the production, and sets at liberty a corresponding portion of the capital employed in the manufacture. This capital, thus withdrawn from the maintenance of velvet-makers, is not the same fund with that which the customer employs in maintaining bricklayers; it is a second fund. There are, therefore, two funds to be employed in the maintenance and remuneration of labour, where before there was only one. There is not a transfer of employment from velvet-makers to bricklayers; there is a new employment created for bricklayers, and a transfer of employment from velvet-makers to some other labourers, most probably those who produce the food and other things which the bricklayers consume.

[m]In answer to this it is said, that though[m] money laid out in buying velvet is not [n] capital, it replaces a capital; that though it does not create a new demand for labour, it is the necessary means of enabling the existing demand to be kept up. The funds (it may be said) of the manufacturer, while locked up in velvet, cannot be directly applied to the maintenance of labour; they do not begin to constitute a demand for labour until the velvet is sold, and the capital which made it replaced from the outlay of the purchaser; and thus, it may be said, the velvet-maker and the velvet-buyer have not two capitals, but only one capital between them, which by the act of purchase the buyer transfers to the manufacturer, and if instead of buying velvet he buys labour, he simply transfers this capital elsewhere, extinguishing as much demand for labour in one quarter as he creates in another.

The premises of this argument are not denied. To set free a capital which would otherwise be locked up in a form useless for the support of labour, is, no doubt, the same thing to the interests of labourers as the creation of a new capital. It is perfectly true that if I expend 1000*l.* in buying velvet, I enable the manufacturer to employ 1000*l.* in the maintenance of labour, which could not have been so employed while the velvet remained unsold: and if it would have remained unsold for ever unless I bought it, then by changing my purpose, and hiring bricklayers instead, I undoubtedly create no new demand for labour: for while I employ 1000*l.* in hiring labour on the one hand, I annihilate for ever 1000*l.* of the velvet-maker's capital on the other. But this is confounding the effects arising from the mere sud-

[m-m]52, 57, 62 It may, no doubt, be said, that though the
[n]52, 57, 62 an addition to

denness of a change with the effects of the change itself. If when the buyer ceased to purchase, the capital employed in making velvet for his use necessarily perished, then his expending the same amount in hiring bricklayers would be no creation, but merely a transfer, of employment. The increased employment which I contend is given to labour, would not be given unless the capital of the velvet-maker *could* be liberated, and would not be given until it *was* liberated. But every one knows that the capital invested in an employment can be withdrawn from it, if sufficient time be allowed. If the velvet-maker had previous notice, by not receiving the usual order, he will have produced 1000*l.* less velvet, and an equivalent portion of his capital will have been already set free. If he had no previous notice, and the article consequently remains on his hands, the increase of his stock will induce him next year to suspend or diminish his production until the surplus is carried off. When this process is complete, the manufacturer will find himself as rich as before, with undiminished power of employing labour in general, though a portion of his capital will now be employed in maintaining some other kind of it. Until this adjustment has taken place, the demand for labour will be merely changed, not increased: but as soon as it has taken place, the demand for labour is increased. Where there was formerly only one capital employed in maintaining weavers to make 1000*l.* [o]worth[o] of velvet, there is now that same capital employed in making something else, and 1000*l.* distributed among bricklayers besides. There are now two capitals employed in remunerating two sets of labourers; while before, one of those capitals, that of the customer, only served as a wheel in the machinery by which the other capital, that of the manufacturer, carried on its employment of labour from year to year.

The proposition for which I am contending is in reality equivalent to the following, which to some minds will appear a truism, though to others it is a paradox: that a person does good to labourers, not by what he consumes on himself, but solely by what he does not so consume. If instead of laying out 100*l.* in wine or silk, I expend it in wages [p] , the demand for commodities is precisely equal in both cases: in the one, it is a demand for 100*l.* worth of wine or silk, in the other, for the same value of bread, beer, labourers' clothing, fuel, and indulgences: but the labourers of the community have in the latter case the value of 100*l.* more of the produce of the community distributed among them. I have consumed that much less, and made over my consuming power to them. If it were not so, my having consumed less would not leave more to be consumed by others; which is a manifest contradiction. When less is not produced, what one person forbears to consume is necessarily added to the share of those to whom he transfers his power of purchase. In the case supposed I do not

[o-o]+62, 65, 71 [p]52, 57, 62 or in alms

necessarily consume less ultimately, since the labourers whom I pay may build a house for me, or make something else for my future consumption. But I have at all events postponed my consumption, and have turned over part of my share of the present produce of the community to the labourers. If after an interval I am indemnified, it is not from the existing produce, but from a subsequent addition made to it. I have therefore left more of the existing produce to be consumed by others; and have put into the possession of labourers the power to consume it. [q]

[r]There cannot be a better *reductio ad absurdum* of the opposite doctrine than that afforded by the Poor Law. If it be equally for the benefit of the labouring classes whether I consume my means in the form of things purchased for my own use, or set aside a portion in the shape of wages or alms for their direct consumption, on what ground can the policy be justified of taking my money from me to support paupers? since my unproductive expenditure would have equally benefited them, while I should have enjoyed it too. If society can both eat its cake and have it, why should it not be allowed the double indulgence? But common sense tells every one in his own case (though he does not see it on the larger scale), that the poor rate which he pays is really subtracted from his own consumption, and that no shifting of payment backwards and forwards will enable two persons to eat the same food. If he had not been required to pay the rate, and had consequently laid out the amount on himself, the poor would have had as much less for their share of the total produce of the country, as he himself would have consumed more.[r] [l] *

*[49 *in text*; 52, 57, 62, 65, 71 *footnote*] The following case, which presents the argument in a somewhat different shape, may serve for still further illustration. [49 The preceding explanations having been found insufficient by some readers, I shall endeavour to carry them along with me in a different mode of stating the argument.]

Suppose that a rich individual, A, expends a certain amount daily in wages or alms, which, as soon as received, is expended and consumed, in the form of coarse food, by the receivers. A dies, leaving his property to B, who discontinues this item of expenditure, and expends in lieu of it the same sum each day in delicacies for his own table. I have chosen this supposition [49 this illustration], in order that the two cases may be similar in all their circumstances, except that which is the subject of comparison. In order not to obscure the essential facts of the case by exhibiting them through the hazy medium of a money transaction, let us further suppose that A, and B after him, are landlords of the estate on which both the food consumed by the recipients of A's disbursements, and the articles of luxury supplied for B's table, are produced; and that their rent is paid to them in kind, they giving previous notice what description of produce they shall require. The question is, whether B's expenditure gives as much employment or as much food to his poorer neighbours as A's gave.

From the case as stated, it seems to follow that while A lived, that portion

[q]52, 57, 62 *next footnote in* 65, 71 *occurs here* [r-r]+65, 71

[s]It appears, then,[s] that a demand delayed until the work is completed, and furnishing no advances, but only reimbursing advances made by others, contributes nothing to the demand for labour; and that what is so expended, is, in all its effects, so far as regards the employment of the labouring class, a mere nullity; it does not and cannot create any employment except at the expense of other employment which existed before.

---

of his income which he expended in wages or alms, would be drawn by him from the farm in the shape of food for labourers, and would be used as such; while B, who came after him, would require, instead of this, an equivalent value in expensive articles of food, to be consumed in his own household: that the farmer, therefore, would, under B's régime, produce that much less of ordinary food, and more of expensive delicacies, for each day of the year, than was produced in A's time, and that there would be that amount less of food shared, throughout the year, among the labouring and poorer classes. This is what would be conformable to the principles laid down in the text [49 conformable to our fourth theorem]. Those who think differently, must, on the other hand, suppose that the luxuries required by B would be produced, not instead of, but in addition to, the food previously supplied to A's labourers, and that the aggregate produce of the country would be increased in amount. But when it is asked, how this double production would be effected—how the farmer, whose capital and labour were already fully employed, would be enabled to supply the new wants of B, without producing less of other things; the only mode which presents itself is, that he should *first* produce the food, and then, giving that food to the labourers whom A formerly fed, should by means of their labour, produce the luxuries wanted by B. This, accordingly, when the objectors are hard pressed, appears to be really their meaning. But it is an obvious answer, that on this supposition, B must wait for his luxuries till the second year, and they are wanted this year. By the original hypothesis, he consumes his luxurious dinner day by day, *pari passu* with the rations of bread and potatoes formerly served out by A to his labourers. There is not time to feed the labourers first, and supply B afterwards: he and they cannot both have their wants ministered to: he can only satisfy his own demand for commodities, by leaving as much of theirs, as was formerly supplied from that fund, unsatisfied.

It may, indeed, be rejoined by an objector, that since, on the present showing, time is the only thing wanting to render the expenditure of B consistent with as large an employment to labour as was given by A, why may we not suppose that B postpones his increased consumption of personal luxuries until they can be furnished to him by the labour of the persons whom A employed? In that case, it may be said, he would employ and feed as much labour as his predecessors. Undoubtedly he would; but why? Because his income would be expended in exactly the same manner as his predecessor's; it would be expended in wages. A reserved from his personal consumption a fund which he paid away directly to labourers; B does the same, only instead of paying it to them himself, he leaves it in the hands of the farmer, who pays it to them for him. On this supposition, B, in the first year, neither expending the amount,

[s-s]MS, 48 [no *paragraph*], 49 Thus, in whatever manner the question is stated, we are brought back to the conclusion

[t]But though[t] a demand for velvet does nothing more in regard to the employment [u]for[u] labour and capital, than to determine so much of the employment [v]which[v] already existed, into that particular channel instead of any other; still, to the producers already engaged in the velvet manufacture, and not intending to quit it, this is of the utmost importance. To them, a falling off in the demand is a real loss, and one which, even if none of their goods finally perish unsold, may mount to any height, up to that which would make them choose, as the smaller evil, to retire from the business. On the contrary, an increased demand enables them to extend their transactions—to make a profit on a larger capital, if they have it, or can borrow it; and, turning over their capital more rapidly, they [w]will[w] employ their labourers more constantly, or employ a greater number than before. So that an increased demand for a commodity does really, in the particular department, often cause a greater employment to be given to labour by the same capital. The mistake lies in not perceiving that in the cases supposed, this advantage is given to labour and capital in one

---

as far as he is personally concerned, in A's manner nor in his own, really saves that portion of his income, and lends it to the farmer. And if, in subsequent years, confining himself within the year's income, he leaves the farmer in arrears to that amount, it becomes an additional capital, with which the farmer may permanently employ and feed A's labourers. Nobody pretends that such a change as this, a change from spending an income in wages of labour, to saving it for investment, deprives any labourers of employment. What is affirmed to have that effect is, the change from hiring labourers to buying commodities for personal use; as represented by our original hypothesis.

In our illustration we have supposed no buying and [49, 52 buying or] selling, or use of money. But the case as we have put it, corresponds with actual fact in everything except the details of the mechanism. The whole of any country is virtually a single farm and manufactory, from which every member of the community draws his appointed share of the produce, having a certain number of counters, called pounds sterling, put into his hands, which, at his convenience, he brings back and exchanges for such goods as he prefers, up to the limit of the amount. He does not, as in our imaginary [49 our suppositious] case, give notice beforehand what things he shall require; but the dealers and producers are quite capable of finding it out by observation, and any change in the demand is promptly followed by an adaptation of the supply to it. If a consumer changes from paying away a part of his income in wages, to spending it that same day (not some subsequent and distant day) in things for his own consumption, and perseveres in this altered practice until production has had time to adapt itself to the alteration of demand, there will from that time be less food and other articles for the use of labourers, produced in the country, by exactly the value of the extra luxuries now demanded; and the labourers, as a class, will be worse off by the [49, 52 by that] precise amount.

[t-t]MS, 48, 49 The error, nevertheless, is a most natural one, and has first appearances strongly on its side. Although
[u-u]MS of
[v-v]MS, 48, 49 that
[w-w]MS really

department, only by being withdrawn from another; and that when the change has produced its natural effect of attracting into the employment additional capital proportional to the increased demand, the advantage itself ceases.

[x]The grounds of a proposition, when well understood, usually give a tolerable indication of the limitations of it. The general principle, now stated, is that demand for commodities determines merely the direction of labour, and the kind of wealth produced, but not the quantity or efficiency of the labour, or the aggregate of wealth. But to this there are two exceptions. First, when labour is supported, but not fully occupied, a new demand for something which it can produce, may stimulate the labour thus supported to increased exertions, of which the result may be an increase of wealth, to the advantage of the labourers themselves and of others. Work which can be done in the spare hours of persons subsisted from some other source, can (as before remarked) be undertaken without withdrawing capital from other occupations, beyond the amount (often very small) required to cover the expense of tools and materials, and even this will often be provided by savings made expressly for the purpose. The reason of our theorem thus failing, the theorem itself fails, and employment of this kind may, by the springing up of a demand for the commodity, be called into existence without depriving labour of an equivalent amount of employment in any other quarter. The demand does not, even in this case, operate on labour any otherwise than through the medium of an existing capital, but it affords an inducement which causes that capital to set in motion a greater amount of labour than it did before.[x]

[y]The second exception, of which I shall speak at length in a subsequent chapter, consists in the known effect of an extension of the market for a commodity, in rendering possible an increased development of the division of labour, and hence a more effective distribution of the productive forces

[x-x]MS [*footnote to* . . . existed before.* (85.6)] *The grounds of a proposition, when well understood, usually give a tolerable indication of the limitations of it. There is a case in which a demand for commodities *may* create employment for labour, namely, when the labourer is already fed, without being employed. Work which can be done in the spare hours of persons subsisted from some other source, can (as we before remarked) be undertaken without withdrawing capital from other occupations, beyond the amount (often very small) required to repay the expense of tools and materials. The reason of our principle thus failing, the principle itself fails, and employment of this kind may, by the springing up of a demand for the commodity, be called into existence without depriving labour of an equivalent amount of employment in any other quarter. The demand does not, even in this case, operate on labour any otherwise than through the medium of an existing capital, but it affords an inducement which causes that capital to set in motion a greater amount of labour than it did before.] 48, 49 *as* MS . . . being fully employed . . . in another quarter . . . *as* MS] 52, 57 *as* 48 . . . (as before . . . our theorem thus . . . the theorem itself . . . *as* 48] 62 *as* 52 . . . required to cover the . . . *as* 52

[y-y]88+65, 71

of society. This, like the former, is more an exception in appearance than it is in reality. It is not the money paid by the purchaser, which remunerates the labour; it is the capital of the producer: the demand only determines in what manner that capital shall be employed, and what kind of labour it shall remunerate; but if it determines that the commodity shall be produced on a large scale, it enables the same capital to produce more of the commodity, and may by an indirect effect in causing an increase of capital, produce an eventual increase of the remuneration of the labourer.[y]

The demand for commodities is a consideration of importance rather in the theory of exchange, than in that of production. Looking at things in the aggregate, and permanently, the remuneration of the producer is derived from the productive power of his own capital. The sale of the produce for money, and the subsequent expenditure of the money in buying other commodities, are a mere exchange of equivalent values for mutual accommodation. It is true that, the division of employments being one of the principal means of increasing the productive power of labour, the power of exchanging gives rise to a great increase of the produce; but even then it is production, not exchange, which remunerates labour and capital. We cannot too strictly represent to ourselves the operation of exchange, whether conducted by barter or through the medium of money, as the mere mechanism by which each person transforms the remuneration of his labour or of his capital into the particular shape in which it is most convenient to him to possess it; but in no wise the source of the remuneration itself.

§ 10. [*Fallacy respecting Taxation*] The preceding principles demonstrate the fallacy of many popular arguments and doctrines, which are continually reproducing themselves in new forms. For example, it has been contended, and by some from whom better things might have been expected, that the argument for the income-tax, grounded on its falling on the higher and middle classes only, and sparing the poor, is an error; some have gone so far as to say, an imposture; because in taking from the rich what they would have expended among the poor, the tax injures the poor as much as if it had been directly levied from them. Of this doctrine we now know what to think. So far, indeed, as what is taken from the rich in taxes, would, if not so taken, have been saved and converted into capital, or even expended in the maintenance and wages of servants or of any class of unproductive labourers, to that extent the demand for labour is no doubt diminished, and the poor injuriously affected, by [a]the[a] tax on the rich; and as these effects are almost always produced in a greater or less degree, it is impossible so to tax the rich as that no portion whatever of the tax can fall

[a-a]MS, 48, 49, 52, 57 any

on the poor. But even here the question arises, whether the government, after receiving the amount, will not lay out as great a portion of it in the direct purchase of labour, as the taxpayers would have done. In regard to all that portion of the tax, which, if not paid to the government, would have been consumed in the form of commodities (or even expended in services if the payment has been advanced by a capitalist), this, according to the principles we have investigated, falls definitively on the rich, and not at all on the poor. There is exactly the same demand for labour, so far as this portion is concerned, after the tax, as before it. The capital which hitherto employed the labourers of the country, remains, and is still capable of employing the same number. There is the same amount of produce paid in wages, or allotted to defray the feeding and clothing of labourers.

If those against whom I am now contending were in the right, it would be impossible to tax anybody except the poor. If it is taxing the labourers, to tax what is laid out in the produce of labour, the labouring classes pay all the taxes. The same argument, however, equally proves, that it is impossible to tax the labourers at all; since the tax, being laid out either in labour or in commodities, comes all back to them; so that taxation has the singular property of falling on nobody. On the same showing, it would do the labourers no harm to take from them all they have, and distribute it among the other members of the community. It would all be "spent among them," which on this theory comes to the same thing. The error is produced by not looking directly at the realities of the phenomena, but attending only to the outward mechanism of paying and spending. If we look at the effects produced not on the money, which merely changes hands, but on the commodities which are used and consumed, we see that, in consequence of the income-tax, the classes who pay it do really diminish their consumption. Exactly so far as they do this, they are the persons on whom the tax falls. It is defrayed out of what they would otherwise have used and enjoyed. So far, on the other hand, as the burthen falls, not on what they would have consumed, but on what they would have saved to maintain production, or spent in maintaining or paying unproductive labourers, to that extent the tax forms a deduction from what would have been used and enjoyed by the labouring classes. But if the government, as is probably the fact, expends fully as much of the amount as the tax-payers would have done in the direct employment of labour, as in hiring sailors, soldiers, and policemen, or in paying off debt, by which last operation it even increases capital; the labouring classes not only do not lose any employment by the tax, but may possibly gain some, and the whole of the tax falls exclusively where it was intended.

All that portion of the produce of the country which any one[b], not a

[b-b]90+52, 57, 62, 65, 71

labourer,[b] actually and literally consumes for his own use, does not contribute in the smallest degree to the maintenance of labour. No one is benefited by mere consumption, except the person who consumes. And a person cannot [c]both[c] consume his income himself, and make it over to be consumed by others. Taking away a certain portion by taxation cannot deprive both him and them of it, but only him *or* them. To know which is the sufferer, we must understand whose consumption will have to be retrenched in consequence: this, whoever it be, is the person on whom the tax really falls.

[c-c]MS *both*

CHAPTER VI

[a]On[a] Circulating and Fixed Capital

§ 1. [*Fixed and Circulating Capital, what*] To complete our explanations on the subject of capital, it is necessary to say something of the two species into which it is usually divided. The distinction is very obvious, and though not named, has been often adverted to, in the [b]two[b] preceding chapters: but it is now proper to define it accurately, and to point out a few of its consequences.

Of the capital engaged in the production of any commodity, there is a part which, after being once used, exists no longer as capital; is no longer capable of rendering service to production, or at least not the same service, [c]nor[c] to the same sort of production. Such, for example, is the portion of capital which consists of materials. The tallow and alkali of which soap is made, once used in the manufacture, are destroyed as alkali and tallow; and cannot be employed any further in the soap manufacture, though in their altered condition, as soap, they are capable of being used as a material or an instrument in other branches of manufacture. In the same division must be placed the portion of capital which is paid as the wages, or consumed as the subsistence, of labourers. [d]The[d] part of the capital of a cotton-spinner which he pays away to his work-people, once so paid, exists no longer as his capital, or as a cotton-spinner's capital: such portion of it as the workmen consume, no longer exists as capital at all: even if they save any part, it [e]may now be more properly regarded[e] as a fresh capital, the result of a second act of accumulation. Capital which in this manner fulfils the whole of its office in the production in which it is engaged, by a single use, is called Circulating Capital. The term, which is not very appropriate, is derived from the circumstance, that this portion of capital requires to be constantly renewed by the sale of the finished product, and when renewed is perpetually parted with in buying materials and paying wages; so that it does its work, not by being kept, but by changing hands.

[a-a]MS Of
[b-b][*cancelled in* MS]
[c-c]MS, 48, 49, 52 or
[d-d]MS, 48, 49, 52, 57, 62, 65 That
[e-e]MS, 48, 49 exists not as the same but

Another large portion of capital, however, consists in instruments of production, of a more or less permanent character; which produce their effect not by being parted with, but by being kept; and the efficacy of which is not exhausted by a single use. To this [f]class[f] belong buildings, machinery, and all or most things known by the name of implements or tools. The durability of some of these is considerable, and their function as productive instruments is prolonged through many repetitions of the productive operation. In this class must likewise be included capital sunk (as the expression is) in permanent improvements of land. So also the capital expended once for all, in the commencement of an undertaking, to prepare the way for subsequent operations: the expense of opening a mine, for example: of cutting canals, of making roads or docks. Other examples might be added, but these are sufficient. Capital which exists in any of these durable shapes, and the return to which is spread over a period of corresponding duration, is called Fixed Capital.

Of fixed capital, some kinds require to be occasionally or periodically renewed. Such are all implements and buildings: they require, at intervals, partial renewal by means of repairs, and are at last entirely worn out, and cannot be of any further service as buildings and implements, but fall back into the class of materials. In other cases, the capital does not, unless as a consequence of some unusual accident, require entire renewal: but there is always some outlay needed, either regularly or at least occasionally, to keep it up. A dock or a canal, once made, does not require, like a machine, to be made again, unless purposely destroyed, or unless an earthquake [g]or some similar catastrophe[g] has filled it up: but regular and frequent outlays are necessary to keep it in repair. The cost of opening a mine needs not be incurred a second time; but unless some one goes to the expense of keeping the mine clear of water, it is soon rendered useless. The most permanent of all kinds of fixed capital is that employed in giving increased productiveness to a natural agent, such as land. The draining of marshy or inundated tracts like the Bedford Level, the reclaiming of land from the sea, or its protection by embankments, are improvements calculated for perpetuity; but drains and dykes require frequent repairs. The same character of perpetuity belongs to the improvement of land by subsoil draining, which adds so much to the productiveness of the clay soils; or by permanent manures, that is, by the addition to the soil, not of the substances which enter into the composition of vegetables, and which are therefore consumed by vegetation, but of those which merely alter the relation of the soil to air and water; as sand and lime on the heavy soils, clay and marl on the light. Even such works, however, require some, though it may be very little, occasional outlay to maintain their full effect.

[f-f]+62, 65, 71 [g-g][*cancelled in* MS]

These improvements, however, by the very fact of their deserving that title, produce an increase of return, which, after defraying all expenditure necessary for keeping them up, still leaves a surplus. This surplus forms the return to the capital sunk in the first instance, and that return does not, as in the case of machinery, terminate by the wearing out of the machine, but continues for ever. The land, thus increased in productiveness, bears a value in the market, proportional to the increase: and hence it is usual to consider the capital which was invested, or sunk, in making the improvement, as still existing in the increased value of the land. There must be no mistake, however. The capital, like all other capital, has been consumed. It was consumed in maintaining the labourers who executed the improvement, and in the wear and tear of the tools by which they were assisted. But it was consumed productively, and has left a permanent result in the improved productiveness of an appropriated natural agent, the land. We may call the increased produce the joint result of the land and of a capital fixed in the land. But as the capital, having in reality been consumed, cannot be withdrawn, its productiveness is thenceforth indissolubly blended with that arising from the original qualities of the soil; and the remuneration for the use of it thenceforth depends, not upon the laws which govern the returns to labour and capital, but upon those which govern the recompense for natural agents. What these are, we shall see hereafter.*

§ 2. [*Increase of fixed capital, when at the expense of circulating, might be detrimental to the labourers*] There is a great difference between the effects of circulating and those of fixed capital, on the amount of the gross produce of the country. Circulating capital being destroyed as such, or at any rate finally lost to the owner, by a single use; and the product resulting from that one use being the only source from which the owner can replace the capital, or obtain any remuneration for its productive employment; the product must of course be sufficient for those purposes, or in other words, the result of a single use must be a reproduction equal to the whole amount of the circulating capital used, and a profit besides. This, however, is by no means necessary in the case of fixed capital. Since machinery, for example, is not wholly consumed by one use, it is not necessary that it should be wholly replaced from the product of that use. The machine answers the purpose of its owner if it brings in, during each interval of time, enough to cover the expense of repairs, and the deterioration in value which the machine has sustained during the same time, with a surplus sufficient to yield the ordinary profit on the entire value of the machine.

From this it follows that all increase of fixed capital, when taking place

*Infra, book ii. chap. xvi. *On Rent.* [Vol. I, pp. 416–29.]

at the expense of circulating, must be, at least temporarily, prejudicial to the interests of the labourers. This is true, not of machinery alone, but of all improvements by which capital is sunk; that is, rendered permanently incapable of being applied to the maintenance and remuneration of labour. Suppose that a person farms his own land, with a capital of two thousand quarters of corn, employed in maintaining labourers during one year (for simplicity we omit the consideration of seed and tools), whose labour produces him annually two thousand four hundred quarters, being a profit of twenty per cent. This profit we shall suppose that he annually consumes, carrying on his operations from year to year on the original capital of two thousand quarters. Let us now suppose that by the expenditure of half his capital he effects a permanent improvement of his land, which is executed by half his labourers, and occupies them for a year, after which he will only require, for the effectual cultivation of [a]his[a] land, half as many labourers as before. The remainder of his capital he employs as usual. In the first year there is no difference in the condition of the labourers, except that part of them have received the same pay for [b]an operation on[b] the land, which they previously obtained for ploughing, sowing, and reaping. At the end of the year, however, the improver has not, as before, a capital of two thousand quarters of corn. Only one thousand quarters of his capital have been reproduced in the usual way: he has now only those thousand quarters and his improvement. He will employ, in the next and in each following year, only half the number of labourers, and will divide among them only half the former quantity of subsistence. The loss [c]will[c] soon be made up to them if the improved land, with the diminished quantity of labour, [d]produces[d] two thousand four hundred quarters as before, because so enormous an accession of gain [e]will[e] probably induce the improver to save a part, add it to his capital, and become a larger employer of labour. [f]But it is conceivable that this may not[f] be the case; for (supposing, as we may do, that the improvement will last indefinitely, without any outlay worth mentioning to keep it up) the improver will have gained largely by his improvement if the land now yields, not two thousand four hundred, but one thousand five hundred quarters; since this will replace the one thousand quarters forming his present circulating capital, with a profit of twenty-five per cent (instead of twenty as before) on the whole capital, fixed and circulating together. The improvement, therefore, may be a very profitable one to him, and yet very injurious to the labourers.

[a–a]MS the
[b–b]MS, 48 trenching or tile-draining or manuring
[c–c]MS, 48 would
[d–d]MS, 48 produced
[e–e]MS, 48 would
[f–f]MS, 48 But this may not, and often will not,

[g]The supposition, in the terms in which it has been stated, is purely ideal; or at most applicable only to such a case as that of the conversion of arable land into pasture, which, though formerly a [h]frequent[h] practice, is regarded by modern agriculturists as the reverse of an improvement.* [i] But this does not affect the substance of the argument. Suppose that the improvement does not operate in the manner supposed—does not enable a part of the labour previously employed on the land to be dispensed with—but only enables the same labour to raise a greater produce.[g] Suppose, too, that the greater produce, which by means of the improvement can be raised from the soil with the same labour, is all wanted, and will find purchasers. The improver will in that case require the same number of labourers as before, at the same wages. But where will he find the means of paying them? He has no longer his original capital of two thousand quarters disposable for the purpose. One thousand of them are lost and gone—consumed in making the improvement. If he is to employ as many labourers as before, and pay them as highly, he must borrow, or obtain from some other source, a thousand quarters to supply the deficit. But these thousand quarters already maintained, or were destined to maintain, an equivalent quantity of labour. They are not a fresh creation; their destination is only changed from one productive employment to another; and though the agriculturist has made up the deficiency in his own circulating capital, the breach in the circulating capital of the community remains unrepaired.

*[65] The clearing away of the small farmers in the North of Scotland, within the present century, was, however, a case of it; and Ireland, since the potato famine and the repeal of the corn laws, is another. The remarkable decrease which has lately attracted notice in the gross produce of Irish agriculture, is, to all appearance, partly attributable to the diversion of land from maintaining human labourers to feeding cattle; and it could not have taken place without the removal of a large part of the Irish population by emigration or death. We have thus two recent instances, in which what was regarded as an agricultural improvement, has diminished the power of the country to support its population. The effect, however, of all the improvements due to modern science is to increase, or at all events, not to diminish, the gross produce.

[g-g]MS, 48 It will perhaps be objected that agricultural improvements do not operate in the manner supposed—do not enable a part of the labour previously employed on the land to be dispensed with—but only enable the same labour to raise a greater produce. This is true of some kinds of agricultural improvement; but the contrary is true of others. Suppose, however, that the case were as the objection assumes it to be.

[h-h]49, 52 common

[i]49, 52, 57, 62 The effect of the agricultural improvements of the present day (of those, at least, which operate on the soil itself,)* is to increase, not to diminish the gross produce. [*footnote*:] *For the distinction between these and the other kind of improvements, which do not take effect upon the soil itself, but upon the operation of cultivating it, see infra, chap. xii. of the present book, § 3. [Vol. I, pp. 177–85.]

[j]The[j] argument relied on by most of those who contend that machinery can never be injurious to the labouring class, [k]is[k], that by cheapening production it creates such an increased demand for the commodity, as enables, ere long, a greater number of persons than ever to find employment in producing it. [l]This argument does not seem to me to have the weight commonly ascribed to it.[l] The fact, though too broadly stated, is, no doubt, often true. The copyists who were thrown out of employment by the invention of printing, were doubtless soon outnumbered by the compositors and pressmen who took their place; and the number of labouring persons now occupied in the cotton manufacture is many times greater than were so occupied previously to the inventions of Hargreaves and Arkwright, which shows that besides the enormous fixed capital now embarked in the manufacture, it also employs a far larger circulating capital than at any former time. But if this capital was drawn from other employments; if the funds which took the place of the capital sunk in costly machinery, were supplied not by [m]any[m] additional saving consequent on the improvements, but by drafts on the general capital of the community; what better [n]were[n] the labouring classes for the mere transfer? In what manner [o]was[o] the loss they sustained by the conversion of circulating into fixed capital made up to them by a mere shifting of part of the remainder of the circulating capital from its old employments to a new one?

All attempts to make out that the labouring classes as a collective body *cannot* suffer [p]temporarily[p] by the introduction of machinery, or by the sinking of capital in permanent improvements, are, I conceive, necessarily fallacious. That they would suffer in the particular department of industry to which the change [q]applies[q], is generally admitted, and obvious to common sense; but it is often said, that though employment is withdrawn from labour in one department, an exactly equivalent employment is opened for it in others, because what the consumers save in the increased cheapness of one particular article enables them to augment their consumption of others, thereby increasing the demand for other kinds of labour. This is plausible, but, as [r]was shown[r] in the last chapter, involves a fallacy; demand for commodities being a totally different thing from demand for labour. It is true, the consumers have now additional [s]means of buying[s] other things; but this will not create the other things, unless there is capital to produce them, and the improvement has not set at liberty any capital, if even it has not absorbed some from other employments. The supposed increase of production and of employment for labour in other departments therefore

[j-j]MS, 48, 49 I cannot assent to the
[k-k]MS, 48, 49 namely
[l-l]+52, 57, 62, 65, 71
[m-m]48, 49, 52, 57 an
[n-n]MS, 48, 49, 52, 57, 62, 65 are
[o-o]MS, 48, 49, 52, 57, 62, 65 is
[p-p]+52, 57, 62, 65, 71
[q-q]MS applied
[r-r]MS, 48, 49 we saw
[s-s]MS, 48, 49 money to buy

will not take place; and the increased demand for commodities by some consumers, will be balanced by a cessation of demand on the part of others, namely, the labourers who were superseded by the improvement, and who will now be maintained, if at all, by sharing, either in the way of competition or of charity, in what was previously consumed by other people.

§ 3. [*But this detriment to the labourers seldom if ever occurs*] Nevertheless, I do not believe that as things are actually transacted, improvements in production are often, if ever, injurious, even temporarily, to the labouring classes in the aggregate. They would be so if they took place suddenly to a great amount, because much of the capital sunk must necessarily in that case be provided from funds already employed as circulating capital. But improvements are always introduced very gradually, and are seldom or never made by withdrawing circulating capital from actual production, but [a]are made[a] by the employment of the annual increase. [b]There are few if any examples[b] of a great increase of fixed capital, at a time and place where circulating capital was not rapidly increasing likewise. It is not in poor or backward countries that great and costly improvements in production are made. To sink capital in land for a permanent return—to introduce expensive machinery—are acts involving immediate sacrifice for distant objects; and indicate, in the first place, tolerably complete security of property; in the second, [c] considerable activity of industrial enterprise; and in the third, a high standard of what has been called the "effective desire of accumulation:" which three things are the elements of a society rapidly progressive in its amount of capital. Although, therefore, the labouring classes must suffer, not only if the increase of fixed capital takes place at the expense of circulating, but even if it is so large and rapid as to retard that ordinary increase to which the growth of population has habitually adapted itself; yet, in point of fact, this is very unlikely to happen, since there is probably no country whose fixed capital increases in a ratio more than proportional to its circulating. If the whole of the railways which[d], during the speculative madness of 1845,[d] obtained the sanction of Parliament, [e]had been[e] constructed in the times fixed for the completion of each, this improbable contingency would, most likely, [f]have been[f] realized; but this very case [g]has afforded a striking[g] example of the difficulties which oppose the diversion into new channels, of any [h]considerable[h] portion of the capital that supplies the old: difficulties generally much more than

[a-a]+48, 49, 52, 57, 62, 65, 71
[b-b]MS, 48, 49, 52, 57, 62 I doubt if there would be found a single example
[c]MS, 48, 49, 52 a
[d-d]MS, 48, 49 have lately] 52 lately
[e-e]MS, 48, 49 were
[f-f]MS, 48, 49 be
[g-g]MS, 48, 49 is even now affording an
[h-h]MS material

sufficient to prevent enterprises that involve the sinking of capital, from extending themselves with such rapidity as to impair the sources of the existing employment for labour.

To these considerations must be added, that even if improvements did for a time decrease the aggregate produce and the circulating capital of the community, they would not the less tend in the long run to augment both. They increase the return to capital; and of this increase the benefit must necessarily accrue either to the capitalist in greater profits, or to the [i]customer[i] in diminished prices; affording, in either case, an augmented fund from which accumulation may be made, while enlarged profits also hold out an increased inducement to accumulation. In the case we before selected, in which the immediate result of the improvement was to diminish the gross produce from two thousand four hundred quarters to one thousand five hundred, yet the profit of the capitalist being now five hundred quarters instead of four hundred, the extra one hundred quarters, if regularly saved, [j]would[j] in a few years replace the one thousand quarters subtracted from his circulating capital. Now the extension of business which almost certainly follows in any department in which an improvement has been made, affords a strong inducement to those engaged in it to add to their capital; and hence, at the slow pace at which improvements are usually introduced, a great part of the capital which the improvement ultimately absorbs, is drawn from the increased profits and increased savings which it has itself called forth.

This tendency of improvements in production to cause increased accumulation, and thereby ultimately to increase the gross produce, even if temporarily diminishing it, will assume a still more decided character if it should appear that there are assignable limits both to the accumulation of capital, and to the increase of production from the land, which limits once attained, all further increase of produce must stop; but that improvements in production, whatever may be their other effects, tend to throw one or both of these limits farther off. Now, these are truths which will appear in the clearest light in a subsequent stage of our investigation. It will be seen, that the quantity of capital which will, or even which can, be accumulated in any country, and the amount of gross produce which will, or even which can, be raised, bear a proportion to the state of the arts of production there existing; and that every improvement, even if for the time it diminish the circulating capital and the gross produce, ultimately makes room for a larger amount of both, than could possibly have existed otherwise. It is this which is the conclusive answer to the objections against machinery; and the proof thence arising of the ultimate [k]benefit[k] [l]to labourers of mechanical

[i-i]MS, 48, 49, 52, 57 consumer
[j-j]MS, 48, 49 will
[k-k]MS benefits
[l-l]MS, 48, 49 of mechanical inventions to the human race

inventions even in the existing state of society[l], will hereafter be seen to be conclusive.* But this does not discharge governments from the obligation of alleviating, and if possible preventing, the evils of which this source of ultimate benefit is or may be productive to an existing generation. If the sinking or fixing of capital in machinery or useful works were ever to proceed at such a pace as to impair materially the funds for the maintenance of labour, it would be incumbent on legislators to take measures for moderating its rapidity: and since improvements which do not diminish employment on the whole, almost always throw some particular class of labourers out of it, there cannot be a more legitimate object of the legislator's care than the interests of those who are thus sacrificed to the gains of their fellow-citizens and of posterity.

To return to the theoretical distinction between fixed and circulating capital. Since all wealth which is destined to be employed for reproduction comes within the designation of capital, there are parts of capital which do not agree with the definition of either species of it; for instance, the stock of finished goods which a manufacturer or dealer at any time possesses unsold in his warehouses. But this, though capital as to its destination, is not yet capital in actual exercise: it is not engaged in production, but has first to be sold or exchanged, that is, converted into an equivalent value of some other commodities; and therefore is not yet either fixed or circulating capital; but will become either one or the other, or be eventually divided between them. With the proceeds of his finished goods, a manufacturer will partly pay his work-people, partly replenish his stock of the materials of his manufacture, and partly provide new buildings and machinery, or repair the old; but how much will be devoted to one purpose, and how much to another, depends on the nature of the manufacture, and the requirements of the particular moment.

It should be observed further, that the portion of capital [m] consumed in the form of seed or material, though, unlike fixed capital, it requires to be at once replaced from the gross produce, stands yet in the same relation to the employment of labour, as fixed capital does. What is expended in materials is as much withdrawn from the maintenance and remuneration of labourers, as what is fixed in machinery; and if capital now expended in wages were diverted to the providing of materials, the effect on the labourers would be as prejudicial as if it were converted into fixed capital. This, however, is a kind of change which [n]seldom, if ever,[n] takes place. The tendency of improvements in production is always to economize, never to increase, the expenditure of seed or material for a given produce; and the interest of the labourers has no detriment to apprehend from this source.

*Infra, book iv. chap. v. [Vol. II, pp. 747–51.]

[m]MS, 48, 49 which is
[n-n]MS, 48, 49, 52, 57, 62, 65 never

CHAPTER VII

On What Depends the Degree of Productiveness of Productive Agents

§ 1. [*Land, labour, and capital, are of different productiveness at different times and places*] We have concluded our general survey of the requisites of production. We have found that they may be reduced to three: labour, capital, and the materials and motive forces afforded by nature. Of these, labour and the raw material of the globe are primary and indispensable. Natural motive powers may be called in to the assistance of labour, and are a help, but not an essential, of production. The remaining requisite, capital, is itself the product of labour: its instrumentality in production is therefore, in reality, that of labour in an indirect shape. It does not the less require to be specified separately. A previous application of labour to produce the capital required for consumption during the work, is no less essential than the application of labour to the work itself. Of capital, again, one, and by far the largest, portion, conduces to production only by sustaining in existence the labour which produces: the remainder, namely the instruments and materials, contribute to it directly, in the same manner with natural agents, and the materials supplied by nature.

We now advance to the second great question in political economy; on what the degree of productiveness of these agents depends. For it is evident that their productive efficacy varies greatly at various times and places. With the same population and extent of territory, some countries have a much larger amount of production than others, and the same country at one time a greater amount than itself at another. Compare England either with a similar extent of territory in Russia, or with an equal population of Russians. Compare England now with England in the Middle Ages; Sicily, Northern Africa, or Syria at present, with the same countries [a]at[a] the time of their greatest prosperity, before the Roman Conquest. Some of the causes which contribute to this difference of productiveness are obvious; others not so much so. We proceed to specify several of them.

[a-a]MS, 48, 49 in

§ 2. [*Causes of superior productiveness. Natural advantages*] The most evident cause of superior productiveness is what are called natural advantages. These are various. Fertility of soil is one of the principal. In this there are great varieties, from the deserts of Arabia to the alluvial plains of the Ganges, the Niger, and the Mississippi. A favourable climate is even more important than a rich soil. There are countries capable of being inhabited, but too cold to be compatible with agriculture. Their inhabitants cannot pass beyond the nomadic state; they must live, like the Laplanders, by the domestication of the rein-deer, if not by hunting or fishing, like the miserable Esquimaux. There are countries where oats will ripen, but not wheat, such as the North of Scotland; others where wheat can be grown, but from excess of moisture and want of sunshine, affords but a precarious crop; as in parts of Ireland. With each advance towards the [a]south[a], or, in the European temperate region, towards the east, some new branch of agriculture becomes first possible, then advantageous; the vine, maize, [b]silk, figs, olives[b], rice, dates, successively present themselves, until we come to the sugar, coffee, cotton, spices, &c. of climates which also afford, of the more common agricultural products, and with only a slight degree of cultivation, two or even three harvests in a year. Nor is it in agriculture alone that differences of climate are important. Their influence is felt in many other branches of production: in the durability of all work which is exposed to the air; of buildings, for example. If the temples of Karnac and Luxor had not been injured by men, they might have subsisted in their original perfection almost for ever, for the inscriptions on some of them, though anterior to all authentic history, are fresher than is in our climate an inscription fifty years old: while at St. Petersburg, the most massive works, solidly executed in granite hardly a generation ago, are already, as travellers tell us, almost in a state to require reconstruction, from [c]alternate exposure to[c] summer heat and intense frost. The superiority of the woven fabrics of Southern Europe over those of England in the richness and clearness of many of their colours, is ascribed to the superior quality of the atmosphere, for which neither the knowledge of chemists nor the skill of dyers has been able to provide, in our hazy and damp climate, a complete equivalent.

Another part of the influence of climate consists in lessening the physical requirements of the producers. In hot regions, mankind can exist in comfort with less perfect housing, less clothing; fuel, that [d]absolute[d] necessary of life in cold climates, they can almost dispense with, except for industrial uses[e]. They also[e] require less aliment; as experience had proved, long before

[a-a]MS north
[b-b]MS, 48, 49, 52, 57, 62, 65 figs, olives, silk
[c-c]MS the alternations to which they have been exposed between
[d-d]MS, 48, 49 essential
[e-e]MS ; & they

theory had accounted for it by ascertaining that most of what we consume as food is not required for the actual nutrition of the organs, but for keeping up the animal heat, and for supplying the necessary stimulus to the vital functions, which in hot climates is almost sufficiently supplied by air and sunshine. Much, therefore, of the labour elsewhere expended to procure the mere necessaries of life, not being required, more remains disposable for its higher uses and its enjoyments; if the character of the inhabitants does not rather induce them to use up these advantages in over-population, or in the indulgence of repose.

Among natural advantages, besides soil and climate, must be mentioned abundance of mineral productions, in convenient situations, and capable of being worked with moderate labour. Such are the coal-fields of Great Britain, which do so much to compensate its inhabitants for the disadvantages of climate; and the scarcely inferior [f]resource[f] possessed by this country and the United States, in a copious supply of an easily reduced iron ore, at no great depth below the earth's surface, and in close proximity to coal deposits available for working it. In mountain and hill districts, the abundance of natural water-power makes considerable amends for the usually inferior fertility of those regions. But perhaps a greater advantage than all these is a maritime situation, especially when accompanied with good natural harbours; and, next to it, great navigable rivers. These advantages consist indeed wholly in saving of cost of carriage. But few who have not considered the subject, have any adequate notion how great an extent of economical advantage this comprises; nor, without having considered the influence exercised on production by exchanges, and by what is called the division of labour, can it be fully estimated. So important is it, that it often does more than counterbalance sterility of soil, and almost every other natural inferiority; especially in that early stage of industry in which labour and science have not yet provided artificial means of communication capable of rivalling the natural. In the ancient world, and in the Middle Ages, the most prosperous communities were not those which had the largest territory, or the most fertile soil, but rather those which had been forced by natural sterility to make the utmost [g] use of a convenient maritime situation; as Athens, Tyre, Marseilles, Venice, the free cities on the Baltic, and the like.

§ 3. [*Causes of superior productiveness. Greater energy of labour*] So much for natural advantages; the value of which, *cæteris paribus*, is too obvious to be ever underrated. But experience testifies that natural advantages scarcely ever do for a community, no more than fortune and station

[f-f]MS, 48, 49, 52 resources
[g]MS, 48 possible

do for an individual, anything like what it lies in their nature, or in their capacity, to do. [a] Neither now nor in former ages have the nations possessing the best climate and soil, been either the richest or the most powerful; but (in so far as regards the mass of the people) generally among the poorest, though, in the midst of poverty, probably on the whole the most enjoying. Human life in those countries can be supported on so little, that the poor seldom suffer from anxiety, and in climates in which mere existence is a pleasure, the luxury which they prefer is that of repose. Energy, at the call of passion, they possess in abundance, but not that which is manifested in sustained and persevering labour: and as they seldom concern themselves enough about remote objects to establish good political institutions, the incentives to industry are further weakened by imperfect protection of its fruits. Successful production, like most other kinds of success, depends more on the qualities of the human agents, than on the circumstances in which they work: and it is difficulties, not facilities, that nourish bodily and mental energy. Accordingly the tribes of mankind who have overrun and conquered others, and compelled them to labour for their benefit, have been mostly reared amidst hardship. They have either been bred in the forests of northern climates, or the deficiency of natural hardships has been supplied, as among the Greeks and Romans, by the artificial ones of a rigid military discipline. [b]From the time when[b] the circumstances of modern society [c] permitted the discontinuance of that discipline, the South has no longer produced conquering nations; military vigour, as well as speculative thought and industrial energy, have all had their principal seats in the less favoured North.

As the second, therefore, of the causes of superior productiveness, we may rank the greater energy of labour. By this is not to be understood occasional, but regular and habitual energy. No one undergoes, without murmuring, a greater amount of occasional fatigue and hardship, or has his [d]bodily powers, and such faculties of mind as he possesses,[d] kept longer at their utmost stretch, than the North American Indian; yet his indolence is proverbial, whenever he has a brief respite from the pressure of present wants. Individuals, or [e]nations[e], do not differ so much in the efforts they are able and willing to make under strong immediate incentives, as in their capacity of present exertion for a distant object; and in the thoroughness of

[a]MS The greatest advantages gratuitously bestowed, generally become disadvantages. To be able to live in ease & enjoyment with little labour, is almost more unfavourable to the active faculties than the extremity of hardship.] 48, 49 *as* MS . . . disadvantages. Neither . . . *as* 71

[b-b]MS Since

[c]MS have

[d-d]MS faculties of mind & body

[e-e]MS, 48, 49 races

their application to work on ordinary occasions. [f]Some amount of these qualities is[f] a necessary condition of any great improvement among mankind. [g] To civilize a savage, he must be inspired with new wants and desires, even if not of a very elevated kind, provided that their gratification can be a motive to [h]steady and regular[h] bodily and mental exertion. If the negroes of Jamaica and Demerara, after their emancipation, had contented themselves, as it was predicted they would do, with the necessaries of life, and abandoned all labour beyond the little which in a tropical climate, with a thin population and [i] abundance of the richest land, is sufficient to support existence, they would have sunk into a condition more barbarous, though [j]less unhappy[j], than their previous state of slavery. The motive which was most relied on for inducing them to work was their love of fine clothes and personal ornaments. No one will stand up for this taste as [k] worthy of being cultivated, and in most societies its indulgence tends to impoverish rather

[f-f]MS In this last quality, the English, and perhaps the Anglo-Americans, appear at present to surpass every other people. This efficiency of labour is connected with their whole character; with their defects, as much as with their good qualities. The majority of Englishmen and Americans have no life but in their work; that alone stands between them and ennui. Either from original temperament, climate, or want of development, they are too deficient in senses to enjoy mere existence in repose; and scarcely any pleasure or amusement is pleasure or amusement to them. Except, therefore, those who are alive to some of the nobler interests of humanity (a small minority in all countries), they have little to distract their attention from work, or to divide the dominion over them with the one propensity which is the passion of those who have no other, and the satisfaction of which comprises all that they imagine of success in life—the desire of growing richer, and getting on in the world. This last characteristic applies chiefly to those who are in a condition superior to day labourers; but the absence of any taste for amusement, or enjoyment of repose, is characteristic of all classes. Whether this or anything else be the cause, the same steadiness and persistency of labour is common to the most improvident of the English working classes—those who never think of saving, or improving their condition. It has become the habit of the country; and life in England is more governed by habit, and less by personal inclination and will, than in any other country, except perhaps China or Japan. The effect is, that where hard labour is the thing required, there are no labourers like the English; though in natural intelligence, and even in manual dexterity, they have many superiors.

Energy of labour, though not an unqualified good, nor one which it is desirable to nourish at the expense of other valuable attributes of human nature, is yet, in a certain measure,] 48, 49 *as* MS . . . characteristic belongs chiefly . . . is common to all classes. Whether from this or any other cause, the national . . . labour extends to . . . *as* MS] 52 This last quality is the principal industrial excellence of the English people. This efficiency . . . *as* 48 . . . majority of Englishmen have . . . countries, and particularly so in this), . . . there are no better labourers than . . . *as* 48

[g]MS A state of mere indolence is the most fruitless & hopeless condition of a human being. It is the most obstinate of hindrances to improvement; almost any means are good for getting rid of it.

[h-h]+57, 62, 65, 71

[i]MS, 48, 49, 52, 57 an

[j-j]52, 57 happier

[k]MS, 48, 49 in itself

than to enrich; but in the state of mind of the negroes it [l]might[l] have been the only incentive that could make them voluntarily undergo systematic labour, and so acquire or maintain habits of [m]voluntary[m] industry which may be converted to more valuable ends. [n]In England[n], it is not the desire of wealth that needs to be taught, but the use of wealth, and appreciation of the objects of desire which wealth cannot purchase, or for attaining which it is not required. Every real improvement in the character of the English [o], whether it consist in giving them higher aspirations, or only [p]a juster estimate of the value of their present objects of desire, must necessarily moderate the ardour of their devotion to the pursuit of wealth.[p] There is no need, however, that it should diminish [q]the[q] strenuous and businesslike application to the matter in hand, which [r]is found in the best English workmen, and is their most valuable quality.[r]

[s] The desirable medium is one which mankind have not often known how

[l-l]MS, 48, 49 may

[m-m]+52, 57, 62, 65, 71

[n-n]MS, 48, 49 As much as the industrial spirit required to be stimulated in their case, so much does it require to be moderated in such countries as England and the United States. There

[o]MS, 48, 49 or Americans

[p-p]MS, 48, 49 more numerous and better pleasures, must necessarily moderate the all-engrossing torment of their industrialism; must diminish, therefore, so far as it depends on that cause alone, the aggregate productiveness of their labour.] 52 *as* MS . . . industrialism. There . . . *as* 71

[q-q]MS, 48, 49 that

[r-r]MS, 48, 49 is one of their most precious characteristics. "Whoever" (says Mr. Laing*) "looks into the social economy of an English or Scotch manufacturing district, in which the population has become thoroughly imbued with the spirit of productiveness, will observe that it is not merely the expertness, despatch, and skill of the operative himself, that are concerned in the prodigious amount of his production in a given time, but the labourer who wheels coal to his fire, the girl who makes ready his breakfast, the whole population, in short, from the potboy who brings his beer, to the banker who keeps his employer's cash, are inspired with the same alert spirit, are in fact working to his hand with the same quickness and punctuality as he works himself. English workmen taken to the Continent always complain that they cannot get on with their work as at home, because of the slow, unpunctual, pipe-in-mouth working habits of those who have to work to their hands, and on whom their own activity and productiveness mainly depend."

Foreigners are generally quite unaware that to these qualities in English industry the wealth and power which they seek to emulate are in reality owing, and not to the "ships, colonies, and commerce" which these qualities have called into being, and which, even if annihilated, would leave England the richest country in the world. An Englishman, of almost every class, is the most efficient of all labourers, because, to use a common phrase, his heart is in his work. But it is surely quite possible to put heart into his work without being incapable of putting it into anything else. [*footnote*:] **Notes of a Traveller*, p. 290. [Laing, Samuel (the elder). *Notes of a Traveller, on the Social and Political State of France, Prussia, Switzerland, Italy, and other Parts of Europe, During the present Century*. London: Longman, Brown, Green, and Longmans, 1842.]

[s]MS, 48, 49 [*no paragraph*]

to hit: when they [t] labour, to do it with all their might, and especially with all their mind; but to devote to labour, for mere pecuniary gain, fewer hours in the day, fewer days in the year, and fewer years of life.

§ 4. [*Causes of superior productiveness. Superior skill and knowledge*] The third element which determines the productiveness of the labour of a community, is the skill and knowledge therein existing; whether it be the skill and knowledge of the labourers themselves, or of those who direct their labour. No illustration is requisite to show how the efficacy of industry is promoted by the manual dexterity of those who perform mere routine processes; by the intelligence of those engaged in operations in which the mind has a considerable part; and by the amount of knowledge of natural powers and [a]of[a] the properties of objects, which is turned to the purposes of industry. That the productiveness of the labour of a people is limited by their knowledge of the arts of life, is self-evident; and that any progress in those arts, any improved application of the objects or powers of nature to industrial uses, enables the same quantity and intensity of labour to raise a greater produce.

One principal department of these improvements consists in the invention and use of tools and machinery. The manner in which these serve to increase production and to economize labour, needs not be specially detailed in a work like the present: it will be found explained and exemplified, in a manner at once scientific and popular, in Mr. Babbage's well-known "Economy of Machinery and Manufactures." An entire chapter of Mr. Babbage's book is composed of instances of the efficacy of machinery in "exerting forces too great for human power, and executing operations too delicate for human touch."[*] But to find examples of work which could not be performed at all by unassisted labour, we need not go so far. Without pumps, worked by steam-engines or otherwise, the water which collects in mines could not in many situations be got rid of at all, and the mines, after being worked to a little depth, must be abandoned: without ships or boats the sea could never have been crossed; without tools of some sort, trees could not be cut down, nor rocks excavated; a plough, or at least a [b]hoe[b], is necessary to any tillage of the ground. Very simple and rude instruments, however, are sufficient to render literally possible most works hitherto executed by [c]mankind[c]; and subsequent inventions have chiefly served to enable the work to be performed in greater perfection, and, above

[*Babbage, Charles. *On the Economy of Machinery and Manufactures.* 3rd ed. London: Knight, 1832 (1833?). The passage quoted is the title of chapter vii.]

[t]MS, 48, 49, 52, 57, 62 do
[a-a]+48, 49, 52, 57, 62, 65, 71
[b-b]MS, 48, 49, 52, 57, 62 spade
[c-c]MS, 48, 49 man

all, with a greatly diminished quantity of labour: the labour thus saved becoming disposable for other [d]employments[d].

The use of machinery is far from being the only mode in which the effects of knowledge in aiding production are exemplified. In agriculture and horticulture, machinery [e]is only now beginning to show that it can do anything[e] of importance, beyond the invention and progressive improvement of the plough and a few other simple instruments. The greatest agricultural inventions have consisted in the direct application of more judicious processes to the land itself, and [f]to[f] the plants growing on it: such as rotation of crops, to avoid the necessity of [g]leaving the land uncultivated[g] for one season in every two or three; improved manures, to renovate its fertility when exhausted by cropping; [h]ploughing and draining the subsoil as well as the surface;[h] conversion [i] of bogs and marshes into cultivable land; such modes of pruning, and of training and propping up plants and trees, as experience has shown to deserve the preference; in the case of the more expensive cultures, planting the [j]roots or seeds[j] further apart, and more completely pulverizing the soil in which they are placed, &c. In manufactures and commerce, some of the most important improvements consist in economizing time; in making the return follow more speedily upon the labour and outlay. There are others of which the advantage consists in economy of material.

§ 5. [*Causes of superior productiveness. Superiority of intelligence and trustworthiness in the community generally*] But the effects of the increased knowledge of a community in increasing its wealth, need the less illustration as they have become familiar to the most uneducated, from such conspicuous instances as railways and steam-ships. A thing not yet [a] so well understood and recognised, is the economical value of the general diffusion of intelligence among the people. The number of persons fitted to direct and superintend any industrial enterprise, or even to execute any process which cannot be reduced almost to an affair of memory and routine, is always far short of the demand; as is evident from the enormous difference between the salaries paid to such persons, and the wages of ordinary labour. The deficiency of practical good sense, which renders the majority of the labouring class [b] such bad calculators—which makes, for instance, their domestic economy so improvident, lax, and irregular—must disqualify them for any but a low grade of intelligent labour, and render their industry far less productive than with equal energy it otherwise might be. The

[d-d]MS, 48, 49, 52, 57, 62 employment
[e-e]MS, 48, 49 has done little
[f-f]+52, 57, 62, 65, 71
[g-g]MS letting the land rest
[h-h]+65, 71
[i]MS , by drainage,
[j-j]MS, 48 seeds or roots
[a]MS, 48, 49 , perhaps,
[b]MS, 48, 49 , in this and many other countries,

importance, even in this limited aspect, of popular education, is well worthy of the attention of politicians, especially in England; since competent observers, accustomed to employ labourers of various nations, testify that in the workmen of other countries they often find great intelligence wholly apart from instruction, but that if an English labourer is anything but a hewer of wood and [c]a[c] drawer of water, he is indebted [d]for it to education, which in his case is almost always self-education.[d] Mr. Escher, of Zurich (an engineer and cotton manufacturer employing nearly two thousand working men of many different nations), in his evidence annexed to the Report of the Poor Law Commissioners, in 1840, on the training of pauper children, gives a character of English as contrasted with Continental workmen, which all persons of similar experience will, I believe, confirm.

"The Italians' quickness of perception is shown in rapidly comprehending any new descriptions of labour put into their hands[e], in a power[e] of quickly comprehending the meaning of their employer, of adapting themselves to new circumstances, much beyond what any other classes have. The French workmen have the like natural characteristics, only in a somewhat lower degree. The English, Swiss, German, and Dutch workmen, we find, have all much slower natural comprehension. As workmen *only*, the preference is undoubtedly due to the English; because, as we find them, they are all trained to special branches, on which they have had comparatively superior training, and have concentrated all their thoughts. As men of business or of general usefulness, and as men with whom an employer would best like to be surrounded, I should, however, decidedly prefer the Saxons and the Swiss, but more especially the Saxons, because they have had a very careful general education, which has extended their capacities beyond any special employment, and rendered them fit to take up, after a short preparation, any employment to which they may be called. If I have an English workman engaged in the erection of a steam-engine, he will understand that, and nothing else; and for other circumstances or other branches of mechanics, however closely allied, he will be comparatively helpless to adapt himself to all the circumstances that may arise, to make arrangements for them, and give sound advice or write clear statements and letters on his work in the various related branches of mechanics."

On the connexion between mental cultivation and moral trustworthiness in the labouring class, the same witness says, "The better educated work-

[c-c]+62, 65, 71

[d-d]MS, 48, 49 to education (though often to self-education) for it.* [*footnote*:] *Extracts from the evidence of Mr. Escher, of Zurich, (an engineer and cotton manufacturer employing nearly two thousand working men of many different nations), annexed to the Report of the Poor Law Commissioners in 1840, on the training of pauper children.

"The Italians' . . . *as text of* 71 . . . [109.25] useless. The educated English workmen in a short time comprehend their position, and adopt an appropriate behaviour."

[e-e]+48, 49, 52, 57, 62, 65, 71 [*not in* Source]

men, we find, are distinguished by superior moral habits in every respect. In the first place, they are entirely sober; they are discreet in their enjoyments, which are of a more rational and refined kind; they have a taste for much better society, which they approach respectfully, and consequently find much readier admittance to it; they cultivate music; they read; they enjoy the pleasures of scenery, and make parties for excursions into the country; they are economical, and their economy extends beyond their own purse to the stock of their master; they are, consequently, honest and trustworthy." And in answer to a question respecting the English workmen, "Whilst in respect to the work to which they have been specially trained they are the most skilful, they are in conduct the most disorderly, debauched, and unruly, and least respectable and trustworthy of any nation whatsoever whom we have employed; and in saying this, I express the experience of every manufacturer on the Continent to whom I have spoken, and especially of the English manufacturers, who make the loudest complaints. These characteristics of depravity do not apply to the English workmen who have received an education, but attach to the others in the degree in which they are in want of it. When the uneducated English workmen are released from the bonds of iron discipline in which they have been restrained by their employers in England, and are treated with the urbanity and friendly feeling which the more educated workmen on the Continent expect and receive from their employers, they, the English workmen, completely lose their balance: they do not understand their position, and after a certain time become totally unmanageable and useless."* [f]This result of observation is borne out by experience in England itself. As soon as any idea of equality enters the mind of an [g]uneducated[g] English working man, his head is turned by it. When he ceases to be servile, he becomes insolent.[f]

The moral qualities of the labourers are fully as important to the efficiency and worth of their labour, as the intellectual. Independently of the effects of intemperance upon their bodily and mental faculties, and of flighty, unsteady habits upon the energy and continuity of their work (points so easily understood as not to require being insisted upon), it is well worthy of meditation, how much of the aggregate effect of their labour

*[MS, 48, 49 *in text*] The whole [MS I strongly recommend to attention the entire] 48, 49 The entire] evidence of this [MS this very] intelligent and experienced employer of labour is deserving of attention; as well as [MS employer of labour, & much] much testimony on similar points by other witnesses, contained in the same volume. ["Report to the Secretary of State for the Home Department, from the Poor Law Commissioners, on the Training of Pauper Children," *House of Lords Sessional Papers*, 1841, XXXIII. The passages are from pp. 16, 16–7, 19.]

f–f+52, 57, 62, 65, 71
*g–g*52, 57, 62 ordinary

depends on their trustworthiness. All the labour [h]now[h] expended in watching that they fulfil their engagement, or in verifying that they have fulfilled it, is so much withdrawn from the real business of production, [i]to be devoted[i] to a subsidiary function rendered needful not by the necessity of things, but by the dishonesty of men. Nor are the greatest outward precautions [j]more than very imperfectly efficacious, where, as is now almost invariably the case with hired labourers, the slightest relaxation of vigilance is an opportunity eagerly seized for eluding performance of their contract. The advantage to mankind of being[j] able to trust one another, penetrates into every crevice and cranny of human life: the economical is perhaps the smallest part of it, yet even this is incalculable. To consider only the [k]most obvious part of the[k] waste of wealth occasioned to society by human improbity; there is in all rich communities a predatory population, who live [l] by pillaging or overreaching other people; their numbers cannot be authentically ascertained, but on the lowest estimate, in a country like England, it is [m]very large[m]. The support of these persons is a direct burthen on the national industry. The police, and the whole apparatus of punishment, and of criminal and partly of civil justice, are a second burthen rendered necessary by the first. The [n]exorbitantly-paid[n] profession of lawyers[o], so far as their work is not created by defects in the law, of their own contriving,[o] are required and supported principally by the dishonesty of mankind. As the standard of integrity in a community [p]rises higher, all these expenses become[p] less. But this positive saving [q]would be[q] far outweighed [r]by the immense increase in the produce of all kinds of labour, and saving of time and expenditure, which would be obtained if the labourers honestly performed what they undertake; and[r] by the increased spirit, the feeling of power and confidence, with which works of all sorts [s]would be[s] planned and carried on by those who [t]felt[t] that all whose aid [u]was[u] required [v]would[v] do their part faithfully according to their contracts. Conjoint action is possible just in proportion as human beings can rely on each other. There are countries in Europe, of first-rate industrial capabilities, where the most serious impediment to conducting business concerns on a large scale, is the rarity of persons who are supposed fit to be trusted with the receipt and expenditure of large sums of money. There are nations whose commodities are looked shily upon by merchants, because they cannot depend on finding the quality of the article conformable to that

[h-h]+52, 57, 62, 65, 71

[i-i]+48, 49, 52, 57, 62, 65, 71

[j-j]MS, 48, 49 comparable in efficacy to the monitor within. The advantage that it is to mankind to be

[k-k]MS direst] 48, 49 direct

[l]MS wholly

[m-m]MS enormous

[n-n]MS, 48, 49 highly paid

[o-o]+52, 57, 62, 65, 71

[p-p]MS, 48, 49 is higher, so are all these expenses

[q-q]MS, 48, 49 is

[r-r]+52, 57, 62, 65, 71

[s-s]MS, 48, 49 are

[t-t]MS, 48, 49 feel

[u-u]MS, 48, 49 is

[v-v]MS, 48, 49 will

of the sample. Such short-sighted frauds are far from unexampled [w] in English exports. Every one has heard of "devil's dust:" and among other instances given by Mr. Babbage, is one in which a branch of export trade was for a long time actually stopped by the forgeries and frauds which had occurred in it. On the other hand, the substantial advantage derived in business transactions from proved trustworthiness, is not less remarkably exemplified in the same work. "At one of our largest towns, sales and purchases on a very extensive scale are made daily in the course of business without any of the parties ever exchanging a written document."[*] Spread over a [x] year's transactions, how great a return, in saving of time, trouble, and expense, is brought in to the producers and dealers of such a town from their own integrity. "The influence of established character in producing confidence operated in a very remarkable manner at the time of the exclusion of British manufactures from the Continent during the last war. One of our largest establishments had been in the habit of doing extensive business with a house in the centre of Germany; but on the closing of the Continental ports against our manufactures, heavy penalties were inflicted on all those who contravened the Berlin and Milan decrees. The English manufacturer continued, nevertheless, to receive orders, with directions how to consign them, and appointments for the time and mode of payment, in letters, the handwriting of which was known to him, but which were never signed except by the Christian name of one of the firm, and even in some instances they were without any signature at all. These orders were executed, and in no instance was there the least irregularity in the payments." * [y]

[*Babbage, pp. 219–20.]

* Some minor instances noticed by Mr. Babbage may be cited in further illustration of the waste occasioned to society through the inability of its members to trust one another.

"The cost to the purchaser is the price he pays for any article, added to

[w]MS, 48, 49 even [x]MS, 48, 49, 52, 57, 62 whole

[y]MS [*paragraph*] In a book recently published, "De la Liberté du Travail," [*ou simple exposé des conditions dans lesquelles les forces humaines s'exercent avec le plus de puissance*. 3 vols. Paris: Guillaumin, 1845] by a distinguished member of the administrative body in France, M. Charles Dunoyer, a comprehensive survey is taken of all the great branches of industry, for the express object of pointing out the personal qualities, moral, intellectual, and practical, which must exist in individuals, or be diffused through society, to enable each particular branch to be carried on with success. It would swell unreasonably the bulk of the present treatise were I to illustrate minutely one half of the principles I introduce, & I am glad when, as in this case, I can direct the reader to another work in which what is here left undone, has been done so amply that if I had room to spare I should only have to transcribe or abridge. In M. Dunoyer's work will be found, what we in general vainly seek from political economists, a clear view of the relation between the political economy of any society & its state of general intelligence & of moral & social improvement; nor am I aware of any other work in which this important relation is traced out in anything like similar detail.

§ 6. [*Causes of superior productiveness. Superior security*] Among the secondary causes which determine the productiveness of productive agents, the most important is Security. By security I mean the completeness of the protection which society affords to its members. This consists of protection *by* the government, and protection *against* the government. The latter is the more important. Where a person known to possess anything worth taking away, can expect nothing but to have it torn from him, with every circumstance of tyrannical violence, by the agents of a rapacious government, it is not likely that many will exert themselves to produce much more than necessaries. This is the acknowledged explanation of the poverty of many fertile tracts of Asia, which were once prosperous and populous. From this to the degree of security enjoyed in the best governed

---

the cost of verifying the fact of its having that degree of goodness for which he contracts. In some cases, the goodness of the article is evident on mere inspection; and in those cases there is not much difference of price at different shops. The goodness of loaf sugar, for instance, can be discerned almost at a glance; and the consequence is, that the price is so uniform, and the profit upon it so small, that no grocer is at all anxious to sell it; whilst on the other hand, tea, of which it is exceedingly difficult to judge, and which can be adulterated by mixture so as to deceive the skill even of a practised eye, has a great variety of different prices, and is that article which every grocer is most anxious to sell to his customers. The difficulty and expense of verification are in some instances so great, as to justify the deviation from well-established principles. Thus it is a general maxim that Government can purchase any article at a cheaper rate than that at which they can manufacture it themselves. But it has, nevertheless, been considered more economical to build extensive flour-mills (such as those at Deptford), and to grind their own corn, than to verify each sack of purchased flour, and to employ persons in devising methods of detecting the new modes of adulteration which might be continually resorted to." [Pp. 134–5.] A similar want of confidence might deprive a nation, such as the United States, of a large export trade in flour.

Again: "Some years since, a mode of preparing old clover and trefoil seeds by a process called *doctoring* became so prevalent as to excite the attention of the House of Commons. It appeared in evidence before a Committee, that the old seed of the white clover was doctored by first wetting it slightly, and then drying it by the fumes of burning sulphur; and that the red clover seed had its colour improved by shaking it in a sack with a small quantity of indigo; but this being detected after a time, the *doctors* then used a preparation of logwood, fined by a little copperas, and sometimes by verdigris; thus at once improving the appearance of the old seed, and diminishing, if not destroying, its vegetative power, already enfeebled by age. Supposing no injury had resulted to good seed so prepared, it was proved that, from the improved appearance, the market price would be enhanced by this process from five to twenty-five shillings a hundred-weight. But the greatest evil arose from the circumstance of these processes rendering old and worthless seed equal in appearance to the best. One witness had tried some doctored seed, and found that not above one grain in a hundred grew, and that those which did vegetate died away after-parts of Europe, there are numerous gradations. In [a]many provinces of[a] France, before the Revolution, a vicious system of taxation on the land, and still more the absence of redress against the arbitrary exactions which were made under colour of the taxes, rendered it the interest of every cultivator to appear poor, and therefore to cultivate badly. The only insecurity which is altogether paralysing to the active energies of producers, is that arising from the government, or from persons invested with its authority. Against all other depredators there is a hope of defending oneself. Greece and the Greek colonies in the ancient world, Flanders and Italy in the Middle Ages, by no means enjoyed what any one with modern ideas would call security: the state of society was most unsettled and turbulent; person and property were exposed to a thousand dangers. But they were free countries; they were [b]in general[b] neither arbitrarily oppressed, nor systematically plundered by their governments. Against other enemies

---

wards; whilst about eighty or ninety per cent of good seed usually grows. The seed so treated was sold to retail dealers in the country, who of course endeavoured to purchase at the cheapest rate, and from them it got into the hands of the farmers, neither of these classes being capable of distinguishing the fraudulent from the genuine seed. Many cultivators in consequence diminished their consumption of the articles [Source, MS, 48, 49 the article], and others were obliged to pay a higher price to those who had skill to distinguish the mixed seed, and who had integrity and character to prevent them from dealing in it." [Pp. 135–6.]

The same writer states that Irish flax, though in natural quality inferior to none, sells, or did lately sell, in the market at a penny to twopence per pound less than foreign or British flax; part of the difference arising from negligence in its preparation, but part from the cause mentioned in the evidence of Mr. Corry, many years Secretary to the Irish Linen Board: "The owners of the flax, who are almost always people in the lower classes of life, believe that they can best advance their own interests by imposing on the buyers. Flax being sold by weight, various expedients are used to increase it; and every expedient is injurious, particularly the damping of it; a very common practice, which makes the flax afterwards heat. The inside of every bundle (and the bundles all vary in bulk) is often full of pebbles, or dirt of various kinds, to increase the weight. In this state it is purchased and exported to Great Britain." [Quoted by Babbage, p. 137.]

It was given in evidence before a Committee of the House of Commons that the lace trade at Nottingham had greatly fallen off, from the making of fraudulent and bad articles: that "a kind of lace called *single-press* was manufactured," (I still quote Mr. Babbage,) "which although good to the eye, became nearly spoiled in washing by the slipping of the threads; that not one person in a thousand could distinguish the difference between single-press and double-press lace; that even workmen and manufacturers were obliged to employ a magnifying-glass for that purpose; and that in another similar article, called warp-lace, such aid was essential." [P. 138.]

[a-a]+49, 52, 57, 62, 65, 71
[b-b]+52, 57, 62, 65, 71

the individual energy which their institutions called forth, enabled them to make successful resistance: their labour, therefore, was eminently productive, and their riches, while they remained free, [c]were[c] constantly on the increase. The Roman despotism, putting an end to wars and internal conflicts throughout the empire, relieved the subject population from much of the former insecurity: but because it left them under the grinding yoke of its own rapacity, they became enervated and impoverished, until they were an easy prey to barbarous but free invaders. They would neither fight nor labour, because they were no longer suffered to enjoy that for which they fought and laboured.

Much of the security [d]of[d] person and property in modern nations is the effect of manners and opinion rather than of law. There are[e], or lately were,[e] countries in Europe where the monarch [f]was[f] nominally absolute, but where, from the restraints imposed by established usage, no subject [g]felt[g] practically in the smallest danger of having his possessions arbitrarily seized or a contribution levied on them by the government. There must, however, be in such governments much petty plunder and other tyranny by subordinate agents, for which redress is not obtained, owing to the want of publicity which is the ordinary character of absolute governments. In England the people are tolerably well protected, both by institutions and manners, against the agents of government; but, for the security they enjoy against other evil-doers, they are very little indebted to their institutions. The laws cannot be said to afford protection to property, when they afford it only at such a cost as renders submission to injury in general the better calculation. The security of property in England is owing (except as regards open violence) to opinion, and the fear of exposure, much more than to [h]the direct operation of[h] the law and the courts of justice. [i]

Independently of all imperfection in the bulwarks which society purposely throws round what it recognises as property, there are various other modes in which defective institutions impede the employment of the productive resources of a country to the best advantage. We shall have occasion for noticing many of these in the progress of our subject. It is sufficient here to remark, that the efficiency of industry may be expected to be great, in proportion as the fruits of industry are insured to the person exerting it: and that all social arrangements are conducive to useful exertion, accord-

[c-c]62 was
[d-d]62 to
[e-e]+49, 52, 57, 62, 65, 71
[f-f]MS, 48 is
[g-g]MS, 48 feels
[h-h]+65, 71
[i]MS, 48, 49 Of late, indeed, law has thrown a part of its weight into the other scale, by a course of legislation on the subject of insolvent debtors, which is almost a direct encouragement to repudiation of engagements.

ing as they provide that the reward of every one for his labour shall be proportioned as much as possible to the benefit which it produces. All laws or usages which favour one class or sort of persons to the disadvantage of others; which chain up the efforts of any part of the community in pursuit of their own good, or stand between those efforts and their natural fruits—are (independently of all other grounds of condemnation) violations of the fundamental principles of economical policy; [j]tending[j] to make the aggregate productive powers of the community productive in a less degree than they would otherwise be.

[j-j]MS, 48, 49, 52, 57 and tend

CHAPTER VIII

Of Co-operation, or the Combination of Labour

§ 1. [*Combination of Labour a principal cause of superior productiveness*] In the enumeration of the circumstances which promote the productiveness of labour, we have left one untouched, which, because of its importance, and of the many topics of discussion which it involves, requires to be treated apart. This is, co-operation, or the combined action of numbers. Of this great aid to production, a single department, known by the name of Division of Labour, has engaged a large share of the attention of political economists; most deservedly indeed, but to the exclusion of other cases and exemplifications of the same comprehensive law. Mr. Wakefield was, I believe, the first to point out, that a part of the subject had, with injurious effect, been mistaken for the whole; that a more fundamental principle lies beneath that of the division of labour, and comprehends it.

Co-operation, he observes,* is "of two distinct kinds: first, such co-operation as takes place when several persons help each other in the same employment; secondly, such co-operation as takes place when several persons help each other in different employments. These may be termed Simple Co-operation and Complex Co-operation.

"The advantage of simple co-operation is illustrated by the case of two greyhounds running together, which, it is said, will kill more hares than four greyhounds running separately. In a vast number of simple operations performed by human exertion, it is quite obvious that two men working together will do more than four, or four times four men, each of whom should work alone. In the lifting of heavy weights, for example, in the felling of trees, in the sawing of timber, in the gathering of much hay or corn during a short period of fine weather, in draining a large extent of land during the short season when such a work may be properly conducted,

*Note to Wakefield's edition of Adam Smith, vol. i. p. 26[–8]. [Smith, Adam. *An Inquiry into the Nature and Causes of the Wealth of Nations.* With a Commentary by the Author of "England and America" [E. G. Wakefield]. 6 vols. London: Knight, 1835.]

in the pulling of ropes on board ship, in the rowing of large boats, in some mining operations, in the erection of a scaffolding for building, and in the breaking of stones for the repair of a road, so that the whole of the road shall always be kept in good order: in all these simple operations, and thousands more, it is absolutely necessary that many persons should work together, at the same time, in the same place, and in the same way. The savages of New Holland never help each other, even in the most simple operations; and their condition is hardly superior, in some respects it is inferior, to that of the wild animals which they now and then catch. Let any one imagine that the labourers of England should suddenly desist from helping each other in simple employments, and he will see at once the prodigious advantages of simple co-operation. In a countless number of employments, the produce of labour is, up to a certain point, in proportion to such mutual assistance amongst the workmen. This is the first step in social improvement." The second is, when "one body of men having combined their labour to raise more food than they require, another body of men are induced to combine their labour for the purpose of producing more clothes than they require, and with those surplus clothes buying the surplus food of the other body of labourers; while, if both bodies together have produced more food and clothes than they both require, both bodies obtain, by means of exchange, a proper capital for setting more labourers to work in their respective occupations." To simple co-operation is thus superadded what Mr. Wakefield terms Complex Co-operation. The one is the combination of several labourers to help each other in the same set of operations; the other is the combination of several labourers to help one another by a division of operations.

There is "an important distinction between simple and complex co-operation. Of the former, one is always conscious at the time of practising it: it is obvious to the most ignorant and vulgar eye. Of the latter, but a very few of the vast numbers who practise it are in any degree conscious. The cause of this distinction is easily seen. When several men are employed in lifting the same weight, or pulling the same rope, at the same time, and in the same place, there can be no sort of doubt that they co-operate with each other; the fact is impressed on the mind by the mere sense of sight; but when several men, or bodies of men, are employed at different times and places, and in different pursuits, their co-operation with each other, though it may be quite as certain, is not so readily perceived as in the other case: in order to perceive it, a complex operation of the mind is required."[*]

In the present state of society the breeding and feeding of sheep is the occupation of one set of people, dressing the wool to prepare it for

[* *Wealth of Nations*, ed. Wakefield, I, 30.]

the spinner is that of another, spinning it into thread of a third, weaving the thread into broadcloth of a fourth, dyeing the cloth of a fifth, making it into a coat of a sixth, without counting the multitude of carriers, merchants, factors, and retailers, put in requisition at the successive stages of this progress. All these persons, without knowledge of one another or previous understanding, co-operate in the production of the ultimate result, a coat. But these are far from being all who co-operate in it; for each of these persons requires food, and many other articles of consumption, and unless he could have relied that other people would produce these for him, he could not have devoted his whole time to one step in the succession of operations which produces one single commodity, a coat. Every person who took part in producing food or erecting houses for this series of producers, has, however unconsciously on his part, combined his labour with theirs. It is by a real, though unexpressed, concert, "that the body who raise more food than they want, can exchange with the body who raise more clothes than they want; and if the two bodies were separated, either by distance or disinclination—unless the two bodies should virtually form themselves into one, for the common object of raising enough food and clothes for the whole—they could not divide into two distinct parts the whole operation of producing a sufficient quantity of food and clothes."[*]

§ 2. [*Effects of separation of employments analyzed*] The influence exercised on production by the separation of employments, is more fundamental than, from the mode in which the subject is usually treated, a reader might be induced to suppose. It is not merely that when the production of different things becomes the sole or principal occupation of different persons, a much greater quantity of each kind of article is produced. The truth is much beyond this. Without some separation of employments, very few things would be produced at all.

Suppose a set of persons, or a number of families, all employed [a]precisely in[a] the same manner; each family settled on a piece of its own land, on which it grows by its labour the food required for its own sustenance, and as there are no persons to buy any surplus produce where all are producers, each family [b]has to[b] produce within itself whatever other articles it consumes. In such circumstances, if the soil was tolerably fertile, and population did not tread too closely on the heels of subsistence, there would be, no doubt, some kind of domestic manufactures; clothing for the family might perhaps be spun and woven within it, by the labour probably of the women (a first step in the separation of employments); and a dwelling of some sort would be erected and kept in repair by their united labour.

[* *Wealth of Nations*, ed. Wakefield, I, 29.]

[a-a]MS, 48, 49, 52, 57 in precisely [b-b]MS must

But beyond simple food (precarious, too, from the variations of the seasons), coarse clothing, and very imperfect lodging, it would be scarcely possible that the family should produce anything more. They would, in general, require their utmost exertions to accomplish so much. Their power even of extracting food from the soil would be kept within narrow limits by the quality of their tools, which would necessarily be of the most wretched description. To do almost anything in the way of producing for themselves articles of convenience or luxury, would require too much time, and, in many cases, their presence in a different place. Very few kinds of industry, therefore, would exist; and that which did exist, namely the production of necessaries, would be extremely inefficient, not solely from imperfect implements, but because, when the ground and the domestic industry fed by it had been made to supply the necessaries of a single family in tolerable abundance, there would be little motive, while the numbers of the family remained the same, to make either the land or the labour produce more.

But suppose an event to occur, which would amount to a revolution in the circumstances of this little settlement. Suppose that a company of artificers, provided with tools, and with food sufficient to maintain them [c]for[c] a year, arrive in the country and establish themselves in the midst of the population. These new settlers occupy themselves in producing articles of use or ornament adapted to the taste of a simple people; and before their food is exhausted they have produced these in considerable quantity, and are ready to exchange them for more food. The economical position of the landed population is now most materially altered. They have an opportunity given them of acquiring comforts and luxuries. Things which, while they depended solely on their own labour, they never could have obtained, because they could not have produced, are now accessible to them if they can succeed in producing an additional quantity of food and necessaries. They are thus incited to increase the productiveness of their industry. Among the conveniences for the first time made accessible to them, better tools are probably one: and apart from this, they have a motive to labour more assiduously, and [d]to[d] adopt contrivances for making their labour more effectual. By these means they will generally succeed in compelling their land to produce, not only food for themselves, but a surplus for the new comers, wherewith to buy from them the products of their industry. The new settlers constitute what is called a *market* for surplus agricultural produce: and their arrival has enriched the settlement not only by the manufactured [e]article[e] which they produce, but by the food which would not have been produced unless they had been there to consume it.

[c-c]+48, 49, 52, 57, 62, 65, 71
[d-d]+57, 62, 65, 71

[e-e]MS, 48, 49, 52, 57, 62 articles

There is no inconsistency between this doctrine, and the [f]proposition we before maintained[f], that a market for commodities does not constitute employment for labour.* The labour of the agriculturists was already provided with employment; they are not indebted to the demand of the new comers for being able to maintain themselves. What that demand does for them is, to call their labour into increased vigour and efficiency; to stimulate them, by new motives, to new exertions. Neither do the new comers owe their maintenance and employment to the demand of the agriculturists: with a year's subsistence in store, they could have settled side by side with the former inhabitants, and produced a similar scanty stock of food and necessaries. Nevertheless we see of what supreme importance to the productiveness of the labour of producers, is the existence of other producers within reach, employed in a different kind of industry. The power of exchanging the products of one kind of labour for those of another, is a condition, but for which, there would almost always be a smaller quantity of labour altogether. When a new market is opened for any product of industry, and a greater quantity of the article is consequently produced, the increased production is not always obtained at the expense of some other product; it is often a new creation, the result of labour which would otherwise have remained unexerted; or of assistance rendered to labour by improvements or by modes of co-operation to which recourse would not have been had if an inducement had not been offered for raising a larger produce.

§ 3. [*Combination of labour between town and country*] From these considerations it appears that a country will seldom have a productive agriculture, unless it has a large town population, or the only available substitute, a large export trade in agricultural produce to supply a population elsewhere. I use the phrase town population for shortness, to imply a population non-agricultural; which will generally be collected in towns or large villages, for the sake of combination of labour. The application of this truth by Mr. Wakefield to the theory of colonization, has excited much attention, and is doubtless destined to excite much more. It is one of those great practical discoveries, which, once made, appears so obvious that the merit of making them seems less than it is. Mr. Wakefield was the first to point out that the mode of planting new settlements, then commonly practised—setting down a number of families side by side, each on its piece of land, [a] all employing themselves in exactly the same manner,—though [b]in[b] favourable circumstances it may assure to those families a rude

*Supra, pp. 78–88.

[f-f]MS, 48, 49, 52, 57 principle we have laid down
[a]MS, 48, 49, 52, 57 and [b-b]MS, 48 under

abundance of mere necessaries, can never be other than unfavourable to great production or rapid growth: and his system consists of arrangements for securing that every colony shall have from the first a town population bearing due proportion to its agricultural, and that the cultivators of the soil shall not be so widely scattered as to be deprived by distance, of the benefit of that town population as a market for their produce. The principle on which the scheme is founded, does not depend on any theory respecting the [c]superior[c] productiveness of land held in large portions, and cultivated by hired labour. Supposing it true that land yields the greatest produce when divided into small properties and cultivated by peasant proprietors, a town population [d]will[d] be just as necessary to induce those proprietors to raise that larger produce: and if they were too far from the nearest seat of non-agricultural industry to use it as a market for disposing of their surplus, and thereby supplying their other wants, neither that surplus nor any equivalent for it would, generally speaking, be produced.

It is, above all, the deficiency of town population which limits the productiveness of the industry of a country like India. The agriculture of India is conducted entirely on the system of small holdings. There is, however, a considerable amount of combination of labour. The village institutions and customs, which are the real framework of Indian society, make provision for joint action in the cases in which it is seen to be necessary; or where they fail to do so, the government (when tolerably well administered) steps in, and by an outlay from the revenue, executes by combined labour the tanks, embankments, and works of irrigation, which are indispensable. The implements and processes of agriculture are however so wretched, that the produce of the soil, in spite of great natural fertility and a climate highly favourable to vegetation, is miserably small: and the land might be made to yield food in abundance for many more than the present number of inhabitants, without departing from the system of small holdings. But to this the stimulus is wanting, which a large town population, connected with the rural districts by easy and unexpensive means of communication, would afford. That town population, again, does not grow up, because the few wants and unaspiring spirit of the cultivators (joined until lately with great insecurity of property, from military and fiscal rapacity) prevent them from attempting to become consumers of town produce. In these circumstances the best chance of an early development of the productive resources of India, consists in the [e] rapid growth of its export of agricultural produce (cotton, indigo, sugar, coffee, &c.) to the markets of Europe. The producers of these articles are consumers of food

[c-c]48 inferior [*printer's error?*]
[d-d]MS, 48, 49, 52, 57, 62, 65 would
[e]MS, 48, 49 now

supplied by their fellow-agriculturists in India; and the market thus opened for surplus food will, if accompanied by good government, raise up by degrees more extended wants and desires, directed either towards European commodities, or towards things which will require for their production in India a larger manufacturing population.

§ 4. [*The higher degrees of the division of labour*] Thus far of the separation of employments, a form of the combination of labour without which there cannot be the first rudiments of industrial civilization. But when this separation is thoroughly established; when it has become the general practice for each producer to supply many others with one commodity, and to be supplied by others with most of the things which he consumes; reasons not less real, though less imperative, invite to a further extension of the same principle. It is found that the productive power of labour is increased by carrying the separation further and further; by breaking down more and more every process of industry into parts, so that each labourer shall confine himself to an ever smaller number of simple operations. And thus, in time, arise those remarkable cases of what is called the division of labour, with which all readers on subjects of this nature are familiar. Adam Smith's illustration from pin-making, though so well known, is so much to the point, that I will venture once more to transcribe it. "The business of making a pin is divided into about eighteen distinct operations. [a] One man draws out the wire, another straights it, a third cuts it, a fourth points it, a fifth grinds it at the top for receiving the head; to make the head requires two or three distinct operations; to put it on, is a peculiar business; to whiten the pins is another; it is even a trade by itself to put them into the paper. . . . . I have seen a small manufactory where ten men only were employed, and where some of them, consequently, performed two or three distinct operations. But though they were very poor, and therefore but indifferently accommodated with the necessary machinery, they could, when they exerted themselves, make among them about twelve pounds of pins in a day. There are in a pound upwards of four thousand pins of a middling size. Those ten persons, therefore, could make among them upwards of forty-eight thousand pins in a day. Each person, therefore, making a tenth part of forty-eight thousand pins, might be considered as making four thousand eight hundred pins in a day. But if they had all wrought separately and independently, and without any of them having been educated to this peculiar business, they certainly could not each of them have made twenty, perhaps not one pin in a day."[*]

[* *Wealth of Nations*, ed. Wakefield, I, 8.]

[a]MS [*ellipsis indicated by*] . .

M. Say furnishes a still stronger example of the effects of division of labour—from a not very important branch of industry certainly, the manufacture of playing cards. "It is said by those engaged in the business, that each card, that is, a piece of pasteboard of the size of the hand, before being ready for sale, does not undergo fewer than seventy [b] operations,* every one of which might be the occupation of a distinct class of workmen. And if there are not seventy classes of work-people in each card manufactory, it is because the division of labour is not carried so far as it might be; because the same workman is charged with two, three, or four distinct operations. The influence of this distribution of [c]employment[c] is immense. I have seen a card manufactory where thirty workmen produced daily fifteen thousand five hundred cards, being above five hundred cards for each labourer; and it may be presumed that if each of these workmen were obliged to perform all the operations himself, even supposing him a practised hand, he would not perhaps complete two cards in a day: and the thirty workmen, instead of fifteen thousand five hundred cards, would make only sixty."[*]

* "Ce ne sont point les mêmes ouvriers qui préparent le papier dont on fait les cartes, ni les couleurs dont on les empreint; et en ne fesant attention qu'au seul emploi de ces matières, nous trouverons qu'un jeu de cartes est le résultat de plusieurs opérations dont chacune occupe une série distincte d'ouvriers et [Source, MS d'ouvriers ou] d'ouvrières qui s'appliquent toujours à la même opération. Ce sont des personnes différentes, et toujours les mêmes, qui épluchent les bouchons et grosseurs qui se trouvent dans le papier et nuiraient à l'égalité d'épaisseur; les mêmes qui collent ensemble les trois feuilles de papier dont se compose le carton et qui le mettent en presse; [Source, MS, 48, 49, 52, 57 presse; les mêmes qui colorent le coté destiné à former le dos des cartes;] les mêmes qui impriment en noir le dessin des figures; d'autres ouvriers impriment les couleurs des mêmes figures; d'autres font sécher au réchaud les cartons une fois qu'ils sont imprimés; d'autres s'occupent de les lisser dessus et dessous. C'est une occupation particulière que de les couper d'égale dimension; c'en est une autre de les assembler pour en former des jeux; une autre encore d'imprimer les enveloppes des jeux, et une autre encore de les envelopper; sans compter les fonctions des personnes chargées des ventes et des achats, de payer les ouvriers et de tenir les écritures."—Say, *Cours d'Economie Politique*, vol. i. p. 340[–1]. [Say, Jean-Baptiste. *Cours complet d'économie politique pratique; ouvrage destiné à mettre sous les yeux des hommes d'état, des propriétaires fonciers et des capitalistes, des savans, des agriculteurs, des manufacturiers, des négocians, et en général de tous les citoyens, l'économie des sociétés*. Tome premier. Paris: Rapilly, 1828.]

It is a remarkable proof of the economy of labour occasioned by this minute division of occupations, that an article, the production of which is the result of such a multitude of manual operations, can be sold for a trifling sum.

[**Translated from* ibid., I, 341.]

[b]Source, MS different
[c–c]Source, MS, 48, 49, 52, 57, 62 employments

In watchmaking, as Mr. Babbage observes, "it was stated in evidence before a Committee of the House of Commons, that there are a hundred and two distinct branches of this art, to each of which a boy may be put apprentice; and that he only learns his master's department, and is unable, after his apprenticeship has expired, without subsequent instruction, to work at any other branch. The watch-finisher, whose business [d]it[d] is to put together the scattered parts, is the only one, out of the hundred and two persons, who can work in any other department than his own."*

§ 5. [*Analysis of the advantages of the division of labour*] The causes of the increased efficiency given to labour by the division of employments are some of them too familiar to require specification; but it is worth while to attempt a complete enumeration of them. By Adam Smith they are reduced to three. "First, the increase of dexterity in every particular workman; secondly, the saving of the time which is commonly lost in passing from one species of work to another; and lastly, the invention of a great number of machines which facilitate and abridge labour, and enable one man to do the work of many."[*]

Of these, the increase of dexterity of the individual workman is the most obvious and universal. It does not follow that because a thing has been done oftener it will be done better. That depends on the intelligence of the workman, and on the degree in which his mind works along with his hands. But it will be done more easily. The organs themselves acquire greater power: the muscles employed grow stronger by frequent exercise, the sinews more pliant, and the mental powers more efficient, and less sensible of fatigue. What can be done easily has at least a better chance of being done well, and is sure to be done more expeditiously. What was at first done slowly comes to be done quickly; what was at first done slowly with accuracy is at last done quickly with equal accuracy. This is as true of mental operations as of bodily. Even a child, after much practice, sums up a column of figures with a rapidity which resembles intuition. The act of speaking any language, of reading fluently, of playing music at sight, are cases as remarkable as they are familiar. Among bodily acts, dancing, gymnastic exercises, ease and brilliancy of execution on a musical instrument, are examples of the rapidity and facility acquired by repetition. In simpler manual operations the effect is of course still sooner produced. "The rapidity," Adam Smith observes, "with which some of the operations of certain manufactures are performed, exceeds what the human hand could, by those who had never seen them, be supposed capable of

**Economy of Machinery and Manufactures*, 3rd Edition, p. 201[–2].

[**Wealth of Nations*, ed. Wakefield, I, 12–3.]

d–d+48, 49, 52, 57, 62, 65, 71

acquiring."* This skill is, naturally, attained after shorter practice, in proportion as the division of labour is more minute; and will not be attained in the same degree at all, if the workman has a greater variety of operations to execute than allows of a sufficiently frequent repetition of each. The advantage is not confined to the greater efficiency ultimately attained, but includes also the diminished loss of time, and waste of material, in learning the art. "A certain quantity of material," says Mr. Babbage,† "will in all cases be consumed unprofitably, or spoiled, by every person who learns an art; and as he applies himself to each new process, he will waste some of the raw material, or of the partly manufactured commodity. But if each man commit this waste in acquiring successively every process, the quantity of waste will be much greater than if each person confine his attention to one process." And in general each will be much sooner qualified to execute his one process, if he be not distracted while learning it, by the necessity of [a]learning[a] others.

The second advantage enumerated by Adam Smith as arising from the division of labour, is one on which I cannot help thinking that more stress is laid by him and others than it deserves. To do full justice to his opinion, I will quote his own exposition of it. "The advantage which is gained by saving the time commonly lost in passing from one sort of work to another, is much greater than we should at first view be apt to imagine it. It is impossible to pass very quickly from one kind of work to another, that is carried on in a different place, and with quite different tools. A country weaver, who cultivates a small farm, must lose a good deal of time in passing from his loom to the field, and from the field to his loom. When the two trades can be carried on in the same workhouse, the loss of time is no doubt much less. It is even in this case, however, very considerable. A man commonly saunters a little in turning his hand from one sort of employment to another. When he first begins the new work, he is seldom very

*[*Ibid.*, I, 14.] [49] "In astronomical observations, the senses of the operator are rendered so acute by habit, that he can estimate differences of time to the tenth of a second; and adjust his measuring instrument to graduations of which five thousand occupy only an inch. It is the same throughout the commonest processes of manufacture. A child who fastens on the heads of pins will repeat an operation requiring several distinct motions of the muscles one hundred times a minute for several successive hours. In a recent Manchester paper it was stated that a peculiar sort of twist or 'gimp,' which cost three shillings making when first introduced, was now manufactured for one penny; and this not, as usually, by the invention of a new machine, but solely through the increased dexterity of the workman."—*Edinburgh Review* for January 1849, p. 81 ["The Progress of Mechanical Invention." *Edinburgh Review*, LXXXIX (Jan., 1849)].

†Page 171.

[a-a]MS, 48, 49, 52 acquiring

keen and hearty; his mind, as they say, does not go to it, and for some time he rather trifles than applies to good purpose. The habit of sauntering and of indolent careless application, which is naturally, or rather necessarily acquired by every country workman who is obliged to change his work and his tools every half hour, and to apply his hand in twenty different ways almost every day of his life, renders him almost always slothful and lazy, and incapable of any vigorous application even on the most pressing occasions."[*] This is surely a most exaggerated description of the inefficiency of country labour, where it has any adequate motive to exertion. Few workmen change their work and their tools oftener than a gardener; is he usually incapable of vigorous application? Many of the higher description of artisans have to perform a great multiplicity of operations with a variety of tools. They do not execute each of these with the rapidity with which a factory workman performs his single operation; but they are, except in a merely manual sense, more skilful labourers, and in all senses whatever more energetic.

Mr. Babbage, following in the track of Adam Smith, says, "When the human hand, or the human head, has been for some time occupied in any kind of work, it cannot instantly change its employment with full effect. The muscles of the limbs employed have acquired a flexibility during their exertion, and those not in action a stiffness during rest, which renders every change slow and unequal in the commencement. Long habit also produces in the muscles exercised a capacity for enduring fatigue to a much greater degree than they could support under other circumstances. A similar result seems to take place in any change of mental exertion; the attention bestowed on the new subject not being so perfect at first as it becomes after some exercise. The employment of different tools in the successive processes, is another cause of the loss of time in changing from one operation to another. If these tools are simple, and the change is not frequent, the loss of time is not considerable; but in many processes of the arts, the tools are of great delicacy, requiring accurate adjustment every time they are used; and in many cases, the time employed in adjusting bears a large proportion to that employed in using the tool. The sliding-rest, the dividing and the drilling engine are of this kind: and hence, in manufactories of sufficient extent, it is found to be good economy to keep one machine constantly employed in one kind of work: one lathe, for example, having a screw motion to its sliding-rest along the whole length of its bed, is kept constantly making cylinders; another, having a motion for equalizing the velocity of the work at the point at which it passes the tool, is kept for facing surfaces; whilst a third is constantly employed in cutting wheels."[†]

[* *Wealth of Nations*, ed. Wakefield, I, 14–5.]
[†Babbage, pp. 171–2.]

I am very far from implying that these different considerations are of no weight; but I think there are counter-considerations which are overlooked. If one kind of muscular or mental labour is different from another, for that very reason it is to some extent a rest from that other; and if the greatest vigour is not at once obtained in the second occupation, neither could the first have been indefinitely prolonged without some relaxation of energy. It is a matter of common experience that a change of occupation will often afford relief where complete repose would otherwise be necessary, and that a person can work many more hours without fatigue at a succession of occupations, than if confined during the whole time to one. Different occupations employ different muscles, or different [b]energies[b] of the mind, some of which rest and are refreshed while others work. Bodily labour itself rests from mental, and conversely. [c]The[c] variety itself has an invigorating effect on what, for want of a more philosophical appellation, we must term the animal spirits; so important to the efficiency of all work not mechanical, and not unimportant even to that. The comparative weight due to these considerations is different with different individuals; some are more fitted than others for persistency in one occupation, and less fit for change; they require longer to get the steam up (to use a metaphor now common); the irksomeness of setting to work lasts longer, and it requires more time to bring their faculties into full play, and therefore when this is once done, they do not like to leave off, but go on long without intermission, even to the injury of their health. Temperament has something to do with these differences. There are people whose faculties seem by nature to come slowly into action, and to accomplish little until they have been a long time employed. Others, again, get into action rapidly, but cannot, without exhaustion, continue long. In this, however, as in most other things, though natural differences are something, habit is much more. The habit of passing rapidly from one occupation to another may be acquired, like other habits, by early cultivation; and when it is acquired, there is none of the sauntering which Adam Smith speaks of, after each change; no want of energy and interest, but the workman comes to each part of his occupation with a freshness and a spirit which he does not retain if he persists in any one part (unless in case of unusual excitement) beyond the length of time to which he is accustomed. Women are usually (at least in their present social circumstances) of far greater versatility than men; and the present topic is an instance among multitudes, how little the ideas and experience of women have yet counted for, in forming the opinions of mankind. There are few women who would not reject the idea that work is made vigorous by being protracted, and is inefficient for some time after changing to a new thing. Even in this case, habit, I believe, much more than nature, is

[b-b]MS, 48, 49, 52, 57 faculties [c-c]MS, 48, 49 Even the

the cause of the difference. The occupations of nine out of every ten men are special, those of nine out of every ten women general, embracing a multitude of details, each of which requires very little time. Women are in the constant practice of passing quickly from one manual, and still more from one mental operation to another, which therefore rarely costs them either effort or loss of time, while a man's occupation generally consists in working steadily for a long time at one thing, or one very limited class of things. But the situations are sometimes reversed, and with them the characters. Women are not found less efficient than men for the uniformity of factory work, or they would not so generally be employed for it; and a man who has cultivated the habit of turning his hand to many things, far from being the slothful and lazy person described by Adam Smith, is usually remarkably lively and active. It is [d]true, however,[d] that change of occupation may be too frequent even for the most versatile. Incessant variety is even more fatiguing than perpetual sameness.

The third advantage attributed by Adam Smith to the division of labour, is, to a certain extent, real. Inventions tending to save labour in a particular operation, are more likely to occur to any one in proportion as his thoughts are intensely directed to that occupation, and continually employed upon it. A person is not so likely to make practical improvements in one department of things, whose attention is very much diverted to others. But, in this, much more depends on general intelligence and habitual activity of mind, than on exclusiveness of occupation; and if that exclusiveness is carried to a degree unfavourable to the cultivation of intelligence, there will be more lost in this kind of advantage, than gained. We may add, that whatever may be the cause of making inventions, when they are once made, the increased efficiency of labour is owing to the invention itself, and not to the division of labour.

The greatest advantage (next to the [e] dexterity of the workmen) derived from the minute division of labour which takes place in modern manufacturing industry, is [f] one not mentioned by Adam Smith, but to which attention has been drawn by Mr. Babbage; the more economical distribution of labour, by classing the work-people according to their capacity. Different parts of the same series of operations require unequal degrees of skill and bodily strength; and those who have skill enough for the most difficult, or strength enough for the hardest parts of the labour, are made much more useful by being employed solely in them; the operations [g]which everybody is capable of[g], being left to those who are fit for no others.

[d-d]MS , however, true
[e]MS increased
[f]MS, 48, 49 probably
[g-g]MS, 48, 49 of which inferior workmen are capable

Production is most efficient when the precise quantity of skill and strength, which is required for each part of the process, is employed in it, and no more. The operation of pin-making requires, it seems, in its different parts, such different degrees of skill, that the wages earned by the persons employed vary from fourpence halfpenny a day to six shillings; and if the workman who is paid at that highest rate had to perform the whole process, he would be working a part of his time with a waste per day equivalent to the difference between six shillings and fourpence halfpenny. Without reference to the loss sustained in quantity of work done, and supposing even that he could make a pound of pins in the same time in which ten workmen combining their labour can make ten pounds, Mr. Babbage computes that they would cost, in making, three times and three-quarters as much as they now do by [h]means[h] of the division of labour. In needle-making, he adds, the difference would be still greater, for in that, the scale of remuneration for different parts of the process varies from sixpence to twenty shillings a day.

To the advantage which consists in extracting the greatest possible amount of utility from skill, may be added the analogous one, of extracting the utmost possible utility from tools. "If any man," says an able writer,* "had all the tools which many different occupations require, at least three-fourths of them would constantly be idle and useless. It were clearly then better, were any society to exist where each man had all these tools, and alternately carried on each of these occupations, that the members of it should, if possible, divide them amongst them, each restricting himself to some particular employment. [i] The advantages of the change to the whole community, and therefore to every individual in it, are great. In the first place, the various implements being in constant employment, yield a better return for what has been laid out in procuring them. In consequence their owners can afford to have them of better quality and more complete construction. The result of both events is, that a larger provision is made for the future wants of the whole society."

§ 6. [*Limitations of the division of labour*] The division of labour, as all writers on the subject have remarked, is limited by the extent of the market. If, by the separation of pin-making into ten distinct employments, forty-eight thousand pins can be made in a day, this separation will only be advisable if the number of accessible consumers is such as to require,

**Statement of some New Principles on the subject of Political Economy* [*Exposing the Fallacies of the System of Free Trade, and of some other Doctrines mentioned in the "Wealth of Nations"*], by John Rae, (Boston, U.S. [: Hilliard, Gray and Co., 1834]) p. 164[–5].

[h-h]MS the application [i]MS [*ellipsis indicated by*] . . .

every day, something like forty-eight thousand pins. If there is only a demand for twenty-four thousand, the division of labour can only be advantageously carried to the extent which will every day produce that smaller number. This, therefore, is a further mode in which an accession of demand for a commodity tends to increase the efficiency of the labour employed in its production. The extent of the market may be limited by several causes: too small a population; the population too scattered and distant to be easily accessible; deficiency of roads and water carriage; or, finally, the population too poor, that is, their collective labour too little effective, to admit of their being large consumers. Indolence, want of skill, and want of combination of labour, among those who would otherwise be buyers of a commodity, limit, therefore, the [a]practical[a] amount of combination of labour among its producers. In an early stage of civilization, when the demand of any particular locality was necessarily small, industry only flourished among those who by their command of the sea-coast or of a navigable river, could have the whole world, or all that part of it which lay on coasts or navigable rivers, as a market for their productions. The increase of the general riches of the world, when accompanied with freedom of commercial intercourse, improvements in navigation, and inland communication by roads, canals, or railways, tends to give increased productiveness to the labour of every nation in particular, by enabling each locality to supply with its special products so much larger a market, that a great extension of the division of labour in their production is an ordinary consequence.

The division of labour is also limited, in many cases, by the nature of the employment. Agriculture, for example, is not susceptible of so great a division of occupations as many branches of manufactures, because its different operations cannot possibly be simultaneous. One man cannot be always ploughing, another sowing, and another reaping. A workman who only practised one agricultural operation would be idle eleven months of the year. The same person may perform them all in succession, and have, in [b]most climates[b], a considerable amount of unoccupied time. [c] To execute a great agricultural improvement, it is often necessary that many labourers should work together; but in general, except the few whose business is superintendence, they all work in the same manner. A canal or a railway embankment cannot be made without a combination of many labourers; but they are all excavators, except the [d]engineers[d] and [e]a few[e] clerks.

[a-a]MS, 48, 49, 52, 57, 62, 65 practicable

[b-b]MS, 48, 49, 52, 57, 62 almost every climate

[c]MS, 48, 49, 52 The combination of labour, of which agricultural industry is susceptible, is chiefly that which Mr. Wakefield terms Simple Co-operation; many persons employed together in the same work.

[d-d]MS, 48, 49, 52, 57, 62 engineer

[e-e]MS, 48 his

CHAPTER IX

Of Production on a Large, and Production on a Small Scale

§ 1. [*Advantages of the large system of production in manufactures*] From the importance of combination of labour, it is an obvious conclusion, that there are many cases in which production is made much more effective by being conducted on a large scale. Whenever it is essential to the greatest efficiency of labour that many labourers should combine, even though only in the way of Simple Co-operation, the scale of the enterprise must be such as to bring many labourers together, and the capital must be large enough to maintain them. Still more needful is this when the nature of the employment allows, and the extent of the possible market encourages, a considerable division of labour. The larger the enterprise, the [a]farther[a] the division of labour may be carried. This is one of the principal causes of large manufactories. Even when no additional subdivision of the work would follow an enlargement of the operations, there will be good economy in enlarging them to the point at which every person to whom it is convenient to assign a special occupation, will have full employment in that occupation. This point is well illustrated by Mr. Babbage.*

"If machines be kept working through the twenty-four hours," (which is evidently the only economical mode of employing them,) "it is necessary that some person shall attend to admit the workmen at the time they relieve each other; and whether the porter or other [b]person[b] so employed admit one person or twenty, his rest will be equally disturbed. It will also be necessary occasionally to adjust or repair the machine; and this can be done much better by a workman accustomed to machine-making, than by the person who uses it. Now, since the good performance and the duration of machines depend, to a very great extent, upon correcting every shake or imperfection in their parts as soon as they appear, the prompt attention of a workman resident on the spot will considerably reduce the expenditure arising from the wear and tear of the machinery. But in the case of a single

*Page 214 et seqq. [Pp. 214–6.]

[a-a]MS, 48, 49, 52 further   [b-b]Source, MS, 48, 49, 52, 57, 62 servant

lace-frame, or a single loom, this would be too expensive a plan. Here then arises another circumstance which tends to enlarge the extent of a factory. It ought to consist of such a number of machines as shall occupy the whole time of one workman in keeping them in order: if extended beyond that number, the same principle of economy would point out the necessity of doubling or tripling the number of machines, in order to employ the whole time of two or three skilful workmen.

"[c]When[c] one portion of the workman's labour consists in the exertion of mere physical force, as in weaving, and in many similar arts, it will soon occur to the manufacturer, that if that part were executed by a steam-engine, the same man might, in the case of weaving, attend to two or more looms at once: and, since we already suppose that one or more operative engineers have been employed, the number of looms may be so arranged that their time shall be fully occupied in keeping the steam-engine and the looms in order. [d]

"Pursuing the same principles, the manufactory becomes gradually so enlarged, that the expense of lighting during the night amounts to a considerable sum: and as there are already attached to the establishment persons who are up all night, and can therefore constantly attend to it, and also engineers to make and keep in repair any machinery, the addition of an apparatus for making gas to light the factory leads to a new extension, at the same time that it contributes, by diminishing the expense of lighting, and the risk of accidents from fire, to reduce the cost of manufacturing.

"Long before a factory has reached this extent, it will have been found necessary to establish an accountant's department, with clerks to pay the workmen, and to see that they arrive at their stated times; and this department must be in communication with the agents who purchase the raw produce, and with those who sell the manufactured article." It will cost these clerks and accountants little more time and trouble to pay a large number of workmen than a small number; to check the accounts of large transactions, than of small. If the business doubled itself, it would probably be necessary to increase, but certainly not to double, the number either of accountants, or of buying and selling agents. Every increase of business would enable the whole to be carried on with a [e]proportionately[e] smaller amount of labour.

As a general rule, the expenses of a business do not increase by any means proportionally to the quantity of business. Let us take as an example, a set of operations which we are accustomed to see carried on by one great establishment, that of the Post Office. Suppose that the business, let us say

[c-c]Source, MS, 48, 49, 52, 57 Where
[d]MS [*ellipsis indicated by*] . . . .
[e-e]MS, 48, 49, 52, 57, 62, 65 proportionally

only of the London letter-post, instead of being centralized in a single concern, were divided among five or six [f]competing companies[f]. Each of these would be obliged to maintain almost as large an establishment as is now sufficient for the whole. Since each must arrange for receiving and delivering letters in all parts of the town, each must send letter-carriers into every street, and almost every alley, and this too as many times in the day as is now done by the Post Office, if the service is to be as well performed. Each must have an office for receiving letters in every neighbourhood, with all subsidiary arrangements for collecting the letters from the different offices and re-distributing them. [g]To this must be added[g] the much greater number of superior officers who would be required to check and control the subordinates, implying not only a greater cost in salaries for such responsible officers, but the necessity, perhaps, of being satisfied in many instances with an inferior standard of qualification, and so failing in the object.

Whether or not the advantages obtained by operating on a large scale preponderate in any particular case over the more watchful attention, and greater regard to minor gains and losses, usually found in small establishments, can be ascertained, in a state of free competition, by an unfailing test. Wherever there are large and small establishments in the same business, that one of the two which in existing circumstances carries on the production at greatest advantage will be able to undersell the other. The power of permanently underselling can only[h], generally speaking,[h] be derived from increased effectiveness of labour; and this, when obtained by a more extended division of employment, or by a classification tending to a better economy of skill, always implies a greater produce from the same labour, and not merely the same produce from less labour: it increases not the surplus only, but the gross produce of industry. If an increased quantity of the particular article is not required, and [i] part of the labourers in consequence lose their employment, the capital which maintained and employed them is also set at liberty; and the general produce of the country is increased by some other application of their labour.

Another of the causes of large manufactories, however, is the introduction of processes requiring expensive machinery. Expensive machinery supposes a large capital; and is not resorted to except with the intention of producing, and the hope of selling, as much of the article as comes up to the full powers of the machine. For both these reasons, wherever costly machinery [j]is[j] used, the large system of production is inevitable. But the

[f-f]+48, 49, 52, 57, 62, 65, 71
[g-g]MS, 48, 49, 52, 57 I say nothing of
[h-h]+52, 57, 62, 65, 71
[i]MS, 48, 49 a
[j-j]MS, 48 are

power of underselling is not in this case so unerring a test as in the former, of the beneficial effect on the total production of the community. The power of underselling does not depend on the absolute increase of produce, but on its bearing an increased proportion to the expenses; which, as was shown in a former chapter,* it may do, consistently with even a diminution of the gross annual produce. By the adoption of machinery, a circulating capital, which was perpetually consumed and reproduced, has been converted into a fixed capital, requiring only a small annual expense to keep it up: and a much smaller produce will suffice for merely covering that expense, and replacing the remaining circulating capital of the producer. The machinery therefore [k]might[k] answer perfectly well to the manufacturer, and [l] enable him to undersell his competitors, though the effect on the production of the country [m]might[m] be not an increase but a diminution. It is true, the article will be sold cheaper, and therefore, of that single article, there will probably be not a smaller, but a greater quantity sold; since the loss to the community collectively has fallen upon the work-people, and they are not the principal customers, if customers at all, of most branches of manufacture. But though that particular branch of industry may extend itself, it will be by replenishing its diminished circulating capital from that of the community generally; and if the labourers employed in that department escape loss of employment, it is because the loss will spread itself over the labouring people at large. If any of them are reduced to the condition of unproductive labourers, supported by voluntary or legal charity, the gross produce of the country is to that extent permanently diminished, until the ordinary progress of accumulation makes it up; but if the condition of the labouring classes enables them to bear a temporary reduction of wages, and the superseded labourers become absorbed in other employments, their labour is still productive, and the breach in the gross produce of the community is repaired, though not the detriment to the labourers. I have restated this exposition, which has already been made in a former place, to impress more strongly the truth, that a mode of production does not of necessity increase the productive effect of the collective labour of a community, because it enables a particular commodity to be sold cheaper. The one consequence generally accompanies the other, but not necessarily. I will not here repeat the reasons I formerly gave, nor anticipate those which will be given more fully hereafter, for deeming the exception to be rather a case abstractedly possible, than one which is frequently realized in fact.

A considerable part of the saving of labour effected by substituting the

*Supra, chap. vi. p. 94.

[k-k]MS may
[l]MS may
[m-m]MS may

large system of production for the small, is the saving in the labour of the capitalists themselves. If a hundred producers with small capitals carry on separately the same business, the superintendence of each concern will probably require the whole attention of the person conducting it, sufficiently at least to hinder his time or thoughts from being disposable for anything else: while a single manufacturer possessing a capital equal to the sum of theirs, with ten or a dozen clerks, could conduct the whole of their amount of business, and have leisure too for other occupations. The small capitalist, it is true, generally combines with the business of direction some portion of the details, which the other leaves to his subordinates: the small farmer follows his own plough, the small tradesman serves in his own shop, the small weaver plies his own loom. But in this very union of functions there is, in a great proportion of cases, a want of economy. The principal in the concern is either wasting, in the routine of a business, qualities suitable for the direction of it, or he is only fit for the former, and then the latter will be ill done. I must observe, however, that I do not attach, to this saving of labour, the importance often ascribed to it. There is undoubtedly much more labour expended in the superintendence of many small capitals than in that of one large capital. For this labour however the small producers have generally a full compensation, in the feeling of being their own masters, and not servants of an employer. It may be said, that if they value this independence they will submit to pay a price for it, and to sell at the reduced rates occasioned by the competition of the great dealer or manufacturer. But they cannot always do this and continue to gain a living. They thus gradually disappear from society. After having consumed their little capital in prolonging the unsuccessful struggle, they either sink into the condition of hired labourers, or become dependent on others for support.

§ 2. [*Advantages and disadvantages of the joint-stock principle*] Production on a large scale is greatly promoted by the practice of forming a large capital by the combination of many small contributions; or, in other words, by the formation of joint stock companies. The [a]advantages[a] of the joint stock principle are numerous and important.

In the first place, many undertakings require an amount of capital beyond the means of the richest individual or private partnership. No individual could have made a railway from London to Liverpool; it is doubtful if any individual could even work the traffic on it, now when it is made. The government indeed could have done both; and in countries where the practice of co-operation is only in the earlier stages of its growth, the government can alone be looked to for any of [b]the[b] works for which a great combination of means is requisite; because it can obtain those means

[a–a]MS recommendations [b–b]MS, 48, 49, 52, 57, 62 those

by compulsory taxation, and is already accustomed to the conduct of large operations. For reasons, however, which are tolerably well known, and of which we shall treat fully hereafter, government agency for the conduct of industrial operations is generally one of the least eligible of resources, when any other is available.

Next, there are undertakings which individuals are not absolutely incapable of performing, but which they cannot perform on the scale and with the continuity which [c]are[c] ever more and more required by the exigencies of a society in an advancing state. Individuals are quite capable of despatching ships from England to any or every part of the world, to carry passengers and letters; the thing was done before joint stock companies [d]for the purpose[d] were heard of. But when, from the increase of population and transactions, as well as of means of payment, the public will no longer content themselves with occasional opportunities, but require the certainty that packets shall start regularly, for some places once or even twice a day, for others once a week, for others that a steam ship of [e]great[e] size and expensive construction shall depart on fixed days twice in each month, it is evident that to afford an assurance of keeping up with punctuality such a circle of costly operations, requires a much larger capital and a much larger staff of qualified subordinates than can be commanded by an individual capitalist. There are other cases, again, in which though the business might be perfectly well transacted with small or moderate capitals, the guarantee of a great subscribed stock is necessary or desirable as a security to the public for the fulfilment of pecuniary engagements. This is especially the case when the nature of the business requires that numbers of persons should be willing to trust the concern with their money: as in the business of banking, and that of insurance: to both of which the joint stock principle is eminently adapted. It is an instance of the folly and jobbery of the rulers of mankind, that until [f]a late period[f] the joint stock principle, as a general resort, was in this country interdicted by law to these two modes of business; to banking altogether, and to insurance in the department of sea risks; in order to bestow a lucrative monopoly on particular establishments which the government was pleased exceptionally to license, namely the Bank of England, and two insurance companies, the London and the Royal Exchange.

[g]Another advantage of joint stock or associated management, is its incident of publicity. This is not an invariable, but it is a natural consequence of the joint stock principle, and might be, as in some important cases it

[c-c]MS is
[d-d]+48, 49, 52, 57, 62, 65, 71
[e-e]MS enormous
[f-f]MS, 48, 49, 52, 57 very lately
[g-g137]+65, 71

already is, compulsory. In banking, insurance, and other businesses which depend wholly on confidence, publicity is a still more important element of success than a large subscribed capital. A heavy loss occurring in a private bank may be kept secret; even though it were of such magnitude as to cause the ruin of the concern, the banker may still carry it on for years, trying to retrieve its position, only to fall in the end with a greater crash: but this cannot so easily happen in the case of a joint stock company, whose accounts are published periodically. The accounts, even if cooked, still exercise some check; and the suspicions of shareholders, breaking out at the general meetings, put the public on their guard.[g]

These are some of the advantages of joint stock over individual management. But if we look to the other side of the question, we shall find that individual management has also [h]very great[h] advantages over joint stock. The chief of these is the much keener interest of the managers in the success of the undertaking.

The administration of a joint stock association is, in the main, administration by hired servants. Even the committee, or board of directors, who are supposed to superintend the management, and who do really appoint and remove the managers, have no pecuniary interest in the good working of the concern beyond the shares they individually hold, which are always a very small part of the capital of the association, and in general but a small part of the fortunes of the directors themselves; and the part they take in the management usually divides their time with many other occupations, of as great or greater importance to their own interest; the business being the principal concern of no one except those who are hired to carry it on. But experience shows, and proverbs, the expression of popular experience, attest, how inferior is the quality of hired [i]servants[i], compared with the ministration of those personally interested in the work, and how indispensable, when hired service must be employed, is "the master's eye" to watch over it.

The successful conduct of an industrial enterprise requires two quite distinct qualifications: fidelity, and zeal. The fidelity of the hired managers of a concern it is possible to secure. When their work admits of being reduced to a definite set of rules, the violation of these is a matter on which conscience cannot easily blind itself, and on which responsibility may be enforced by the loss of employment. But to carry on a great business successfully, requires a hundred things which, as they cannot be defined beforehand, it is impossible to convert into distinct and positive obligations. First and principally, it requires that the directing mind should be incessantly occupied with the subject; should be continually laying schemes by

[h-h]MS enormous
[i-i]MS, 48, 49, 52 service

which greater profit may be obtained, or expense saved. This intensity of interest in the subject it is seldom to be expected that any one should feel, who is conducting a business as the hired servant and for the profit of another. There are experiments in human [j]affairs which are[j] conclusive on the point. Look at the whole class of rulers, and ministers of state. The work they are entrusted with, is among the most interesting and exciting of all occupations; the personal share which they themselves reap of the national benefits or misfortunes which befal the state under their rule, is far from trifling, and the rewards and punishments which they may expect from public estimation are of the plain and palpable kind which are most keenly felt and most widely appreciated. Yet how rare a thing is it to find a statesman in whom mental indolence is not stronger than all these inducements. How infinitesimal is the proportion [k] who trouble themselves to form, or even to attend to, plans of public improvement, unless [l]when[l] it is made still more troublesome to them to remain inactive; or who have any other real desire than that of rubbing on, so as to escape general blame. On a smaller scale, all who have ever employed hired labour have had ample experience of the efforts made to give as little labour in exchange for the wages, as is compatible with not being turned off. The universal neglect by domestic servants of their employer's interests, wherever these are not protected by some fixed rule, is matter of common remark; unless where long continuance in the same service, and reciprocal good offices, have produced either personal attachment, or some feeling of a common interest.

Another of the disadvantages of joint stock concerns, which is in some degree common to all concerns on a large scale, is disregard of small gains and small savings. In the management of a great capital and great transactions, especially when the managers have not much interest in it of their own, small sums are apt to be counted for next to nothing; they never seem worth the care and trouble which it costs to attend to them, and the credit of liberality and openhandedness is cheaply bought by a disregard of such trifling considerations. But small profits and small expenses often repeated, amount to great gains and losses: and of this a large capitalist is often a sufficiently good calculator to be practically aware; and to arrange his business on a *system*, which if enforced by a sufficiently vigilant superintendence, precludes the possibility of the habitual waste, otherwise incident to a great business. But the managers of a joint stock concern seldom devote themselves sufficiently to the work, to enforce unremittingly, even if introduced, through every detail of the business, a really economical system.

From considerations of this nature, Adam Smith was led to enunciate as

[j-j]MS, 48, 49 nature which are quite
[k]MS of them
[l-l]+49, 52, 57, 62, 65, 71

a principle, that joint stock companies could never be expected to maintain themselves without an exclusive privilege, except in branches of business which, like banking, insurance, and some others, admit of being, in a considerable degree, reduced to fixed rules. This, however, is one of those over-statements of a true principle, often met with in Adam Smith. In his days there were few instances of joint stock companies which had been permanently successful without a monopoly, except the class of cases which he referred to; but since his time there have been many; and the regular increase both of the spirit of combination and of the ability to combine, will doubtless produce many more. Adam Smith fixed his observation too exclusively on the superior energy and more unremitting attention brought to a business in which the whole stake and the whole gain belong to the persons conducting it; and he overlooked various countervailing considerations which go a great way towards neutralizing even that great point of superiority.

Of these one of the most important is that which relates to the intellectual and active qualifications of the directing head. The stimulus of individual interest [m]is some security for[m] exertion, but [n] exertion is of little avail if the intelligence exerted is of an inferior order, which it must necessarily be in the majority of concerns carried on by the persons chiefly interested in them. Where the concern is large, and can afford a remuneration sufficient to attract a class of candidates superior to the common average, it is possible to select for the general management, and for all the skilled employments of a subordinate kind, persons of a degree of acquirement and cultivated intelligence which more than compensates for their inferior interest in the result. Their greater perspicacity enables them, with even a part of their minds, to see probabilities of advantage which never occur to the ordinary run of men by the continued exertion of the whole of theirs; [o]and their superior knowledge,[o] and [p] habitual rectitude of perception and of judgment, [q]guard[q] them against blunders, the [r]fear[r] of which would prevent the others from hazarding their interests in any attempt out of the ordinary routine.

It must [s]be further[s] remarked, that it is not a necessary consequence of joint stock management, that the persons employed, whether in superior or in subordinate offices, should be paid wholly by fixed salaries. There are modes of connecting more or less intimately the interest of the employés with the pecuniary success of the concern. There is a long series of intermediate positions, between working wholly on one's own account, and

[m-m]MS, 48, 49 secures the greatest amount of
[n]MS, 48, 49 that
[o-o]+57, 62, 65, 71
[p]MS, 48, 49, 52 their
[q-q]MS, 48, 49, 52 guards
[r-r]MS, 48, 49, 52, 57 apprehension
[s-s]MS, 48, 49 further be

working by the day, week, or year for an invariable payment. Even in the case of ordinary unskilled labour, there is such a thing as task-work, or working by the piece: and the superior efficiency of this is so well known, that judicious employers always resort to it when the work admits of being put out in definite portions, without the necessity of too troublesome a surveillance to guard against inferiority in the execution. In the case of the managers of joint stock companies, and of the superintending and controlling officers in many private establishments, it is a common enough practice to connect their pecuniary interest with the interest of their employers, by giving them part of their remuneration in the form of a percentage on the profits. The personal interest thus given to hired servants is not comparable in intensity to that of the owner of the capital; but it is sufficient to be a very material stimulus to zeal and carefulness, and, when added to the advantage of superior intelligence, often raises the quality of the service much above that which the generality of masters are capable of rendering to themselves. The ulterior extensions of which this principle of remuneration is susceptible, being of great social as well as economical importance, will be more particularly adverted to in a subsequent stage of the present inquiry.

As I have already remarked of large establishments generally, when compared with small ones, whenever competition is free its results will show whether individual or joint stock agency is best adapted to the particular case, since that which is most efficient and most economical will always in the end succeed in underselling the other.

§ 3. [*Conditions necessary for the large system of production*] The possibility of substituting the large system of production for the small, depends, of course, in the first place, on the extent of the market. The large system can only be advantageous when a large amount of business is to be done: it implies, therefore, either a populous and flourishing community, or a great opening for exportation. Again, this as well as every other change in the system of production is greatly favoured by a progressive condition of capital. It is chiefly when the capital of a country is receiving a great annual increase, that there is a large amount of capital seeking for investment: and a new enterprise is much sooner and more easily entered upon by new capital, than by withdrawing capital from existing employments. The change is also much facilitated by the existence of large capitals in few hands. It is true that the same amount of capital can be raised by bringing together many small sums. But this (besides that it is not equally well suited to all branches of industry) supposes a much greater degree of commercial confidence and enterprise diffused through the community, and belongs altogether to a more advanced stage of industrial progress.

In the countries in which there are the largest markets, the widest diffusion of commercial confidence and enterprise, the greatest annual increase of capital, and the greatest number of large capitals owned by individuals, there is a tendency to substitute more and more, in one branch of industry after another, large establishments for small ones. In England, the [a]chief[a] type of all these characteristics, there is [b]a perpetual growth not only[b] of large manufacturing establishments, but also, wherever a sufficient number of purchasers are assembled, of shops and warehouses for conducting retail business on a large scale. These are almost always able to undersell the smaller tradesmen, partly, it is understood, by means of division of labour, and the economy occasioned by limiting the employment of skilled agency to cases where skill is required; and partly, no doubt, by the saving of labour arising from the great scale of the transactions; as it costs no more time, and not much more exertion of mind, to make a large purchase, for example, than a small one, and very much less than to make a number of small ones.

With a view merely to production, and to the greatest efficiency of labour, this change is wholly beneficial. In some cases it is attended with drawbacks, rather social than economical, the nature of which has been already hinted at. But whatever disadvantages may be supposed to attend on the change from a small to a large system of production, they are not applicable to the change from a large to a still larger. When, in any employment, the régime of independent small producers has either never been possible, or has been superseded, and the system of many [c]work-people[c] under one management has become fully established, from that time any further enlargement in the scale of production is generally an unqualified benefit. It is obvious, for example, how great an economy of labour would be obtained if London were supplied by a single gas or water company instead of the existing plurality. While there are even as many as two, this implies double establishments of all sorts, when one only, with a small increase, could probably perform the whole operation equally well; double sets of machinery and works, when the whole of the gas or water required could generally be produced by one set only; even double sets of pipes, if the companies did not prevent this needless expense by agreeing upon a division of the territory. Were there only one establishment, it could make lower charges, consistently with obtaining the rate of profit now realized. But would it do so? Even if it did not, the community in the aggregate would still be a gainer: since the shareholders are [d]a[d] part of the community, and they

[a-a]MS, 48, 49 great
[b-b]MS, 48 not only a perpetual growth
[c-c]MS, 48, 49 workmen
[d-d]+57, 62, 65, 71

would obtain higher profits [e]while[e] the consumers paid only the same. It is, however, an error to suppose that the prices are [f]ever permanently[f] kept down by the competition of these companies. Where competitors are so few, they always [g]end by agreeing[g] not to compete. They may run a race of cheapness to ruin a new candidate, but as soon as he has established his footing they come to terms with him. When, therefore, a business of real public importance can only be carried on advantageously upon so large a scale as to render the liberty of competition almost illusory, it is an unthrifty dispensation of the public resources that several costly sets of arrangements should be kept up for the purpose of rendering to the community this one service. It is much better to treat it at once as a public function; and if it be not such as the government itself could beneficially undertake, it should be made over entire to the company or association which will perform it on the best terms for the public. In the case of railways, for example, no one can desire to see the enormous waste of capital and land (not to speak of increased nuisance) involved in the construction of a second railway to connect the same places already united by an existing one; while the two would not do the work better than it could be done by one, and after a short time [h]would probably[h] be amalgamated. Only one [i]such[i] line ought to be permitted, but the control over that line never ought to be parted with by the State, unless on a temporary concession, as in France; and the vested right which Parliament has allowed to be acquired by the existing companies, like all other proprietary rights which are opposed to public utility, is morally valid only as a claim to compensation.

§ 4. [*Large and small farming compared*] The question between the large and the small [a]systems[a] of production as applied to agriculture—between large and small farming, the *grande* and the *petite culture*—stands, in many respects, on different grounds from the general question between great and small industrial establishments. In its social aspect, and as an element in the Distribution of Wealth, this question will occupy us hereafter: but even as a question of production, the superiority of the large system in agriculture is by no means so clearly established as in manufactures.

I have already remarked, that the operations of agriculture are little susceptible of benefit from the division of labour. There is but little separation of employments even on the largest farm. The same persons may not in general attend to the live stock, to the marketing, and to the cultivation

[e-e]52, 57 when
[f-f]MS, 48, 49 really
[g-g]MS, 48, 49 agree
[h-h]MS, 48 they would certainly] 49 would certainly
[i-i]+52, 57, 62, 65, 71
[a-a]MS, 48, 49 system

of the soil; but much beyond that primary and simple classification the subdivision is not carried. The combination of labour of which agriculture is susceptible, is chiefly that which Mr. Wakefield terms Simple Co-operation; several persons helping one another in the same work, at the same time and place. But I confess it seems to me that this able writer attributes more importance to that kind of co-operation, in reference to agriculture properly so called, than it deserves. None of the common farming operations require much of it. There is no particular advantage in setting a [b]great[b] number of people to work together in ploughing or digging or sowing the same field, or even in mowing or reaping it unless time presses. A single family can generally supply all the combination of labour necessary for these purposes. And in the works in which an union of many efforts is really needed, there is seldom found any impracticability in obtaining it where farms are small.

The waste of productive power by subdivision of the land often amounts to a great evil, but this applies chiefly to a subdivision so minute, that the cultivators have not enough land to occupy their time. Up to that point the same principles which recommend large [c]manufactories[c] are applicable to agriculture. For the greatest productive efficiency, it is generally desirable (though even this proposition must be received with qualifications) that no family who have any land, should have less than they could cultivate, or than will fully employ their cattle and tools. These, however, are not the dimensions of large farms, but of what are reckoned in England very small ones. The large farmer has some advantage in the article of buildings. It does not cost so much to house a great number of cattle in one building, as to lodge them equally well in several buildings. There is also some advantage in implements. A small farmer is not so likely to possess expensive instruments. But the principal agricultural implements, even when of the best construction, are not expensive. It may not answer to a small farmer to own a threshing machine, for the small quantity of corn he has to thresh; but there is no reason why such a machine should not in every neighbourhood be owned in common, or provided by some person to whom the others pay a consideration for its use[d]; especially as, when worked by steam, they are so constructed as to be moveable[d].* The large farmer can

*[52] The observations in the text may hereafter require some degree of modification from inventions such as the steam plough and the reaping machine. The effect, however, of these improvements on the relative advantages of large and small farms, will not depend [52 will depend not] on the efficiency of the instruments, but on their costliness. I see no reason to expect that this will be such as to make them inaccessible to small farmers, or combinations of small farmers.

[b-b]+57, 62, 65, 71 [c-c]MS, 48 factories [d-d]+62, 65, 71

make some saving in cost of carriage. There is nearly as much trouble in carrying a small portion of produce to market, as a much greater produce; in bringing home a small, as a much larger quantity of [e]manures[e], and articles of daily consumption. There is also the greater cheapness of buying things in large quantities. These various advantages must count for something, but it does not seem that they ought to count for very much. In England, for some generations, there has been little experience of small farms; but in Ireland the experience has been ample, not merely under the worst but under the best management; and the highest Irish authorities may be cited in opposition to the opinion which on this subject commonly prevails in England. Mr. Blacker, for example, one of the most experienced agriculturists and successful improvers in the North of Ireland, whose experience [f]was[f] chiefly in the best cultivated, which are also the most minutely divided parts of the country, [g]was[g] of opinion, that tenants holding farms not exceeding from five to eight or ten acres, [h]could[h] live comfortably and pay as high a rent as any large farmer whatever. "I am firmly persuaded," (he says,*) "that the small farmer who holds his own plough and digs his own ground, if he follows a proper rotation of crops, and feeds his cattle in the house, can undersell the large farmer, or in other words can pay a rent which the other cannot afford; and in this I am confirmed by the opinion of many practical men who have well considered the subject. . . The English farmer of 700 to 800 acres is a kind of man approaching to what is known by the name of a gentleman farmer. He must have his horse to ride, and his gig, and perhaps an overseer to attend to his labourers; he certainly cannot superintend himself the labour going on in a farm of 800 acres." After a few other remarks, he adds, "Besides all these drawbacks, which the small farmer knows little about, there is the great expense of carting out the manure from the homestead to such a great distance, and again carting home the crop. A single horse will consume the produce of more land than would feed a small farmer and his wife and two children. And what is more than all, the large farmer says to his labourers, *go* to your work; but when the small farmer has occasion to hire them, he says, *come*; the intelligent reader will, I dare say, understand the difference."

One of the objections most urged against small farms is, that they do not and cannot maintain, proportionally to their extent, so great a number of cattle as large farms, and that this occasions such a deficiency of manure, that a soil much subdivided must always be impoverished. It will be found,

*Prize Essay on the Management of Landed Property in Ireland, by William Blacker, Esq. (1837,) [Dublin: Curry, 1834,] p. 23 [23n–24n].

[e-e]MS, 48, 49, 52, 57, 62 manure
[f-f]MS, 48, 49 lies
[g-g]MS, 48, 49 is
[h-h]MS, 48, 49 can

however, that subdivision only produces this effect when it throws the land into the hands of cultivators so poor as not to possess the amount of live stock suitable to the size of their farms. A small farm and a badly stocked farm are not synonymous. To make the comparison fairly, we must suppose the same amount of capital which is possessed by the large farmers to be disseminated among the small ones. When this condition, or even any approach to it, exists, and when stall feeding is practised (and stall feeding now begins to be considered good economy even on large farms), experience, far from bearing out the assertion that small farming is unfavourable to the multiplication of cattle, conclusively establishes the very reverse. The abundance of cattle, and copious use of manure, on the small farms of Flanders, are the most striking features in that Flemish agriculture which is the admiration of all competent judges, whether in England or on the Continent.*

* "The number of beasts fed on a farm of which the whole is arable land," (says the elaborate and intelligent treatise on Flemish Husbandry, from personal observation and the best sources, published in the Library of the Society for the Diffusion of Useful Knowledge,) "is surprising to those who are not acquainted with the mode in which the food is prepared for the cattle. A beast for every three acres of land is a common proportion, and in very small occupations where much spade husbandry is used, the proportion is still greater. [MS *ellipsis indicated by* . .] After comparing the accounts given in a variety of places and situations of the average quantity of milk which a cow gives when fed in the stall, the result is, that it greatly exceeds that of our best dairy farms, and the quantity of butter made from a given quantity of milk is also greater. [MS *ellipsis indicated by* . . .] It appears astonishing that the occupier of only ten or twelve acres of light arable land should be able to maintain four or five cows, but the fact is notorious in the Waes country." (pp. 59, 60.) [Rham, William Lewis. *Outlines of Flemish Husbandry*, in Burke, John L. (ed.) *British Husbandry*. Vol. III. London: Baldwin and Cradock, 1840.]

This subject is treated very intelligently in the work of [MS, 48 intelligently by] M. [MS M. Hippolite] Passy, [MS, 48 Passy, a distinguished politician and high economical authority, whose treatise] "Des Systêmes de Culture et de leur Influence sur l'Economie Sociale [Paris: Guillaumin, 1846]," [MS, 48 is one] one of the most impartial discussions, as between the two systems, which has yet appeared in France.

"Sans nul doute, c'est l'Angleterre qui, à superficie égale, nourrit le plus d'animaux; la Hollande et quelques parties de la Lombardie pourraient seules lui disputer cet avantage: mais est-ce là un résultat des formes de l'exploitation, et des circonstances de climat et de situation locale ne concourent-elles pas à le produire? C'est, à notre avis, ce qui ne saurait être contesté. En effet, quoiqu'on en ait dit, partout où la grande et la petite culture se rencontrent sur les mêmes points, c'est celle-ci qui, bien qu'elle ne puisse entretenir autant de moutons, possède, tout compensé, le plus grand nombre d'animaux producteurs d'engrais. Voici, par exemple, ce qui ressort des informations fournies par la Belgique.

"Les deux provinces où règne la plus petite culture sont celles d'Anvers et de la Flandre orientale, et elles possèdent en moyenne, par 100 hectares de terres

The disadvantage, when disadvantage there is, of small or rather of peasant farming, as compared with capitalist farming, must chiefly consist in inferiority of skill and knowledge; but it is not true, as a general fact, that such inferiority exists. Countries of small farms and peasant farming, Flanders and Italy, had a good agriculture many generations before England, and theirs is still, as a whole, probably the best agriculture in the world. [i] The empirical skill, which is the effect of daily and close observa-

---

cultivées, 74 bêtes bovines et 14 moutons. Les deux provinces où se trouvent les grandes fermes sont celles de Namur et du Hainaut, et elles n'ont en moyenne, pour 100 hectares de terres cultivées, que 30 bêtes bovines et 45 moutons. Or, en comptant, suivant l'usage, 10 moutons comme l'équivalent d'une tête de gros bétail, nous rencontrons d'un côté, 76 animaux servant à maintenir la fécondité du sol; de l'autre, moins de 35, différence à coup sûr énorme. (D'après les documents statistiques publiés par le Ministre de l'Intérieur, 3me publication officielle.) Il est à remarquer, au surplus, que le nombre des animaux n'est pas, dans la partie de la Belgique dont le sol est divisé en très-petites fermes, beaucoup moindre qu'en Angleterre. En l'évaluant dans cette dernière contrée à raison seulement du territoire en culture, il y existe, par centaine d'hectares, 65 bêtes à corne et près de 260 moutons, c.-à-d. l'équivalent de 91 des premiers, ou seulement 15 de plus que dans l'autre. Et encore est-il juste d'observer qu'en Belgique presque rien n'est perdu des engrais donnés par des animaux nourris à peu près toute l'année à l'étable, tandis qu'en Angleterre la pâture en plein air affaiblit considérablement les quantités qu'il devient possible de mettre entièrement à profit.

"Dans le département du Nord aussi, ce sont les arrondissements dont les fermes ont la moindre contenance qui entretiennent le plus d'animaux. Tandis que les arrondissements de Lille et de Hazebrouck, outre un plus grand nombre de chevaux, nourissent, l'un l'équivalent de 52 têtes de gros bétail, l'autre l'équivalent de 46; les arrondissements où les exploitations sont les plus grandes, ceux de Dunkerque et d'Avesnes, ne contiennent, le premier, que l'équivalent de 44 bêtes bovines, l'autre, que celui de 40. (D'après la Statistique de la France publiée par le Ministre du Commerce: *Agriculture*, t. i.)

"Pareilles recherches étendues sur d'autres points de la France offriraient des résultats analogues. S'il est vrai que dans la banlieue des villes, la petite culture s'abstienne de garder des animaux, au produit desquels elle supplée facilement par des achats d'engrais, il ne se peut que le genre de travail qui exige le plus de la terre ne soit pas celui qui en entretienne le plus activement la fertilité. Assurément il n'est pas donné aux petites fermes de posséder de nombreux troupeaux de moutons, et c'est un inconvénient; mais, en revanche, elles nourrissent plus de bêtes bovines que les grandes. C'est là une nécessité à laquelle elles ne sauraient se soustraire dans aucun des pays où les besoins de la consommation les ont appelées à fleurir; elles périraient si elles ne réussissaient pas à y satisfaire.

"Voici, au surplus, sur ce point des détails dont l'exactitude nous paraît pleinement attestée par l'excellence du travail où nous les avons puisés. Ces détails, contenus dans la statistique de la commune de Vensat (Puy de Dôme),

[i]MS Notwithstanding all that is said of the backwardness of French agriculture, there are some parts of France which can almost vie with them.

tion, peasant farmers often possess in an eminent degree. The traditional knowledge, for example, of the culture of the vine, possessed by the peasantry of the countries where the best wines are produced, is extraordinary. There is no doubt an absence of science, or at least of theory; and to some extent a deficiency of the spirit of improvement, so far as relates to the introduction of new processes. There is also a want of means to make experiments, which can seldom be made with advantage except by rich proprietors or capitalists. As for those systematic improvements which operate on a large tract of country at once (such as great works of draining or irrigation) or which for any other [j]reasons[j] do really require large numbers of workmen combining their labour, these are not in general to be expected from small farmers, or even small proprietors, though combination among them for such purposes is by no means unexampled, and will become more common as their intelligence is more developed.

Against these disadvantages is to be placed, where the tenure of land is of the requisite kind, an ardour of industry absolutely unexampled in any other condition of agriculture. This is a subject on which the testimony of competent witnesses is unanimous. The working of the *petite culture*

---

publiée récemment par M. le docteur Jusseraud, maire de la commune, sont d'autant plus précieux, qu'ils mettent dans tout leur jour la nature des changements que le développement de la petite culture a, dans le pays dont il s'agit, apportés au nombre et à l'espèce des animaux dont le produit en engrais soutient et accroît la fertilité des terres. Dans la commune de Vensat, qui comprend 1612 hectares divisés en 4600 parcelles appartenant à 591 propriétaires, le territoire exploité se compose de 1466 hectares. Or, en 1790, 17 fermes en occupaient les deux tiers et 20 autres tout le reste. Depuis lors, les cultures se sont morcelées, et maintenant leur petitesse est extrême. Quelle a été l'influence du changement sur la quantité des animaux? Une augmentation considérable. En 1790, la commune ne possédait qu'environ 300 bêtes à cornes, et de 1800 à 2000 bêtes à laine; aujourd'hui elle compte 676 des premières, et 533 seulement des secondes. Ainsi pour remplacer 1300 moutons elle a acquis 376 bœufs et vaches, et tout compensé, la somme des engrais s'est accrue dans la proportion de 490 à 729, ou de plus de 48 pour cent. Et encore est-il à remarquer que, plus forts et mieux nourris à présent, les animaux contribuent bien davantage à entretenir la fertilité des terres.

"Voilà ce que les faits nous apprennent sur ce point: il n'est donc pas vrai que la petite culture ne nourrisse pas autant d'animaux que les autres; loin de là, à conditions locales pareilles, c'est elle qui en possède le plus, et il ne devait pas être difficile de le présumer; car, du moment où c'est elle qui demande le plus aux terres, il faut bien qu'elle leur donne des soins d'autant plus réparateurs qu'elle en exige davantage. Que l'on prenne un à un les autres reproches; qu'on les examine à la clarté de faits bien appréciés, on s'appercevra bientôt qu'ils ne sauraient être mieux fondés, et qu'ils n'ont été formulés que parce qu'on a comparé l'état des cultures dans des contrées où les causes de la prospérité agricole n'agissaient pas avec la même énergie." (pp. 116–120.)

[j-j]MS, 48, 49, 52, 62, 65 reason

cannot be fairly judged where the small cultivator is merely a tenant, and not even a tenant on fixed conditions, but ([k]as until lately in[k] Ireland) at a nominal rent greater than can be paid, and therefore practically at a varying rent always amounting to the utmost that can be paid. To understand the subject, it must be studied where the cultivator is the proprietor, or at least a *métayer* with a permanent tenure; where the labour he exerts to increase the produce and value of the land avails wholly, or at least partly, to his own benefit and that of his descendants. In another division of our subject, we shall discuss at some length the important subject of tenures of land, and I defer till then any citation of evidence on the marvellous industry of peasant proprietors. It may suffice here to appeal to the immense amount of gross produce which, even without a permanent tenure, English labourers generally obtain from their little allotments; a produce beyond comparison greater than a large farmer extracts, or would find it his interest to extract, from the same piece of land.

And this I take to be the true reason why large cultivation is generally most advantageous as a mere investment for profit. Land occupied by a large farmer is not[l], in one sense of the word,[l] farmed so highly. There is not nearly so much labour expended on it. This is not on account of any economy arising from combination of labour, but because, by employing less, a greater return is obtained in proportion to the outlay. It does not answer to any one to pay others for exerting all the labour which the peasant, or even the allotment-holder, gladly undergoes when the fruits are to be wholly reaped by himself. This labour, however, is not unproductive: it all adds to the gross produce. With anything like equality of skill and knowledge, the large farmer does not obtain nearly so much from the soil as the small proprietor, or the small farmer with adequate motives to exertion: but though his returns are less, the labour is less in a still greater degree, and as whatever labour *he* employs must be paid for, it does not suit his purpose to employ more.

But although the gross produce of the land is greatest, *cæteris paribus*, under small cultivation, and although, therefore, a country is able on that system to support a larger aggregate population, it is generally assumed by English writers that what is termed the net produce, that is, the surplus after feeding the cultivators, [m]must[m] be smaller; that therefore, the population disposable for all other purposes, for manufactures, for commerce and navigation, for national defence, for the promotion of knowledge, for the liberal professions, for the various functions of government, for the arts and literature, all of which are [n] dependent on this surplus for their existence as occupations, must be less numerous; and that the nation, therefore (waving all question as to the condition of the actual cultivators), must be

[k-k]MS, 48, 49, 52 as in] 57 as hitherto in
[l-l]+62, 65, 71 [m-m]MS *must* [n]MS, 48, 49 entirely

inferior in the principal elements of national power, and in many of those of general well-being. This, however, has been taken for granted much too readily. Undoubtedly the non-agricultural population will bear a less ratio to the agricultural, under small than under large cultivation. But that it will be less numerous absolutely, is by no means a consequence. If the total population, agricultural and non-agricultural, is greater, the non-agricultural portion may be more numerous in itself, and may yet be a smaller proportion of the whole. If the gross produce is larger, the net produce may be larger, and yet bear a smaller ratio to the gross produce. Yet even Mr. Wakefield sometimes [o]appears to confound[o] these distinct ideas. In France it is computed that two-thirds of the whole population are agricultural. In England, at most, one-third. Hence Mr. Wakefield infers, that "as in France only three people are supported by the labour of two cultivators, while in England the labour of two cultivators supports six people, English agriculture is twice as productive as French agriculture," owing to the superior efficiency of large farming through combination of labour. But in the first place, the facts themselves are overstated. The labour of two persons in England does not quite support six people, for there is not a little food imported from foreign countries, and from Ireland. In France, too, the labour of two cultivators does much more than supply the food of three persons. It provides the three persons, and occasionally foreigners, with flax, hemp, and to a certain extent with silk, oils, tobacco, and latterly sugar, which in England are wholly obtained from abroad; nearly all the timber used in France is of home growth, nearly all which is used in England is imported; the principal fuel of France is procured and brought to market by persons reckoned among agriculturists, in England by persons not so reckoned. I do not take into calculation hides and wool, these products being common to both countries, nor wine or brandy produced for home consumption, since England has a corresponding production of beer and spirits; but England has no material export of either article, and a great importation of the last, while France supplies wines and spirits to the whole world. I say nothing of fruit, eggs, and such minor [p]articles of agricultural produce, in which the export trade of France is enormous[p]. But not to lay undue stress on these abatements, we will take the statement as it stands. Suppose that two persons, in England, do *bonâ fide* produce the food of six, while in France, for the same purpose, the labour of four is requisite. Does it follow that England must have a larger surplus for the support of a non-agricultural population? No; but merely that she can devote two-thirds of her whole produce to the purpose, instead of one-third. Suppose the produce to be twice as great, and the one-third will amount to as much as the two-thirds. The fact might be, that owing

[o-o]MS confounds
[p-p]MS, 48, 49, 52, 57, 62 exportable articles of agricultural produce

to the greater quantity of labour employed on the French system, the same land would produce food for twelve persons which on the English system would only produce it for six: and if this were so, which would be quite consistent with the conditions of the hypothesis, then although the food for twelve was produced by the labour of eight, while the six were fed by the labour of only two, there would be the same number of hands disposable for other employment in the one country as in the other. I am not contending that the fact is so. I know that the gross produce per acre in France [q]as a whole (though not in its most improved districts)[q] averages much less than in England, and that, in proportion to the extent and fertility of the two countries, England has, in the sense we are now speaking of, much the largest disposable population. But the disproportion certainly is not [r]to be measured by Mr. Wakefield's simple criterion[r]. As well might it be said that agricultural labour in the United States, where, by [s]a late[s] census, four families in every five [t]appeared[t] to be engaged in agriculture, must be still more inefficient than in France.

The inferiority of French cultivation (which, taking the country as a whole, must be allowed to be real, though much exaggerated) is probably more owing to the lower general average of industrial skill and energy in that country, than to any special cause; and even if partly the effect of minute subdivision, it does not prove that small farming is disadvantageous, but only (what is undoubtedly the fact) that farms in France are very frequently *too* small, and, what is worse, broken up into an almost incredible number of patches or *parcelles*, most inconveniently dispersed and parted from one another.

As a question, not of gross, but of net produce, the comparative merits of the *grande* and the *petite culture*, especially when the small farmer is also the proprietor, cannot be looked upon as decided. It is a question on which good judges at present differ. The current of English opinion is in favour of large farms: on the Continent, the weight of authority seems to be on the other side. Professor Rau, of Heidelberg, the author of one of the most comprehensive and elaborate of extant treatises on political economy, and who has that large acquaintance with facts and authorities on his own subject, which generally characterises his countrymen, lays it down as a settled truth, that small or moderate-sized farms yield not only a larger gross but a larger net produce: though, he adds, it is desirable there should be some great proprietors, to lead the way in new improvements.*

*See pp. 352 and 353 [48, 49, 52, 57 335] of a French translation published at Brussels in 1839, by M. Fred. de Kemmeter, of Ghent. [Rau, C. H. *Traité d'économie nationale*. Trans. F. de Kemmeter, from the 3rd ed. Brussels: Hauman, 1839, pp. 332, 335.]

[q-q]+62, 65, 71
[r-r]MS, 48 nearly so great, as Mr. Wakefield's simple criterion would represent it
[s-s]MS, 48, 49 the last [t-t]52, 57 appear

The most apparently impartial and discriminating judgment that I have met with is that of M. Passy, who (always speaking with reference to *net* produce) gives his verdict in favour of large farms for grain and forage; but, for the kinds of culture which require much labour and attention, places the advantage wholly on the side of small cultivation; including in this description, not only the vine and the olive, where a considerable amount of care and labour must be bestowed on each individual plant, but also roots, leguminous plants, and those which furnish the materials of manufactures. The small size, and consequent multiplication, of farms, according to all authorities, are extremely favourable to the abundance of many minor products of agriculture.*

It is evident that every labourer who extracts from the land more than his own food, and that of any family he may have, increases the means of supporting a non-agricultural population. Even if his surplus is no more than enough to buy [u]clothes[u], the labourers who make the clothes are a non-agricultural population, enabled to exist by food which he produces. Every agricultural family, therefore, which produces its own necessaries, adds to the net produce of agriculture; and so does every person born on the land, who by employing himself on it, adds more to its gross produce than the mere food which he eats. It is questionable whether, even in the most subdivided districts of Europe which are cultivated by the proprietors, the multiplication of hands on the soil has approached, or tends to approach, within a great distance of this limit. In France, though the subdivision is confessedly too great, there is proof positive that it is far from having reached the point at which it would begin to diminish the power of supporting a non-agricultural population. This is demonstrated by the great increase of the towns; which have of late increased in a much greater ratio than the population generally,† showing (unless the condition of the town labourers is becoming rapidly deteriorated, which there is no reason to believe) that even by the unfair and inapplicable test of proportions, the productiveness of agriculture must be on the increase. This, too, concurrently with the amplest evidence that in the more improved districts of France, and in some which, until lately, were among the unimproved, there is a considerably increased consumption of country produce by the country population itself.

*"Dans le département du Nord," says M. Passy, "une ferme de 20 hectares recueille en veaux, laitage, œufs, et volailles, parfois pour un millier de francs dans l'année; et, les frais défalqués, c'est l'équivalent d'une addition au produit net de 15 à 20 francs par hectare." *Des Systèmes de Culture*, p. 114[n].

†[57] During the interval between the census of 1851 and that of 1856, the increase of the population of Paris alone, exceeded the aggregate increase of all France; while nearly all the other large towns likewise showed [57, 62 show] an increase.

[u-u]MS him clothes] 48, 49 clothes for him

[v]Impressed with the conviction that, of all faults which can be committed by a scientific writer on political and social subjects, exaggeration, and [w]assertion[w] beyond the evidence, most require to be guarded against, I limited myself in the early editions of this work to the foregoing very moderate statements. I little knew how much stronger my language might have been without exceeding the truth, and how much the actual progress of French agriculture surpassed anything which I had at that time sufficient grounds to affirm. The investigations of that eminent authority on agricultural statistics, M. Léonce de Lavergne, undertaken by desire of the Academy of Moral and Political Sciences of the Institute of France, have led to the conclusion that since the Revolution of 1789, the total produce of French agriculture has doubled; profits and wages having both increased in about the same, and rent in a still greater ratio. M. de Lavergne, whose impartiality is one of his greatest merits, is, moreover, so far in this instance from the suspicion of having a case to make out, that he is labouring to show, not how much French agriculture has accomplished, but how much still remains for it to do. "We have required" (he says) "no less than seventy years to bring into cultivation two million hectares" (five million English acres) "of waste land, to suppress half our fallows, double our agricultural products, increase our population by 30 per cent, our wages by 100 per cent, our rent by 150 per cent. At this rate we shall require three quarters of a century more to arrive at the point which England has already attained."*

After this evidence, we have surely now heard the last of the incompatibility of small properties and small farms with agricultural improvement. The only question which remains open is one of degree; the comparative [x]rapidity[x] of agricultural improvement under the two systems; and it is the general opinion of those who are equally well acquainted with both, that improvement is greatest under a due admixture between them.[v]

In the present chapter, [y]I[y] do not enter on the question [z]between great[z] and small cultivation in any other respect than as a question of production, and of the efficiency of labour. We shall return to it hereafter as affecting the distribution of the produce, and the physical and social well-being of the cultivators themselves; in which aspects it deserves, and requires, a still more particular examination.

*[62] *Economie Rurale de la France depuis* 1789. Par M. Léonce de Lavergne [Louis Gabriel Léonce, Guilhaud de Lavergne], Membre de l'Institut et de la Société Centrale d'Agriculture de France. 2me éd. [Paris: Guillaumin, 1861,] p. 59.

v–v+62, 65, 71
w–w62 assertions
x–x62 *rapidity*
y–yMS, 48, 49, 52, 57, 62 we
z–zMS, 48 of great] 49 great

CHAPTER X

Of the Law of the Increase of Labour

§ 1. [*The law of the increase of production depends on those of three elements, Labour, Capital, and Land*] We have now successively considered each of the agents or conditions of production, and of the means by which the [a]efficacy[a] of these various agents is promoted. In order to come to an end of the questions which relate exclusively to production, one more, of primary importance, remains.

Production is not a fixed, but an increasing thing. When not kept back by bad institutions, or a low state of the arts of life, the produce of industry has usually tended to increase; stimulated not only by the desire of the producers to augment their means of consumption, but by the increasing number of the consumers. Nothing in political economy can be of more importance than to ascertain the law of this increase of production; the conditions to which it is subject: whether it has practically any limits, and what these are. There is also no subject in political economy which is popularly less understood, or on which the errors committed are of a character to produce, and do produce, greater mischief.

We have seen that the essential requisites of production are three—labour, capital, and natural agents; the term capital including all external and physical requisites which are products of labour, the term natural agents all those which are not. But among natural agents we need not take into account those which, existing in unlimited quantity, being incapable of appropriation, and never altering in their qualities, are always ready to lend an equal degree of assistance to production, whatever may be its extent; as air, and the light of the sun. Being now about to consider the impediments to production, not the facilities for it, we need advert to no other natural agents than those which are liable to be deficient either in quantity or in productive power. These may be all represented by the term land. Land, in the narrowest acceptation, as the source of agricultural produce, is the chief of them; and if we extend the term to mines and fisheries—to

[a-a]MS efficiency

what is found in the earth itself, or in the waters which partly cover it, as well as to what is grown or fed on its surface, it embraces everything with which we need at present concern ourselves.

We may say, then, without a greater stretch of language than under the necessary [b]explanation[b] is permissible, that the requisites of production are Labour, Capital, and Land. The increase of production, therefore, depends on the properties of these elements. It is a result of the increase either of the elements themselves, or of their productiveness. The law of [c]the[c] increase of production must be a consequence of the laws of these elements; the limits to the increase of production must be the limits, whatever they are, set by those laws. We proceed to consider the three elements successively, with reference to this effect; or in other words, the law of the increase of production, viewed in respect of its dependence, first on Labour, secondly on Capital, and lastly on Land.

§ 2. [*The Law of Population*] The increase of labour is the increase of mankind; of population. On this subject the discussions excited by [a]the Essay of Mr. Malthus[a] have made the truth, though by no means universally admitted, yet so fully known, that a briefer examination of the question than would otherwise have been necessary will probably on the present occasion suffice.

The power of multiplication inherent in all organic life may be regarded as infinite. There is no one species of vegetable or animal, which, if the earth were entirely abandoned to it, and to the things on which it feeds, would not in a small number of years overspread every region of the globe, of which the climate was compatible with its existence. The degree of possible rapidity is different in different orders of beings; but in all it is sufficient, for the earth to be very speedily filled up. There are [b]many[b] species of vegetables of which a single plant will produce in one year the germs of a thousand; if only two come to maturity, in fourteen years the two will have multiplied to sixteen thousand and more. [c]It is but a moderate case of fecundity in animals to be capable[c] of quadrupling their numbers in a single year; if they only do as much in half a century, ten thousand will have swelled within two centuries to upwards of two millions and a half. The capacity of increase is necessarily in a geometrical progression: the numerical ratio alone is different.

To this property of organized beings, the human species forms no exception. Its power of increase is indefinite, and the actual multiplication would be extraordinarily rapid, if [d]the[d] power were exercised to the utmost.

[b-b]MS, 48, 49, 52, 57, 62 explanations
[c-c]+62, 65, 71

[a-a]MS, 48, 49 Mr. Malthus' Essay
[b-b]+52, 57, 62, 65, 71
[c-c]MS, 48, 49 Many animals have the power
[d-d]MS, 48, 49 that

It never is exercised to the utmost, and yet, in the most favourable circumstances known to exist, which are those of a fertile region colonized from an industrious and civilized community, population has continued, for several generations, independently of fresh immigration, to double itself in not much more than twenty years.* That [e]the capacity of multiplication in the human species exceeds[e] even this, is evident if we consider how great is the ordinary number of children to a family, where the climate is good and early marriages usual; and how small a proportion of them die before the age of maturity, in the present state of hygienic knowledge, where the locality is healthy, and the family adequately provided with the means of living. It is a very low estimate of the capacity of increase, if we only assume, that in a good sanitary condition of the people, each generation may be double the number of the generation which preceded it.

Twenty or thirty years ago, these propositions might still have required considerable enforcement and illustration; but the evidence of them is so ample and incontestable, that they have made their way against all kinds of opposition, and may now be regarded as axiomatic: though the extreme reluctance felt to admitting them, every now and then gives birth to some ephemeral theory, speedily forgotten, of a different law of increase in different circumstances, through a providential adaptation of the fecundity of the human species to the exigencies of society.† The obstacle to a just

*[65] This has been disputed; but the highest estimate I have seen of the term which population requires for doubling itself in the United States, independently of immigrants and of their progeny—that of Mr. Carey—does not exceed thirty years.

†[52] One of these theories, that of Mr. Doubleday [Doubleday, Thomas. *The True Law of Population shewn to be connected with the Food of the People*. London: Simpkin, Marshall, & Co., 1842], may be thought to require a passing notice, because it has of late obtained some followers [52, 57 some disciples], and because it derives a semblance of support from the general analogies of organic life. This theory maintains that the fecundity of the human animal, and of all other living beings, is in inverse proportion to the quantity of nutriment: that an underfed population multiplies rapidly, but that all classes in comfortable circumstances are, by a physiological law, so unprolific, as seldom to keep up their numbers without being recruited from a poorer class. There is no doubt that a positive excess of nutriment, in animals as well as in fruit trees, is unfavourable to reproduction; and it is quite possible, though by no means proved, that the physiological conditions of fecundity may exist in the greatest degree when the supply of food is somewhat stinted. But any one who might be inclined to draw from this, even if admitted, conclusions at variance with the principles [52, 57, 62 the principle] of Mr. Malthus, needs only be invited to look through a volume of the Peerage, and observe the enormous families, almost universal in that class; or call to mind the large families of the English clergy, and generally of the middle classes of England. [52, 57, 62

[e-e]MS, 48, 49 there is a capacity of multiplication in the human species beyond

understanding of the subject does not arise from these theories, but from too confused a notion of the causes which, at most times and places, keep the actual increase of mankind so far behind the capacity.

§ 3. [*By what checks the increase of population is practically limited*] Those causes, nevertheless, are in no way mysterious. What prevents the population of hares and rabbits from overstocking the earth? Not want of fecundity, but causes very different: many enemies, and insufficient subsistence; not enough to eat, and liability to [a]be[a] eaten. In the human race, which is not generally subject to the latter inconvenience, the equivalents for it are war and disease. If the multiplication of mankind proceeded [b]only[b], like that of the other animals, from a blind instinct, it would be limited in the same manner with theirs; the births would be as numerous as the physical constitution of the species admitted of, and the population would be kept down by deaths.* But the conduct of human creatures is

England. Whatever the limit to the increase of population among the richer classes in Great Britain may be, it certainly is not the small number of births to a marriage.]

[65] It is, besides, well remarked by Mr. Carey, that, to be consistent with Mr. Doubleday's theory, the increase of the population of the United States, apart from immigration, ought to be one of the slowest on record.

Mr. Carey has a theory of his own, also grounded on a physiological truth, that the total sum of nutriment received by an organized body directs itself in largest proportion to the parts of the system which are most used; from which he anticipates a diminution in the fecundity of human beings, not through more abundant feeding, but throught the greater use of their brains incident to an advanced civilization. There is considerable plausibility in this speculation, and experience may hereafter confirm it. But the change in the human constitution which it supposes, if ever realized, will conduce to the expected effect rather by rendering physical self-restraint easier, than by dispensing with its necessity; since the most rapid known rate of multiplication is quite compatible with a very sparing employment of the multiplying power.

*[65] Mr. Carey expatiates on the absurdity of supposing that matter tends to assume the highest form of organization, the human, at a more rapid rate than it assumes the lower forms, which compose human food; that human beings multiply faster than turnips and cabbages. But the limit to the increase of mankind, according to the doctrine of Mr. Malthus, does not depend on the power of increase of turnips and cabbages, but on the limited quantity of the land on which they can be grown. So long as the quantity of land is practically unlimited, which it is in the United States, and food, consequently, can be increased at the highest rate which is natural to it, mankind also may, without augmented difficulty in obtaining subsistence, increase at their highest rate. When Mr. Carey can show, not that turnips and cabbages, but that the soil itself, or the nutritive elements contained in it, tend naturally to multiply, and that too at a rate exceeding the most rapid possible increase of mankind, he will have said something to the purpose. Till then, this part at least of his argument may be considered as non-existent.

[a-a]MS, 48, 49, 52, 57, 62, 65 being   [b-b]+52, 57, 62, **65**, **71**

[c] more or less influenced by foresight of consequences, and by [d] impulses superior to mere animal instincts: and they do not, therefore, propagate like swine, but are capable, though in very unequal degrees, of being withheld by prudence, or by the social affections, from giving existence to beings born only to misery and premature death. In proportion as mankind rise above the condition of [e]the[e] beasts, population is restrained by the fear of want rather than by want itself. Even where there is no question of starvation, [f]many[f] are similarly acted upon by the apprehension of losing what have come to be regarded as the decencies of their situation in life. Hitherto no other motives than these two have been found strong enough, in the generality of mankind, to counteract the tendency to increase. It has been the practice of a great majority of the middle and the poorer classes, whenever free from external control, to marry as early, and in most countries to have as many children, as was consistent with maintaining themselves in the condition of life which they were born to, or were accustomed to consider as theirs. Among the middle classes, in many individual instances, there is an additional restraint exercised from the desire of doing more than maintaining their circumstances—of improving them; but such a desire is rarely found, or rarely has that effect, in the labouring classes. If they can bring up a family as they were themselves brought up, even the prudent among them are usually satisfied. Too often they do not think even of that, but rely on fortune, or on the resources to be found in legal or voluntary charity.

In a very backward state of society, like that of Europe in the Middle Ages, and many parts of Asia at present, population is kept down by actual starvation. The starvation does not take place in ordinary years, but in seasons of scarcity, which in those states of society are much more frequent and more extreme than Europe is now accustomed to. In these seasons actual want, or the maladies consequent on it, carry off numbers of the population, which in a succession of favourable years again expands, to be again cruelly decimated. In a more improved state, few, even among the poorest of the people, are limited to [g]actual[g] necessaries, and to a bare sufficiency of those: and the increase is kept within bounds, not by excess of deaths, but by limitation of births. The limitation is brought about in various ways. In some countries, it is the result of prudent or conscientious self-restraint. There is a condition to which the labouring people are habituated; they perceive that by having too numerous families, they must sink below that condition, or fail to transmit it to their children; and this they do not choose to submit to. The countries in which, so far as is known, [h]a great[h] degree of voluntary prudence [i]has been longest[i] practised on this

[c]MS, 48, 49 everywhere
[d]MS, 48, 49, 52, 57, 62 some
[e-e]MS brute
[f-f]MS, 48, 49 most persons
[g-g]MS, 48, 49, 52 absolute
[h-h]MS the greatest
[i-i]MS is

subject, are Norway and parts of Switzerland. Concerning both, there happens to be unusually authentic information; many facts were carefully brought together by Mr. Malthus, and much additional evidence has been obtained since his time. In both these countries the increase of population is very slow; and what checks it, is not multitude of deaths, but fewness of births. Both the births and the deaths are remarkably few in proportion to the population; the average duration of life is the longest in Europe; the population contains fewer children, and a greater proportional number of persons in the vigour of life, than is known to be the case in any other part of the world. The paucity of births tends directly to prolong life, by keeping the people in comfortable circumstances; and the same prudence is doubtless exercised in avoiding causes of disease, as in keeping clear of the principal [j]cause[j] of poverty. It is worthy of remark that the two countries thus honourably distinguished, are countries of small landed proprietors.

There are other cases in which the prudence and forethought, which perhaps might not be exercised by the people themselves, are exercised by the state for their benefit; marriage not being permitted until the contracting parties can show that they have the prospect of a comfortable support. Under these laws, of which I shall speak more fully hereafter, the condition of the people is reported to be good, and the illegitimate births not so numerous as might be expected. There are places, again, in which the restraining cause seems to be not so much individual prudence, as some general and perhaps even accidental habit of the country. In the rural districts of England, during the last century, the growth of population was very effectually repressed by the difficulty of obtaining a cottage to live in. It was the custom for unmarried labourers to lodge and board with their employers; it was the custom for married labourers to have a cottage: and the rule of the English poor laws by which a parish was charged with the support of its unemployed poor, rendered landowners averse to promote marriage. About the end of the century, the great demand for men in war and manufactures, made it be thought a patriotic thing to encourage population: and about the same time the growing inclination of farmers to live like rich people, favoured as it was by a long period of high prices, made them desirous of keeping inferiors at a greater distance, and, pecuniary motives arising from abuses of the poor laws being superadded, they gradually drove their labourers into cottages, which the landlords now no longer refused permission to build. [k] In some countries an old standing custom that a girl should not marry until she had spun and woven for

[j-j]62 causes

[k]MS But when a young man had a cottage to himself he wished for a wife to make it comfortable: and hence, partly, the rapid start which the agricultural population made during the generation which followed.

herself an ample *trousseau* [l](destined for the supply of her whole subsequent life,)[l] is said to have acted as a substantial check to population. In England, at present, the influence of prudence in keeping down multiplication is seen by the diminished number of marriages in the manufacturing districts in years when trade is bad.

But whatever be the causes by which population is anywhere limited to a comparatively slow rate of increase, [m]an acceleration of the rate very speedily follows any diminution of the motives to restraint[m]. It is but rarely that improvements in the condition of the labouring classes do anything more than give a temporary margin, speedily filled up by an increase of their numbers. The use they commonly choose to make of any advantageous change in their circumstances, is to take it out in the form which, by augmenting the population, deprives the succeeding generation of the benefit. Unless[n], either by their general improvement in intellectual and moral culture, or at least by raising their habitual standard of comfortable living, they can be taught to make a better use of favourable circumstances[n], nothing permanent can be done for them; the most promising schemes end only in having a more numerous, but not a happier people. By their habitual standard, I mean that [o](when any such there is)[o] down to which they will multiply, but not lower. Every advance they make in education, civilization, and social improvement, tends to raise this standard; and there is no doubt that it is gradually, though slowly, rising in the more advanced countries of Western Europe. Subsistence and employment in England have never increased more rapidly than in the last [p]forty[p] years, but [q]every census since 1821 showed a smaller proportional increase of population than that of the period preceding[q]; and the produce of French agriculture and industry is increasing in a progressive ratio, while the population exhibits in every quinquennial census, a smaller proportion of births to the population.

The subject, however, of population, in its connexion with the condition of the labouring classes, will be considered in another place: in the present we have to do with it solely as one of the elements of Production: and in that character we could not dispense with pointing out the unlimited extent of its natural powers of increase, and the causes owing to which so small a portion of that unlimited power is for the most part actually exercised. After this brief indication, we shall proceed to the other elements.

[l-l]+65, 71

[m-m]MS, 48, 49 there is always an immense residuary power behind, ready to start into activity as soon as the pressure which restrained it is taken off

[n-n]MS their idea and habitual standard of comfortable living can be raised] 48, 49 *as* MS . . . and their habitual . . . *as* MS

[o-o]+52, 57, 62, 65, 71

[p-p]MS, 48, 49 sixteen] 52, 57 thirty

[q-q]MS, 48, 49 the census of 1841 shewed a smaller proportional increase of population than that of 1831

CHAPTER XI

Of the Law of the Increase of Capital

§ 1. [*Means and motives to saving, on what dependent*] The requisites of production being labour, capital, and land, it has been seen from the preceding chapter that the impediments to the increase of production do not arise from the first of these elements. On the side of labour there is no obstacle to an increase of production, indefinite in extent and of unslackening rapidity. Population has the power of increasing in an uniform and rapid geometrical ratio. If the only essential condition of production were labour, the produce might, and naturally would, increase in the same ratio; and there would be no limit, until the numbers of mankind were brought to a stand from actual want of space.

But production has other requisites, and of these, the one which we shall next consider is Capital. There cannot be more people in any country, or in the world, than can be supported from the produce of past labour until that of present labour comes in. There will be no greater number of productive labourers in any country, or in the world, than can be supported from that portion of the produce of past labour, which is spared from the enjoyments of its possessor for purposes of reproduction, and is termed Capital. We have next, therefore, to inquire into the conditions of the increase of capital: the causes by which the rapidity of its increase is determined, and the necessary limitations of that increase.

Since all capital is the product of saving, that is, of abstinence from present consumption for the sake of a future good, the increase of capital must depend upon two things—the amount of the fund from which saving can be made, and the strength of the dispositions which prompt to it.

The fund from which saving can be made, is the surplus of the produce of labour, after supplying the necessaries of life to all concerned in the production: (including those employed in replacing the materials, and keeping the fixed capital in repair.) More than this surplus cannot be saved under any circumstances. As much as this, though it never is saved, always might be. This surplus is the fund from which the enjoyments, as distinguished from the necessaries, of the producers are provided; it is the fund from which all are subsisted, who are not themselves engaged in production; and from which all additions are made to capital. It is the real net produce of the country. The phrase, net produce, is often taken in a more limited sense, to denote only the profits of the capitalist and the rent of the landlord, under the idea that nothing can be included in the net produce of capital, but what is returned to the owner of the capital after replacing his expenses. But this is too narrow an acceptation of the term. The capital of the employer forms the revenue of the labourers, and if this exceeds the necessaries of life, it gives them a surplus which they may either expend in enjoyments, or save. For every purpose for which there can be occasion to speak of the net produce of industry, this surplus ought to be included in it. When this is included, and not otherwise, the net produce of the country is the measure of its effective power; of what it can spare for any [a]purposes[a] of public utility, or private indulgence; the portion of its produce of which it can dispose at pleasure; which can be drawn upon to attain any ends, or gratify any wishes, either of the government or of individuals; which it can either spend for its satisfaction, or save for future advantage.

The amount of this fund, this net produce, this excess of production above the physical necessaries of the producers, is one of the elements that determine the amount of saving. The greater the produce of labour after supporting the labourers, the more there is which *can* be saved. The same thing also partly contributes to determine how much *will* be saved. A part of the motive to saving consists in the prospect of deriving an income from savings; in the fact that capital, employed in production, is capable of not only reproducing itself but yielding an increase. The greater the profit that can be made from capital, the stronger is the motive to its accumulation. That indeed which forms the inducement to save, is not the whole of the fund which supplies the means of saving, not the whole net produce of the land, capital, and labour of the country, but only a part of it, the part which forms the remuneration of the capitalist, and is called profit of stock. It will however be readily enough understood, even previously to the explanations which will be given hereafter, that when the general productiveness of labour and capital is great, the returns to the capitalist are likely to be large, and that some proportion, though not an uniform one, will commonly obtain between the two.

§ 2. [*Causes of diversity in the effective strength of the desire of accumulation*] But the disposition to save does not wholly depend on the external inducement to it; on the amount of profit to be made from savings.

[a-a]MS, 48 purpose

With the same pecuniary inducement, the inclination is very different, in different persons, and in different communities. The [a]effective desire of accumulation[a] is of unequal strength, not only according to the varieties of individual character, but to the general state of society and civilization. Like all other moral attributes, it is one in which the human race exhibits great differences, conformably to the diversity of its circumstances and the stage of its progress.

On topics which if they were to be fully investigated would exceed the bounds that can be allotted to them in this treatise, it is satisfactory to be able to refer to other works in which the necessary developments have been presented more at length. On the subject of Population this valuable service has been rendered by the celebrated Essay of Mr. Malthus; and on the point which now occupies us I can refer with equal confidence to another, though a less known work, "New Principles of Political Economy," by [b]Dr.[b] Rae.* In no other book known to me is so much light thrown, both from principle and history, on the causes which determine the accumulation of capital [c] .

All accumulation involves the sacrifice of a present, for the sake of a future good. But the expediency of such a sacrifice varies very much in

*This treatise is an example, such as not unfrequently presents itself, how much more depends on accident, than on the qualities of a book, in determining its reception. Had it appeared at a suitable time, and been favoured by circumstances, it would have had every requisite for great success. The author, a Scotchman settled in the United States, unites much knowledge, an original vein of thought, a considerable turn for philosophic generalities, and a manner of exposition and illustration calculated to make ideas tell not only for what they are worth, but for more than they are worth, and which sometimes, I think, has that effect in the writer's own mind. The principal fault of the book is the position of antagonism in which, with the controversial spirit apt to be found in those who have new thoughts on old subjects, he has placed himself towards Adam Smith. I call this a fault, (though I think many of the criticisms just, and some of them far-seeing,) because there is much less [MS, 48, 49, 52, 57 less of] real difference of [MS, 48, 49, 52 difference in] opinion than might be supposed from Dr. [MS, 48, 49, 52, 57, 62 Mr.] Rae's animadversions; and because what he has found vulnerable in his great predecessor is chiefly the "human *too much*" in his premises; the portion of them that is over and above what was either required or is actually used for [MS, 48, 49, 52 used in] the establishment of his conclusions. [MS conclusions.—Yet such are the conditions of celebrity, that if this author had attained it, the polemical character of his book would probably have been the hinge on which would have turned the accident of its exciting attention.]

[a-a]MS "effective desire of accumulation" [*quoted from Rae*; *see* Vol. I, p. 165]
[b-b]MS, 48, 49, 52, 57, 62 Mr.
[c]MS ; & in the much more abridged view which can here be taken of that subject, I shall frequently find it advisable to adopt his words

different states of circumstances; and [d]the[d] willingness to make it, varies still more.

In weighing the future against the present, the uncertainty of all things future is a leading element; and that uncertainty is of very different degrees. "All circumstances" therefore, "increasing the probability of the provision we make for futurity being enjoyed by ourselves or others, tend" justly and reasonably "to give strength to the effective desire of accumulation. Thus a healthy climate or occupation, by increasing the probability of life, has a tendency to add to this desire. When engaged in safe occupations, and living in healthy countries, men are much more apt to be frugal, than in unhealthy or hazardous occupations, and in climates pernicious to human life. Sailors and soldiers are prodigals. In the West Indies, New Orleans, the East Indies, the expenditure of the inhabitants is profuse. The same people, coming to reside in the healthy parts of Europe, and not getting into the vortex of extravagant fashion, live economically. War and pestilence have always waste and luxury among the other evils that follow in their train. For similar reasons, whatever gives security to the affairs of the community is favourable to the strength of this principle. In this respect the general prevalence of law and order, and the prospect of the continuance of peace and tranquillity, have considerable influence."* The more perfect the security, the greater will be the effective strength of the desire of accumulation. Where property is less safe, or the vicissitudes ruinous to fortunes are more frequent and severe, fewer persons will save at all, and of those who do, many will require the inducement of a higher rate of profit on capital, to make them prefer a doubtful future to the [e]temptation[e] of present enjoyment.

These are considerations which affect the expediency, in the eye of reason, of consulting future interests at the expense of present. But [f]the[f] inclination to make [g]the[g] sacrifice does not solely depend upon its expediency. The disposition to save is often far short of what reason would dictate: and at other times is liable to be in excess of it.

[h]Deficient strength of the desire of accumulation may arise from improvidence, or from want of interest in others. Improvidence may be connected with intellectual as well as moral causes.[h] Individuals and communities of a very low state of intelligence are always improvident. A

*Rae, p. 123.

[d-d]MS, 48, 49 men's
[e-e]MS, 48, 49, 52 temptations
[f-f]MS, 48, 49 men's
[g-g]MS, 48, 49, 52, 57, 62, 65 this
[h-h]MS The causes of deficient strength of the desire of accumulation may be distinguished into improvidence & selfishness. The influence of improvidence needs no explanation. The vice to which that name is appropriated, may be connected with intellectual as well as moral causes.

certain measure of intellectual development seems necessary to enable absent things, and especially things future, to act with any force on the imagination and will. [i]The effect of want of interest in others in diminishing accumulation will be admitted, if we considered how much saving at present takes place, which[i] has for its object the interest of others rather than of ourselves; the education of children, their advancement in life, the future interests of other personal connexions, the [j]power[j] of promoting, by the bestowal of money or time, objects of public or private usefulness. If mankind were generally in the state of mind to which some approach was seen in the declining period of the Roman Empire—caring nothing for their heirs, as well as nothing for friends, the public, or any object which survived them—they would seldom deny themselves any [k] indulgence for the sake of saving[l], beyond what was necessary for their own future years; which they would place[l] in life annuities, or in some other form which would make its existence and their lives terminate together.

§ 3. [*Examples of deficiency in the strength of the desire of accumulation*] From [a]these various causes[a], intellectual and moral, there is, in different portions of the human race, a greater diversity than is usually adverted to, in the strength of the effective desire of accumulation. A backward state of general civilization is often more the effect of deficiency in this particular, than in many others which attract more attention. [b]In the circumstances, for example, of a hunting tribe, "[b]man may be said to be necessarily improvident, and regardless of futurity, because, in [c]this

[i-i]MS Besides, plans for future benefit suppose some degree of reasoning, some calculation of distant consequences: & to be able to make such a calculation, or to have faith in the results of it when made, is beyond the capacity of a very weak or a wholly unexercised understanding. It is beyond the compass of many a mind (as is often observed in savage life) which is by no means without acuteness & contrivance for the attainment of an immediate object. With mental faculties in some respects by no means undeveloped, a person may be, from circumstance & habit, so entirely unused to employ those faculties for any purpose requiring a looking beyond the moment, as amounts to an intellectual disqualification from forethought.

It may not at first sight be equally clear in what manner selfishness operates to diminish the desire of accumulation; & it is not every kind of selfishness which does so. The selfishness that embraces descendants & family connexions generally in its conception of self, is one of the most potent of all causes of accumulation. But pure individualism, entire want of care for others, saps it at the root; as we must admit if we consider, how great a portion of all the saving that takes place,

[j-j]MS, 48, 49, 52, 57, 62 desire

[k]MS costly

[l-l]MS ; or if they saved anything for their own future years, they would place it

[a-a]MS, 48, 49 various degrees of these deficiencies

[b-b]MS Mr. Rae has illustrated the point by examples, some of which are too interesting & characteristic to be omitted. One of these is the American Indian. After shewing by a survey of the circumstances which surround a hunting tribe, that "in this state

[c-c]Source, MS it

state[c], the future presents nothing which can be with certainty either foreseen or governed[d]. . . . . .[d] Besides a want of the motives exciting to provide for the needs of futurity through means of the abilities of the present, there is a want of the habits of perception and action, leading to a constant connexion in the mind of those distant points, and of the series of events serving to unite them. Even, therefore, if motives be awakened capable of producing the exertion necessary to effect this connexion, there remains the task of training the mind to think and act so as to establish it."

For instance: "Upon the banks of the St. Lawrence there are several little Indian villages. They are surrounded, in general, by a good deal of land, from which the wood seems to have been long extirpated, and have, besides, attached to them, extensive tracts of forest. The cleared land is rarely, I may almost say never, cultivated, nor are any inroads made in the forest for such a purpose. The soil is, nevertheless, fertile, and were it not, manure lies in heaps by their houses. Were every family to inclose half an acre of ground, till it, and plant [e]it in[e] potatoes and maize, it would yield a sufficiency to support them one half the year. They suffer, too, every now and then, extreme want, insomuch that, joined to occasional intemperance, it is rapidly reducing their numbers. This, to us, so strange apathy proceeds not, in any great degree, from repugnance to labour; on the contrary, they apply very diligently to it when its reward is immediate. Thus, besides their peculiar occupations of hunting and fishing, in which they are ever ready to engage, they are much employed in the navigation of the St. Lawrence, and may be seen labouring at the oar, or setting with the pole, in the large boats used for the purpose, and always furnish the greater part of the additional hands necessary to conduct rafts through some of the rapids. Nor is the obstacle aversion to agricultural labour. This is no doubt a prejudice of theirs; but mere prejudices always yield, principles of action cannot be created. When the returns from agricultural labour are speedy and great, they are also agriculturists. Thus, some of the little islands on Lake St. Francis, near the Indian village of St. Regis, are favourable to the growth of maize, a plant yielding a return of a hundredfold, and forming, even when half ripe, a pleasant and substantial repast. Patches of the best land on these islands are therefore every year cultivated by them for this purpose. As their situation renders them inaccessible to cattle, no fence is required; were this additional outlay necessary, I suspect they would be neglected, like the commons adjoining their village. These had apparently, at one time, been under crop. The cattle of the neighbouring settlers would now, however, destroy any crop not securely fenced, and this additional necessary outlay consequently bars their culture. It removes them to an order of instruments of slower return than that which corresponds to the strength of the effective desire of accumulation in this little society.

[d–d]MS , "he adds"   [e–e]Source, MS, 48, 49, 52 in it

"It is here deserving of notice, that what instruments of this kind they do form, are completely formed. The small spots of corn they cultivate are thoroughly weeded and hoed. A little neglect in this part would indeed reduce the crop very much; of this experience has made them perfectly aware, and they act accordingly. It is evidently not the necessary labour that is the obstacle to more extended culture, but the distant return from that labour. I am assured, indeed, that among some of the more remote tribes, the labour thus expended much exceeds that given by the whites. The same portions of ground being cropped without remission, and manure not being used, they would scarcely yield any return, were not the soil most carefully broken and pulverized, both with the hoe and the hand. In such a situation a white man would clear a fresh piece of ground. It would perhaps scarce repay his labour the first year, and he would have to look for his reward in succeeding years. On the Indian, succeeding years are too distant to make sufficient impression; though, to obtain what labour may bring about in the course of a few months, he toils even more assiduously than the white man."*

This view of things is confirmed by the experience of the Jesuits, in their interesting [f]efforts[f] to civilize the Indians of Paraguay. They gained the confidence of these savages in a most extraordinary degree. They acquired influence over them sufficient to make them change their whole manner of life. They obtained their absolute submission and obedience. They established peace. They taught them all the operations of European agriculture, and many of the more difficult arts. There were everywhere to be seen, according to Charlevoix, "workshops of gilders, painters, sculptors, goldsmiths, watchmakers, carpenters, joiners, dyers," [*] &c. These occupations were not practised for the personal gain of the artificers: the produce was at the absolute disposal of the missionaries, who ruled the people by a voluntary despotism. The obstacles arising from aversion to labour were therefore very completely overcome. The real difficulty was the improvidence of the people; their inability to think for the future: and the necessity accordingly of the most unremitting and minute superintendence on the part of their instructors. "Thus at first, if these gave up to them the care of the oxen with which they ploughed, their indolent thoughtlessness would probably leave them at evening still yoked to the implement. Worse than this, instances occurred where they cut them up for supper, thinking, when reprehended, that they sufficiently excused themselves by saying they were hungry. . . . These fathers, says Ulloa, have to visit the houses, to examine what is really wanted: for without this care, the Indians would never look after anything.

*Rae, p. 136 [131–7].

[**Ibid.*, p. 141.]

[f-f]MS effort

They must be present, too, when animals are slaughtered, not only that the meat may be equally divided, but that nothing may be lost." "But notwithstanding all this care and superintendence," says Charlevoix, "and all the precautions which are taken to prevent any want of the necessaries of life, the missionaries are sometimes much embarrassed. It often happens that they" (the Indians,) "do not reserve to themselves a sufficiency of grain, even for seed. As for their other provisions, were they not well looked after, they would soon be without wherewithal to support life."*

As an example intermediate, in the strength of the effective desire of accumulation, between the state of things thus depicted and that of modern Europe, [g]the case of the Chinese deserves attention. From[g] various circumstances in their personal habits and social [h]condition,[h] it might be anticipated that they would possess a degree of prudence and self-control greater than other Asiatics, but inferior to most European nations[i]; and the following evidence is adduced[i] of the fact.

"Durability is one of the chief qualities, marking a high degree of the effective desire of accumulation. The testimony of travellers ascribes to the instruments formed by the Chinese, [j] a very inferior durability to similar instruments constructed by Europeans. The houses, we are told, unless of the higher ranks, are in general of unburnt bricks, of clay, or of hurdles plastered with earth; the roofs, of reeds fastened to laths. We can scarcely conceive more unsubstantial or temporary fabrics. Their partitions are of paper, requiring to be renewed every year. A similar observation may be made concerning their implements of husbandry, and other utensils. They are almost entirely of wood, the metals entering but very sparingly into their construction; consequently they soon wear out, and require frequent renewals. A greater degree of strength in the effective desire of accumulation, would cause them to be constructed of materials requiring a greater present expenditure but being far more durable. From the same cause, much land, that in other countries would be cultivated, lies waste. All travellers take notice of large tracts of [k]lands[k], chiefly swamps, which continue in a state of nature. To bring a swamp into tillage is generally a process, to complete which, requires several years. It must be previously drained, the surface long exposed to the sun, and many operations performed, before it can be made capable of bearing a crop. Though yielding, probably, a very

*Ibid. p. 140 [–41].

[g-g]MS Mr. Rae bestows considerable attention on the case of the Chinese. After pointing out

[h-h]MS condition from which

[i-i]MS , he adduces the following evidence

[j]MS (Mr. Rae understands by instruments not tools only, but all things constructed to serve as means for human purposes)

[k-k]Source, MS, 48, 49, 52 land

considerable return for the labour bestowed on it, that return is not made until a long time has elapsed. The cultivation of such land implies a greater strength of the effective desire of accumulation than exists in the empire.

"The produce of the harvest is, as we have remarked, always an instrument of some order or another; it is a provision for future want, and regulated by the same laws as those to which other means of attaining a similar end conform. It is there chiefly rice, of which there are two harvests, the one in June, the other in October. The period then of eight months between October and June, is that for which provision is made each year, and the different estimate they make of to-day and this day eight months will appear in the self-denial they practise now, in order to guard against want then. The amount of this self-denial would seem to be small. The father Parennin, indeed, (who seems to have been one of the most intelligent of the Jesuits, and spent a long life among the Chinese of all classes,) asserts, that it is their great deficiency in forethought and frugality in this respect, which is the cause of the scarcities and famines that frequently occur."

That it is defect of providence, not defect of industry, that limits production among the Chinese, is still more obvious than in the case of the semi-agriculturized Indians. "Where the returns are quick, where the instruments formed require but little time to bring the events for which they were formed to an issue," it is well known that "the great progress which has been made in the knowledge of the arts suited to the nature of the country and the wants of its inhabitants" makes industry energetic and effective. "The warmth of the climate, the natural fertility of the country, the knowledge which the inhabitants have acquired of the arts of agriculture, and the discovery and gradual adaptation to every soil of the most useful vegetable productions, enable them very speedily to draw from almost any part of the surface, what is there esteemed an equivalent to much more than the labour bestowed in tilling and cropping it. They have commonly double, sometimes treble harvests. These, when they consist of a grain so productive as rice, the usual crop, can scarce fail to yield to their skill, from almost any portion of soil that can be at once brought into culture, very ample returns. Accordingly there is no spot that labour can immediately bring under cultivation that is not made to yield to it. Hills, even mountains, are ascended and formed into terraces; and water, in that country the great productive agent, is led to every part by drains, or carried up to it by the ingenious and simple hydraulic machines which have been in use from time immemorial among this singular people. They effect this the more easily, from the soil, even in these situations, being very deep and covered with much vegetable mould. But what yet more than this marks the readiness with which labour is forced to form the most difficult materials into instruments, where these instruments soon bring to an issue the events for which they are formed, is the frequent occurrence on many of their lakes and rivers, of structures resembling the floating gardens of the Peruvians, rafts covered with vegetable soil and cultivated. Labour in this way draws from the materials on which it acts very speedy returns. Nothing can exceed the luxuriance of vegetation when the quickening powers of a genial sun are ministered to by a rich soil and abundant moisture. It is otherwise, as we have seen, in cases where the [l]return[l], though copious, is distant. European travellers are surprised at meeting these little floating farms by the side of swamps which only require draining to render them tillable. It seems to them strange that labour should not rather be bestowed on the solid earth, where its fruits might endure, than on structures that must decay and perish in a few years. The people they are among think not so much of future years as of the present time. The effective desire of accumulation is of very different strength in the one, from what it is in the other. The views of the European extend to a distant futurity, and he is surprised at the Chinese, condemned through improvidence, and want of sufficient prospective care, to incessant toil, and as he thinks, insufferable wretchedness. The views of the Chinese are confined to narrower bounds; he is content [m] to live from day to day, and has learnt to conceive even a life of toil a blessing."*

When a country has carried production as far as in the existing state of knowledge it can be carried with an amount of return corresponding to the average strength of the effective desire of accumulation in that country, it has reached what is called the stationary state; the state in which no further addition will be made to capital, unless there takes place either some improvement in the arts of production, or an increase in the strength of the desire to accumulate. In the stationary state, though capital does not on the whole increase, some persons grow richer and others poorer. Those whose degree of providence is below the usual standard, become impoverished, their capital perishes, and makes room for the savings of those whose effective desire of accumulation exceeds the average. These become the natural purchasers of the lands, manufactories, and other instruments of production owned by their less provident countrymen.

What the causes are which make the return to capital greater in one country than in another, and which, in certain circumstances, make it impossible for any additional capital to find investment unless at diminished returns, will appear clearly hereafter. In China, if that country has really attained, as it is supposed to have done, the stationary state, accumulation has stopped when the returns to capital are still as high as is indicated by a rate of interest legally twelve per cent, and practically varying (it is said)

*Rae, pp. 151–5.

[l-l]48 returns [*printer's error?*]

[m]Source, MS, 48, 49 , as we say,

between eighteen and thirty-six. It is to be presumed therefore that no greater amount of capital than the country already possesses, can find employment at this high rate of profit, and that any lower rate does not hold out to a Chinese sufficient temptation to induce him to abstain from present enjoyment. What a contrast with Holland, where, during the most flourishing period of its history, the government was able habitually to borrow at two per cent, and private individuals, on good security, at three. Since China is not a country like Burmah or the native states of India, where an enormous interest is but an indispensable compensation for the risk incurred from the bad faith or poverty of the state, and of almost all private borrowers; the fact, if fact it be, that the increase of capital has come to a stand while the returns to it are still so large, denotes a much less degree of the effective desire of accumulation, in other words a much lower estimate of the future relatively to the present, than that of most European nations.

§ 4. [*Exemplification of excess in the strength of the desire of accumulation*] We have hitherto spoken of countries in which the average strength of the desire to accumulate is short of that which, [a]in[a] circumstances of any tolerable security, reason and sober calculation would approve. We have now to speak of others in which it decidedly surpasses that standard. In the more prosperous countries of Europe, [b]there are to be found abundance of prodigals;[b] in some of them (and in none more than [c] England) the ordinary degree of economy and providence among those who live by manual labour cannot be considered high: still, in a very numerous portion of the community, the professional, manufacturing, and trading classes, being those who, generally speaking, unite more of the means with more of the motives for saving than any other class, the spirit of accumulation is so strong, that the signs of rapidly increasing wealth meet every eye: and the great amount of capital seeking investment excites astonishment, whenever peculiar circumstances turning much of it into some one channel, such as railway construction or foreign speculative adventure, [d]bring[d] the largeness of the total amount into evidence.

There are many circumstances, which, in England, give a peculiar force to the accumulating propensity. The long exemption of the country from the ravages of war, and the far earlier period than elsewhere at which property was secure from military violence or arbitrary spoliation, have produced a long-standing and hereditary confidence in the safety of funds when trusted out of the owner's hands, which in most other countries is of much more

[a-a]MS, 48 under
[b-b]MS, 48, 49 although in them also are to be found abundance of prodigals, and
[c]MS, 48 in
[d-d]MS brings

recent origin, and less firmly established. The geographical causes which have made industry rather than war the natural source of power and importance to Great Britain, have turned an unusual proportion of the most enterprising and energetic characters into the direction of manufactures and commerce; into supplying their wants and gratifying their ambition by producing and saving, rather than by appropriating what has been produced and saved. Much also depended on the better political institutions of this country, which by the scope they have allowed to individual freedom of action, have encouraged personal activity and self-reliance, while by the liberty they confer of association and combination, they facilitate industrial enterprise on a large scale. The same institutions in another of their aspects, give a most direct and potent stimulus to the desire of acquiring wealth. The earlier decline of feudalism having removed or much weakened [e] invidious distinctions between the originally trading classes and those who had been accustomed to despise them; and a polity having grown up which made wealth the real source of political influence; its acquisition was invested with a [f]factitious[f] value, independent of its intrinsic utility. It became synonymous with power; and since power with the common herd of mankind *gives* power, wealth became the chief source of personal consideration, and the measure and stamp of success in life. To get out of [g]one[g] rank in society into the next above it, is the great aim of English [h]middle-class[h] life, and the acquisition of wealth the means. And inasmuch as to be rich without industry, [i]has always hitherto constituted[i] a step in the social scale above those who are rich by means of industry, it becomes the object of ambition to save not merely as much as will afford a large income while in business, but enough to retire from business and live in affluence on realized gains. These causes [j]have, in England, been[j] greatly aided by that extreme [k]incapacity of the people for[k] personal enjoyment, which is a characteristic of [l] countries over which puritanism has passed. But if accumulation is, on one hand, rendered easier by the absence of a taste for pleasure, it is, on the other, made more difficult by the presence of a very real taste for expense. So strong is the association between personal consequence and the signs of wealth, that the silly desire for the appearance of a large expenditure [m]has the force of[m] a passion, among large classes of a nation which derives less pleasure than perhaps any other in the world from what it

[e]MS all
[f-f]48 fictitious [*printer's error?*]
[g-g]MS one's
[h-h]MS, 48, 49, 52, 57, 62 bourgeois
[i-i]MS, 48, 49 constitutes
[j-j]MS, 48, 49, 52, 57, 62 are, in England
[k-k]MS, 48, 49 indifference of the people to
[l]MS, 48, 49 all
[m-m]MS amounts to

spends. Owing to this circumstance, the effective desire of accumulation has never reached so high a pitch in England as it did in Holland, where, there being no rich idle class to set the example of a reckless expenditure, and the mercantile classes, who possessed the substantial power on which social influence always waits, being left to establish their own scale of living and standard of propriety, their habits remained frugal and unostentatious.

In England and Holland, then, for a long time past, and now in most other countries [n]in[n] Europe (which are rapidly following England in the same race), the desire of accumulation does not require, to make it effective, the copious returns which it requires in Asia, but is sufficiently called into action by a rate of profit so low, that instead of slackening, accumulation seems now to proceed more rapidly than ever; and the second requisite of increased production, increase of capital, shows no tendency to become deficient. So far as that element is concerned, production is susceptible of an increase without any assignable bounds.

[o] The progress of accumulation would no doubt be considerably checked, if the returns to capital were to be reduced still lower than at present. But why should any possible increase of capital have that effect? This question carries the mind forward to the remaining one of the three requisites of production. The limitation to production, not consisting in any necessary limit to the increase of the other two elements, labour and capital, must turn upon the properties of the only element which is inherently, and in itself, limited in quantity. It must depend on the properties of land.

[n-n]MS of
[o]MS *[no paragraph here; paragraph indicated at next sentence]*

CHAPTER XII

Of the Law of the Increase of Production from Land

§ 1. [*The limited quantity and limited productiveness of land are the real limits to production*] Land differs from the other elements of production, labour and capital, in not being susceptible of indefinite increase. Its extent is limited, and the extent of the more productive kinds of it more limited still. It is also evident that the quantity of produce capable of being raised on any given piece of land is not indefinite. This limited quantity of land, and limited productiveness of it, are the real limits to the increase of production.

That they are the ultimate limits, must always have been clearly seen. But since the final barrier has never in any instance been reached; since there is no country in which all the land, capable of yielding food, is so highly cultivated that a larger produce could not (even without supposing any fresh advance in agricultural knowledge) be obtained from it, and since a large portion of the earth's surface still remains entirely uncultivated; it is commonly thought, and is very natural at first to suppose, that for the present all limitation of production or population from this source is at an indefinite distance, and that ages must elapse before any practical necessity arises for taking the limiting principle into serious consideration.

I apprehend this to be not only an error, but the most serious one, to be found in the whole field of political economy. The question is more important and fundamental than any other; it involves the whole subject of the causes of poverty, in a rich and industrious community: and unless this one matter be thoroughly understood, it is to no purpose proceeding any further in our inquiry.

§ 2. [*The law of production from the soil is a law of diminishing return in proportion to the increased application of labour and capital*] The limitation to production from the properties of the soil, is not like the obstacle opposed by a wall, which stands immovable in one particular spot, and offers no hindrance to motion short of stopping it entirely. We may rather compare it to a highly elastic and extensible band, which is hardly ever so violently stretched that it could not possibly be stretched any more, yet the pressure of which is felt long before the final limit is reached, and felt more severely the nearer that limit is approached.

After a certain, and not very advanced, stage in the progress of [a]agriculture, it[a] is the law of production from the land, that in any given state of agricultural skill and knowledge, by increasing the labour, the produce is not increased in an equal degree; doubling the labour does not double the produce; or, to express the same thing in other words, every increase of produce is obtained by a more than proportional increase in the application of labour to the land.

This general law of agricultural industry is the most important proposition in political economy. Were the law different, nearly all the phenomena of the production and distribution of wealth would be other than they are. The most fundamental errors which still prevail on our subject, result from not perceiving this law at work underneath the more superficial agencies on which attention fixes itself; but mistaking those agencies for the ultimate causes of effects of which they may influence the form and mode, but of which it alone determines the essence.

When, for the purpose of raising an increase of produce, recourse is had to inferior land, it is evident that, so far, the produce does not increase in the same proportion with the labour. The very meaning of inferior land, is land which with equal labour returns a smaller amount of produce. Land may be inferior either in fertility or in situation. The one requires a greater proportional amount of labour for growing the produce, the other for carrying it to market. If the land A yields a thousand quarters of wheat, to a given outlay in wages, manure, &c., and in order to raise another thousand recourse must be had to the land B, which is either less fertile or more distant from the market, the two thousand quarters will cost more than twice as much labour as the original thousand, and the produce of agriculture will be increased in a less ratio than the labour employed in procuring it.

Instead of cultivating the land B, it would be possible, by higher cultivation, to make the land A produce more. It might be ploughed or harrowed twice instead of once, or three times instead of twice; it might be dug instead of being ploughed; after ploughing, it might be gone over with a hoe instead of a harrow, and the soil more completely pulverized; it might be oftener or more thoroughly weeded; [b] the implements used might be of higher finish, [c]or[c] more elaborate construction; a greater quantity or more

[a-a]MS, 48, 49 agriculture; as soon, in fact, as men have applied themselves to cultivation with any energy, and have brought to it any tolerable tools; from that time it] 52, 57, 62 *as* MS . . . as mankind have . . . *as* MS

[b]MS the seed might be put into the ground by drill instead of broadcast; [*omitted by printer?*]

[c-c]MS, 48 and

expensive kinds of manure might be applied, or when applied, they might be more carefully mixed and incorporated with the soil. These are some of the modes by which the same land may be made to yield a greater produce; and when a greater produce must be had, some of these are among the means usually employed for obtaining it. But, that it is obtained at a more than proportional increase of expense, is evident from the fact that inferior lands are cultivated. Inferior lands, or lands at a greater distance from the market, of course yield an inferior return, and an increasing demand cannot be supplied from them unless at an augmentation of cost, and therefore of price. If the additional demand could continue to be supplied from the superior lands, by applying additional labour and capital, at no greater proportional cost than that at which they yield the quantity first demanded of them, the owners or farmers of those lands could undersell all others, and engross the whole market. Lands of a lower degree of fertility or in a more remote situation, might indeed be cultivated by their proprietors, for the sake of subsistence or independence; but it never could be the interest of any one to farm them for profit. That a profit can be made from them, sufficient to attract capital to such an investment, is a proof that cultivation on the more eligible lands has reached a point, beyond which any greater application of labour and capital would yield, at the best, no greater return than can be obtained at the same expense from less fertile or less favourably situated lands.

The careful cultivation of a well-farmed district of England or Scotland is a symptom and an effect of the more unfavourable terms which the land has begun to exact for any increase of its fruits. Such elaborate cultivation costs much more in proportion, and requires a higher price to render it profitable, than farming on a more superficial system; and would not be adopted if access could be had to land of equal fertility, previously unoccupied. Where there is the choice of raising the increasing supply which society requires, from fresh land of as good quality as that already cultivated, no attempt is made to extract from land anything approaching to what it will yield on what are esteemed the best European modes of [d]cultivating[d]. The land is tasked up to the point at which the greatest return is obtained in proportion to the labour employed, but no further: any additional labour is carried elsewhere. "It is long," says [e]an intelligent traveller[e] in the United States,* "before an English eye becomes reconciled

*Letters from America, by John Robert Godley [2 vols. London: Murray, 1844], vol. i. p. 42. [48] See also Lyell's Travels in America [Lyell, Charles. *Travels in North America; with Geological Observations on the United States, Canada, and Nova Scotia.* 2 vols. London: Murray, 1845], vol. ii. p. 83.

[d-d]MS cultivation
[e-e]MS, 48, 49 one of the latest travellers] 52, 57, 62 a late traveller

to the lightness of the crops and the careless farming (as we should call it) which is apparent. One forgets that where land is so plentiful and labour so dear as it is here, a totally different principle must be pursued to that which prevails in populous countries, and that the consequence will of course be a want of tidiness, as it were, and finish, about everything which requires labour." [f]Of the two causes mentioned, the plentifulness of land seems to me the true explanation, rather than the dearness of labour[f]; for, however dear labour may be, when food is wanted, labour will always be applied to producing it in preference to anything else. But this labour is more effective for its end by being applied to fresh soil, than if it were employed in bringing the soil already occupied into higher cultivation. Only when no soils remain to be broken up but such as either from distance or inferior quality require a considerable rise of price to render their cultivation profitable, can it become advantageous to apply the high farming of Europe to any American lands; except, perhaps, in the immediate vicinity of towns, where saving in cost of carriage may compensate for great inferiority in the return from the soil itself. As American farming is to English, so is the [g]ordinary[g] English to that of Flanders, Tuscany, or the Terra di Lavoro; where by the application of a far greater quantity of labour there is obtained a considerably larger gross produce, but on such terms as would never be advantageous to a mere speculator for profit, unless made so by much higher [h] prices of agricultural produce.

The principle which has now been stated must be received, no doubt, with certain explanations and limitations. Even after the land is so highly cultivated that the mere application of additional labour, or [i]of[i] an additional amount of ordinary dressing, would yield no return proportioned to the expense, it may still happen that the application of a much greater additional labour and capital to improving the soil itself, by draining or permanent manures, would be as liberally remunerated by the produce, as any portion of the labour and capital already employed. It would sometimes be much more amply remunerated. This could not be, if capital always sought and found the most advantageous employment; but if the most advantageous employment has to wait longest for its remuneration, it is only in a rather advanced stage of industrial development that the preference will be given to it; and even in that advanced stage, the laws or usages connected with property in land and the tenure of farms, are often such as to prevent the disposable capital of the country from flowing freely into the channel of agricultural improvement: and hence the increased

[f-f]MS I do not think that the dearness of labour has anything to do with the matter

[g-g]MS best

[h]MS than the existing

[i-i]+48, 49, 52, 57, 62, 65, 71

supply, required by increasing population, is sometimes raised at an augmenting cost by higher cultivation, when the means of producing it without increase of cost are known and accessible. There can be no doubt, that if capital were forthcoming to execute, within the next year, all known and recognised improvements in the land [j]of[j] the United Kingdom which would pay [k] at the existing prices, that is, which would increase the produce in as great or a greater ratio than the expense; the result would be such (especially if we include Ireland in the supposition) that inferior land would not for a long time require to be brought under tillage: probably a considerable part of the less productive lands now cultivated, which are not particularly favoured by situation, would go out of culture; or (as the improvements in question are not so much applicable to good land, but operate rather by converting bad land into good) the contraction of cultivation might principally take place by a less high dressing and less elaborate tilling of land generally; a falling back to something nearer the character of American farming; such only of the poor lands being altogether abandoned as were not found susceptible of improvement. And thus the aggregate produce of the whole cultivated land would bear a larger proportion than before to the labour expended on it; and the general law of diminishing return from land would have undergone, to that extent, a temporary supersession. No one, however, can suppose that even in these circumstances, the whole produce required for the country could be raised exclusively from the best lands, together with those possessing advantages of situation to place them on a par with the best. Much would undoubtedly continue to be produced under less advantageous conditions, and with a smaller proportional return, than that obtained from the best soils and situations. And [l]in proportion as the further increase of population required[l] a still greater addition to the supply, the general law would resume its course, and the further augmentation would be obtained at a more than proportionate expense of labour and capital.

§ 3. [*Antagonist principle to the law of diminishing return; the progress of improvements in production*] That the produce of land increases, *cæteris paribus*, in a diminishing ratio to the increase in the labour employed, is [a]a truth more often ignored or disregarded than actually

[j-j]49 in
[k]MS, 48, 49 (as the phrase is)
[l-l]MS as a further increase of population came to require
[a-a179]MS , we have said, (allowing for occasional and temporary exceptions,) the universal law of agricultural industry. This principle, however, has been denied, and experience confidently appealed to, in proof that the returns from land are not less, but greater, in an advanced, than in an early, stage of cultivation—when much capital, than when little, is applied to agriculture. So much so, indeed, that (it is affirmed) the worst land now in cultivation produces as much food per acre, and even

denied. It has, however, met with a direct impugner in the well-known American political economist, Mr. H. C. Carey, who maintains that the real law of agricultural industry is the very reverse; the produce increasing in a greater ratio than the labour, or in other words affording to labour a perpetually increasing return. To substantiate this assertion, he argues that cultivation does not begin with the better soils, and extend from them, as the demand increases, to the poorer, but begins with the poorer, and does not, till long after, extend itself to the more fertile. Settlers in a new country invariably commence on the high and thin lands; the rich but swampy soils of the river bottoms cannot at first be brought into cultivation, by reason of their unhealthiness, and of the great and prolonged labour required for clearing and draining them. As population and wealth increase, cultivation travels down the hill sides, clearing them as it goes, and the most fertile soils, those of the low grounds, are generally (he even says universally) the latest cultivated. These propositions, with the inferences which Mr. Carey draws from them, are set forth at much length in his latest and most elaborate treatise, "Principles of Social Science;" and he considers them as subverting the very foundation of what he calls the English political economy, with all its practical consequences, especially the doctrine of free trade.

As far as words go, Mr. Carey has a good case against several of the highest authorities in political economy, who certainly did enunciate in too universal a manner the law which they laid down, not remarking that it is not true of the first cultivation in a newly settled country. Where population is thin and capital scanty, land which requires a large outlay to render it fit for tillage must remain untilled; though such lands, when their time has come, often yield a greater produce than those earlier cultivated, not only absolutely, but proportionally to the labour employed, even if we include that which had been expended in originally fitting them for culture. But it is not pretended that the law of diminishing return was operative from the very beginning of society: and though some political economists may have believed it to come into operation earlier than it does, it begins quite early enough to support the conclusions they founded on it. Mr. Carey will hardly assert that in any old country—in England or France, for example—the lands left waste are, or have for centuries been, more naturally fertile than

as much to a given amount of labour, as our barbarous ancestors contrived to extract from the richest soils in England.

It is very possible that this may be true; and even if not true to the letter, to a great extent it certainly is so. Unquestionably a much smaller proportion of the population is now occupied in producing food for the whole, than in the early times of our history. This, however, does not prove that the law of which we have been speaking does not exist, but only that there is some antagonizing principle at work, capable for a time of making head against the law. Such an agency there is] 48, 49, 52, 57, 62 , as we have . . . *as* MS . . . our ancestors . . . *as* MS

those under tillage. Judging even by his own imperfect test, that of local situation—how imperfect I need not stop to point out—is it true that in England or France at the present day the uncultivated part of the soil consists of the plains and valleys, and the cultivated, of the hills? Every one knows, on the contrary, that it is the high lands and thin soils which are left to nature, and when the progress of population demands an increase of cultivation, the extension is from the plains to the hills. Once in a century, perhaps, a Bedford Level may be drained, or a Lake of Harlem pumped out: but these are slight and transient exceptions to the normal progress of things; and in old countries which are at all advanced in civilization, little of this sort remains to be done.*

Mr. Carey himself unconsciously bears the strongest testimony to the reality of the law he contends against: for one of the propositions most strenuously maintained by him is, that the raw products of the soil, in an advancing community, steadily tend to rise in price. Now, the most elementary truths of political economy show that this could not happen, unless the cost of production, measured in labour, of those products, tended to rise. If the application of additional labour to the land was, as a general rule, attended with an increase in the proportional return, the price of produce, instead of rising, must necessarily fall as society advances, unless the cost of production of gold and silver fell still more: a case so rare, that there are only two periods in all history when it is known to have taken place; the one, that which followed the opening of the Mexican and Peruvian mines; the other, that in which we now live. At all known periods, except these two, the cost of production of the precious metals has been either stationary or rising. If, therefore, it be true that the tendency of agricultural produce is to rise in money price as wealth and population increase, there needs no other evidence that the labour required for raising it from the soil tends to augment when a greater quantity is demanded.

I do not go so far as Mr. Carey: I do not assert that the cost of production, and consequently the price, of agricultural produce, always and necessarily rises as population increases. It tends to do so; but the tendency may be, and sometimes is, even during long periods, held in check. The effect does not depend on a single principle, but on two antagonizing principles. There is another agency[a], in habitual antagonism to the law of diminishing return from land; and to the consideration of this we shall now proceed. It is no other than the progress of civilization. I use this general

*[65] Ireland may be alleged as an exception; a large fraction of the entire soil of that country being still incapable of cultivation for want of drainage. But though Ireland is an old country, unfortunate social and political circumstances have kept it a poor and backward one. Neither is it at all certain that the bogs of Ireland, if drained and brought under tillage, would take their place along with Mr. Carey's fertile river bottoms, or among any but the poorer soils.

and somewhat vague expression, because the things to be included are so various, that hardly any term of a more restricted signification would comprehend them all.

Of these, the most obvious is the progress of agricultural knowledge, skill, and invention. Improved processes of agriculture are of two kinds: some enable the land to yield a greater absolute produce, without an equivalent increase of labour; others have not the power of increasing the produce, but have that of diminishing the labour and expense by which it is obtained. Among the first are to be reckoned the disuse of fallows, by means of the rotation of crops; and the introduction of new articles of cultivation capable of entering advantageously into the rotation. The change made in British agriculture towards the close of the last century, by the introduction of turnip husbandry, is spoken of as amounting to a revolution. These improvements operate not only by enabling the land to produce a crop every year, instead of remaining idle one year in every two or three to renovate its powers, but also by direct increase of its productiveness; since the great addition made to the number of cattle by the increase of their food, affords more abundant manure to fertilize the corn lands. Next in order comes the introduction of new articles of food, containing a greater amount of sustenance, like the potato, or more productive species or varieties of the same plant, such as the Swedish turnip. In the same class of improvements must be placed a better knowledge of the properties of manures, and of the most effectual [b]modes[b] of applying them; the introduction of new and more powerful fertilizing agents, such as guano, and the conversion to the same purpose, of substances previously wasted; inventions like subsoil-ploughing or tile-draining [c] ; improvements in the breed or feeding of labouring cattle; augmented stock of the animals which consume and convert into human food what would otherwise be wasted; and the like. The other sort of improvements, those which diminish labour, but without increasing the capacity of the land to produce, are such as the improved construction of tools; the introduction of new instruments which spare manual labour, as the winnowing and threshing machines; a more skilful and economical application of muscular exertion, such as the introduction, so slowly accomplished in England, of Scotch ploughing, with two horses abreast and one man, instead of three or four horses in a team and two men, &c. These improvements do not add to the productiveness of the land, but they are equally calculated with the former to counteract the tendency in the cost of production of agricultural produce, to rise with the progress of population and demand.

[b-b]MS mode

[c]MS, 48 , by which the produce of some kinds of land is so greatly multiplied] 49, 52, 57, 62 *as* MS . . . kinds of lands is . . . *as* MS

Analogous in effect to this second class of agricultural improvements, are improved means of communication. Good roads are equivalent to good tools. It is of no consequence whether the economy of labour takes place in extracting the produce from the soil, or in conveying it to the place where it is to be consumed. Not to say in addition, that the labour of cultivation itself is diminished by whatever lessens the cost of bringing manure from a distance, or facilitates the many operations of transport from place to place which occur within the bounds of the farm. Railways and canals are virtually a diminution of the cost of production of all things sent to market by them; and literally so of all those, the appliances and aids for producing which, they serve to transmit. By their means land can be cultivated, which [d]could[d] not otherwise have remunerated the cultivators without a rise of price. Improvements in navigation have, with respect to food or materials brought from beyond sea, a corresponding effect.

From similar considerations, it appears that many purely mechanical improvements, which [e]have, apparently at least,[e] no peculiar connexion with agriculture, nevertheless enable a given amount of food to be obtained with a smaller expenditure of labour. A great improvement in the process of smelting iron, would tend to cheapen agricultural implements, diminish the cost of railroads, of waggons and carts, ships, and perhaps buildings, and many other things to which iron is not at present applied, because it is too costly; and would thence diminish the cost of production of [f] food. The same effect would follow from [g]an[g] improvement in those processes of what may be termed manufacture, to which the material of food is subjected after it is separated from the ground. The first application of wind or water power to grind corn, tended to cheapen bread as much as a very important discovery in agriculture would have done; and any great improvement in the construction of corn-mills, would have, in proportion, a similar influence. The effects of cheapening locomotion have been already considered. There are also engineering inventions which facilitate all great operations on the earth's surface. An improvement in the art of taking levels is of importance to draining, not to mention canal and railway making. The fens of Holland, and of some parts of England, are drained by pumps worked by the wind or by steam. Where [h]canals[h] of irrigation, or where tanks or embankments are necessary, mechanical skill is a great resource for cheapening production.

Those manufacturing improvements which cannot be made instrumental to facilitate, in any of its stages, the actual production of food, and therefore do not help to counteract or retard the diminution of the proportional return

[d-d]MS, 48, 49, 52, 57, 62 would
[e-e]MS, 48, 49, 52, 57 have (apparently at least)] 62 have, apparently, at least,
[f]49 the
[g-g]MS, 48, 49, 52, 57 any
[h-h]MS, 48, 49, 52, 57 works

to labour from the soil, have, however, another effect, which is practically equivalent. What they do not prevent, they yet, in some degree, compensate for.

The materials of [i]manufacture[i] being all drawn from the land, and many of them from agriculture, which supplies in particular the entire material of clothing; the general law of production from the land, the law of diminishing return, must in the last resort be applicable to manufacturing as well as to agricultural [j]history[j]. As population increases, and the power of the land to yield increased produce is strained harder and harder, any additional supply of material, as well as of food, must be obtained by a more than proportionally increasing expenditure of labour. But the cost of the material [k]forming generally a very small portion of the entire cost of the manufacture,[k] the agricultural labour concerned in the production of manufactured goods is but a small fraction of the whole labour worked up in the commodity. All the rest of the labour tends constantly and strongly towards diminution, as the amount of production increases. Manufactures are vastly more susceptible than agriculture, of mechanical improvements, and contrivances for saving labour; and it has already been seen how greatly the division of labour, and its skilful and economical distribution, depend on the extent of the market, and on the possibility of production in large masses. In manufactures, accordingly, the causes tending to increase the productiveness of industry, preponderate greatly over the one cause which tends to diminish it: and the increase of production, called forth by the progress of society, takes place, not at an increasing, but [l]at[l] a continually diminishing proportional cost. This fact has manifested itself in the progressive fall of the prices and values of almost every kind of manufactured goods during two centuries past; a fall accelerated by the mechanical inventions of the last [m]seventy or eighty[m] years, and susceptible of being prolonged and extended beyond any limit which it would be safe to specify.

Now it is quite conceivable that the efficiency of agricultural labour might be undergoing, with the increase of produce, a gradual diminution; that the price of food, in consequence, might be progressively rising, and an ever growing proportion of the population might be needed to raise food for the whole; while yet the productive power of labour in all other branches of industry might be so rapidly augmenting, that the required amount of labour could be spared from manufactures, and nevertheless a greater produce be obtained, and the aggregate wants of the community be on the whole better supplied, than before. The benefit might even extend to the

[i-i]MS, 48, 49, 52, 57, 62 manufactures
[j-j]MS, 48, 49, 52, 57 industry
[k-k]MS forms . . . *as* 71 . . . manufacture;
[l-l]+48, 49, 52, 57, 62, 65, 71
[m-m]MS, 48, 49, 52, 57 sixty or seventy

poorest class. The increased cheapness of clothing and lodging might make up to them for the augmented cost of their food.

There is, thus, no possible improvement in the arts of production which does not in one or another mode exercise an antagonist influence to the law of diminishing return to agricultural labour. Nor is it only industrial improvements which have this effect. Improvements in government, and almost every kind of moral and social [n]advancement[n], operate in the same [o]manner[o]. Suppose a country in the condition of France before the Revolution: taxation imposed [p]almost[p] exclusively on the [q]industrial[q] classes, and on such a principle as to be an actual penalty on production; and no redress obtainable for any injury to property or person, when inflicted by people of rank, or court influence. Was not the hurricane which swept away this system of things, even if we look no further than to its effect in augmenting the productiveness of labour, equivalent to many industrial inventions? The removal of a fiscal burthen on agriculture, such as [r] tithe, has the same effect as if the labour necessary for obtaining the existing produce were suddenly reduced one-tenth. The abolition of corn laws, or of any other restrictions which prevent commodities from being produced where [s]the cost of their[s] production is lowest, amounts to a vast improvement in production. When fertile land, previously reserved as hunting ground, or for any other purpose of amusement, is set free for culture, the aggregate productiveness of agricultural industry is increased. It is well known what has been the effect in England of badly administered poor laws, and the still worse effect in Ireland of a bad system of tenancy, in rendering agricultural labour slack and ineffective. No improvements [t]operate[t] more directly upon the productiveness of labour, than those in the tenure of farms, and in the laws relating to landed property. The breaking up of entails, the cheapening of the transfer of property, and whatever else promotes the natural tendency of land in a system of freedom, to pass out of hands which can make little of it into those which can make more; the substitution of long leases for tenancy at will, and of any tolerable system of tenancy whatever for the wretched cottier system; above all, the acquisition of a [u]permanent[u] interest in the soil by the cultivators of it; all these things are as real, and some of them as great, improvements in production, as the invention of the spinning-jenny or the steam-engine.

We may say the same of improvements in education. The intelligence of the workman is a most important element in the productiveness of labour. So low, in some of the most civilized countries, is the present standard

[n-n]49, 52, 57 advantage
[o-o]MS direction
[p-p]+62, 65, 71
[q-q]MS, 48, 49, 52, 57, 62 industrious
[r]MS, 48, 49, 52, 57 the
[s-s]MS, 48 their cost of
[t-t]MS act
[u-u]MS, 48, 49, 52 fixed

of [v] intelligence, that there is hardly any source from which a more indefinite amount of improvement may be looked for in productive power, than by endowing with brains those who now have only hands. The carefulness, economy, and general trustworthiness of labourers are as important as their intelligence. Friendly relations, and a community of interest and feeling between labourers and employers, are eminently so: I should rather say, would be: for I know not where any such sentiment of friendly alliance now exists. Nor is it only in the labouring class that improvement of mind and character operates with beneficial effect even on industry. In the rich and idle classes, increased mental energy, more solid instruction, and stronger feelings of [w]conscience, public spirit[w], or philanthropy, would qualify them to originate and promote the most valuable improvements, both in the economical resources of their country, and in its institutions and customs. To look no further than the most obvious phenomena; the backwardness of French agriculture in the precise points in which benefit might be expected from the influence of an educated class, is partly accounted for by the exclusive devotion of the richer landed proprietors to town interests and town pleasures. There is scarcely any possible amelioration of human affairs which would not, among its other benefits, have a favourable operation, direct or indirect, upon the productiveness of industry. The intensity of devotion to industrial occupations would indeed in many cases be moderated by a more liberal and genial mental culture, but the labour actually bestowed on those occupations would almost always be rendered more effective.

[x]Before pointing out the principal inferences to be drawn[x] from the nature of the two antagonist forces by which the productiveness of agricultural industry is determined, we must observe that what we have said of agriculture, is true with little variation, of the other occupations which it represents; of all the arts which extract materials from the globe. Mining industry, for example, usually yields an increase of produce at a more than proportional increase of expense. It does worse, for even its customary annual produce requires to be extracted by a greater and greater expenditure of labour and capital. As a mine does not reproduce the coal or [y] ore taken from it, not only are all mines at last exhausted, but even when they as yet show no signs of exhaustion, they must be worked at [z]a continually[z] increasing cost; shafts must be sunk deeper, galleries driven farther, greater power applied to keep them clear of water; the produce must be lifted from a greater depth, or conveyed a greater distance. The law of diminishing return applies therefore to mining, in a still more unqualified sense than to

[v]MS, 48, 49 that
[w-w]MS patriotism, conscience
[y]MS, 48, 49 the
[x-x]MS Before drawing any inferences
[z-z]MS, 48, 49 an ever

agriculture: but the antagonizing agency, that of improvements in production, also applies in a still greater degree. Mining operations are more susceptible of mechanical improvements than agricultural: the first great application of the steam-engine was to mining; and there are unlimited possibilities of improvement in the chemical processes by which the metals are extracted. There is another contingency, of no unfrequent occurrence, which avails to counterbalance the progress of all existing mines towards exhaustion: this is, the discovery of new ones, equal or superior in richness.

To resume; all natural agents which are limited in quantity, are not only limited in their ultimate productive power, but, long before that power is stretched to the utmost, they yield to any additional demands on progressively harder terms. This law may however be suspended, or temporarily controlled, by whatever adds to the general power of mankind over nature; and especially by any extension of their knowledge, and their consequent command, of the properties and powers of natural agents.

CHAPTER XIII

Consequences of the Foregoing Laws

§ 1. [*Remedies when the limit to production is the weakness of the principle of accumulation*] From the preceding exposition it appears that the limit to the increase of production is two-fold; from deficiency of capital, or of land. Production comes to a pause, either because the effective desire of accumulation is not sufficient to give rise to any further increase of capital, or because, however disposed the possessors of surplus income may be to save a portion of it, the limited land at the disposal of the community does not permit additional capital to be employed with such a return, as would be an equivalent to them for their abstinence.

In countries where the principle of accumulation is as weak as it is in the various nations of Asia; where people will neither save, nor work to obtain the means of saving, unless under the inducement of enormously high profits, nor even then if it is necessary to wait [a] a considerable time for them; where either productions remain scanty, or drudgery great, because there is neither capital forthcoming nor forethought sufficient for the adoption of the contrivances by which natural agents are made to do the work of human labour; the desideratum for such a country, economically considered, is an increase of industry, and of the effective desire of accumulation. The means are, first, a better government: more complete security of property; moderate taxes, and freedom from arbitrary exaction under the name of taxes; a more permanent and more advantageous tenure of land, securing to the cultivator as far as possible the undivided benefits of the industry, skill, and economy he may exert. Secondly, improvement of the public intelligence: the decay of usages or superstitions which interfere with the effective employment of industry; and the growth of [b] mental activity, making the people alive to new objects of desire. Thirdly, the introduction of foreign arts, which raise the returns derivable from additional capital, to a rate corresponding to the low strength of the desire of accumulation: and the importation of foreign capital, which renders the increase of pro-

[a]49 for [b]MS a

duction no longer exclusively dependent on the thrift or providence of the inhabitants themselves, while it places before them a stimulating example, and by instilling new ideas and breaking the chains of habit, if not by improving the actual condition of the population, tends to create in them new wants, increased ambition, and greater thought for the future. These considerations apply more or less to all the Asiatic populations, and to the less civilized and industrious parts of Europe, as Russia, [c]Turkey[c], Spain, and Ireland.

§ 2. [*Necessity of restraining population not confined to a state of inequality of property*] But there are other countries, and England is at the head of them, in which neither the spirit of industry nor the effective desire of accumulation need any encouragement; where the people will toil hard for a small remuneration, and save much for a small profit; where, though the general thriftiness of the labouring class is much below what is desirable, the spirit of accumulation in the more prosperous part of the community requires abatement rather than increase. In these countries there would never be any deficiency of capital, if its increase were never checked or brought to a stand by too great a diminution of its returns. It is the tendency of the returns to a progressive diminution, which causes the increase of production to be [a] often attended with a deterioration in the condition of the producers; and this tendency, which would in time put an end to increase of production altogether, is a result of the necessary and inherent conditions of production from the land.

In all countries which have passed [b]beyond a rather[b] early stage in the progress of agriculture, every increase in the demand for food, occasioned by increased population, will always, unless there is a simultaneous improvement in production, diminish the share which on a fair division would fall to each individual. An increased production, in [c]default[c] of unoccupied tracts of fertile land, [d]or of fresh improvements tending to[d] cheapen commodities, can never be obtained but by increasing the labour in more than the same proportion. The population must either work harder, or eat less, or obtain their usual food by sacrificing [e]a part[e] of their other [f]customary[f] comforts. Whenever this necessity is postponed, [g]notwithstanding an increase of population,[g] it is because the improvements which facilitate production [h]continue progressive[h]; because the contrivances of mankind for

[c-c]MS, 48, 49, 52, 57, 62 Hungary
[a]MS so
[b-b]MS, 48, 49 a very] 52, 57, 62 beyond a very
[c-c]MS the absence
[d-d]MS & in a stationary state of the improvements which
[e-e]MS something
[f-f]MS accustomed [g-g]+65, 71 [h-h]MS are *not* stationary

making their labour more effective, keep up an equal struggle with nature, and extort fresh resources from her reluctant powers as fast as human necessities occupy and engross the old.

From this, results the important corollary, that the necessity of restraining population is not, as many persons believe, peculiar to a condition of great inequality of property. A greater number of people cannot, in any given state of civilization, be collectively so well provided for as a smaller. The niggardliness of nature, not the injustice of society, [i]is[i] the cause of the penalty attached to over-population. An unjust distribution of wealth does not even aggravate the evil, but, at most, causes it to be somewhat earlier felt. It is in vain to say, that all mouths which the increase of mankind calls into existence, bring [j]with them[j] hands. The new mouths require as much food as the old ones, and the hands do not produce as much. If all instruments of production were held in joint property by the whole people, and the produce divided with perfect equality among them, and if, in a society thus constituted, industry were as energetic and the produce as ample as at present, there would be enough to make all the existing population extremely comfortable; but when that population had doubled itself, as, with the existing habits of the people, under such an encouragement, it undoubtedly would in little more than twenty years, what would then be their condition? Unless the arts of production were in the same time improved in [k]an almost unexampled degree,[k] the inferior soils which must be resorted to, and the more laborious and scantily remunerative cultivation which must be employed on the superior [l]soils[l], to procure food for so much larger a population, would, by an insuperable necessity, render every individual in the community poorer than before. If the population continued to increase at the same rate, a time would soon arrive when no one would have more than mere necessaries, and, soon after, a time when no one would have a sufficiency of those, and the further increase of population would be arrested by death.

Whether, at the present or any other time, the produce of industry proportionally to the labour employed, is increasing or diminishing, and the average condition of the people improving or deteriorating, depends upon whether population is advancing faster than improvement, or improvement than population. After a degree of density has been attained, sufficient to allow the principal benefits of combination of labour, all further increase tends in itself to mischief, so far as regards the average condition of the people; but the progress of improvement has a counteracting operation, and

[i-i]MS, 48, 49 are
[j-j]49, 52 them with
[k-k]MS, 48, 49 so unexampled a degree as to double the productive power of labour—
[l-l]+48, 49, 52, 57, 62, 65, 71

allows of increased numbers without any deterioration, and even consistently with a higher average of comfort. Improvement must here be understood in a wide sense, including not only new industrial inventions, or an extended use of those already known, but improvements in institutions, education, opinions, and human affairs generally, provided they tend, as almost all improvements do, to give new motives or new facilities to production. If the productive powers of the country increase as rapidly as advancing numbers call for an augmentation of produce, it [m] is not necessary to obtain that augmentation by [n]the cultivation of[n] soils more sterile than the worst already under culture, [o]or[o] by applying additional labour to the old soils at a diminished advantage; or at all events this loss of power is compensated by the increased efficiency with which, in the progress of improvement, labour is employed in manufactures. In one way or the other, the increased population is provided for, and all are as well off as before. But if the growth of human power over nature is suspended or slackened, and population does not slacken its increase; if, with only the existing command over natural agencies, those agencies are called upon for an increased produce; [p]this[p] greater produce will not be afforded to the increased population, without either demanding on the average a greater effort from each, or on the average reducing each to a smaller ration out of the aggregate produce.

As a matter of fact, at some periods the progress of population has been the [q]more[q] rapid of the two, at others that of improvement. In England during a long interval preceding the French Revolution, population increased slowly; but the progress of improvement, at least in agriculture, would seem to have been still slower, since though nothing occurred to lower the value of the precious metals, the price of corn rose considerably, and England, from an exporting, became an importing country. This evidence, however, is [r]short of[r] conclusive, inasmuch as the extraordinary number of abundant seasons during the first half of the century[s], not continuing[s] during the last, was a cause of increased price in the [t]later[t] period, [u] extrinsic to the ordinary progress of society. Whether during the same period improvements in manufactures, or diminished cost of imported commodities, made amends for the diminished productiveness of labour on the land, is uncertain. But ever since the great mechanical inventions of Watt, Arkwright, and their [v]cotemporaries[v], the return to labour has probably increased as fast as the population; and would [w] have out-

[m]MS either
[n-n]MS cultivating
[o-o]MS nor
[p-p]MS, 48, 49 that
[q-q]MS, 48, 49 most
[r-r]MS, 48, 49, 52, 57, 62 not quite
[s-s]MS which did not continue
[t-t]MS, 48, 49, 52, 57 latter
[u]MS (compared with the former)
[v-v]MS, 48 contemporaries
[w]MS, 48, 49, 52, 57, 62 even

stripped it, if that very augmentation of return had not called forth an additional portion of the [x]inherent[x] power of multiplication in the human species. During the [y]twenty or thirty[y] years last elapsed, so rapid has been the extension of improved processes of agriculture, that even the land yields a greater produce in proportion to the labour employed; the average price of corn [z]had become[z] decidedly lower, [a]even before the repeal of the corn laws had so materially lightened, for the time being, the pressure of population upon production[a]. But though improvement may during [b]a[b] certain space of time keep up with, or even surpass, the actual increase of population, it assuredly never comes up to the rate of increase of which population is capable; and nothing could have prevented a general deterioration in the condition of the human race, were it not that population has in fact been restrained. Had it been restrained still more, and the same improvements taken place, there would have been a larger dividend than there now is, for the nation or the species at large. The new ground wrung from nature by the [c]improvements[c] would not have been all used up in the support of mere numbers. Though the gross produce would not have been so great, there would have been a greater produce per head of the population.

§ 3. [*Necessity of restraining population not superseded by free trade in food*] When the growth of numbers outstrips the progress of improvement, and a country is driven to obtain the means of subsistence on terms more and more unfavourable, by the inability of its land to meet additional demands except on more onerous conditions; there are two expedients by which it may hope to mitigate that disagreeable necessity, even though no change should take place in the habits of the people with respect to their rate of increase. One of these expedients is the importation of food from abroad. The other is emigration.

The admission of cheaper food from a foreign country, is equivalent to an agricultural invention by which food could be raised at a similarly diminished cost at home. It equally increases the productive power of labour. The return was before, so much food for so much labour employed in the growth of food: the return is now, a greater quantity of food, for the same labour employed in producing cottons or hardware or some other

[x-x]MS dormant
[y-y]MS, 48, 49 fifteen or twenty] 52 twenty or twenty-five
[z-z]MS, 48, 49 is
[a-a]MS and the country more nearly feeds its own population without foreign aid than it did in 1827] 48 *as* MS . . . 1828] 49 *as* MS . . . country, in ordinary years, . . . *as* 48
[b-b]MS some
[c-c]MS, 48 improvement

commodity, to be given in exchange for [a]food[a]. The one improvement, like the other, throws back the decline of the productive power of labour by a certain distance: but in the one case as in the other, it immediately resumes its course; the tide which has receded, instantly begins to re-advance. It might seem, indeed, that when a country draws its supply of food from so wide a surface as the whole habitable globe, so little [b]impression[b] can be produced on that great expanse by any increase of mouths in one small corner of it, that the inhabitants of the country may double and treble their numbers, without feeling the [c]effect[c] in any increased tension of the springs of production, or any enhancement of the price of food throughout the world. But in this calculation several things are overlooked.

In the first place, the foreign regions from which corn can be imported do not comprise the whole globe, but those parts of it [d]principally[d] which are in the immediate neighbourhood of coasts or navigable rivers. The coast is the part of most countries which is earliest and most thickly peopled, and has seldom any food to spare. The chief source of supply, therefore, is the strip of country along the banks of some navigable river, as the Nile, the Vistula, or the Mississippi; and of such there is not, in the productive regions of the earth, so great a multitude as to suffice during an indefinite time for a rapidly growing demand, without an increasing strain on the productive powers of the soil. To obtain auxiliary supplies of corn from the interior in any abundance, [e]is[e], in the existing state of the communications, [f]in most cases impracticable[f]. By improved roads, and [g]by canals and railways, the obstacle will eventually[g] be so reduced as not to be insuperable: but this is a slow progress; in all the food-exporting countries except America, a very slow progress; and one which cannot keep pace with population, unless the increase of the last is very effectually restrained.

In the next place, even if the supply were drawn from the whole instead of a small part of the surface of the exporting countries, the quantity of food would still be limited, which could be obtained from them without an increase of the proportional cost. The countries which export food may be divided into two classes; those in which the effective desire of accumulation is strong, and those in which it is weak. In Australia and the United States of America, the effective desire of accumulation is strong; capital increases fast, and the production of food might be very rapidly extended.

[a-a]MS it
[b-b]MS effect
[c-c]MS consequence
[d-d]MS, 48, 49, 52, 57, 62, 65 almost alone,
[e-e]MS, 48, 49, 52, 57, 62, 65 would
[f-f]MS, 48, 49, 52, 57, 62, 65 be hopeless
[g-g]MS, 48, 49, 52, 57 ultimately by canals and railways, the obstacle will] 62 often by . . . *as* MS] 65 eventually by . . . *as* MS

But in such countries population also increases with extraordinary rapidity. Their agriculture has to provide for their own expanding numbers, as well as for those of the importing countries. They must, therefore, from the nature of the case, be rapidly driven, if not to less fertile, at least what is equivalent, to remoter and less accessible lands, and to modes of cultivation like those of old countries, less productive in proportion to the labour and expense.

But the countries which have at the same time cheap food and great industrial prosperity are few, being only those in which the arts of civilized life have been transferred full-grown to a rich and uncultivated soil. Among old countries, those which are able to export food, are able only because their industry is in a very backward state; because capital, and hence population, have never increased sufficiently to make food rise to a higher price. Such countries are Russia, Poland, and [h]the plains of the Danube[h]. In those regions the effective desire of accumulation is weak, the arts of production most imperfect, capital scanty, and its increase, especially from domestic sources, slow. When an increased demand arose for food to be exported to [i]other countries[i], it would only be very gradually that food could be produced to meet it. The capital needed could not be obtained by transfer from other employments, for such do not exist. The [j]cottons[j] or hardware which would be received from England in exchange for corn, the Russians and Poles do not now produce in the country: they go without them. Something might in time be expected from the increased exertions to which producers would be stimulated by the market opened for their produce; but to such increase of exertion, the [k]habits[k] of countries whose agricultural population consists of serfs, [l]or of peasants [m]who have but just emerged from a[m] servile condition,[l] are the reverse of favourable, and even in this age of movement these [n]habits[n] do not rapidly change. If a greater outlay of capital is relied on as the source from which the produce is to be increased, the means must either be obtained by the slow process of saving, under the impulse given by new commodities [o]and[o] more extended intercourse (and in that case the population would most likely increase as fast), or must be brought in from foreign countries. If England is to obtain a rapidly increasing supply of corn from Russia or Poland, English capital must go there to produce it. This, however, is attended with so many difficulties, as are equivalent to great positive disadvantages. It is opposed by [p]differences[p] of language, differences of manners, and a thousand obstacles arising from the institutions and social relations of the country; and after

[h-h]MS, 48, 49, 52, 57, 62 Hungary
[i-i]MS, 48, 49, 52, 57 England
[j-j]MS clothes
[k-k]MS, 48, 49, 52, 57, 62 institutions
[l-l]+52, 57, 62, 65, 71
[m-m]52, 57, 62 in an almost
[n-n]MS, 48, 49, 52, 57, 62 institutions
[o-o]MS or
[p-p]MS, 48, 49, 52, 57 difference

all it would inevitably so stimulate population on the spot, that nearly all the increase of food produced by its means would [q]probably[q] be consumed without leaving the country: so that, if it were not the almost only mode of introducing foreign arts and ideas, and giving an effectual spur to the backward civilization of those countries, little reliance could be placed on it for increasing the exports, and supplying other countries with a progressive and indefinite increase of food. But to improve the civilization of a country is a slow process, and gives time for so great an increase of population both in the country itself, and in those supplied from it, that its effect in keeping down the price of food against the increase of demand, is not likely to be more decisive on the scale of all Europe, than on the smaller one of a particular nation.

The law, therefore, of diminishing return to industry, whenever population makes a more rapid progress than improvement, is not solely applicable to countries which are fed from their own soil, but in substance applies quite as much to those which are willing to draw their food from any accessible quarter that can afford it cheapest. [r]A sudden and great cheapening of food, indeed, in whatever manner produced, would, like any other sudden improvement in the arts of life,[r] throw the natural tendency of affairs a stage or two further back, [s]though without[s] altering its course. [t]There is one contingency[t] connected with freedom of importation, which may [u]yet[u] produce temporary effects [v]greater[v] than were ever contemplated either by the bitterest enemies or the most ardent adherents of free-trade in food. Maize, or Indian corn, is a product capable of being supplied in quantity sufficient to feed the whole country, at a cost, allowing for difference of nutritive quality, cheaper even than the potato. If maize should ever substitute itself for wheat as the staple food of the poor, the productive power of labour in obtaining food would be so enormously increased, and the expense of maintaining a family so diminished, that it

[q-q]+52, 57, 62, 65, 71

[r-r]MS, 48, 49 If, indeed, the release of the corn trade from restriction had produced, or should still produce, a sudden cheapening of food, this, like any other sudden improvement in the arts of life, would

[s-s]MS, 48, 49 but without at all

[t-t]MS There would be more for everybody in the first instance; but this more, would begin immediately and continue always to grow less, so long as population went on increasing, unaccompanied by other events of a countervailing tendency.

Whether the repeal of the corn laws is likely, even temporarily, to give any considerable increase of margin for population to fill up, it would be premature as yet to attempt to decide. All the elements of the question have been thrown into temporary disorder by the consequences of bad harvests and of the potatoe failure. But as far as can be foreseen, there seems little reason to expect an importation of the customary articles of food either so great in itself, or capable of such rapid increase, as to interfere much with the operation of the general law. One contingency there is,] 48, 49 *as* MS . . . but this *more* . . . *as* MS

[u-u]+52, 57, 62, 65, 71

[v-v]MS more gigantic

would require perhaps some generations for population, even if it started forward at an American pace, to overtake this great accession to the facilities of its support.

§ 4. [*Necessity of restraining population not* [a]*in general*[a] *superseded by emigration*] Besides the importation of corn, there is another resource which can be invoked by a nation whose increasing numbers press hard, not against their capital, but against the productive capacity of their land: I mean Emigration, especially in the form of Colonization. Of this remedy the efficacy as far as it goes is real, since it consists in seeking elsewhere those unoccupied tracts of fertile land, which if they existed at home would enable the demand of an increasing population to be met without any falling off in the productiveness of labour. Accordingly, when the region to be colonized is near at hand, and the habits and tastes of the people sufficiently migratory, this remedy is completely effectual. The migration from the older parts of the American Confederation to the new territories, which is to all intents and purposes colonization, is what enables population to go on unchecked throughout the Union without having yet diminished the return to industry, or increased the difficulty of earning a subsistence. If Australia or the interior of Canada were as near to Great Britain as Wisconsin and Iowa to New York; if the superfluous people could remove to it without [b]crossing the sea[b], and were of as adventurous and restless a character, and as little addicted to staying at home, as their kinsfolk of New England, those unpeopled continents would render the same service to the United Kingdom which the old states of America derive from the new. But, these things being as they are—though a judiciously conducted emigration is a most important resource for suddenly lightening the pressure of population by a single effort—[c]and though in such an extraordinary case as that of Ireland under the threefold operation of the potato failure, the poor law, and the general turning out of tenantry throughout the country, spontaneous emigration may at a particular crisis remove greater multitudes than it was ever proposed to remove at once by any national scheme;[c] [d]it still remains to be shown by experience whether a permanent stream of emigration can[d] be kept up, sufficient to take off, as in America, all that portion of the annual increase (when proceeding at its greatest rapidity) which being in excess of the progress made during the same short period in the arts of life, tends to render living more difficult for every averagely-situated individual in the community. And unless this

[a-a]+65, 71
[b-b]MS changing their country
[c-c]+52, 57, 62, 65, 71
[d-d]MS, 48, 49, 52, 57, 62 there is no probability that even under the most enlightened arrangements a permanent stream of emigration could

can be done, emigration cannot[e], even in an economical point of view,[e] dispense with the necessity of checks to population. Further than this we have not to speak of it in this place. The general subject of colonization as a practical question, its importance to [f]old countries[f], and the principles on which it should be conducted, will be [g]discussed at some length in a subsequent portion of this Treatise[g].

[e-e]MS, 48, 49 even temporarily
[f-f]MS, 48, 49, 52 this country
[g-g]MS touched incidentally in many passages of this work, and systematically treated in a chapter devoted to the purpose] 48 *as* MS . . . and treated of in . . . *as* MS

BOOK II

DISTRIBUTION

CHAPTER I

Of Property

§ 1. [*Introductory remarks*] The principles which have been set forth in the first part of this Treatise, are, in certain respects, strongly distinguished from those, on the consideration of which we are now about to enter. The laws and conditions of the production of wealth partake of the character of physical truths. There is nothing optional or arbitrary in them. Whatever mankind produce, must be produced in the modes, and under the conditions, imposed by the constitution of external things, and by the inherent properties of their own bodily and mental structure. Whether they like it or not, their [a]productions[a] will be limited by the amount of their previous accumulation, and, that being given, it will be proportional to their energy, their skill, the perfection of their machinery, and their judicious use of the advantages of combined labour. Whether they like it or not, a double quantity of labour will not raise, on the same land, a double quantity of food, unless some improvement takes place in the processes of cultivation. Whether they like it or not, the unproductive expenditure of individuals will *pro tanto* tend to impoverish the community, and only their productive expenditure will enrich it. The opinions, or the wishes, which may exist on these different matters, do not control the things themselves. We cannot, indeed, foresee to what extent the modes of production may be altered, or the productiveness of labour increased, by future extensions of our knowledge of the laws of nature, suggesting new processes of industry of which we have at present no conception. But howsoever we may succeed in making for ourselves more space within the limits set by the constitution of things, [b]we know that there must be limits. We cannot alter the ultimate properties either of matter or mind, but can only employ those properties more or less successfully, to bring about the events in which we are interested[b].

It is not so with the Distribution of Wealth. That is a matter of human institution solely. The things once there, mankind, individually or collectively, can do with them as they like. They can place them at the disposal

[a-a]MS, 48 production
[b-b]MS, 48, 49 those limits exist; there are ultimate laws, which we did not make, which we cannot alter, and to which we can only conform

of whomsoever they please, and on whatever terms. Further, in the social state, in every state except total solitude, any disposal whatever of them can only take place by the [c] consent of society[d], or rather of those who dispose of its active force[d]. Even what a person has produced by his individual toil, unaided by any one, he cannot keep, unless [e]by the permission of society[e]. Not only can society take it from him, but individuals could and would take it from him, if society only remained passive; if it did not either interfere *en masse*, or employ and pay people for the purpose of [f]preventing[f] him from being disturbed in the possession. The distribution of wealth, therefore, depends on the laws and customs of society. The rules by which it is determined, are what the opinions and feelings [g]of the ruling portion[g] of the community make them, and are very different in different ages and countries; and might be still more different, if mankind so chose.

The opinions and feelings of mankind, doubtless, are not a matter of chance. They are consequences of the fundamental laws of human nature, [h]combined with the existing state of knowledge and experience, and the existing condition of social institutions and intellectual and moral culture[h]. But the laws of the generation of human opinions are not within our present subject. They are part of the general theory of human progress, a far larger and more difficult subject of inquiry than political economy. We have here to consider, not the causes, but the consequences, of the rules according to which wealth may be distributed. Those, at least, are as little arbitrary, and have as much the character of physical laws, as the laws of production. Human beings can control their own acts, but not the consequences of their acts [i]either to themselves or to others[i]. Society can subject the distribution of wealth to whatever rules it thinks best: but what practical results [j]will[j] flow from the operation of those rules, [k]must be discovered, like any other physical or mental truths, by observation and reasoning[k].

We proceed, then, to the consideration of the different modes of distributing the produce of land and labour, which have been adopted in practice, or may be conceived in theory. Among these, our attention is first claimed by that primary and fundamental institution, on which, unless in some exceptional and very limited cases, the economical arrangements of society have always rested, though in its secondary features it has varied,

[c]MS, 48, 49 general
[d-d]+52, 57, 62, 65, 71
[e-e]MS, 48, 49 it is the will of society that he should
[f-f]MS, 48, 49 interfering, to prevent
[g-g]+52, 57, 62, 65, 71
[h-h]MS, 48, 49 and of the constitution of the planet which we inhabit, modified by local or special peculiarities
[i-i]MS, 48, 49 , even on their own minds
[j-j]MS, 48, 49 shall
[k-k]MS, 48, 49 society cannot choose, but must be content to learn

and is liable to vary. I mean, of course, the institution of individual property.

§ 2. [*Statement of the question concerning Property*] Private property, as an institution, did not owe its origin to any of those considerations of utility, which plead [a] for the maintenance of it when established. Enough is known of rude ages, both from history and from analogous states of society in our own time, to show, that tribunals (which always precede laws) were originally established, not to determine rights, but to repress violence and terminate quarrels. With this object chiefly in view, they naturally enough gave legal effect to first occupancy, by treating as the aggressor the person who first commenced violence, by turning, or attempting to turn, another out of possession. The preservation of the peace, which was the original object of civil government, was thus attained; while by confirming, to those who already possessed it, even what was not the fruit of personal exertion, a guarantee was incidentally given to them and others that they would be protected in what was so.

In considering the institution of property as a question in social philosophy, we must leave out of consideration its actual origin in any of the existing nations of Europe[b]. We[b] may suppose a community unhampered by any previous possession; a body of colonists, occupying for the first time an uninhabited country; bringing nothing with them but what belonged to them in common, and having a clear field for the adoption of the institutions and polity which they judged most expedient; [c]required[c], therefore, to choose whether they would conduct the work of production on the principle of individual property, or on some system of common ownership and collective agency.

If private property were adopted, we must presume that it would be accompanied by none of the initial inequalities and injustices which obstruct the beneficial operation of the principle in old societies. Every full grown man or woman, we must suppose, would be secured in the unfettered use and disposal of his or her bodily and mental faculties; and the instruments of production, the land and tools, would be divided fairly among them, so that all might start, in respect to outward appliances, on equal terms. It is [d]possible also[d] to conceive that in this original apportionment, compensation might be made for the injuries of nature, and the balance redressed by assigning to the less robust members of the community advantages in the distribution, sufficient to put them on a par with the rest. But the division, once made, would not again be interfered with; individuals would be left to their own exertions and to the ordinary chances, for making

[a]MS, 48 so strongly
[b-b]MS, 48, 49 , and we
[c-c]MS, 48, 49 free
[d-d]MS, 48, 49 even possible

an advantageous use of what was assigned to them. If individual property, on the contrary, were excluded, the plan which must be adopted would be to hold the land and all instruments of production as the joint property of the community, and to carry on the operations of industry on the common account. The direction of the labour of the community would devolve upon a magistrate or magistrates, whom we may suppose elected by the suffrages of the community, and whom we must assume to be voluntarily obeyed by them. The division of the produce would in like manner be a public act. The principle might either be that of complete equality, or of apportionment to the necessities or deserts of individuals, in whatever manner might be conformable to the ideas of justice or policy prevailing in the community.

Examples of such associations, on a small scale, are the monastic orders, the Moravians, the followers of Rapp, and others: and from the [e]hopes which they hold out of relief from[e] the miseries and iniquities of a state of much inequality of wealth, schemes for a larger application of the same idea have reappeared and become popular at all periods of active speculation on the first principles of society. In an age like the present, when a general reconsideration of all first principles is felt to be inevitable, and when [f]more than at any former period of history the[f] suffering portions of the community have a voice in the discussion, it was impossible but that ideas of this nature should spread far and wide. [g]The late revolutions in Europe have thrown up a great amount of speculation of this character, and an unusual share of attention has consequently been drawn to the various forms which these ideas have assumed[h]: nor is this attention likely to diminish, but on the contrary, to increase more and more[h].

The assailants of the principle of individual property may be divided into

[e-e]MS, 48, 49 plausible remedies which they hold out for

[f-f]MS, 48, 49 for the first time in history the most

[g-g203]MS Owenism, or Socialism, in this country, and Communism on the Continent, are the most prevailing forms of the doctrine. These suppose a democratic government of the industry and funds of society, and an equal division of the fruits. In a more refined and elaborate form of the same scheme, which attained a temporary celebrity under the name of St. Simonism, the administering authority was supposed to be a monarchy or aristocracy, not of birth but of capacity; the remuneration of each member of the community being by salary, proportioned to the importance of the services supposed to be rendered by each to the general body.] 48 *as* MS . . . In the more . . . *as* MS

[h-h]49 . This attention is not likely to diminish; attacks on the institution of property being, in the existing state of human intellect, a natural expression of the discontent of all those classes on whom, in whatever manner, the present constitution of society bears hardly: and it is a safe prediction that unless the progress of the human mind can be checked, such speculations will never cease, until the laws of property are freed from whatever portion of injustice they contain, and until whatever is well grounded in the opinions, and legitimate in the aims of its assailants, is adopted into the framework of society

two classes: those whose scheme implies absolute equality in the distribution of the physical means of life and enjoyment, and those who admit inequality, but grounded on some principle, or supposed principle, of justice or general expediency, and not, like so many of the existing social inequalities, dependent on accident alone. At the head of the first class, as the earliest [i] of those belonging to the present generation, must be placed Mr. Owen and his followers. M. Louis Blanc and M. Cabet have more recently become conspicuous as apostles of similar doctrines (though the former advocates equality of distribution only as a transition to a still higher standard of [j] justice, that all should work according to their capacity, and receive according to their wants). The characteristic name for this economical system is Communism, a word of continental origin, only of late introduced into this country. The word Socialism, which originated among the English Communists, and was assumed by them as a name to designate their own doctrine, is now, on the Continent, employed in a larger sense; not necessarily implying Communism, or the entire abolition of private property, but applied to any system which requires that the land and the instruments of production should be the property, not of individuals, but of communities or associations, or of the government. Among such systems, the two of highest intellectual pretension are those which, from the names of their real or [k]reputed[k] authors, have been called St. Simonism and Fourierism; the former defunct as a system, but which during the few years of its public promulgation, sowed the seeds of nearly all the Socialist tendencies which have since spread so widely in France: the second, [l]still[l] flourishing in the number, talent, and zeal of its adherents.[g]

[a] § 3. [*Examination of Communism*] Whatever may be the merits or defects of these various schemes, they cannot be truly said to be impracticable. No reasonable person can doubt that a village community, composed of a few thousand inhabitants cultivating in joint ownership the same extent of land which at present feeds that number of people, and producing by combined labour and the most improved processes the manufactured articles which they required, could raise an amount of productions sufficient to maintain them in comfort; and would find the means of obtaining, and if need be, exacting, the quantity of labour necessary for this purpose, from every member of the association who was capable of work.

The objection ordinarily made to a system of community of property

[i]49 in date
[j]49 abstract
[k-k]49, 52, 57 imputed
[l-l]49, 52, 57, 62 now
[a][*For* MS, 48, 49 *versions of the remainder of this chapter, see* Appendix A.]

and equal distribution of the produce, that each person would be incessantly occupied in evading his fair share of the work, points, undoubtedly, to a real difficulty. But those who urge this objection, forget to how [b]great[b] an extent the same difficulty exists under the system on which nine-tenths of the business of society is now conducted. The objection supposes, that honest and efficient labour is only to be had from those who are themselves individually to reap the benefit of their own exertions. But how small a part of all the labour performed in England, from the lowest-paid to the highest, is done by persons working for their own [c]benefit.[c] From the Irish reaper or hodman to the chief justice or the minister of state, nearly all the work of society is remunerated by day wages or fixed salaries. A factory operative has less personal interest in his work than a member of a Communist association, since he is not, like him, working for a partnership of which he is himself a member. It will no doubt be [d]said[d], that though the labourers themselves have not, in most cases, a personal interest in their work, they are watched and superintended, and their labour directed, and the mental part of the labour performed, by persons who have. Even this, however, is far from being universally the fact. In all public, and many of the largest and most successful private undertakings, not only the labours of detail but the control and superintendence are entrusted to salaried officers. And though the "master's eye," when the master is vigilant and intelligent, is of proverbial value, it must be remembered that in a Socialist farm or manufactory, each labourer would be under the eye not of one master, but of the whole community. In the extreme case of obstinate perseverance in not performing the due share of work, the community would have the same resources which society now has for compelling conformity to the necessary conditions of the association. Dismissal, the only remedy at present, is no remedy when any other labourer who may be engaged does no better than his predecessor: the power of dismissal only enables an employer to obtain [e]from his workmen[e] the customary amount of labour, but that customary labour may be of any degree of inefficiency. Even the labourer who loses his employment by idleness or negligence, has nothing worse to suffer, in the most unfavourable case, than the discipline of a workhouse, and if the desire to avoid this be a sufficient motive in the one system, it would be sufficient in the other. I am not undervaluing the strength of the incitement given to labour when the whole or a large share of the benefit of extra exertion belongs to the labourer. But under the present system of industry this incitement, in the great majority of cases, does not exist. If Communistic labour might be less vigorous than that of a peasant proprietor, or a workman labouring on his own account, it would

[b-b]52 vast
[c-c]52 benefit?
[d-d]52, 57 objected
[e-e]+62, 65, 71

probably be more energetic than that of a labourer for hire, who has no personal interest in the matter at all. The neglect by the uneducated classes of labourers for hire, of the duties which they engage to perform, is in the present state of society most flagrant. Now it is an admitted condition of the Communist scheme that all shall be educated: and this being supposed, the duties of the members of the association would doubtless be as diligently performed as those of the generality of salaried officers in the middle or higher classes; who are not supposed to be necessarily unfaithful to their trust, because so long as they are not dismissed, their pay is the same in however lax a manner their duty is fulfilled. Undoubtedly, as a general rule, remuneration by fixed salaries does not in any class of functionaries produce the maximum of zeal: and this is as much as can be reasonably alleged against Communistic labour.

That even this [f]inferiority would necessarily exist[f], is by no means so certain as is assumed by those who are little used to carry their minds beyond the state of things with which they are familiar. Mankind are capable of a far greater amount of public spirit than the present age is accustomed to suppose possible. History bears witness to the success with which large bodies of human beings may be trained to feel the public interest their own. And no soil could be more favourable to the growth of such a feeling, than a Communist association, since all the ambition, and the bodily and mental activity, which are now exerted in the pursuit of separate and self-regarding interests, would require another [g]sphere[g] of employment, and would naturally find it in the pursuit of the general benefit of the community. The same cause, so often assigned in explanation of the devotion of the Catholic priest or monk to the interest of his order—that he has no interest apart from it—would, under Communism, attach the citizen to the community. And independently of the public motive, every member of the association would be amenable to the most universal, and one of the strongest, of personal motives, that of public opinion. The force of this motive in deterring from any act or omission positively reproved by the community, no one is likely to deny; but the power also of emulation, in exciting to the most strenuous exertions for the sake of the approbation and admiration of others, is borne witness to by experience in every situation in which human beings publicly compete with one another, even if it be in things frivolous, or from which the public derive no benefit. A contest, who can do most for the common good, is not the kind of competition which Socialists repudiate. To what extent, therefore, the energy of labour would be diminished by Communism, or whether in the long run it would be diminished at all, must be considered for the present an undecided question.

f-f52 consequence would necessarily follow
g-g52 field

Another of the objections to Communism is similar to that, so often urged against poor-laws: that if every member of the community were assured of subsistence for himself and any number of children, on the sole condition of willingness to work, prudential restraint on the multiplication of mankind would be at an end, and population would start forward at a rate which would reduce the community, through successive stages of increasing discomfort, to actual starvation. There would certainly be much ground for this apprehension if Communism provided no motives to restraint, equivalent to those which it would take away. But Communism is precisely the state of things in which opinion might be expected to declare itself with greatest intensity against this kind of selfish intemperance. Any augmentation of numbers which diminished the comfort or increased the toil of the mass, would then cause (which now it does not) immediate and unmistakeable inconvenience to every individual in the association; inconvenience which could not then be imputed to the avarice of employers, or the unjust privileges of the rich. In such altered circumstances opinion could not fail to reprobate, and if reprobation did not suffice, to repress by penalties of some description, this or any other culpable self-indulgence at the expense of the community. The Communistic scheme, instead of being peculiarly open to the objection drawn from danger of over-population, has the recommendation of tending in an especial degree to the prevention of that evil.

A more real difficulty is that of fairly apportioning the labour of the community among its members. There are many kinds of work, and by what standard are they to be measured one against another? Who is to judge how much cotton spinning, or distributing goods from the stores, or bricklaying, or chimney sweeping, is equivalent to so much ploughing? The difficulty of making the adjustment between different qualities of labour is so strongly felt by Communist writers, that they have usually thought it necessary to provide that all should work by turns at every description of useful labour: an arrangement which, by putting an end to the division of employments, would sacrifice so much of the advantage of co-operative production as greatly to diminish the productiveness of labour. Besides, even in the same kind of work, nominal equality of labour would be so great a real inequality, that [h]the feeling of[h] justice would revolt against its being enforced. All persons are not equally fit for all labour; and the same quantity of labour is an unequal burthen on the weak and the strong, the hardy and the delicate, the quick and [i]the[i] slow, the dull and the intelligent.

But these difficulties, though real, are not [j]necessarily[j] insuperable. The apportionment of work to the strength and capacities of individuals, the mitigation of a general rule to provide for cases in which it would operate

[h-h]+62, 65, 71 [i-i]+62, 65, 71 [j-j]+62, 65, 71

harshly, are not problems to which human intelligence, guided by a sense of justice, would be inadequate. And the worst and most unjust arrangement which could be made of these points, under a system aiming at equality, would be so far short of the inequality and injustice with which labour (not to speak of remuneration) is now apportioned, as to be scarcely worth counting in the comparison. We must remember too, that Communism, as a system of society, exists only in idea; that its difficulties, at present, are much better understood than its resources; and that the intellect of mankind is only beginning to contrive the means of organizing it in detail, so as to overcome the one and derive the greatest advantage from the other. [k]

If[l], therefore,[l] the choice were to be made between Communism with all its chances, and the present state of society with all its sufferings and injustices; if the institution of private property necessarily carried with it as a consequence, that the produce of labour should be apportioned as we now see it, almost in an inverse ratio to the labour—the largest portions to those who have never worked at all, the next largest to those whose work is almost nominal, and so in a descending scale, the remuneration dwindling as the work grows harder and more disagreeable, until the most fatiguing and exhausting bodily labour cannot count with certainty on being able to earn even the necessaries of life; if this or Communism were the alternative, all the difficulties, great or small, of Communism would be but as dust in the balance. But to make the comparison applicable, we must compare Communism at its best, with the régime of individual property, not as it is, but as it might be made. The principle of private property has never yet had a fair trial in any country; and less so, perhaps, in this country than in some others. The social arrangements of modern Europe commenced from a distribution of property which was the result, not of just partition, or acquisition by industry, but of conquest and violence: and notwithstanding what industry has been doing for many centuries to modify the work of force, the system still retains many and large traces of its origin. The laws of property have never yet conformed to the principles on which the justification of private property rests. They have made property of things which never ought to be property, and absolute property where only a qualified property ought to exist. They have not held the balance fairly between human beings, but have heaped impediments upon some, to give advantage to others; they have purposely fostered inequalities, and prevented all from starting fair in the race. That all should indeed start on perfectly equal terms, is inconsistent with any law of private property: but

[k]52 The impossibility of foreseeing and prescribing the exact mode in which its difficulties should be dealt with, does not prove that it may not be the best and the ultimate form of human society. [l-l]+57, 62, 65, 71

if as much pains as has been taken to aggravate the inequality of chances arising from the natural working of the principle, had been taken to temper that inequality by every means not subversive of the principle itself; if the tendency of legislation had been to favour the diffusion, instead of the concentration of wealth—to encourage the subdivision of the large masses, instead of striving to keep them together; the principle of individual property would have been found to have no necessary connexion with the physical and social evils which almost all Socialist writers assume to be inseparable from it.

Private property, in every defence made of it, is supposed to mean, the guarantee to individuals of the fruits of their own labour and abstinence. The guarantee to them of the fruits of the labour and abstinence of others, transmitted to them without any merit or exertion of their own, is not of the essence of the institution, but a mere incidental consequence, which, when it reaches a certain height, does not promote, but conflicts with, the ends which render private property legitimate. To judge of the final destination of the institution of property, we must suppose everything rectified, which causes the institution to work in a manner opposed to that equitable principle, of proportion between remuneration and exertion, on which in every vindication of it that will bear the light, it is assumed to be grounded. We must also suppose two conditions realized, without which neither Communism nor any other laws or institutions could make the condition of the mass of mankind other than degraded and miserable. One of these conditions is, universal education; the other, a due limitation of the numbers of the community. With these, there could be no poverty, even under the present social institutions: and these being supposed, the question of Socialism is not, as generally stated by Socialists, a question of flying to the sole refuge against the evils which now bear down humanity; but a mere question of comparative advantages, which futurity must determine. We are too ignorant either of what individual agency in its best form, or Socialism in its best form, can accomplish, to be qualified to decide which of the two will be the ultimate form of human society.

If a conjecture may be hazarded, the decision will probably depend mainly on one consideration, viz. which of the two systems is consistent with the greatest amount of human liberty and spontaneity. After the means of subsistence are assured, the next in strength of the personal wants of human beings is liberty; and (unlike the physical wants, which as civilization advances become more moderate and more amenable to control) it increases instead of diminishing in intensity, as the intelligence and the moral faculties are more developed. The perfection both of social arrangements and of practical morality would be, to secure to all persons complete independence and freedom of action, subject to no restriction but that of not doing injury to others: and the education which taught or the social institutions which required them to exchange the control of their own actions for any amount of comfort or affluence, or to renounce liberty for the sake of equality, would deprive them of one of the most elevated characteristics of human nature. It remains to be discovered how far the preservation of this characteristic would be found compatible with the Communistic organization of society. No doubt, this, like all the other objections to the Socialist schemes, is vastly exaggerated. The members of the association need not be required to live together more than they do now, nor need they be controlled in the disposal of their individual share of the produce, and of the probably large amount of leisure which, if they limited their production to things really worth producing, they would possess. Individuals need not be chained to an occupation, or to a particular locality. The restraints of Communism would be freedom in comparison with the present condition of the majority of the human race. The generality of labourers in this and most other countries, have as little choice of occupation or freedom of locomotion, are practically as dependent on fixed rules and on the will of others, as they could be on any system short of actual slavery; to say nothing of the entire domestic subjection of one half the species, to which it is the signal honour of Owenism and most other forms of Socialism that they assign equal rights, in all respects, with those of the hitherto dominant sex. But it is not by comparison with the present bad state of society that the claims of Communism can be estimated; nor is it sufficient that it should promise greater personal and mental freedom than is now enjoyed by those who have not enough of either to deserve the name. The question is, whether there would be any asylum left for individuality of character; whether public opinion would not be a tyrannical yoke; whether the absolute dependence of each on all, and surveillance of each by all, would not grind all down into a tame uniformity of thoughts, feelings, and actions. This is already one of the glaring evils of the existing state of society, notwithstanding a much greater diversity of education and pursuits, and a much less absolute dependence of the individual on the mass, than would exist in the Communistic régime. No society in which eccentricity is a matter of reproach, can be in a wholesome state. It is yet to be ascertained whether the Communistic scheme would be [m]consistent with[m] that multiform development of human nature, those manifold unlikenesses, that diversity of tastes and talents, and variety of intellectual points of view, which not only form a great part of the interest of human life, but by bringing intellects into stimulating collision, and by presenting to each innumerable notions that he would not have conceived of himself, are the mainspring of mental and moral progression.

[m-m]52 favourable to

§ 4. [*Examination of St. Simonism and Fourierism*] I have thus far confined my observations to the Communistic doctrine, which forms the extreme limit of Socialism; according to which not only the instruments of production, the land and capital, are the joint property of the community, but the produce is divided and the labour apportioned, as far as possible, equally. The objections, whether well or ill grounded, to which Socialism is liable, apply to this form of it in their greatest force. The other varieties of Socialism mainly differ from Communism, in not relying solely on what M. Louis Blanc calls the point of honour of industry, but retaining more or less of the incentives to labour derived from private pecuniary interest. Thus it is already a modification of the strict theory of Communism, when the principle is professed of proportioning remuneration to labour. The attempts which have been made [a]in France[a] to carry Socialism into practical effect, by associations of workmen manufacturing on their own account, [b] mostly began by sharing the remuneration equally, without regard to the quantity of work done by the individual: but in almost every case this plan was after a short time abandoned, and recourse was had to working by the piece. The original principle appeals to a higher standard of justice, and is adapted to a much higher moral condition of human nature. The proportioning of remuneration to work done, is really just, only in so far as the more or less of the work is a matter of choice: when it depends on natural difference of strength or capacity, this principle of remuneration is in itself an injustice: it is giving to those who have; assigning most to those who are already most favoured by nature. Considered, however, as a compromise with the selfish type of character formed by the present standard of morality, and fostered by the existing social institutions, it is highly expedient; and until education shall have been entirely regenerated, is far more likely to prove immediately successful, than an attempt at a higher ideal.

The two elaborate forms of non-communistic Socialism known as St. Simonism and Fourierism, are totally free from the objections usually urged against Communism; and though they are open to others of their own, yet by the great intellectual power which in many respects distinguishes them, and by their large and philosophic treatment of some of the fundamental problems of society and morality, they may justly be counted among the most remarkable productions of the past and present age.

The St. Simonian scheme does not contemplate an equal, but an unequal division of the produce; it does not propose that all should be occupied alike, but differently, according to their vocation or capacity; the function of each being assigned, like grades in a regiment, by the choice of the

[a-a]+57, 62, 65, 71
[b]52 which are now very numerous and in some cases very successful in France,

directing authority, and the remuneration being by salary, proportioned to the importance, in the eyes of that authority, of the function itself, and the merits of the person who fulfils it. For the constitution of the ruling body, different plans might be adopted, consistently with the essentials of the system. It might be appointed by popular suffrage. In the idea of the original authors, the rulers were supposed to be persons of genius and virtue, who obtained the voluntary adhesion of the rest by the force of mental superiority. That the scheme might in some peculiar states of society work with advantage, is not improbable. There is indeed a successful experiment, of a somewhat similar kind, on record, to which I have once alluded; that of the Jesuits in Paraguay. A race of savages, belonging to a portion of mankind more averse to consecutive exertion for a distant object than any other authentically known to us, was brought under the mental dominion of civilized and instructed men who were united among themselves by a system of community of goods. To the absolute authority of these men they reverentially submitted themselves, and were induced by them to learn the arts of civilized life, and to practise labours for the community, which no inducement that could have been offered would have prevailed on them to practise for themselves. This social system was of short duration, being prematurely destroyed by diplomatic arrangements and foreign force. That it could be brought into action at all was probably owing to the immense distance in point of knowledge and intellect which separated the few rulers from the whole body of the ruled, without any intermediate orders, either social or intellectual. In any other circumstances it would probably have been a complete failure. It supposes an absolute despotism in the heads of the association; which would probably not be much improved if the depositaries of the despotism (contrary to the views of the authors of the system) were varied from time to time according to the result of a popular canvass. But to suppose that one or a few human beings, howsoever selected, could, by whatever machinery of subordinate agency, be qualified to adapt each person's work to his capacity, and proportion each person's remuneration to his merits—to be, in fact, the dispensers of distributive justice to every member of a community; or that any use which they could make of this power would give general satisfaction, or would be submitted to without the aid of force—is a supposition almost too chimerical to be reasoned against. A fixed rule, like that of equality, might be acquiesced in, and so might chance, or an external necessity; but that a handful of human beings should weigh everybody in the balance, and give more to one and less to another at their sole pleasure and judgment would not be borne, unless from persons believed to be more than men, and backed by supernatural terrors.

The most skilfully combined, and with the greatest foresight of objections, of all the forms of Socialism, is that commonly known as Fourierism. This system does not contemplate the abolition of private property, nor even of inheritance; on the contrary, it avowedly takes into consideration, as an element in the distribution of the produce, capital as well as labour. It proposes that the operations of industry should be carried on by associations of about two thousand members, combining their labour on a district of about a square league in extent, under the guidance of chiefs selected by themselves. In the distribution, a certain minimum is first assigned for the subsistence of every member of the community, whether capable or not of labour. The remainder of the produce is shared in certain proportions, to be determined beforehand, among the three elements, Labour, Capital, and Talent. The capital of the community may be owned in unequal shares by different members, who would in that case receive, as in any other joint-stock company, proportional dividends. The claim of each person on the share of the produce apportioned to talent, is estimated by the grade or rank which the individual occupies in the several groups of labourers to which he or she belongs; these grades being in all cases conferred by the choice of his or her companions. The remuneration, when received, would not of necessity be expended or enjoyed in common; there would be separate *ménages* for all who preferred them, and no other community of living is contemplated, than that all the members of the association should reside in the same pile of buildings; for saving of labour and expense, not only in building, but in every branch of domestic economy; and in order that, the whole [c]of the[c] buying and selling operations of the community being performed by a single agent, the enormous portion of the produce of industry now carried off by the profits of mere distributors might be reduced to the smallest amount possible.

This system, unlike Communism, does not, in theory at least, withdraw any of the motives to exertion which exist in the present state of society. On the contrary, if the arrangement worked according to the intentions of its contrivers, it would even strengthen those motives; since each person would have much more certainty of reaping individually the fruits of increased skill or energy, bodily or mental, than under the present social arrangements can be felt by any but those who are in the most advantageous positions, or to whom the chapter of accidents is more than ordinarily favourable. The Fourierists, however, have still another resource. They believe that they have solved the great and fundamental problem of rendering labour attractive. That this is not impracticable, they contend by very strong arguments; in particular by one which they have in common with the Owenites, viz., that scarcely any labour, however severe, undergone by human beings for the sake of subsistence, exceeds in intensity that which

[c-c]+65, 71

other human beings, whose subsistence is already provided for, are found ready and even eager to undergo for pleasure. This certainly is a most significant fact, and one from which the student in social philosophy may draw important instruction. But the argument founded on it may easily be stretched too far. If occupations full of discomfort and fatigue are freely pursued by many persons as amusements, who does not see that they are amusements exactly because they are pursued freely, and may be discontinued at pleasure? The liberty of quitting a position often makes the whole difference between its being painful and pleasurable. Many a person remains in the same town, street, or house from January to December, without a wish or a thought tending towards removal, who, if confined to that same place by the mandate of authority, would find the imprisonment absolutely intolerable.

According to the Fourierists, scarcely any kind of useful labour is naturally and necessarily disagreeable, unless it is either regarded as dishonourable, or is immoderate in degree, or destitute of the stimulus of sympathy and emulation. Excessive toil needs not, they contend, be undergone by any one, in a society in which there would be no idle class, and no labour wasted, as so enormous an amount of labour is now wasted, in useless things; and where full advantage would be taken of the power of association, both in increasing the efficiency of production, and in economizing consumption. The other requisites for rendering labour attractive would, they think, be found in the execution of all labour by social groups, to any number of which the same individual might simultaneously belong, at his or her own choice: their grade in each being determined by the degree of service which they were found capable of rendering, as appreciated by the suffrages of their comrades. It is inferred from the diversity of tastes and talents, that every member of the community would be attached to several groups, employing themselves in various kinds of occupation, some bodily, others mental, and would be capable of occupying a high place in some one or more; so that a real equality, or something more nearly approaching to it than might at first be supposed, would practically result: not, from the compression, but, on the contrary, from the largest possible development, of the various natural superiorities residing in each individual.

Even from so brief an outline, it must be evident that this system does no violence to any of the general laws by which human action, even in the present imperfect state of moral and intellectual cultivation, is influenced; and that it would be extremely rash to pronounce it incapable of success, or unfitted to realize a great part of the hopes founded on it by its partisans. With regard to this, as to all other varieties of Socialism, the thing to be desired, and to which they have a just claim, is opportunity of trial. They are all capable of being tried on a moderate scale, and at no risk, either personal or pecuniary, to any except those who try them. It is for experience to determine how far or how soon any one or more of the possible systems of community of property will be fitted to substitute itself for the "organization of industry" based on private ownership of land and capital. In the meantime we may, without attempting to limit the ultimate capabilities of human nature, affirm, that the political economist, for a considerable time to come, will be chiefly concerned with the conditions of existence and progress belonging to a society founded on private property and individual competition; and that the object to be principally aimed at in the present stage of human improvement, is not the subversion of the system of individual property, but the improvement of it, and the full participation of every member of the community in its benefits.

CHAPTER II

The Same Subject Continued

§ 1. [*The institution of property implies freedom of acquisition by contract*] It is next to be considered, what is included in the idea of private property, and by what considerations the [a]application[a] of the principle [b]should be[b] bounded.

The institution of property, [c]when limited[c] to its essential elements, consists in the recognition, in each person, of a right to the exclusive disposal of what he or she have produced by their own exertions, or received [d]either[d] by gift or [e]by[e] fair agreement, without force or fraud, from those who produced it. The foundation of the whole is, the right of producers to what they themselves have produced. It may be objected, therefore, [f]to the institution as it now exists, that it[f] recognises rights of property in individuals over things which they have not produced. For example (it may be said) the operatives in a manufactory create, by their labour and skill, the whole produce; yet, instead of its belonging to them, the law gives them only their stipulated hire, and transfers the produce to some one who has merely supplied the funds, without perhaps contributing anything to the work itself, even in the form of superintendence. The answer to this is, that the labour of manufacture is only one of the conditions which must combine for the production of the commodity. The labour cannot be carried on without materials and machinery, nor without a stock of necessaries provided in advance, to maintain the labourers during the production. All these things are the fruits of previous labour. If the labourers were possessed of them, they would not need to divide the produce with any one; but [g]while[g] they have them not, an equivalent must be given to those who have, both for the antecedent labour, and for the abstinence by which the produce of that labour, instead of being expended on indulgences, has been reserved for this use. The capital may not have been, and in most

[a-a]MS, 48, 49 applicability
[b-b]MS, 48, 49 is
[c-c]MS, 48, 49 reduced
[d-d]+52, 57, 62, 65, 71
[e-e]+52, 57, 62, 65, 71
[f-f]MS, 48, 49, 52, 57 that the institution as it now exists,
[g-g]MS, 48, 49 since

cases was not, created by the labour and abstinence of the present possessor; but it was created by the labour and abstinence of some former person, who [h]may indeed have been wrongfully dispossessed of it, but who, in the present age of the world, much more probably transferred his claims to the present capitalist by gift or voluntary contract:[h] and the abstinence at least must have been continued by each successive owner, down to the present. [i]If it be said, as it may with truth, that those who have inherited the savings of others have an advantage which they may have in no way deserved, over the industrious whose predecessors have not left them anything; I not only admit, but strenuously contend, that this unearned advantage should be curtailed, as much as is consistent with justice to those who thought fit to dispose of their savings by giving them to their descendants. But while it is true that the labourers are at a disadvantage compared with those whose predecessors have saved, it is also true that the labourers are far better off than if those predecessors had not saved. They share in the advantage, though not to an equal extent with the inheritors.[i] The terms of co-operation between present labour and the fruits of past labour [j]and saving[j], are a subject for adjustment between the two parties. Each is necessary to the other. The [k]capitalists[k] can do nothing without labourers, nor the labourers without capital. [l] If the labourers compete for employment, the capitalists on their part compete for labour, to the full extent of the circulating capital of the country. [m]Competition is often spoken of as if it were necessarily a cause of misery and degradation to the labouring class; as if high wages were not precisely as much a product of competition as low wages. The remuneration of labour is as much the result of the law of competition in the United States, as it is in Ireland[n], and much more completely so than in England[n].[m]

[h-h]MS, 48, 49 , by gift or contract, transferred his claims to the present capitalist;
[i-i]+52, 57, 62, 65, 71
[j-j]+52, 57, 62, 65, 71
[k-k]MS, 48, 49, 52, 57 capitalist
[l]MS, 48, 49 It may be said, they do not meet on an equal footing: the capitalist, as the richer, can take advantage of the labourer's necessities, and make his conditions as he pleases. He could do so, undoubtedly, if he were but one. The capitalists collectively could do so, if they were not too numerous to combine, and act as a body. But, as things are, they have no such advantage. Where combination is impossible, the terms of the contract depend on competition, that is, on the amount of capital which the collective abstinence of society has provided, compared with the number of the labourers.

[m-m]MS, 48 A joint administration on account of the state, would not make the fund go further, or afford better terms to the labourers, unless either by enforcing, on the society collectively, greater abstinence, or by limiting more strictly the number of the labouring population. It is impossible to increase the quotient that falls to the share of each labourer, without either augmenting the dividend, or diminishing the divisor.

[n-n]+52, 57, 62, 65, 71

The right of property includes then, the freedom of acquiring by contract. The right of each to what he has produced, implies a right to what has been produced by others, if obtained by their free consent [o]; since the producers must either have given it from good will, or exchanged it for what they esteemed an equivalent, and to prevent them from doing so would be to infringe their right of property in the product of their own industry.

§ 2. [*The institution of property implies the validity of prescription*] Before proceeding to consider the things which the principle of individual property does [a]not[a] include, we must specify one more thing which it does include: and this is that a title, after a certain period, should be given by prescription. According to the fundamental idea of property, indeed, nothing ought to be treated as such, which has been acquired by force or fraud, or appropriated in ignorance of a prior title vested in some other person; but it is necessary to the security of rightful possessors, that they should not be molested by charges of wrongful acquisition, when by the lapse of time witnesses must have perished or been lost sight of, and the real character of the transaction can no longer be cleared up. Possession which has not been legally questioned within a moderate number of years, ought to be, as by the laws of all nations it is, a complete title. Even when the acquisition was wrongful, the dispossession, after a generation has elapsed, of the probably *bonâ fide* possessors, by the revival of a claim which had been long dormant, would generally be a greater injustice, and almost always a greater private and public mischief, than leaving the original wrong without atonement. It may seem hard that a claim, originally just, should be defeated by mere lapse of time; but there is a time after which (even looking at the individual case, and without regard to the general effect on the security of possessors), the balance of hardship turns the other way. With the injustices of men, as with the convulsions and disasters of nature, the longer they remain unrepaired, the greater become the obstacles to repairing them, arising from the aftergrowths which would have to be torn up or broken through. In no human transactions, not even in the simplest and clearest, does it follow that a thing is fit to be done now, because it was fit to be done sixty years ago. It is scarcely needful to remark, that these reasons for not disturbing acts of injustice of old date, cannot apply to unjust systems or institutions; since a bad law or usage is not one bad act, in the remote past, but a perpetual repetition of bad acts[b], as[b] long as the law or usage lasts.

Such, then, being the essentials of private property, it is now to be considered, to what extent the forms in which the institution has existed in

[o]MS, 48, 49 , and without fraud
[a-a]MS, 48, 49 *not*
[b-b]MS so

different states of society, or still exists, are necessary consequences of its principle, or are recommended by the reasons on which it is grounded.

§ 3. [*The institution of property implies the power of bequest, but not the right of inheritance. Question of inheritance examined*] Nothing is implied in property but the right of each to his [a](or her)[a] own faculties, to what he can produce by them, and to whatever he can get for them in a fair market; together with his right to give this to [b]any other[b] person if he chooses, and the right of that other to receive and enjoy it.

It follows, therefore, that although the right of bequest, or gift after death, forms part of the idea of private property, the right of inheritance, as distinguished from bequest, does not. That the property of [c]persons who have[c] made no disposition of it during [d]their[d] lifetime, should pass first to [e]their[e] children, and failing them, to [f]the[f] nearest relations, may be a proper arrangement or not, but is no consequence of the principle of private property. Although there belong to the decision of such questions many considerations besides those of political economy, it is not foreign to the plan of this work to suggest, for the judgment of thinkers, the view of them which most recommends itself to the writer's mind.

No presumption in favour of existing ideas on this subject is to be derived from their antiquity. In early ages, the property of a deceased person passed to his children and nearest relatives by so natural and obvious an arrangement, that no other [g]was likely to be even[g] thought of in competition with it. In the first place, they were usually present on the spot: they were in possession, and if they had no other title, had that, so important in an early state of society, of first occupancy. Secondly, they were already, in a manner, joint owners of his property during his life. If the property was in land, it had generally been conferred by the State on a family rather than on an individual: if it consisted of cattle or moveable goods, it had probably been acquired, and was certainly protected and defended, by the united efforts of all members of the family who were of an age to work or fight. Exclusive individual property in the modern sense, scarcely entered into the ideas of the time; and when the first magistrate of the association died, he really left nothing vacant but his own share in the division, which devolved on the member of the family who succeeded to his authority. To have disposed of the property otherwise, would have been to break up a little commonwealth, united by ideas, interest, and habits, and to cast them adrift on the world. These considerations, though rather felt than reasoned about, had so great an influence on the minds of man-

[a-a]+52, 57, 62, 65, 71
[b-b]MS, 48, 49 another
[c-c]MS, 48, 49 a person who has
[d-d]MS, 48, 49 his
[e-e]MS, 48, 49 his
[f-f]MS, 48, 49 his
[g-g]MS, 48, 49 could ever have been

kind, as to create the idea of an inherent right in the children to the possessions of their ancestor; a right which it was not competent to himself to defeat. Bequest, in a primitive state of society, was seldom recognised; a clear proof, were there no other, that property was conceived in a manner totally different from the conception of it in the present time.*

But the feudal family, the last historical form of patriarchal life, has long perished, and the unit of society is not now the family or clan, composed of all the reputed descendants of a common ancestor, but the individual; or at most a pair of individuals, with their unemancipated children. Property is now inherent in individuals, not in families: the children when grown up do not follow the occupations or fortunes of the parent: if they participate in [h]the parent's[h] pecuniary means it is at his [i]or her[i] pleasure, and not by a voice in the ownership and government of the whole, but generally by the exclusive enjoyment of a part; and in this country at least (except as far as entails or [j] settlements are an obstacle) it is in [k]the power of parents[k] to disinherit even [l]their[l] children, and leave [m]their[m] fortune to strangers. More distant relatives are in general almost as completely detached from the family and its interests as if they were in no way connected with it. [n]The[n] only claim they are supposed to have on their richer relations, is to a preference, *cæteris paribus*, in good offices, and some aid [o] in case of actual necessity.

So great a change in the constitution of society must make a considerable difference in the grounds on which the disposal of property by inheritance should rest. The reasons usually assigned by modern writers for giving the property of a person who dies intestate, to the children, or nearest relatives, are, first, the supposition that in so disposing of it, the law is more likely than in any other mode to do what the proprietor [p] would have done, if he had done anything; and secondly, the hardship, to those who lived with their [q]parents[q] and partook in [r]their[r] opulence, of being cast down from the enjoyments of wealth into poverty and privation.

There is [s]some[s] force in both these arguments. The law [t]ought, no doubt,[t] to do for the children or dependents of an intestate, whatever it was the

*[62] See, for admirable illustrations of this and many kindred points, Mr. Maine's profound work on Ancient Law and its relation to Modern Ideas [Maine, Henry J. S. *Ancient Law: its Connection with the Early History of Society, and its Relation to Modern Ideas.* London: Murray, 1861].

[h-h]MS, 48, 49 his
[i-i]+52, 57, 62, 65, 71
[j]MS, 48, 49, 52, 57 other
[k-k]MS, 48, 49 his power
[l-l]MS, 48, 49 his
[m-m]MS, 48, 49 his
[n-n]MS Except on failure of children, the
[o]MS in money or money's worth
[p]MS, 48, 49 himself
[q-q]MS, 48, 49 parent
[r-r]MS, 48, 49 his
[s-s]+52, 57, 62, 65, 71
[t-t]MS, 48, 49 certainly ought

duty of the parent or protector to have done, [u]so far as this can be known by any one besides himself. Since, however, the law cannot decide on individual claims, but must proceed by general rules, it is next to be considered what these rules should be[u].

We may first remark, that in regard to collateral [v]relatives[v], it is not, unless [w]on grounds personal to the particular individual[w], the duty of any one to make a pecuniary provision for them. No one now expects it, unless there happen to be no direct heirs; nor would it be expected even then, if the expectation were not created by the [x]provisions of the law in case of intestacy[x]. I see, therefore, no reason why collateral inheritance should exist at all. Mr. Bentham long ago proposed, and other high authorities have agreed in the opinion, that if there are no heirs either in the descending or in the ascending line, the property, in case of intestacy, should escheat to the State. [y]With respect to the more remote degrees of collateral relationship, the point is not very likely to be disputed. Few will maintain that there is any[y] good reason why the accumulations of some childless miser should on his death (as every now and then happens) go to enrich a distant relative who never saw him, who perhaps never knew himself to be related to him until there was something to be gained by it, and who had no moral claim upon him of any kind, more than the most entire stranger. [z]But the reason of the case applies alike to all collaterals, even in the nearest degree. Collaterals have no real claims, but [a]such as may be equally[a] strong in the case of non-relatives; and in the one case as in the other, where [b]valid[b] claims exist, the proper mode of paying regard to them is by bequest.[z]

The claims of children are of a different nature: they are real, and indefeasible. But even of these, I venture to think that the measure usually

[u-u]MS, 48, 49 but from accident or negligence or worse causes he failed to do. Whether it would be possible, by means of a public administrator of intestate estates, to take cognizance of special claims and see justice done in detail, is a question of some difficulty into which I forbear to enter. I shall only consider what might with best reason be laid down as a general rule

[v-v]MS, 48, 49, 52 relations

[w-w]MS, 48, 49 from special and peculiar causes

[x-x]MS law

[y-y]MS, 48, 49 There is no

[z-z]MS, 48, 49 Where collaterals have real claims, those claims are personal, and the proper mode of paying regard to them is by bequest. That duty may be neglected, but is not more likely to be so in the case of relatives than of strangers, who may have just as strong claims of the same nature. If any near relatives, known to be such, were in a state of indigence, a donation, or a small pension, according to circumstances, might, in case of intestacy, be assigned to them when the State appropriated the inheritance. This would be a justice, or a generosity, which they do not experience from the present law, since that gives all to the nearest collaterals, however great may be the necessities of those more distant.

[a-a]52 in cases which may be just as

[b-b]+57, 62, 65, 71

taken is an erroneous one: what is due to children is in some respects underrated, in others, as it appears to me, exaggerated. One of the most binding of all obligations, that of not bringing children into the world unless they can be maintained in comfort [c]during childhood[c], and brought up with a likelihood of [d]supporting themselves when of full age[d], is both disregarded in practice and made light of in theory in a manner disgraceful to human intelligence. On the other hand, when the parent possesses property, the claims of the children upon it seem to me to be the subject of an opposite error. Whatever fortune a parent may have inherited, or still more, may have acquired, I cannot admit that he owes to his children, merely because they are his children, to leave them rich, without the necessity of any exertion. I could not admit it, even if to be so left were always, and certainly, for the good of the children themselves. But this is in the highest degree uncertain. It depends on individual character. Without supposing extreme cases, it may be affirmed that in a majority of instances the good not only of society but of the individuals would be better consulted by bequeathing to them a moderate, than a large provision. This, which is a commonplace of moralists ancient and modern, is felt to be true by many intelligent parents, and would be acted upon much more frequently, if they did not allow themselves to consider less what really is, than what will be thought by others to be, advantageous to the children.

The duties of parents to their children are those which are indissolubly attached to the fact of causing the existence of a human being. The parent owes to society to endeavour to make the child a good and valuable member of it, and owes to [e]the[e] children to provide, so far as depends on him, such education, and such appliances and means, as will enable them to start with a fair chance of [f]achieving by their own exertions[f] a successful life. To this every child has a claim; and I cannot admit, that as a child he has a claim to more. There is a case in which these obligations present themselves [g]in their true light[g], without any extrinsic circumstances to disguise or confuse them: it is that of [h] an illegitimate child. To such a child it is generally felt that there is due from the parent, the amount of provision for his welfare which will [i]enable him to make his life on the whole[i] a desirable one. I hold that to no child, merely as such, anything more is due, than what is admitted to be due to an illegitimate child: and that no child for whom thus much has been done, has, unless on the score of previously raised expectations, any grievance, if the remainder of the parent's fortune is devoted to

[c-c]+52, 57, 62, 65, 71
[d-d]MS, 48, 49 its continuance
[e-e]MS, 48, 49 his
[f-f]+52, 57, 62, 65, 71
[g-g]MS, 48, 49 nakedly
[h]MS the father of
[i-i]MS make him feel the gift of life to have been

public uses, or to the benefit of individuals on whom in the parent's opinion it is better bestowed.

In order to give the children that fair chance of a desirable existence, to which they are entitled, it is generally necessary that they should not be brought up from childhood in habits of luxury which they will not have the means of indulging in after-life. This, again, is a duty often flagrantly violated by possessors of terminable incomes, who have little property to leave. When the children of rich parents have lived, as [j] it is natural they should do, in habits corresponding to the scale of expenditure in which the parents indulge, it is generally the duty of the parents to make a greater provision for them, than would suffice for children otherwise brought up. I say generally, because even here there is another side to the question. It is a proposition quite capable of being maintained, that to a strong nature which has to make its way against narrow circumstances, to have known early some of the feelings and experiences of wealth, is [k] an advantage both in the formation of character and in the happiness of life. But [l]allowing[l] that children have a just ground of complaint, who have been brought up [m]to require luxuries which they are not afterwards likely to obtain, and that their[m] claim, therefore, is good to a provision bearing some relation to the mode of their bringing up[n]; this[n], too, is a claim which [o] is particularly liable to be stretched further than its reasons warrant. The case is exactly that of the younger children of the nobility and landed gentry, the bulk of whose fortune passes to the eldest son. The other sons, who are usually numerous, are brought up in the same habits of luxury as the future heir, and they receive as a younger brother's portion, generally what the reason of the case dictates, namely, enough to support, in the habits of life to which they are accustomed, themselves, but not a wife [p]or[p] children. It really is no grievance to any man, that for the means of marrying and of supporting a family, he has to depend on his own exertions.

A provision, then, such as is admitted to be reasonable in the case of illegitimate children, [q]for[q] younger children, wherever in short the justice of the case, and the real interests of the individuals and of society, are the only things considered, is, I conceive, all that parents owe to their children, and all, therefore, which the State owes to the children of those who die intestate. The surplus, if any, I hold that it may rightfully appro-

[j]MS, 48, 49 to a certain degree
[k]MS, 48, 49 on the whole
[l-l]MS, 48, 49 ordinary rules of conduct are not framed to suit strong natures, and it is mostly true,
[m-m]MS, 48, 49 more luxuriously than they are afterwards enabled to live. Their
[n-n]MS, 48, 49 . But this
[o]MS, 48, 49 , though just in itself,
[p-p]MS, 48, 49 and
[q-q]MS, 48, 49, 52, 57, 62, 65 of

priate to the general purposes of the community. I would not, however, [r] be supposed to recommend that parents should [s]never[s] do more for their children than what, merely as children, they have a moral right to. In some cases it is imperative, in many laudable, and in all allowable, to do much more. For this, however, the means are afforded by the liberty of bequest. It is due, not to the children but to the parents, that they should have the power of showing marks of affection, of requiting services and sacrifices, and of bestowing their wealth according to their own preferences, or their own judgment of fitness.

§ 4. [*Should the right of bequest be limited, and how?*] Whether the power of bequest should itself be subject to limitation, is an ulterior question of [a]great[a] importance. Unlike inheritance *ab intestato*, bequest is one of the attributes of property: the ownership of a thing cannot be looked upon as complete without the power of bestowing it, at death or during life, at the owner's pleasure: and all the reasons, which recommend that private property should exist, recommend *pro tanto* this extension of it. But property is only a means to an end, not itself the end. Like all other proprietary rights, and even in a greater degree than most, the power of bequest [b]may be so exercised as to conflict with the permanent interests of the human race[b]. It does so, when, not content with bequeathing an estate to A, the testator prescribes that on A's death it shall pass to his eldest son, and to that son's son, and so on for ever. No doubt, persons have occasionally exerted themselves more strenuously to acquire a fortune from the hope of founding a family in perpetuity; but the mischiefs to society of such perpetuities outweigh the value of this incentive to exertion, and the incentives in the case of those who have the opportunity of making large fortunes are strong enough without it. A similar abuse of the power of bequest is committed when a person who does the meritorious act of leaving property for public uses, attempts to prescribe the details of its application in perpetuity; when in founding a place of education (for instance) he dictates, for ever, what doctrines shall be taught. It being impossible that any one should know what doctrines will be fit to be taught after he has been dead for centuries, the law ought [c]not[c] to give effect to such dispositions of property, [d]unless[d] subject to the perpetual revision (after a certain interval has elapsed) of a fitting authority.

These are obvious limitations. But even the simplest exercise of the right

[r]MS, 48, 49 be so far misunderstood as to
[s-s]MS, 48, 49 not
[a-a]MS, 48, 49 no little
[b-b]MS, 48, 49 is liable to conflict with objects still more important
[c-c]MS only
[d-d]+48, 49, 52, 57, 62, 65, 71

of bequest, that of determining the person to whom property shall pass immediately on the death of the testator, has always been reckoned among the privileges which might be limited or varied, according to views of expediency. The limitations, hitherto, have been almost solely in favour of children. In England the right is in principle unlimited, almost the only impediment being that arising from a settlement by a former proprietor, in which case the holder for the time [e]being[e] cannot indeed bequeath his possessions, but only because there is nothing to bequeath, he having merely a life interest. By the Roman law, on which the civil legislation of the Continent of Europe is principally founded, bequest originally was not permitted at all, and even after it was introduced, a *legitima portio* was compulsorily reserved for each child; and such is still the law in some of the Continental nations. By the French law since the Revolution, the parent can only dispose by will, of a portion equal to the share of one child, each of the children taking an equal portion. This entail, as it may be called, of the bulk of every one's property upon the children collectively, seems to me as little defensible in principle as an entail in favour of one child, though it does not shock so directly the [f]idea[f] of justice. [g]I cannot admit that parents should be compelled[g] to leave to their children even that provision which, as children, I have contended that they have a moral claim to. Children may forfeit that claim by general unworthiness, or particular ill-conduct to the parents: they may have other resources or prospects: what has been previously done for them, in the way of education and advancement in life, may fully satisfy their moral claim; or others may have claims superior to theirs. [h]

The extreme restriction of the power of bequest in French law, was adopted as a democratic expedient, to break down the custom of primogeniture, and counteract the tendency of inherited property to collect in large masses. I agree in thinking these objects eminently desirable; but the means used are not, I think, the most judicious. Were I framing a code of laws according to what seems to me best in itself, without regard to exist-

[e-e]+62, 65, 71

[f-f]MS, 48, 49 sentiment

[g-g]MS There are strong reasons against compelling parents] 48, 49 It is questionable whether parents . . . *as* 71

[h]MS If they are of age and strength to provide, however humbly, for themselves, the maintenance of some authority in the parent by the power of disinheriting, is probably on the whole the most expedient, as, when the property was acquired by the parent's own exertions, it is unquestionably the most just. But however the case may be as to a mere provision, I hold that justice and expediency are wholly against compelling anything beyond. That a person should be certain from childhood of succeeding to a large fortune independently of the good will and affection of any human being, is, unless under very favourable influences of other kinds, almost a fatal circumstance in his education.] 48, 49 *as* MS . . . is perhaps expedient. But . . . *as* MS

ing opinions and sentiments, I should prefer to restrict, not what any one might bequeath, but what any one should be permitted to acquire, by bequest or inheritance. Each person should have power to dispose by will of his [i]or her[i] whole property; but not to lavish it in enriching some one individual, beyond a certain maximum, which should be fixed sufficiently high to afford the means of comfortable independence. The inequalities of property which arise from unequal industry, frugality, perseverance, talents, and [j]to a certain extent[j] even opportunities, are inseparable from the principle of private property, and if we accept the principle, we must bear with these consequences of it: but I see nothing objectionable in fixing a limit to what any one may acquire by the mere favour of others, without any exercise of his faculties, and in requiring that if he desires any further accession of fortune, he shall work for it.* I do not conceive that the degree of limitation which this would impose on the right of bequest, would be felt as a burthensome restraint by any testator who estimated a large fortune at its true value, that of the pleasures and advantages that can be purchased with it: on even the most extravagant estimate of which, it must be apparent to every one, that the difference to the happiness of the possessor between a moderate independence and five times as much, is insignificant when weighed against the enjoyment that might be given, and the permanent benefits diffused, by some other disposal of the four-fifths. So long indeed as the opinion practically prevails, that the best thing which can be done for [k]objects[k] of affection is to heap on [l]them[l] to satiety [m]those intrinsically worthless things on which large fortunes are mostly expended[m], there might be little use in enacting such a law, even if it were possible to get it passed, since if there were the inclination, there would generally be the power of evading it. The law would be unavailing unless the popular sentiment went energetically along with it; which (judging from the tenacious adherence of public opinion in France to the law of compulsory division) it would

*[65] In the case of capital employed, in the hands of the owner himself, in carrying on any of the operations of industry, there are strong grounds for leaving to him the power of bequeathing to one person the whole of the funds actually engaged in a single enterprise. It is well that he should be enabled to leave the enterprise under the control of whichever of his heirs he regards as best fitted to conduct it virtuously and efficiently: and the necessity (very frequent and inconvenient under the French law) would be thus obviated, of breaking up a manufacturing or commercial establishment at the death of its chief. In like manner, it should be allowed to a proprietor who leaves to one of his successors the moral burthen of keeping up an ancestral mansion and park or pleasure-ground, to bestow along with them as much other property as is required for their sufficient maintenance.

[i-i]+52, 57, 62, 65, 71
[j-j]+52, 57, 62, 65, 71
[k-k]MS, 48, 49 an object
[l-l]MS, 48, 49 him
[m-m]MS, 48, 49 all the external good things of life

in some states of society and government be very likely to do, however much the contrary may be the fact in England and at the present time. If the restriction could be made practically effectual, the benefit would be great. Wealth which could no longer be employed in [n]over-[n]enriching a few, would either be devoted to objects of public usefulness, or if bestowed on individuals, would be distributed among a larger number. While those enormous fortunes which no one needs for any [o]personal[o] purpose but ostentation or improper power, would become much less numerous, there would be a great multiplication of [p]persons[p] in easy circumstances, with the advantages of leisure, and all the real enjoyments which wealth can give, except those of vanity; a class by whom the services which a nation [q]having leisured classes is entitled to expect from them[q], either by their direct exertions or by the tone they give to the feelings and tastes of the public, would be rendered in a much more beneficial manner than at present. A large portion also of the accumulations of successful industry would probably be devoted to public uses, either by direct bequests to the State, or by the endowment of institutions; as is already done very largely in the United States, where the ideas and practice in the matter of inheritance seem to be unusually rational and beneficial.*

§ 5. [*Grounds of property in land are different from those of property in moveables*] The next point to be considered is, whether the reasons on which the institution of property rests, are applicable to all things in which

*"Munificent bequests and donations for public purposes, whether charitable or educational, form a striking feature in the modern history of the United States, and especially of New England. Not only is it common for rich capitalists to leave by will a portion of their fortune towards the endowment of national institutions, but individuals during their lifetime make magnificent grants of money for the same objects. There is here no compulsory law for the equal partition of property among children, as in France, and on the other hand, no custom of entail or primogeniture, as in England, so that the affluent feel themselves at liberty to share their wealth between their kindred and the public; it being impossible to found a family, and parents having frequently the happiness of seeing all their children well provided for and independent long before their death. I have seen a list of bequests and donations made during the last thirty years for the benefit of religious, charitable, and literary institutions in the state of Massachusetts alone, and they amounted to no less a sum than six millions of dollars, or more than a million sterling."—Lyell's *Travels in America*, vol. i. p. 263 [–64].

[52] In England, whoever leaves anything beyond trifling legacies for public or beneficent objects when he has any near relatives living, does so at the risk of being declared insane by a jury after his death, or at the least, of having the property wasted in a Chancery suit to set aside the will.

[n-n]+52, 57, 62, 65, 71   [o-o]+49, 52, 57, 62, 65, 71   [p-p]MS, 48, 49 families
[q-q]MS, 48, 49 is entitled to expect from its leisured classes

a right of exclusive ownership is at present recognised; and if not, on what other grounds the recognition is defensible.

The essential principle of property being to assure to all persons what they have produced by their labour and accumulated by their abstinence, this principle cannot apply to what is not the produce of labour, the raw material of the earth. If the land derived its productive power wholly from nature, and not at all from industry, or if there were any means of discriminating what is derived from each source, it not only would not be necessary, but it would be the height of injustice, to let the gift of nature be engrossed by [a]individuals[a]. The use of the land in agriculture must indeed, for the time being, be of necessity exclusive; the same person who has ploughed and sown must be permitted to reap: but the land might be occupied [b]for one season only[b], as among the ancient Germans; or might be periodically redivided as population increased: or the State might be the universal landlord, and the cultivators tenants under it, either on lease or at will.

But though land is not the produce of industry, most of its valuable qualities are so. Labour is not only requisite for using, but almost equally so for fashioning, the instrument. Considerable labour is often required at the commencement, to clear the land for cultivation. In many cases, even when cleared, its productiveness is wholly the effect of labour and art. The Bedford Level produced little or nothing until artificially drained. The bogs of Ireland, until the same thing is done to them, can produce little besides fuel. One of the barrenest soils in the world, composed of the material of the Goodwin Sands, the Pays de Waes in Flanders, has been so fertilized by industry, as to have become one of the most productive in Europe. Cultivation also requires buildings and fences, which are wholly the produce of labour. The fruits of this industry cannot be reaped in a short period. The labour and outlay are immediate, the benefit is spread over many years, perhaps over all future time. A holder will not incur this labour and outlay when [c]strangers[c] and not himself will be benefited by it. If he undertakes such improvements, he must have a [d]sufficient[d] period before him in which to profit by them: and [e]he is in no way so sure of having always a sufficient period as when his tenure is[e] perpetual.*

*"Ce qui donnait à l'homme l'intelligence et la constance dans ses travaux, qui [48 ce qui] lui faisait diriger tous ses efforts vers un but utile à sa race, c'était le sentiment de la perpétuité. Les terrains les plus fertiles sont toujours ceux que les eaux ont déposés le long de leur cours, mais ce sont aussi ceux

[a-a]MS, 48, 49 a few
[b-b]MS in turns
[c-c]MS, 48, 49, 52 his successors
[d-d]MS, 48, 49 long
[e-e]MS, 48, 49 he cannot continue always to have a long time before him, unless his tenure is] 52, 57 in order that he may be sure of having always a sufficient period, it has been thought necessary that his tenure should be

§ 6. [*Grounds of property in land are only valid on certain conditions, which are not always realized. The limitations considered*] These are the reasons which form the justification in an economical point of view, of property in land. It is seen, that they are only valid, in so far as the proprietor of land is its improver. Whenever, in any country, the proprietor, generally speaking, ceases to be the improver, political economy has nothing to say in defence of landed property, as there established. In no sound theory of private property was it ever contemplated that the proprietor of land should be merely a sinecurist quartered on it.

In Great Britain, the landed proprietor is not unfrequently an improver. But it cannot be said that he is generally so. And in the majority of cases he grants the liberty of cultivation on such terms, as to prevent improvements from being made by any one else. In the southern parts of the island, as there are usually no leases, permanent improvements can scarcely be made except by the landlord's capital; accordingly the South, compared with the North of England, and with the Lowlands of Scotland, is [a]still[a] extremely backward in agricultural improvement. The truth is, that any very general improvement of land by the landlords, is hardly compatible with

---

qu'elles menacent de leurs inondations ou qu'elles corrompent par des marécages. Avec la garantie de la perpétuité, l'homme entreprit de longs et pénibles travaux pour donner aux marécages un écoulement, pour élever des digues contre les inondations, pour répartir par des canaux d'arrosement des eaux fertilisantes sur les mêmes champs que les mêmes eaux condamnaient à la stérilité. Sous la même garantie, l'homme, ne se contentant plus des fruits annuels de la terre, a démêlé parmi la végétation sauvage les plantes vivaces, les arbustes, les arbres qui pouvaient lui être utiles, il les a perfectionnés par la culture, il a changé en quelque sorte leur essence, et il les a multipliés. Parmi les fruits, en effet, on en reconnaît que des siècles de culture ont seuls pu amener à la perfection qu'ils ont atteinte aujourd'hui, tandis que d'autres ont été importés des régions les plus lointaines. L'homme en même temps a ouvert la terre jusqu'à une grande profondeur, pour renouveler son sol, et le fertiliser par le mélange de ses parties et les impressions de l'air; il a fixé sur les collines la terre qui s'en échappait, et il a couvert la face entière de la campagne d'une végétation partout abondante, et partout utile à la race humaine. Parmi ses travaux, il y en a dont il ne recueillera le fruit qu'au bout de dix ou de vingt ans; il y en a d'autres dont ses derniers neveux jouiront encore dans plusieurs siècles. Tous ont concouru à augmenter la force productive de la nature, à donner à la race humaine un revenu infiniment plus abondant, un revenu dont une portion considérable est consommée par ceux qui n'ont point part à la propriété territoriale, et qui cependant n'auraient point trouvé de nourriture sans ce partage du sol qui semble les avoir deshérités."—Sismondi, *Etude sur l'Economie Politique*, Troisième Essai, De la Richesse Territoriale [Sismondi, J. C. L. Simonde de. *Etudes sur l'économie politique*. Tome premier. Paris: Treuttel et Würtz, 1837, pp. 165–7].

[a-a]+62, 65, 71

[b]a law or[b] custom of primogeniture. When the land goes wholly to the heir, it generally goes to him severed from the pecuniary resources which would enable him to improve it, the personal property being absorbed by the provision for younger children, and the land itself often heavily burthened for the same purpose. There is therefore but a small proportion of landlords who have the means of making expensive improvements, unless they do it with borrowed money, and by adding to the mortgages with which in most cases the land was already burthened when they received it. But the position of the owner of a deeply mortgaged estate is so precarious; economy is so unwelcome to one whose apparent fortune greatly exceeds his real means, and the vicissitudes of rent and price which only trench upon the margin of his income, are so formidable to one who can call little more than [c]the[c] margin his own, that it is no wonder if few landlords find themselves in a condition to make immediate sacrifices for the sake of future profit. Were they ever so much inclined, those alone can prudently do it, who have seriously studied the principles of scientific agriculture: and great landlords have seldom seriously studied anything. They might at least hold out inducements to the farmers to do what they will not or cannot do themselves; but even in granting leases, it is in England a general complaint that they tie up their tenants by covenants grounded on the practices of an obsolete and exploded agriculture; while most of them, by withholding leases altogether, and giving the farmer no guarantee of possession beyond a single harvest, keep the land on a footing little more favourable to improvement than in the time of our barbarous ancestors,

——— immetata quibus jugera liberas
Fruges et Cererem ferunt,
Nec cultura placet longior annuâ.

Landed property in England is thus very far from completely fulfilling the conditions which render its existence economically justifiable. But if insufficiently realized even in England, in Ireland those conditions are not complied with at all. With individual exceptions (some of them very honourable ones), the owners of Irish estates do nothing for the land but drain it of its produce. What has been epigrammatically said in the discussions on "peculiar burthens" is literally true when applied to them; that the greatest "burthen on land" is the landlords. Returning nothing to the soil, they consume its whole produce, minus the potatoes strictly necessary to keep the inhabitants from dying of famine; and when they have any [d]purpose[d] of improvement, [e]the preparatory step usually[e] consists in not leaving even this pittance, but turning out the people to beggary if not to

[b-b]MS the law &
[c-c]MS, 48, 49 that
[d-d]MS, 48, 49 notion
[e-e]MS, 48 it] 49 it usually

starvation.* When landed property has placed itself upon this footing it ceases to be defensible, and the time has come for making some new arrangement of the matter.

When the "sacredness of property" is talked of, it should always be remembered, that [f]any such[f] sacredness does not belong in the same degree to landed property. No man made the land. It is the original inheritance of the whole species. [g]Its appropriation is wholly a question of general expediency. When private property in land is not expedient, it is unjust.[g] It is no hardship to any one, to be excluded from what others have produced: they were not bound to produce it for his use, and he loses nothing by not sharing in what otherwise would not have existed at all. But it is some hardship to be born into the world and to find all nature's gifts previously engrossed, and no place left for the new-comer. To reconcile people to this, after they have once admitted into their minds the idea that any moral rights belong to them as human beings, it will always be necessary to convince them that the exclusive appropriation is good for mankind on the whole, themselves included. But this is what no sane human being could be persuaded of if the relation between the landowner and the cultivator were the same everywhere as it [h]has been[h] in Ireland.

Landed property is felt, even by those most tenacious of its rights, to be a different thing from other property; and where the bulk of the community have been disinherited of their share of it, and it has become the exclusive attribute of a small minority, men have generally tried to reconcile it, at least in theory, to their sense of justice, by endeavouring to attach duties to it, and erecting it into a sort of magistracy, either moral or legal. But if the state is at liberty to treat the possessors of land as public functionaries, it is only going one step further to say, that it is at liberty to discard them. The claim of the landowners to the land is altogether subordinate to the general policy of the state. The principle of property gives them no right to the land, but only a right to compensation for whatever portion of their interest in the land it may be the policy of the state to deprive them of. To that, their claim is indefeasible. It is due to landowners, and to owners of any property whatever, recognised as such by the state, that they should not be dispossessed of it without receiving [i]its[i] pecuniary value,

*[62] I must beg the reader to bear in mind that this paragraph was written more than twenty [62 written fifteen] 65 written eighteen] years ago. So wonderful are the changes, both moral and economical, taking place in our age, that, without perpetually re-writing a work like the present, it is impossible to keep up with them.

[f-f]MS, 48, 49 this
[g-g]MS, 48, 49 Public reasons exist for its being appropriated. But if those reasons lost their force, the thing would be unjust.
[h-h]MS, 48, 49, 52, 57 is
[i-i]MS , at their choice, either its full] 48, 49 its full

or an annual income equal to what they derived from it. This is due on the general principles on which property rests. If the land was bought with the produce of the labour and abstinence of themselves or their ancestors, compensation is due to them on that ground; even if otherwise, it is still due on the ground of prescription. Nor can it ever be necessary for accomplishing an object by which the community altogether will gain, that a particular portion of the community should be immolated. When the property is of a kind to which peculiar affections attach themselves, the compensation ought to exceed a bare pecuniary equivalent. But, subject to this proviso, the state is at liberty to deal with landed property as the general interests of the community may require, even to the extent, if it so happen, of doing with the whole, what is done with a part whenever a bill is passed for a railroad or a new street. [j] The community has too much at stake in the proper cultivation of the land, and in the conditions annexed to the occupancy of it, to leave these things to the discretion of a class of persons called landlords, when they have shown themselves unfit for the trust. The legislature, which if it pleased might convert the whole body of landlords into fundholders or pensioners, might, *à fortiori*, commute the average receipts of Irish landowners into a fixed rent charge, and raise the tenants into proprietors; supposing always [k] that the full market value of the land was tendered to the landlords, in case they preferred that to accepting the conditions proposed.

There will be another place for discussing the various modes of landed property and tenure, and the advantages and inconveniences of each; in this chapter our concern is with the right itself, the grounds which justify it, and (as a corollary from [l]these[l]) the conditions by which it should be limited. To me it seems almost an axiom that property in land should be interpreted strictly, and that the balance in all cases of doubt should incline against the proprietor. The reverse is the case with property in moveables, and in all things the product of labour: over these, the owner's power both of use and of exclusion should be absolute, except where positive evil to [m]others[m] would result from it: but in the case of land, no exclusive right should be permitted in any individual, which cannot be

[j]MS, 48 I do not pretend that occasions can often arise in which so drastic a measure would be fit to be taken into serious consideration, or that it should be thought of as anything else than an extreme remedy, which may happen to be the only suitable one for an extreme case. But even if this ultimate prerogative of the state could never require to be actually exercised, it ought nevertheless to be asserted, because the principle which permits the greater of two things permits the less, and though to do all which the principle would sanction might never be advisable, to do much less than all not only may be so, but often is so in a very high degree.] 49 *as* MS . . . arise on which . . . consideration. But . . . state should never . . . sanction should never . . . *as* MS

[k]MS, 48, 49 (without which these acts would be nothing better than robbery)

[l–l]MS, 48, 49 those grounds

[m–m]MS, 48, 49 society

shown to be productive of positive good. To be allowed any exclusive right at all, over a portion of the common inheritance, while there are others who have no portion, is already a [n] privilege. No quantity of moveable goods which a person can acquire by his labour, prevents others from acquiring the like by the same means; but from the very nature of the case, whoever owns land, keeps [o]others out of the enjoyment of it[o]. The privilege, or monopoly, is only defensible as a necessary evil; it becomes an injustice when carried to any point to which the compensating good does not follow it.

For instance, the exclusive right to the land for purposes of cultivation does not imply an exclusive right to it for purposes of access; and no such right ought to be recognised, except to the extent necessary to protect the produce against damage, and the owner's privacy against invasion. The pretension of two Dukes to shut up a part of the Highlands, and exclude the rest of mankind from many square miles of mountain scenery to prevent disturbance to wild animals, is an abuse; it exceeds the legitimate bounds [p]of the right[p] of landed property. When land is not intended to be cultivated, no good reason can in general be given for its being private property at all; and if any [q]one[q] is permitted to call it his, he ought to know that he holds it by sufferance of the community, and on an implied condition that his ownership, since it cannot possibly do them any good, at least shall not deprive them of any, which could have derived from the land if it had been unappropriated. Even in the case of cultivated land, a man whom, though only one among millions, the law permits to hold thousands of acres as his single share, is not entitled to think that all this is given to him to use and abuse, and deal with as if it concerned nobody but himself. The rents or profits which he can obtain from it are [r]at his sole disposal[r]; but with regard to the land, in everything which he does with it, and in everything which he abstains from doing, he is morally bound, and should whenever the case admits be legally compelled, to make his interest and pleasure consistent with the public good. The species at large still retains, of its original claim to the soil of the planet which it inhabits, as much as is compatible with the purposes for which it has parted with the remainder.

§ 7. [*Rights of property in abuses*] Besides property in the produce of labour, and property in land, there are other things which are or have been subjects of property, in which no proprietary rights ought to exist at all.

[n]52, 57 questionable
[o-o]MS, 48, 49 it from somebody else
[p-p]+52, 57, 62, 65, 71
[q-q]MS, 48 man
[r-r]MS, 48, 49 his, and his only

But as the civilized world has in general made up its mind on most of these, there is no necessity for dwelling on them in this place. At the head of them, is property in human beings. It is almost superfluous to observe, that this institution can have no place in any society even pretending to be founded on justice, or on fellowship between human creatures. But, iniquitous as it is, yet when the state has expressly legalized it, and human beings, for generations, have been bought, sold, and inherited under sanction of law, it is another [a]wrong, in abolishing the property, not to make[a] full compensation. This wrong was avoided by the great measure of justice in 1833, [b]one of the most virtuous acts[b], as well as [c] the most practically beneficent, ever done collectively by a nation. Other examples of property which ought not to have been created, are properties in public trusts; such as judicial offices under the old French régime, and the heritable jurisdictions which, in countries not wholly emerged from feudality, pass with the land. Our own country affords, as cases in point, that of a commission in the army, and of an advowson, or right of nomination to an ecclesiastical benefice. A property is also sometimes created in a right of taxing the public; in a monopoly, for instance, or other exclusive privilege. These abuses prevail most in semibarbarous countries but are not without example in the most civilized. In France there are several important trades and professions, including notaries, attorneys, brokers, appraisers, printers, [d]and (until lately) bakers and butchers[d], of which the numbers are limited by law. The *brevet* or privilege of one of the permitted number consequently brings a high price in the market. [e]When such is the case[e], compensation probably could not with justice be refused, on the abolition of the privilege. There are other cases in which this would be more doubtful. The question would turn upon what, in the peculiar circumstances, was sufficient to constitute prescription; and whether the legal recognition which the abuse had obtained, was sufficient to constitute it an institution, or amounted only to an occasional licence. It would be absurd to claim compensation for losses caused by changes in a tariff, a thing confessedly variable from year to year; or for monopolies like those granted to individuals by [f]the Tudors[f], favours of a despotic authority, which the power that gave was competent at any time to recal.

[a-a]MS, 48, 49 iniquity to abolish the property without
[b-b]MS, 48, 49 probably the most virtuous act
[c]MS, 48, 49 one of
[d-d]MS, 48, 49, 52, 57 even bakers and butchers] 62 even bakers, and (until lately) butchers
[e-e]MS There is in England at least one court of justice (the Palace Court at Westminster) in which the number of barristers permitted to practise is restricted to four, who buy their places from their predecessors. In these various cases] 48, 49 *as* MS . . . England a court . . . *as* MS] 52, 57, 62 In these cases
[f-f]MS, 48, 49, 52, 57, 62 Queen Elizabeth

So much on the institution of property, a subject of which, for the purposes of political economy, it was indispensable to treat, but on which we could not usefully confine ourselves to economical considerations. We have now to inquire on what principles and with what results the distribution of the produce of land and labour is effected, under the relations which this institution creates among the different members of the community. [g]

[g]MS [*paragraph*] This will be the object of the ensuing chapters.

CHAPTER III

Of the Classes Among Whom the Produce Is Distributed

§ 1. [*The produce is sometimes shared among three classes*] Private property being assumed as a fact, we have next to enumerate the different classes of persons to whom it gives rise; whose concurrence, or at least whose permission, is necessary to production, and who are therefore able to stipulate for a share of the produce. We have to inquire, according to what laws the produce distributes itself among these classes, by the spontaneous action of the interests of those concerned: after which, a further question will be, what effects are or might be produced by laws, institutions, and measures of government, in superseding or modifying that spontaneous distribution.

The three requisites of production, as has been so often repeated, are labour, capital, and land: understanding by capital, the means and appliances which are the accumulated results of previous labour, and by land, the materials and instruments supplied by nature, whether contained in the interior of the earth, or constituting its surface. Since each of these elements of production may be separately appropriated, the industrial community may be considered as divided into landowners, capitalists, and productive labourers. Each of these classes, as such, obtains a share of the produce: no other person or class obtains anything, except by concession from them. The remainder of the community is, in fact, supported at their expense, giving, if any equivalent, one consisting of unproductive services. These three classes, therefore, are considered in political economy as making up the whole community.

§ 2. [*The produce sometimes belongs undividedly to one*] But although these three sometimes exist as separate classes, dividing the produce among them, they do not necessarily or always so exist. The fact is so much otherwise, that there are only one or two communities in which the complete separation of these classes is the general rule. England and Scotland, with parts of Belgium and Holland, are almost the only countries in the world, where the land, capital, and labour employed in agriculture, are generally the property of separate owners. The ordinary case is, that the same person owns either two of these requisites, or all three.

The case in which the same person owns all three, embraces the two extremes of [a]existing[a] society, in respect to the independence and dignity of the labouring class. First, when the labourer himself is the proprietor. This is the commonest case in the Northern States of the American Union; one of the commonest in France, Switzerland, the three Scandinavian kingdoms, and parts of Germany;* and a common case in parts of Italy and in Belgium. In all these countries there are, no doubt, large landed properties, and a still greater number which, without being large, require the occasional or constant aid of hired labourers. Much, however, of the land is owned in portions too small to require any other labour than that of the peasant and his family, or fully to occupy even that. The capital employed is not always that of the peasant proprietor, many of these small properties being mortgaged to obtain the means of cultivating; but the capital is invested at [b]the peasant's[b] risk, and though he pays interest for it, it gives to no one any right of interference, except, perhaps, eventually to take possession of the land, if the interest ceases to be paid.

The other case in which the land, labour, and capital, belong to the same person, is the case of slave countries, in which the labourers themselves

*"The Norwegian return" (say the Commissioners of Poor Law Enquiry, to whom information was furnished from nearly every country in Europe and America by the ambassadors and consuls there) "states that at the last census in 1825, out of a population of 1,051,318 persons, there were 59,464 freeholders. As by 59,464 freeholders must be meant 59,464 heads of families, or about 300,000 individuals; the freeholders must form more than a fourth of the whole population. Mr. Macgregor states that in Denmark (by which Zealand and the adjoining islands are probably meant) out of a population of 926,110, the number of landed proprietors and farmers is 415,110, or nearly one-half. In Sleswick-Holstein, out of a population of 604,085, it is 196,017, or about one-third. The proportion of proprietors and farmers to the whole population is not given in Sweden; but the Stockholm return estimates the average quantity of land annexed to a labourer's habitation at from one to five acres; and though the Gottenburg return gives a lower estimate, it adds, that the peasants possess much of the land. In Wurtemburg we are told that more than two-thirds of the labouring population are the proprietors of their own habitations, and that almost all own at least a garden of from three-quarters of an acre to an acre and a half." In some of these statements, proprietors and farmers are not discriminated; but "all the returns concur in stating the number of day-labourers to be very small."—(*Preface to Foreign Communications*, ["Appendix F to the Report from His Majesty's Commissioners for inquiring into the Administration and Practical Operation of the Poor Laws," *Parliamentary Papers*, 1834, XXXIX,] p. xxxviii.) As the general *status* of the labouring people, the condition of a workman for hire is almost peculiar to Great Britain.

[a-a]+52, 57, 62, 65, 71 [b-b]MS, 48, 49 his

are owned by the landowner. Our West India colonies before emancipation, and the sugar colonies of the nations by whom a similar act of justice is still unperformed, are examples of large establishments for agricultural and manufacturing labour (the production of sugar and rum is a combination of both) in which the land, the factories (if they may be so called), the machinery, and the degraded labourers, are all the property of a capitalist. In this case, as well as in its extreme opposite, the case of the peasant proprietor, there is no division of the produce.

§ 3. [*The produce is sometimes divided between two*] When the three requisites are not all owned by the same person, it often happens that two of them are so. Sometimes the same person owns the capital and the land, but not the labour. The landlord makes his engagement directly with the labourer, and supplies [a]the whole or part of[a] the stock necessary for cultivation. This system is the usual one in those parts of Continental Europe, in which the labourers are neither serfs on the one hand, nor proprietors on the other. It was [b]very common[b] in France before the Revolution, and is still much practised in some parts of that country, when the land is not the property of the cultivator. It prevails generally in the level districts of Italy, except those [c]principally[c] pastoral, such as the Maremma of Tuscany and the Campagna of Rome. On this system the division of the produce is between two classes, the landowner and the labourer.

In other cases again the labourer does not own the land, but owns the little stock employed on it, the landlord not being in the habit of supplying any. This [d]system[d] generally prevails in Ireland. It is nearly universal in India, and in most countries of the East; whether the government retains, as it generally does, the ownership of the soil, or allows portions to become, either absolutely or in a qualified sense, the property of individuals. In India, however, things are so far better than in Ireland, that the owner of land is in the habit of making advances to the cultivators, if they cannot cultivate without them. For these advances the native landed proprietor usually demands high interest; but the principal landowner, the government, makes them gratuitously, recovering the advance after the harvest, together with the rent. The produce is here divided as before, between the same two classes, the landowner and the labourer.

These are the principal variations in the classification of those among whom the produce of agricultural labour is distributed. In the case of

[a-a]+52, 57, 62, 65, 71
[b-b]MS, 48, 49, 52 the common system
[c-c]MS, 48, 49 purely
[d-d]MS , the most wretched system of all (except personal slavery),

manufacturing industry there never are more than two classes, the labourers and the capitalists. The original artisans in all countries were either slaves, or the women of the family. In the manufacturing establishments of the ancients, whether on a large or on a small scale, the labourers were [e]usually[e] the property of the [f]capitalist[f]. [g]In general, if[g] any manual labour was thought compatible with the dignity of a freeman, it was only agricultural labour. The converse system, in which the capital was owned by the labourer, was coeval with free labour, and under it the first great advances of manufacturing industry were achieved. The artisan owned the loom or the few tools he used, and worked on his own account; or at least ended by doing so, though he usually worked for another, first as apprentice and next as journeyman, for a certain number of years before he could be admitted a master. But the *status* of a permanent journeyman, all his life a hired labourer and nothing more, had no place in the crafts and guilds of the middle ages. In country villages, where a carpenter or a blacksmith cannot live and support hired labourers on the returns of his business, he is even now his own workman; and shopkeepers in similar circumstances are their own shopmen, or shopwomen. But wherever the extent of the market admits of it, the distinction is now fully established between the class of capitalists, or employers of labour, and the class of labourers; the capitalists, in general, contributing no other labour than that of direction and superintendence.

e–e+52, 57, 62, 65, 71
f–fMS capitalists
g–gMS, 48, 49 If

CHAPTER IV

Of Competition, and Custom

§ 1. [*Competition is not the sole regulator of the division of the produce*] Under the rule of individual property, the division of the produce is the result of two determining agencies: Competition, and Custom. It is important to ascertain the amount of influence which belongs to each of these causes, and in what manner the operation of one is modified by the other.

Political economists generally, and English political economists above others, [a]have been[a] accustomed to lay almost exclusive stress upon the first of these agencies; to exaggerate the effect of competition, and [b]to[b] take into little account the other and conflicting principle. They are apt to express themselves as if they thought that competition actually does, in all cases, whatever it can be shown to be the tendency of competition to do. This is partly intelligible, if we consider that only through the principle of competition has political economy any pretension to the character of a science. So far as rents, profits, wages, prices, are determined by competition, laws may be assigned for them. Assume competition to be their exclusive regulator, and principles of broad generality and scientific precision may be laid down, according to which they will be regulated. The political economist justly deems this his proper business: and as an abstract or hypothetical science, political economy cannot be required to do[c], and indeed cannot do,[c] anything more. But it would be a great misconception of the actual course of human affairs, to suppose that competition exercises in fact this unlimited sway. I am not speaking of monopolies, either natural or artificial, or of any interferences of authority with the liberty of production or exchange. Such disturbing causes have always been allowed for by political economists. I speak of cases in which there is nothing to restrain competition; no hindrance to it either in the nature of the case or in artificial obstacles; yet in which the result is not determined by competition, but by custom or usage; competition either not taking place at all, or producing its effect in quite a different manner from that which is ordinarily assumed to be natural to it.

[a-a]MS, 48, 49 are
[b-b]+62, 65, 71
[c-c]+52, 57, 62, 65, 71

§ 2. [*Influence of custom on rents, and on the tenure of land*] Competition, in fact, has only become in any considerable degree the governing principle of contracts, at a comparatively modern period. The farther we look back into history, the more we see all transactions and engagements under the influence of fixed customs. The reason is evident. Custom is the most powerful protector of the weak against the strong; their sole protector where there are no laws or government adequate to the purpose. Custom is a barrier which, even in the most oppressed condition of mankind, tyranny is forced in some degree to respect. To the industrious population, in a turbulent military community, freedom of competition is a vain phrase; they are never in a condition to make terms for themselves by it: there is always a master who throws his sword into the scale, and the terms are such as he imposes. But though the law of the strongest decides, it is not the interest nor in general the practice of the strongest to strain that law to the utmost, and every relaxation of it has a tendency to become a custom, and every custom to become a right. Rights thus originating, and not competition in any shape, determine, in a rude state of society, the share of the produce enjoyed by those who produce it. The relations, more especially, between the landowner and the cultivator, and the payments made by the latter to the former, are, in all states of society but the most modern, determined by the usage of the country. Never until late times have the conditions of the occupancy of land been (as a general rule) an affair of competition. The occupier for the time has very commonly been considered to have a right to retain his holding, while he fulfils the customary requirements; and has thus become, in a certain sense, a co-proprietor of the soil. Even where the holder has not acquired this fixity of tenure, the terms of occupation have often been fixed and invariable.

In India, for example, and other Asiatic communities similarly constituted, the ryots, or peasant-farmers, are not regarded as tenants at will, [a]nor[a] even as tenants by virtue of a lease. In most villages there are indeed some ryots on this precarious footing, consisting of those, or the descendants of those, who have settled in the place at a known and comparatively recent period; but all who are looked upon as descendants or representatives of the original inhabitants, [b]and even many mere tenants of ancient date,[b] are thought entitled to retain their land, as long as they pay the customary rents. What these customary rents are, or ought to be, has indeed, in most cases, become a matter of obscurity; usurpation, tyranny, and foreign conquest having to a great degree obliterated the evidences of them. But when an old and purely Hindoo principality falls under the dominion of the British Government, or the management of its officers,

[a-a]MS, 48, 49 or
[b-b]+52, 57, 62, 65, 71

and when the details of the revenue system come to be inquired into, it is [c]usually[c] found that though the demands of the great landholder, the State, have been swelled by fiscal rapacity until all limit is practically lost sight of, it has yet been thought necessary to have a distinct name and a separate pretext for each increase of exaction; so that the demand has sometimes come to consist of thirty or forty different items, in addition to the nominal rent. This circuitous mode of increasing the payments assuredly would not have been resorted to, if there had been an acknowledged right in the landlord to increase the rent. Its adoption is a proof that there was once an effective limitation, a real customary rent; and that the understood right of the ryot to the land, so long as he paid rent according to custom, was at some time or other more than nominal.* The British Government of India always simplifies the tenure by consolidating the various assessments into one, thus making the rent nominally as well as really an arbitrary thing, or at least a matter of specific agreement: but it scrupulously respects the right of the ryot to the land, [d] though [e]until the reforms of the present generation (reforms even now only partially carried into effect) it seldom left[e] him much more than a bare subsistence [f].

In modern Europe the cultivators have gradually emerged from a state of personal slavery. The barbarian conquerors of the Western Empire found that the easiest mode of managing their conquests would be to leave [g]the occupation of[g] the land in the hands in which they found it, and to save themselves a labour so uncongenial as the superintendence of troops of slaves, by allowing the slaves to retain in a certain degree the control of their own actions, under an obligation to furnish the lord with provisions and labour. A common expedient was to assign to the serf, for his exclusive use, as much land as was thought sufficient for his support, and to make him work on the other lands of his lord whenever required. By degrees these indefinite obligations were transformed into a definite one, of supplying a fixed quantity of provisions or a fixed quantity of labour: and as the lords, in time, became inclined to employ their income in the purchase of luxuries rather than in the maintenance of retainers, the payments in kind were commuted for payments in money. Each concession, at first volun-

*The ancient law books of the Hindoos mention in some cases one-sixth, in others one-fourth of the produce, as a proper rent; but there is no evidence that the rules laid down in those books were, at any period of history, really acted upon.

[c-c]MS, 48, 49 often
[d]MS &
[e-e]MS, 48, 49, 52 it seldom leaves
[f]MS , it does not, like Irish landlords, turn him out, & let the land over his head, to a higher bidder
[g-g]+62, 65, 71

tary and revocable at pleasure, gradually acquired the force of custom, and was at last recognised and enforced by the tribunals. In this manner the serfs progressively rose into a free tenantry, who held their land in perpetuity on fixed conditions. The conditions were sometimes very onerous, and the people very miserable. But their obligations were determined by the usage or law of the country, and not by competition.

Where the cultivators had never been, strictly speaking, in personal bondage, or after they had ceased to be so, the exigencies of a poor and little advanced society gave rise to another arrangement, which in some parts of Europe, even highly improved parts, has been found sufficiently advantageous to be continued to the present day. I speak of the métayer system. Under this, the land is divided, in small farms, among single families, the landlord generally supplying the stock which the agricultural system of the country is considered to require, and receiving, in lieu of rent and profit, a fixed proportion of the produce. This proportion, which is generally paid in kind, is usually, (as is implied in the words *métayer*, *mezzaiuolo*, and *medietarius*,) one-half. There are places, however, such as the rich volcanic soil of the province of Naples, where the landlord takes two-thirds, and yet the cultivator by means of an excellent agriculture contrives to live. But whether the proportion is two-thirds or one-half, it is a fixed proportion; not variable from farm to farm, or from tenant to tenant. The custom of the country is the universal rule; nobody thinks of raising or lowering rents, or of letting land on other than the customary conditions. Competition, as a regulator of rent, has no existence.

§ 3. [*Influence of custom on prices*] Prices, whenever there was no monopoly, came earlier under the influence of competition, and are much more universally subject to it, than rents: but that influence is by no means, even in the present [a]activity of mercantile[a] competition, so absolute as is sometimes assumed. There is no proposition which meets us in the field of political economy oftener than this—that there cannot be two prices in the same market. Such undoubtedly is the natural effect of unimpeded competition; yet every one knows that there are, [b]almost always[b], two prices in the same market. Not only are there in every large town, and in almost every trade, cheap shops and dear shops, but the same shop often sells the same article at different prices to different customers: and, as a general rule, each retailer adapts his scale of prices to the class of customers whom he expects. The wholesale trade, in the great articles of commerce, is really under the dominion of competition. There, the buyers as well as sellers are traders or manufacturers, and their purchases are not influenced by indo-

[a-a]MS, 48, 49 state of intense
[b-b]MS, 48, 49 very often

lence or vulgar finery, [c]nor depend on the smaller motives of personal convenience,[c] but are business transactions. In the wholesale markets therefore it is true as a general proposition, that there are not two prices at one time for the same thing: there is at each time and place a market price, which can be quoted in a price-current. But retail price, the price paid by the actual consumer, seems to feel very slowly and imperfectly the effect of competition; and when competition does exist, it often, instead of lowering prices, merely divides the gains of the high price among a greater number of dealers. Hence it is that, of the price paid by the consumer, so large a proportion is absorbed by the gains of retailers; and any one who [d]inquires into[d] the amount which reaches the hands of those who made the things he buys, will often be astonished at its smallness. When indeed the market, being that of a great city, holds out a sufficient inducement to large capitalists to engage in retail operations, it is generally found a better speculation to attract a large business by underselling others, than merely to divide the field of employment with them. This influence of competition is making itself felt more and more through the principal branches of retail trade in the large towns; and the rapidity and cheapness of transport, by making consumers less dependent on the dealers in their immediate neighbourhood, are tending to assimilate more and more the whole country to a large town: but hitherto it is only in the great centres of business that retail transactions have been chiefly, or even much, determined, by competition. Elsewhere it rather acts, when it acts at all, as an occasional disturbing influence; the habitual regulator is custom, modified from time to time by notions existing in the minds of purchasers and sellers, of some kind of equity or justice.

In many trades the terms on which business is done are a matter of positive arrangement among the trade, who use the means they always possess of making the situation of any member of the body who departs from its fixed customs, inconvenient or disagreeable. It is well known that the bookselling trade [e]was, until lately,[e] one of these, and that notwithstanding the active spirit of rivalry in the trade, competition [f]did[f] not produce its natural effect in breaking down the trade rules. All professional remuneration is regulated by custom. The fees of physicians, surgeons, and barristers, the charges of attorneys, are nearly invariable. Not certainly for want of abundant competition in those professions, but because the competition operates by diminishing each competitor's chance of fees, not by lowering the fees themselves.

[c-c]+65, 71
[d-d]MS either takes pains to find out, or accidentally lear[ns? *binding pasted over*]
[e-e]MS, 48, 49, 52 is
[f-f]MS, 48, 49, 52 does

Since custom stands its ground against competition to so considerable an extent, even where, from the multitude of competitors and the general energy in the pursuit of gain, the spirit of competition is strongest, we may be sure that this is much more the case where people are content with smaller gains, and estimate their pecuniary interest at a lower rate when balanced against their ease or their pleasure. I believe it will often be found, in Continental Europe, that prices and charges, of some or of all sorts, are much higher in some places than in others not far distant, without its being possible to assign any other cause than that it has always been so: the customers are used to it, and acquiesce in it. An enterprising competitor, with sufficient capital, might force down the charges, and make his fortune during the process; but there are no enterprising competitors; those who have capital prefer to leave it where it is, or to make less profit by it in a more quiet way.

These observations must be received as a general correction to be applied whenever relevant, whether expressly mentioned or not, to the conclusions contained in the subsequent portions of this treatise. Our reasonings must, in general, proceed as if the known and natural effects of competition were actually produced by it, in all cases in which it is not restrained by some positive obstacle. Where competition, though free to exist, does not exist, or where it exists, but has its natural consequences overruled by any other agency, the conclusions will fail more or less of being applicable. To escape error, we ought, in applying the conclusions of political economy to the actual affairs of life, to consider not only what will happen supposing the maximum of competition, but how far the result will be affected if competition falls short of the maximum.

The states of economical relation which stand first in order to be discussed and appreciated, are those in which competition has no part, the arbiter of transactions being either brute force or established usage. These will be the subject of the next four chapters.

CHAPTER V

Of Slavery

§ 1. [*Slavery considered in relation to the slaves*] Among the forms which society assumes under the influence of the institution of property, there are, as I have already remarked, two, otherwise of a widely dissimilar character, but resembling in this, that the ownership of the land, the labour, and the capital, is in the same hands. One of these cases is that of slavery, the other is that of peasant proprietors. In the one, the landowner owns the labour, in the other the labourer owns the land. We begin with the first.

In this system all the produce belongs to the landlord. The food and other necessaries of his labourers are part of his expenses. The labourers possess nothing but what he thinks fit to give them, and until he thinks fit to take it back: and [a]they[a] work as hard as he chooses, or is able, to compel them. Their wretchedness is only limited by his humanity, or his [b]pecuniary interest.[b] With the first consideration, we have on the present occasion nothing to do. What the second in so detestable a constitution of society may dictate, depends on the facilities for importing fresh slaves. If full-grown able-bodied slaves can be procured in sufficient numbers, and imported at a moderate expense, [c] self-interest will recommend working the slaves to death, and replacing them by importation in preference to the slow and expensive process of breeding them. Nor are the slave-owners generally backward in learning this lesson. It is notorious that such was the practice in our [d] slave colonies, while the slave trade was legal; and it is said to be so still [e]in Cuba[e].

When, as among the ancients, the slave-market could only be supplied by captives either taken in war, or kidnapped from thinly scattered tribes on the remote confines of the known world, it was generally more profitable to keep up the number by breeding, which necessitates a far better treatment of them; and for this reason, joined with several others, the condition of slaves, notwithstanding occasional enormities, was probably much less

[a-a]+48, 49, 52, 57, 62, 65, 71
[b-b]MS, 48, 49 "enlightened self-interest."
[c]MS, 48, 49 enlightened
[d]MS, 48, 49, 52, 57 own
[e-e]MS in those States of the American Union which receive a regular supply of negroes from other States] 48, 49, 52 in Cuba, and in . . . *as* MS

bad in the ancient world, than in the colonies of modern nations. The Helots are usually cited as the type of the most hideous form of personal slavery, but with how little truth appears from the fact that they were regularly armed (though not with the panoply of the hoplite) and formed an integral part of the military strength of the State. They were doubtless an inferior and degraded caste, but their slavery seems to have been one of the least onerous varieties of serfdom. Slavery appears in far more frightful colours among the Romans, during the period in which the Roman aristocracy was gorging itself with the plunder of a newly-conquered world. The Romans were a cruel people, and the worthless nobles sported with the lives of their myriads of slaves with the same reckless prodigality with which they squandered any other part of their ill-acquired possessions. Yet, slavery is divested of one of its worst features when it is compatible with hope: enfranchisement was easy and common: enfranchised slaves obtained at once the full rights of citizens, and instances were frequent of their acquiring not only riches, but latterly even honours. By the progress of milder legislation under the Emperors, much of the protection of law was thrown round the slave, he became capable of possessing property, and the evil altogether assumed a considerably gentler aspect. Until, however, slavery assumes the mitigated form of villenage, in which not only the [f]slaves have[f] property and legal rights, but [g]their[g] obligations are more or less limited by usage, and [h]they partly labour for their[h] own benefit; [i]their[i] condition is seldom such as to produce a rapid growth [j]either of population or of production.

§ 2. [*Slavery in relation to production*] So long as slave countries are[j] underpeopled in proportion to their cultivable land, the labour of the slaves, [a] under any tolerable management, produces much more than is sufficient for their support; especially as the great amount of superinten-

[f-f]MS, 48, 49 slave has
[g-g]MS, 48, 49 his
[h-h]MS, 48, 49 he partly labours for his
[i-i]MS, 48, 49 his
[j-j]MS of population. This cannot be from physical privation, for no slave-labourers are worse fed, clothed, or lodged, than the free peasantry of Ireland. The cause usually assigned, is the great disproportion of the sexes which almost always exists where slaves are not bred but imported: this explanation however is not sufficient, as the negro population of our West India colonies continued nearly stationary, after the slave-trade to those colonies was suppressed. It is perhaps the general weakness of family ties among slaves, which causes fewer children to be born, or a greater proportion of those born to perish in infancy. Whatever be the cause, a slave-population is seldom a rapidly increasing one. Slave countries, unless of very small extent or limited natural resources, are generally] 48, 49 *as* MS . . . imported: this cannot however be the sole cause, as . . . suppressed. Whatever be the causes, a . . . *as* MS
[a]MS, 48, 49 therefore,

dence which their labour requires, preventing the dispersion of the population, insures some of the advantages of combined labour. Hence, in a good soil and climate, and with reasonable care of his own interests, the owner of many slaves has the means of being rich. [b] The influence, however, of such a state of society on production, is perfectly well understood. It is a truism to assert, that labour extorted by fear of punishment is inefficient and unproductive. It is true that in some circumstances, human beings can be driven by the lash to attempt, and even to accomplish, things which they would not have undertaken for any payment which it could have been worth while to an employer to offer them. And it is likely that productive operations which require much combination of labour, the production of sugar for example, would not have taken place so soon in the American colonies, if slavery had not existed to keep masses of labour together. There are also savage tribes so averse from regular industry, that industrial life is scarcely able to introduce itself among them until they are either conquered [c]and[c] made slaves of, or become conquerors and make others so. But after allowing the full value of these considerations, it remains certain that slavery [d] is incompatible with any high state of the arts of life, and any [e]great[e] efficiency of labour. For all products which require much skill, slave countries are [f]usually[f] dependent on foreigners. Hopeless slavery effectually brutifies the intellect; and intelligence in the slaves, though often encouraged in the ancient world and in the East, is in a more advanced state of society a source of so much danger and an object of so much dread to the masters, that in some [g]of the States of America it was[g] a highly penal offence to teach a slave to read. All processes carried on by slave labour are conducted in the rudest and most unimproved manner. And even the animal strength of the slave is, on an average, not half exerted. [h]The unproductiveness and wastefulness of the industrial system in the Slave States [i] is instructively displayed in the valuable writings of Mr. Olmsted.[h] The mildest form of slavery is certainly the condition of the serf, who is attached to the soil, supports himself from his [j] allotment, and works a certain number of days in the week for his lord. Yet there is but one opinion on the extreme inefficiency of serf labour. The following passage is from Professor Jones,* whose Essay on the Distribution of Wealth (or rather on Rent), is a

**Essay on the Distribution of Wealth and on the Sources of Taxation.* By the Rev. Richard Jones [London: Murray, 1831]. Page 50 [–51].

[b]MS, 48, 49 [§ 2 *begins*] [c-c]48 or [*printer's error?*]
[d]MS, 48 , even in the most mitigated form,
[e-e]MS, 48, 49, 52, 57 real
[f-f]MS, 48, 49 always
[g-g]MS, 48, 49, 52, 57, 62 countries it is] 65 of the States of America it is
[h-h]+62 [*as footnote to* exerted], 65, 71
[i]62 of North America, [j]MS own

copious repertory of valuable facts on the landed tenures of different countries.

"The Russians, or rather those German writers who have observed the manners and habits of Russia, state some strong facts on this point. Two Middlesex mowers, they say, will mow in a day as much grass as six Russian serfs, and in spite of the dearness of provisions in England and their cheapness in Russia, the mowing a quantity of hay which would cost an English farmer half a copeck, will cost a Russian proprietor three or four copecks.* The Prussian counsellor of state, Jacob, is considered to have proved, that in Russia, where everything is cheap, the labour of a serf is doubly as expensive as that of a labourer in England. M. Schmalz gives a startling account of the unproductiveness of serf labour in Prussia, from his own knowledge and observation.† In Austria, it is distinctly stated, that the labour of a serf is equal to only one-third of that of a free hired labourer. This calculation, made in an able work on agriculture (with some extracts from which I have been favoured), is applied to the practical purpose of deciding on the number of labourers necessary to cultivate an estate of a given magnitude. So palpable, indeed, are the ill effects of labour rents on the industry of the agricultural population, that in Austria itself, where proposals [k]of[k] changes of any kind do not readily make their way, schemes and plans for the commutation of labour rents are as popular as in the more stirring German provinces of the North."‡

What is wanting in the quality of the labour itself, is not made up by any excellence in the direction and superintendence. As the same writer§ remarks, the landed proprietors "are necessarily, in their character of cultivators of their own domains, the only guides and directors of the industry of the agricultural population," since there can be no intermediate class of capitalist farmers where the labourers are the property of the lord. Great landowners are everywhere an idle class, or if they labour at all, addict themselves only to the more exciting kinds of exertion; that lion's

*[MS *square-bracketed in text*] "Schmalz, *Economie Politique*, French translation [by M. Fritob. Paris: Bertrand, 1826], vol. i. p. 66."

†[MS *square-bracketed in text*] "Vol. ii. p. 107."

‡[52] The Hungarian revolutionary government, during its brief existence, bestowed on that country one of the greatest benefits it could receive, and one which the tyranny that succeeded [52, 57 that has succeeded] did not dare [52, 57, 62, 65 has not dared] to take away: it freed the peasantry from what remained of the bondage of serfdom, the labour rents; decreeing compensation to the landlords at the expense of the state, and not at that of the liberated peasants.

§Jones, pp. 53, 54.

[k-k]Source, MS, 48, 49, 52, 57 for

share which superiors always reserve for themselves. "It would," as Mr. Jones observes, "be hopeless and irrational to expect, that a race of noble proprietors, fenced round with privileges and dignity, and attracted to military and political pursuits by the advantages and habits of their station, should ever become attentive cultivators as a body." Even in England, if the cultivation of every estate depended upon its proprietor, any one [l]can[l] judge what would be the result. There would be a few cases of great science and energy, and numerous individual instances of moderate success, but the general state of agriculture would be contemptible.

§ 3. [*Emancipation considered in relation to the interest of the slave-owners*] Whether the proprietors themselves would lose by the emancipation of their slaves, is a different question from the comparative effectiveness of free and slave labour to the community. There has been much discussion of this question as an abstract thesis; as if it could possibly admit of any universal solution. Whether slavery or free labour is most profitable to the employer, depends on the wages of the free labourer. These, again, depend on the numbers of the labouring population, compared with the capital and the land. Hired labour is generally so much more efficient than slave labour, that the employer can pay a considerably greater value in wages, than the maintenance of his slaves cost him before, and yet be a gainer by the change: but he cannot do this without limit. The decline of serfdom in Europe, and its [a]destruction[a] in the Western nations, [b]were[b] doubtless hastened by the changes which the growth of population must have made in the pecuniary interests of the master. As population pressed harder upon the land, without any improvement in agriculture, the maintenance of the serfs necessarily became more costly, and their labour less valuable. With the rate of wages such as it is in Ireland, or in England (where, in proportion to its efficiency, [c]labour is quite as cheap[c] as in Ireland), no one can for a moment imagine that slavery could be profitable. If the Irish peasantry were slaves, their masters would be as willing, as their landlords now are, to pay large sums merely to get rid of them. In the rich and underpeopled soil of the West India islands, there is just as little doubt that the balance of profits between free and slave labour was greatly on the side of slavery, and that the compensation granted to the slave-owners for its abolition was not more, [d]perhaps even[d] less, than an equivalent for their loss.

[l-l]52, 57 could
[a-a]MS, 48, 49, 52, 57, 62 extinction
[b-b]MS, 48, 49, 52, 57, 62 was
[c-c]MS it is quite as low
[d-d]MS, 48, 49, 52, 57 but in all probability

More needs not be said here on a cause so completely judged and decided as that of slavery. [e]Its demerits are no longer a question requiring argument; though the temper of mind manifested by the larger part of the influential classes in Great Britain respecting the struggle [f] in America, shows how grievously the feelings of the present generation of Englishmen, on this subject, [g]had[g] fallen behind the positive acts of the generation which preceded them. That the sons of the deliverers of the West Indian Negroes should [h]expect[h] with complacency, and encourage by their sympathies, the [i]establishment[i] of a great and powerful military commonwealth, pledged by its principles and driven by its strongest interests to be the armed propagator of slavery through every region of the earth into which its power [j]could[j] penetrate, discloses a mental state in the leading portion of our higher and middle classes which it is melancholy to see, and will be a lasting blot in English history. Fortunately they [k] stopped short of actually aiding, otherwise than by words, the nefarious enterprise to which they [l]were[l] not ashamed of wishing success; and [m] at the expense of the best blood of the Free States, but to their immeasurable elevation in mental and moral worth, the curse of slavery [n]has been[n] cast out from the great American republic, to find its last temporary refuge in Brazil and Cuba. No European country, except Spain alone, any longer participates in the enormity. Even

[e–e251]MS It will be curious to see how long the other nations possessing slave colonies will be content to remain behind England in a matter of such concernment both to justice, which decidedly is not at present a fashionable virtue, and to philanthropy, which certainly is so. Europe is far more inexcusable than America in tolerating an enormity, of which she could rid herself with so much greater ease. I speak of negro-slavery, not of the servage of the Slavonic nations, who have not yet advanced beyond a state of civilization corresponding to the age of villenage in Western Europe, and must emerge from it in the same gradual manner, however much accelerated by that salutary influence of the ideas of more advanced countries, which is so important to those more backward, in enabling them to make up for lost time.] 48 *as* MS . . . Europe, and can only be expected to emerge . . . by the salutary . . . advanced countries.] 49 *as* MS . . . is so.* [*footnote*:] *Denmark has the honour of being the first Continental nation which followed the example of England; and the emancipation of the slaves was one of the earliest acts of the French Provisional Government. Still more recently, the progress of the American mind towards a determination to rid itself of this odious stain has been manifested by very gratifying symptoms. [*end of note; text resumes:*] . . . *as* 48] 52, 57 *as* 49 . . . acts of the heroic and calumniated Provisional Government of France . . . Western Europe, and who, to all appearance, will be indebted for their liberation from this great evil, to the influence of the ideas of the more advanced countries, rather than to the rapidity of their own progress in improvement.] 62 *as* 52 . . . of France. The Dutch Government is now seriously engaged in the same beneficent enterprise . . . *as* 52

[f]65 now taking place
[g–g]65 have
[h–h]65 see
[i–i]65 foundation
[j–j]65 can
[k]65 have
[l–l]65 have not been
[m]65 it is now probable that,
[n–n]65 will be

serfage has now ceased to have a legal existence in Europe. Denmark has the honour of being the first Continental nation which imitated England in liberating its colonial slaves; and the abolition of slavery was one of the earliest acts of the heroic and calumniated Provisional Government of France. The Dutch Government was not long behind, and its colonies and dependencies are now, I believe without exception, free from actual slavery, though forced labour for the public authorities is still a recognised institution in Java, soon, we may hope, to be exchanged for complete personal freedom.[e]

CHAPTER VI

Of Peasant Proprietors

§ 1. [*Difference between English and Continental opinions respecting peasant properties*] In the régime of peasant properties, as in that of slavery, the whole produce belongs to a single owner, and the distinction of rent, profits, and wages, does not exist. In all other respects, the two states of society are the extreme opposites of each other. The one is the state of greatest oppression and degradation to the labouring class. The other is that in which they are the most uncontrolled arbiters of their own lot.

The advantage, however, of small properties in land, is one of the most disputed questions in the range of political economy. On the Continent, though there are some dissentients from the prevailing opinion, the benefit of having a numerous proprietary population exists in the minds of most people in the form of an axiom. But English authorities are either unaware of the judgment of Continental agriculturists, or are content to put it aside, on the plea of their having no experience of large properties in favourable circumstances: the advantage of large properties being only felt where there are also large farms; and as this, in arable districts, implies a greater accumulation of capital than usually exists on the Continent, the great Continental estates, except in the case of grazing farms, are mostly let out for cultivation in small portions. There is some truth in this; but the argument admits of being retorted; for if the Continent knows little, by experience, of cultivation on a large scale and by large capital, the generality of English writers are no better acquainted practically with peasant proprietors, and have almost always the most erroneous ideas of their social condition and mode of life. Yet the old traditions even of England are on the same side with the general opinion of the Continent. The "yeomanry" who were vaunted as the glory of England while they existed, and have been so much mourned over since they disappeared, were either small proprietors or small farmers, and if they were mostly the last, the character they bore for sturdy independence is the more noticeable. There is a part of England, unfortunately a very small part, where peasant proprietors are still common; for such are the "statesmen" of Cumberland and Westmoreland, though they pay, I believe, generally if not universally, certain customary dues, which, being fixed, no more affect their character of [a]proprietor[a], than the land-tax does. There is but one voice, among those acquainted with the country, on the admirable effects of this tenure of land in those counties. No other agricultural population in England could have furnished the originals of Wordsworth's peasantry.*

The general system, however, of English cultivation, affording no experience to render the nature and operation of peasant properties familiar, and [b]Englishmen being in general profoundly ignorant of the agricultural economy of other countries,[b] the very idea of peasant proprietors is strange to the English mind, and does not easily find access to it. Even the forms of language stand in the way: the familiar designation for owners of land being "landlords," a term to which "tenants" is always understood as a correlative. When, [c]at the time of the famine[c], the suggestion of peasant properties as a means of Irish improvement found its way into parliamentary and newspaper discussions, there were writers of pretension to whom

*In Mr. Wordsworth's little descriptive work on the scenery of the Lakes, he speaks of the upper part of the dales as having been for centuries "a perfect republic of shepherds and agriculturists, proprietors, for the most part, of the lands which they occupied and cultivated. [*MS ellipsis indicated by* . .] The plough of each man was confined to the maintenance of his own family, or to the occasional accommodation of his neighbour. Two or three cows furnished each family with milk and cheese. The chapel was the only edifice that presided over these dwellings, the supreme head of this pure commonwealth; the members of which existed in the midst of a powerful empire, like an ideal society, or an organized community, whose constitution had been imposed and regulated by the mountains which protected it. Neither high-born nobleman, knight, nor esquire was here; but many of these humble sons of the hills had a consciousness that the land which they walked over and tilled had for more than five hundred years been possessed by men of their name and blood. . . . Corn was grown in these vales sufficient upon each estate to furnish bread for each family, no more. The storms and moisture of the climate induced them to sprinkle their upland property with outhouses of native stone, as places of shelter for their sheep, where, in tempestuous weather, food was distributed to them. Every family spun from its own flock the wool with which it was clothed; a weaver was here and there found among them, and the rest of their wants was supplied by the produce of the yarn, which they carded and spun in their own houses, and carried to market either under their arms, or more frequently on packhorses, a small train taking their way weekly down the valley, or over the mountains, to the most commodious town."—*A Description of the Scenery of the Lakes in the North of England*, 3rd edit. [London: Longman, Hurst, Rees, Orme, and Brown, 1822, pp. 63–5, 51–2,] pp. 50 to 53 and 63 to 65.

[a–a]MS, 48, 49, 52, 57, 62, 65 proprietors

[b–b]MS it being one of the faults of Englishmen to be both ignorant and careless of any other social, economical, & political experience than their own,

[c–c]MS, 48, 49, 52, 57 very recently

the word "proprietor" was so far from conveying any distinct idea, that they mistook the small holdings of Irish cottier tenants for peasant properties. The subject being so little understood, I think it important, before entering into the theory of it, to do something towards showing how the case stands as to [d]matter[d] of fact; by exhibiting, at greater length than would otherwise be admissible, some of the testimony which exists respecting the state of cultivation, and the comfort and happiness of the cultivators, in those countries and parts of countries, in which the greater part of the land has neither landlord nor farmer, other than the labourer who tills [e]the[e] soil.

§ 2. [*Evidence respecting peasant properties in Switzerland*] I lay no stress on the condition of North America, where, as is well known, the land, [a]except in the former Slave States[a], is almost universally owned by the same person who holds the plough. A country combining the natural fertility of America with the knowledge and arts of modern Europe, is so peculiarly circumstanced, that scarcely anything, except insecurity of property or a tyrannical government, could materially impair the prosperity of the industrious classes. I might, with Sismondi, insist more strongly on the case of ancient Italy, especially Latium, that Campagna which then swarmed with inhabitants in the very regions which under a contrary régime have become uninhabitable from malaria. But I prefer taking the evidence of the same writer on things known to him by personal observation.

"C'est surtout la Suisse," says M. de Sismondi, "qu'il faut parcourir, qu'il faut étudier, pour juger du bonheur des paysans propriétaires. C'est la Suisse qu'il faut apprendre à connaître pour se convaincre que l'agriculture pratiquée par ceux-là même qui en recueillent les fruits suffit pour procurer une grande aisance à une population très nombreuse; une grande indépendance de caractère, fruit de l'indépendance des situations; un grand commerce de consommation, conséquence du bien-être de tous les habitans, même dans un pays dont le climat est rude, dont le sol est médiocrement fertile, et où les gelées tardives et l'inconstance des saisons détruisent souvent l'espoir du laboureur. On ne saurait voir sans admiration ces maisons de bois du moindre paysan, si vastes, si bien closes, si bien construites, si couvertes de sculpture. Dans l'intérieur, de grands corridors dégagent chaque chambre de la nombreuse famille; chaque chambre n'a qu'un lit, et il est abondamment pourvu de rideaux, de couvertures, et du linge le plus blanc; des meubles soignés l'entourent; les armoires sont remplies de linge, la laiterie est vaste, aérée, et d'une netteté exquise; sous

[d-d]MS matters [? MS *blotted*]
[e-e]MS its
[a-a]MS, 48, 49, 52, 57, 62, 65 wherever free from the curse of slavery

le même toit on trouve de grands approvisionnemens de blé, de viande salée, de fromage et de bois; dans les étables on voit le bétail le mieux soigné et le plus beau de l'Europe; le jardin est planté de fleurs, les hommes comme les femmes sont chaudement et proprement habillés, les dernières conservent avec orgueil leur antique costume; tous portent sur leur visage l'empreinte de la vigueur et de la santé. [b] Que d'autres nations vantent leur opulence, la Suisse pourra toujours leur opposer avec orgueil ses paysans."*

The same eminent writer thus expresses his opinion on peasant proprietorship in general.

"Partout où l'on retrouve les paysans propriétaires, on retrouve aussi cette aisance, cette sécurité, cette confiance dans l'avenir, cette indépendance qui assurent en même temps le bonheur et la vertu. Le paysan qui fait avec ses enfans tout l'ouvrage de son petit héritage, qui ne paie de fermage à personne au-dessus de lui, ni de salaire à personne au-dessous, qui règle sa production sur sa consommation, qui mange son propre blé, boit son propre vin, se revêt de son chanvre et de ses laines, se soucie peu de connaître les prix du marché; car il a peu à vendre et peu à acheter, et il n'est jamais ruiné par les révolutions du commerce. Loin de craindre pour l'avenir, il le voit s'embellir dans son espérance; car il met à profit pour ses enfans, pour les siècles qui viendront, chacun des instans que ne requiert pas de lui le travail de l'année. Il lui a suffi de donner peu de momens de travail pour mettre en terre le noyau qui dans cent ans sera un grand arbre, pour creuser l'aquéduc qui séchera à jamais son champ, pour former le conduit qui lui amènera une source d'eau vive, pour améliorer par des soins souvent répétés mais dérobés sur les instans perdus, toutes les espèces d'animaux et de végétaux dont il s'entoure. Son petit patrimoine est une vraie caisse d'épargnes, toujours prête à recevoir tous ses petits profits, à utiliser tous ses momens de loisir. La puissance toujours agissante de la nature les féconde, et les lui rend au centuple. Le paysan a vivement le sentiment de ce bonheur attaché à la condition de propriétaire. Aussi est-il toujours empressé de la terre à tout prix. Il la paie plus qu'elle ne vaut, plus qu'elle ne lui rendra peut-être; mais combien n'a-t-il pas raison d'estimer à un haut prix l'avantage de placer désormais toujours avantageusement son travail, sans être obligé de l'offrir au rabais; de trouver toujours au besoin son pain, sans être obligé de le payer à l'enchère.

"Le paysan propriétaire est de tous les cultivateurs celui qui tire le plus de parti du sol; parceque c'est celui qui songe le plus à l'avenir, tout comme

**Etudes sur l'Economie Politique*, Essai III [pp. 171–3]. [MS 48, 49 See also to the same effect Laing's *Notes of a Traveller*, p. 354.]

[b]MS [*ellipsis indicated by* . .]

celui qui a été le plus éclairé par l'expérience; c'est encore lui qui met le mieux à profit le travail humain, parceque répartissant ses occupations entre tous les membres de sa famille, il en réserve pour tous les jours de l'année, de manière à ce qu'il n'y ait de chômage pour personne: de tous les cultivateurs il est le plus heureux, et en même temps, sur un espace donné, la terre ne nourrit bien, sans s'épuiser, et n'occupe jamais tant d'habitans que lorsqu'ils sont propriétaires; enfin de tous les cultivateurs le paysan propriétaire est celui qui donne le plus d'encouragement au commerce et à l'industrie, parcequ'il est le plus riche."*

This picture of unwearied assiduity, and what may be called affectionate interest in the land, is borne out in regard to the more intelligent Cantons of Switzerland by English observers. "In walking anywhere in the neighbourhood of Zurich," says Mr. Inglis, "in looking to the right or to the left, one is struck with the extraordinary industry of the inhabitants; and if we learn that a proprietor here has a return of ten per cent, we are inclined to say, 'he deserves it.' I speak at present of country labour, though I believe that in every kind of trade also, the people of Zurich are remarkable for their assiduity; but in the industry they show in the cultivation of their land I may safely say they are unrivalled. When I used to open my casement between four and five in the morning to look out upon the lake and the distant Alps, I saw the labourer in the fields; and when I returned from an evening walk, long after sunset, as late, perhaps, as half-past eight, there was the labourer mowing his grass, or tying up his vines. . . . It is impossible to look at a field, a garden, a hedging, scarcely even a tree, a flower, or a vegetable,

*And in another work (*Nouveaux Principes d'Economie Politique*, [*ou de la Richesse dans Rapports avec la Population*. 2nd ed. 2 vols. Paris: Delaunay, 1827,] liv. iii. ch. 3 [pp. 168–9]) he says: "Quand on traverse la Suisse presqu'entière, plusieurs provinces de France, d'Italie, et d'Allemagne, il n'est pas besoin de demander, en regardant chaque partie de terre, si elle appartient à un cultivateur propriétaire ou à un fermier. Les soins bien entendus, les jouissances préparées au laboureur, la parure que la campagne a reçue de ses mains, indiquent bien vite le premier. Il est vrai qu'un gouvernement oppressif peut détruire l'aisance et abrutir l'intelligence que devait donner la propriété, que l'impôt peut enlever le plus net du produit des champs, que l'insolence des agens du pouvoir peut troubler la sécurité des paysans, que l'impossibilité d'obtenir justice contre un puissant voisin peut jeter le découragement dans l'âme, et que, dans le beau pays qui a été rendu à l'administration du Roi de Sardaigne, un propriétaire porte aussi bien qu'un journalier l'uniforme de la misère." He was [MS, 48, 49, 52, 57, 62 he is] here speaking of Savoy, where the peasants are generally proprietors; and according to authentic (though not recent) accounts [MS, 48, 49, 52, 57, 62, 65 authentic accounts], extremely miserable. But, as M. de Sismondi continues, "On a beau se conformer à une seule des règles de l'économie politique, elle ne peut pas opérer le bien à elle seule; du moins elle diminue le mal."

without perceiving proofs of the extreme care and industry that are bestowed upon the cultivation of the soil. If, for example, a path leads through or by the side of a field of grain, the corn is not, as in England, permitted to hang over the path, exposed to be pulled or trodden down by every passer by; it is everywhere bounded by a fence, stakes are placed at intervals of about a yard, and, about two, or three feet from the ground, boughs of trees are passed longitudinally along. If you look into a field towards evening, where there are large beds of cauliflower or cabbage, you will find that every single plant has been watered. In the gardens, which around Zurich are extremely large, the most punctilious care is evinced in every production that grows. The vegetables are planted with seemingly mathematical accuracy; not a single weed is to be seen, [c]not[c] a single stone. Plants are not earthed up as with us, but are planted in a small hollow, into each of which a little manure is put, and each plant is watered daily. Where seeds are sown, the earth directly above is broken into the finest powder; every shrub, every flower is tied to a stake, and where there is wall-fruit a trellice is erected against the wall, to which the boughs are fastened, and there is not a single [d]thing[d] that has not its appropriate resting place."*

Of one of the remote valleys of the High Alps the same writer thus expresses himself.†

"In the whole of the Engadine the land belongs to the peasantry, who, like the inhabitants of every other place where this state of things exists, vary greatly in the extent of their possessions. . . . Generally speaking, an Engadine peasant lives entirely upon the produce of his land, with the exception of the few articles of foreign growth required in his family, such as coffee, sugar, and wine. [e] Flax is grown, prepared, spun, and woven, without ever leaving his house. He has also his own wool, which is converted into a blue coat, without passing through the hands of either the dyer or the tailor. The country is incapable of greater cultivation than it has received. All has been done for it that industry and an extreme love of gain can devise. There is not a foot of waste land in the Engadine, the lowest part of which is not much lower than the top of Snowdon. Wherever grass will grow, there it is; wherever a rock will bear a blade, verdure is seen upon it; wherever an ear of rye will ripen, there it is to be found. Barley

**Switzerland, the South of France, and the Pyrenees, in* 1830. [2 vols. Edinburgh: Constable, 1831.] By H. D. Inglis ["Derwent Conway"]. Vol. i. ch. 2 [pp. 32–3].

†Ibid. ch. 8 and 10 [pp. 110, 111, 113, 146, 109].

[c–c]Source, MS, 48, 49, 52, 57 nor
[d–d]Source, MS twig
[e]MS [*ellipsis indicated by* . .]

and oats have also their appropriate spots; and wherever it is possible to ripen a little patch of wheat, the cultivation of it is attempted. In no country in Europe will be found so few poor as in the Engadine. In the village of Suss, which contains about six hundred inhabitants, there is not a single individual who has not wherewithal to live comfortably, not a single individual who is indebted to others for one morsel that he eats."

Notwithstanding the general prosperity of the Swiss peasantry, this total absence of pauperism and (it may almost be said) of poverty, cannot be predicated of the whole country; the largest and richest canton, that of Berne, being an example of the contrary; for although, in the parts of it which are occupied by peasant proprietors, their industry is as remarkable and their ease and comfort as conspicuous as elsewhere, the canton is burthened with a numerous pauper population, through the operation of the worst regulated system of poor-law administration in Europe, except that of England before the new Poor Law.* Nor is Switzerland in some other respects a favourable example of all that peasant properties might effect. There exists a series of statistical accounts of the Swiss Cantons, drawn up mostly with great care and intelligence, containing detailed information, of tolerably recent date, respecting the condition of the land and of the people. From these, the subdivision appears to be often so minute, that it can hardly be supposed not to be excessive: and the indebtedness of the proprietors in the flourishing canton of Zurich "borders," as the writer expresses it, "on the incredible;"† so that "only the intensest industry, frugality, temperance, and complete freedom of commerce enable them to stand their ground." Yet the general conclusion deducible from these books is that since the beginning of the century, and concurrently with the subdivision of many great estates which belonged to nobles or to the

*[52] There have been considerable changes in the Poor Law administration and legislation of the Canton of Berne since the sentence in the text was written. But I am not sufficiently acquainted with the nature and operation of these changes to speak more particularly of them here.

†"Eine an das unglaubliche gränzende Schuldenmasse" is the expression. (*Historisch-geographisch-statistische[s] Gemälde der Schweiz. Erster Theil. Der Kanton Zürich.* Von Gerold Meyer Von Knonau, [St. Gall: Huber,] 1834, pp. 80–1.) There are villages in Zurich, he adds, in which there is not a single property unmortgaged. It does not, however, follow that each individual proprietor is deeply involved because the aggregate mass of encumbrances is large. In the Canton of Schaffhausen, for instance, it is stated that the landed properties are almost all mortgaged, but rarely for more than one-half their registered value (*Zwölfter Theil. Der Kanton Schaffhausen*, von Edward Im-Thurn, 1840, p. 52), and the mortgages are often for the improvement and enlargement of the estate. (*Siebenzehnter Theil. Der Kanton Thürgau*, von J. A. Pupikofer, 1837, p. 209.)

cantonal governments, there has been a striking and rapid improvement in almost every department of agriculture, as well as in the houses, the habits, and the food of the people. The writer of the account of Thürgau goes so far as to say, that since the subdivision of the feudal estates into peasant properties, it is not uncommon for a third or a fourth part of an estate to produce as much grain, and support as many head of cattle, as the whole estate did before.*

§ 3. [*Evidence respecting peasant properties in Norway*] One of the countries in which peasant proprietors are of oldest date, and most numerous in proportion to the population, is Norway. Of the social and economical condition of that country [a]an[a] interesting account has been given by Mr. Laing. His testimony in favour of small landed properties both there and elsewhere, is given with great decision. I shall quote a few passages.

"If small proprietors are not good farmers, it is not from the same cause here which we are told makes them so in Scotland—indolence and want of exertion. The extent to which irrigation is carried on in these glens and valleys shows a spirit of exertion and *co-operation*" (I request particular attention to this point), "to which the latter can show nothing similar. Hay being the principal winter support of live stock, and both it and corn, as well as potatoes, liable, from the shallow soil and powerful reflexion of sunshine from the rocks, to be burnt and withered up, the greatest exertions are made to bring water from the head of each glen, along such a level as will give the command of it to each farmer at the head of his fields. This is done by leading it in wooden troughs (the half of a tree roughly scooped) from the highest perennial stream among the hills, through woods, across ravines, along the rocky, often perpendicular, sides of the glens, and from this main trough giving a lateral one to each farmer in passing the head of his farm. He distributes this supply by moveable troughs among [b]the[b] fields; and at this season waters each rig successively with scoops like those used by bleachers in watering cloth, laying his trough between every two rigs. One would not believe, without seeing it, how very large an extent of land is traversed expeditiously by these artificial showers. The extent of the main troughs is very great. In one glen I walked ten miles, and found it troughed on both sides: on one, the chain is continued down the main valley for forty

*"Denselben Erfolg hat die Vertheilung der ehemaligen grossen Lehenhöfe in mehrere kleinere eigenthümliche Bauerngüter. Es ist gar nicht selten, dass ein Drittheil oder Viertheil eines solchen Hofes nun eben so viel Getreide liefert und eben so viel Stück Vieh unterhält als vormals der ganze Hof." (*Thürgau*, p. 72.)

[a-a]MS a most [b-b]MS, 48, 49, 52, 57, 62 his

miles.* Those may be bad farmers who do such things; but they are not indolent, nor ignorant of the principle of working in concert, and keeping up establishments for common benefit. They are undoubtedly, in these respects, far in advance of any community of cottars in our Highland glens. They feel as proprietors, who receive the advantage of their own exertions. The excellent state of the roads and bridges is another proof that the country is inhabited by people who have a common interest to keep [c]them[c] under repair. There are no tolls." [d] †

*[52] Reichensperger (*Die Agrarfrage*) quoted by Mr. Kay ("Social Condition and Education of the People in England and Europe,") observes, "that the parts of Europe where the most extensive and costly plans for watering the meadows and lands have been carried out in the greatest perfection, are those where the lands are very much subdivided, and are in the hands of small proprietors. He instances the plain round Valencia, several of the southern departments of France, particularly those of Vaucluse and Bouches du Rhône, Lombardy, Tuscany, the districts of Sienna, Lucca, and Bergamo, Piedmont, many parts of Germany, &c., in all which parts of Europe the land is very much subdivided among small proprietors. In all these parts great and expensive systems and plans of general irrigation have been carried out, and are now being supported by the small proprietors themselves; thus showing how they are able to accomplish, by means of combination, work requiring the expenditure of great quantities of capital." *Kay*, i. 126 [–7]. [Kay, Joseph. *The Social Condition and Education of the People in England and Europe; shewing the results of the Primary Schools, and of the Division of Landed Property, in Foreign Countries*. 2 vols. Vol. I. *The Peasant Proprietors*. London: Longman, Brown, Green, and Longmans, 1850.]

†Laing, *Journal of a Residence in Norway*, pp. 36, 37 [MS, 48, 49 pp. 36–40].

[c–c]+Source, MS, 49, 52, 57, 62, 65, 71

[d]MS, 48, 49 [*paragraph*] "It is, I am aware, a favourite and constant observation of our agricultural writers, that these small proprietors make the worst farmers. It may be so; but a population may be in a wretched condition, although their country is very well farmed; or they may be happy, although bad cultivators. . . . Good farming is a phrase composed of two words which have no more application to the happiness or well-being of a people than good weaving or good iron-founding. That the human powers should be well applied, and not misapplied, in the production of grain, or iron, or clothing, is, no doubt, an object of great importance; but the happiness or well-being of a people does not entirely depend upon it. *It has more effect on their numbers than on their condition.* The producer of grain who is working for himself only, who is owner of his land, and has not a third of its produce to pay as rent, can afford to be a worse farmer by one-third, than a tenant, and is, notwithstanding, in a preferable condition. Our agricultural writers tell us, indeed, that labourers in agriculture are much better off as farm-servants than they would be as small proprietors. We have only the master's word for this. Ask the servant. The colonists told us the same thing of their slaves. If property is a good and desirable thing, I suspect that the smallest quantity of it is good and desirable; and that the state of society in which it is most widely diffused is the best constituted."* [*footnote:*] *[Samuel] Laing's *Journal of a Residence in Norway*, [*during the years 1834, 1835, and 1836; made with a view to inquire into the moral and political economy*

On the effects of peasant proprietorship on the Continent generally, the same writer expresses himself as follows.*

"If we listen to the large farmer, the scientific agriculturist, the" [English] "political economist, good farming must perish with large farms; the very idea that good farming can exist, unless on large farms cultivated with great capital, they hold to be absurd. Draining, manuring, economical arrangement, cleaning the land, regular rotations, valuable stock and implements, all belong exclusively to large farms, worked by large capital, and by hired labour. This reads very well; but if we raise our eyes from their books to their fields, and coolly compare what we see in the best districts farmed in large farms, with what we see in the best districts farmed in small farms, we see, and there is no blinking the fact, better crops on the ground in Flanders, East Friesland, Holstein, in short, on the whole line of the arable land of equal quality of the Continent, from the Sound to Calais, than we see on the line of British coast opposite to this line, and in the same latitudes, from the [e]Frith[e] of Forth all round to Dover. Minute labour on small portions of arable ground gives evidently, in equal soils and climate, a superior productiveness, where these small portions belong in property, as in Flanders, Holland, Friesland, and Ditmarsch in Holstein, to the farmer. It is not pretended by our agricultural writers, that our large farmers, even in Berwickshire, Roxburghshire, or the Lothians, approach to the garden-like cultivation, attention to manures, drainage, and clean state of the land, or in productiveness from a small space of soil not originally rich, which distinguish the small farmers of Flanders, or their system. In the best-farmed parish in Scotland or England, more land is wasted in the corners and borders of the fields of large farms, in the roads through them, unnecessarily wide because they are bad, and bad because they are wide, in neglected commons, waste spots, useless belts and clumps of sorry trees, and such unproductive areas, [f]than[f] would maintain the poor of the parish, if they were all laid together and cultivated. But large capital applied to farming is of course only applied to the very best of the soils of a country. It cannot touch the small unproductive spots which require more time and labour to fertilize them than is consistent with a quick return of capital. But although hired time and labour cannot be applied beneficially to such cultivation, the owner's own time and labour may. He is working for no higher [g]terms[g] at first from his land than a bare living. But in the course of generations fertility and value are produced; a better living, and even very

**Notes of a Traveller*, pp. 299 et seqq. [Pp. 299–300.]

of that country, and the condition of its inhabitants. London: Longman, Rees, Orme, Brown, Green, and Longman, 1836,] pp. 36–40 [36–8].

[e–e]Source, MS Firth

[f–f]Source, MS, 48 as

[g–g]Source, MS, 48, 49 returns

improved processes of husbandry, are attained. Furrow draining, stall feeding all summer, liquid manures, are universal in the husbandry of the small farms of Flanders, Lombardy, Switzerland. Our most improving districts under large farms are but beginning to adopt them. Dairy husbandry even, and the manufacture of the largest cheeses by the co-operation of many small farmers,* the mutual assurance of property against fire and hail-storms, by the co-operation of small farmers—the most scientific and expensive of all agricultural operations in modern times, the manufacture of beet-root sugar—the supply of the European markets with flax and hemp, by the husbandry of small farmers—the abundance of legumes, fruits, poultry, in the usual diet even of the lowest classes abroad, and the total want of such variety at the tables even of our middle classes, and this variety and abundance essentially connected with the husbandry of small farmers—all these are features in the occupation of a country by small proprietor-farmers, which must make the inquirer pause before he admits the dogma of our land doctors at home, that large farms worked by hired labour and great capital can alone bring out the greatest productiveness of the soil and furnish the greatest supply of the necessaries and conveniences of life to the inhabitants of a country."

§ 4. [*Evidence respecting peasant properties in Germany*] Among the many flourishing regions of Germany in which peasant properties prevail, I select the Palatinate, for the advantage of quoting, from an English source, the results of recent personal observation of its agriculture and its

* The manner in which the Swiss peasants combine to carry on cheese-making by their united capital deserves to be noted. "Each parish in Switzerland hires a man, generally from the district of Gruyère in the canton of Freyburg, to take care of the herd, and make the cheese. [MS *ellipsis indicated by* . .] One cheeseman, one pressman or assistant, and one cowherd are considered necessary for every forty cows. The owners of the cows get credit each of them, in a book daily for the quantity of milk given by each cow. The cheeseman and his assistants milk the cows, put the milk all together, and make cheese of it, and at the end of the season each owner receives the weight of cheese proportionable to the quantity of milk his cows have delivered. By this co-operative plan, instead of the small-sized unmarketable cheeses only, which each could produce out of his three or four cows' milk, he has the same weight in large marketable cheese superior in quality, because made by people who attend to no other business. The cheeseman and his assistants are paid so much per head of the cows, in money or in cheese, or sometimes they hire the cows, and pay the owners in money or cheese." *Notes of a Traveller*, p. 351 [p. 352]. A similar system exists in the French Jura. See, for full details, Lavergne, *Economie Rurale de la France*, 2nd ed., pp. 139 et seqq. One [MS, 48, 49, 52, 57 Jura. One] of the most remarkable points in this interesting case of combination of labour, is the confidence which it supposes, and which experience must justify, in the integrity of the persons employed.

people. Mr. Howitt, a writer whose habit it is to see all English objects and English socialities *en beau*, and who, in treating of the Rhenish peasantry, certainly does not [a]underrate[a] the rudeness of their implements, and the inferiority of their ploughing, nevertheless shows that under the invigorating influence of the feelings of proprietorship, they make up for the imperfections of their apparatus by the intensity of their application. "The peasant harrows and clears his land till it is in the nicest order, and it is admirable to see the crops which he obtains."* "The peasants† are the great and ever-present objects of country life. They are the great population of the country, because they themselves are the possessors. This country is, in fact, for the most part, in the hands of the people. It is parcelled out [b]among[b] the multitude. . . . . . The peasants are not, as with us, for the most part, totally cut off from property in the soil they cultivate, totally dependent on the labour afforded by others—they are themselves the proprietors. It is, perhaps, from this cause that they are probably the most industrious peasantry in the world. They labour busily, early and late, because they feel that they are labouring for themselves. . . . . . The German peasants work hard, but they have no actual want. Every man has his house, his orchard, his roadside trees, commonly so heavy with fruit, that he is obliged to prop and secure them all ways, or they would be torn to pieces. He has his corn-plot, his plot for mangel-wurzel, for hemp, and so on. He is his own master; and he, and every member of his family, have the strongest motives to labour. You see the effect of this in that unremitting diligence which is beyond that of the whole world besides, and his economy, which is still greater. The Germans, indeed, are not so active and lively as the English. You never see them in a bustle, or as though they meant to knock off a vast deal in a little time. . . . . . They are, on the contrary, slow, but for ever doing. They plod on from day to day, and year to year—the most patient, untirable, and persevering of animals. The English peasant is so cut off from the idea of property, that he comes habitually to look upon it as a thing from which he is warned by the laws of the large proprietors, and becomes, in consequence, spiritless, purposeless. . . . . . The German bauer, on the contrary, looks on the country as made for him and his fellow-men. He feels himself a man; he has a stake in the country, as good as that of the bulk of his neighbours; no man can threaten him with ejection, or the workhouse, so long as he is active and economical. He walks, therefore,

* [Howitt, William.] *Rural and Domestic Life of Germany* [*with Characteristic Sketches of its Cities and Scenery, collected in a general Tour, and during a Residence in the Country in the years 1840, 41 and 42*. London: Longman, Brown, Green, and Longmans, 1842], p. 27.

† Ibid. p. 40 [–2].

[a-a]MS understate [b-b]Source, MS amongst

with a bold step; he looks you in the face with the air of a free man, but of a respectful one."

Of their industry, the same writer thus further speaks: "There is not an hour of the year in which they do not find unceasing occupation. In the depth of winter, when the weather permits them by any means to get out of doors, they are always finding something to do. They carry out their manure to their lands while the frost is in them. If there is not frost, they are busy cleaning ditches and felling old fruit trees, or such as do not bear well. Such of them as are too poor to lay in a sufficient stock of wood, find plenty of work in ascending into the mountainous woods, and bringing thence fuel. It would astonish the English common people to see the intense labour with which the Germans earn their firewood. In the [c]depths[c] of frost and snow, go into any of their hills and woods, and there you [d]will[d] find them hacking up stumps, cutting off branches, and gathering, by all means which the official wood-police will allow, boughs, stakes, and pieces of wood, which they convey home with the most incredible toil and patience."* After a description of their careful and laborious vineyard culture, he continues,† "In England, with its great quantity of grass lands, and its large farms, so soon as the grain is in, and the fields are shut up for hay grass, the country seems in a comparative state of rest and quiet. But here they are everywhere, and for ever, hoeing and mowing, planting and cutting, weeding and gathering. They have a succession of crops like a market-gardener. They have their carrots, poppies, hemp, flax, saintfoin, lucerne, rape, colewort, cabbage, rotabaga, black turnips, Swedish and white turnips, teazles, Jerusalem artichokes, mangel-wurzel, parsnips, kidney-beans, field beans, and peas, vetches, Indian corn, buckwheat, madder for the manufacturer, potatoes, their great crop of tobacco, millet—all, or the greater part, under the family management, in their own family allotments. They have had these things first to sow, many of them to transplant, to hoe, to weed, to clear [e]of[e] insects, to top; many of them to mow and gather in successive crops. They have their water-meadows, of which kind almost all their meadows are, to flood, to mow, and reflood; watercourses to reopen and to make anew: their early fruits to gather, to bring to market with their green crops of vegetables; their cattle, sheep, calves, foals, most of them prisoners, and poultry to look after; their vines, as they shoot rampantly in the summer heat, to prune, and thin out the leaves [f]when[f] they are too thick: and any one may imagine what a scene of incessant labour it is."

* *Rural and Domestic Life of Germany*, p. 44.
† Ibid. p. 50 [–1].

[c–c]Source, MS, 48, 49, 52, 57, 62 depth
[d–d]+71 [*not in* Source]
[e–e]Source, MS, 48, 49, 52, 57, 62, 65 off [*printer's error?*]
[f–f]Source, MS where

This interesting sketch, to the general truth of which any observant traveller in that highly cultivated and populous region can bear witness, accords with the more elaborate delineation by a distinguished inhabitant, Professor Rau, in his little treatise "On the Agriculture of the Palatinate."* [g]Dr.[g] Rau bears testimony not only to the industry, but to the skill and intelligence of the peasantry; their judicious employment of manures, and excellent rotation of crops; the progressive improvement of their agriculture for generations past, and the spirit of further improvement which is still active. "The indefatigableness of the country people, who may be seen in activity all the day and all the year, and are never idle, because they make a good distribution of their labours, and find for every interval of time a suitable occupation, is as well known as their zeal is praiseworthy in turning to use every circumstance which presents itself, in seizing upon every useful novelty which offers, and even in searching out new and advantageous methods. One easily perceives that the peasant of this district has reflected much on his occupation: he can give reasons for his modes of proceeding, even if those reasons are not always tenable; he is as exact an observer of proportions as it is possible to be from memory, without the aid of figures: he attends to such general signs of the times as appear to augur him either benefit or harm."†

[h]The experience of all other parts of Germany is similar. "In Saxony," says Mr. Kay, "it is a notorious fact, that during the last thirty years, and since the peasants became the proprietors of the land, there has been a rapid and continual improvement in the condition of the houses, in the manner of living, in the dress of the peasants, and particularly in the culture of the land. I have twice walked through that part of Saxony called Saxon Switzerland, in company with a German guide, and on purpose to see the state of the villages and of the farming, and I can safely challenge contradiction when I affirm that there is no farming in all Europe superior to the laboriously careful cultivation of the valleys of that part of Saxony. There, as in the cantons of Berne, Vaud, and Zurich, and in the Rhine provinces, the farms are singularly flourishing. They are kept in beautiful condition, and are always neat and well managed. The ground is cleared as if it were a garden. No hedges or brushwood encumber it. Scarcely a rush or thistle or a bit of rank grass is to be seen. The meadows are well watered every spring with liquid manure, saved from the drainings of the farm yards. The grass is so free from weeds that the Saxon meadows reminded me more of English lawns than of anything else I had seen. The

* *Ueber die Landwirthschaft der Rheinpfalz, und insbesondere in der Heidelberger Gegend.* Von D. Karl Heinrich Rau. Heidelberg [: Winter], 1830.

† [*Translated from*] Rau, pp. 15, 16.

[g-g]MS, 48, 49, 52 M.

[h-h267]+52, 57, 62, 65, 71

peasants endeavour to outstrip one another in the quantity and quality of the produce, in the preparation of the ground, and in the general cultivation of their respective portions. All the little proprietors are eager to find out how to farm so as to produce the greatest results: they diligently seek after improvements; they send their children to the agricultural schools in order to fit them to assist their fathers; and each proprietor soon adopts a new improvement introduced by any of his neighbours."* If this be not overstated, it denotes a state of intelligence very different not only from that of English labourers but of English farmers.

Mr. Kay's book, published in 1850, contains a mass of evidence gathered from observation and inquiries in many different parts of Europe, together with attestations from many distinguished writers, to the beneficial effects of peasant properties. Among the testimonies which he cites respecting their effect on agriculture, I select the following.

"Reichensperger, himself an inhabitant of that part of Prussia where the land is the most subdivided, has published a long and very elaborate work to show the admirable consequences of a system of freeholds in land. He expresses a very decided opinion that not only are the *gross* products of any given number of acres held and cultivated by small or peasant proprietors, greater than the gross products of an equal number of acres held by a few great proprietors, and cultivated by tenant farmers, but that the *net* products of the former, after deducting all the expenses of cultivation, are also greater than the net products of the latter. . . . He mentions one fact which seems to prove that the fertility of the land in countries where the properties are small, must be rapidly increasing. He says that the price of the land which is divided into small properties in the Prussian Rhine provinces, is much higher, and has been rising much more rapidly, than the price of land on the great estates. He and Professor Rau both say that this rise in the price of the small estates would have ruined the more recent purchasers, unless the productiveness of the small estates had increased in at least an equal proportion; and *as the small proprietors have been gradually becoming more and more prosperous* notwithstanding the increasing prices they have paid for their land, he argues, with apparent justness, that this would seem to show that not only the gross profits of the small estates, but the net profits also have been gradually increasing, and that the net profits per acre, of land, when farmed by small proprietors, are greater than the net profits per acre of land farmed by a great proprietor. He says,

* [52] *The Social Condition and Education of the People in England and Europe; showing the results of the Primary Schools, and of the division of Landed Property in Foreign Countries.* By Joseph Kay, Esq., M.A. Barrister-at-Law, and late Travelling Bachelor of the University of Cambridge. Vol. i. pp. 138–40.

with seeming truth, that the increasing price of land in the small estates cannot be the mere effect of competition, or it would have diminished the profits and the prosperity of the small proprietors, and that this result has not followed the rise.

"Albrecht Thaer, another celebrated German writer on the different systems of agriculture, in one of his later works (Grundsätze der rationellen Landwirthschaft) expresses his decided conviction, that the *net produce* of land is greater when farmed by small proprietors than when farmed by great proprietors or their tenants. . . . This opinion of Thaer is all the more remarkable, as, during the early part of his life, he was very strongly in favour of the English system of great estates and great farms."

Mr. Kay adds from his own observation, "The peasant farming of Prussia, Saxony, Holland, and Switzerland is the most perfect and economical farming I have ever witnessed in any country." *[h]

§ 5. [*Evidence respecting peasant properties in Belgium*] But the most decisive example in opposition to the English prejudice against cultivation by peasant proprietors, is the case of Belgium. The soil is originally one of the worst in Europe. "The provinces," says Mr. M'Culloch,† "of West and East Flanders, and Hainault, form a far stretching plain, of which the luxuriant vegetation indicates the indefatigable care and labour bestowed upon its cultivation; for the natural soil consists almost wholly of barren sand, and its great fertility is entirely the result of very skilful management and judicious application of various manures." There exists a carefully prepared [a]and comprehensive[a] treatise on Flemish Husbandry, in the Farmer's Series of the Society for the Diffusion of Useful Knowledge. The writer observes‡ that the Flemish agriculturists "seem to want nothing but a space to work upon: whatever be the quality or texture of the soil, in time they will make it produce something. The [b]sands[b] in the Campine can be compared to nothing but the [c]sand[c] on the sea-shore, which they probably were originally. It is highly interesting to follow step by step the progress of improvement. Here you see a cottage and rude cow-shed erected on a spot of the most unpromising aspect. The loose white sand blown into irregular mounds is only kept together by the roots of the heath: a small

* [52] Kay, i. 116–8 [114–8].

† *Geographical Dictionary*, art. "Belgium." [McCulloch, J. R. *A Dictionary, Geographical, Statistical, and Historical, of the various Countries, Places, and Principal Natural Objects in the World.* 2 vols. London: Longman, Orme, Brown, Green, and Longmans, 1851, I, 324.]

‡ Pp. 11–14.

[a-a]MS, 48, 49 systematic
[b-b]Source, MS, 48, 49, 52, 57, 62, 65 sand [*printer's error?*]
[c-c]Source, MS, 48, 49, 52, 57, 62, 65 sands [*printer's error?*]

spot only is levelled and surrounded by a ditch: part of this is covered with young broom, part is planted with potatoes, and perhaps a small patch of diminutive clover may show itself:" but manures, both solid and liquid, are collecting, "and this is the nucleus from which, in a few years, a little farm will spread around. . . . If there is no manure at hand, the only thing that can be sown, on [d]pure[d] sand, at first is broom: this grows in the most barren soils; in three years it is fit to cut, and produces some return in faggots for the bakers and brickmakers. The leaves which have fallen have somewhat enriched the soil, and the fibres of the roots have given a [e]slight[e] degree of compactness. It may now be ploughed and sown with buckwheat, or even with rye without manure. By the time this is reaped, some manure may have been collected, and a regular course of cropping may begin. As soon as clover and potatoes enable the farmer to keep cows and make manure, the improvement goes on rapidly; in a few years the soil undergoes a complete change: it becomes mellow and retentive of moisture, and enriched by the vegetable matter afforded by the decomposition of the roots of clover and other plants. . . . After the land has been gradually brought into a good state, and is cultivated in a regular manner, there appears much less difference between the soils which have been originally good, and those which have been made so by labour and industry. At least the crops in both appear more nearly alike at harvest, than is the case in soils of different qualities in other countries. This is a great proof of the excellency of the Flemish system; for it shows that the land is in a constant state of improvement, and that the deficiency of the soil is compensated by greater attention to tillage and manuring, especially the latter."

The people who labour thus intensely [f]on their small properties or farms[f], have practised for centuries those principles of rotation of crops and economy of manures, which in England are counted among modern discoveries: and even now the superiority of their agriculture, as a whole, to that of England, is admitted by competent judges. "The cultivation of a poor light soil, [g]or a moderate soil[g]," says the writer last quoted,* "is generally superior in Flanders to that of the most improved farms of the same kind in Britain. We surpass the Flemish farmer greatly in capital, in varied implements of tillage, in the choice and breeding of cattle and sheep," (though, according to the same authority,† they are much "before us in the feeding of their cows,") "and the British farmer is in general a man of superior

* *Flemish Husbandry*, p. 3.
† Ibid. p. 13.

[d-d]Source, MS poor
[e-e]Source, MS, 48, 49, 52, 57, 62, 65 certain
[f-f]MS, 48, 49, 52, 57, 62, 65 , because labouring for themselves
[g-g]Source, MS on a moderate scale

education to the Flemish peasant. But in the minute attention to the qualities of the soil, in the management and application of manures of different kinds, in the judicious succession of crops, and especially in the economy of land, so that every part of it shall be in a constant state of production, we have still something to learn from the Flemings," and not from an instructed and enterprising Fleming here and there, but from the general practice.

Much of the most highly cultivated part of the country consists of peasant properties, managed by the proprietors, always either wholly or partly by spade [h]industry[h].* "When the land is cultivated entirely by the spade, and no horses are kept, a cow is kept for every three acres of land, and entirely fed on artificial grasses and roots. This mode of cultivation is principally adopted in the Waes district, where properties are very small. All the labour is done by the different members of the family;" children soon beginning "to assist in various minute operations, according to their age and strength, such as weeding, hoeing, feeding the cows. If they can raise rye and wheat enough to make their bread, and potatoes, turnips, carrots and clover, for the cows, they do well; and the produce of the sale of their rape-seed, their flax, their hemp, and their butter, after deducting the expense of manure purchased, which is always considerable, gives them a very good profit. [i]Suppose[i] the whole extent of the land to be six acres, which is not an uncommon occupation, and which one man can manage;" then (after describing the cultivation), "if a man with his wife and three young children are considered as equal to three and a half grown up men, the family will require thirty-nine bushels of grain, forty-nine bushels of potatoes, a fat hog, and the butter and milk of one cow: an acre and a half of land will produce the grain and potatoes, and allow some corn to finish the fattening of the hog, which has the extra buttermilk: another acre in clover, carrots, and potatoes, together with the stubble turnips, will more than feed the cow; consequently two and a half acres of land is sufficient to feed this family, and the produce of the other three and a half may be sold to pay the rent or the interest of purchase-money, wear and tear of implements, extra manure, and clothes for the family. But these acres are the most profitable on the farm, for the hemp, flax, and colza are included; and by having another acre in clover and roots, a second cow can be kept, and its produce sold. We have, therefore, a solution of the problem, how a family can live and thrive on six acres of moderate land." After showing by calculation that this extent of land can be cultivated in the most perfect manner by the family without any aid from hired labour, the writer continues, "In a farm

* *Flemish Husbandry*, pp. 73 *et seq.* [73–5].

[h-h]MS, 48, 49, 52, 57 husbandry [i-i]Source, MS, 48 Supposing

of *ten* acres entirely cultivated by the spade, the addition of a man and a woman to the members of the family will render all the operations more easy; and with [j] horse and cart to carry out the manure, and bring home the produce, and occasionally draw the harrows, *fifteen* acres may be very well cultivated. . . . Thus it will be seen," (this is the result of some pages of details and calculations,*) "that by spade husbandry, an industrious man with a small capital, occupying only fifteen acres of good light land, may not only live and bring up a family, *paying a good rent*, but may accumulate a considerable sum in the course of his life." But the indefatigable industry by which he accomplishes this, and of which so large a portion is expended not in the mere cultivation, but in the improvement, for a distant return, of the soil itself—has that industry no connexion with *not* paying rent? Could it exist, without presupposing [k]either a virtually permanent tenure, or the certain prospect, by labour and economy on hired land, of becoming one day a landed proprietor[k]?

As to their mode of living, "the Flemish farmers and labourers live much more economically than the same class in England: they seldom eat meat, except on Sundays and in harvest: buttermilk and potatoes with brown bread is their daily food."[*] It is on this kind of evidence that English travellers, as they hurry through Europe, pronounce the peasantry of every Continental country poor and miserable, its agricultural and social system a failure, and the English the only régime under which labourers are well off. It is, truly enough, the only régime under which labourers, whether well off or not, never attempt to be better. So little are English [l]labourers[l] accustomed to consider it possible that a labourer should not spend all he earns, that they habitually mistake the signs of economy for those of poverty. Observe the true interpretation of the phenomena.

"Accordingly *they are gradually acquiring capital*, and their great ambition is to have land of their own. They eagerly seize every opportunity of purchasing a small farm, and the price is so raised by [m] competition, that land pays little more than two per cent interest for the purchase money. Large properties gradually disappear, and are divided into small portions, which sell at a high rate. But the wealth and industry of the population is continually increasing, being rather diffused through the masses than accumulated in individuals."[†]

* *Flemish Husbandry*, p. 81.

[**Ibid.*]

[†*Ibid.*]

[j]Source, MS, 48, 49, 52, 57, 62, 65 a

[k-k]MS , at least, a permanent tenure] 48, 49, 52, 57, 62, 65 *as* MS . . . a virtually permanent . . . *as* MS

[l-l]MS, 48 observers

[m]Source, MS, 48 the

With facts like these, known and accessible, it is not a little surprising to find the case of Flanders referred to not in recommendation of peasant properties, but as a warning against them; on no better ground than a presumptive excess of population, inferred from the distress which existed among the peasantry of Brabant and East Flanders in the disastrous year 1846–47. The evidence which I have cited from a writer conversant with the subject, and having no economical theory to support, shows that the distress, whatever may have been its severity, arose from no insufficiency in these little properties to supply abundantly, in any ordinary circumstances, the wants of all whom they have to maintain. It arose from the essential condition to which those are subject who employ land of their own in growing their own food, namely, that the vicissitudes of the seasons must be borne by themselves, and cannot, as in the case of large farmers, be shifted from them to the consumer. When we remember the season of 1846, a partial failure of all kinds of grain, and an almost total one of the potato, it is no wonder that in so unusual a calamity the produce of six acres, half of them sown with flax, hemp, or oil seeds, should fall short of a year's provision for a family. But we are not to contrast the distressed Flemish peasant with an English capitalist who farms several hundred acres of land. If the peasant were an Englishman, he would not be that capitalist, but a day labourer under a capitalist. And is there no distress, in times of dearth, among day labourers? Was there none, that year, in countries where small proprietors and small farmers are unknown? [n]I am aware of no reason for believing[n] that the distress was greater in Belgium, than corresponds to the proportional extent of the failure of crops compared with other [o]countries.[o]*

[a]§ 6. [*Evidence respecting peasant properties in the Channel Islands*] The evidence of the beneficial operation of peasant properties in the Channel Islands is of so decisive a character, that I cannot help adding to

*[49] As much of the distress lately complained of in Belgium, as partakes in any degree of a permanent character, appears to be almost confined to the portion [49, 52, 57 that portion] of the population who carry on manufacturing labour, either by itself or in conjunction with agricultural; and to be occasioned by a diminished demand for Belgic manufactures.

[52] To the preceding testimonies respecting Germany, Switzerland, and Belgium, may be added the following from Niebuhr, respecting the Roman Campagna. In a letter from Tivoli, he says, "Wherever you find hereditary farmers, or small proprietors, there you also find industry and honesty. I believe that a man who would employ a large fortune in establishing small freeholds might put an end to robbery in the mountain districts."—*Life and Letters of Niebuhr*, [2 vols. London: Chapman and Hall, 1852,] vol. ii. p. 149.

[n–n]MS, 48, 49 Is there any reason whatever to believe
[o–o]MS, 48, 49 countries?
[a–a273]+49, 52, 57, 62, 65, 71

the numerous citations already made, part of a description of the economical condition of those islands, by a writer who combines personal observation with an attentive study of the information afforded by others. Mr. William Thornton, in his "Plea for Peasant Proprietors," a book which by the excellence both of its materials and of its execution, deserves to be regarded as the standard work on that side of the question, speaks of the island of Guernsey in the following terms: "Not even in England is nearly so large a quantity of produce sent to market from a tract of such limited extent. This of itself might prove that the cultivators must be far removed above poverty, for being absolute owners of all the produce raised by them, they of course sell only what they do not themselves require. But the satisfactoriness of their condition is apparent to every observer. 'The happiest community,' says Mr. Hill, 'which it has ever been my lot to fall in with, is to be found in this little island of Guernsey.' 'No matter,' says Sir George Head, 'to what point the traveller may choose to bend his way, comfort everywhere prevails.' What most surprises the English visitor in his first walk or drive beyond the bounds of St. Peter's Port is the appearance of the habitations with which the landscape is thickly studded. Many of them are such as in his own country would belong to persons of middle rank; but he is puzzled to guess what sort of people live in the [b]other[b], which, though in general not large enough for farmers, are almost invariably much too good in every respect for day labourers. . . Literally, in the whole island, with the exception of a few fishermen's huts, there is not one so mean as to be likened to the ordinary habitation of an English farm labourer. . . . 'Look,' says a late Bailiff of Guernsey, Mr. De L'Isle Brock, 'at the hovels of the English, and compare them with the cottages of our peasantry.' . . . Beggars are utterly unknown. . . . Pauperism, able-bodied pauperism at least, is nearly as rare as mendicancy. The Savings Banks accounts also bear witness to the general abundance enjoyed by the labouring classes of Guernsey. In the year 1841, there were in England, out of a population of nearly fifteen millions, less than 700,000 depositors, or one in every twenty persons, and the average amount of the deposits was 30*l*. In Guernsey, in the same year, out of a population of 26,000, the number of depositors was 1920, and the average amount of the deposits 40*l*."* The evidence as to Jersey and Alderney is of a similar character.

Of the efficiency and productiveness of agriculture on the small properties of the Channel Islands, Mr. Thornton produces ample evidence, the result of which he sums up as follows: "Thus it appears that in the two

**A Plea for Peasant Proprietors* [*; with the Outlines of a Plan for their Establishment in Ireland*. London: Murray, 1848]. By William Thomas Thornton, pp. 99–104.

[b-b]Source, 49, 52, 57, 62 others

principal Channel Islands, the agricultural population is, in the one twice, and in the other, three times, as dense as in Britain, there being in the latter country, only one cultivator to twenty-two acres of cultivated land, while in Jersey there is one to eleven, and in Guernsey one to seven acres. Yet the agriculture of these islands maintains, besides cultivators, non-agricultural populations, respectively four and five times as dense as that of Britain. This difference does not arise from any superiority of soil or climate possessed by the Channel Islands, for the former is naturally rather poor, and the latter is not better than in the southern counties of England. It is owing entirely to the assiduous care of the farmers, and to the abundant use of manure."* "In the year 1837," he says in another place,† "the average yield of wheat in the large farms of England was only twenty-one bushels, and the highest average for any one county was no more than twenty-six bushels. The highest average since claimed for the whole of England is thirty bushels. In Jersey, where the average size of farms is only sixteen acres, the average produce of wheat per acre was stated by Inglis in 1834 to be thirty-six bushels; but it is proved by official tables to have been forty bushels in the five years ending with 1833. In Guernsey, where farms are still smaller, four quarters per acre, according to Inglis, is considered a good, but still a very common crop." "Thirty shillings ‡ an acre would be thought in England a very fair rent for middling land; but in the Channel Islands, it is only very inferior land that would not let for at least 4*l*."[a]

[a]§ 7.[a] [*Evidence respecting peasant properties in France*] It is from France, [b] that impressions unfavourable to peasant properties are generally drawn; it is in France that the system is so often asserted to have brought forth its fruit in the most wretched possible agriculture, and to be rapidly reducing, if not to have already reduced the peasantry, by subdivision of land, to the verge of starvation. It is difficult to account for the general prevalence of impressions so much the reverse of [c] truth. The agriculture of France was wretched and the peasantry in great indigence before the Revolution. At that time they were not, [d]so universally as at present[d], landed proprietors. There were, however, considerable districts of France where the land, even then, was to a great extent the property of the peasantry, and among these were many of the most conspicuous exceptions to the general bad agriculture and to the general poverty. An authority, on this point, not to be disputed, is Arthur Young, the inveterate enemy of small farms, the coryphæus of the modern English school of agriculturists;

*Ibid. p. 38. †Ibid. p. 9 [–10]. ‡Ibid. p. 32.

[a–a]MS, 48 § 6.
[b]MS, 48 however,
[c]MS, 48 the
[d–d]MS, 48, 49, 52 generally speaking

who yet, travelling over nearly the whole of France in 1787, 1788, and 1789, when he finds remarkable excellence of cultivation, never hesitates to ascribe it to peasant property. "Leaving Sauve," says he,* "I was much struck with a large tract of land, seemingly nothing but huge rocks; yet most of it enclosed and planted with the most industrious attention. Every man has an olive, a mulberry, an almond, or a peach tree, and vines scattered among them; so that the whole ground is covered with the oddest mixture of these plants and bulging rocks, that can be conceived. The inhabitants of this village deserve encouragement for their industry; and if I were a French minister they should have it. They would soon turn all the deserts around them into gardens. Such a knot of active husbandmen, who turn their rocks into scenes of fertility, because I suppose *their own*, would do the same by the wastes, if animated by the same omnipotent principle." Again:† "Walk to Rossendal," (near Dunkirk) "where M. le Brun has an improvement on the Dunes, which he very obligingly showed me. Between the town and that place is a great number of neat little houses, built each with its garden, and one or two fields enclosed, of most wretched blowing *dune* sand, naturally as white as snow, but improved by industry. The magic of *property* turns sand to gold." And again:‡ "Going out of Gange, I was surprised to find by far the greatest exertion in irrigation which I had yet seen in France; and then passed by some steep mountains, highly cultivated in terraces. Much watering at St. Lawrence. The scenery very interesting to a farmer. From Gange, to the mountain of rough ground which I crossed, the ride has been the most interesting which I have taken in France; the efforts of industry the most vigorous; the animation the most lively. An activity has been here, that has swept away all difficulties before it, and has clothed the very rocks with verdure. It would be a disgrace to common sense to ask the cause; the enjoyment of property *must* have done it. Give a man the secure possession of a bleak rock, and he will turn it into a garden; give him a nine years' lease of a garden, and he will convert it into a desert."

In his description of the country at the foot of the Western Pyrenees, he speaks no longer from surmise, but from knowledge. "Take§ the road to Moneng, and come presently to a scene which was so new to me in France, that I could hardly believe my own eyes. A succession of many well-built, tight, and *comfortable* farming cottages built of stone and covered with tiles; each having its little garden, enclosed by clipt thorn-hedges, with plenty of peach and other fruit-trees, some fine oaks scattered in the hedges,

*Arthur Young's *Travels in France*, vol. i. p. 50. [Young, Arthur. *Travels during the Years 1787, 1788, & 1789; undertaken more particularly with a view of ascertaining the cultivation, wealth, resources, and national prosperity of the Kingdom of France*. 2nd ed. 2 vols. London: Richardson, 1794.]

†Ibid. p. 88. ‡Ibid. p. 51. §Ibid. p. 56.

and young trees nursed up with so much care, that nothing but the fostering attention of the owner could effect anything like it. To every house belongs a farm, perfectly well enclosed, with grass borders mown and neatly kept around the corn-fields, with gates to pass from one enclosure to another. There are some parts of England (where small yeomen still remain) that resemble this country of Béarn; but we have very little that is equal to what I have seen in this ride of twelve miles from Pau to Moneng. It is all in the hands of little proprietors, without the farms being so small as to occasion a vicious and miserable population. An air of neatness, warmth, and comfort breathes over the whole. It is visible in their new built houses and stables; in their little gardens; in their hedges; in the courts before their doors; even in the coops for their poultry, and the sties for their hogs. A peasant does not think of rendering his pig comfortable, if his own happiness hang by the thread of a nine years' lease. We are now in Béarn, within a few miles of the cradle of Henry IV. Do they inherit these blessings from that good prince? The benignant genius of that good monarch seems to reign still over the country; each peasant has *the fowl in the pot*." He frequently notices the excellence of the agriculture of French Flanders, where the farms "are all small, and much in the hands of little proprietors."* In the Pays de Caux, also a country of small properties, the agriculture was miserable; of which his explanation was that it "is a manufacturing country, and farming is but a secondary pursuit to the cotton fabric, which spreads over the whole of it."† The same district is still a seat of manufactures, and a country of small proprietors, and is now, whether we judge from the appearance of the crops or from the official returns, one of the best cultivated in France. In "Flanders, Alsace, and part of Artois, as well as on the banks of the Garonne, France possesses a husbandry equal to our own."‡ [e]Those[e] countries, and a considerable part of Quercy, "are cultivated more like gardens than farms. Perhaps they are too much like gardens, from the smallness of properties."§ In those districts the admirable rotation of crops, so long practised in Italy, but at that time generally neglected in France, was already universal. "The rapid succession of crops, the harvest of one being but the signal of sowing immediately for a second," (the same fact which [f]strikes[f] all observers in the valley of the Rhine) "can scarcely be carried to greater perfection: and this is a point, perhaps, of all others the most essential to good husbandry, when such crops are so justly distributed as we generally find them in these provinces; cleaning and ameliorating ones being made the preparation for such as foul and exhaust."

It must not, however, be supposed, that Arthur Young's testimony on the

*Young, pp. 322–4 [p. 322].
†Ibid. p. 325.
‡Ibid. p. 357.
§Ibid. p. 364.

[e–e]MS, 48 These
[f–f]MS, 48, 49, 52 must strike

subject of peasant properties is uniformly favourable. In Lorraine, Champagne, and elsewhere, he finds the agriculture bad, and the small proprietors very miserable, in consequence, as he says, of the extreme subdivision of the land. His opinion is thus summed up:*—"Before I travelled, I conceived that small farms, in property, were very susceptible of good cultivation; and that the occupier of such, having no rent to pay, might be sufficiently at his ease to work improvements, and carry on a vigorous husbandry; but what I have seen in France, has greatly lessened my good opinion of them. In Flanders, I saw excellent husbandry on properties of 30 to 100 acres; but we seldom find here such small patches of property as are common in other provinces. In Alsace, and on the Garonne, that is, on soils of such exuberant fertility as to demand no exertions, some small properties also are well cultivated. In Béarn, I passed through a region of little farmers, whose appearance, neatness, ease, and happiness charmed me; it was what property alone could, on a small scale, effect; but these were by no means contemptibly small; they are, as I judged by the distance from house to house, from 40 to 80 acres. Except these, and a very few other instances, I saw nothing respectable on small properties, except a most unremitting industry. Indeed, it is necessary to impress on the reader's mind, that though the husbandry I met with, in a great variety of instances on little properties, was as bad as can [g]be well[g] conceived, yet the industry of the possessors was so conspicuous, and so meritorious, that no commendations would be too great for it. It was sufficient to prove that property in land is, of all others, the most active instigator to severe and incessant labour. And this truth is of such force and extent, that I know no way so sure of carrying tillage to a mountain top, as by permitting the adjoining villagers to acquire it in property; in fact, we see that in the mountains of Languedoc, &c., they have conveyed earth in baskets, on their backs, to form a soil where nature had denied it."

The experience, therefore, of this celebrated agriculturist, and apostle of [h]the[h] *grande culture*, may be said to be, that the effect of small properties, cultivated by peasant proprietors, is admirable when they are not *too* small: so small, namely, as not fully to occupy the time and attention of the family; for he often complains, with great apparent reason, of the quantity of idle time which the peasantry had on their hands when the land was in very small portions, notwithstanding the ardour with which they toiled to improve their little patrimony in every way which their knowledge or ingenuity could suggest. He recommends, accordingly, that a limit of subdivision should be fixed by law; and this is by no means an indefensible

*Young, vol. i. p. 412.

[g-g]Source, MS, 48, 49 well be   [h-h]MS, 48, 49, 52, 57, 62 *la*

proposition in countries, if such there are, where the *morcellement*, having already gone farther than the state of capital and the nature of the staple articles of cultivation render advisable, still continues progressive. That each peasant should have a patch of land, even in full property, if it is not sufficient to support him in comfort, is a system with all the disadvantages, and scarcely any of the benefits, of small properties; since he must either live in indigence on the produce of his land, or depend as habitually as if he had no landed possessions, on the wages of hired labour: which, besides, if all the holdings[i] surrounding him are [j]of similar dimensions[j], he has little prospect of finding. The benefits of peasant properties are conditional on their not being too much subdivided; that is, on their not being required to maintain too many persons, in proportion to the produce that can be raised from them by those persons. The question resolves itself, like most questions respecting the condition of the labouring classes, into one of population. Are small properties a stimulus to undue multiplication, or a check to it?

[i-i]MS, 48, 49 lands
[j-j]MS, 48, 49 held in a similar manner

CHAPTER VII

Continuation of the Same Subject

§ 1. [*Influence of peasant properties in stimulating industry*] Before examining the influence of peasant properties on the ultimate economical interests of the labouring class, as determined by the increase of population, let us note the points respecting the moral and social influence of that territorial arrangement, which may be looked upon as established, either by the reason of the case, or by the facts and authorities cited in the preceding chapter.

The reader new to the subject must have been struck with the powerful impression made upon all the witnesses to whom I have referred, by what a Swiss statistical writer calls the "almost superhuman industry" of peasant proprietors.* On this point at least, authorities are unanimous. Those who have seen only one country of peasant properties, always think the inhabitants of that country the most industrious in the world. There is as little doubt among observers, with what feature in the condition of the peasantry this pre-eminent industry is connected. It is [a]the "magic[a] of property" which, in the words of Arthur Young, "turns sand into gold." The idea of property does not, however, necessarily imply that there should be no rent, any more than that there should be no taxes. It merely implies that the rent should be a fixed charge, not liable to be raised against the possessor by his own improvements, or by the will of a landlord. A tenant at a quit-rent is, to all intents and purposes, a proprietor; a copyholder is not less so than a freeholder. What is wanted is [b]permanent[b] possession on fixed terms. "Give a man the secure possession of a bleak rock, and he will turn it into a garden; give him a nine years' lease of a garden, and he will convert it into a desert."

The details which have been cited, and those, still more minute, to be found in the same authorities, concerning the habitually elaborate system of cultivation, and the thousand devices of the peasant proprietor for making every superfluous hour and odd moment instrumental to some in-

* "*Fast übermenschliche Fleiss.*" Der Canton Schaffhausen (ut supra) [*see* p. 258n *above*], p. 53.

[a-a]MS, 48, 49, 52, 57, 62, 65 "the magic
[b-b]MS, 48, 49 perpetuity of

crease in the future produce and value of the land, will explain what has been said in a previous chapter* respecting the far larger gross produce which, with anything like parity of agricultural knowledge, is obtained from the same quality of soil on small farms, at least when they are the property of the cultivator. The treatise on "Flemish Husbandry" is especially instructive respecting the means by which untiring industry does more than outweigh inferiority of resources, imperfection of implements, and ignorance of scientific theories. The peasant cultivation of Flanders and Italy is affirmed to produce heavier crops, in equal circumstances of soil, than the best cultivated districts of Scotland and England. It produces them, no doubt, with an amount of labour which, if paid for by an employer, would make the cost to him more than equivalent to the benefit; but to the peasant it is not cost, it is the devotion of time which he can spare, to a favourite pursuit, if we should not rather say a ruling passion.†

[c]We have seen, too, that it is not solely by superior exertion that the Flemish cultivators succeed in obtaining these brilliant results. The same motive which gives such intensity to their industry, placed them earlier in possession of an amount of agricultural knowledge, not attained until much later in countries where agriculture was carried on solely by hired labour.

* Supra, Book i. ch. ix. § 4. [Pp. 142–52.]

† Read the graphic description [MS the description] by the historian Michelet, [MS Michelet, in his quaint manner,] of the feelings of a peasant proprietor towards his land.

"Si nous voulons connaître la pensée intime, la passion, du paysan de France, cela est fort aisé. Promenons-nous le dimanche dans la campagne, suivons-le. Le voilà qui s'en va là-bas devant nous. Il est deux heures; sa femme est à vêpres; il est endimanché; je réponds qu'il va voir sa maîtresse.

"Quelle maîtresse ? sa terre.

"Je ne dis pas qu'il y aille tout droit. Non, il est libre ce jour-là, il est maître d'y aller ou de n'y pas aller. N'y va-t-il pas assez tous les jours de la semaine? Aussi, il se détourne, il va ailleurs, il a affaire ailleurs. Et pourtant, il y va.

"Il est vrai qu'il passait bien près; c'était une occasion. Il la regarde, mais apparemment il n'y entrera pas; qu'y ferait-il?—Et pourtant il y entre.

"Du moins, il est probable qu'il n'y travaillera pas; il est endimanché; il a blouse et chemise blanches.—Rien n'empêche cependant d'ôter quelque mauvaise herbe, de rejeter cette pierre. Il y a bien encore cette souche qui gêne, mais il n'a pas sa pioche, ce sera pour demain.

"Alors, il croise ses bras et s'arrête, regarde, sérieux, soucieux. Il regarde longtemps, très-longtemps, et semble s'oublier. A la fin, s'il se croit observé, s'il apperçoit un passant, il s'éloigne à pas lents. A trente pas encore, il s'arrête, se retourne, et jette sur sa terre un dernier regard, regard profond et sombre; mais pour qui sait bien voir, il est tout passionné, ce regard, tout de cœur, plein de dévotion."—*Le Peuple*, par J. Michelet, 1re partie, ch. 1 [Paris: Comptoire des Imprimeurs-Unis, 1846, pp. 1–2].

*c–c*280+62, 65, 71

An equally high testimony is borne by M. de Lavergne* to the agricultural skill of the small proprietors in those parts of France to which the *petite culture* is really suitable. "In the rich plains of Flanders, on the banks of the Rhine, the Garonne, the Charente, the Rhone, all the practices which fertilize the land and increase the productiveness of labour are known to the very smallest cultivators, and practised by them, however considerable may be the advances which they require. In their hands, abundant manures, collected at great cost, repair and incessantly increase the fertility of the soil, in spite of the activity of cultivation. The races of cattle are superior, the crops magnificent. Tobacco, flax, colza, madder, beetroot, in some places; in others, the vine, the olive, the plum, the mulberry, only yield their abundant treasures to a population of industrious labourers. Is it not also to the *petite culture* that we are indebted for most of the garden produce obtained by dint of great outlay in the neighbourhood of Paris?"[c]

§ 2. [*Influence of peasant properties in training intelligence*] Another aspect of peasant properties, in which it is essential that they should be considered, is that of an instrument of popular education. [a] Books and schooling are absolutely necessary to education; but not all-sufficient. The mental faculties will be most developed where they are most exercised; and what gives more exercise to them than the having a multitude of interests, none of which can be neglected, and which can be provided for only by varied efforts of will and intelligence? Some of the disparagers of small properties lay great stress on the cares and anxieties which beset the peasant proprietor of the Rhineland or Flanders. It is precisely those cares and anxieties which tend to make him a superior being to an English day-labourer. It is, to be sure, rather abusing the [b]privileges[b] of fair argument to represent the condition of a day-labourer as not an anxious one. I can conceive no circumstances in which he is free from anxiety, where there is a possibility of being out of employment; unless he has access to a profuse dispensation of parish pay, and no shame or reluctance in demanding it[c]. The[c] day-labourer has, in the existing state of society and population, many of the anxieties which have [d]not[d] an invigorating effect on the mind,

*[62] [*Translated from*] *Essai sur l'Economie Rurale de l'Angleterre, de l'Ecosse, et de l'Irlande*, 3me éd. [Paris: Guillaumin, 1858,] p. 127.

[a]MS, 48, 49 It is difficult to imagine what theory of education that can be, which can attach no importance to such an instrument.

[b-b]48, 49, 52 privilege

[c-c]MS, 48, 49 : then indeed he may feel with the old doggrel,

Hang sorrow, cast away care,
The parish is bound to find us.

[*paragraph*] But unless so shielded, the

[d-d]MS *not*

and none of those which have. The position of the peasant proprietor of [e]Continental Europe[e] is the reverse. From the anxiety which chills and paralyses—the uncertainty of having food to eat—few persons are more exempt: it requires as rare a concurrence of circumstances as the potato failure combined with an universal bad harvest, to bring him within reach of that danger. His anxieties are the ordinary vicissitudes of [f]more and less[f]; his cares are that he takes his fair share of the business of life; that he is a free human being, and not perpetually a child, which seems to be the approved condition of the labouring classes according to the prevailing philanthropy. He is no longer a being of a different order from the middle classes; he has pursuits and objects like those which occupy them, and give to their intellects the greatest part of [g]such cultivation as[g] they receive. If there is a first principle in intellectual education, it is this—that the discipline which does good to the mind is that in which the mind is active, not that in which it is passive. The secret for developing the faculties is to give them much to do, and much inducement to do it. [h] This detracts nothing from the importance, and even necessity, of other kinds of mental cultivation. The possession of property will not prevent the peasant from being coarse, selfish, and narrow-minded. These things depend on other influences, and other kinds of instruction. But this great stimulus to one kind of mental activity, in no way impedes any other means of intellectual development. On the contrary, by cultivating the habit of turning to practical use every fragment of knowledge acquired, it helps to render that schooling and reading fruitful, which without some such auxiliary influence are in too many cases like seed thrown on a rock.

§ 3. [*Influence of peasant properties in promoting forethought and self-control*] It is not [a]on[a] the intelligence alone, that the situation of a peasant proprietor [b]exercises an improving influence[b]. It is no less propitious to the moral virtues of prudence, temperance, and self-control. [c] Day-labourers, where the labouring class mainly consists of them, are usually improvident:

[e-e]MS, 48, 49, 52, 57, 62, 65 Flanders
[f-f]MS, 48, 49, 52, 57 *more* and *less*
[g-g]MS, 48, 49 the cultivation which
[h]MS, 48, 49 Few things surpass in this respect the occupations and interests created by the ownership and cultivation of land.
[a-a]MS, 48, 49 to
[b-b]MS, 48, 49 is full of improving influences
[c]MS, 48, 49 The labourer who possesses property, "whether he can read and write, or not, has," as Mr. Laing remarks,* "an educated mind: he has forethought, caution, and reflection guiding every action; he knows the value of restraint, and is in the constant habitual practice of it." It is remarkable how this general proposition is borne out by the character of the rural population in almost every civilized country where peasant properties are frequent. [*footnote:*] **Residence in Norway*, p. 20 [p. 21].

they spend carelessly to the full extent of their means, and let the future shift for itself. This is so notorious, that many persons [d]strongly interested in the welfare of[d] the labouring classes, hold it as a fixed opinion that an increase of wages would do them little good, unless accompanied by at least a corresponding improvement in their tastes and habits. The tendency of peasant proprietors, and of those who hope to become proprietors, is to the contrary extreme; to take even too much thought for the morrow. They are oftener accused of penuriousness than of prodigality. They deny themselves reasonable indulgences, and live wretchedly in order to economize. In Switzerland almost everybody saves, who has any means of saving; the case of the Flemish farmers [e]has been[e] already noticed: among the French, though a pleasure-loving and reputed to be a self-indulgent people, the spirit of thrift is diffused through the rural population in a manner most gratifying as a whole, and which in individual instances errs rather on the side of excess than defect. [f]Among those[f] who, from the hovels in which they live, and the herbs and roots which constitute their diet, are mistaken by travellers for proofs and specimens of general indigence, [g]there are[g] numbers who have hoards in [h]leathern[h] bags, consisting of sums, in five-franc pieces, which they keep by them perhaps [i]for[i] a whole generation, unless brought out to be expended in their most cherished gratification—the purchase of land. If there is a moral inconvenience attached to a state of society in which the peasantry have land, it is the danger of their being [j]too[j] careful of their pecuniary concerns; of its making them crafty, and "calculating" in the objectionable sense. The French peasant is no simple countryman, no downright "paysan du Danube;" both in fact and in fiction he is now "le rusé paysan." That is the stage which he has reached in the progressive development which the constitution of things has imposed on human intelligence and human emancipation. But some excess in this direction is a small and a passing evil compared with recklessness and improvidence in the labouring classes, and a cheap price to pay for the inestimable worth of the virtue of self-dependence, as the general characteristic of a people: a virtue which is one of the first conditions of excellence in [k]the[k] human character—the stock on which if the other virtues are not grafted, they have seldom any firm root; a quality indispensable in the case of a labouring class, even to any tolerable degree of physical comfort; and by which the peasantry of France, and of most European countries of peasant proprietors, are distinguished beyond any other labouring population.

[d-d]MS, 48, 49 otherwise well affected to
[e-e]MS, 48, 49 I have
[f-f]MS Those
[g-g]MS include
[h-h]MS, 48 leather
[i-i]+62, 65, 71
[j-j]MS *too*
[k-k]MS, 48, 49, 52, 57, 62, 65 a

§ 4. [*Their effect on population*] Is it likely that a state of economical relations so conducive to frugality and prudence in every other respect, should be prejudicial to it in the cardinal point of increase of population? That it is so, is the opinion expressed by most of those English political economists who have written anything about the matter. Mr. M'Culloch's opinion is well known. Mr. Jones affirms,* that [a]a "peasant[a] population raising their own wages from the soil, and consuming them in kind, are universally acted upon very feebly by internal checks, or by motives disposing them to restraint. The consequence is, that unless some external cause, quite independent of their will, forces such peasant cultivators to slacken their rate of increase, they will, in a limited territory, very rapidly approach a state of want and penury, and will be stopped at last only by the physical impossibility of procuring subsistence." He elsewhere† speaks of such a peasantry as "exactly in the condition in which the animal disposition to increase their numbers is checked by the fewest of those balancing motives and desires which regulate the increase of superior ranks or [b] more civilized people." The "causes of this peculiarity," Mr. Jones [c]promised[c] to point out in a subsequent work, which [d]never[d] made its appearance. I am totally unable to conjecture from what theory of human nature, and of the motives which influence human conduct, he [e]would have derived[e] them. Arthur Young assumes the same "peculiarity" as a fact; but, though not much in the habit of qualifying his opinions, he does not push his doctrine to so violent an extreme as Mr. Jones; having, as we have seen, himself testified to various instances in which peasant populations such as Mr. Jones speaks of, were not tending to "a state of want and penury," and were in no danger whatever of coming [f]into[f] contact with "physical impossibility of procuring subsistence."

That there should be discrepancy of experience on this matter, is easily to be accounted for. Whether the labouring people live by land or by wages, they have always hitherto multiplied up to the limit set by their habitual standard of comfort. When that standard was low, not exceeding a scanty subsistence, the size of properties, as well as the rate of wages, has been kept down to what would barely support life. Extremely low ideas of what is necessary for subsistence, are perfectly compatible with peasant properties; and if a people have always been used to poverty, and habit has reconciled them to it, there will be over-population, and excessive subdivision of land. But this is not to the purpose. The true question is, supposing a peasantry to possess land not insufficient but sufficient for their

* *Essay on the Distribution of Wealth,* p. 146. †Ibid. p. 68.

[a-a]MS, 48, 49, 52 "a peasant
[b]Source, MS, 48 of
[c-c]MS, 48, 49, 52 promises
[d-d]MS, 48, 49, 52 has never yet
[e-e]MS, 48, 49, 52 will derive
[f-f]MS, 48, 49, 52, 57, 62, 65 in

comfortable support, are they more, or less, likely to fall from this state of comfort through improvident multiplication, than if they were living in an equally comfortable manner as hired labourers? All *à priori* considerations are in favour of their being less likely. The dependence of wages on population is a matter of speculation and discussion. That wages would fall if population were much increased is often a matter of real doubt, and always a thing which requires some exercise of the [g]thinking[g] faculty for its intelligent recognition. But every peasant can satisfy himself from evidence which he can fully appreciate, whether his piece of land can be made to support several families in the same comfort [h]as[h] it supports one. Few people like to leave to their children a worse lot in life than their own. The parent who has land to leave, is perfectly able to judge whether the children can live upon it or not: but people who are supported by wages, see no reason why their sons should be unable to support themselves in the same way, and trust accordingly to chance. "In even the most useful and necessary arts and manufactures," says Mr. Laing,* "the demand for labourers is not a seen, known, steady, and appreciable demand: but it is so in husbandry" under small properties. "The labour to be done, the subsistence that labour will produce out of his portion of land, are seen and known elements in a man's calculation upon his means of subsistence. Can his square of land, or can it not, subsist a family? Can he marry or not? are questions which every man can answer without delay, doubt, or speculation. It is the depending on chance, where judgment has nothing clearly set before it, that causes reckless, improvident marriages in the lower, as in the higher classes, and produces among us the evils of over-population; and chance necessarily enters into every man's calculations, when certainty is removed altogether; as it is, where certain subsistence is, by our distribution of property, the lot of but a small portion instead of about two-thirds of the people."

There never has been a writer more keenly sensible of the evils brought upon the labouring classes by excess of population, than Sismondi, and this is one of the grounds of his earnest advocacy of peasant properties. He had ample opportunity, in more countries than one, for judging of their effect on population. Let us see his testimony. "In the countries in which cultivation by small proprietors still continues, population increases regularly and rapidly until it has attained its natural limits; that is to say, inheritances continue to be divided and subdivided among several sons, as long as, by an increase of labour, each family can extract an equal income from a smaller portion of land. A father who possessed a vast extent of natural pasture, divides it among his sons, and they turn it into fields and meadows;

* *Notes of a Traveller*, p. 46.

[g-g]MS, 48, 49 reflecting [h-h]MS, 48, 49, 52, 57, 62 in which

his sons divide it among their sons, who abolish fallows: each improvement in agricultural knowledge admits of another step in the subdivision of property. But there is no danger lest the proprietor should bring up his children to make beggars of them. He knows exactly what inheritance he has to leave them; he knows that the law will divide it equally among them; he sees the limit beyond which this division would make them descend from the rank which he has himself filled, and a just family pride, common to the peasant and to the nobleman, makes him abstain from summoning into life, children for whom he cannot properly provide. If more are born, at least they do not marry, or they agree among themselves, which of several brothers shall perpetuate the family. It is not found that in the Swiss Cantons, the patrimonies of the peasants are ever so divided as to reduce them below an honourable competence; though the habit of foreign service, by opening to the children a career indefinite and uncalculable, sometimes calls forth a super-abundant population." *

There is similar testimony respecting Norway. Though there is no law or custom of primogeniture, and no manufactures to take off a surplus population, the subdivision of property is not carried to an injurious extent. "The division of the land among children," says Mr. Laing,† "appears not, during the thousand years it has been in operation, to have had the effect of reducing the landed properties to the minimum size that will barely support human existence. I have counted from five-and-twenty to forty cows upon farms, and that in a country in which the farmer must, for at least seven months in the year, have winter provender and houses provided for all the cattle. It is evident that some cause or other, operating on aggregation of landed property, counteracts the dividing effects of partition among children. That cause can be no other than what I have long conjectured would be effective in such a social arrangement; viz. that in a country where land is held, not in tenancy merely, as in Ireland, but in full ownership, its aggregation by the deaths of co-heirs, and by the marriages of [t]the[t] female heirs among the body of landholders, will balance its subdivision by the equal succession of children. The whole mass of property will, I conceive, be found in such a state of society to consist of as many estates of the class of 1000*l.*, as many of 100*l.*, as many of 10*l.*, a year, at one period as [j] another." That this should happen, supposes diffused through society a very efficacious prudential check to population; and it is reasonable to give part of the credit of this prudential restraint to the peculiar adaptation of the peasant-proprietary system for fostering it.

*[MS Translated from the] *Nouveaux Principes*, Book iii. ch. 3 [Vol. I, pp. 170–1].

† *Residence in Norway*, p. 18 [–9].

[t-t]+49, 52, 57, 62, 65, 71 [*not in* Source]

[j]Source, MS, 48, 49, 52, 57, 62, 65 at

[k]"In some parts of Switzerland," says Mr. Kay,* "as in the canton of Argovie for instance, a peasant never marries before he attains the age of twenty-five years, and generally much later in life; and in that canton the women very seldom marry before they have attained the age of thirty. . . . Nor do the division of land and the cheapness of the mode of conveying it from one man to another, encourage the providence of the labourers of the rural districts only. They act in the same manner, though perhaps in a less degree, upon the labourers of the smaller towns. In the smaller provincial towns it is customary for a labourer to own a small plot of ground outside the town. This plot he cultivates in the [l]evening[l] as his kitchen garden. He raises in it vegetables and fruits for the use of his family during the winter. After his day's work is over, he and his family repair to the garden for a short time, which they spend in planting, sowing, weeding, or preparing for sowing or harvest, according to the season. The desire to become possessed of one of these gardens operates very strongly in strengthening prudential habits and in restraining improvident marriages. Some of the manufacturers in the canton of Argovie told me that a townsman was seldom contented until he had bought a garden, or a garden and house, and that the town labourers generally deferred their marriages for some years, in order to save enough to purchase either one or both of these luxuries."

The same writer shows by statistical evidence† that in Prussia the average age of marriage is not only much later than in England, but "is gradually becoming later than it was formerly," while at the same time "fewer illegitimate children are born in Prussia than in any other of the European countries." "Wherever I travelled," says Mr. Kay,‡ "in North Germany and Switzerland, I was assured by all that the desire to obtain land, which was felt by all the peasants, was acting as the strongest possible check upon undue increase of population." § [k]

*[52] Vol. i. pp. 67–9.
†[52] Ibid. pp. 75–9 [pp. 75 & 79].
‡[52] Ibid. p. 90.
§[52] The Prussian minister of statistics, in a work (Der Volkswohlstand im Preussischen Staate) which I am obliged to quote at second hand from Mr. Kay, after proving by figures the great and progressive increase of the consumption of food and clothing per head of the population, from which he justly infers a corresponding increase of the productiveness of agriculture, continues: "The division of estates has, since 1831, proceeded more and more throughout the country. There are now many more small independent proprietors than formerly. Yet, however many complaints of pauperism are heard among the dependent labourers, we never hear it complained that pauperism is increasing among the peasant proprietors."—Kay, i. 262–6 [*the quoted passage is on* 266].

[k-k]+52, 57, 62, 65, 71
[l-l]Source, 52, 57 evenings

[m]In Flanders, according to Mr. Fauche, the British Consul at Ostend,* "farmers' sons and those who have the means to become farmers will delay their marriage until they get possession of a farm." Once a farmer, the next object is to become a proprietor. "The first thing a Dane does with his savings," says Mr. Browne, the Consul at Copenhagen,† "is to purchase a clock, then a horse and cow, which he hires out, and which pays a good interest. Then his ambition is to become a petty proprietor, and this class of persons is better off than any in Denmark. Indeed, I know of no people in any country who have more easily within their reach all that is really necessary for life than this class, which is very large in comparison with that of labourers."[m]

But the experience which most decidedly contradicts the asserted tendency of peasant proprietorship to produce excess of population, is the case of France. In that country the experiment is [n]not tried in the most favourable[n] circumstances[o], a large proportion of the properties being too small[o]. The number of landed proprietors in France is not exactly ascertained, but on no estimate does it fall much short of five millions; which, on the lowest calculation of the number of persons [p]of[p] a family (and for France it ought to be a low calculation), shows much more than half the population as either possessing, or entitled to inherit, landed property. A majority of the properties are [q]so small as not[q] to afford a subsistence to the proprietors, of whom, according to some computations, as many as three millions are obliged to eke out their means of support either by working for hire, or by taking additional land, generally on metayer tenure. When the property possessed is not sufficient to relieve the possessor from dependence on wages, the condition of a proprietor loses much of its characteristic efficacy as a check to over-population: and if the prediction so often made in England had been realized, and France had become a "pauper warren," the experiment would have proved nothing against the tendencies of the same system of agricultural economy in other circumstances. But what is the fact? That the rate of increase of the French population is the slowest in Europe. During the generation which the Revolution raised from the extreme of hopeless wretchedness to sudden abundance, a great increase of population took place. But a generation has grown up, which, having been born in improved circumstances, has not learnt to be miserable; and upon them the spirit of thrift operates most conspicuously, in keeping the in-

*In a communication to the Commissioners of Poor Law Enquiry, p. 640[–1] of their Foreign Communications, Appendix F to their First Report [*Parliamentary Papers*, 1834, XXXIX].

†Ibid. 268.

[m–m]MS, 48, 49 [*in §5 below; see* p. 295[k]]

[n–n]MS tried in most unfavourable

[o–o]+48, 49, 52, 57, 62, 65, 71

[p–p]MS, 48, 49, 52, 57 to

[q–q]MS too small

crease of population within the increase of national wealth. In a table, drawn up by Professor Rau,* [r] of the rate of annual increase of the popu-

* The following is the table (see p. 168 of the Belgian translation of Mr. [MS, 48 M.] Rau's large work [MS Rau's great work] [Translated from *Traité d'économie nationale.*]):

		Per cent			Per cent
United States	1820–30	2.92	Scotland	1821–31	1.30
Hungary (according to Rohrer)		2.40	Saxony	1815–30	1.15
England	1811–21	1.78	Baden	1820–30 (Heunisch)	1.13
England	1821–31	1.60	Bavaria	1814–28	1.08
Austria (Rohrer)		1.30	Naples	1814–24	0.83
Prussia	1816–27	1.54	France	1817–27 (Mathieu)	0.63
Prussia	1820–30	1.37	and more recently (Moreau de		
Prussia	1821–31	1.27	Jonnès)		0.55
Netherlands	1821–28	1.28			

But the number given by Moreau de Jonnès, he adds, is not entitled to implicit confidence.

The following table given by M. Quetelet (*Sur l'Homme et le Développement de ses Facultés,* [*ou Essai de Physique Social.* Paris: Bachelier, 1835] vol. i. ch. 7 [p. 292]), also on the authority of Rau, contains additional matter, and differs in some items from the preceding, probably from the author's having taken, in those cases, an average of different years:

	Per cent		Per cent
Ireland	2.45	Bavaria	1.08
Hungary	2.40	Netherlands	0.94
Spain	1.66	Naples	0.83
England	1.65	France	0.63
Rhenish Prussia	1.33	Sweden	0.58
Austria	1.30	Lombardy	0.45

A [MS, 48, 49 A recent and] very carefully prepared statement, by M. Legoyt ["Recensement de la population de la France en 1846 et du mouvement de la population en Europe"], in the *Journal des Economistes* for May 1847 [Vol. XVII, p. 174], which brings up the results for France to the census of the preceding year 1846, is summed up in the following table:

	According to the census	According to the excess of births over deaths		According to the census	According to the excess of births over deaths
	per cent	per cent		per cent	per cent
Sweden	0.83	1.14	Wurtemburg	0.01	1.00
Norway	1.36	1.30	Holland	0.90	1.03
Denmark	—	0.95	Belgium	—	0.76
Russia	—	0.61	Sardinia	1.08	—
Austria	0.85	0.90	Great Britain		
Prussia	1.84	1.18	(exclusive of Ireland)	1.95	1.00
Saxony	1.45	0.90			
Hanover	—	0.85	France	0.68	0.50
Bavaria	—	0.71	United States	3.27	—

[r]MS [*footnote occurs at the end of this sentence*]

lations of various countries, that of France, from 1817 to 1827, is stated at $^{63}/_{100}$ per cent, that of England during a similar decennial period being $1^{6}/_{10}$ annually, and that of the United States nearly 3. According to the official returns as analysed by M. Legoyt,* the increase of the population, which from 1801 to 1806 was at the rate of 1.28 per cent annually, averaged only 0.47 per cent from 1806 to 1831; from 1831 to 1836 it averaged 0.60 per cent; from 1836 to 1841, 0.41 per cent, and from 1841 to 1846, 0.68 per [s]cent.†[s] [t]At the census of 1851 the rate of annual increase shown was only 1.08 per cent [u]in[u] the five years, or 0.21 annually; and at the census of 1856 only 0.71 per cent in five years, or 0.14 annually: so that, in the words of M. de Lavergne, "la population ne s'accroît presque plus en France." ‡ [t] Even this slow increase is wholly the effect of a diminution of deaths; the number of births not increasing at all, while the proportion of the births to the population is constantly diminishing.§ This

**Journal des Economistes* for March and May 1847 [*ibid.*, Vols. XVI & XVII].

†[MS, 48, 49, 52 *in text following* cent; but] M. Legoyt is of opinion that the population was understated in 1841, and the increase between that time and 1846 consequently overstated, and that the real increase during the whole period was something intermediate between the last two averages, or not much more than one in two hundred.

‡[57] *Journal des Economistes* for February 1847. [65] In the Journal for January 1865, M. Legoyt gives some of the numbers slightly altered, and I presume corrected. The series of percentages is 1.28, 0.31, 0.69, 0.60, 0.41, 0.68, 0.22, and 0.20. The last census in the table, that [65 census, that] of 1861, shows a slight reaction, the percentage, independently of the newly acquired departments, being 0.32.

§The following are the numbers given by M. Legoyt: [MS, 48, 49, 52 numbers:]

From 1824 to 1828 annual number of births 981,914, being 1 in 32.30 of the population.
From 1829 to 1833 annual number of births 965,444, being 1 in 34.00
From 1834 to 1838 annual number of births 972,993, being 1 in 34.39 [Source, MS, 48 34.49]
From 1839 to 1843 annual number of births 970,617, being 1 in 35.27
From 1844 and 1845 annual number of births 983,573, being 1 in 35.58

In the last two years the births, according to M. Legoyt, were swelled by the effects of a considerable immigration. "Cette diminution des naissances," he observes, "en présence d'un accroissement constant, quoique peu rapide, de la population générale et des mariages, ne peut être attribué qu'aux progrès de l'esprit d'ordre et de prévision dans les familles. C'est d'ailleurs la conséquence prévue de nos institutions civiles et sociales, qui, en amenant chaque jour une plus grande subdivision de la fortune territoriale et mobilière de la France, développent au sein des populations les instincts de conservation et de bien-être."

In four departments, among which are two of the most thriving in Normandy, the deaths even then exceeded [MS, 48, 49, 52 deaths actually exceed] the births. [57] The census of 1856 [57, 62 census, that of 1856,] exhibits the

[s-s]MS, 48, 49, 52 cent; but
[t-t]+57, 62, 65, 71 [u-u]57 on

slow growth of the numbers of the people, while capital increases much more rapidly, has caused a noticeable improvement in the condition of the labouring class. The circumstances of that portion of the class who are landed proprietors are not easily ascertained with precision, being of course extremely variable; but the mere labourers, who derived no direct benefit from the changes in landed property which took place at the Revolution, have unquestionably much improved in condition since that period.* [v]Dr.[v]

remarkable fact of a positive diminution in the population of 54 out of the 86 departments. A significant comment on the pauper-warren theory. See M. de Lavergne's analysis of the returns.

*"Les classes de notre population qui n'ont que leur salaire, celles qui, par cette raison, sont les plus exposées à l'indigence, sont aujourd'hui beaucoup mieux pourvues des objets nécessaires à la nourriture, au logement et au vêtement, qu'elles ne l'étaient au commencement du siècle. . . . On peut appuyer [ce fait] du témoignage de toutes les personnes qui ont souvenir de la première des époques comparées. . . . S'il restait des doutes à cet égard, on pourrait facilement les dissiper en consultant les anciens cultivateurs et les anciens ouvriers, ainsi que nous l'avons fait nous-mêmes dans diverses localités, sans rencontrer un seul témoignage contradictoire; on peut invoquer aussi les renseignemens recueillis à ce sujet par un observateur exact, M. Villermé (*Tableau de l'Etat Physique et Moral des Ouvriers*, [Paris: Renouard, 1840,] liv. ii. ch. i.)" From an intelligent work published in 1846, *Recherches sur les Causes de l'Indigence* [Paris: Guillaumin, 1846], par A. Clément, pp. 84–5. The same writer speaks (p. 118) of "la hausse considérable qui s'est manifesté depuis 1789 dans le taux du salaire de nos cultivateurs journaliers;" and adds the following evidence of a higher standard of habitual requirements, even in that portion of the town population, the state of which is usually represented as most deplorable. "Depuis quinze à vingt ans, un changement considérable s'est manifesté dans les habitudes des ouvriers de nos villes manufacturières: ils dépensent aujourd'hui beaucoup plus que par le passé pour le vêtement et la parure. . . . . . Les ouvriers de certaines classes, tels que les anciens *canuts* de Lyon," (according to all representations, like their counterpart, our handloom weavers, the very worst paid class of artizans,) "ne se montrent plus comme autrefois couverts de sales haillons." (Page 164.)

[49, 52, 57 Much stronger statements to the same effect are found in the recent work "On Property," by M. Thiers [Thiers, A. *De la Propriété*. Paris: Paulin, L'Heureux et Cie., 1848]; but as that work is written to make out a case, and overstates nearly every argument which the subject affords, I do not venture to rely implicitly on its statements, even in matters of fact.] [62] The preceding statements were given in former editions of this work, being the best to which I had at the time access; but evidence, both of a more recent, and of a more minute and precise character, will now be found in the important work of M. Léonce de Lavergne, *Economie Rurale de la France depuis* 1789. According to that pains-taking, well-informed, and most impartial enquirer, the average daily wages of a French labourer have risen, since the commencement of the Revolution, in the ratio of 19 to 30, while, owing to the more constant employment, the total earnings have increased in a still greater ratio, not short of double. The following are the words of M. de Lavergne (2nd ed. p. 57 [–8]):

[v-v]MS Mr] 48, 49, 52 M.

Rau testifies to a similar fact in the case of another country in which the subdivision of [w]the[w] land is [x]probably[x] excessive, the Palatinate.*

I am not aware of a single authentic instance which supports the assertion that rapid multiplication is promoted by peasant properties. Instances may undoubtedly be cited of its not being prevented by them, and one of the principal of these is Belgium; the [y]prospects[y] of which, in respect to population, [z]are at present a matter of considerable uncertainty[z]. Belgium has the most rapidly increasing population on the Continent; and when the circumstances of the country require, as they must soon do, that this

"Arthur Young évalue à *dix-neuf sols* le prix moyen de la journée du travail, qui doit être aujourd'hui *d'un franc cinquante centimes*, et cette augmentation ne représente encore qu'une partie du gain réalisé. Bien que la nation rurale soit restée à peu près la même, l'excédant de population survenu depuis 1789 s'étant concentré dans les villes, le nombre effectif des journées de travail a grossi, d'abord parce que la vie moyenne s'étant allongée, le nombre des hommes valides s'est élevé, et ensuite parce que le travail est mieux organisé, soit par la suppression de plusieurs fêtes chômées, soit par le seul effet d'une demande plus active. En tenant compte de l'accroissement du nombre des journées, le gain annuel de l'ouvrier rural doit avoir doublé. . . . Cette augmentation dans le salaire se traduit pour l'ouvrier en une augmentation au moins correspondante de bien-être, puisque le prix des principaux objets nécessaires à la vie a peu changé, et que celui des objets fabriqués, des tissus [62 *des tissus*], par exemple, a sensiblement baissé. L'habitation est également devenue meilleure, sinon partout, du moins dans la plupart de nos provinces."

M. de Lavergne's estimate of the average amount of a day's wages is grounded on a careful comparison, in this and all other economical points of view, of all the different provinces of France.

*In his little book on the Agriculture of the Palatinate, already cited. He says that the daily wages of labour, which during the last years of the war were unusually high, and so continued until 1817, afterwards sank to a lower money-rate, but that the prices of many commodities having fallen in a still greater proportion, the condition of the people was unequivocally improved. The food given to farm labourers by their employers has also greatly improved in quantity and quality. "Sie heutigen Tages bedeutend besser ist, als vor ungefähr 40 Jahren, wo das Gesinde weniger Fleisch und Mehlspeisen, keinen Käse zum Brote u. dgl. erhielt." (p. 20.) "Such an increase of wages" (adds the Professor) "which must be estimated not in money, but in the quantity of necessaries and conveniences which the labourer is enabled to procure, is, by universal admission, a proof that the mass of capital must have increased." [Translated from Rau, p. 18.] It proves not only this, but also that the labouring population has not increased in an equal degree; and that in this instance as well as in that of France [MS, 48, 49, 52, 57, 62, 65 in France], the division [MS, 48, 49, 52, 57, 62 the *morcellement*] of the land, even when excessive, has been compatible with a strengthening of the prudential checks to population.

w-w+49, 52, 57, 62, 65, 71
x-xMS, 48, 49 really
y-yMS state
z-zMS will be a subject of rather anxious contemplation, to the political philosopher for some time to come

rapidity should be checked, there will be a considerable strength of existing habit to be broken through. One of the unfavourable circumstances is the great power possessed over the minds of the people by the Catholic priesthood, whose influence is [a]everywhere strongly exerted against restraining[a] population. As yet, however, it must be remembered that the indefatigable industry and great agricultural skill of the people have rendered the existing rapidity of increase practically innocuous; the great number of large estates still undivided affording by their gradual dismemberment, a resource for the necessary augmentation of the gross produce; and there are, besides, many [b]large[b] manufacturing towns, and mining and coal districts, which attract and employ a [c]considerable[c] portion of the annual increase of population.

§ 5. [*Their effect on the subdivision of land*] But even where peasant properties are accompanied by an excess of numbers, this evil is not necessarily attended with the additional economical disadvantage of too great a subdivision of the land. It does not follow because landed [a]property[a] is minutely divided, that [b]farms[b] will be so. As large properties are perfectly compatible with small farms, so are small properties with farms of an adequate size; and a subdivision of occupancy is not an inevitable consequence of even undue multiplication among peasant proprietors. As might be expected from their admirable intelligence in things relating to their occupation, the Flemish peasantry have long learnt this lesson. "The habit of not dividing properties," says [c]Dr.[c] Rau,* "and the opinion that this is advantageous, have been so completely preserved in Flanders, that even now, when a peasant dies leaving several children, they do not think of dividing his patrimony, though it be neither entailed nor settled in trust; they prefer selling it entire, and sharing the proceeds, considering it as a jewel which loses its value when it is divided." That the same feeling must prevail widely even in France, is shown by the great frequency of sales of land, amounting in ten years to a fourth part of the whole soil of the country: and M. Passy, in his tract "On the Changes in the Agricultural Condition of the Department of the Eure since the year 1800,"† states other

*[*Translated from*] Page 334 [n.] of the Brussels translation [MS translation of his great work] [*Traité d'économie nationale.*]. He cites as an authority, Schwerz, *Landwirthschaftliche Mittheilungen*, i. 185.

†[*The following passage is translated by JSM from* "Des changements survenus dans la situation agricole du Département de l'Eure depuis l'année 1800," *Journal des Economistes*, I (1842), p. 63.] One of the many important [MS, 48, 49, 52, 57 the important] papers which have appeared in the *Journal*

[a-a]MS almost everywhere exerted in furtherance of
[b-b]MS, 48 thriving [c-c]MS, 48 large

[a-a]MS, 48, 49, 52, 57, 62 *property*
[b-b]MS, 48, 49, 52, 57, 62 *farms* [c-c]MS Mr] 48, 49, 52 M.

facts tending to the same conclusion. "The example," says he, "of this department attests that there does not exist, as some writers have imagined, between the distribution of property and that of cultivation, a connexion which tends invincibly to assimilate them. In no portion of it have changes of ownership had a perceptible influence on the size of holdings. While, in districts of small farming, lands belonging to the same owner are ordinarily distributed among many tenants, so neither is it uncommon, in places where the *grande culture* prevails, for the same farmer to rent the lands of several proprietors. In the plains of Vexin, in particular, many active and rich cultivators do not content themselves with a single farm; others add to the lands of their principal holding, all those in the neighbourhood which they are able to hire, and in this manner make up a total extent which in some cases reaches or exceeds two hundred hectares" (five hundred English acres). "The more the estates are dismembered, the more frequent do this sort of arrangements become: and as they conduce to the interest of all concerned, it is probable that time will confirm them."

[d]"In some places," says M. de Lavergne,* "in the neighbourhood of Paris, for example, where the advantages of the *grande culture* become evident, the size of farms tends to increase, several farms are thrown together into one, and farmers enlarge their holdings by renting *parcelles* from a number of different proprietors. Elsewhere farms as well as properties of too great extent, tend to division. Cultivation spontaneously finds out the organization which suits it best." It is a striking fact, stated by the same eminent writer,† that the departments which have the greatest number of small *côtes foncières*, are the Nord, the Somme, the Pas de Calais, the Seine Inférieure, the Aisne, and the Oise; all of them among the richest and best cultivated, and the first-mentioned of them the very richest and best cultivated, in France.[d]

Undue subdivision, and excessive smallness of holdings, are undoubtedly a prevalent evil in some countries of peasant proprietors, and particularly in parts of Germany and France. The governments of Bavaria and Nassau have thought it necessary to impose a legal limit to subdivision, and the

---

des Economistes, the [MS, 48, 49 the monthly] organ of the principal [MS, 48 the enlightened] political economists of France, and doing great and increasing honour [MS, 48, 49 great honour] to their knowledge and ability [MS, 48, 49 abilities]. M. Passy's [52, 57 France. M. Passy's] essay has been reprinted separately as a pamphlet.

*[*Translated from*] *Economie Rurale de la France, p.* 455.

†P. 117 [–8]. See, for facts of a similar tendency, pp. 141, 250, and other passages of the same important treatise: which, on the other hand, equally abounds with evidence of the mischievous effect of subdivision when too minute, or when the nature of the soil and of its products is not suitable to it.

[d–d]+62, 65, 71

Prussian Government unsuccessfully proposed the [e]same measure[e] to the [f]Estates[f] of its Rhenish Provinces. But I do not think it will anywhere be found that the *petite culture* is the system of the peasants, and the *grande culture* that of the great landlords: on the contrary, wherever the small properties are divided among too many proprietors, I believe it to be true that the large properties also are parcelled out among too many farmers, and that the cause is the same in both cases, a backward state of capital, skill, and agricultural enterprise. There is reason to believe that the subdivision in France is not more excessive than is accounted for by this cause; that it is diminishing, not increasing; and that the terror expressed in some quarters, at the progress of the *morcellement*, is one of the most groundless of real or pretended panics.*

If peasant properties have any effect in promoting subdivision beyond the

[48, 49 See the Appendix to the present volume [pp. 433–51].] [52] Mr. Laing, in his latest publication, "Observations on the Social and Political State of the European People in 1848 and 1849" [; being the Second Series of the Notes of a Traveller*. London: Longman, Brown, Green, and Longmans, 1850], a book devoted to the glorification of England, and the disparagement of everything elsewhere which others, or even he himself in former works, had thought worthy of praise, argues that "although the land itself is not divided and subdivided" on the death of the proprietor, "the value of the land is, and with effects almost as prejudicial to social progress. The value of each share becomes a debt or burden upon the land." Consequently the condition of the agricultural population is retrograde; "each generation is worse off than the preceding one, although the land is neither less nor more divided, nor worse cultivated." And this he gives as the explanation of the great indebtedness of the small landed proprietors in France (pp. 97–9 [97 & 99]). If these statements were correct, they would invalidate all which Mr. Laing affirmed so positively in other writings, and repeats in this, respecting the peculiar efficacy of the possession of land in preventing over-population. But he is entirely mistaken as to the matter of fact. In the only country of which he speaks from actual residence, Norway, he does not pretend that the condition of the peasant proprietors is deteriorating. The facts already cited prove that in respect to Belgium, Germany, and Switzerland, the assertion is equally wide of the mark; and what has been shown respecting the slow increase of population in France, demonstrates that if the condition of the French peasantry was deteriorating, it could not be from the cause supposed by Mr. Laing. The truth I believe to be that in every country without exception, in which peasant properties prevail, the condition of the people is improving, the produce of the land and even its fertility increasing, and from the larger surplus which remains after feeding the agricultural classes, the towns are augmenting both in population and in the well-being of their inhabitants. On this question, as well as on that of the *morcellement*, so far as regards France, [52, 57 France, some] additional facts and observations, brought up to a later date, will [52, 57 observations will] be found in the Appendix. [*See* pp. 433–51 *below*.]

[e-e]MS, 48 same,
[f-f]MS, 48, 49, 52, 57 States

degree which corresponds to the agricultural practices of the country, and which is customary on its large estates, the cause must lie in one of the salutary influences of the system; the eminent degree in which it promotes providence on the part of those who, not being yet peasant proprietors, hope to become so. In England, where the [g]agricultural[g] labourer has no investment for his savings but the savings bank, and no position [h]to which he can rise[h] by any exercise of economy, except perhaps that of a petty shopkeeper, with its chances of bankruptcy, there is nothing at all resembling the intense spirit of thrift which takes possession of [i]one who,[i] from being a day labourer, can raise himself by saving to the condition of a landed proprietor. According to almost all authorities, the real cause of the *morcellement* is the higher price which can be obtained for land by selling it to the peasantry, as an investment for their small accumulations, than by disposing of it entire to some rich purchaser who has no object but to live on its income, without improving it. The hope of obtaining such an investment is the most powerful of inducements, to those who are without land, to practise the industry, frugality, and self-restraint, on which their success in this object of [j] ambition is dependent. [k]

As the result of this enquiry into the direct operation and indirect influences of peasant properties, I conceive it to be established, that there is no necessary connexion between this form of landed property and an imperfect state of the arts of production; that it is favourable in quite as many respects as it is unfavourable, to the most effective use of the powers of the soil; that no other existing state of agricultural economy has so beneficial an effect on the industry, the intelligence, the frugality, and prudence of the population, nor tends on the whole so much to discourage an improvident increase of their numbers; and that no [l]existing state[l], therefore, is on the whole so favourable [m] both to their moral and [n] their

[g-g]+65, 71
[h-h]MS which he can rise to
[i-i]MS him who
[j]MS, 48, 49 rational
[k]MS, 48, 49 In Flanders, according to Mr. Fauche, the British Consul at Ostend,* "farmers' sons and those who have the means to become farmers will delay their marriage until they get possession of a farm." Once a farmer, the next object is to become a proprietor. "The first thing a Dane does with his savings," says Mr. Browne, the Consul at Copenhagen,† "is to purchase a clock, then a horse and cow, which he hires out, and which pays a good interest. Then his ambition is to become a petty proprietor, and this class of persons is better off than any in Denmark. Indeed I know of no people in any country who have more easily within their reach all that is really necessary for life than this class, which is very large in comparison with that of labourers." [*footnotes:*] *In a communication to the Commissioners of Poor Law Enquiry, p. 640 of their Foreign Communications, Appendix F to their First Report. †Ib. 268. [*in* § 4 *above; see* p. 287[m-m]]
[l-l]MS, 48, 49 other
[m]MS, 48, 49 , in the present state of their education, [n]MS to

physical welfare. °Compared with the English system of cultivation by hired labour, it must be regarded as eminently beneficial to the labouring class.* We are not on the present occasion called upon to compare it with the joint ownership of the land by associations of labourers.°

*[MS, 48, 49, 52, 57 *in text*, II, x, § 3; *see* Appendix C, II.1004^{l-l} *below*.] [62] French history strikingly confirms these conclusions. Three times during the course of ages the peasantry have been purchasers of land; and these times immediately preceded the three principal eras of French agricultural prosperity.

"Aux temps les plus mauvais," says the historian Michelet, (*Le Peuple*, 1re partie, ch. 1, [pp. 5–6]) "aux moments de pauvreté universelle, où le riche même est pauvre et vend par force, alors le pauvre se trouve en état d'acheter; nul acquéreur ne se présentant, le paysan en guenilles arrive avec sa pièce d'or, et il acquiert un bout de terre. Ces moments de désastre où le paysan a pu acquérir la terre à bon marché, ont toujours été suivis d'un élan subit de fécondité qu'on ne s'expliquait pas. Vers 1500, par exemple, quand la France épuisée par Louis XI. semble achever sa ruine en Italie, la noblesse qui part est obligée de vendre; la terre, passant à de nouvelles mains, refleurit tout-à-coup; on travaille, on bâtit. Ce beau moment (dans le style de l'histoire monarchique) s'est appelé *le bon Louis XII.*

"Il dure peu, malheureusement. La terre est à peine remise en bon état, le fisc fond dessus; les guerres de religion arrivent, qui semblent raser tout jusqu'au sol, misères horribles, famines atroces où les mères mangeaient leurs enfants. Qui croirait que le pays se relève de là? Eh bien, la guerre finit à peine, de ce champ ravagé, de cette chaumière encore noire et brulée, sort l'épargne du paysan. Il achète; en dix ans, la France a changé de face; en vingt ou trente, tous les biens ont doublé, triplé de valeur. Ce moment encore baptisé d'un nom royal, s'appelle *le bon Henri IV.* et le grand Richelieu."

Of the third era it is needless again to speak: it was that of the Revolution. Whoever would study the reverse of the picture, may compare these historic periods, characterized by the dismemberment of large and the construction of small properties, with the wide-spread national suffering which accompanied, and the permanent deterioration of the condition of the labouring classes which followed, the "clearing" away of small yeomen to make room for large grazing farms, which was the grand economical event of English history during the sixteenth century.

$^{o-o}$MS Whether and in what these considerations admit of useful application to any of the social questions of our time, will be considered further on.] 48 *as* MS . . . considered in a future chapter.] 49 *as* MS . . . the practical questions . . . *as* 48

CHAPTER VIII

Of Metayers

§ 1. [*Nature of the metayer system, and its varieties*] From the case in which the produce of land and labour belongs undividedly to the labourer, we proceed to the cases in which it is divided, but between two classes only, the labourers and the landowners: the character of [a]capitalists[a] merging in the one or the other, as the case may be. It is possible indeed to conceive that there might be only two classes of persons to share the produce, and that a class of capitalists might be one of them; the character of labourer and that of landowner being united to form the other. This might occur in two ways. The labourers, though owning the land, might let it to a tenant, and work under him as hired servants. But this arrangement, even in the very rare cases which could give rise to it, would not require any particular discussion, since it would not differ in any material respect from the threefold system of labourers, capitalists, and landlords. The other case is the not uncommon one, in which a peasant proprietor owns and cultivates the land, but raises the little capital required, by a mortgage upon it. Neither does this case present any important peculiarity. There is but one person, the peasant himself, who has any right or power of interference in the management. He pays a fixed annuity as interest to a capitalist, as he pays another fixed sum in taxes to the government. Without dwelling further on these cases, we pass to those which [b] present marked features of peculiarity.

When the two parties sharing in the produce are the labourer or labourers and the landowner, it is not a very material circumstance in the case, which of the two furnishes the stock, or whether, as sometimes happens, they furnish it, in a determinate proportion, between them. The essential difference does not lie in this, but in another circumstance, namely, whether the division of the produce between the two is regulated by custom or by competition. We will begin with the former case; of which the metayer culture is the principal, and in Europe almost the sole, example.

The principle of the metayer system, is that the labourer, or peasant, makes his engagement directly with the landowner, and pays, not a fixed rent, either in money or in kind, but a certain proportion of the produce,

[a-a]MS, 48, 49, 52 capitalist [b]MS, 48, 49 do

or rather of what remains of the produce after deducting what is considered necessary to keep up the stock. The proportion is usually, as the name imports, one-half; but in several districts in Italy it is two-thirds. Respecting the supply of stock, the custom varies from place to place; in some places the landlord furnishes the whole, in others half, in others some particular part, as for instance the cattle and seed, the labourer providing the implements.* "This connexion," says Sismondi, speaking chiefly of Tuscany,† "is often the subject of a contract, to define certain services and certain occasional payments to which the metayer binds himself; nevertheless the differences in the obligations of one such contract and another are inconsiderable; usage governs alike all these engagements, and supplies the stipulations which have not been expressed; and the landlord who attempted to depart from usage, who exacted more than his neighbour, who took for the basis of the agreement anything but the equal division of the crops, would render himself so odious, he would be so sure of not obtaining a metayer who was an honest man, that the contract of all the metayers may be considered as identical, at least in each province, and never gives rise to any competition among peasants in search of [c] employment, or any offer to cultivate the soil on cheaper terms than one another." To the same effect Châteauvieux,‡ speaking of the metayers of Piedmont. "They consider it," (the farm) "as a patrimony, and never think of renewing the lease, but go on from generation to generation, on the same terms, without writings or registries."§

*In France before the Revolution, according to Arthur Young (i. 403) there was great local diversity in this respect. In Champagne "the landlord commonly finds half the cattle and half the seed, and the metayer, labour, implements, and taxes; but in some districts the landlord bears a share of these. In Roussillon, the landlord pays half the taxes; and in Guienne, from Auch to Fleuran, many landlords pay all. Near Aguillon, on the Garonne, the metayers furnish half the cattle. At Nangis, in the Isle of France, I met with an agreement for the landlord to furnish live stock, implements, harness, and taxes; the metayer found labour and his own capitation tax: the landlord repaired the house and gates; the metayer the windows: the landlord provided seed the first year, the metayer the last; in the intervening years they supply half and half. In the Bourbonnois the landlord finds all sorts of live stock, yet the metayer sells, changes, and buys at his will; the steward keeping an account of these mutations, for the landlord has half the product of sales, and pays half the purchases." In Piedmont, he says, "the landlord commonly pays the taxes and repairs the buildings, and the tenant provides cattle, implements, and seed." (II. 151.)

†[*Translated from*] *Etudes sur l'Economie Politique,* 6me essai: De la Condition des Cultivateurs en Toscane [p. 290].

‡*Letters from Italy.* I quote from Dr. Rigby's translation [Lullin de Châteauvieux, J. F. *Italy, its Agriculture, &c.* Norwich: Hunter, 1819] (p. 22).

§This virtual fixity of tenure is not however universal even in Italy; and it is

[c]MS an

§ 2. [*Its advantages and inconveniences*] When the partition of the produce is a matter of fixed usage, not of varying convention, political economy has no laws of distribution to investigate. It has only to consider, as in the case of peasant proprietors, the effects of the system first on the condition of the peasantry, morally and physically, and secondly, on the efficiency of [a]the[a] labour. In both these particulars the metayer system has the characteristic advantages of peasant properties, but has them in a less degree. The metayer has less motive to exertion than the peasant proprietor, since only half the fruits of his industry, instead of the whole, are his own. But he has a much stronger motive than a day labourer, who has no other interest in the result than not to be dismissed. If the metayer cannot be turned out except for some violation of his contract, he has a stronger motive to exertion than any tenant-farmer who has not a lease. The metayer is at least his landlord's partner, and a half-sharer in their joint gains. Where, too, the permanence of his tenure is guaranteed by custom, he acquires local attachments, and much of the feelings of a proprietor. I am supposing that [b]this[b] half produce is sufficient to yield him a comfortable support. Whether it is so, depends (in any given state of agriculture) on the degree of subdivision of the land; which depends on the operation of the population principle. A multiplication of people, beyond the number that can be properly supported on the land or taken off by manufactures, is incident even to a peasant proprietary, and of course not less but rather more incident to a metayer population. The tendency, however, which we noticed in the proprietary system, to promote prudence on this point, is in no small degree common to it with the metayer system. There, also, it is a matter of easy and exact calculation whether a family can be supported or not. If it is easy to see whether the owner of the whole produce can increase the production so as to maintain a greater number of persons equally well, it is a not less simple problem whether the owner of half the produce can do so.* There is one check which this system seems to

to its absence that Sismondi attributes the inferior condition of the metayers in some provinces of Naples, in Lucca, and in the Riviera of Genoa; where the landlords obtain a larger (though still a fixed) share of the produce. In those countries the cultivation is splendid, but the people wretchedly poor. "The same misfortune would probably have befallen the people of Tuscany if public opinion did not protect the cultivator; but a proprietor would not dare to impose conditions unusual in the country, and even in changing one metayer for another he alters nothing in the terms of the engagement." [*Translated from*] *Nouveaux Principes*, liv. iii. ch. 5 [pp. 199–200].

*M. Bastiat [MS, 48, 49 A high authority among French political economists, M. Frédéric Bastiat,] affirms that even in France, incontestably the least

[a-a]MS their
[b-b]MS, 48 his

offer, over and above those held out even by the proprietary system; there is a landlord, who may exert a controlling power, by refusing his consent to a subdivision. I do not, however, attach great importance to this check, because the farm may be loaded with superfluous hands without being subdivided; and because, so long as the increase of hands increases the gross produce, which is almost always the case, the landlord, who receives half the produce, is an immediate gainer, the inconvenience falling only on the labourers. The landlord is no doubt liable in the end to suffer from their poverty, by being forced to make advances to them, especially in bad seasons; and a foresight of this ultimate inconvenience may operate beneficially on such landlords as prefer future security to present profit.

The characteristic disadvantage of the metayer system is very fairly stated by Adam Smith. After pointing out that metayers "have a plain interest that the whole produce should be as great as possible, in order that their own proportion may be so," he continues,* "it could never, however, be the interest of this species of cultivators to lay out, in the further improvement of the land, any part of the little stock which they might save from their own share of the produce, because the lord who laid out nothing, was to get one-half of whatever it produced. The tithe, which is but a tenth of the produce, is found to be a very great hindrance to improvement. A tax, therefore, which amounted to one-half, must have been an effectual bar to it. It might be the interest of a metayer to make the land produce as much as could be brought out of it by means of the stock furnished by the proprietor; but it could never be his interest to mix any part of his own with it. In France, where five parts out of six of the whole

---

favourable example of the metayer system, its effect in repressing population is conspicuous.

"Un fait bien constaté, c'est que la tendance à une multiplication désordonnée se manifeste principalement au sein de cette classe d'hommes qui vit de salaires. Cette prévoyance qui retarde les mariages a sur elle peu d'empire, parce que les maux qui résultent de l'excès de concurrence ne lui apparaissent que très-confusément, et dans un lointain en apparence peu redoutable. C'est donc la circonstance la plus favorable pour un pays d'être organisé de manière à exclure le salariat. Dans les pays de métairies, les mariages sont déterminés principalement par les besoins de la culture; ils se multiplient quand, par quelque circonstance, les métairies offrent des vides nuisibles aux travaux; ils se ralentissent quand les places sont remplies. Ici, un état de choses facile à constater, savoir, le rapport entre l'étendue du domaine et le nombre des bras, opère comme la prévoyance et plus sûrement qu'elle. Aussi voyons-nous que si aucune circonstance n'intervient pour ouvrir des débouchés à une population surnuméraire, elle demeure stationnaire. Nos départements méridionaux en sont la preuve."—Considérations sur le Métayage, *Journal des Economistes* for February 1846 [Vol. XIII, pp. 236–7].

**Wealth of Nations*, book iii. ch. 2. [Ed. Wakefield, III, 20–2.]

kingdom are said to be still occupied by this species of cultivators, the proprietors complain that their metayers take every opportunity of employing the master's cattle rather in carriage than in cultivation; because in the one case they get the whole profits to themselves, in the other they share them with their landlord."

It is indeed implied in the very nature of the tenure, that all improvements which require expenditure of capital must be made with the capital of the landlord. This, however, is essentially the case even in England, whenever the farmers are tenants-at-will: or (if Arthur Young is right) even on a "nine years' lease." If the landlord is willing to provide capital for improvements, the metayer has the strongest interest in promoting them, since half the benefit of them will accrue to himself. As however the perpetuity of tenure which, in the case [c] we are discussing, he enjoys by custom, renders his consent a necessary condition; the spirit of routine, and dislike of innovation, characteristic of an agricultural people when not corrected by education, are no doubt, as the advocates of the system seem to admit, a serious hindrance to [d]improvement[d].

§ 3. [*Evidence concerning its effects in different countries*] The metayer system has met with no mercy from English authorities. "There is not one word to be said in favour of the practice," says Arthur Young,* [a]and a "thousand[a] arguments that might be used against it. The hard plea of necessity can alone be urged in its favour; the poverty of the farmers being so great, that the landlord must stock the farm, or it could not be stocked at all: this is a most cruel burden to a proprietor, who is thus obliged to run much of the hazard of farming in the most dangerous of all methods, that of trusting his property absolutely in the hands of people who are generally ignorant, many careless, and some undoubtedly wicked. . . . In this most miserable of all the modes of letting land, the defrauded landlord receives a contemptible rent; the farmer is in the lowest state of poverty; the land is miserably cultivated; and the nation suffers as severely as the parties themselves. . . . Wherever† this system prevails, it may be taken for granted that a useless and miserable population is found. . . . Wherever the country (that I saw) is poor and unwatered, in the Milanese, it is in the hands of metayers:" they are almost always in debt to their landlord for seed or food, and "their condition is more wretched than that of a day labourer. . . . There ‡ are but few districts" (in Italy) "where lands are let

***Travels*, vol. i. pp. 404–5.

†Ibid. ii. 151–3.

‡Ibid. 217.

[c]MS, 48, 49, 52, 57 which

[d-d]MS improvements

[a-a]MS, 48, 49, 52, 57, 62 "and a thousand

to the occupying tenant at a money-rent; but wherever it is found, their crops are greater; a clear proof of the imbecility of the metaying system." "Wherever it" (the [b]metayer[b] system) "has been adopted," says Mr. M'Culloch,* "it has put a stop to all improvement, and has reduced the cultivators to the most abject poverty." Mr. Jones† shares the common opinion, and quotes Turgot and Destutt-Tracy in support of it. The impression, however, of all these writers (notwithstanding Arthur Young's occasional references to Italy) seems to be chiefly derived from France, and France before the Revolution.‡ Now the situation of French metayers under the old régime by no means represents the typical form of the contract. It is essential to that form, that the proprietor pays all the taxes. But in France the exemption of the noblesse from direct taxation had led the Government to throw the whole burthen of their ever-increasing fiscal exactions upon the occupiers: and it is to these exactions that Turgot ascribed the extreme wretchedness of the metayers: a wretchedness in some cases so excessive, that in Limousin and Angoumois (the provinces which he administered) they had seldom more, according to him, after deducting all burthens, than from twenty-five to thirty livres (20 to 24 shillings) per head for their whole annual consumption: "je ne dis pas en argent, mais en comptant tout ce qu'ils consomment en nature sur ce qu'ils ont récolté." §

**Principles of Political Economy* [*: with some Inquiries Respecting their Application, and a Sketch of the Rise and Progress of the Science*], 3rd ed. [Edinburgh: Tait, 1843,] p. 471.

†*Essay on the Distribution of Wealth*, pp. 102–4.

‡M. de Tracy is partially an exception, inasmuch as his experience reaches lower down than the revolutionary period; but he admits (as Mr. Jones has himself stated in another place) that he is acquainted only with a limited district, of great subdivision and unfertile soil.

M. Passy is of opinion, that a French peasantry must be in indigence and the country badly cultivated on a metayer system, because the proportion of the produce claimable by the landlord is too high; it being only in more favourable climates that any land, not of the most exuberant fertility, can pay half its gross produce in rent, and leave enough to peasant farmers to enable them to grow successfully the more expensive and valuable products of agriculture. (*Systèmes de Culture*, p. 35 [35n–36n].) This is an objection only to a particular numerical proportion, which is indeed the common one, but is not essential to the system.

§See the "Mémoire sur la Surcharge des Impositions qu'éprouvait la Généralité de Limoges, adressé au Conseil d'Etat en 1766," pp. 260–304 of the fourth volume of Turgot's Works. The occasional engagements of landlords (as mentioned by Arthur Young) to pay a part of the taxes, were according to Turgot, of recent origin, under the compulsion of actual necessity. "Le propriétaire ne s'y prête qu'autant qu'il ne peut trouver de métayer autrement; ainsi, même dans ce cas-là, le métayer est toujours réduit à ce qu'il faut précisément pour ne pas mourir de faim." (p. 275.)

[b-b]49 metaying

When we add that they had not the virtual fixity of tenure of the metayers of Italy, ("in Limousin," says Arthur Young,* "the metayers are considered as little better than menial servants, removable at pleasure, and obliged to conform in all things to the will of the landlords,") it is evident that their case affords no argument against the metayer system in its better form. A population who could call nothing their own, who, like the Irish cottiers, could not in any contingency be worse off, had nothing to restrain them from multiplying, and subdividing the land, until stopped by actual starvation.

We shall find a very different picture, by the most accurate authorities, of the metayer cultivation of Italy. In the first place, as to subdivision. In Lombardy, according to Châteauvieux,† there are few farms which exceed [c]fifty[c] acres, and few which have less than ten. These farms are all occupied by metayers at half profit. They invariably display "an extent‡ and a richness in buildings [d]rarely[d] known in any other country in Europe." Their plan "affords the greatest room with the least extent of building; is best adapted to arrange and secure the crop; and is, at the same time, the most economical, and the least exposed to accidents by fire." The court-yard "exhibits a whole so regular and commodious, and a system of such care and good order, that our dirty and ill-arranged farms can convey no adequate idea of." The same description applies to Piedmont. The rotation of crops is excellent. "I should think§ no country can bring so large a portion of its produce to market as Piedmont." Though the soil is not naturally very fertile, "the number of cities is prodigiously great." The agriculture must, therefore, be eminently favourable to the net as well as to the gross produce of the land. "Each plough works thirty-two acres in the season. . . . Nothing can be more perfect or neater than the hoeing and moulding up the maize, when in full growth, by a single plough, with a pair of oxen, without injury to a single plant, while all the weeds are effectually destroyed." So much for agricultural skill. "Nothing can be so excellent as the crop which precedes and that which follows it." The wheat "is thrashed by a cylinder, drawn by a horse, and guided by a boy, while the labourers turn over the straw with forks. This process lasts nearly a fortnight; it is quick and economical, and completely gets out the grain. . . . . In no part of the world are the economy and [e]the[e] management of the land

*Vol. i. p. 404.
†*Letters from Italy*, translated by Rigby, p. 16
‡Ibid. pp. 19, 20.
§Ibid. pp. 24–31.

[c-c]Source, MS, 48, 49, 52, 57, 62 sixty
[d-d]Source, MS scarcely
[e-e]+48, 49, 52, 57, 62, 65, 71 [*not in* Source]

better understood than in Piedmont, and this explains the phenomenon of its great population, and immense export of provisions." All this under metayer cultivation.

Of the valley of the Arno, in its whole extent, both above and below Florence, the same writer thus speaks:*—"Forests of olive-trees covered the lower parts of the mountains, and by their foliage concealed an infinite number of small farms, which peopled these parts of the mountains; chestnut-trees raised their heads on the higher slopes, their healthy verdure contrasting with the pale tint of the olive-trees, and spreading a brightness over this amphitheatre. The road was bordered on each side with village-houses, not more than a hundred paces from each other. . . . . They are placed at a little distance from the road, and separated from it by a wall, and a terrace of some feet in extent. On the wall are commonly placed many vases of antique forms, in which flowers, aloes, and young orange-trees are growing. The house itself is completely covered with vines. . . . . . Before these houses we saw groups of peasant females dressed in white linen, silk corsets, and straw-hats, ornamented with flowers. . . . . These houses being so near each other, it is evident that the land annexed to them must be small, and that property, in these valleys, must be very much divided; the extent of these domains being from three to ten acres. The land lies round the houses, and is divided into fields by small canals, or rows of trees, some of which are mulberry-trees, but the greatest number poplars, the leaves of which are eaten by the cattle. Each tree supports a vine. . . . . These divisions, [f]arrayed[f] in oblong squares, are large enough to be cultivated by a plough without wheels, and a pair of oxen. There is a pair of [g]oxen[g] between ten or twelve of the farmers; they employ them successively in the cultivation of all the farms. . . . . Almost every farm maintains a well-looking horse, which goes in a small two-wheeled cart, neatly made, and painted red; they serve for all the purposes of draught for the farm, and also to convey the farmer's daughters to mass and to balls. Thus, on holidays, hundreds of these little carts are seen flying in all directions, carrying the young women, decorated with flowers and ribbons."

This is not a picture of poverty; and so far as agriculture is concerned, it effectually redeems metayer cultivation, as existing in these countries, from the reproaches of English writers; but with respect to the condition of the cultivators, Châteauvieux's testimony is, in some points, not so favourable. "It is† neither the natural fertility of the soil, nor the abundance

* Pp. 78–9. [MS Ib. pp. 73–6.] [Pp. 73–7.]
† Pp. 73–6. [MS *reads correctly* Ib. pp. 78–9.]

*f–f*Source, MS arranged
*g–g*Source, MS, 48, 49, 52, 57 them

[h]which[h] strikes the eye of the traveller, which constitute the well-being of its inhabitants. It is the number of individuals among whom the total produce is divided, which fixes the portion that each is enabled to enjoy. Here it is very small. I have thus far, indeed, exhibited a delightful country, well watered, fertile, and covered with a perpetual vegetation; I have shown it divided into countless enclosures, which, like so many beds in a garden, display a thousand varying productions; I have shown, that to all these enclosures are attached well-built houses, clothed with vines, and decorated with flowers; but, on entering them, we find a total want of all the conveniences of life, a table more than frugal, and a general appearance of privation." Is not Châteauvieux here unconsciously contrasting the condition of the metayers with that of the farmers of other countries, when the proper standard with which to compare it is that of the agricultural day-labourers?

Arthur Young says,* "I was assured that these metayers are (especially near Florence) much at their ease; that on holidays they are dressed remarkably well, and not without objects of luxury, as silver, gold, and silk; and live well, on plenty of bread, wine, and legumes. In some instances this may possibly be the case, but the general fact is contrary. It is absurd to think that metayers, upon such a farm as is cultivated by a pair of oxen, can live at their ease; and a clear proof of their poverty is this, that the landlord, who provides half the live stock, is often obliged to lend the peasant money to procure his half. . . . . The metayers, not in the vicinity of the city, are so poor, that landlords even lend them corn to eat: their food is black bread, made of a mixture with vetches; and their drink is very little wine, mixed with water, and called *aquarolle*; meat on Sundays only; their dress very ordinary." Mr. Jones admits the superior comfort of the metayers near Florence, and attributes it partly to straw-platting, by which the women of the peasantry can earn, according to Châteauvieux,† from fifteen to twenty pence a day. But even this fact tells in favour of the metayer system: for in those parts of England in which either straw-platting or lace-making is carried on by the women [i]and children[i] of the labouring class, as in Bedfordshire and Buckinghamshire, the condition of the class is not better, but rather worse than elsewhere, the wages of agricultural labour being depressed by a full equivalent.

In spite of Châteauvieux's statement respecting the poverty of the metayers, his opinion, in respect to Italy at least, is given in favour of the system. "It occupies‡ and constantly interests the proprietors, which is never the case with great proprietors who lease their estates at fixed rents. It

* *Travels*, vol. ii. p. 156. † *Letters from Italy*, p. 75. ‡Ibid. pp. 295–6.

[h-h]Source, MS, 48 that [i-i]+49, 52, 57, 62, 65, 71

establishes a community of interests, and relations of kindness between the proprietors and the metayers; a kindness which I have often witnessed, and from which result great advantages in the moral condition of society. The proprietor, under this system, always interested in the success of the crop, never refuses to make an advance upon it, which the land promises to repay with interest. It is by these advances and by the hope thus inspired, that the rich proprietors of land have gradually perfected the whole rural economy of Italy. It is to them that it owes the numerous systems of irrigation which water its soil, as also the establishment of the terrace culture on the hills: gradual but permanent improvements, which common peasants, for want of means, could never have affected, and which could never have been accomplished by the farmers, nor by the great proprietors who let their estates at fixed rents, because they are not sufficiently interested. Thus the interested system forms of itself that alliance between the rich proprietor, whose means provide for the improvement of the culture, and the metayer whose care and [j]labour[j] are directed, by a common interest, to make the most of these advances."

But the testimony most favourable to the system is that of Sismondi, which has the advantage of being specific, and from accurate knowledge; his information being not that of a traveller, but of a resident proprietor, intimately acquainted with rural life. His statements apply to Tuscany generally, and more particularly to the Val di Nievole, in which his own property lay, and which is not within the supposed privileged circle immediately round Florence. It is one of the districts in which the size of farms appears to be the smallest. The following is his description of the dwellings and mode of life of the metayers of that district.*

"Cette maison, bâtie en bonnes murailles à chaux et à ciment, a toujours au moins un étage, quelquefois deux, au-dessus du rez-de-chaussée. Le plus souvent on trouve à ce rez-de-chaussée la cuisine, une étable pour deux bêtes à corne, et le magasin, qui prend son nom, *tinaia*, des grandes cuves (*tini*) où l'on fait fermenter le vin, sans le soumettre au pressoir: c'est là encore que le métayer enferme sous clé ses tonneaux, son huile, et son blé. Presque toujours il possède encore un hangar appuyé contre la maison, pour qu'il puisse y travailler à couvert à raccommoder ses outils, ou à hacher le fourrage pour son bétail. Au premier et au second étage sont deux, trois, et souvent quatre chambres à lit. . . . La plus spacieuse et la mieux aérée de ces chambres est en général destinée par le métayer, pendant les mois de Mai et de Juin, à l'éducation des vers à soie: de grands coffres pour enfermer les habits et le linge, et quelques chaises de bois, sont les

* From his Sixth Essay [pp. 295–8], formerly referred to.

[j-j]Source, MS, 48, 49, 52, 57, 62 labours

principaux meubles de ces chambres; mais une nouvelle épouse y apporte toujours sa commode de bois de noyer. Les lits sont sans rideaux, sans tour de lit; mais sur chacun, outre un bon garde-paille rempli de la paille élastique du blé de Turquie, on voit un ou deux matelas en laine, ou, chez les plus pauvres, en étoupe, une bonne couverture piquée, des draps de forte toile de chanvre, et sur le meilleur lit de la famille, un tapis de bourre de soie qu'on étale les jours de fête. Il n'y a de cheminée qu'à la cuisine; dans la même pièce on trouve toujours la grande table de bois où dîne la famille, avec ses bancs; le grand coffre, qui sert en même temps d'armoire pour conserver le pain et les provisions, et de pétrin; un assortiment assez complet et fort peu coûteux de pots, de plats et d'assiettes en terre cuite; une ou deux lampes de laiton, un poids à la romaine, et au moins deux cruches en cuivre rouge pour puiser et pour conserver l'eau. Tout le linge et tous les habits de travail de la famille ont été filés par les femmes de la maison. Ces habits, tant pour les hommes que pour les femmes, sont de l'étoffe qu'ils nomment *mezza lana* si elle est épaisse, *mola* si elle est légere. La trame est un gros fil ou de chanvre ou [k]d'étoupe[k], le remplissage est de laine ou de coton; elle est teinte par les mêmes paysannes qui l'ont filée. On se figurerait difficilement combien, par un travail assidu, les paysannes savent accumuler et de toile et de *mezza lana*; combien de draps se trouvent au dépôt commun: combien chaque membre de la famille a de chemises, de vestes, de pantalons, de jupons, et de robes. Pour le faire comprendre, nous joignons en note une partie de l'inventaire de la famille de paysans que nous connaissons le mieux; elle n'est ni parmi les plus pauvres ni parmi les plus riches, et elle vit heureuse par son travail sur la moitié des récoltes de moins de dix arpens de terre. [l] * Cette épouse

*"Inventaire du trousseau de Jeanne, fille de Valente Papini, à son mariage avec Giovacchino Landi, le 29 Avril 1835, à Porta Vecchia, près Pescia:

"28 chemises, 3 robes de bourre de soie en couleur, 4 robes de fleuret de soie en couleur, 7 robes d'indienne ou toile de coton, 2 robes de travail d'hiver (*mezza lana*), 3 robes et jupons de travail d'été (*mola*), 3 jupes blanches, 5 tabliers de toile peinte, 1 tablier de soie noir, 1 tablier de mérinos noir, 9 tabliers de travail (*mola*) en couleur, 4 mouchoirs blancs, 8 mouchoirs en couleur, 3 mouchoirs de soie, 2 voiles brodés et 1 voile de tulle, 3 essuie-mains, 14 paires de bas, 2 chapeaux, l'un de feutre, l'autre de paille fine: 2 camées d'or, 2 boucles d'oreilles en or, 1 chapelet avec deux piastres romaines, 1 collier de corail avec sa croix d'or. . . . . Toutes les épouses plus riches ont de plus *la veste di seta*, la grande robe de toilette, de soie, qu'elles ne portent que quatre ou cinq fois dans leur vie.

"Les hommes n'ont point de trousseaux; l'époux en se mariant n'avait que 14 chemises, et le reste en proportion. Il n'a encore à présent que 13 paires de draps, tandis que dans la famille de sa femme il y en a 30 paires."

[k-k]Source, MS d'étoupes
[l]MS [*ellipsis indicated by . . .*]

avait eu 50 écus de dot, dont 20 payés comptant, et le reste à terme, à 2 écus par année. L'écu de Toscane vaut 6 francs. La dot la plus commune pour les paysannes, dans le reste de la Toscane où les métairies sont plus grandes, est de 100 écus, 600 francs."

Is this poverty, or consistent with poverty? When a common, M. de Sismondi even says *the* common, marriage portion of a metayer's daughter is 24*l.* English money, equivalent to at least 50*l.* in Italy and in that rank of life; when one whose dowry is only half that amount, has the [m]wardrobe[m] described, which is represented by Sismondi as a fair average; [n]the class must[n] be fully comparable, in general condition, to a large proportion even of capitalist farmers in other [o]countries;[o] and incomparably above the day-labourers of any country, except a new colony, or the United States. Very little can be inferred, against such evidence, from a traveller's impression of the poor quality of their food. Its unexpensive character may be rather the effect of economy than of necessity. Costly feeding is not the favourite luxury of a southern people; their diet in all classes is principally vegetable, and no peasantry on the Continent has the superstition of the English labourer respecting white bread. But the nourishment of the Tuscan peasant, according to Sismondi, "is wholesome and various: its basis is an excellent wheaten bread, brown, but pure from bran and from all mixture." "Dans la mauvaise saison, il ne fait que deux repas par jour: à dix heures du matin il mange sa pollenta, à l'entrée de la nuit il mange la soupe, puis du pain avec quelque assaisonnement (*companatico*). En été il fait trois repas, à huit heures, à une heure, et au soir, mais il n'allume de feu qu'une seule fois par jour, pour son dîner, qui se compose de soupe, puis d'un plat ou de viande salée ou de poisson sec, ou de haricots, ou d'herbages, qu'il mange avec du pain. La viande salée n'entre que pour une quantité bien minime dans cet ordinaire, car il estime que quarante livres de porc salé par individu suffisent amplement à sa provision de l'année; il en met deux fois par semaine un petit morceau dans son potage. Le dimanche il a toujours sur sa table un plat de viande fraîche, mais un morceau qui ne pèse qu'une livre ou une livre et demie suffit à toute la famille, quelque nombreuse qu'elle soit. Il ne faut point oublier que le paysan Toscan récolte en général de l'huile d'olive pour son usage: il s'en sert, non seulement pour s'éclairer, mais pour assaisonner tous les végétaux qu'il apprête pour sa table, et qui deviennent ainsi bien plus savoureux et plus nutritifs. A déjeuner il mange du pain, et quelquefois du fromage et des fruits; à souper, du pain et de la salade. Sa boisson se compose du vin inférieur du pays, et de la vinelle ou piquette fait d'eau fermentée sur le marc du raisin.

[m-m]MS, 48, 49 trousseau just
[n-n]MS, 48, 49 must not the class
[o-o]MS, 48, 49 countries?

Il réserve cependant toujours quelque peu de son meilleur vin pour le jour où il battra son grain, et pour quelques fêtes qui se célèbrent en famille. Il estime à dix barils de vinelle par année (environ cinquante bouteilles) et à cinq sacs de froment (environ mille livres de pain) la portion requise pour un homme fait." [*]

The remarks of Sismondi on the moral influences of this state of society are not less worthy of attention. The rights and obligations of the metayer being fixed by usage, and all taxes and rates being paid by the proprietor, "le métayer a les avantages de la propriété sans l'inconvénient de la défendre. C'est au propriétaire qu'avec la terre appartient la guerre: pour lui il vit en paix avec tous ses voisins; il n'a à leur égard aucun motif de rivalité ou de défiance; il conserve la bonne harmonie avec eux, comme avec son maître, avec le fisc et avec l'église: il vend peu, il achète peu, il touche peu d'argent, mais personne ne lui en demande. On a souvent parlé du caractère doux et bienveillant des Toscans, mais on n'a point assez remarqué la cause qui a le plus contribué à préserver cette douceur: c'est celle qui a soustrait tous les agriculteurs, formant plus des trois quarts de la population, à presque toute occasion de querelle."[†] The fixity of tenure which the metayer, so long as he fulfils his known obligations, possesses by usage, though not by law, gives him the local attachments, and almost the strong sense of personal interest, characteristic of a proprietor. "Le métayer vit sur sa métairie comme sur son héritage, l'aimant d'affection, travaillant à la bonifier sans cesse, se confiant dans l'avenir, et comptant bien que ses champs seront travaillés après lui par ses enfans et les enfans de ses enfans. En effet, le plus grand nombre des métayers vivent de génération en génération sur la même terre; ils la connaissent en détail avec une précision que le sentiment seul de la propriété peut donner. . . Les champs élevés en terrasses les uns au-dessus des autres n'ont souvent pas plus de quatre pieds de largeur, mais il n'y en a pas un dont le métayer n'ait étudié en quelque sorte le caractère. Celui-ci est sec, celui-là froid et humide; ici la terre est profonde, là ce n'est qu'une croûte qui couvre à peine le roc; le froment prospère mieux sur l'un, le seigle sur l'autre; ici ce serait peine perdue de semer du blé de Turquie, ailleurs la terre se refuse aux fèves et aux lupins, plus loin le lin viendra à merveille, et le bord de ce ruisseau sera propre au chanvre: ainsi l'on apprend du métayer, avec étonnement, que dans une espace de dix arpens, le sol, les aspects, et l'inclinaison du terrain, présentent plus de variété qu'un riche fermier n'en sait en général distinguer dans une ferme de cinq cents acres d'étendue. C'est que le dernier sent qu'il n'est là que de passage, que de plus il doit se conduire par des règles générales, et negliger les détails. Mais

[*Sismondi, *Etudes*, pp. 305–6.]
[†*Ibid.*, p. 294.]

le métayer, avec l'expérience du passé, a senti son intelligence éveillée par l'intérêt et l'affection pour devenir le meilleur des observateurs, et avec tout l'avenir devant lui, il ne songe pas à lui seulement, mais à ses enfans et à ses petits enfans. Aussi lorsqu'il plante l'olivier, arbre séculaire, et qu'il ménage au fond du creux qu'il fait pour lui un écoulement aux eaux qui pourraient lui nuire, il étudie toutes les couches de terrain qu'il est appelé à défoncer."*

§ 4. [*Is its abolition desirable?*] I do not offer these quotations as evidence of the intrinsic excellence of the metayer system; but they surely suffice to prove that neither "land miserably cultivated" nor a people in "the most abject poverty" have any necessary connexion with it, and that the unmeasured vituperation lavished upon the system by English writers, is grounded on an extremely narrow view of the subject. I look upon the rural economy of Italy as simply so much additional evidence in favour of small occupations with [a]permanent[a] tenure. It is an example of what can be accomplished by those two elements, even under the disadvantage of the peculiar nature of the metayer contract, in which the motives to exertion on the part of the tenant are only half as strong as if he farmed the land on the same footing of perpetuity at a money-rent, either fixed, or varying according to some rule which would leave to the tenant the whole benefit of his own exertions. The metayer tenure is not one which we should be anxious to introduce where the exigencies of society had not naturally given birth to it; but neither ought we to be eager to abolish it on a mere *à priori* view of its disadvantages. If the system in Tuscany works as well in

*[*Etudes*, pp. 292–3] Of the intelligence of this [MS, 48, 49 this most] interesting people, M. de Sismondi speaks in the most favourable terms. Few of them can read; but there is often one member of the family destined for the priesthood, who reads to them on winter evenings. Their language differs little from the purest Italian. The taste for improvisation in verse is general. "Les paysans du val de Nievole fréquentent le spectacle les jours de fête, en été, de neuf à onze heures du soir: leur admission ne leur coûte guère que cinq sols de France. Alfieri est leur auteur de prédilection; toute l'histoire des Atrides est familière à ces hommes qui ne savent pas lire, et qui vont demander à ce poète austère un délassement de leurs rudes travaux." [P. 312.] Unlike most rustics, they find pleasure in the beauty of their country. "Dans les collines du val de Nievole on trouve devant chaque maison, l'aire pour battre le blé, qui a rarement plus de vingt-cinq à trente toises carrées, c'est le plus souvent le seul espace de niveau qu'on rencontre dans toute la métairie. En même temps c'est une terrasse qui domine les plaines et la vallée, et d'où la vue s'étend sur un pays ravissant. Presque jamais je ne m'y suis arrêté pour l'admirer, sans que le métayer soit venu jouir de mon admiration, et m'indiquer du doigt les beautés qu'il croyait pouvoir m'avoir échappé." [Pp. 308–9.]

[a-a]MS, 48, 49 perpetuity of

practice as it is represented to do, with every appearance of minute knowledge, by so competent an authority as Sismondi; if the mode of living of the people, and the size of farms, have for ages maintained and still maintain themselves* such as they are said to be by him, it were to be regretted that a state of rural well-being so much beyond what is realized in most European countries, should be put to hazard by an attempt to introduce, under the guise of agricultural improvement, a system of money-rents and capitalist farmers. Even where the metayers are poor, and the subdivision great, it is not to be assumed as of course, that the change would be for the better. The enlargement of farms, and the introduction of what are called agricultural improvements, usually diminish the number of labourers employed on the land; and unless the growth of capital in trade and manufactures affords an opening for the displaced population, or unless there [b]are[b] reclaimable wastes on which they can be located, competition will so reduce wages, that they will probably be worse off as day-labourers than they were as metayers.

Mr. Jones very properly objects against the French Economists of the last century, that in pursuing their favourite object of introducing money-rents, they turned their minds solely to putting farmers in the place of metayers, instead of transforming the existing metayers into farmers; which, as he justly remarks, can scarcely be effected, unless, to enable the metayers to save and become owners of stock, the proprietors submit for a considerable time to a diminution of income, instead of expecting an increase of it, which has generally been their immediate motive [c]for[c] making the attempt. If this transformation were effected, and no other change made in the metayer's condition; if, preserving all the other rights which usage insures to him, he merely got rid of the landlord's claim to half the produce, paying in lieu of it a moderate fixed rent; he would be so far in a better position than at present, [d]as[d] the whole, instead of only half the fruits of any improvement he made, would now belong to himself; but even so, the benefit would not be without alloy; for a metayer, though not himself a

*"On ne voit jamais," says Sismondi, "une famille de métayers proposer à son maître de partager sa métairie, à moins que le travail ne soit réellement supérieur à ses forces, et qu'elle ne sente la certitude de conserver les mêmes jouissances sur un moindre espace de terrain. On ne voit jamais dans une famille plusieurs fils se marier en même temps, et former autant de ménages nouveaux; un seul prend une femme et se charge des soins du ménage; aucun de ses frères ne se marie, à moins que lui-même n'ait pas d'enfans, ou que l'on n'offre à cet autre frère une nouvelle métairie."—*Nouveaux Principes*, liv. iii. ch. 5 [p. 198].

[b-b]MS be
[c-c]MS to
[d-d]MS that

capitalist, [e] has a capitalist for his partner, and has the use, in Italy at least, of a considerable capital, as is proved by the excellence of the farm buildings: and it is not probable that the landowners would any longer consent to peril their moveable property on the hazards of agricultural enterprise, when assured of a fixed money income without it. Thus would the question stand, even if the change left undisturbed the metayer's virtual fixity of tenure, and converted him, in fact, into a peasant proprietor at a quitrent. But if we suppose him converted into a mere tenant, displaceable at the landlord's will, and liable to have his rent raised by competition to any amount which any unfortunate being in search of subsistence can be found to offer or promise for it; he would lose all the features in his condition which preserve it from being deteriorated; he would be cast down from his present position of a kind of half proprietor of the land, and would sink into a cottier tenant. [f]

[e]MS he
[f]MS What the cottier tenure is, we shall now see.

CHAPTER IX

Of Cottiers

§ 1. [*Nature and operation of cottier tenure*] By the general appellation of cottier tenure I shall designate all cases without exception in which the labourer makes his contract for land without the intervention of a capitalist farmer, and in which the conditions of the contract, especially the amount of rent, are determined not by custom but by competition. The principal European example of this tenure is Ireland, and it is from that country that the term cottier is derived.* [a]By far the greater part of the[a] agricultural population of Ireland [b]might until very lately have been[b] said to be cottier-tenants; except so far as the Ulster tenant-right [c]constituted[c] an exception. There [d]was[d], indeed, a numerous class of labourers who (we may presume through the refusal either of proprietors or of tenants in possession to permit any further subdivision) [e]had[e] been unable to obtain even the smallest patch of land as permanent tenants. But, from the deficiency of capital, the custom of paying wages in land [f]was[f] so universal, that even those who [g]worked[g] as casual labourers for the cottiers or for such larger farmers as [h]were[h] found in the country, [i]were[i] usually paid not in money, but by permission to cultivate for the season a piece of ground, which [j]was[j] generally delivered to them by the farmer ready manured, and [k]was[k] known by the name of conacre. For this they [l]agreed[l] to pay a money rent,

*In its original acceptation, the word "cottier" designated [MS, 48, 49, 52, 57 designates] a class of subtenants, who rent a cottage and an acre or two of land from the small farmers. But the usage of writers has long since stretched the term to include those small farmers themselves, and generally all peasant farmers whose rents are determined by competition.

a–aMS, 48, 49, 52, 57, 62 Nearly the whole
b–bMS, 48, 49, 52, 57 may be
c–cMS, 48, 49, 52, 57 constitutes
d–dMS, 48, 49, 52, 57 is
e–eMS, 48, 49, 52, 57 have
f–fMS, 48, 49, 52, 57 is
g–gMS, 48, 49, 52, 57 work
h–hMS, 48, 49, 52, 57 are
i–iMS, 48, 49, 52, 57 are
j–jMS, 48, 49, 52, 57 is
k–kMS, 48, 49, 52, 57 is
l–lMS, 48, 49, 52, 57 agree

often of several pounds an acre, but no money actually [m]passed[m], the debt being worked out in labour, at a money valuation. [n]

The produce, on the cottier system, being divided into two portions, rent, and the remuneration of the labourer; the one is evidently determined by the other. The labourer has whatever the landlord does not take: the condition of the labourer depends on the amount of rent. But rent, being regulated by competition, depends upon the relation between the demand for land, and the supply of it. The demand for land depends on the number of competitors, and the competitors are the whole rural population. The effect, therefore, of this tenure, is to bring the principle of population to act directly on the land, and not, as in England, on capital. Rent, in this state of things, depends on the proportion between population and land. As the land is a fixed quantity, while population has an unlimited power of increase; unless something checks that increase, the competition for land soon forces up rent to the highest point consistent with keeping the population alive. The effects, therefore, of cottier tenure depend on the extent to which the capacity of population to increase is controlled, either by custom, by individual prudence, or by starvation and disease.

It would be an exaggeration to affirm, that cottier tenancy is absolutely incompatible with a prosperous condition of the labouring class. If we could suppose it to exist among a people to whom a high standard of comfort was habitual; whose requirements were such, that they would not offer a higher rent for land than would leave them an ample subsistence, and whose moderate increase of numbers left no unemployed population to force up rents by competition, save when the increasing produce of the land from increase of skill would enable a higher rent to be paid without inconvenience; the cultivating class might be as well remunerated, might have as large a share of the necessaries and comforts of life, on this system of tenure as on any other. They would not, however, while their rents were arbitrary, enjoy any of the peculiar advantages which metayers on the Tuscan system derive from their connexion with the land. They would neither have the use of a capital belonging to their landlords, nor would

[m-m]MS, 48, 49, 52, 57 passes

[n]49 [*footnote:*] *It should be borne in mind, that this chapter and the next following were written at a time when the great change in the agricultural economy of Ireland, which must necessarily arise from the joint operation of the potato failure and the poor law of 1847, had not yet begun to take effect. The form which the industrial system of Ireland is tending to assume, remains still in such uncertainty, that no speculations grounded on it can at present be hazarded with any prospect of advantage. The chapters, therefore, are left as they originally stood.] 52, 57 [*footnote:*] *Conacre is understood to have fallen into disuse in Ireland since the famine of 1846 and 1847. But in an attempt to describe and characterize the cottier system, conacre, as a natural incident and outgrowth of cottier tenure, must retain its place. The text, therefore, is left as it originally stood.

the want of this be made up by the intense motives to bodily and mental exertion which act upon the peasant who has [o]a permanent tenure[o]. On the contrary, any increased value given to the land by the exertions of the tenant, would have no effect but to raise the rent against himself, either the next year, or at farthest when his lease expired. The landlords might have justice or good sense enough not to avail themselves of the advantage which competition would give them; and different landlords would do so in different degrees. But it is never safe to expect that a class or body of men will act [p]in opposition[p] to their immediate pecuniary interest; and even a doubt on the subject would be almost as fatal as a certainty, for when a person is considering whether [q]or not to[q] undergo a present exertion or sacrifice for a comparatively remote future, the scale is turned by a very small probability that the fruits of the exertion or of the sacrifice will be taken away from him. The only safeguard against these uncertainties would be the growth of a custom, insuring a permanence of tenure in the same occupant, without liability to any other increase of rent than might happen to be sanctioned by the general sentiments of the community. The Ulster tenant-right is such a custom. The very considerable sums which outgoing tenants obtain from their successors, for the goodwill of their farms,* in the first place actually limit the competition for land to persons who have such sums to offer: while the same fact also proves that full advantage is not taken by the landlord of even that more limited competition, since the landlord's rent does not amount to the whole of what the incoming tenant not only offers but actually pays. He does so in the full confidence that the rent will not be raised; and for this he has the guarantee of a custom, not recognised by law, but deriving its binding force from another sanction, perfectly well understood in Ireland.† Without one or other of these

*"It is not uncommon for a tenant without a lease to sell the bare privilege of occupancy or possession of his farm, without any visible sign of improvement having been made by him, at from ten to sixteen, up to twenty and even forty years' purchase of the rent."—(*Digest of Evidence taken by Lord Devon's Commission*, Introductory Chapter [2 vols. Dublin: Thorn, 1847–8, vol. I, p. 1].) The compiler adds, "the comparative tranquillity of that district" (Ulster) "may [MS district may] perhaps be mainly attributable to this fact."

†"It is in the great majority of cases not a reimbursement for outlay incurred, or improvements effected on the land, but a mere life insurance or purchase of immunity from outrage."—(*Digest, ut supra.* [Vol. I, p. 2.]) "The present tenant-right of Ulster" (the writer judiciously remarks) "is an embryo *copyhold.*" [*Ibid.*] "Even there, if the tenant-right be disregarded, and a tenant be ejected [Source, MS be evicted] without having received the price of his goodwill, outrages are generally the consequence."—(Ch. viii. [*Ibid.*, p. 319.]) "The

[o-o]MS, 48, 49 assurance of a perpetuity
[p-p]MS, 48, 49 contrary
[q-q]MS, 48, 49 he shall

supports, a custom limiting the rent of land is not likely to grow up in any progressive community. If wealth and population were stationary, rent also would generally be stationary, and after remaining a long time unaltered, would probably come to be considered unalterable. But all progress in wealth and population tends to a rise of rents. Under a metayer system there is an established mode in which the owner of land is sure of participating in the increased produce drawn from it. But on the cottier system he can only do so by a readjustment of the contract, while that readjustment, in a progressive community, would almost always be to his advantage. His interest, therefore, [r]is[r] decidedly opposed to the growth of any custom commuting rent into a fixed demand.

§ 2. [*In an overpeopled country its necessary consequence is nominal rents*] Where the amount of rent is not limited, either by law or custom, a cottier system has the disadvantages of the worst metayer system, with scarcely any of the advantages by which, in the best forms of that tenure, they are compensated. It is scarcely possible that cottier agriculture should be other than miserable. There is not the same necessity that the condition of the cultivators should be so. Since by a sufficient restraint on population competition for land could be kept down, and extreme poverty prevented; habits of prudence and a high standard of comfort, once established, would have a fair chance of maintaining themselves: though even in these favourable circumstances the motives to prudence would be considerably weaker than in the case of metayers, protected by custom (like those of Tuscany) from being deprived of their [a]farms[a]: since a metayer family, thus protected, could not be impoverished by any other improvident multiplication than their own, but a cottier family, however prudent and self-restraining, may have the rent raised against it by the consequences of the multiplication of other families. Any protection to the [b]cottiers[b] against this evil could only be derived from a salutary sentiment of duty or dignity, pervading the class. From this source, however, [c]they[c] might derive considerable protection. If the habitual standard of requirement among the class were high, a young man might not choose to offer a rent which would leave him in a worse [d]condition[d] than the preceding tenant; or it might be the general custom, as it actually is in some countries, not to marry until a farm [e]is[e] vacant.

disorganized state of Tipperary, and the agrarian combination throughout Ireland, are but a methodized war to obtain the Ulster tenant-right." [*Ibid.*, pp. 3–4.]

[r–r]MS, 48, 49 would be
[a–a]MS, 48, 49 lands
[b–b]MS, 48, 49 cottier
[c–c]MS, 48, 49 he
[d–d]MS, 48, 49, 52, 57 situation
[e–e]MS, 48, 49 was

But it is not where a high standard of comfort has rooted itself in the habits of the labouring class, that we are ever called upon to consider the effects of a cottier system. That system is found only where the habitual requirements of the rural labourers are the lowest possible; where as long as they are not actually starving, they will multiply: and population is only checked by the diseases, and the shortness of life, consequent on insufficiency of [f]merely[f] physical necessaries. This [g]was[g] the state of the largest portion of the Irish peasantry. When a people have sunk into this state, and still more when they have been in it from time immemorial, the cottier system is an almost insuperable obstacle to their emerging from it. When the habits of the people are such that their increase is never checked but by the impossibility of obtaining a bare support, and when this support can only be obtained from land, all stipulations and agreements respecting amount of rent are merely nominal; the competition for land makes the tenants undertake to pay more than it is possible they should pay, and when they have paid all they can, more almost always remains due.

"As it may fairly be said of the Irish peasantry," [h]said[h] Mr. Revans, the Secretary to the Irish Poor Law Enquiry Commission,* "that every family which has not sufficient land to yield its food has one or more of its members supported by begging, it will easily be conceived that every endeavour is made by the peasantry to obtain small holdings, and that they are not influenced in their biddings by the fertility of the land, or by their ability to pay the rent, but solely by the offer which is most likely to gain them possession. The rents which they promise, they are almost invariably incapable of paying; [i]and[i] consequently they become indebted to those under whom they hold, almost as soon as they take possession. They give up, in the shape of rent, the whole produce of the land with the exception of a sufficiency of potatoes for a subsistence; but as this is rarely equal to the promised rent, they constantly have against them an increasing balance. In some cases, the largest quantity of produce which their holdings ever yielded, or which, under their system of tillage, they could in the most favourable seasons be made to yield, would not be equal to the rent bid; consequently, if the peasant fulfilled his engagement with his landlord, which he is rarely able to accomplish, he would till the ground for nothing, and give his landlord a premium for being allowed to till it. On the sea-

*[Revans, John.] *Evils of the State of Ireland, their Causes and their Remedy.* [2nd ed. London: Hatchard, 1837.] Page 10 [-1]. A pamphlet containing, among other things, an excellent digest and selection of evidence from the mass collected by the Commission presided over by Archbishop Whately.

[f-f]MS, 48, 49 mere
[g-g]MS, 48, 49, 52, 57 is unhappily
[h-h]MS, 48, 49, 52, 57 says
[i-i]+48, 49, 52, 57, 62, 65, 71 [*not in* Source]

coast, fishermen, and in the northern counties those who have looms, frequently pay more in rent than the market value of the whole produce of the land they hold. It might be supposed that they would be better without land under such circumstances. But fishing might fail during a week or two, and so might the demand for the produce of the loom, when, did they not possess the land upon which their food is grown, they might starve. The full amount of the rent bid, however, is rarely paid. The peasant remains constantly in debt to his landlord; his miserable possessions—the wretched clothing of himself and of his family, the two or three stools, and the few pieces of crockery, which his wretched hovel contains, would not, if sold, liquidate the standing and generally accumulating debt. The peasantry are mostly a year in arrear, and their excuse for not paying more is destitution. Should the produce of the holding, in any year, be more than usually abundant, or should the peasant by any accident become possessed of any property, his comforts cannot be increased; he cannot indulge in better food, nor in a greater quantity of it. His furniture cannot be increased, neither can his wife or children be better clothed. The acquisition must go to the person under whom he holds. The accidental addition will enable him to reduce his arrear of rent, and thus to defer ejectment. But this must be the bound of his expectation."

As an extreme instance of the intensity of competition for land, and of the monstrous height to which it occasionally [j]forced[j] up the nominal rent; we may cite from the evidence taken by Lord Devon's Commission,* [k] a fact attested by Mr. Hurly, Clerk of the Crown for Kerry: "I have known a tenant bid for a farm that I was perfectly well acquainted with, worth 50*l.* a year: I saw the competition get up to such an extent, that he was declared the tenant at 450*l.*"

§ 3. [*Nominal rents are inconsistent with industry, frugality, or restraint on population*] In such a condition, what can a tenant gain by any amount of industry or prudence, and what lose by any recklessness? If the landlord at any time exerted his full legal rights, the cottier would not be able even to live. If by extra exertion he doubled the produce of his bit of land, or if he prudently abstained from producing mouths to eat it up, his only gain would be to have more left to pay [a]to his landlord[a]; while, if he had twenty children, they would still be fed first, and the landlord could only take what was left. Almost alone [b]amongst[b] mankind the [c] cottier is in this condition,

**Evidence*, [*Parliamentary Papers*, 1845, XX,] p. 851.

[j-j]MS, 48, 49, 52, 57 forces
[k]MS [*footnote occurs at end of sentence*]
[a-a]MS his landlord with
[b-b]MS, 48, 49 among
[c]MS, 48, 49, 52, 57 Irish

that he can scarcely be either better or worse off by any act of his own. If he [d]were[d] industrious or prudent, nobody but his landlord would gain; if he is lazy [e]or[e] intemperate, it is at his landlord's expense. A situation more devoid of motives to either labour or self-command, imagination itself cannot conceive. The inducements of free human beings are taken away, and those of a slave not substituted. He has nothing to hope, and nothing to fear, except being dispossessed of his holding, and against this he protects himself by the *ultima ratio* of a defensive civil war. Rockism and Whiteboyism [f]were[f] the determination of a people who [g]had[g] nothing that [h]could[h] be called theirs but a daily meal of the lowest description of food, not to submit to being deprived of that for other people's convenience.

Is it not, then, a bitter satire on the mode in which opinions are formed on the most important problems of human nature and life, to find [i] public instructors [j]of the greatest pretension,[j] imputing the backwardness of Irish industry, and the want of energy of the Irish people in improving their condition, to a peculiar indolence and *insouciance* in the Celtic race? Of all vulgar modes of escaping from the consideration of the effect of social and moral influences on the human mind, the most vulgar is that of attributing the diversities of conduct and character to inherent natural differences. What race would not be indolent and insouciant when things are so arranged, that they derive no advantage from forethought or exertion? If such are the arrangements in the midst of which they live and work, what wonder if the listlessness and indifference so engendered are not shaken off the first moment an opportunity offers when exertion would really be of use? It is very natural that a pleasure-loving and sensitively organized people like the Irish, should be less addicted to steady routine labour than the English, because life has more excitements for them independent of it; but they are not less fitted for it than their Celtic brethren the French, [k]nor[k] less so than the Tuscans, or the ancient Greeks. An excitable organization is precisely that in which, by adequate inducements, it is easiest to kindle a spirit of animated exertion. It speaks nothing against the capacities of industry in human beings, that they will not exert themselves [l]without[l] motive. No labourers work harder, in England or America, than the Irish; but not under a cottier system.

§ 4. [*Ryot tenancy of India*] The multitudes who till the soil of India, are in a condition sufficiently analogous to the cottier system, and at the same time sufficiently different from it, to render the comparison of the two

[d-d]MS, 48 was
[e-e]MS &
[f-f]MS, 48, 49, 52, 57 are
[g-g]MS, 48, 49, 52, 57 have
[h-h]MS, 48, 49, 52, 57 can
[i]MS, 48, 49 grave
[j-j]+52, 57, 62, 65, 71
[k-k]MS, 48 not
[l-l]MS, 48, 49, 52, 57 when they have no

a source of some instruction. In most parts of India there are, and [a]perhaps have[a] always been, only two contracting parties, the landlord and the peasant: the landlord being generally the sovereign, except where he has, by a special instrument, conceded his rights to an individual, who becomes his representative. The payments, however, of the peasants, or ryots as they are termed, have seldom if ever been regulated, as in Ireland, by competition. Though the customs locally obtaining were infinitely various, and though practically no custom [b]could be maintained[b] against the sovereign's will, there was always a rule of some sort common to a neighbourhood; the collector did not make his separate bargain with [c]the[c] peasant, but assessed each according to the rule adopted for the rest. The idea was thus kept up of a right of property in the tenant, or at all events, of a right to permanent possession; and the anomaly arose of a fixity of tenure in the peasant-farmer, co-existing with an arbitrary power of increasing the rent.

When the Mogul government substituted itself throughout the greater part of India for the Hindoo rulers, it proceeded on a different principle. A minute survey was made of the land, and upon that survey an assessment was founded, fixing the specific payment due to the government from each field. If this assessment had never been exceeded, the ryots would have been in the comparatively advantageous position of peasant-proprietors, subject to a heavy, but a fixed quit-rent. The absence, however, of any real protection against illegal extortions, rendered this improvement in their condition rather nominal than real; and, except during the occasional accident of a humane and vigorous local administrator, the exactions had no practical limit but the inability of the ryot to pay more.

It was to this state of things that the English rulers of India succeeded; and they were, at an early period, struck with the importance of putting an end to this arbitrary character of the land-revenue, and imposing a fixed limit to the government demand. They did not attempt to go back to the Mogul valuation. It has been in general the very rational practice of the English Government in India, to pay little regard to what was laid down as the theory of the native institutions, but to inquire into the rights which existed and were respected in practice, and to protect and enlarge those. For a long time, however, it blundered grievously about matters of fact, and grossly misunderstood the usages and rights which it found existing. Its mistakes arose from the inability of ordinary minds to imagine a state of social relations fundamentally different from those with which they are practically familiar. England being accustomed to great estates and great landlords, the English rulers took it for granted that India must possess the like; and looking round for some set of people who might be [d]taken[d] for the objects of their search, they pitched upon a sort of tax-gatherers called

[a-a]MS, 48 have] 49 seem to have
[b-b]MS, 48, 49, 52, 57 existed
[c-c]MS, 48 every
[d-d]MS, 48 mistaken

zemindars. "The zemindar," says the philosophical historian of India,* "had some of the attributes which belong to a landowner; he collected the rents of a particular district, he governed the cultivators of that district, lived in comparative splendour, and his son succeeded him when he died. The zemindars, therefore, it was inferred without delay, were the proprietors of the soil, the landed nobility and gentry of India. It was not considered that the zemindars, though they collected the rents, did not keep them; but paid them all away with a small deduction to the government. It was not considered that if they governed the ryots, and in many respects exercised over them despotic power, they did not govern them as tenants of theirs, holding their lands either at will or by contract under them. The possession of the ryot was an hereditary possession; from which it was unlawful for the zemindar to displace him; for every farthing which the zemindar drew from the ryot, he was bound to account; and it was only by fraud, if, out of all that he collected, he retained an *ana* more than the small proportion which, as pay for collection, he was permitted to receive."

"There was an opportunity in India," continues the historian, "to which the history of the world presents not a parallel. Next after the sovereign, the immediate cultivators had, by far, the greatest portion of interest in the soil. For the rights (such as they were) of the zemindars, a complete compensation might have easily been made. The generous resolution was adopted, of sacrificing to the improvement of the country, the proprietary rights of the sovereign. The motives to improvement which property gives, and of which the power was so justly appreciated, might have been bestowed upon those upon whom they would have operated with a force incomparably greater than that with which they could operate upon any other class of men: they might have been bestowed upon those from whom alone, in every country, the principal improvements in agriculture must be derived, the immediate cultivators of the soil. And a measure worthy to be ranked among the noblest that ever were taken for the improvement of any country, might have helped to compensate the people of India for the miseries of that misgovernment which they had so long endured. But the legislators were English aristocrats; and aristocratical prejudices prevailed."

The measure proved a total failure, as to the main effects which its well-meaning promoters expected from it. Unaccustomed to estimate the mode in which the operation of any given [e]institution[e] is modified even by such variety of circumstances as exists within a single kingdom, they flattered themselves that they had created, throughout the Bengal provinces, English landlords, and it proved that they had only created Irish ones. The new

*[James] Mill's *History of British India*, [London: Baldwin, Cradock, and Joy, 1817. Vol. III, pp. 271, 277,] book vi, ch. 8. [MS, 48, 49 *read correctly* ch. 5.]

[e-e]MS, 48, 49, 52 institutions

landed aristocracy disappointed every expectation built upon them. They did nothing for the improvement of their estates, but everything for their own ruin. The same pains not being taken, as [f]had[f] been taken in Ireland, to enable landlords to defy the consequences of their improvidence, [g]nearly[g] the whole land of Bengal had to be sequestrated and sold, for debts or arrears of revenue, and in one generation [h]most of[h] the ancient zemindars had ceased to exist. Other families, mostly the descendants of Calcutta money dealers, [i]or of native officials who had enriched themselves under the British government,[i] now occupy their place; and live as useless drones on the soil which has been given up to them. Whatever the government has sacrificed of its pecuniary claims, for the creation of such a class, has at the best been wasted. [j]

In the parts of India into which the British rule has been more recently introduced, the blunder has been avoided of endowing a useless body of great landlords with gifts from the public revenue[k]. In most parts of the Madras and in part of the Bombay Presidency, the rent is paid directly to the government by the immediate cultivator[l]. In the North-Western Provinces, the government makes its engagement with the village community collectively, determining the share to be paid by each individual, but holding them jointly responsible for each other's default[l]. But in[k] the greater part of India, the immediate cultivators have [m]not[m] obtained a perpetuity of tenure at a fixed rent. The government manages the land on the principle on which a good Irish landlord manages his estate: not putting it up to competition, not asking the cultivators what they will promise to pay, but determining for itself what they can afford to pay, and defining its demand accordingly. In [n]many districts a portion of the cultivators are considered as tenants of the rest, the government making its demand from those only (often a numerous body) who are looked upon as the successors of the original settlers or conquerors of the village[n]. Sometimes the rent is fixed

[f-f]MS, 48, 49, 52 has

[g-g]+62, 65, 71 [h-h]+52, 57, 62, 65, 71 [i-i]+52, 57, 62, 65, 71

[j]MS, 48, 49 [*paragraph*] But in this ill judged measure there was one redeeming point, to which may probably be ascribed all the progress which the Bengal provinces have since made in production and in amount of revenue. The ryots were reduced, indeed, to the rank of tenants of the zemindar; but tenants with fixity of tenure. The rents were left to the zemindars to fix at their discretion; but once fixed, were never more to be altered. This is now the law and practice of landed tenure, in the most flourishing part of the British Indian dominions. [*paragraph*]

[k-k]MS, 48, 49 ; but along with the evil, the good also has been left undone. The government has done less for the ryots than it has required to be done for them by the landlords of its creation. In

[l-l]52 , and the rate on each class of land is fixed in perpetuity

[m-m]MS, 48, 49 never yet

[n-n]MS, 48, 49 some places it makes its arrangements with the ryots individually, in others with the village communities, leaving them to apportion the demand according to usage or agreement

only for one year, sometimes for three or five; but the [o]uniform[o] tendency of [p]present[p] policy is towards long leases, extending, in the northern provinces of India, to a term of thirty years [q] . This arrangement has not existed for a sufficient time to have shown by experience, how far the motives [r]to improvement[r] which the long lease creates in the minds of the cultivators, fall short of the [s] influence of a perpetual settlement.* But the two plans, of annual settlements and of short leases, are irrevocably condemned. They can only be said to have succeeded, in comparison with the unlimited oppression which [t]existed[t] before. They are approved by nobody, and were never looked upon in any other light than as temporary arrangements, to be abandoned when a more complete knowledge of the capabilities of the country should afford data for something more permanent.

*[65] Since this was written, the resolution has been adopted by the Indian government of converting the long leases of the northern provinces into perpetual tenures at fixed rents.

[o-o]+57, 62, 65, 71
[p-p]MS, 48, 49, 52 recent
[q]MS, 48, 49 , with conditional renewal for twenty more
[r-r]+52, 57, 62, 65, 71
[s]MS, 48, 49 beneficial
[t-t]MS prevailed

CHAPTER X

Means of Abolishing Cottier Tenancy

[a] § 1. [*Irish cottiers should be converted into peasant proprietors*] When the first edition of this work was written and published, the question, what is to be done with a cottier population, was to the English Government the most urgent of practical questions. The majority of a population of eight millions, having long grovelled in helpless inertness and abject poverty under the cottier system, reduced by its operation to mere food of the cheapest description, and to an incapacity of either doing or willing anything for the improvement of their lot, had at last, by the failure of that lowest quality of food, been plunged into a state in which the alternative seemed to be either death, or to be permanently supported by other people, or a radical change in the economical arrangements under which it had hitherto been their misfortune to live. Such an emergency had compelled attention to the subject from the legislature and from the nation, but it could hardly be said with much result; for, the evil having originated in a system of land tenancy which withdrew from the people every motive to industry or thrift except the fear of starvation, the remedy provided by Parliament was to take away even that, by conferring on them a legal claim to eleemosynary support: while, towards correcting the cause of the mischief, nothing was done, beyond vain complaints, though at the price to the national treasury of ten millions sterling for the delay.

"It is needless," (I observed) "to expend any argument in proving that the very foundation of the economical evils of Ireland is the cottier system; that while peasant rents fixed by competition are the practice of the country, to expect industry, useful activity, any restraint on population but death, or any the smallest diminution of poverty, is to look for figs on thistles and grapes on thorns. If our practical statesmen are not ripe for the recognition of this fact; or if while they acknowledge it in theory, they have not a sufficient feeling of its reality, to be capable of founding upon it any course of conduct; there is still another, and a purely physical consideration, from which they will find it impossible to escape. If the one crop on which the people have hitherto supported themselves continues to be precarious, either some new and great impulse must be given to

[a][*For* MS, 48, 49 *versions of this chapter, see* Appendices B *and* C]

agricultural skill and industry, or the soil of Ireland can no longer feed anything like its present population. The whole produce of the western half of the island, leaving nothing for rent, will not now keep permanently in existence the whole of its people: and they will necessarily remain an annual charge on the taxation of the empire, until they are reduced either by emigration or by starvation to a number corresponding with the low state of their industry, or unless the means are found of making that industry much more productive."

Since these words were written, events unforeseen by any one have saved the English rulers of Ireland from the embarrassments which would have been the just [b]penalty[b] of their indifference and want of foresight. Ireland, under cottier agriculture, could no longer supply food to its population: Parliament, by way of remedy, applied a stimulus to population, but none at all to production; the help, however, which had not been provided for the people of Ireland by political wisdom, came from an unexpected source. Self-supporting emigration—the Wakefield system, brought into effect on the voluntary principle and on a gigantic scale (the expenses of those who followed being paid from the earnings of those who went before) has[c], for the present, reduced[c] the population down to the number for which the existing agricultural system can find employment and support. The census of 1851, compared with that of 1841, showed in round numbers a diminution of population of a million and a half. [d]The subsequent census (of 1861) shows a further diminution of about half a million.[d] The Irish having thus found the way to that flourishing continent which for generations will be capable of supporting in undiminished comfort the increase of the population of the whole world; the peasantry of Ireland having learnt to fix their eyes on a terrestrial paradise beyond the ocean, as a sure refuge both from the oppression of the Saxon and from the tyranny of nature; there can be little doubt that however much the employment for agricultural labour may hereafter be diminished by the general introduction throughout Ireland of English farming—or even if, like the county of Sutherland, all Ireland should be turned into a grazing farm—the superseded people would migrate to America with the same rapidity, and as free of cost to the nation, as the million of Irish who [e]went[e] thither during the [f]three years previous to 1851[f]. Those who think that the land of a country exists for the sake of a few thousand landowners, and that as long as rents are paid, society and government have fulfilled their function, may see in this consummation a happy end to Irish difficulties.

[b-b]52, 57 penalties
[c-c]52 reduced or is reducing
[d-d]+62, 65, 71
[e-e]52 have gone
[f-f]52 last three years

But this is not a time, nor is the human mind now in a condition, in which such insolent pretensions can be maintained. The land of Ireland, the land of every country, belongs to the people of that country. The individuals called landowners have no right, in morality and justice, to anything but the rent, or compensation for its saleable value. With regard to the land itself, the paramount consideration is, by what mode of appropriation and of cultivation it can be made most useful to the collective body of its inhabitants. To the owners of the rent it may be very convenient that the bulk of the inhabitants, despairing of justice in the country where they and their ancestors have lived and suffered, should seek on another continent that property in land which is denied to them at home. But the legislature of the empire ought to regard with other eyes the forced expatriation of millions of people. When the inhabitants of a country quit the country *en masse* because its Government will not make it a place fit for them to live in, the Government is judged and condemned. [g] There is no necessity for depriving the landlords of one farthing of the pecuniary value of their legal rights; but justice requires that the actual cultivators should be enabled to become in Ireland what they will become in America—proprietors of the soil which they cultivate.

Good policy requires it no less. Those who, knowing neither Ireland nor any foreign country, take as their sole standard of social and economical excellence English practice, propose as the single remedy for Irish wretchedness, the transformation of the cottiers into hired labourers. But this is rather a scheme for the improvement of Irish agriculture, than of the condition of the Irish people. The status of a day-labourer has no charm for infusing forethought, frugality, or self-restraint, into a people devoid of them. If the Irish peasantry could be [h]universally[h] changed into receivers of wages, the [i]old[i] habits and mental characteristics of the people remaining, we should merely see four or five millions of people living as day-labourers in the same wretched manner in which as cottiers they lived before; equally passive in the absence of every comfort, equally reckless in multiplication, and even, perhaps, equally listless at their work; since they could not be dismissed [j]in a body[j], and if they could, dismissal would now be simply remanding them to the poor-rate. Far other would be the effect of making them peasant proprietors. A people who in industry and providence have everything to learn—who are confessedly among the most backward of European populations in the industrial virtues—require for their regeneration the most powerful incitements by which those virtues can be stimulated: and there is no stimulus as yet comparable to property

[g]52, 57 It is the duty of Parliament to reform the landed tenure of Ireland.
[h-h]52, 57 instantaneously
[i-i]52, 57 present
[j-j]52, 57, 62 *en masse*

in land. A permanent interest in the soil to those who till it, is almost a guarantee for the most unwearied laboriousness: against over-population, thought not infallible, it is the best preservative yet known, and where it failed, any other plan would probably fail much more egregiously; the evil would be beyond the reach of merely economic remedies.

The case of Ireland is similar in its requirements to that of India. In India, though great errors have from time to time been committed, no one ever proposed, under the name of agricultural improvement, to eject the ryots or peasant farmers from their possession; [k] the improvement that has been looked for, has been through making their tenure more secure to them, and the sole difference of opinion is between those who contend for perpetuity, and those who think that long leases will suffice. The same question exists as to Ireland: and it would be idle to deny that long leases, under such landlords as are sometimes to be found do effect wonders, even in Ireland. But then they must be leases at a low rent. Long leases are in no way to be relied on for getting rid of cottierism. During the existence of cottier tenancy, leases have always been long; twenty-one years and three lives concurrent, was a usual term. But the rent being fixed by competition, at a higher amount than could be paid, so that the tenant neither had, nor could by any exertion acquire, a beneficial interest in the land, the advantage of a lease was [l]nearly[l] nominal. In India, the government, where it has not imprudently made over its proprietary rights to the zemindars, is able to prevent this evil, because, being itself the landlord, it can fix the rent according to its own judgment; but under individual landlords, while rents are fixed by competition, and the competitors are a peasantry struggling for subsistence, nominal rents are inevitable, unless the population is so thin, that the competition itself is only nominal. The majority of landlords will grasp at immediate money and immediate power; and so long as they find cottiers eager to offer them everything, it is useless to rely on them for tempering the vicious practice by a considerate self-denial.

A perpetuity is a stronger stimulus to improvement than a long lease: not only because the longest lease, before coming to an end, passes through all the varieties of short leases down to no lease at all; but for more fundamental reasons. It is very shallow, even in pure economics, to take no account of the influence of imagination: there is a virtue in "for ever" beyond the longest term of years; even if the term is long enough to include children, and all whom a person individually cares for, yet until he has reached that high degree of mental cultivation at which the public good (which also includes perpetuity) acquires a [m]paramount[m] ascendancy

[k]52 all
[l-l]52 merely
[m-m]52 permanent

over his feelings and desires, he will not exert himself with the same ardour to increase the value of an estate, his interest in which diminishes in value every year. Besides, while perpetual tenure is the general rule of landed property, as it [n] is in all the countries of Europe, a tenure for a limited period, however long, is sure to be regarded as [o]a[o] something of inferior consideration and dignity, and inspires less of ardour to obtain it, and of attachment to it when obtained. But where a country is under cottier tenure, the question of perpetuity is quite secondary to the more important point, a limitation of the rent. Rent paid by a capitalist who farms for profit, and not for bread, may safely be abandoned to competition; rent paid by labourers cannot, unless the labourers were in a state of civilization and improvement which labourers have nowhere yet reached, and cannot easily reach under such a tenure. Peasant rents ought never to be arbitrary, never at the discretion of the landlord: either by custom or law, it is imperatively necessary that they should be fixed; and where no mutually advantageous custom, such as the metayer system of Tuscany, has established itself, reason and experience recommend that they should be fixed by authority: thus changing the rent into a quit-rent, and the farmer into a peasant proprietor.

[p] For carrying this change into effect on a sufficiently large scale to accomplish the complete abolition of cottier tenancy, the mode which most obviously suggests itself is the direct one of doing the thing outright by Act of Parliament; making the whole land of Ireland the property of the tenants, subject to the rents now really paid (not the nominal [q]rent[q]), as a fixed rent charge. This, under the name of "fixity of tenure," was one of the demands of the Repeal Association during the most successful period of their agitation; and was better expressed by Mr. Conner, its earliest, most enthusiastic, and most indefatigable apostle,* by the words, "a valuation and a perpetuity." [r] In such a measure there would not [s]have been[s] any injustice, provided the landlords were compensated for the present value of the chances of increase which they [t]were[t] prospectively required to

*Author of numerous pamphlets, entitled "True Political Economy of Ireland," "Letter to the Earl of Devon," "Two Letters on the Rackrent Oppression of Ireland," and others. Mr. Conner has been an agitator on the subject since 1832. [The phrase occurs in the third pamphlet listed, *Two letters to the Editor of the Times, on the Rackrent Oppression of Ireland, its Source—its Evils— and its Remedy*. Dublin: Machen, 1846, p. iii.]

[n]52, 57 still [o-o]+71 [p]52, 57 §2.
[q-q]52, 57, 62, 65 rents
[r]52 Within the last two years an association has been formed under the name of the Tenant Right League, for the purpose of directing public opinion towards this object.] 57 Of late years . . . *as* 52 . . . purpose, among others, of . . . *as* 52
[s-s]52, 57 be [t-t]52, 57, 62 would be

forego. The rupture of existing social relations would hardly [u]have been[u] more violent than that effected by the ministers Stein and Hardenberg when, by a series of edicts, in the early part of the present century, they revolutionized the state of landed property in the Prussian monarchy, and left their names to posterity among the greatest benefactors of their country. To enlightened foreigners writing on Ireland, Von Raumer and Gustave de Beaumont, a remedy of this sort [v]seemed[v] so exactly and obviously what the disease [w]required[w], that they [x]had[x] some difficulty in comprehending how it [y]was[y] that the thing [z]was[z] not yet done.

[a]This, however, would have been, in the first place,[a] a complete expropriation of the higher classes of Ireland: which, if there is any truth in the principles we have laid down, would be perfectly warrantable, but only if it were the sole means of effecting a great public good. In the second place, that there should be none but peasant proprietors, is in itself far from desirable. Large farms, cultivated by large [b]capital[b], and owned by persons of the best education which the country can give, persons qualified by instruction to appreciate scientific discoveries, and able to bear the delay and risk of costly experiments, are an important part of a good agricultural system. Many such landlords there are even in Ireland; and it would be a public misfortune to drive them from their [c]posts[c]. A large proportion also of the present holdings are [d]probably still[d] too small to try the proprietary system under the greatest advantages; nor are the tenants always the persons one would desire to select as the first occupants of peasant-properties. There are numbers of them on whom it would have a more beneficial effect to give them the hope of acquiring a landed property by industry and frugality, than the property itself in immediate possession.

[e]There are, however, much milder measures, not open to similar objections, and[e] which, if pushed to the utmost extent of which they are sus-

[u-u]52, 57 be [v-v]52, 57 seems [w-w]52, 57 requires
[x-x]52, 57 have [y-y]52, 57 is [z-z]52, 57 is

[a-a]52, 57 Though this measure is not beyond the competence of a just legislature, and would be no infringement of property if the landlords had the option allowed them of giving up their lands at the full value, reckoned at the ordinary number of years purchase; I am not unaware of the serious nature of the objections to it. In the first place, it is

[b-b]52 capitals [c-c]52, 57 post [d-d]+57, 62, 65, 71

[e-e]52, 57 But though the most direct and drastic mode of creating a peasant proprietary is not in all respects the best, it is far better than no mode at all. If the rulers of Ireland do not exert themselves in time to effect this great public end by means less subversive of existing social relations, they will probably find it extorted from them by the compulsion of circumstances, when they will no longer have any power of controlling its conditions. But if they were sincerely desirous to confer this benefit upon Ireland, and only solicitous about the means of conferring it with the least disturbance of individual positions and expectations, there are measures within their reach, liable to none of the objections urged against the proposal of the Tenant League, but

ceptible, would realize in no inconsiderable degree the object sought. One of them would be, to enact that whoever reclaims waste land becomes the owner of it, at a fixed quit-rent equal to a moderate interest on its mere value as waste. It would of course be a necessary part of this measure, to make compulsory on landlords the surrender of waste lands (not of an ornamental character) whenever required for reclamation. [f] Another expedient, and one in which individuals could co-operate, would be to buy as much as possible of the land offered for sale [g], and sell it again in small portions as peasant-properties. A Society for this purpose was [h]at one time[h] projected [i](though the attempt to establish it proved unsuccessful)[i] on the principles, so far as applicable, of the Freehold Land Societies which have been so successfully established in England, not primarily for agricultural, but for electoral purposes.

This is a mode in which private capital may be employed in renovating the social and agricultural economy of Ireland, not only without sacrifice but with considerable profit to its owners. The remarkable success of the Waste Land Improvement Society, which proceeded on a plan far less advantageous to the tenant, is an instance of what an Irish peasantry can be stimulated to do, by a sufficient assurance that what they do will be for their own advantage. It is not even indispensable to adopt perpetuity as the rule; long leases at moderate rents, like those of the Waste Land Society, would suffice, if a prospect were held out to the farmers of being allowed to purchase their farms with the capital which they might acquire, as the Society's tenants were so rapidly acquiring under the influence of its beneficent system.* When the lands were sold, the funds of the association would be liberated, and it might recommence operations in some other quarter.

*[52] Though this society, during the years succeeding the famine [52, 57 during the recent calamitous years], was forced to wind up its affairs, the memory of what it accomplished ought to be preserved. The following is an

[f]52, 57 [*footnote:*] *"The profit of reclaiming waste land," says the Digest of Evidence to Lord Devon's Commission (p. 570) "will be best understood from a practice not uncommon in Ireland, to which farmers sometimes resort. This consists in giving the use of a small portion of it to a poor cottier or herdsman for the first three crops, after which this improved portion is given up to the farmer, and a fresh piece of the waste land is taken on the same terms by the cottier." Well may the compiler say, "Here we have the example of the very poorest class in Ireland obtaining a livelihood by the cultivation of waste land under the most discouraging and the least remunerative circumstances that can well be imagined." It is quite worthy of the spirit which pervades the wretched attempts as yet made to do good to Ireland, that this spectacle of the poorest of mankind making the land valuable by their labour for the profit of other people, who have done nothing to assist them, does not once strike Lord Devon and his Commission as a thing which ought not to be.

[g]52, 57 under the orders of the Encumbered Estates Commission

[h-h]52 lately

[i-i]52, 57, 62 under the auspices of the Tenant Right League, and

[a] § 2. [[b]*Present state of this question*[b]] Thus far I had written in 1856. [c]Since that time the great crisis of Irish industry has made further progress, and it is necessary to consider how its present state affects the opinions, on prospects or on practical measures, expressed in the previous part of this chapter.

---

extract in the Proceedings of Lord Devon's Commission [*Parliamentary Papers*, 1845, XX] (page 84 [–5]), from the report made to the society in 1845, by their intelligent manager, Colonel Robinson:—

"Two hundred and forty-five tenants, many of whom were a few years since in a state bordering on pauperism, the occupiers of small holdings of from ten to twenty plantation acres each, have, by their own free labour, with the society's aid, improved their farms to the value of 4396*l.*; 605*l.* having been added during the last year, being at the rate of 17*l.* 18*s.* per tenant for the whole term, and 2*l.* 9*s.* for the past year; the benefit of which improvements each tenant will enjoy during the unexpired term of a thirty-one years' lease.

"These 245 tenants and their families have, by spade industry [Source, 52, 57 spade husbandry], reclaimed and brought into cultivation 1032 plantation acres of land, previously unproductive mountain waste, upon which they grew, last year, crops valued by competent practical persons at 3896*l.*, being in the proportion of 15*l.* 18*s.* each tenant; and their live stock, consisting of cattle, horses, sheep, and pigs, now actually upon the estates, is valued, according to the present prices of the neighbouring markets, at 4162*l.*, of which 1304*l.* has been added since February 1844, being at the rate of 16*l.* 19*s.* for the whole period, and 5*l.* 6*s.* for the last year; during which time their stock has thus increased in value a sum equal to their present annual rent; and by the statistical

[a][*For* MS, 48, 49, 52, 57 *versions of the remainder of the chapter, see* Appendix C]
[b-b]62 *Inapplicability of this advice to present circumstances*
[c-c336] 62 I have not changed any of the opinions I then expressed. But I feel that they are no longer susceptible of practical application. The new state of things created in Ireland by the vast decrease of her population, and by the effects of that greatest of boons ever conferred on her by any Government, the Encumbered Estates Act, has rendered the introduction, on a large scale, of the English agricultural system for the first time possible in that country. The present population of Ireland is now not greater than can be supported on that system in a state of comfort probably equal to the average lot of English farm labourers. The general improvement in agriculture is already most striking; and the improved scale of subsistence which is now becoming habitual to the people, together with the familiarity they have now acquired with the resource of expatriation, will probably prevent them for a considerable time from relapsing, through improvident multiplication, into their former degraded state. Ireland, therefore, is not now in a condition to require what are called heroic remedies. The benefits to that country of peasant proprietorship would be as great as ever; but they are no longer indispensable; a prospect has opened to her of making a great advance in civilization without that aid. But though she can now do without peasant-properties, she cannot do without the total extinction of cottier tenancy. Unless that is rooted out, the whole fruits of the improvement now in course of being effected, will be and remain precarious. The lapse of another generation will show whether the landlords of Ireland, now weeded of the reckless and bankrupt portion who formerly held so much of the land, and recruited by the substitution of a more moral and intelligent class, will improve the opportunity by the successful accomplishment of this the only real, permanent, and radical reform in the social economy of that long-suffering country.

The principal change in the situation consists in the great diminution, holding out a hope of the entire extinction, of cottier tenure. The enormous decrease in the number of small holdings, and increase in those of a medium size, attested by the statistical returns, sufficiently proves the general fact, and all testimonies show that the tendency still continues.* It is

---

tables [Source, 52, 57 table] and returns referred to in previous reports, it is proved that the tenants, in general, improve their little farms, and increase their cultivation and crops, in nearly direct proportion to the number of available working persons of both sexes, of which their families consist."

There cannot be a stronger testimony to the superior amount of gross, and even of net produce, raised by small farming under any tolerable system of landed tenure; and it is worthy of attention that the industry and zeal were greatest among the smaller holders; Colonel Robinson noticing, as exceptions to the remarkable and rapid progress of improvement, some tenants who were "occupants of larger farms than twenty acres, a class too often deficient in the enduring industry indispensable for the successful prosecution of mountain improvements."

*There is, however, a partial counter-current, of which I have not seen any public notice. "A class of men, not very numerous, but sufficiently so to do much mischief, have, through the Landed Estates Court, got into possession of land in Ireland, who, of all classes, are least likely to recognise the duties of a landlord's position. These are small traders in towns, who by dint of sheer parsimony, frequently combined with money-lending at usurious rates, have succeeded, in the course of a long life, in scraping together as much money as will enable them to buy fifty or a hundred acres of land. These people never think of turning farmers, but, proud of their position as landlords, proceed to turn it to the utmost account. An instance of this kind came under my notice lately. The tenants on the property were, at the time of the purchase, some twelve years ago, in a tolerably comfortable state. Within that period their rent has been raised three several times; and it is now, as I am informed by the priest of the district, nearly double its amount at the commencement of the present proprietor's reign. The result is that the people, who were formerly in tolerable comfort, are now reduced to poverty: two of them have left the property and squatted near an adjacent turf bog, where they exist trusting for support to occasional jobs. If this man is not shot, he will injure himself through the deterioration of his property, but meantime he has been getting eight or ten per cent on his purchase-money. This is by no means a rare case. The scandal which such occurrences cause, casts its reflection on transactions of a wholly different and perfectly legitimate kind, where the removal of the tenants is simply an act of mercy for all parties.

"The anxiety of landlords to get rid of cottiers is also to some extent neutralized by the anxiety of middlemen to get them. About one-fourth of the whole land of Ireland is held under long leases; the rent received, when the lease is of long standing, being generally greatly under the real value of the land. It rarely happens that the land thus held is cultivated by the owner of the lease: instead of this, he sublets it at a rack rent to small men, and lives on the excess of the rent which he receives over that which he pays. Some of these leases are always running out; and as they draw towards their close, the middleman has no other interest in the land than, at any cost of permanent deteriora-

probable that the repeal of the corn laws, necessitating a change in the exports of Ireland from the products of tillage to those of pasturage, would of itself have sufficed to bring about this revolution in tenure. A grazing farm can only be managed by a capitalist farmer, or by the landlord. But a change involving so great a displacement of the population, has been immensely facilitated and made more rapid by the vast emigration, as well as by that greatest boon ever conferred on Ireland by any Government, the Encumbered Estates Act; the best provisions of which have since, through the Landed Estates Court, been permanently incorporated into the social system of the country. The greatest part of the soil of Ireland, there is reason to believe, is now farmed either by the landlords, or by small capitalist farmers. That these farmers are improving in circumstances, and accumulating capital, there is considerable evidence, in particular the great increase of deposits in the banks of which they are the principal customers. So far as that class is concerned, the chief thing still wanted is security of tenure, or assurance of compensation for improvements. The means of supplying these wants are now engaging the attention of the most competent minds; Judge Longfield's address, in the autumn of 1864, and the sensation created by it, are an era in the subject, and a point has now been reached when we may confidently expect that within a very few years something effectual will be done.

But what, meanwhile, is the condition of the displaced cottiers, so far as they have not emigrated; and of the whole class who subsist by agricultural labour, without the occupation of any land? As yet, their state is one of great poverty, with but slight prospect of improvement. Many wages, indeed, have risen much above the wretched level of a generation ago: but the cost of subsistence has also risen so much above the old potato standard, that the real improvement is not equal to the nominal; and according to the best information to which I have access, there is little appearance of an improved standard of living among the class. The population, in fact, reduced though it be, is still far beyond what the country

---

tion, to get the utmost out of it during the unexpired period of the term. For this purpose the small cottier tenants precisely answer his turn. Middlemen in this position are as anxious to obtain cottiers as tenants, as the landlords are to be rid of them; and the result is a transfer of this sort of tenant from one class of estates to the other. The movement is of limited dimensions, but it does exist, and so far as it exists, neutralizes the general tendency. Perhaps it may be thought that this system will reproduce itself; that the same motives which led to the existence of middlemen will perpetuate the class; but there is no danger of this. Landowners are now perfectly alive to the ruinous consequences of this system, however convenient for a time; and a clause against sub-letting is now becoming a matter of course in every lease."— (*Private Communication from Professor Cairnes.*) [*See* Appendix H, II.1077[41].]

can support as a mere grazing district of England. It may not, perhaps, be strictly true that, if the present number of inhabitants are to be maintained at home, it can only be either on the old vicious system of cottierism, or as small proprietors growing their own food. The lands which will remain under tillage would, no doubt, if sufficient security for outlay were given, admit of a more extensive employment of labourers by the small capitalist farmers; and this, in the opinion of some competent judges, might enable the country to support the present number of its population in actual existence. But no one will pretend that this resource is sufficient to maintain them in any condition in which it is fit that the great body of the peasantry of a country should exist. Accordingly the emigration, which for a time had fallen off, has, under the additional stimulus of bad seasons, revived in all its strength. It is calculated that within the year 1864 not less than 100,000 emigrants left the Irish shores. As far as regards the emigrants themselves and their posterity, or the general interests of the human race, it would be folly to regret this result. The children of the immigrant Irish receive the education of Americans, and enter, more rapidly and completely than would have been possible in the country of their descent, into the benefits of a higher state of civilization. In twenty or thirty years they are not mentally distinguishable from other Americans. The loss, and the disgrace, are England's: and it is the English people and government whom it chiefly concerns to ask themselves, how far it will be to their honour and advantage to retain the mere soil of Ireland, but to lose its inhabitants. With the present feelings of the Irish people, and the direction which their hope of improving their condition seems to be permanently taking, England, it is probable, has only the choice between the depopulation of Ireland, and the conversion of a part of the labouring population into peasant proprietors. The truly insular ignorance of her public men respecting a form of agricultural economy which predominates in nearly every other civilized country, makes it only too probable that she will choose the worse side of the alternative. Yet there are germs of a tendency to the formation of peasant proprietors on Irish soil, which require only the aid of a friendly legislator to foster them; as is shown in the following extract from a private communication by my eminent and valued friend, Professor Cairnes:—

"On the sale, some eight or ten years ago, of the Thomond, Portarlington, and Kingston estates, in the Encumbered Estates Court, it was observed that a considerable number of occupying tenants purchased the fee of their farms. I have not been able to obtain any information as to what followed that proceeding—whether the purchasers continued to farm their small properties, or under the mania of landlordism tried to escape from their former mode of life. But there are other facts which have a bearing on this question. In those parts of the country where tenant-right prevails, the prices given for the goodwill of a farm are enormous. The following figures, taken from the schedule of an estate in the neighbourhood of Newry, now passing through the Landed Estates Court, will give an idea, but a very inadequate one, of the prices which this mere customary right generally fetches.

"Statement showing the prices at which the tenant-right of certain farms near Newry was sold:—

Lot	Acres	Rent	Purchase-money of tenant-right
1	23	£74	£ 33
2	24	77	240
3	13	39	110
4	14	34	85
5	10	33	172
6	5	13	75
7	8	26	130
8	11	33	130
9	2	5	5
	110	£334	£980

"The prices here represent on the whole about three years' purchase of the rental: but this, as I have said, gives but an inadequate idea of that which is frequently, indeed of that which is ordinarily, paid. The right, being purely customary, will vary in value with the confidence generally reposed in the good faith of the landlord. In the present instance, circumstances have come to light in the course of the proceedings connected with the sale of the estate, which give reason to believe that the confidence in this case was not high; consequently, the rates above given may be taken as considerably under those which ordinarily prevail. Cases, as I am informed on the highest authority, have in other parts of the country come to light, also in the Landed Estates Court, in which the price given for the tenant-right was equal to that of the whole fee of the land. It is a remarkable fact that people should be found to give, say twenty or twenty-five years' purchase, for land which is still subject to a good round rent. Why, it will be asked, do they not purchase land out and out for the same, or a slightly larger, sum? The answer to this question, I believe is to be found in the state of our land laws. The cost of transferring land in small portions is, relatively to the purchase money, very considerable, even in the Landed Estates Court; while the goodwill of a farm may be transferred without any cost at all. The cheapest conveyance that could be drawn in that Court, where the utmost economy, consistent with the present mode of remunerating legal services, is strictly enforced, would, irrespective of stamp duties, cost 10*l.*—a very sensible addition to the purchase of a small peasant estate: a conveyance to transfer a thousand acres might not cost more, and would probably not cost much more. But in truth, the mere cost of conveyance represents but the least part of the obstacles which exist to obtaining land in small portions. A far more serious impediment is the complicated state of the ownership of land, which renders it frequently impracticable to subdivide a property into such portions as would bring the land within the reach of small bidders. The remedy for this state of things, however, lies in measures of a more radical sort than I fear it is at all probable that any House of Commons we are soon likely to see would even with patience consider. A registry of titles may succeed in reducing this complex condition of ownership to its simplest expression; but where real complication exists, the difficulty is not to be got rid of by mere simplicity of form; and a registry of titles—while the powers of disposition at present enjoyed by landowners remain undiminished, while every settlor and testator has an almost unbounded licence to multiply interests in land, as pride, the passion for dictation, or mere whim may suggest—will, in my opinion, fail to reach the root of the evil. The effect of these circumstances is to place an immense premium upon large dealings in land—indeed in most cases practically to preclude all other than large dealings; and while this is the state of the law, the experiment of peasant proprietorship, it is plain, cannot be fairly tried. The facts, however, which I have stated, show, I think, conclusively, that there is no obstacle in the disposition of the people to the introduction of this system."[c] [*]

I have concluded a discussion, which has occupied a space almost disproportioned to the dimensions of this work; and I here close the examination of those simpler forms of social economy in which the produce of the land either belongs undividedly to one class, or is shared only between two classes. We now proceed to the hypothesis of a threefold division of the produce, among labourers, landlords, and capitalists; and in order to connect the coming discussions as closely as possible with those which have now for some time occupied us, I shall commence with the subject of Wages.

[*See Appendix H, II.1082[43].]

CHAPTER XI

Of Wages

§ 1. [*Wages depend on the demand and supply of labour—in other words, on population and capital*] Under the head of Wages are to be considered, first, the causes which determine or influence the wages of labour generally, and secondly, the differences that exist between the wages of different employments. It is convenient to keep these two classes of considerations separate; and in discussing the law of wages, to proceed in the first instance as if there were no other kind of labour than common unskilled labour, of the average degree of hardness and disagreeableness.

Wages, like other things, may be regulated either by competition or by custom[a]. In this country there are few kinds of labour of which the remuneration would not be lower than it is, if the employer took the full advantage of competition. Competition, however, must be regarded, in the present state of society, as the principal regulator of wages, and custom or individual character only as a modifying circumstance, and that in a comparatively slight degree.[a]

Wages, then, depend [b]mainly[b] upon the demand and supply of labour; or as it is often expressed, on the proportion between population and capital. By population is here meant the number only of the labouring class, or rather of those who work for hire; and by capital only circulating capital, and not even the whole of that, but the part which is expended in the direct purchase of labour. To this, however, must be added all funds which, without forming a part of capital, are paid in exchange for labour, such as the wages of soldiers, domestic servants, and all other unproductive labourers. There is unfortunately no mode of expressing by one familiar term, the aggregate of what [c]has been[c] called the wages-fund of a country:

[a-a]MS, 48 : but the last is not a common case. A custom on the subject, even if established, could not easily maintain itself unaltered in any other than a stationary state of society. An increase or a falling off in the demand for labour, an increase or diminution of the labouring population, could hardly fail to engender a competition which would break down any custom respecting wages, by giving either to one side or the other a strong direct interest in infringing it. We may at all events speak of the wages of labour as determined, in ordinary circumstances, by competition.]
49 *as* MS . . . side or to the . . . as MS
[b-b]+52, 57, 62, 65, 71
[c-c]MS, 48, 49, 52, 57, 62, 65 may be

and as the wages of productive labour form nearly the whole of that fund, it is usual to overlook the smaller and less important part, and to say that wages depend on population and capital. It will be convenient to employ this expression, remembering, however, to consider it as elliptical, and not as a literal statement of the entire truth.

With these limitations of the terms, wages not only depend upon the relative amount of capital and population, but cannot[d], under the rule of competition,[d] be affected by anything else. Wages (meaning, of course, the general rate) cannot rise, but by an increase of the aggregate funds employed in hiring labourers, or a diminution in the number of the competitors for hire; nor fall, except either by a diminution of the funds devoted to paying labour, or by an increase in the number of labourers to be paid.

§ 2. [*Examination of some popular opinions respecting wages*] There are, however, some facts in apparent contradiction to this doctrine, which it is incumbent on us to consider and explain.

For instance, it is a common saying that wages are high when trade is good. The demand for labour in any particular employment is more pressing, and higher wages are paid, when there is a brisk demand for the commodity produced; and the contrary when there is what is called a stagnation: then workpeople are dismissed, and those who are retained must submit to a reduction of wages: though in these cases there is neither more nor less capital than before. This is true; and is one of those complications in the concrete phenomena, which obscure and disguise the operation of general causes: but it is not really inconsistent with the principles laid down. Capital which the owner does not employ in purchasing labour, but keeps idle in his hands, is the same thing to the labourers, for the time being, as if it did not exist. All capital is, from the variations of trade, occasionally in this state. A manufacturer, finding a slack demand for his commodity, forbears to employ labourers in increasing a stock which he finds it difficult to dispose of; or if he goes on until all his capital is locked up in unsold goods, then at least he must of necessity pause until he can get paid for some of them. But no one expects either of these states to be permanent; if he did, he would at the first opportunity remove his capital to some other occupation, in which it would still continue to employ labour. The capital remains unemployed for a time, during which the labour market is overstocked, and wages fall. Afterwards the demand revives, and perhaps becomes unusually brisk, enabling the manufacturer to sell his commodity even faster than he can produce it: his whole capital is then brought into complete efficiency, and if he is able, he borrows [a] capital in addition, which would otherwise have gone into some

[d-d]+52, 57, 62, 65, 71 [a]MS other

other employment. At such times wages, in his particular occupation, rise. If we suppose, what in strictness is not absolutely impossible, that one of these fits of briskness or of stagnation should affect all occupations at the same time, wages altogether might undergo a rise or a fall. These, however, are but temporary fluctuations: the capital now lying idle will next year be in active employment, that which is this year unable to keep up with the demand will in its turn be locked up in crowded warehouses; and wages in these several departments will ebb and flow accordingly: but nothing can permanently alter general wages, except [b] an increase or a diminution of capital itself (always meaning by the term, the funds of all sorts, [c]devoted to[c] the payment of labour) compared with the quantity of labour offering itself to be hired.

Again, it is another common [d]notion[d] that high prices make high wages; because the producers and dealers, being better off, can afford to pay more to their labourers. I [e]have already said[e] that a brisk demand, which causes temporary high prices, causes also [f] temporary high wages. But high prices, in themselves, can only raise wages if the dealers, receiving more, are induced to save more, and make an addition to their capital, or at least to their purchases of labour. This is indeed likely enough to be the case; and if the high prices came direct from heaven, or even from abroad, the labouring class might be benefited, not by the high prices themselves, but by the increase of capital occasioned by them. The same effect, however, is often attributed to a high price which is the result of restrictive laws, or which is in some way or other to be paid by the remaining members of the community; they having no greater means than before to pay it with. High prices of this sort, if they benefit one class of labourers, can only do so at the expense of others; since if the dealers by receiving high prices are enabled to make greater savings, or otherwise increase their purchases of labour, all other people by paying those high prices have their means of saving, or of purchasing labour, reduced in an equal degree; and it is a matter of accident whether the one alteration or the other will have the greatest effect on the labour market. Wages will probably be temporarily higher in the employment in which prices have risen, and somewhat lower in other employments: in which case, [g]while[g] the first half of the phenomenon excites notice, the other is generally overlooked, or if observed, is not ascribed to the cause which really produced it. Nor will the partial rise of wages last long: for though the dealers in that one employment gain

[b]MS, 48, 49, 52 either
[c-c]MS, 48, 49, 52, 57, 62, 65 destined for
[d-d]MS idea
[e-e]MS admit
[f]MS , in the manner just pointed out,
[g-g]+48, 49, 52, 57, 62, 65, 71

more, it does not follow that there is room to employ a greater amount of savings in their own business: their increasing capital will probably flow over into other employments, and [h]there counterbalance[h] the diminution previously made in the demand for labour by the diminished savings of other classes.

Another opinion often maintained is, that wages [i](meaning of course money wages)[i] vary with the price of food; rising when it rises, and falling when it falls. This opinion is, I conceive, only partially true; and in so far as true, in no way affects the dependence of wages on the proportion between capital and labour: since the price of food, when it affects wages at all, affects them through that law. Dear or cheap food, caused by variety of seasons, does not affect wages (unless they are artificially adjusted to it by law or charity): or rather, it has some tendency to affect them in the contrary way to that supposed; since in times of scarcity people generally [j]compete more violently for employment[j], and lower the labour market against themselves. But dearness or cheapness of food, when of a permanent character, and capable of being calculated on beforehand, may affect wages. In the first place, if the labourers have, as is often the case, no more than enough to keep them in working condition, and enable them barely to support the ordinary number of children, it [k]follows[k] that if food grows permanently dearer without a rise of wages, a greater number of the children will prematurely die; and thus wages will ultimately be higher, but only because the number of people will be smaller, than if food had remained cheap. But, secondly, even though wages were high enough to admit of food's becoming more costly without depriving the labourers and their families of necessaries; though they could bear, physically speaking, to be worse off, perhaps they would not consent to be so. They [l]might[l] have habits of comfort which [m]were[m] to them as necessaries, and sooner than forego which, they would put an additional restraint on their power of multiplication; so that wages would rise, not by increase of deaths but by diminution of births. In these cases, [n]then[n], wages do adapt themselves to the price of food, though after an interval of almost a generation. Mr. Ricardo considers these two cases to comprehend all cases. He assumes, that there is everywhere a minimum rate of wages: either the lowest with which it is physically possible to keep up the population, or the lowest with which the people will choose to do so. To this minimum he assumes that the general rate of wages always tends; that they can never be lower, beyond the length of time required for a diminished rate of increase to make itself

[h-h]MS counterbalance there
[i-i]+49, 52, 57, 62, 65, 71
[j-j]MS, 48, 49, 52, 57 work harder
[k-k]MS is evident
[l-l]MS, 48, 49 may
[m-m]MS, 48, 49 are
[n-n]MS, 48, 49 therefore

felt, and can never long continue higher. This assumption contains sufficient truth to render it admissible for the purposes of abstract science; and the conclusion which Mr. Ricardo draws from it, namely, that wages in the long run rise and fall with the permanent price of food, is, like almost all his conclusions, true hypothetically, that is, granting the suppositions from which he sets out. But in the application to practice, it is necessary to consider that the minimum of which he speaks, especially when it is not a physical, but what may be termed a moral minimum, is itself liable to vary. If wages were previously so high that they could bear reduction, to which the obstacle was a high standard of comfort habitual among the labourers, a rise [o]in[o] the price of food, or any other disadvantageous change in their circumstances, may operate in two ways: it may correct itself by a rise of wages brought about through a gradual effect on the prudential check to population; or it may permanently lower the standard of living of the class, in case their previous habits in respect of population prove stronger than their previous habits in respect of comfort. In that case the injury done to them will be permanent, and their deteriorated condition will become a new minimum, tending to perpetuate itself as the more ample minimum did before. It is to be feared that of the two modes in which the cause may operate, the last is the most frequent, or at all events sufficiently so, to render all propositions ascribing a self-repairing quality to the calamities which befal the labouring classes, practically of no validity. There is considerable evidence that the circumstances of the agricultural labourers in England have more than once in our history sustained great permanent deterioration, from causes which operated by diminishing the demand for labour, and which, if population had exercised its power of self-adjustment in obedience to the previous standard of comfort, could only have had a temporary effect: but unhappily the poverty in which the class was plunged during a long series of years brought that previous standard into disuse; and the next generation, growing up without having possessed those pristine comforts, multiplied in turn without any attempt to retrieve them.*

The converse case occurs when, by improvements in agriculture, the repeal of corn laws, or other such causes, the necessaries of the [p]labourers[p] are cheapened, and [q]they are[q] enabled, with the same wages, to command

*See the historical sketch of the condition of the English peasantry, prepared from the best authorities by Mr. William Thornton [MS, 48, 49 Mr. Thornton], in his work entitled *Over-Population and its Remedy* [MS, 48, 49 work on *Over-Population*]: a work honourably distinguished from most others which have been published in the present generation [52 published during the last few years], by its rational treatment of questions affecting the economical condition of the labouring classes.

[o-o]MS, 48, 49, 52, 57, 62 of
[p-p]MS, 48, 49 labourer
[q-q]MS, 48, 49 he is

greater comforts than before. Wages will not fall immediately; it is even possible that they may rise; but they will fall at last, so as to leave the labourers no better off than before, unless during this interval of prosperity the standard of comfort regarded as indispensable by the class, is permanently raised. Unfortunately this salutary effect is by no means to be counted upon; it is a much more difficult thing to raise, than to lower, the scale of living which the [r]labourer[r] will consider as more indispensable than marrying and having a family. If they content themselves with enjoying the greater comfort while it lasts, but do not learn to require it, they will people down to their old scale of living. If from poverty their children had previously been insufficiently fed or improperly nursed, a greater number will now be reared, and the competition of these, when they grow up, will depress wages, probably in full proportion to the greater cheapness of food. If the effect is not produced in this mode, it will be produced by earlier and more numerous marriages, or by an increased number of births to a marriage. According to all experience, a great increase invariably takes place in the number of marriages, in seasons of cheap food and full employment. I cannot, therefore, agree in the importance so often attached to the repeal of the corn laws, considered merely as a [s]labourers'[s] question, or to any of the schemes, of which some one or other is at all times in vogue, for making the labourers a very little better off. Things which only affect them a very little, make no permanent impression upon their habits and requirements, and they [t] soon slide back into their former state. To produce permanent advantage, the temporary cause operating upon them must be sufficient to make a great change in their condition—a change such as will be felt for many years, notwithstanding any stimulus which it may give during one generation to the increase of people. When, indeed, the improvement is of this signal character, and a generation grows up which has always been used to an improved scale of comfort, the habits of this new generation in respect to population become formed upon a higher minimum, and the improvement in their condition becomes permanent. Of cases in point, the most remarkable is France after the Revolution. The majority of the population being suddenly raised from misery, to independence and comparative comfort; the immediate effect was that population, notwithstanding the destructive wars of the period, started forward with unexampled rapidity, partly because improved circumstances enabled many children to be reared who would otherwise have died, and partly from increase of births. The succeeding generation however grew up with habits [u]considerably[u] altered; and though the country was never before in

[r-r]MS, 48, 49, 52, 57, 62, 65 labourers
[s-s]MS labourer's
[t]MS very
[u-u]MS, 48, 49, 52, 57 entirely

so prosperous a state, the annual number of births is now nearly stationary,* and the increase of population extremely slow.†

§ 3. [*Certain rare circumstances excepted, high wages imply restraints on population*] Wages depend, then, on the proportion between the number of the labouring population, and the capital or other funds devoted to the purchase of labour; we will say, for shortness, the capital. If wages are higher at one time or place than at another, if the subsistence and comfort of the class of hired labourers are more ample, it is [a] for no other reason than because capital bears a greater proportion to population. It is not the absolute amount of accumulation or of production, that is of importance to the labouring class; it is not the amount even of the funds destined for distribution among the labourers: it is the proportion between those funds and the numbers among whom they are shared. The condition of the class can be bettered in no other way than by altering that proportion to their advantage; and every scheme for their benefit, which does not proceed on this as its foundation, is, for all permanent purposes, a delusion.

In countries like North America and the Australian colonies, where the knowledge and arts of civilized life, and a high effective desire of accumula-

*Supra, pp. 287 to 291.

†A similar, though not an equal improvement in the standard of living took place among the labourers of England during the remarkable fifty years from 1715 to 1765, which were distinguished by such an extraordinary succession of fine harvests (the years of decided deficiency not exceeding five in all that period) that the average price of wheat during those years was much lower than during the previous half century. Mr. Malthus computes that on the average of sixty years preceding 1720, the labourer could purchase with a day's earnings only two-thirds of a peck of wheat, while from 1720 to 1750 he could purchase a whole peck. The average price of wheat, according to the Eton tables, for fifty years ending with 1715, was 41*s.* 7¾*d.* per quarter [MS, 48, 49, 52, 57, 62 the quarter], and for the last twenty-three of these, 45*s.* 8*d.*, while for the fifty years following, it was no more than 34*s.* 11*d.* So considerable an improvement in the condition of the labouring class, though arising from the accidents of seasons, yet continuing for more than a generation, had time to work a change in the habitual requirements of the labouring class; and this period is always noted as the date of "a marked improvement of the quality of the food consumed, and a decided elevation in the standard of their comforts and conveniences."—(Malthus, *Principles of Political Economy* [*considered with a view to their practical application*. London: Murray, 1820. P. 254], p. 225 [MS, 48, 49, 52 255].) For the character of the period, see Mr. Tooke's excellent *History of Prices*, [*and of the State of the Circulation from 1793–1837*. 2 vols. London: Longman, Orme, Brown, Green and Longmans, 1838,] vol. i. pp. 38 to 61, and for the prices of corn, the Appendix to that work [Vol. II, Appendix A, pp. 289–95].

[a]MS, 48, 49 , and can be,

tion, co-exist with a boundless extent of unoccupied land, the growth of capital easily keeps pace with the utmost possible increase of population, and is chiefly retarded by the impracticability of obtaining labourers enough. All, therefore, who can possibly be born, can find employment without overstocking the market: every labouring family enjoys in abundance the necessaries, many of the comforts, and some of the luxuries of life; and, unless in case of individual misconduct, or actual inability to work, poverty does not, and dependence [b]need[b] not, exist. A similar advantage, though in a less degree, is occasionally enjoyed by some special class of labourers in old countries, from an [c]extraordinarily[c] rapid growth, not of capital generally, but of the capital employed in a particular occupation. So gigantic has been the progress of the cotton manufacture since the inventions of Watt and Arkwright, that the capital engaged in it has probably quadrupled in the time which population requires for doubling. While, therefore, it has attracted from other employments nearly all the hands which geographical circumstances and the habits or inclinations of the people rendered available; and while the demand it created for infant labour has enlisted the immediate pecuniary interest of the operatives in favour of promoting, instead of restraining, the increase of population; nevertheless wages in the great seats of the manufacture are [d]generally[d] so high, that the collective earnings of a family amount[e], on an average of years,[e] to a very satisfactory sum; and there is, as yet, no sign of [f]permanent[f] decrease, while the effect has also been felt in raising the general standard of agricultural wages in the [g]counties adjoining[g].

But those circumstances of a country, or of an occupation, in which population can with impunity increase at its utmost rate, are rare, and transitory. Very few are the countries presenting the needful union of conditions. Either the industrial arts are backward and stationary, and capital therefore increases slowly; or the effective desire of accumulation being low, the increase soon reaches its limit; or, even though both these elements are at their highest known degree, the increase of capital is checked, because there is not fresh land to be resorted to, of as good [h] quality as that already occupied. Though capital should for a time double itself simultaneously with population, if all this capital and population are to find employment on the same land, they cannot without an unexampled succession of agricultural inventions continue doubling the produce; therefore, if wages [i]do[i] not fall, profits must; and when profits fall, increase of capital is slackened. Besides, even if wages did not fall, the

[b-b]MS, 48, 49, 52, 57, 62 needs
[c-c]52 extraordinary
[d-d]MS, 48, 49, 52, 57, 62 still
[e-e]+49, 52, 57, 62, 65, 71
[f-f]+65, 71
[g-g]MS, 48, 49, 52, 57 surrounding country
[h]MS, 48, 49, 52, 57 a
[i-i]MS, 48, 49, 52, 57 did

price of food (as will be shown more fully hereafter) would in these circumstances necessarily rise; which is equivalent to a fall of wages.

Except, therefore, in the very peculiar cases which I have just noticed, of which the only one of any practical importance is that of a new colony, or a country in circumstances equivalent to it; it is impossible that population should increase at its utmost rate without lowering wages. Nor will the fall be stopped at any point, short of that which either by its physical or its moral operation, checks the increase of population. In no old country, therefore, does population increase at anything like its utmost rate; in most, at a very moderate rate: in some countries, not at all. These facts are only to be accounted for in two ways. Either the whole number of births which nature admits of, and which [j]happen[j] in some circumstances, do not take place; or if they do, a large proportion of those who are born, die. The retardation of increase results either from mortality or prudence; from Mr. Malthus's positive, or from his preventive check: and one or the other of these must and does exist, and very powerfully too, in all old societies. Wherever population is not kept down by the prudence either of individuals or of the state, it is kept down by starvation or disease.

Mr. Malthus has taken great pains to ascertain, for almost every country in the world, which of these checks it is that operates; and the evidence which he collected on the subject, in his Essay on Population, may even now be read with advantage. Throughout Asia, and formerly in most European countries in which the labouring classes were not in personal bondage, there is, or was, no restrainer of population but death. The mortality was not always the result of poverty: much of it proceeded from unskilful and careless management of children, from uncleanly and otherwise unhealthy habits of life among the adult population, and from the almost periodical occurrence of destructive [k]epidemics[k]. Throughout Europe these causes of shortened life have [l]much diminished,[l] but they have [m]not[m] ceased to exist. Until a period not very remote, hardly any of our large towns kept up [n]its[n] population, independently of the stream always flowing into them from the rural districts: this was still true of Liverpool until very recently; and even in London, the mortality is larger, and the average duration of life shorter, than in rural districts where there is much greater poverty. In Ireland, epidemic fevers, and deaths from the exhaustion of the constitution by insufficient nutriment, [o]have always accompanied[o] even the most moderate deficiency of the potato crop. Nevertheless, it cannot now be said that in any [p]part[p] of Europe, popula-

[j-j]65 happens
[k-k]MS, 48, 49 pestilences
[l-l]MS greatly abated of their intensity;
[m-m]MS, 48, 49 nowhere
[n-n]MS, 48, 49, 52 their
[o-o]MS, 48, 49 accompany
[p-p]MS considerable district

tion is principally kept down by disease, still less by starvation, either in a direct or [q]in[q] an indirect form. The agency by which it is limited is [r]chiefly[r] preventive, not (in the language of Mr. Malthus) positive. But the [s]preventive remedy[s] seldom, I believe, consists in the unaided operation of prudential motives on a class wholly or mainly composed of labourers for hire, and looking forward to no other lot. In England, for example, I much doubt if the generality of agricultural labourers practise any prudential restraint whatever. They generally marry as early, and have as many children to a marriage, as they would or could do if they were settlers in the United States. During the generation which preceded the enactment of the present Poor Law, they received the most direct encouragement to this sort of improvidence: being not only assured of support, on easy terms, whenever out of employment, but, even when in employment, very commonly receiving from the parish a weekly allowance proportioned to their number of children; and the married with large families being always, from a short-sighted economy, employed in preference to the unmarried; which last premium on population still exists. Under such prompting, the rural labourers acquired habits of recklessness, which are so congenial to the uncultivated mind that in whatever manner produced, they in general long survive their immediate causes. There are so many new elements at work in society, even in those deeper strata which are inaccessible to the mere movements on the surface, that it is hazardous to affirm anything positive on the mental state or practical impulses of classes and bodies of men, when the same assertion may be true to-day, and may require great modification in [t]a few[t] years time. It does, however, seem, that if the rate of increase of population depended solely on the agricultural labourers, it would, as far as dependent on births, and unless repressed by deaths, be as rapid in the southern counties of England as in America. The restraining principle lies in the very great proportion of the population composed of the middle classes and the skilled artizans, who in this country almost equal in number the common labourers, and on whom prudential motives do, in a considerable degree, operate.

§ 4. [*Restraints on population are in some cases legal*] Where a labouring class who have no property but their daily wages, and no hope of acquiring it, refrain from over-rapid multiplication, the cause, I believe, has always hitherto been, either actual legal restraint, or a custom of some sort, which, without intention on their part, insensibly moulds their con-

[q-q]+52, 57, 62, 65, 71

[r-r]+62, 65, 71

[s-s]MS specific mode of action of the preventive remedy, is in general, I suspect, not very correctly conceived. It

[t-t]MS, 48, 49, 52, 57 five

duct, or affords immediate inducements not to marry. It is not generally known in how many countries of Europe direct legal obstacles are opposed to improvident marriages. The communications made to the original Poor Law Commission by our foreign ministers and consuls in different parts of Europe, contain a considerable amount of information on this subject. Mr. Senior, in his preface to those communications,* says that in the countries which recognise a legal right to relief, "marriage on the part of persons in the actual receipt of relief appears to be everywhere prohibited, and the marriage of those who are not likely to possess the means of independent support is allowed by very few. Thus we are told that in Norway no one can marry without 'showing to the satisfaction of the clergyman, that he is permanently settled in such a manner as to offer a fair prospect that he can maintain a family.'

"In Mecklenburg, that 'marriages are delayed by conscription in the twenty-second year, and military service for six years; besides, the parties must have a dwelling, without which a clergyman is not permitted to marry them. The men marry at from twenty-five to thirty, the women not much earlier, as both must first gain by service enough to establish themselves.'

"In Saxony, that 'a man may not marry before he is twenty-one years old, if liable to serve in the army. In Dresden, professionists (by which [a]words[a] artizans are probably meant) may not marry until they become masters in their trade.'

"In Wurtemburg, that 'no man is allowed to marry till his twenty-fifth year, on account of his military duties, unless permission be especially obtained or purchased: at that age he must also obtain permission, which is granted on proving that he and his wife would have together sufficient to maintain a family or to establish themselves; in large towns, say from 800 to 1000 florins (from 66*l.* 13*s.* 4*d.* to 84*l.* 3*s.* 4*d.*); in smaller, from 400 to 500 florins; in villages, 200 florins (16*l.* 13*s.* 4*d.*) [b] ' " †

The minister at Munich says, "The great cause why the number of the poor is kept so low in this country arises from the prevention by law of marriages in cases in which it cannot be proved that the parties have reasonable means of subsistence; and this regulation is in all places and at all times strictly adhered to. The effect of a constant and firm observance of this rule has, it is true, a considerable influence in keeping down the

*Forming an Appendix (F) to the General Report of the Commissioners, [*Parliamentary Papers*, 1834, XXXIX,] and also published by authority as a separate volume.

†Preface, p. xxxix.

[a–a]Source, MS, 48 word

[b]Source, MS They must not be persons of disorderly or dissolute lives, drunkards, or under suspicion of crime, & they must not have received any assistance from their parish within the last three years.

population of Bavaria, which is at present low for the extent of country, but it has a most salutary effect in averting extreme poverty and consequent misery."*

At Lubeck, "marriages among the poor are delayed by the necessity a man is under, first, of previously proving that he is in a regular employ, work, or profession, that will enable him to maintain a wife: and secondly, of becoming a burgher, and equipping himself in the uniform of the burgher guard, which together may cost him nearly 4*l*."† At Frankfort, "the government prescribes no age for marrying, but the permission to marry is only granted on proving a livelihood."‡

The allusion, in some of these statements, to military duties, points out an indirect obstacle to marriage, interposed by the laws of some countries in which there is no direct legal restraint. In Prussia, for instance, the institutions which compel every able-bodied man to serve for several years in the army, at the time of life at which imprudent marriages are most likely to take place, are probably a full equivalent, in effect on population, for the legal restrictions of the smaller German states.

[c]"So strongly," says Mr. Kay, "do the people of Switzerland understand from experience the expediency of their sons and daughters postponing the time of their marriages, that the councils of state of four or five of the most democratic of the cantons, elected, be it remembered, by universal suffrage, have passed laws by which all young persons who marry before they have proved to the magistrate of their district that they are able to support a family, are rendered liable to a heavy fine. In Lucerne, Argovie, Unterwalden, and I believe, St. Gall, Schweitz, and Uri, laws of this character have been in force for many years." §[c]

§ 5. [*Restraints on population are in other cases the effect of particular customs*] Where there is no general law restrictive of marriage, there are often customs equivalent to it. When the guilds or trade corporations of the Middle Ages were in vigour, their bye-laws or regulations were conceived with a very vigilant eye to the advantage which the trade derived from limiting competition: and they made it very effectually the interest of artizans not to marry until after passing through the two stages of apprentice and journeyman, and attaining the rank of master.|| In Norway, where

*Preface, p. xxxiii., or p. 554 of the Appendix itself.

†Appendix, p. 419.

‡Ibid. p. 567.

§[52] Kay, op. cit. i. 68.

||"En général," says Sismondi, "le nombre des maîtres était fixé dans chaque communauté, et le maître pouvait seul tenir boutique, acheter et vendre pour

[c-c]+52, 57, 62, 65, 71

the labour is chiefly agricultural, it is forbidden by law to engage a farm-servant for less than a year; which was the general English practice until the poor-laws destroyed it, by enabling the farmer to cast his labourers on parish pay whenever he did not immediately require their labour. In consequence of this custom, and of its enforcement by law, the whole of the rather limited class of agricultural labourers in Norway have an engagement for a year at least, which, if the parties are content with one another, naturally becomes a permanent engagement: hence it is known in every neighbourhood whether there is, or is likely to be, a vacancy, and unless

---

son compte. Chaque maître ne pouvait former qu'un certain nombre d'apprentis, auxquels il enseignait son métier; et dans plusieurs communautés, il n'en pouvait tenir qu'un seul. Chaque maître pouvait de même tenir un nombre limité d'ouvriers, qui portaient le nom de compagnons; et, dans les métiers où l'on ne pouvait avoir qu'un seul apprenti, on ne pouvait avoir non plus qu'un seul, ou que deux compagnons. Aucun homme ne pouvait acheter, vendre, ou travailler dans un métier, s'il n'était apprenti, compagnon, ou maître; aucun homme ne pouvait devenir compagnon s'il n'avait servi un nombre d'années déterminé comme apprenti, ou devenir maître s'il n'avait servi un nombre égal d'années comme compagnon; et s'il n'avait de plus fait son chef-d'œuvre, ou exécuté un travail désigné dans son métier, qui devait être jugé par sa jurande. On voit que cette organisation mettait entièrement dans la main des maîtres le renouvellement des corps de métier. Eux seuls pouvaient recevoir des apprentis; mais ils n'étaient point obligés à en prendre; aussi se faisaient-ils payer cette faveur, et souvent à un prix très-élevé; en sorte qu'un jeune homme ne pouvait entrer dans un métier s'il n'avait, au préalable, la somme qu'il fallait payer pour son apprentissage, et celle qui lui était nécessaire pour se sustenter pendant la durée de cet apprentissage; car pendant quatre, cinq, ou sept ans, tout son travail appartenait à son maître. Sa dépendance de ce maître était tout aussi longtemps absolue; car un seul acte de la volonté, ou même du caprice de celui-ci, pouvait lui fermer l'entrée des professions lucratives. L'apprenti, devenu compagnon, acquérait un peu plus de liberté; il pouvait s'engager avec quel maître il voulait, passer de l'un à l'autre; et comme l'entrée au compagnonage n'était ouverte que par l'apprentissage, il commençait à profiter du monopole dont il avait souffert, et il était à peu près sûr de se faire bien payer un travail que personne ne pouvait faire, si ce n'est lui. Cependant il dépendait de la jurande pour obtenir la maîtrise; aussi ne se regardait-il point encore comme assuré de son sort, comme ayant un état. En général, il ne se mariait point qu'il ne fût *passé maître.*

"Il est bien certain, et comme fait et comme théorie, que l'établissement des corps de métier empêchait et devait empêcher la naissance d'une population surabondante. D'après les statuts de presque tous les corps de métier, un homme ne pouvait être passé maître qu'après vingt-cinq ans; mais s'il n'avait pas un capital à lui, s'il n'avait pas fait des économies suffisantes, il continuait bien plus longtemps à travailler comme compagnon; plusieurs, et peut-être le plus grand nombre des artisans, demeuraient compagnons toute leur vie. Il était presque sans exemple, cependant, qu'ils se mariassent avant d'être reçus maîtres; quand ils auraient été assez imprudens pour le désirer, aucun père n'aurait voulu donner sa fille à un homme qui n'avait point d'état."—*Nouveaux Principes,* book iv. ch. 10. See also Adam Smith, book i. ch. 10, part 2.

there is, a young man does not marry, knowing that he could not obtain employment. The [a] custom still exists in Cumberland and Westmoreland, except that the term is half a year instead of a year; and seems to be still attended with the same consequences. The farm-servants "are lodged and boarded in their [b]masters'[b] houses, which they seldom leave until, through the death of some relation or neighbour, they succeed to the ownership or lease of a cottage farm. What is called surplus labour does not here exist." * I have mentioned in another chapter the check to population in England during the last century, from the difficulty of obtaining a separate dwelling place.† Other customs restrictive of population might be specified: in some parts of Italy, it is the practice, according to Sismondi, among the poor, as it is well known to be in the higher ranks, that all but one of the sons remain unmarried. But such family arrangements are not likely to exist among day-labourers. They are the resource of small proprietors and metayers, for preventing too minute a subdivision of the land.

In England generally there is now scarcely a relic of these indirect checks to population; except that in parishes owned by one or a very small number of landowners, the increase of resident labourers is still occasionally obstructed, by preventing cottages from being built, or by pulling down those which exist; thus restraining the population liable to become locally chargeable, without any material effect on population generally, the work required in those parishes being performed by labourers settled elsewhere. The surrounding districts always feel themselves much aggrieved by this practice, against which they cannot defend themselves by similar means, since a single acre of land owned by any one who does not enter into the combination, enables him to defeat the attempt, very profitably to himself, by covering that acre with cottages. To meet these complaints [c]an Act has within the last few years been passed by Parliament, by which the poor-rate is made a charge not on the parish, but on the whole union. This enactment, in other respects very beneficial, removes[c] the small remnant of what was

*See Thornton on *Over-Population [and its Remedy; or, an Inquiry into the Extent and Causes of the Distress Prevailing among the Labouring Classes of the British Islands, and into the means of remedying it.* London: Longman, Brown, Green, and Longmans, 1846], page 18, and the authorities there cited.

†Supra, p. 158.

[a]MS same

[b-b]48, 49 master's

[c-c]MS, 48, 49, 52, 57, 65 it has already been under the consideration of Parliament to abolish parochial settlements, and make the poor rate a charge not on the parish, but on the whole union. If this proposition be adopted, which for other reasons is very desirable, it will remove] 62 *as* MS . . . union.* [*footnote:*] *An act passed in the session of 1861, though not going to quite this length, has the effect intended in nearly the same degree. . . . *as* MS

once a check to population: the value of which, however, from the [d] narrow limits of its operation, [e]had become very trifling[e].

§ 6. [*Due restriction of population the only safeguard of a labouring class*] In the case, therefore, of the common agricultural labourer, the checks to population may almost be considered as non-existent. If the growth of the towns, and of the capital there employed, by which the factory operatives are maintained at their present average [a]rate[a] of wages notwithstanding their rapid increase, did not also absorb a great part of the annual addition to the rural population, there seems no reason in the present habits of the people why they should not fall into as miserable a condition as the Irish [b]previous to 1846[b]; and if the market for our manufactures should, I do not say fall off, but even cease to expand at the rapid rate of the last fifty years, there is no certainty that this fate may not be [c]reserved[c] for us [d] . Without carrying our anticipations forward to such a calamity, which the great and growing intelligence of the factory population would, it may be hoped, avert, by an adaptation of their habits to their circumstances; the existing condition of the labourers of some of the most exclusively agricultural counties, Wiltshire, Somersetshire, Dorsetshire, Bedfordshire, Buckinghamshire, is sufficiently painful to contemplate. The labourers of [e]these[e] counties, with large families, and [f]eight or perhaps nine[f] shillings for their weekly wages when in full employment, have [g]for some time been[g] one of the stock objects of popular compassion: it is time that they had the benefit also of some application of common sense.

Unhappily, sentimentality rather than common sense [h] usually presides over the discussion of these subjects; and while there is a growing sensitiveness to the hardships of the poor, and a ready disposition to admit claims in them upon the good offices of other people, there is an all but universal unwillingness to face the real difficulty of their position, or advert at all to the conditions which nature has made indispensable to the improvement of their physical lot. Discussions on the condition of the

[d]MS very
[e-e]MS cannot now be considered great] 48, 49, 52, 57, 62, 65 must now be considered very trifling
[a-a]+48, 49, 52, 57, 62, 65, 71
[b-b]+62, 65, 71
[c-c]MS, 48, 49, 52 in reserve
[d]MS, 48, 49, 52, 57 ; especially considering how much the Irish themselves contribute to it, by migrating to this country and underbidding its native inhabitants
[e-e]MS those
[f-f]MS, 48, 49, 52, 57 seven or perhaps eight
[g-g]MS, 48, 49, 52, 57 lately become
[h]MS, 48, 49 is the genius that

labourers, lamentations over its wretchedness, [i]denunciations of all who are supposed to be[i] indifferent to it, projects of one kind or another for improving it, were in no country and in no time of the world so rife as [j]in the present generation;[j] but there is a tacit agreement to ignore totally the law of wages, or to dismiss it in a parenthesis, with such terms as "hard-hearted Malthusianism;" as if it were not a thousand times more hard-hearted to tell human beings that they may, than that they may not, call into existence swarms of creatures who are sure to be miserable, and most likely to be depraved; and forgetting that the conduct, which it is reckoned so cruel to disapprove, is a degrading slavery to a brute instinct in one of the persons concerned, and most commonly, in the other, helpless submission to a revolting abuse of power. [k]

So long as mankind remained in a semi-barbarous state, with the indolence and the few wants of [l]a[l] savage, it probably was not desirable that population should be restrained; the pressure of physical want may have been a necessary stimulus, in that stage of the human mind, to the exertion of labour and ingenuity required for accomplishing that greatest of all past changes in human modes of existence, by which industrial life attained predominance over the hunting, the pastoral, and the military or

[i-i]MS crimination and recrimination for being

[j-j]MS, 48, 49, 52, 57 at present:

[k]MS [*paragraph*] It is not wonderful that the working classes themselves should cherish error on this subject. They obey a common propensity, in laying the blame of their misfortunes, and the responsibility of providing remedies, on any shoulders but their own. They must be above the average level of humanity if they chose the more disagreeable opinion, when nearly all their professed teachers, both in their own and in every other class, either silently reject or noisily declaim against it. The true theory of the causes of poverty seems to answer nobody's peculiar purpose. Those who share the growing and certainly well-grounded discontent with the place filled and the part performed in society by what are called the higher classes, seem to think that acknowledging the necessary dependence of wages on population is removing some blame from those classes, and acquitting them at the bar of public opinion for doing so little for the people; as if anything they could do, either in their present relation to them or in any other, could be of permanent use to the people in their material interests, unless grounded on a recognition of all the facts on which their condition depends. With this class of opponents, the accidents of personal politics have latterly conjoined nearly the whole effective literary strength of the party who proclaim themselves Conservative of existing social arrangements. Any one with whom the cause of the poor is a principle, and not a pretence, or a mere freak of sensibility, must contemplate with unfeigned bitterness the conduct, during ten important years, of a large portion of the Tory party, including nearly all its popular organs; who have studiously fostered the prejudices and inflamed the passions of the democracy, on the points on which democratic opinion is most liable to be dangerously wrong, for the paltry advantage of turning into a handle of popular declamation against their Whig rivals, an enactment most salutary in principle, in which their own party had concurred, but of which those rivals were almost accidentally the nominal authors.] 48, 49 *as* MS . . . depends. To this . . . latterly added . . . *as* MS

[l-l]MS, 48, 49, 52, 57, 62 the

predatory state. Want, in that age of the world, had its uses, as even slavery had; and there may be corners of the earth where those uses are not yet superseded, though they might easily be so were a helping hand held out by more civilized communities. But in Europe the time, if it ever existed, is [m] long past, when a life of privation had the smallest tendency to make men either better workmen or more civilized beings. It is, on the contrary, evident, that if the agricultural labourers were better off, they would both work more efficiently, and be better citizens. I ask, then, is it true, or not, that if their numbers were fewer they would obtain higher wages? This is the question, and no other: and it is idle to divert attention from it, by attacking any incidental position of Malthus or some other writer, and pretending that to refute that, is to disprove the principle of population. Some, for instance, have achieved an easy victory over a passing remark of Mr. Malthus, hazarded chiefly by way of illustration, that the increase of food may perhaps be assumed to take place in an arithmetical ratio, while population increases in a geometrical: when every candid reader knows that Mr. Malthus laid no stress on this unlucky attempt to give numerical precision to things which do not admit of it, and every person capable of reasoning must see that it is wholly superfluous to his argument. Others have [n]attached immense importance to[n] a correction which more recent political economists have made in the mere language of the earlier followers of Mr. Malthus. Several writers [o]had[o] said that it is the tendency of population to *increase faster* than the means of subsistence. The assertion was true in the sense in which they meant it, namely, that population would in most circumstances increase faster than the means of subsistence, if it were not checked either by mortality or by prudence. But inasmuch as these checks act with unequal force at different times and places, it was possible to interpret the language of these writers as if they had meant that population is usually gaining ground upon subsistence, and the poverty of the people becoming greater. Under this interpretation of their meaning, it was urged that the reverse is the truth: that as civilization advances, the prudential check tends to become stronger, and population to slacken its rate of increase, relatively to subsistence; and that it is an error to maintain that population, in any improving community, tends to increase faster than, or even so fast as, subsistence. The word tendency is here used in a totally different sense from that of the writers who affirmed the proposition: but waving the verbal question, is it not allowed on both sides, that in old countries, population presses too closely upon the means of subsistence? And though its pressure diminishes, the more the ideas and

[m]MS now
[n-n]MS, 48, 49, 52, 57 laid immense stress upon
[o-o]57 have

habits of the poorest class of labourers can be improved, to which it is to be hoped that there is always some tendency in a progressive country, yet since that tendency has hitherto been, and still is, extremely faint, and (to descend to particulars) has not yet extended to giving to the Wiltshire labourers higher wages than eight shillings a week, the only thing which it is necessary to consider is, whether that is a sufficient and suitable provision for a labourer? for if not, population does, as an existing fact, bear too great a proportion to the [p]wages-fund[p]; and whether it pressed still harder or not quite so hard at some former period, is practically of no moment, except that, if the ratio is an improving one, there is the better hope that by proper aids and encouragements it may be made to improve more and faster.

It is not, however, against reason, that the argument on this subject has to struggle; but against a feeling of dislike, which will only reconcile itself to the unwelcome truth, when every device is exhausted by which the recognition of that truth can be evaded. It is necessary, therefore, to enter into a detailed examination of these devices, and to force every position which is taken up by the enemies of the population principle in their determination to find some refuge for the [q]labourers[q], some plausible means of improving [r]their[r] condition, without requiring the exercise, either enforced or voluntary, of any self-restraint, or any greater control than at present over the animal power of multiplication. This will be the object of the next chapter.

[p–p]MS, 48, 49 means of subsistence
[q–q]MS, 48, 49 labourer
[r–r]MS, 48, 49 his

CHAPTER XII

Of Popular Remedies for Low Wages

§ 1. [*A legal or customary minimum of wages, with a guarantee of employment*] The simplest expedient which can be imagined for keeping the wages of labour up to the desirable point, would be to fix them by law: and this is virtually the object aimed at in a variety of plans which have at different times been, or still are, current, for remodelling the relation between labourers and employers. No one probably ever suggested that wages should be absolutely fixed; since the interests of all concerned, often require that they should be variable: but some have proposed to fix a minimum of wages, leaving the variations above that point to be adjusted by competition. Another plan which has found many advocates among the leaders of the operatives, is that councils should be formed, which in England have been called local boards of trade, in France "conseils de prud'hommes," and other names; consisting of delegates from the work-people and from the employers, who meeting in [a] conference, should agree upon a rate of wages, and promulgate it from authority, to be binding generally on employers and workmen; the ground of decision being, not the state of the labour-market, but natural equity; [b] to provide that the workmen shall have *reasonable* wages, and the capitalist reasonable profits.

Others again (but these are rather philanthropists interesting themselves for the labouring classes, than the labouring people themselves) are shy of admitting the interference of authority in contracts for labour: they fear that if law intervened, it would intervene rashly and ignorantly; they are convinced that two parties, with opposite interests, attempting to adjust those interests by negotiation through their representatives on principles of equity, when no rule could be laid down to determine what was equitable, would merely exasperate their differences instead of healing them; but what it is useless to attempt by the legal sanction, these persons desire to compass by the moral. Every employer, they think, *ought* to give *sufficient* wages; and if he does it not willingly, should be compelled to it by general

[a]MS, 48, 49, 52, 57 fair [b]MS so

opinion; the test of sufficient wages being their own feelings, or what they suppose to be those of the public. This is, I think, a fair representation of a considerable body of existing opinion on the subject.

I desire to confine my remarks to the principle involved in all these suggestions, without taking into account practical difficulties, serious as these must at once be seen to be. I shall suppose that by one or other of these contrivances, wages could be kept above the point to which they would be brought by competition. This is as much as to say, above the highest rate which can be afforded by the existing capital consistently with employing all the labourers. For it is a mistake to suppose that competition merely keeps down wages. It is equally the means by which they are kept up. When there are any labourers unemployed, [c]these, unless maintained by charity,[c] become competitors for hire, and wages fall; but when all who were out of work have found employment, wages will not, under the freest system of competition, fall lower. There are strange notions afloat concerning the nature of competition. Some people seem to imagine that its effect is something indefinite; that the competition of sellers may lower prices, and the competition of labourers may lower wages, down to zero, or some unassignable minimum. Nothing can be more unfounded. Goods can only be lowered in price by competition, to the point which calls forth buyers sufficient to take them off; and wages can only be lowered by competition until room is made to admit all the labourers to a share in the distribution of the wages-fund. If they fell below this point, a portion of capital would remain unemployed for want of labourers; a counter-competition would commence on the side of capitalists, and wages would rise.

Since, therefore, the rate of wages which results from competition [d] distributes the whole [e]existing[e] wages-fund among the whole labouring population; if law or opinion succeeds in fixing wages above this rate, some labourers are kept out of employment; and as it is not the intention of the philanthropists that these should starve, they must be provided for by a forced increase of the wages-fund; by a compulsory saving. It is nothing to fix a minimum of wages, unless there be a provision that work, or wages at least, be found for all who apply for it. This, accordingly, is always part of the scheme; and is consistent with the ideas of more people than would approve of either a legal or a moral minimum of wages. Popular sentiment looks upon it as the duty of the rich, or of the state, to find employment for all the poor. If the moral influence of opinion does not induce the rich to spare from their consumption enough to set all the poor to work at "reasonable wages," it is supposed to be incumbent on the state to lay on taxes for the purpose, either by local rates or votes of public money. The proportion

[c-c]MS unless maintained by charity, they
[d]MS is that which [e-e]+71

between labour and the wages-fund would thus be modified to the advantage of the labourers, not by restriction of population, but by an increase of capital.

§ 2. [*Such a minimum and guarantee would require as a condition legal measures for repression of population*] If this claim on society could be limited to the existing generation; if nothing more [a]were necessary[a] than a compulsory accumulation, sufficient to provide permanent employment at ample wages for the existing numbers of the people; such a proposition would have no more strenuous supporter than myself. Society mainly consists of those who live by bodily labour; and if society, that is, if the labourers, lend their physical force to protect individuals in the enjoyment of superfluities, they are entitled to do so, and have always done so, with the reservation of a power to tax those superfluities for purposes of public utility; among which purposes the subsistence of the people is the foremost. Since no one is responsible for having been born, no pecuniary sacrifice is too great to be made by those who have more than enough, for the purpose of securing enough to all persons already in existence.

But it is another thing altogether, when those who have produced and accumulated are called upon to abstain from consuming until they have given food and clothing, not only to all who now exist, but to all whom these or their descendants may think fit to call into existence. Such an obligation acknowledged and acted upon, would suspend all checks, both positive and preventive; there would be nothing to hinder population from starting forward at its rapidest rate; and as the natural increase of capital would, at the [b]best[b], not be more rapid than before, taxation, to make up the growing deficiency, must advance with the same gigantic strides. The attempt would of course be made to exact labour in exchange for support. But experience has shown the sort of work to be expected from recipients of public charity. When the pay is not given for the sake of the work, but the work found for the sake of the pay, inefficiency is a matter of certainty: to extract real work from day-labourers without the power of dismissal, is only practicable by the power of the lash. [c]It is conceivable, doubtless, that this objection might be got over. The fund raised by taxation might be spread over the labour market generally, as seems to be intended by the supporters of the *droit au travail* in France; without giving to any unemployed labourer a right to demand support in a particular place or from a particular functionary. The power of dismissal as regards individual labourers, would then remain; the government only undertaking to create additional employment when there was a deficiency, and reserving, like

[a-a]MS was required
[b-b]MS least
[c-c358]+49, 52, 57, 62, 65, 71

other employers, the choice of its own workpeople.[c] But let them work ever so efficiently, the increasing population could not, as we have so often shown, increase the produce proportionally: the surplus, after all were fed, would bear a less and less proportion to the whole produce, and to the population: and the increase of people going on in a constant ratio, while the increase of produce went on in a diminishing ratio, the surplus would in time be wholly absorbed; taxation for the support of the poor would engross the whole income of the country; the payers and the receivers would be melted down into one mass. The check to population either by death or prudence, could not then be staved off any longer, but must [d]come[d] into operation [e]suddenly and[e] at once; everything which places mankind above a nest of ants or a colony of beavers, having perished in the interval.

These consequences have been so often and so clearly pointed out by [f]authors of reputation[f], in writings known and accessible, that ignorance of them on the part of educated persons is no longer pardonable. It is doubly discreditable in any person setting up for a public teacher, to ignore these considerations; to dismiss them silently, and discuss or declaim on wages and poor-laws, not as if these arguments could be refuted, but as if they did not exist. [g]

Every one has a right to live. We will suppose this granted. But no one has a right to bring creatures into life [h], to be supported by other people. Whoever means to stand upon the first of these rights must renounce all pretension to the last. If a man cannot support even himself unless others help him, those others are entitled to say that they do not also undertake the support of [i]any[i] offspring which it is physically possible for him to summon into the world. Yet there are abundance of writers and public speakers, including many of most ostentatious [j]pretensions[j] to high feeling, whose views of life are so truly brutish, that they see hardship in preventing paupers from breeding hereditary paupers in the [k] workhouse itself. Posterity will one day ask with astonishment, what sort of people it could be among whom such preachers could find proselytes.

[l]It would be possible for the state to[l] guarantee employment at ample wages to all who are born. But if it does this, it is bound in self-protection,

[d-d]MS rush
[e-e]+48, 49, 52, 57, 62, 65, 71
[f-f]MS, 48, 49, 52, 57 celebrated authors
[g]MS, 48, 49 Yet such has been the tone of popular and newspaper discussion for some years past.
[h]MS whom nobody wants
[i-i]MS, 48, 49 all the
[j-j]MS pretension
[k]MS, 48, 49, 52 very
[l-l]MS I can conceive a society in which the state should] 48, 49 It is conceivable that the state might

and [m]for the sake[m] of every purpose for which government exists, to provide that no person shall be born without its consent. If the ordinary and [n]spontaneous[n] motives to self-restraint are removed, others must be substituted. Restrictions on marriage, at least equivalent to those existing in some of the German states, or severe penalties on those who have children when unable to support them, would then be indispensable. Society [o]can[o] feed the necessitous, if it takes their multiplication under its control; or [p](if destitute of all moral feeling for the wretched offspring)[p] it [q]can[q] leave the last to their discretion, [r]abandoning[r] the first to their own care. [s] But it cannot [t]with impunity[t] take the feeding upon itself, and leave the multiplying free.

To [u]give profusely[u] to the people, whether under the name of charity or of employment, without placing them under such influences that prudential motives shall act powerfully upon them, is to lavish the means of benefiting mankind, without attaining the object. Leave the people in a situation in which their condition manifestly depends upon their numbers, and the greatest permanent benefit may be derived from any sacrifice made to improve the physical well-being of the present generation, and raise, by that means, the habits of their children. But remove the regulation of their wages from their own control; guarantee [v]to[v] them a certain payment, either by law, or by the feeling of the community; and no amount of comfort that you can give them will make either them or their descendants look to their own self-restraint as the proper means [w]of[w] preserving them in that state. You will only make them indignantly claim the continuance of your guarantee, to themselves and their full complement of possible posterity.

On these grounds some writers have altogether condemned the English poor-law, and any system of relief to the able-bodied, at least when uncombined with systematic legal precautions against over-population. The famous Act [x]of the 43d of[x] Elizabeth [y]undertook[y], on the part of the public, to provide work and wages for all the destitute able-bodied: and there is little doubt that if the intent of that Act had been fully carried out, and no means had been adopted by the administrators of relief to neutralize its natural tendencies, the poor-rate would by this time have absorbed the whole net produce of the land and labour of the country. It is not at all surprising, therefore, that Mr. Malthus and others should at first have

[m-m]MS in the name
[n-n]MS, 48, 49 natural
[o-o]MS, 48, 49 may
[p-p]+52, 57, 62, 65, 71
[q-q]MS, 48, 49 may
[r-r]MS, 48, 49 if it abandons
[s]MS, 48, 49 But it cannot take half of the one course, and half of the other. Let it choose that, which circumstances or the public sentiment render most expedient.
[t-t]+48, 49, 52, 57, 62, 65, 71
[u-u]MS *give*
[v-v]+62, 65, 71
[w-w]MS, 48, 49, 52, 57, 62 for
[x-x]MS, 48, 49, 52, 57 of 43
[y-y]MS, 48, 49, 52, 57 undertakes

concluded against all poor-laws whatever. It required much experience, and careful examination of different modes of poor-law management, to give assurance that the admission of an absolute right to [z]be supported[z] at the cost of other people, could exist in law and in fact, without fatally relaxing the springs of industry and the restraints of prudence. This, however, was fully substantiated, by the investigations of the original Poor Law Commissioners. Hostile as they are unjustly accused of being to the principle of legal relief, they are the first who fully proved the compatibility of any Poor Law, in which a right to relief was recognised, with the permanent interests of the labouring class and of posterity. By a [a]collection[a] of facts, experimentally ascertained in parishes scattered throughout England, it was shown that the guarantee of support could be freed from its injurious effects upon the minds and habits of the people, if the relief, though ample in respect to necessaries, was accompanied with conditions which they disliked, consisting of some restraints on their freedom, and the privation of [b]some[b] indulgences. Under this proviso, it may be regarded as irrevocably established, that the fate of no member of the community needs be abandoned to chance; that society can and therefore ought to insure every individual belonging to it against the extreme of want; that the condition even of those [c]who are unable to find their own support[c], needs not be one of physical suffering, or the dread of it, but only of restricted indulgence, and enforced rigidity of discipline. This is surely something gained for humanity, important in itself, and still more so as a step to something beyond; and humanity has no worse enemies than those who lend themselves, either knowingly or unintentionally, to bring odium on this law, or on the principles in which it originated.

§ 3. [*Allowances in aid of wages*] Next to the attempts to regulate wages, and provide artificially that all who are willing to work shall receive an adequate price for their labour, we have to consider another class of popular remedies, which do not profess to interfere with freedom of contract; which [a]leave wages to be fixed by the competition of the market[a], but, when they are considered insufficient, endeavour by some subsidiary resource to make up to the labourers for the insufficiency. Of this nature [b]was[b] the expedient resorted to by parish authorities during thirty or forty years previous to 1834, generally known as the Allowance System. This was first introduced, when, through a succession of bad seasons, and consequent high prices of food, the wages of labour had become inadequate

[z-z]MS support
[a-a]MS, 48, 49, 52 collation [b-b]MS, 48, 49, 52, 57 certain
[c-c]MS, 48, 49 on the lowest step of the social ladder

[a-a]MS, 48, 49 allow wages to be what the competition of the market makes them
[b-b]MS is

to afford to the families of the agricultural labourers the [c]amount[c] of support to which they had been accustomed. Sentiments of humanity, joined with the idea then inculcated in high quarters, that people ought not to be allowed to suffer for having enriched their country with a multitude of inhabitants, induced the magistrates of the rural districts to commence giving parish relief to persons already in private employment: and when the practice had once been sanctioned, the immediate interest of the farmers, whom it enabled to throw part of the support of their labourers upon the other inhabitants of the parish, led to a great and rapid extension of it. The principle of this scheme being avowedly that of adapting the means of every family to its necessities, it was a natural [d]consequence[d] that more should be given to the married than to the single, and to those who had large families than to those who had not: in fact, an allowance was usually granted for every child. So direct and positive an encouragement to population is not, however, inseparable from the scheme: the allowance in aid of wages might be a fixed thing, given to all labourers alike, and as this is the least objectionable form which the system can assume, we will give it the benefit of the supposition.

It is obvious that this is merely another mode of fixing a minimum of wages; no otherwise differing from the direct mode, than in allowing the employer to buy the labour at its market price, the difference being made up to the labourer from a public fund. The one kind of guarantee is open to all the objections which have been urged against the other[e]. It[e] promises to the labourers that they shall all have a certain amount of wages, however numerous they may be: and removes, therefore, alike the positive and the prudential obstacles to an unlimited increase. But besides the objections common to all attempts to regulate wages without regulating population, the allowance system has a peculiar absurdity of its own. This is, that it inevitably takes from wages with one hand what it adds to them with the other. There is a rate of wages, either the lowest on which the people can, or the lowest on which they will consent, to live. We will suppose this to be seven shillings a week. Shocked at the wretchedness of this pittance, the parish authorities humanely make it up to ten. But the labourers are accustomed to seven, and though they would gladly have more, will live on that (as the fact proves) rather than restrain the instinct of multiplication. Their habits will not be altered for the better by giving them parish pay. Receiving three shillings from the parish, they will be as well off as before though they should increase sufficiently to bring down wages to four shillings. They will accordingly people down to that point;

[c-c]MS, 48, 49 degree
[d-d]MS, 48, 49, 52, 57 corollary
[e-e]MS : it

or perhaps, without waiting for an increase of numbers, there are unemployed labourers enough in the workhouse to produce the effect at once. It is well known that the allowance system did practically operate in the mode described, and that under its influence wages sank to a lower rate than [f]had been[f] known in England before. During the last century, under a rather rigid administration of the poor-laws, population increased slowly, and agricultural wages were considerably above the starvation point. Under the allowance system the people increased so fast, and wages [g]sank[g] so low, that with wages and allowance together, families were worse off than they had been before with wages alone. When the labourer depends solely on wages, there [h]is[h] [i]a virtual[i] minimum. [j]If wages fall below the lowest rate which will enable the population to be kept up, depopulation at least restores them to that lowest rate.[j] But if the deficiency is to be made up by a forced contribution from all who have anything to give, wages may fall below starvation point; they may fall almost to zero. This deplorable system, worse than any other form of poor-law abuse yet invented, inasmuch as it pauperizes not merely the unemployed part of the population but the whole, [k]received a severe check from the Poor Law of 1834: I wish it could be said that there are no signs of[k] its revival. [l]

§ 4. [*The Allotment System*] But while this is [a]generally condemned[a], there is another mode of relief in aid of wages, which is [b]still highly popular[b]; a mode greatly preferable, morally and socially, to parish allowance, but tending, it is to be feared, to a very similar economical result: I mean the much-boasted Allotment System. This, too, is a contrivance to compensate the labourer for the insufficiency of his wages, by giving him something else as a supplement to them: but instead of having them made up from the poor-rate, he is enabled to make them up for himself, by renting a small piece of ground, which he cultivates like a garden by spade labour, raising potatoes and other vegetables for home consumption, with perhaps some additional quantity for sale. If he hires the ground ready manured, he sometimes pays for it at as high a rate as eight pounds an

[f-f]MS was
[g-g]MS, 48 sunk
[h-h]MS, 48, 49, 52, 57 *is* [i-i]MS, 48, 49 an absolute
[j-j]MS, 48, 49 Anything less than what will absolutely support him he will not take, for if he is to starve, he may as well do so without working as with it.
[k-k]MS, 48, 49, 52, 57, 62 has now been abolished, and of this one abuse at least it may be said, that nobody professes to wish for] 65 has been . . . *as* MS
[l]MS, 48, 49 Even the agitators against the New Poor Law have hitherto stopped short of patronizing the Allowance System.
[a-a]MS, 48, 49, 52, 57, 62, 65 (it is to be hoped) exploded
[b-b]MS, 48, 49 at the height of popularity

acre: but getting his own labour and that of his family for nothing, he is able to gain several pounds by it even at so high a rent.* The patrons of the system make it a great point that the allotment shall be in aid of wages, and not a substitute for them; that it shall not be such as a labourer can live on, but only sufficient to occupy the spare hours and days of a man in tolerably regular agricultural employment, with assistance from his wife and children. They usually limit the extent of a single allotment to a quarter, or something between a quarter and half an acre. If it exceeds this, without being enough to occupy him entirely, it will make him, they say, a bad and uncertain workman for hire: if it is sufficient to take him entirely out of the class of hired labourers, and to become his sole means of subsistence, it will make him an Irish cottier: [c]for which assertion[c], at the enormous rents usually demanded, there is some foundation. But in their precautions against cottierism, these well-meaning persons do not perceive, that if the system they patronize is not a cottier system, it is, in essentials, neither more nor less than a system of conacre.

There is no doubt a material difference between eking out insufficient wages by a fund raised by taxation, and doing the same thing by means which make a clear addition to the gross produce of the country. There is also a difference between helping a labourer by means of his own industry, and subsidizing him in a mode which tends to make him careless and idle. On both these points, allotments have an unquestionable advantage over parish allowances. But in their effect on wages and population, I see no reason why the two plans should substantially differ. All subsidies in aid of wages enable the labourer to do with less remuneration, and therefore ultimately bring down the price of labour by the full amount, unless a change be wrought in the ideas and requirements of the [d]labouring class[d]; an alteration in the relative value which [e]they set[e] upon the gratification of [f]their[f] instincts, and upon the increase of [g]their[g] comforts and the comforts of those connected with [h]them[h]. That any such change in [i]their[i] character should be produced by the allotment system, appears to me a thing not to be expected. The possession of land, we are sometimes told, renders the labourer provident. Property in land does so; or what is equivalent to property, occupation on fixed terms and on a permanent tenure. But mere hiring from year to year was never found to have any such effect. [j]Did[j]

*See the Evidence on the subject of Allotments, collected by the Commissioners of Poor Law Enquiry.

c–cMS a proposition for which
d–dMS, 48, 49 labourer
e–eMS, 48, 49 he sets
f–fMS, 48, 49 his
g–gMS, 48, 49 his
h–hMS, 48, 49 him
i–iMS, 48, 49 his
j–jMS, 48, 49, 52 Does

possession of land render the Irishman provident? [k] Testimonies, it is true, abound, and I do not seek to discredit them, of the beneficial change produced in the conduct and condition of labourers, by receiving allotments. Such an effect is to be expected while those who hold them are a small number; a privileged class, having a status above the common level, which they are unwilling to lose. They are also, no doubt, almost always, originally a select class, composed of the most favourable specimens of the labouring people: which, however, is attended with the inconvenience that the persons to whom the system facilitates marrying and having [l]children[l], are precisely those who would otherwise be the most likely to practise prudential restraint. As affecting the general condition of the labouring class, the scheme, as it seems to me, must be either nugatory or mischievous. If only a few labourers have allotments, they are naturally those who could do best without them, and no good is done to the class: while, if the system were general, and every or almost every labourer had an allotment, I believe the effect would be much the same as when every or almost every labourer had an allowance in aid of wages. I think there can be no doubt that if, at the end of the last century, the Allotment instead of the Allowance system had been generally adopted in England, it would equally have broken down the practical restraints on population which at that time did really exist; population would have started forward exactly as in fact it did; and in twenty years, wages [m]plus[m] the allotment would have been, as wages plus the allowance actually were, no more than equal to the former wages without any allotment[n]. The[n] only difference in favour of allotments would have been, that they make the people grow their own poor-rates.

I am at the same time quite ready to allow, that in some circumstances, the possession of land at a fair rent, even without ownership, by the generality of labourers for hire, operates as a cause not of low, but of high wages. This, however, is when their land renders them, to the extent of actual necessaries, independent of the market for labour. There is the greatest difference between the position of people who live by wages, with land as an extra resource, and of people who can, in case of necessity, subsist entirely on their land, and only work for hire to add to their comforts. Wages are likely to be high where none are compelled by necessity to sell their labour. "People who have at home some kind of property to apply their labour to, will not sell their labour for wages that do not afford them a better diet than potatoes and maize, although in saving for themselves, they may live very much on potatoes and maize. We are often surprised

[k]MS Property being, as it were, the sun round which the present social system revolves, one might expect to find its virtues better understood.

[l-l]MS, 48, 49 a family

[m-m]MS *plus* [n-n]MS : & the

in travelling on the Continent, to hear of a rate of day's wages very high, considering the abundance and cheapness of food. It is want of the necessity or [o]the[o] inclination to take work, that makes day-labour scarce, and, considering the price of provisions, dear, in many parts of the Continent, where property in land is widely diffused among the [p]people."*[p] There are parts of the Continent, where, even of the inhabitants of the towns, scarcely one seems to be exclusively dependent on his ostensible employment; and nothing else can explain the high price they put on their services, and the carelessness they evince as to whether they are employed at all. But the effect would be far different if their land or other resources gave them only a fraction of a subsistence, leaving them under an undiminished necessity of selling their labour for wages in an overstocked market. Their land would then merely enable them to exist on smaller wages, and to carry their multiplication so much the further before reaching the point below which they either could not, or would not descend.

To the view I have taken of the effect of allotments, I see no argument which can be opposed, but that employed by Mr. Thornton,† with whom on this subject I am at issue. His defence of allotments is grounded on the general [q]doctrine[q], that it is only the very poor who multiply without regard to consequences, and that if the condition of the existing generation could be greatly improved, which he thinks might be done by the allotment system, their successors would grow up with an increased standard of requirements, and would not have families until they could keep them in as much comfort as [r]that in which[r] they had been brought up themselves. I agree in as much of this argument as goes to prove that a sudden and very great improvement in the condition of the poor, [s]has always[s], through its effect on their habits of life, [t]a chance of becoming[t] permanent. What happened at the time of the French Revolution is an example. But I cannot think that the addition of a quarter or even half an acre to every labourer's cottage, and that too at a rack rent, would (after the fall of wages which would be necessary to absorb the already existing mass of pauper labour) make so great a difference in the comforts of the family for a generation to come, as to raise up from childhood a labouring population with a really higher permanent standard of requirements and habits. So small a portion of land could only be made a permanent benefit, by holding out [u]encouragement[u] to acquire by industry and saving, the means

*Laing's *Notes* [MS, 48, 49, 52, 57 *Notes*] *of a Traveller*, p. 456 [457].

†See Thornton on *Over-Population*, ch. viii.

[o-o]+65, 71 [*not in* Source]
[p-p]MS, 48, 49 people." Thus says Mr. Laing,* and his remark is certainly just.
[q-q]MS, 48, 49 principle
[r-r]+52, 57, 62, 65, 71
[s-s]MS is likely
[t-t]MS to become
[u-u]MS, 48, 49, 52, 57, 62 encouragements

of buying it outright: a permission which, if extensively made use of, would be a kind of education in forethought and frugality to the entire class, the effects of which might not cease with the occasion. The benefit would however arise, not from what was given [v]them[v], but from what they were stimulated to acquire.

No remedies for low wages have the smallest chance of being efficacious, which do not operate on and through the minds and habits of the people. While these are unaffected, any contrivance, even if successful, for temporarily improving the condition of the very poor, would but let slip the reins by which population was previously curbed; and could only, therefore, continue to produce its effect, if, by the whip and spur of taxation, capital were compelled to follow at an equally accelerated pace. But this process could not possibly continue for long together, and whenever it stopped, it would leave the country with an increased number of the poorest class, and a diminished proportion of all except the poorest, or, if it continued long enough,with none at all. For "to this complexion must come at last" all social arrangements, which remove the natural checks to population without substituting any others.

v–v+62, 65, 71

CHAPTER XIII

The Remedies for Low Wages Further Considered

§ 1. [*Pernicious direction of public opinion on the subject of population*] By what means, then, is poverty to be contended against? How is the evil of low wages to be remedied? If the expedients usually recommended for the purpose are not adapted to it, can no others be thought of? Is the problem incapable of solution? Can political economy do nothing, but only object to everything, and demonstrate that nothing can be done?

If this were so, political economy might have a needful, but would have a melancholy, and a thankless task. If the bulk of the human race are always to remain as at present, slaves to toil in which they *have* no interest, and therefore *feel* no interest—drudging from early morning till late at night for bare necessaries, and with all the intellectual and moral deficiencies which that implies—without resources either in mind or feelings—untaught, for they cannot be better taught than fed; selfish, for all their thoughts are required for themselves; without interests or sentiments as citizens and members of society, and with a sense of injustice rankling in their minds, equally for what they have not, and for what others have; I know not what there is which should make a person with any capacity of reason, concern himself about the destinies of the human race[a]. There[a] would be no wisdom for any one but in extracting from life, with Epicurean indifference, as much personal satisfaction [b]to[b] himself and those with whom he sympathizes, as it can yield without injury to any one, and letting the unmeaning bustle of so-called civilized existence roll by unheeded. But there is no ground for such a view of human affairs. Poverty, like most social evils, exists because men follow their brute instincts without due consideration. But society is possible, precisely because man is not necessarily a brute. Civilization in every one of its aspects is a struggle against the animal instincts. Over some even of the strongest of them, it has shown itself capable of acquiring abundant control. It has artificialized large portions of mankind to such an extent, that of many of their most natural inclinations they have scarcely a vestige or a remembrance left. If it has

[a-a]MS ; there [b-b]MS, 48, 49, 52, 57 for

not brought the instinct of population under as much restraint as is needful, we must remember that it has never seriously tried. What efforts it has made, have mostly been in the contrary direction. Religion, morality, and statesmanship have vied with one another in incitements to marriage, and to the multiplication of the species, so it be but in wedlock. Religion has not even yet discontinued its encouragements. The Roman Catholic clergy (of any other clergy it is unnecessary to speak, since no other have any considerable influence over the poorer classes) everywhere think it their duty to promote marriage, in order to prevent fornication. There is still in many minds a strong religious prejudice against the true doctrine. The rich, provided the consequences do not touch themselves, think it impugns the wisdom of Providence to suppose that misery can result from the operation of a natural propensity: the poor think that "God never sends mouths but he sends meat." No one would guess from the language of either, that man had any voice or choice in the matter. So complete is the confusion of ideas on the whole subject; owing in a great degree to the mystery in which it is shrouded by a spurious delicacy, which prefers that right and wrong should be mismeasured and confounded on one of the subjects most momentous to human welfare, rather than that the subject be freely spoken of and discussed. People are little aware of the cost to mankind of this scrupulosity of speech. The diseases of society can, no more than corporal maladies, be prevented or cured without being spoken about in plain language. All experience shows that the mass of mankind never judge of moral questions for themselves, never see anything to be right or wrong until they have been frequently told it; and who tells them that they have any duties in the matter in question, while they keep within matrimonial limits? Who meets with the smallest condemnation, or rather, who does not meet with sympathy and benevolence, for any amount of evil which he may have brought upon himself and those dependent on him, by this species of incontinence? While a man who is intemperate in drink, is discountenanced and despised by all who profess to be moral people, [c]it is one of the chief grounds made use of in appeals to the benevolent, that the applicant has a large family and is unable to maintain them.*[c]

*[49] Little improvement can be expected in morality until the producing large families is regarded with the same feelings as drunkenness [49 as over-fondness for wine,] or any other physical excess. But while the aristocracy and clergy are foremost to set the example of this kind of [49, 52, 57 example of] incontinence, what can be expected from the poor?

[c-c]MS, 48 is it not to this hour the favourite recommendation for any parochial office bestowed by popular election, to have a large family and to be unable to maintain them? Do not the candidates placard their intemperance on walls, and publish it through the town in circulars?] 49 *as* MS . . . placard their enormous families . . . publish them . . . circulars?*

One cannot wonder that silence on this great department of human duty should produce unconsciousness of moral obligations, when it produces oblivion of physical facts. That it is possible to delay marriage, and to live in abstinence while unmarried, most people are willing to allow; but when persons are once married [d] , the idea, in this country, never seems to enter any one's mind that [e]having or not having a family, or the number of which it shall consist[e], is [f] amenable to their own control. One would imagine that children were rained down upon married people, direct from heaven, without their being art or part in the matter; that it was really, as the common phrases have it, God's will, and not their own, which decided the numbers of their offspring. Let us see what is a Continental philosopher's opinion on this point; a [g]man[g] among the most benevolent [h]of his time, and the happiness of whose married life has been celebrated[h].

"Lorsque des préjugés dangereux," says Sismondi,* "ne sont point accrédités, lorsqu'une morale contraire à nos vrais devoirs envers les autres et surtout envers les créatures qui nous doivent la vie, n'est point enseignée au nom de l'autorité la plus sacrée, aucun homme sage ne se marie avant de se trouver dans une condition qui lui donne un moyen assuré de vivre; aucun père de famille n'a plus d'enfans qu'il n'en peut convenablement élever. Ce dernier compte à bon droit que ses enfans devront se contenter du sort dans lequel il a vécu; aussi doit-il désirer que la génération naissante représente exactement celle qui s'en va; qu'un fils et une fille arrivés à l'âge nubile remplacent son père et sa mère; que les enfans de ses enfans le remplacent à son tour avec sa femme; que sa fille trouve dans une autre maison précisément le sort qu'il donnera à la fille d'une autre maison dans la sienne, et que le revenu qui suffisait aux pères suffise aux enfans." In a country increasing in wealth, [i]some increase of numbers[i] would be [j]admissible[j], but that is a question of detail, not of principle. "Une fois que cette famille est formée, la justice et l'humanité exigent qu'il s'impose la même contrainte à laquelle se soumettent les célibataires. Lorsqu'on voit combien est petit, en tout pays, le nombre des enfans naturels, on doit reconnaître que cette contrainte est suffisamment efficace. Dans un pays où la population ne peut pas s'accroître, ou du moins dans lequel son progrès doit être si lent qu'il soit à peine perceptible, quand il n'y a point de places nouvelles pour de nouveaux établissemens, un

**Nouveaux Principes*, liv. vii. ch. 5. [Vol. II, pp. 296–7.]

[d]MS —when law and religion have sanctioned their living together
[e-e]MS the number of their family from that time forward
[f]MS, 48, 49 at all] 52, 57 wholly
[g-g]MS philosopher
[h-h]MS , as well as the [MS *ripped*] most enlightened of his time, & who enjoyed an almost European reputation for the happiness of his married life
[i-i]MS, 48, 49, 52, 57, 62 something more than this
[j-j]MS, 48, 49, 52, 57 allowable

père qui a huit enfans doit compter, ou que six de ses enfans mourront en bas âge, ou que trois de ses contemporains et trois de ses contemporaines, et dans la génération suivante, trois de ses fils et trois de ses filles, ne se marieront pas à cause de lui."

§ 2. [*Grounds for expecting improvement*] Those who think it hopeless that the labouring classes should be induced to practise a sufficient degree of prudence in regard to the increase of their families, because they have hitherto stopt short of that point, show an inability to estimate the ordinary principles of human action. Nothing more would probably be necessary to secure that result, than an opinion generally diffused that it was desirable. As a moral principle, such an opinion has never yet existed in any country: it is curious that it does not so exist in countries in which, from the spontaneous operation of individual forethought, population is, comparatively speaking, efficiently repressed. What is practised as prudence is still not recognised as duty; the talkers and writers are mostly on the other side, even in France, where a sentimental horror of Malthus is almost as rife as in this country. Many causes may be assigned, besides the modern date of the doctrine, for its not having yet gained possession of the general mind. Its truth has, in some respects, been its detriment. One may be permitted to doubt whether, except among the poor themselves (for whose prejudices on this subject there is no difficulty in accounting) there has ever yet been, in any class of society, a sincere and earnest desire that wages should be high. There has been plenty of desire to keep down the poor-rate; but, that done, people have been very willing that the working classes should be ill off. Nearly all who are not labourers themselves, are employers of labour, and are not sorry to get the commodity cheap. It is a fact, that even Boards of Guardians, who are supposed to be official apostles of anti-population doctrines, will seldom hear patiently of anything which they are pleased to designate as Malthusianism. Boards of Guardians [a]in rural districts,[a] principally consist of farmers, and farmers, it is well known, in general dislike even allotments, as making the labourers "too independent." From the gentry, who are in less immediate contact and collision of interest with the labourers, better things might be expected, and the gentry of England are usually charitable. But charitable people have human infirmities, and would, very often, be secretly not a little dissatisfied if no one needed their charity: it is from them one oftenest hears the base doctrine, that God has decreed there shall always be poor. When one adds to this, that nearly every person who has had in him any active spring of exertion for a social object, has had some favourite reform to effect which he thought the admission of this great principle would throw into the shade;

[a-a]+62, 65, 71

has had corn laws to repeal, or taxation to reduce, or small notes to issue, or the charter to carry, or the church [b]to revive or abolish, or[b] the aristocracy to pull down, and looked upon every one as an enemy who thought anything important except his object; it is scarcely wonderful that since the population doctrine was first promulgated, nine-tenths of the talk has always been against it, and the remaining tenth only audible at intervals; and that it has not yet penetrated far among those who might be expected to be the least willing recipients of it, the labourers themselves.

But let us try to imagine what would happen if the idea became general among the labouring class, that the competition of too great numbers was the [c]special[c] cause of their poverty; so that every labourer looked (with Sismondi) upon every other who had more than the number of children which the circumstances of society allowed to each, as doing him a wrong—as filling up the place which he was entitled to share [d] . Any one who supposes that this state of opinion would not have a great effect on conduct, must be profoundly ignorant of human nature; can never have considered how large a portion of the motives which induce the generality of men to take care even of their own interest, is derived from regard for opinion—from the expectation of being disliked or despised for not doing it. [e]In the particular case in question, it is not too much to say that over-indulgence is as much caused by the stimulus of opinion as by the mere animal propensity; since opinion universally, and especially among the most uneducated classes, has connected ideas of spirit and power with the strength of the instinct, and of inferiority with its moderation or absence; a perversion of sentiment caused by its being the means, and the stamp, of a dominion exercised over other human beings. The effect would be great of merely removing this factitious stimulus; and when once opinion shall have turned itself into an adverse direction, a resolution will soon take place in this department of human conduct.[e] We are often told that the most thorough perception of the dependence of wages on population will not influence the conduct of a labouring man, because it is not the [f] children he himself can have that will produce any effect in generally depressing the labour market. True: and it is also true, that one soldier's running away will not lose the battle; accordingly it is not that consideration which keeps each soldier in his rank: it is the disgrace which naturally and inevitably attends on conduct by any one individual, which if pursued by a majority, everybody can see would be fatal. Men are seldom found to brave

[b-b]MS, 48, 49, 52 and
[c-c]MS, 48, 49, 52, 57, 62 principal
[d]MS —as helping to prevent him from marrying, or from having the number of children who would not be a burthen but an advantage to him] 48, 49 *as* MS . . . him from having . . . *as* MS
[e-e]+52, 57, 62, 65, 71 [f]MS few

the general opinion of their class, unless supported either by some principle higher than regard for opinion, or by some [g]strong[g] body of opinion elsewhere.

It must be borne in mind also, that the opinion here in question, as soon as it attained any prevalence, would have powerful auxiliaries in the great majority of women. It is [h]seldom[h] by the choice of the wife that families are too numerous; on her devolves (along with all the physical suffering and at least a full share of the privations) the whole of the intolerable domestic drudgery resulting from the excess. To be relieved from it would be hailed as a blessing by multitudes of women who now never venture to urge such a claim, but who would urge it, if supported by the moral feelings of the community. Among the barbarisms which law and morals have not yet ceased to sanction, the most disgusting surely is, that any human being should be permitted to consider himself as having a *right* to the person of another.

If the opinion were once generally established among the labouring class that their welfare required a due regulation of the numbers of families, the respectable and well-conducted of the body would conform to the prescription, and only those would exempt themselves from it, who were in the habit of making light of [i]social obligations generally[i]; and [j]there would be then an evident justification[j] for converting the moral obligation against bringing children into the world who are a burthen to the community, into a legal [k]one[k]; just as in many other cases of the progress of opinion, the law ends by enforcing against recalcitrant minorities, obligations which to be useful must be general, and which, from a sense of their utility, a large majority have voluntarily consented to take upon themselves. [l]There would be no need, however, of legal sanctions, if women were admitted, as on all other grounds they have the clearest [m]title[m] to be, to the same rights of

[g-g]+48, 49, 52, 57, 62, 65, 71
[h-h]MS, 48, 49, 52, 57, 62 never
[i-i]MS other moral rules
[j-j]MS, 48, 49 it is then that a justification would exist
[k-k]MS obligation
[l-l373]MS, 49 Whether a legal sanction would be ultimately required, or moral sanctions, and the indirect influence of law and policy, would suffice—and if legal measures were necessary, of what nature it would be advantageous that they should be, it would be premature, in the present state of the question to discuss.

The prospects, then, of the existing system of society depend upon this: What chance is there] 48 *as* MS . . . to discuss.* [*footnote:*] *Although, in this place, where the subject under discussion is the causes and remedies of low wages, the question of population is treated chiefly as a labourer's question, the principle contended for includes not only the labouring classes, but all persons, except the few who being able to give to their offspring the means of independent support during the whole of life, do not leave them to swell the competition for employment. . . . *as* MS [*cf.* II, xvi, 2[g], p. 419]
[m-m]52 right

citizenship with men. Let them cease to be confined by custom to one physical function as their means of living and their source of influence, and they would have for the first time an equal voice with men in what concerns that function: and of all the improvements in reserve for mankind which it is now possible to foresee, none [n]might be expected to[n] be so fertile as this in almost every kind of moral and social benefit.

It remains to consider what chance there is[l] that opinions and feelings, grounded on the law of the dependence of wages on population, will arise among the labouring [o]classes;[o] and by what means [p]such opinions and feelings can be called forth.[p] Before considering the grounds of hope on this subject, a hope which many persons, no doubt, will be ready, without consideration, to pronounce chimerical, I will remark, that [q]unless a satisfactory answer can be made to these two questions,[q] the industrial system prevailing in this country, and regarded by many writers as the *ne plus ultra* of civilization—the [r] dependence of the whole labouring class of the community on the wages of hired labour[s], is irrevocably condemned[s]. The question we are considering is, whether, of this state of things, over-population and a degraded condition of the labouring class are the inevitable consequence. [t] If a [u]prudent regulation of population be[u] not reconcilable with the system of hired labour, [v] the system is a nuisance, and [w] the grand object of economical statesmanship should [x]be (by whatever arrangements of property, and alterations in the modes of applying industry), to bring the labouring people under the influence of stronger and more obvious inducements to this kind of prudence, than the relation of workmen and employers [y]can[y] afford[x].

[z]But there exists[z] no such incompatibility. The causes of poverty are not so obvious at first sight to a population of hired labourers, as [a]they are[a] to

[n-n]52 would in my opinion
[o-o]MS, 48, 49 classes?
[p-p]MS, 48, 49 can such opinions and feelings be called forth?
[q-q]MS, 48, 49 on the possibility of making a satisfactory answer to these two questions, depends the acquittal or the condemnation of
[r]MS, 48, 49 permanent
[s-s]+52, 57, 62, 65, 71
[t]MS In countries of peasant proprietors, where the whole agricultural class are either owners of land, or have a prospect of ultimately becoming so, we have seen that a prudent regulation of population is prompted by obvious and strong motives, & in general does, to a very considerable extent, exist.
[u-u]MS similar benefit were] 48, 49 *as* 71 . . . population were
[v]MS, 48, 49 the conclusion would be that
[w]MS, 48, 49 that
[x-x]MS henceforth be, to favour & facilitate the parcelling out of the land among the labourers [*on* MS f.57v, *opposite this uncancelled passage, the* 48 *version appears, without the parenthesis, and with accidental variants*]
[y-y]48, 49 could
[z-z]MS, 48, 49 There is, however,
[a-a]+52, 57, 62, 65, 71

one of proprietors, [b]or as they would be to a socialist community. They are, however,[b] in no way mysterious. The dependence of wages on the number of the competitors for employment, is so far from hard of comprehension, or unintelligible to the labouring classes, that by great bodies of them it is already recognised and habitually acted on. It is familiar to all Trades Unions: every successful combination to keep up wages, owes its success to contrivances for restricting the number of the competitors; all skilled trades are anxious to keep down their own numbers, and many impose, or endeavour to impose, as a condition upon employers, that they shall not take more than a prescribed number of apprentices. There is, of course, a great difference between limiting their numbers by excluding other people, and doing the same thing by a restraint imposed on themselves: but the one as much as the other shows a clear perception of the relation between their numbers and their remuneration. The principle is understood in its application to any one employment, but not to the general mass of employment. For this there are several reasons: first, the operation of causes is more easily and distinctly seen in the more circumscribed field; secondly, skilled artizans are a more intelligent class than ordinary manual labourers: and the habit of concert, and of passing in review their general condition as a trade, keeps up a better understanding of their collective interests: thirdly and lastly, they are the most provident, because they are the best off, and have the most to preserve. What, however, is clearly perceived and admitted in particular instances, it cannot be hopeless to see understood and acknowledged as a general truth. Its recognition, at least in theory, seems a thing which must necessarily and immediately come to pass, when the minds of the labouring classes become capable of taking any rational view of their own aggregate condition. Of this the [c]great[c] majority of them have until now been incapable, either from the uncultivated state of their intelligence, or from poverty, which leaving them neither the fear of worse, nor the smallest hope of better, makes them careless of the consequences of their actions, and without thought for the future.

§ 3. [*Twofold means of elevating the habits of the labouring people: by education*] For the purpose therefore of altering the habits of the labouring people, there is need of a twofold action, directed simultaneously upon their intelligence and their poverty. An effective national education of the children of the labouring class, is the first thing needful: and, coincidently with this, a system of measures which shall (as the Revolution did in France) extinguish extreme poverty for one whole generation.

This is not the place for discussing, even in the most general manner,

[b-b]MS, 48, 49 but they are [c-c]+52, 57, 62, 65, 71

either the principles or the machinery of national education. [a] But [b]it is to be hoped that opinion on the subject is advancing, and[b] that an education of mere words would [c]not[c] now [d]be deemed sufficient[d], slow as our progress is towards [e]providing[e] anything better even [f]for the classes to whom society professes to give the very best education it can devise[f]. Without entering into disputable points, it may be asserted without scruple, that the aim of all intellectual training for the mass of the people, should be to cultivate common sense; to qualify them for forming a sound practical judgment of the circumstances by which they are surrounded. Whatever, in the intellectual department, can be superadded to this, is chiefly ornamental; while this is the indispensable groundwork on which education must rest. Let this object be acknowledged and kept in view as the thing to be first aimed at, and there will be little difficulty in deciding either what to teach, or in what manner to teach it.

An education directed to diffuse good sense among the people, with such knowledge as would qualify them to judge of the tendencies of their actions, would be certain, even without any direct inculcation, to raise up a public opinion by which intemperance and improvidence of every kind would be held discreditable, and the improvidence which overstocks the labour market would be severely condemned, as an offence against the common weal. But though the sufficiency of such a state of opinion, supposing it formed, to keep the increase of population within proper limits, cannot, I think, be doubted; yet, for the formation of the opinion, it would not do to trust to education alone. Education is not compatible with extreme poverty. It is impossible effectually to teach an indigent population. And it is difficult to make those feel the value of comfort who have never enjoyed it, or those appreciate the wretchedness of a precarious subsistence, who have been made reckless by always living from hand to mouth. Individuals often struggle upwards into a condition of ease; but the utmost that can be expected from a whole people is to maintain themselves in it; and [g]improvement in the habits and requirements of the mass of unskilled day-labourers[g] will be difficult and tardy, unless means can be contrived of [h] raising the entire body to a state of tolerable comfort, and maintaining them in it until a new generation grows up.

[a]MS, 48, 49 Of the little which is fit to be said on such a subject in a treatise like the present, the smallest portion only can be alluded to in this part of it.

[b-b]MS opinion on the subject is much more advanced than it was even a few years since, & there needs be no fear

[c-c]+48, 49, 52, 57, 62, 65, 71

[d-d]MS, 48, 49 satisfy us

[e-e]MS, 48, 49 giving

[f-f]MS, 48, 49 to those for whom we profess to do our very best

[g-g]MS the progress of the mass of unskilled day-labourers to a happier state

[h]MS suddenly

[i]Towards effecting this object there[i] are two resources available, without wrong to any one, without any of the liabilities of mischief attendant on voluntary or legal charity, and not only without weakening, but on the contrary strengthening, every incentive to industry, and every motive to forethought.

§ 4. [*Twofold means of elevating the habits of the labouring people: by large measures of immediate relief, through foreign and home colonization*] The first is, a great national measure of colonization. I mean, a grant of public money, sufficient to remove at once, and establish in the colonies, a considerable fraction of the youthful agricultural population. By giving the preference, as Mr. Wakefield proposes, to young couples, or when these cannot be obtained, to families with children nearly grown up, the expenditure would be made to go the farthest possible towards accomplishing the end, while the colonies would be supplied with the greatest amount of what is there in deficiency and here in superfluity, present and prospective labour. [a]It has been shown by others, and the grounds of the opinion will be exhibited in a subsequent [b]part[b] of the present work[a], that colonization on an adequate scale might be so conducted as to cost the country nothing, or nothing that would not be certainly repaid; and that the funds required, even by way of advance, would not be drawn from the capital employed in maintaining labour, but from that surplus which cannot find employment at such profit as constitutes an adequate remuneration for the abstinence of the possessor, and which is therefore sent abroad for investment, or wasted at home in reckless speculations. That portion of the income of the country which is habitually ineffective for any purpose of benefit to the labouring class, would bear any draught which it could be necessary to make on it for the amount of emigration which [c]is here[c] in view.

[d]The[d] second resource would be, to devote all common land, hereafter

[i-i]MS This, happily, is not impracticable, if men would but turn themselves to it in earnest, & cease to think that merely because a scheme promises much, the part of statesmanship is to have nothing to do with it. There

[a-a]MS The subject will be considered in a practical point of view, in a subsequent chapter of the present work: where it will be shewn, as has been shewn by others in the discussions which have from time to time taken place

[b-b]48 chapter

[c-c]MS I have

[d-d]MS, 48, 49 To the case of Ireland, in her present crisis of transition, colonization, as the exclusive remedy, is, I conceive, unsuitable. The Irish are nearly the worst adapted people in Europe for settlers in the wilderness: nor should the founders of nations destined perhaps to be the most powerful in the world, be drawn principally from the least civilized and least improved inhabitants of old countries. It is most fortunate therefore that the unoccupied lands of Ireland herself afford a resource so nearly adequate to the emergency, as reduces emigration to a rank merely subsidiary. In England and Scotland, with a population much less excessive, and better adapted

brought into cultivation, to raising [e] a class of small proprietors. It has long enough been the practice to take these lands from public use for the mere purpose of adding to the domains of the rich. It is time that what is left of them should be retained as an estate sacred to the benefit of the poor. The machinery for administering it already exists, having been created by the General Inclosure Act. What I would propose (though, I confess, with small hope of its being soon adopted) is, that in all future cases in which common land is permitted to be enclosed, such portion should first be sold or assigned as is sufficient to compensate the owners of manorial or common rights, and that the remainder should be divided into sections of five acres or thereabouts, to be conferred in absolute property on [f]individuals[f] of the labouring class who would reclaim and bring them into cultivation by their own labour. The preference should be given to such [g]labourers[g], and there are many of them, as had saved enough to maintain them until their first crop was got in, or whose character [h]was[h] such as to induce some responsible person to advance [i]to[i] them the requisite amount on their personal security. The tools, the manure, and in some cases the subsistence also might be supplied by the parish, or by the state; interest for the advance, at the rate yielded by the public funds, being laid on as a perpetual quit-rent, with power to the peasant to redeem it at any time for a moderate number of years' purchase. These little landed estates might, if it were thought necessary, be made indivisible by law; though, if the plan worked in the manner designed, I should not apprehend any objectionable degree of subdivision. [j]In[j] case of intestacy, and in default of amicable arrangement among the heirs, they [k]might[k] be bought by government at their value, and regranted to some other [l]labourer who[l] [m]would[m] give security for the price. The desire to possess one of these small properties would [n]probably[n] become, as [o] on the Continent, an inducement to prudence and economy pervading the whole labouring population; and that great desideratum among a people of hired labourers would be provided, an intermediate class

to a settler's life, colonization must be the chief resource for easing the labour market, and improving the condition of the existing generation of labourers so materially as to raise the permanent standard of habits in the generation following. But England too has waste lands, though less extensive than those of Ireland: and the

[e]MS, 48, 49, 52, 57 up
[f-f]MS respectable families] 48, 49 families
[g-g]MS, 48, 49 families
[h-h]MS is
[i-i]+52, 57, 62, 65, 71
[j-j]MS I do not recommend that they should be subject to primogeniture, but rather that in
[k-k]MS should
[l-l]MS, 48, 49 labouring family which
[m-m]MS, 48, 49, 52, 57, 62, 65 could
[n-n]+48, 49, 52, 57, 62, 65, 71 [o]MS it is

between them and their employers; affording them the double advantage, of an object for their hopes, and, as there would be good reason to anticipate, an example for their imitation.

It would, however, be of little avail that either or both of these measures of relief should be adopted, unless on such a scale, as would enable the whole body of hired labourers remaining on the soil to obtain not merely employment, but a large addition to the present wages—such an addition as would enable them to live and bring up their children in a degree of comfort and independence to which they have hitherto been strangers. When the object is to raise the permanent condition of a people, small means do not merely produce small effects, they produce no effect at all. Unless comfort can be made as habitual to a whole generation as indigence is now, nothing is accomplished; and [p]feeble half-measures do but fritter away resources[p], far better reserved until the improvement of public opinion and of education shall raise up [q]politicians who will not think that merely because a scheme promises much, the part of statesmanship is to have nothing to do with it[q].

[r]I have left the preceding paragraphs as they were written, since they remain true in principle, though it is no longer urgent to apply these specific recommendations to the present state of this country. The extraordinary cheapening of the means of transport, which is one of the great scientific achievements of the age, and the knowledge which nearly all classes of the people have now acquired, or are in the way of acquiring, of the condition of the labour market in remote parts of the world, have opened up a spontaneous emigration from these islands to the new countries beyond the ocean, which does not tend to diminish, but to increase; and which, without any national measure of systematic colonization, may prove sufficient to effect a material rise of wages in Great Britain, as it has already done in Ireland, and to maintain that rise unimpaired for one or more generations. Emigration, instead of an occasional vent, is becoming a steady outlet for superfluous numbers; and this new fact in modern history, together with the flush of prosperity occasioned by free trade, have granted to this overcrowded country a temporary breathing-time, capable of being employed in accomplishing those moral and intellectual improvements in all classes of the people, the very poorest included, which would render improbable any relapse into the over-peopled state. Whether this golden opportunity will be properly used, depends on the wisdom of our councils;

[p-p]MS any feeble, timid half-attempt would be but frittering away a precious resource

[q-q]MS some politician with heart & intellect, & place the government of the country in his hands

[r-r]379+65, 71

and whatever depends on that, is always in a high degree precarious. The grounds of hope are, that there has been no time in our history when mental progress has depended so little on governments, and so much on the general disposition of the people; none in which the spirit of improvement has extended to so many branches of human affairs at once, nor in which all kinds of suggestions tending to the public good in every department, from the humblest physical to the highest moral or intellectual, were heard with so little prejudice, and had so good a chance of becoming known and being fairly considered.[r]

CHAPTER XIV

Of the Differences of Wages in Different Employments

§ 1. [*Differences of wages arising from different degrees of attractiveness in different employments*] In treating of wages, we have hitherto confined ourselves to the causes which operate on them generally, and *en masse*; the laws which govern the remuneration of ordinary or average labour: without reference to the existence of different kinds of work which are habitually paid at different rates, depending in some degree on different laws. We will now take into consideration these differences, and examine in what manner they affect or are affected by the conclusions already established.

A well-known and very popular chapter of Adam Smith* contains the best exposition yet given of this portion of the subject. I cannot indeed think his treatment so complete and exhaustive as it has sometimes been considered; but as far as it goes, his analysis is [a]tolerably[a] successful.

The differences, he says, arise partly from the policy of Europe, which nowhere leaves things at perfect liberty, and partly "from certain circumstances in the employments themselves, which either really, or at least in the imaginations of men, make up for a small pecuniary gain in some, and counterbalance a great one in others." These circumstances he considers to be: "First, the agreeableness or disagreeableness of the employments themselves; secondly, the easiness and cheapness, or the difficulty and expense of learning them; thirdly, the constancy or inconstancy of employment in them; fourthly, the small or great trust which must be reposed in those who exercise them; and fifthly, the probability or improbability of success in them."

Several of these points he has very copiously illustrated: though his examples are sometimes drawn from a state of facts now no longer existing. "The wages of labour vary with the ease or hardship, the cleanliness or dirtiness, the honourableness or dishonourableness of the employment. Thus, in most places, take the year round, a journeyman tailor earns

**Wealth of Nations*, book i. ch. 10 [ed. Wakefield, Vol. I, pp. 255–7].

[a–a]MS most] 48, 49 on the whole

less than a journeyman weaver. His work is much easier." Things have much altered, as to a weaver's remuneration, since Adam Smith's time; and the artizan whose work was more difficult than that of a tailor, can never, I think, have been the common weaver. "A journeyman weaver earns less than a journeyman smith. His work is not always easier, but it is much cleanlier." A more probable explanation is, that it requires less bodily strength. "A journeyman blacksmith, though an artificer, seldom earns so much in twelve hours as a collier, who is only a labourer, does in eight. His work is not quite so dirty, is less dangerous, and is carried on in day-light, and above ground. Honour makes a great part of the reward of all honourable professions. In point of pecuniary gain, all things considered,[b]" their recompense is, in his opinion, below the average[b]. "Disgrace has the contrary effect. The trade of a butcher is a brutal and an odious business; but it is in most places more profitable than the greater part of common trades. The most detestable of all employments, that of public executioner, is, in proportion to the quantity of work done, better paid than any common trade whatever."

One of the causes which make hand-loom weavers cling to their occupation in spite of the scanty remuneration which it now yields, is said to be a peculiar attractiveness arising from the freedom of action which it allows to the workman. "He can play or idle," says a recent authority,* "as feeling or inclination lead him; rise early or late, apply himself assiduously or carelessly, as he pleases, and work up at any time by increased exertion, hours previously sacrificed to indulgence or recreation. There is scarcely another condition of any portion of our working population thus free from external control. The factory operative is not only mulcted [c]of[c] his wages for absence, but, if of frequent occurrence, discharged altogether from his employment. The bricklayer, the carpenter, the painter, the joiner, the stonemason, the outdoor labourer, have each their appointed daily hours of labour, a disregard of which would lead to the same result." Accordingly, "the weaver will stand by his loom while it will enable him to exist, however miserably; and many, induced temporarily to quit it, have returned to it again, when work was to be had." [d]

*Mr. Muggeridge's Report to the Handloom Weavers Inquiry Commission. [*Parliamentary Papers*, 1841, X, 38.]

[b-b]MS they are generally under-recompensed," (the cases excepted in which the honorable are also the powerful professions, & help themselves)

[c-c]+57, 62, 65, 71 [Source *reads* mulct his; *see* Appendix I]

[d]MS, 48, 49 [*paragraph*] There is no difficulty in understanding the operative principle in all these cases. If, with complete freedom of competition, labour of different degrees of desirableness were paid alike, competitors would crowd into the more attractive employments, and desert the less eligible, thus lowering wages in the first, and raising them in the second, until there would be such a difference of reward

"Employment is much more constant," continues Adam Smith, "in some trades than in others. In the greater part of manufactures, a journeyman may be pretty sure of employment almost every day in the year that he is able to work" (the interruptions of business arising from overstocked markets, or from a suspension of demand, or from a commercial crisis, must be excepted). "A mason or bricklayer, on the contrary, can work neither in hard frost nor in foul weather, and his employment at all other times depends upon the occasional calls of his customers. He is liable, in consequence, to be frequently without any. What he earns, therefore, while he is employed, must not only maintain him while he is idle, but make him some compensation for those anxious and desponding moments which the thought of so precarious a situation must sometimes occasion. When the computed earnings of the greater part of manufacturers, accordingly, are nearly upon a level with the day wages of common labourers, those of masons and bricklayers are generally from one-half more to double those wages. No species of skilled labour, however, seems more easy to learn than that of masons and bricklayers. The high wages of those workmen, therefore, are not so much the recompense of their skill, as the compensation for the inconstancy of their employment.

"When the inconstancy of the employment is combined with the hardship, disagreeableness, and dirtiness of the work, it sometimes raises the wages of the most common labour above those of the most [e]skilled[e] artificers. A collier working by the piece, is supposed, at Newcastle, to earn commonly about double, and in many parts of Scotland about three times, the wages of common labour. His high wages arise altogether from the hardship, disagreeableness, and dirtiness of his work. His employment may, upon most occasions, be as constant as he pleases. The coal-heavers in London exercise a trade which in hardship, dirtiness, and disagreeableness, almost equals that of colliers; and from the unavoidable irregularity in the [f]arrival[f] of coal-ships, the employment of the greater part of them is necessarily very inconstant. If colliers, therefore, commonly earn double and triple the wages of common labour, it ought not to seem unreasonable that coal-heavers should sometimes earn four or five times those wages. In the inquiry made into their condition a few years ago, it was found that at the rate at which they were then paid, they could earn about four times the wages of common labour in London. How extravagant soever [g]these[g]

as to balance in common estimation the difference of eligibility. Under the unobstructed influence of competition, wages tend to adjust themselves in such a manner, that the situation and prospects of the labourers in all employments shall be, in the general estimation, as nearly as possible on a par.

[e-e]Source, MS, 48, 49, 52, 57, 62, 65 skilful

[f-f]Source, MS, 48, 49, 52, 57, 62, 65 arrivals

[g-g]Source, MS those

earnings may appear, if they were more than sufficient to compensate all the disagreeable circumstances of the business, there would soon be so great a number of competitors as, in a trade which has no exclusive privilege, would quickly reduce them to a lower rate."[*]

[h]These inequalities of remuneration, which are supposed to compensate for the disagreeable circumstances of particular employments, would, under certain conditions, be natural consequences of perfectly free competition: and as between employments of about the same grade, and filled by nearly the same description of people, they are, no doubt, for the most part, realized in practice. But it is altogether a false view of the state of facts, to present this as the relation which generally exists between agreeable and disagreeable employments. The really exhausting and the really repulsive labours, instead of being better paid than others, are almost invariably paid the worst of all, because performed by those who have no choice. It would be otherwise in a favourable state of the general labour market. If the labourers in the aggregrate, instead of exceeding, fell short of the amount of employment, work which was generally disliked would not be undertaken, except for more than ordinary wages. But when the supply of labour so far exceeds the demand that to find employment at all is an uncertainty, and to be offered it on any terms a favour, the case is totally the reverse. Desirable labourers, those whom every one is anxious to have, can still exercise a choice. The undesirable must take what they can get. The more revolting the occupation, the more certain it is to receive the minimum of remuneration, because it devolves on the most helpless and degraded, on those who from squalid poverty, or from want of skill and education, are rejected from all other employments. Partly from this cause, and partly from the natural and artificial monopolies which will be spoken of presently, the inequalities of wages are generally in an opposite direction to the equitable principle of compensation erroneously represented by Adam Smith as the general law of the remuneration of labour. The hardships and the earnings, instead of being directly proportional, as in any just arrangements of society they would be, are generally in [i]an[i] inverse ratio to one another.[h]

One of the points best illustrated by Adam Smith, is the influence exercised on the remuneration of an employment by the uncertainty of success in it. If the chances are great of total failure, the reward in case of success must be sufficient to make up, in the general estimation, for those adverse chances. But, owing to another principle of human nature, if the reward comes in the shape of a few great prizes, it usually attracts

[*Smith, *Wealth of Nations*, Vol. I, pp. 262–3.]

[h-h]+52, 57, 62, 65, 71 [i-i]52, 57, 62 the

competitors in such numbers, that the average remuneration may be reduced not only to zero, but even to a negative quantity. The success of lotteries proves that this is possible: since the aggregate body of adventurers in lotteries necessarily lose, otherwise the undertakers could not gain. The case of certain professions is considered by Adam Smith to be similar. "The probability that any particular person shall ever be qualified for the employment to which he is educated, is very different in different occupations. In the greater part of mechanic trades, success is almost certain, but very uncertain in the liberal professions. Put your son apprentice to a shoemaker, there is little doubt of his learning to make a pair of shoes; but send him to study the law, it is at least twenty to one if ever he makes such proficiency as will enable him to live by the business. In a perfectly fair lottery, those who draw the prizes ought to gain all that is lost by those who draw the blanks. In a profession where twenty fail for one that succeeds, that one ought to gain all that should have been gained by the unsuccessful twenty. The counsellor-at-law, who, perhaps, at near forty years of age, begins to make something by his profession, ought to receive the retribution, not only of his own so tedious and expensive education, but of that of more than twenty others who are never likely to make anything by it. How extravagant soever the fees of counsellors-at-law may sometimes appear, their real retribution is never equal to this. Compute in any particular place, what is likely to be annually gained, and what is likely to be annually spent, by all the different workmen in any common trade, such as that of shoemakers or weavers, and you will find that the former sum will generally exceed the latter. But make the same computation with regard to all the counsellors and students of law, in all the different inns of court, and you will find that their annual gains bear but a small proportion to their annual expense, even though you rate the former as high, and the latter as low, as can well be done. [j] "[*]

Whether this is true in our own day, when the gains of the few are incomparably greater than in the time of Adam Smith, but also the unsuccessful aspirants much more numerous, those who have the appropriate information must decide. It does not, however, seem to be sufficiently considered by Adam Smith, that the prizes which he speaks of comprise not the fees of counsel only, but the places of emolument and honour to which their profession gives access, together with the coveted distinction of a conspicuous position in the public eye.

Even where there are no great prizes, the mere love of excitement is

[*Smith, *Wealth of Nations*, Vol. I, pp. 265–6.]

[j]MS The lottery of the law, therefore, is very far from being a perfectly fair lottery: & that, as well as many other liberal & honourable professions, are, in point of pecuniary gain, evidently under-recompensed."

sometimes enough to cause an adventurous employment to be overstocked. This is apparent "in the readiness of the common people to enlist as soldiers, or to go to sea. . . . . The dangers and hair-breadth escapes of a life of adventures, instead of disheartening young people, seem frequently to recommend a trade to them. A tender mother, among the inferior ranks of people, is often afraid to send her son to school at a sea-port town, lest the sight of the ships and the conversation and adventures of the sailors should entice him to go to sea. The distant prospect of hazards from which we can hope to extricate ourselves by courage and address, is not disagreeable to us, and does not raise the wages of labour in any employment. It is otherwise with those in which courage and address can be of no avail. In trades which are known to be very unwholesome, the wages of labour are always remarkably high. Unwholesomeness is a species of disagreeableness, and its effects upon the wages of labour are to be ranked under that general head."[*]

§ 2. [*Differences of wages arising from natural monopolies*] [a]The preceding[a] are cases in which inequality of remuneration is necessary to produce equality of attractiveness, and are examples of the equalizing effect of free competition. The following are cases of real inequality, and arise from a different principle. "The wages of labour vary according to the small or great trust which must be reposed in the workmen. The wages of goldsmiths and jewellers are everywhere superior to those of many other workmen, not only of equal, but of much superior ingenuity; on account of the precious materials with which they are intrusted. We trust our health to the physician, our fortune and sometimes our life and reputation to the lawyer and attorney. Such confidence could not safely be reposed in people of a very mean or low condition. Their reward must be such, therefore, as may give them that rank in society which so important a trust requires."[†]

The superiority of reward is not here the consequence of competition, but of its absence: not a compensation for disadvantages inherent in the employment, but an extra advantage; a kind of monopoly price, the effect not of a legal, but of what has been termed a natural monopoly. If all labourers were trustworthy, it would not be necessary to give extra pay to working goldsmiths on account of the trust. The degree of integrity required being supposed to be uncommon, those who can make it appear that they possess it are able to take advantage of the peculiarity, and obtain higher pay in proportion to its rarity. This opens a class of considerations which Adam Smith, and most other political economists, have

[*Smith, *Wealth of Nations*, Vol. I, pp. 270, 273.]
[†*Ibid.*, p. 246.]

[a-a]MS, 48, 49 All these

taken into far too little account, and from inattention to which, he has given a most imperfect exposition of the wide difference between the remuneration of common labour and that of skilled employments.

Some employments require a much longer time to learn, and a much more expensive course of instruction than others; and to this extent there is, as explained by Adam Smith, an inherent reason for their being more highly remunerated. If an artizan must work several years at learning his trade before he can earn anything, and several years more before becoming sufficiently skilful for its finer operations, he must have a prospect of at last earning enough to pay the wages of all this past labour, with compensation for the delay of payment, and an indemnity for the expenses of his education. His wages, consequently, must yield, over and above the ordinary amount, an annuity sufficient to repay these sums, with the common rate of profit, within the number of years he can expect to live and [b]to[b] be in working condition. This, which is necessary to place the skilled employments, all circumstances taken together, on the same level of advantage with the unskilled, is the smallest difference which can exist for any length of time between the two remunerations, since otherwise no one would learn the skilled employments. And this amount of difference is all which Adam Smith's principles account for. When the disparity is greater, he seems to think that it must be explained by apprentice laws, and the rules of corporations which restrict admission into many of the skilled employments. But, independently of these or any other artificial monopolies, there is a natural monopoly in favour of skilled labourers against the unskilled, which makes the difference of reward exceed, sometimes in a manifold proportion, what is sufficient merely to equalize their advantages. If unskilled labourers had it in their power to compete with skilled, by merely taking the trouble of learning the trade, the difference of wages [c]might[c] not exceed what would compensate them for that trouble, at the ordinary rate at which labour is remunerated. But the fact that a course of instruction is required, of even a low degree of costliness, or that the labourer must be maintained for a considerable time from other sources, suffices everywhere to exclude the great body of the labouring people from the possibility of any such competition. Until lately, all employments which required even the humble education of reading and writing, could be recruited only from a select class, the majority having [d]had[d] no opportunity of acquiring those attainments. All such employments, accordingly, were immensely overpaid, as measured by the ordinary remuneration of labour. Since reading and writing have been brought within the reach of [e]a[e] multitude, the monopoly price of the lower grade of educated employments has

[b-b]+71
[c-c]MS, 48, 49 could
[d-d]+52, 57, 62, 65, 71
[e-e]MS, 48, 49 the

greatly fallen, the competition for them having increased in an almost incredible degree. There is still, however, a much greater disparity than can be accounted for on the principle of competition. A clerk from whom nothing is required but the mechanical labour of copying, gains more than [f]an equivalent for his mere exertion if he receives the wages of a bricklayer's labourer[f]. His work is not a tenth part as hard, it is quite as easy [g] to learn, and his condition is less precarious, a clerk's place being generally a place for life. The higher rate of his remuneration, therefore, must be partly ascribed to monopoly, the small degree of education required being not even yet so generally diffused as to call forth the natural number of competitors; and partly to the remaining influence of an ancient custom, which requires that clerks should maintain the dress and appearance of a more highly paid class. In some manual employments, requiring a nicety of hand which can only be acquired by long practice, it is difficult to obtain at any cost workmen in sufficient numbers, who are capable of the most delicate kind of work; and the wages paid to them are only limited by the price which purchasers are willing to give for the commodity they produce. This is the case with some working watchmakers, and with the makers of [h]some[h] astronomical and optical instruments. If workmen competent to such employments were ten times as numerous as they are, there would be purchasers for all which they could make, not indeed at the present prices, but at those lower prices which would be the natural consequence of lower wages. Similar considerations apply in a still greater degree to employments which it is attempted to confine to persons of a certain social rank, such as what are called the liberal professions; into which a person of what is considered too low a class of society, is not easily admitted, and if admitted, does not easily succeed.

So complete, indeed, has hitherto been the separation, so strongly marked the line of demarcation, between the different grades of labourers, as to be almost equivalent to an hereditary distinction of caste; each employment being [i]chiefly[i] recruited from the children of those already employed in it, or in employments of the same rank with it in social estimation[j], or from the children of persons who, if originally of a lower rank, have succeeded in raising themselves by their exertions[j]. The liberal professions are [k]mostly supplied[k] by the sons of either the professional, or the idle classes: the more highly skilled manual employments are filled up from the sons of skilled artizans, or [l] the class of tradesmen who rank with them: the lower classes of skilled employments are in a similar case; and

[f-f]MS the natural price of his labour if he receives the wages of a plowman
[g]MS or easier
[h-h]+49, 52, 57, 62, 65, 71
[i-i]MS almost exclusively
[j-j]+48, 49, 52, 57, 62, 65, 71
[k-k]MS supplied almost entirely
[l]MS, 48, 49 of

unskilled labourers, with occasional exceptions, remain from father to son in their pristine condition. Consequently the wages of each class have hitherto been regulated by the increase of its own population, rather than of the general population of the country. If the professions are overstocked, it is because the class of society from which they have always mainly been supplied, has greatly increased in number, and because most of that class have numerous families, and bring up some at least of their sons to professions. If the wages of artizans remain so much higher than those of common labourers, it is because artizans are a more prudent class, and do not marry so early or so inconsiderately. The changes, however, now so rapidly taking place in usages and ideas, are undermining all these distinctions; the habits or disabilities which chained people to their hereditary condition are fast wearing away, and every class is exposed to increased and increasing competition from at least the class immediately below it. The general relaxation of conventional barriers, and the increased facilities of education which already are, and will be in a much greater degree, brought within the reach of all, [m]tend[m] to produce, among many excellent effects, one which is the reverse; [n]they tend[n] to bring down the wages of skilled labour. The inequality of remuneration between the skilled and the unskilled is, without doubt, [o]very[o] much greater than is justifiable; but it is desirable that this should be [p]corrected[p] by raising the unskilled, not by lowering the skilled. If, however, the other changes taking place in society are not accompanied by a strengthening of the [q]checks[q] to population on the part of labourers generally, there will be a tendency to bring the lower grades of skilled labourers under the influence of a rate of increase regulated by a lower standard of living than their own, and thus to deteriorate their condition without raising that of the general mass; [r]the stimulus given to the multiplication of the lowest class being[r] sufficient to fill up without difficulty the additional space gained by them from those immediately above.

§ 3. [*Effect on wages of a class of subsidized competitors*] A modifying circumstance still remains to be noticed, which interferes to some extent with the operation of the principles thus far brought to view. While it is true, as a general rule, that the earnings of skilled labour, and especially of any labour which requires school education, are at a monopoly rate, from the impossibility, to the mass of the people, of obtaining that educa-

[m-m]MS tends
[n-n]MS it tends
[o-o]+52, 57, 62, 65, 71
[p-p]MS, 48, 49, 52, 57 remedied
[q-q]MS, 48 check
[r-r]MS there being a residuary capacity of multiplication in the lowest class,

tion; it is also true that the policy of nations[a], or the bounty of individuals, formerly did[a] much to counteract the effect of this limitation of competition, by offering eleemosynary instruction to a much larger class of persons than could have obtained the same advantages by paying their price. Adam Smith has pointed out the operation of this cause in keeping down the remuneration of scholarly or bookish occupations generally, and in particular of clergymen, literary men, and schoolmasters, or other teachers of youth. I cannot better set forth this part of the subject than in his words.

"It has been considered as of so much importance that a proper number of young people should be educated for certain professions, that sometimes the public, and sometimes the piety of private founders, have established many pensions, scholarships, exhibitions, bursaries, &c. for this purpose, which draw many more people into those trades than could otherwise pretend to follow them. In all Christian countries, I believe, the education of the greater part of churchmen is paid for in this manner. Very few of them are educated altogether at their own expense. The long, tedious, and expensive education, therefore, of those who are, will not always procure them a suitable reward, the church being crowded with people who, in order to get employment, are willing to accept of a much smaller recompense than what such an education would otherwise have entitled them to; and in this manner the competition of the poor takes away the reward of the rich. It would be indecent, no doubt, to compare either a curate or a chaplain with a journeyman in any common trade. The pay of a curate or [b]a[b] chaplain, however, may very properly be considered as of the same nature with the wages of a journeyman. They are, all three, paid for their work according to the contract which they may happen to make with their respective superiors. Till after the middle of the fourteenth century, five marks, containing as much silver as ten pounds of our present money, was in England the usual pay of a curate or a stipendiary parish priest, as we find it regulated by the decrees of several different national councils. At the same period fourpence a day, containing the same quantity of silver as a shilling of our present money, was declared to be the pay of a master-mason, and threepence a day, equal to ninepence of our present money, that of a journeyman mason.* The wages of both these labourers, therefore, supposing them to have been constantly employed, were much superior to those of the curate. The wages of the master-mason, supposing him to have been without employment one-third of the year, would have fully equalled them. By the 12th of Queen Anne, c. 12, it is declared, 'That whereas for want of sufficient maintenance and encouragement to curates, the cures have

*"See the Statute of Labourers, 25 Edw. III."

[a-a]MS, 48, 49 has almost everywhere done
[b-b]+62, 65, 71 [*not in* Source]

in several places been meanly supplied, the bishop is therefore empowered to appoint by writing under his hand and seal a sufficient certain stipend or allowance, not exceeding fifty, and not less than twenty pounds a year.' Forty pounds a year is reckoned at present very good pay for a curate, and notwithstanding this act of parliament, there are many curacies under twenty pounds a year. This last sum does not exceed what is frequently earned by common labourers in many country parishes. Whenever the law has attempted to regulate the wages of workmen, it has always been rather to lower them than to raise them. But the law has upon many occasions attempted to raise the wages of curates, and for the dignity of the Church, to oblige the rectors of parishes to give them more than the wretched maintenance which they themselves might be willing to accept of. And in both cases the law seems to have been equally ineffectual, and has never [c]been either[c] able to raise the wages of curates or to sink those of labourers to the degree that was intended, because it has never been able to hinder either the one from being willing to accept of less than the legal allowance, on account of the indigence of their situation and the multitude of their competitors; or the other from receiving more, on account of the contrary competition of those who expected to derive either profit or pleasure from employing them."

"In professions in which there are no benefices, such as law (?) and physic, if an equal proportion of people were educated at the public expense, the competition would soon be so great as to sink very much their pecuniary reward. It might then not be worth any man's while to educate his son to either of those professions at his own expense. They would be entirely abandoned to such as had been educated by those public charities; whose numbers and necessities would oblige them in general to content themselves with a very miserable recompense.

"That unprosperous race of men, commonly called men of letters, are pretty much in the situation which lawyers and physicians probably would be in upon the foregoing supposition. In every part of Europe, the greater part of them have been educated for the church, but have been hindered by different reasons from entering into holy orders. They have generally, therefore, been educated at the public expense, and their numbers are everywhere so great as to reduce the price of their labour to a very paltry recompense.

"Before the invention of the art of printing, the only employment by which a man of letters could make anything by his talents, was that of a public or private teacher, or by communicating to other people the curious and useful knowledge which he had acquired himself: and this is still surely a more honourable, a more useful, and in general even a more profitable

[c–c]MS, 48 either been

employment than that other of writing for a bookseller, to which the art of printing has given occasion. The time and study, the genius, knowledge, and application requisite to qualify an eminent teacher of the sciences, are at least equal to what is necessary for the greatest practitioners in law and physic. But the usual reward of the eminent [d]teacher[d] bears no proportion to that of the lawyer or physician; because the trade of the one is crowded with indigent people who have been brought up to it at the public expense, where those of the other two are encumbered with very few who have not been educated at their own. The usual recompense, however, of public and private teachers, small as it may appear, would undoubtedly be less than it is, if the competition of those yet more indigent men of letters who write for bread was not taken out of the market. Before the invention of the art of printing, a scholar and a beggar seem to have been terms very nearly synonymous. The different governors of the universities before that time appear to have often granted licences to their scholars to beg."

§ 4. [*Effect on wages of the competition of persons with independent means of support*] The demand for literary labour has so greatly increased since Adam Smith wrote, while the provisions for eleemosynary education have nowhere been much added to, and in the countries which have [a]undergone[a] revolutions have been much diminished, that little effect in keeping down the recompense of literary labour can now be ascribed to the influence of those institutions. But an effect nearly equivalent is now produced by a cause somewhat similar—the competition of persons who, by analogy with other arts, may be called amateurs. Literary occupation is one of those pursuits in which [b] success may be attained by persons the greater part of whose time is taken up by other employments; and the education necessary for it, is the common education of all cultivated persons. The inducements to it, independently of money[c], in the present state of the world, to all who have either vanity to gratify, or personal or public objects to promote, are [d] strong[c]. These motives now attract into this career [e] a great and increasing number of persons who do not need its pecuniary fruits, and who would equally resort to it if it afforded no remuneration at all. In our own country (to cite known examples), the most influential, and

[d-d]Source, MS, 48, 49, 52 teachers
[a-a]MS, 48, 49, 52, 57 experienced
[b]MS considerable
[c-c]MS are, in the present state of the world, to persons of suitable qualifications, & of almost every diversity of character, the strongest possible: in case of success, not only greater personal celebrity, & of a kind more flattering to vanity, than in any other pursuit except military or political life, but also greater real power, both for the promotion of personal, & of public objects
[d]48, 49 extremely
[e]MS of distinction

on the whole most eminent philosophical writer of recent times (Bentham), the greatest political economist (Ricardo), the most ephemerally celebrated, and the really greatest poets (Byron and Shelley), and the most successful writer of prose fiction (Scott), were none of them authors by profession; and only two of the five, Scott and Byron, could have supported themselves by the works which they wrote. Nearly all the higher departments of authorship are, to a great extent, similarly filled. In consequence, although the highest pecuniary prizes of successful authorship are incomparably greater than [f] at any former period, yet on any rational calculation of [g]the[g] chances, [h]in[h] the existing competition, [i]scarcely any[i] writer can hope to gain a living by books, and to do so by magazines and reviews becomes daily more difficult. It is only the more troublesome and disagreeable kinds of literary labour, and those which confer no personal celebrity, such as most of those connected with newspapers, or with the smaller periodicals, on which an educated person can now rely for subsistence. Of these, the remuneration is, on the whole, decidedly high; because, though exposed to the competition of what used to be called "poor scholars" (persons who [j]have[j] received a learned education from some public or private charity), they are exempt from that of amateurs, those who have other means of support being seldom candidates for such employments. Whether these considerations are not connected with something radically amiss in the idea of authorship as a profession, and whether any social arrangement under which the teachers of mankind consist of persons giving out doctrines for bread, is suited to be, or can possibly be, a permanent thing—would be a subject well worthy of the attention of thinkers.

The clerical, like the literary profession, is frequently adopted by persons of independent means, either from religious zeal, or for the sake of the honour or usefulness which may belong to it, or for a chance of the high prizes which it holds out: and it is now principally for this reason that the salaries of curates are so low; those salaries, though considerably raised by the influence of public opinion, being still generally insufficient as the sole means of support for one who has to maintain the externals expected from a clergyman of the established church.

When an occupation is carried on chiefly by persons who derive the main portion of their subsistence from other sources, its remuneration may be lower almost to any extent, than the wages of equally severe labour in other employments. The principal example of the kind is domestic manufactures. When spinning and knitting were carried on in every cottage, by families deriving their principal support from agriculture, the price at which their

[f]MS had been heard of
[g-g]+49, 52, 57, 62, 65, 71
[h-h]MS under
[i-i]MS, 48, 49, 52, 57 no
[j-j]MS, 48, 49 had

produce was sold (which constituted the remuneration of the labour) was often so low, that there would have been required great perfection of machinery to undersell it. The amount of the remuneration in such a case, depends chiefly upon whether the quantity of the commodity, produced by this description of labour, suffices to supply the whole of the demand. If it does not, and there is [k]consequently[k] a necessity for some labourers who devote themselves entirely to the employment, the price of the article must be sufficient to pay those labourers at the ordinary rate, and to reward therefore very handsomely the domestic producers. But if the demand is so limited that the domestic manufacture can do more than satisfy it, the price is naturally kept down to the lowest rate at which peasant families think it worth while to continue the production. It is, no doubt, because the Swiss artizans do not depend for the whole of their subsistence upon their looms, that Zurich is able to maintain a competition in the European market [l] with English capital, and English fuel and machinery.* Thus far, as to the remuneration of the subsidiary employment; but the effect to the labourers of having this additional resource, is almost certain to be (unless peculiar counteracting causes intervene) a proportional diminution of the wages of their main occupation. The habits of the people (as has already been so often remarked) everywhere require some particular scale of living, and no more, as the condition [m]without which they will not[m] bring up a family. Whether the income which maintains them in this condition comes from one source or from two, makes no difference: if there is a second source of income, they [n] require less from the first; and [o] multiply (at least this has always hitherto been the case) to a point which leaves them no more from both employments, than they would probably have had from either if it had been their sole occupation.

For the same reason it is found that, *cæteris paribus*, those trades are [p]generally[p] the worst paid, in which the wife and children of the artizan aid in the work. The income which the habits of the class demand, and down to which they are almost sure to multiply, is made up, in those trades, by the earnings of the whole family, while in others the same income must be obtained by the labour of the man alone. It is even probable that their [q]collective[q] earnings will amount to a smaller sum than those of the man

*Four-fifths of the manufacturers of the Canton of Zurich are small farmers, generally proprietors of their farms. The cotton manufacture occupies either wholly or partially 23,000 people, nearly a tenth part of the population; and they consume a greater quantity of cotton per inhabitant than either France or England. See the Statistical Account of Zurich formerly cited, pp. 105, 108, 110.

[k-k]+48, 49, 52, 57, 62, 65, 71
[l]MS, 48, 49 even
[m-m]MS, 48, 49 under which they are willing to
[n]MS, 48, 49 will
[o]MS, 48, 49 will
[p-p]MS, 48, 49 by far
[q-q]+48, 49, 52, 57, 62, 65, 71

alone in other trades; because the prudential restraint on marriage is unusually weak when the only consequence immediately felt is an improvement of circumstances, the joint earnings of the two going further in their domestic economy after marriage than before. Such accordingly is the fact, in the case of hand-loom weavers. In most kinds of weaving, women can and do earn as much as men, and children [r] are employed at a very early age; but the aggregate earnings of a family are lower than in almost any other kind of industry, and the marriages earlier. It is noticeable also that there are certain branches of hand-loom weaving in which wages are much above the rate common in the trade, and that these are the branches in which [s] neither women nor young persons are employed. These facts were authenticated by the inquiries of the Hand-loom Weavers Commission, which made its report in 1841. [t]No argument [u] can be hence derived for the exclusion of women from the liberty of competing in the labour market[v]: since, even[v] when no more is earned by the labour of a man and a woman than would have been earned by the man alone, the advantage to the woman of not depending on a master for subsistence [w]may be[w] more than an equivalent. [x]It cannot, however, be considered desirable as a *permanent* element in the condition of a labouring class, that the mother of the family (the case of [y]a single woman[y] is totally different) should be under the necessity of working for subsistence, at least elsewhere than in their place of abode. In[x] the case of children, who are necessarily dependent, the influence of their competition in depressing the labour market is an important element in the question of limiting their labour, in order to provide better for their education.[t]

§ 5. [*Wages of women, why lower than those of men*] It deserves consideration, why the wages of women are generally lower, and very much lower, than those of men. They are not universally so. Where men and women work at the same employment, if it be one for which they are equally fitted in point of physical power, [a]they are not always[a] unequally

[r]MS, 48, 49 may be and
[s]MS, 48, 49 , from the degree of bodily strength requisite,
[t-t]MS, 48, 49 The case of factory women and children may be quoted on the other side of the question; but that case is an exception to ordinary principles, inasmuch as from successive improvements in machinery, and a consequent progressive cheapening of the manufactured article, the expansion of factory employment has for half a century outstripped even the rapid growth of the factory population.
[u]52, 57, 62 , however,
[v-v]52, 57, 62 . Even
[w-w]52, 57 is
[x-x]52, 57, 62 But in
[y-y]65 single women
[a-a]MS, 48, 49 it does not appear that they are in general

paid. Women, in factories, [b]sometimes[b] earn as much as men; and so they do in hand-loom weaving, which, being paid by the piece, brings their efficiency to a sure test. [c]When the efficiency is equal, but the pay unequal[c], the only explanation that can be given is custom; grounded either in a prejudice, or in the present constitution of society, which, making almost every woman, socially speaking, an appendage of some man, enables men to take systematically the lion's share of whatever belongs to both. [d] But the principal question relates to the peculiar employments of women. The remuneration of these is always, I believe, greatly below that of employments of equal skill and equal disagreeableness, carried on by men. [e]In some of these cases the explanation is evidently that already given: as in the case of domestic servants, whose wages, speaking generally, are not determined by competition, but are greatly in excess of the market value of the labour, and in this excess, as in almost all things which are regulated by custom, the male sex obtains by far the largest share. In the occupations in which employers take full advantage of competition, the low wages of women as compared with the ordinary earnings of men, are a proof that the employments[e] are overstocked: that although so much smaller a number of women, than of men, support themselves by wages, the occupations which law and [f]usage[f] make accessible to them are comparatively so few, that the field of their employment is still more overcrowded. It must be observed, that as matters now stand, a sufficient degree of overcrowding may depress the wages of women to a much lower minimum than those of men. [g]The wages, at least of single women, must[g] be equal to their support, but need not be more than equal to it; the minimum, in their case, is the pittance absolutely requisite for the sustenance of one human being. Now the lowest point to which the most superabundant competition can per-

[b-b]+52, 57, 62, 65, 71

[c-c]MS, 48, 49 If the pay is unequal where the efficiency is equal

[d]MS, 48, 49 When an employment (as is the case with many trades) is divided into several parts, of some of which men alone are considered capable, while women or children are employed in the others, it is natural that those who cannot be dispensed with, should be able to make better terms for themselves than those who can.

[e-e]MS, 48, 49 The explanation of this must be, that they

[f-f]MS, 48, 49 custom

[g-g]MS In the first place, the great majority of women, even of those who work for wages, have a legal claim upon a father, husband, or other male relative for subsistence. They fall therefore under the same principle which has been already illustrated in the case of domestic manufactures. Since it is not a condition of their continuing to work, that they should earn enough to support them, their wages may sink to any rate, however low, for which they, or the men on whom they are dependent, may think it worth while that they should work. Suppose even that the women already provided with a subsistence are not sufficient to supply the whole demand for women's labour, & that there is need of a class of women deriving their entire support from their earnings. The wages of women must then

manently depress the wages of a man, is always somewhat more than this. Where the wife of a labouring man does not by general custom contribute to his earnings, the man's wages must be at least sufficient to support himself, a wife, and a number of children adequate to keep up the population, since if it were less the population would not be kept up. And even if the wife earns something, their joint wages must be sufficient to support not only themselves, but (at least for some years) their children also [h]. The *ne plus ultra* of low wages, therefore (except during some transitory crisis, or in some decaying employment), can [i]hardly[i] occur in any occupation which the person employed has to live by, except the occupations of women.

§ 6. [*Differences of wages arising from restrictive laws, and from combinations*] Thus far, we have, throughout this discussion, proceeded on the supposition that competition is free, so far as regards human interference; being limited only by natural causes, or by unintended effect of general social circumstances. But law or custom may interfere to limit competition. If apprentice laws, or the regulations of corporate bodies, make the access to a particular employment slow, costly, or difficult, the wages of that employment may be kept much above their natural proportion to the wages of common labour[a]. They might be so kept without[a] any assignable limit, were it not that wages which exceed the usual rate require corresponding prices, and that there is a limit to the price at which even a restricted number of producers can dispose of all they produce. In most civilized countries, the restrictions of this kind which once existed have been either abolished or very much relaxed, and will, no doubt, soon disappear entirely. In some trades, however, and to some extent, the combinations of workmen produce a similar effect. Those combinations always fail to uphold wages at an artificial rate, unless they also limit the number of competitors. But they do occasionally succeed in accomplishing this. In several trades the workmen have been able to make it almost impracticable for strangers to obtain admission either as journeymen or as apprentices, except in limited numbers, and under such restrictions as they choose to impose. It was given in evidence to the Hand-loom Weavers Commission, that this is one of the hardships which aggravate the grievous condition of that depressed class. Their own employment is overstocked and almost ruined; but there are many other trades which it would not be difficult for them to learn: to this, however, the combinations of workmen

[h]MS , nor can the woman, during the infancy of the children, be in constant employment
[i-i]MS never
[a-a]MS ; without, indeed,

in those other trades are said to interpose an obstacle hitherto insurmountable.

Notwithstanding, however, the cruel manner in which the exclusive principle of these combinations operates in a case of this peculiar nature, [b][c]the question, whether they are on the whole more useful or mischievous, requires to be decided on an enlarged consideration of consequences, among which such a fact as this is not one of the most important items[b]. Putting aside the atrocities sometimes committed by [d]workmen[d][c] in the way of personal outrage or intimidation, [e] which cannot be too rigidly repressed[f]; if the present state of the general habits of the people were to remain for ever unimproved, these partial combinations, in so far as they do succeed in keeping up the wages of any trade by limiting its numbers, might be looked upon[f] as simply intrenching [g]around[g] a particular spot against the inroads of over-population, and making [h]the wages of the class[h] depend upon their own rate of increase, instead of depending on that of a more reckless and improvident class than themselves. [i] [j]What at first sight seems the injustice of excluding the more numerous [k]body[k] from sharing the gains of a comparatively few, disappears when we consider that by being

[b-b]52, 57 their existence, it is probable, has, in time past, produced more good than evil

[c-c]MS, 48, 49 I find it impossible to wish, in the present state of the general habits of the people, that no such combinations existed. Acts of atrocity are sometimes committed by them,

[d-d]52, 57 them,

[e]52, 57 and

[f-f]MS, 48, 49 : and even their legitimate liberty of refusing to work unless their own terms are conceded to them, they not unfrequently exercise in an injudicious, unenlightened manner, ultimately very injurious to themselves. But in so far as they do succeed in keeping up the wages of any trade by limiting its numbers, I look upon them

[g-g]MS, 48, 49, 52, 57, 62, 65 round

[h-h]MS, 48, 49, 52, 57 their wages

[i]MS, 48, 49 And I should rejoice if by trade regulations, or even by trades unions, the employments thus specially protected could be multiplied to a much greater extent than experience has shown to be practicable.

[j-j][398]52, 57 The time, however, is past when the friends of human improvement can look with complacency on the attempts of small sections of the community, whether belonging to the labouring or any other class, to organize a separate class interest in antagonism to the general body of labourers, and to protect that interest by shutting out, even if only by a moral compulsion, all competitors from their more highly paid department. The mass of the people are no longer to be thrown out of the account, as too hopelessly brutal to be capable of benefiting themselves by any opening made for them, and sure only, if admitted into competition, to lower others to their own level. The aim of all efforts should now be, not to keep up the monopoly of separate knots of labourers against the rest, but to raise the moral state and social condition of the whole body; and of this it is an indispensable part that no one should be excluded from the superior advantages of any skilled employment, who has intelligence enough to learn it, and honesty enough to be entrusted with it.

[k-k]MS, 48, 49 class

admitted they would not be made better off, for more than a short time; the only permanent effect which their admission would produce, would be to lower the others to their own level. [l]To what extent the force of this consideration is annulled when a tendency commences towards diminished over-crowding in the labouring classes generally, and what grounds of a different nature there may be for regarding the existence of trade combinations as rather to be desired than deprecated, will be considered in a subsequent chapter of this work, with the subject of Combination Laws.[j][l]

§ 7. [*Cases in which wages are fixed by custom*] To conclude this subject, I must repeat an observation already made, that there are kinds of labour of which the wages are fixed by custom, and not by competition. Such are the fees or charges of professional persons: of physicians, surgeons, barristers, and even attorneys. These, as a general rule, do not vary, and though competition operates upon those classes as much as upon any others, it is by dividing the business, not[a], in general,[a] by diminishing the rate at which it is paid. The cause of this, [b]perhaps, has been[b] [c]the prevalence of[c] an opinion [d] that such persons are more trustworthy if paid highly in proportion to the work they perform; insomuch that if a lawyer or a physician offered his services at less than the ordinary rate, instead of gaining more practice, he would probably lose that which he already had. For analogous reasons it is usual to pay greatly beyond the market price of their labour, all persons in whom the employer wishes to place peculiar trust, or from whom he requires something besides their mere services. For example, most persons who can afford it, pay to their domestic servants higher wages than would purchase in the market the labour of persons fully

[l-l]MS, 48, 49 If indeed the general mass of the people were so improved in their standard of living, as not to press closer against the means of employment than those trades do; if, in other words, there were no greater degree of overcrowding outside the barrier, than within it—there would be no need of a barrier, and if it had any effects at all, they must be bad ones; but in that case the barrier would fall of itself, since there would no longer be any motive for keeping it up. On similar grounds, if there were no other escape from that fatal immigration of Irish, which has done and is doing so much to degrade the condition of our agricultural, and some classes of our town population, I should see no injustice, and the greatest possible expediency, in checking that destructive inroad by prohibitive laws. But there is a better mode of putting an end to this mischief, namely, by improving the condition of the Irish themselves; and England owes an atonement to Ireland for past injuries, which she ought to suffer almost any inconvenience rather than fail to make good, by using her power in as determined a manner for the elevation of that unfortunate people, as she used it through so many dreary centuries for their abasement and oppression.

[a-a]+48, 49, 52, 57, 62, 65, 71

[b-b]MS, 48, 49 no doubt, is

[c-c]+62, 65, 71

[d]MS, 48, 49 prevailing in the community,

as competent to the work required. They do this, not [e]merely from[e] ostentation, but [f]also[f] from [g]more[g] reasonable motives; [h]either[h] because they desire that those they employ should serve them cheerfully, and be anxious to remain in their service; [i]or[i] because they do not like to drive a hard bargain with people whom they are in constant intercourse with; [j]or[j] because they dislike to have near their persons, and continually in their sight, people with the appearance and habits which are the usual accompaniments of a mean remuneration. Similar feelings operate in the minds of persons in business, with respect to their clerks, and other employés. Liberality, generosity, and the credit of the employer, are motives which, to whatever extent they operate, preclude taking the utmost advantage of competition: and doubtless such motives might, and even now do, operate on employers of labour in all the great departments of industry; and most desirable is it that they should. But they can never raise the average wages of labour beyond the ratio of population to capital[k]. By[k] giving more to each person employed, they limit the power of giving employment to numbers; and however excellent their moral effect, they do little good economically, unless the pauperism of those who are shut out, leads indirectly to a readjustment by means of an increased restraint on population.

[e-e]MS, 48, 49 from mere
[f-f]+52, 57, 62, 65, 71
[g-g]+52, 57, 62, 65, 71
[h-h]+52, 57, 62, 65, 71
[i-i]+52, 57, 62, 65, 71
[j-j]MS, 48, 49 and
[k-k]MS ; by

CHAPTER XV

Of Profits

§ 1. [*Profits resolvable into three parts; interest, insurance, and wages of superintendence*] Having treated of the labourer's share of the produce, we next proceed to the share of the capitalist; the profits of capital or stock; the gains of the person who advances the expenses of production—who, from funds in his possession, pays the wages of the labourers, or supports them during the work; who supplies the requisite buildings, materials, and tools or machinery; and to whom, by the usual terms of the contract, the produce belongs, to be disposed of at his pleasure. After indemnifying him for his outlay, there commonly remains a surplus, which is his profit; the net income from his capital: the amount which he can afford to [a]spend[a] in necessaries or pleasures, or from which by further saving he can add to his wealth.

As the wages of the labourer are the remuneration of labour, so the profits of the capitalist are properly, according to Mr. Senior's well-chosen expression, the remuneration of abstinence. They are what he gains by forbearing to consume his capital for his own uses, and allowing it to be consumed by productive labourers for their uses. For this forbearance he requires a recompense. Very often in personal enjoyment he would be a gainer by squandering his capital, the capital amounting to more than the sum of the profits which it will yield during the years he can expect to live. But while he retains it undiminished, he has always the power of consuming it if he wishes or needs; he can bestow it upon others at his death; and in the meantime he derives from it an income, which he can without impoverishment apply to the satisfaction of his own wants or inclinations.

Of the gains, however, which the possession of a capital enables a person to make, a part only is properly an equivalent for the use of the capital itself; namely, as much as [b]a solvent[b] person would be willing to pay for the loan of it. This, which as everybody knows is called interest, is all that a person is enabled to get by merely abstaining from the immediate consumption of his capital, and allowing it to be used for productive purposes by others. The remuneration which is obtained in any country for mere abstinence, is measured by the current rate of interest on the best

[a-a]MS, 48, 49, 52, 57, 62 expend [b-b]MS, 48, 49, 52, 57 another

security; such security as precludes any appreciable chance of losing the principal. What a person expects to gain, who superintends the employment of his own capital, is always more, and generally much more, than this. The rate of profit greatly exceeds the rate of interest. The surplus is partly compensation for risk. By lending his capital, on unexceptionable security, he runs little or no risk. But if he embarks in business on his own account, he always exposes his capital to some, and in many cases to very great, danger of [c]partial or total[c] loss. For this danger he must be compensated, otherwise he will not incur it. He must likewise be remunerated for the devotion of his time and labour. The control of the operations of industry usually belongs to the person who supplies the whole or the greatest part of the funds by which they are carried on, and who, according to the ordinary arrangement, is either alone interested, or is the person most interested (at least directly), in the result. To exercise this control with efficiency, if the concern is large and complicated, requires great assiduity, and often, no ordinary skill. This assiduity and skill must be remunerated.

The gross profits from capital, the gains returned to those who supply the funds for production, must suffice for these three purposes. They must afford a sufficient [d]equivalent[d] for abstinence, indemnity for risk, and remuneration for the labour and skill required for superintendence. These different compensations may be either paid to the same, or to different persons. The capital, or some part of it, may be borrowed: may belong to some one who does not undertake the risks or the trouble of business. In that case, the lender, or owner, is the person who practises the abstinence; and is remunerated for it by the interest paid to him, while the difference between the interest and the gross [e]profits[e] remunerates the exertions and risks of the undertaker.* Sometimes, again, the capital, or a part of it, is supplied by what is called a sleeping partner; who shares the risks of the employment, but not the trouble, and who, in consideration of those risks, receives not a mere interest, but a stipulated share of the gross profits. Sometimes the capital is supplied and the risk incurred by one person, and the business carried on exclusively in his name, while the trouble of management is made over to another, who is engaged for that purpose at a fixed salary. Management, however, by hired servants, who have no interest in the result but that of preserving their salaries, is proverbially inefficient, unless they act under the inspecting eye, if not the controlling

*It is to be regretted that this word, in this sense, is not familiar to an English ear. French political economists enjoy a great advantage in being able to speak currently of *les profits de l'entrepreneur*.

[c-c]MS, 48, 49 total or partial
[d-d]MS, 48, 49 reward
[e-e]MS, 48, 49, 52, 57, 62, 65 profit

hand, of the person chiefly interested: and prudence almost always recommends giving to a manager not thus controlled, a remuneration partly dependent on the profits; which virtually reduces the case to that of a sleeping partner. Or finally, the same person may own the capital, and conduct the business; adding, if he will and can, to the management of his own capital, that of as much more as the owners may be willing to trust him with. But under any or all of these arrangements, the same three things require their remuneration, and must obtain it from the gross profit: abstinence, risk, exertion. And the three parts into which profit may be considered as resolving itself, may be described respectively as interest, insurance, and wages of superintendence.

§ 2. [*The minimum of profits; and the variations to which it is liable*] The lowest rate of profit which can permanently exist, is that which is barely adequate, at the given place and time, to afford an equivalent for the abstinence, risk, and exertion implied in the employment of capital. From the gross profit, has first to be deducted as much as will form a fund sufficient on the average to cover all losses incident to the employment. Next, it must afford such an equivalent to the owner of the capital for forbearing to consume it, as is then and there a sufficient motive to him to persist in his abstinence. How much will be required to form this equivalent, depends on the comparative value placed, in the given society, upon the present and the future: [a] (in the words formerly used) on the strength of the effective desire of accumulation. Further, after covering all losses, and remunerating the owner for [b]forbearing to consume[b], there must be something left to recompense the labour and skill of the person who devotes his time to the business. This recompense too must be sufficient to enable at least the owners of the larger capitals to receive for their trouble, or to pay to some manager for his, what to them or him will be a sufficient inducement for undergoing it. If the surplus is no more than this, none but large masses of capital will be employed productively; and if it [c]did not even amount to[c] this, capital would be withdrawn from production, and unproductively consumed, until, by an indirect consequence of its diminished amount, to be explained hereafter, the rate of profit was raised.

Such, then, is the minimum of profits: but that minimum is exceedingly variable, and at some times and places extremely low; on account of the great variableness of two out its three elements. That the rate of necessary remuneration for abstinence, or in other words the effective desire of accumulation, differs widely in different states of society and civilization, has been seen in a former chapter. There is a still wider difference in the

[a]MS, 48 or,
[b–b]MS, 48, 49 his self-denial
[c–c]MS were not even

element which consists in compensation for risk. I am not now speaking of the differences in point of risk between different employments of capital in the same society, but of the very different degrees of security of property in different states of society. Where, as in [d]many[d] of the governments of Asia, property is in perpetual danger of spoliation from a tyrannical government, or from its rapacious and ill-controlled officers; where to possess or to be suspected of possessing wealth, is to be a mark not only for plunder, but perhaps for personal ill-treatment to extort the disclosure and surrender of hidden valuables; or where, as in the European Middle Ages, the weakness of the government, even when not itself inclined to oppress, [e]leaves[e] its subjects exposed without protection or redress to active spoliation, or audacious withholding of just rights, by any powerful individual; the rate of profit which persons of average dispositions will require, to make them forego the immediate enjoyment of what they happen to possess, for the purpose of exposing it and themselves to these perils, must be something very considerable. And these contingencies affect those who live on the mere interest of their capital, in common with those who personally engage in production. In a generally secure state of society, the risks which may be attendant on the nature of particular employments seldom fall on the person who lends his capital, if he lends on good security; but in a state of society like that of [f]many parts of[f] Asia, no security (except perhaps the actual pledge of gold or jewels) is good: and the mere possession of a hoard, when known or suspected, exposes it and the possessor to risks, for which scarcely any profit he could expect to obtain would be an equivalent; so that there would be still less accumulation than there is, if a state of insecurity did not also multiply the occasions on which the possession of a treasure may be the means of saving life or averting serious calamities. Those who lend, under these wretched governments, do it at the utmost peril of never being paid. In most of the native states of India, the lowest terms on which any one will lend money, even to the government, are such, that if the interest is paid only for a few years, and the principal not at all, the lender is tolerably well indemnified. If the accumulation of principal and compound interest is ultimately compromised at a few shillings in the pound, he has generally made an advantageous bargain.

§ 3. [*Differences of profits arising from the nature of the particular employment*] The remuneration of capital in different employments, [a]much more than[a] the remuneration of labour, varies according to the circumstances which render one employment more attractive, or more repulsive, than another. The profits, for example, of retail trade, in proportion to the

[d-d]MS, 48, 49 most
[e-e]MS, 48 left
[f-f]+52, 57, 62, 65, 71
[a-a]MS, 48, 49 like

capital employed, exceed those of wholesale dealers or manufacturers, for this reason among others, that there is less consideration attached to the employment. The greatest[b], however, of these differences,[b] is that caused by difference of risk. The profits of a gunpowder manufacturer must be considerably greater than the average, to make up for the peculiar risks to which he and his property are constantly exposed. When, however, as in the case of marine adventure, the peculiar risks are capable of being, and commonly are, commuted for a fixed payment, the premium of insurance takes its regular place among the charges of production, and the compensation which the owner of the ship or cargo receives for that payment, does not appear in the estimate of his profits, but is included in the replacement of his capital.

The portion, too, of the gross profit, which forms the remuneration for the labour and skill of the dealer or producer, is very different in different employments. This is the explanation always given of the extraordinary rate of apothecaries' profit; the greatest part, as Adam Smith observes, being frequently no more than the reasonable wages of professional attendance; for which, until a late alteration of the law, the apothecary could not demand any remuneration, except in the prices of his drugs. Some occupations require a considerable amount of scientific or technical education, and can only be carried on by persons who combine with that education a considerable capital. Such is the business of an engineer, both in the original sense of the term, a machine-maker, and in its popular or derivative sense, an undertaker of public works. These are always the most profitable employments. There are cases, again, in which a considerable amount of labour and skill [c]is[c] required to conduct a business necessarily of limited extent. In such cases, a higher than common rate of profit is necessary to yield only the common rate of remuneration. "In a small seaport-town," says Adam Smith, "a little grocer will make forty or fifty per cent upon a stock of a single hundred pounds, while a considerable wholesale merchant in the same place will scarce make eight or ten per cent upon a stock of ten thousand. The trade of the grocer may be necessary for the conveniency of the inhabitants, and the narrowness of the market may not admit the employment of a larger capital in the business. The man, however, must not only live by his trade, but live by it suitably to the qualifications which it requires. Besides possessing a little capital, he must be able to read, write, and account, and must be a tolerable judge, too, of perhaps fifty or sixty different sorts of goods, their prices, qualities, and the markets where they are to be had cheapest. Thirty or forty pounds a year cannot be considered as too great a recompense for the labour of a person so accomplished. Deduct this from the seemingly great profits of

[b-b]MS difference however [c-c]MS, 48, 49, 52, 57 are

his capital, and little more will remain, perhaps, than the ordinary profits of stock. The greater part of the apparent profit is, in this case, too, real wages."[*]

All the natural monopolies (meaning thereby those which are created by circumstances, and not by law) which produce or aggravate the disparities in the remuneration of different kinds of labour, operate similarly between different employments of capital. If a business can only be advantageously carried on by a large capital, this in most countries limits so narrowly the class of persons who can enter into the employment, that they are enabled to keep their rate of profit above the general level. A trade may also, from the nature of the case, be confined to so few hands, that profits may admit of being kept up by a combination among the dealers. It is well known that even among so numerous a body as the London booksellers, this sort of combination [d]long continued to exist[d]. I have already mentioned the case of the gas and water companies.

§ 4. [*General tendency of profits to an equality*] After due allowance is made for these various causes of inequality, namely, differences in the risk or agreeableness of different employments, and natural or artificial monopolies; the rate of profit on capital in all employments tends to an equality. Such is the proposition usually laid down by political economists, and under proper explanations it is true.

That portion of profit which is properly interest, and which forms the real remuneration for abstinence, is strictly the same, at the same time and place, whatever be the employment. The rate of interest on equally good security, does not vary according to the destination of the [a]principal[a], though it does vary from time to time very much, according to the circumstances of the market. There is no employment in which, in the present state of industry, competition is so active and incessant as [b]in[b] the lending and borrowing of money. All persons in business are occasionally, and most of them constantly, borrowers: while all persons not in business, who possess monied property, are lenders. Between these two great bodies there is a numerous, keen, and intelligent class of middlemen, composed of bankers, stockbrokers, discount brokers, and others, alive to the slightest breath of probable gain. The smallest circumstance, or the most transient impression on the public mind, which tends to an increase or diminution of the demand for loans either at the time or prospectively, operates immediately on the rate of interest: and circumstances in the general state of

[*Smith, *Wealth of Nations*, Vol. I, pp. 275–6.]

[d-d]MS, 48, 49, 52 exists; though individual interest is often too strong for its rules, nor, indeed, does the combination itself include the whole trade

[a-a]MS funds [b-b]+48, 49, 52, 57, 62, 65, 71

trade, really tending to cause this difference of demand, are continually occurring, sometimes to such an extent, that the rate of interest on the best mercantile bills has been known to vary [c]in little more than[c] a year (even without the occurrence of the great derangement called a commercial crisis) from [d]four, or less, to eight or nine[d] per cent. But, at the same time and place, the rate of interest is the same, to all who can give equally good security. The market rate of interest is at all times a known and definite thing.

It is far otherwise with gross profit; which, though (as will presently be seen) it does not vary much from employment to employment, varies very greatly from individual to individual, and can scarcely be in any two cases the same. It depends on the knowledge, talents, economy, and energy of the capitalist himself, or of the agents whom he employs; on the accidents of personal connexion; and even on chance. Hardly any two dealers in the same trade, even if their commodities are equally good and equally cheap, [e] carry on their business at the same expense, or turn over their capital in the same time. That equal capitals give equal profits, as a general maxim of trade, would be as false as that equal age or size gives equal bodily strength, or that equal reading or experience gives equal knowledge. The effect depends as much upon twenty other things, as upon the single cause specified.

But though profits thus vary, the parity on the whole, of different modes of employing capital (in the absence of any natural or artificial monopoly) is, in a certain, and a very important sense, maintained. On an average (whatever may be the occasional fluctuations) the various employments of capital are on such a footing as to hold out, not equal profits, but equal [f]expectations[f] of profit, to persons of average abilities and advantages. By equal, I mean after making compensation for any inferiority in the agreeableness or safety of an employment. If the case were not so; if there were, evidently, and to common experience, more favourable chances of pecuniary success in one business than in others, more persons would engage their capital in the business, or would bring up their sons to it; which in fact always happens when a business, like that of an engineer at present, or like any newly established and prosperous manufacture, is seen to be a growing and [g] thriving one. If, on the contrary, a business is not considered thriving; if the chances of profit in it are thought to be inferior to those in other employments; capital gradually leaves it, or at least new capital is not attracted to it; and by this change in the distribution of capital

[c-c]MS, 48, 49, 52, 57, 62 within
[d-d]MS, 48, 49, 52, 57, 62 less than four to more than six
[e]MS either
[f-f]MS, 48, 49, 52, 57 chances
[g]MS, 48, 49 a

between the less profitable and the more profitable employments, a sort of balance is restored. The expectations of profit, therefore, in different employments, cannot long continue very different: they tend to a common average, though they are generally oscillating from one side to the other side of the medium.

This equalizing process, commonly described as the transfer of capital from one employment to another, is not necessarily the onerous, slow, and almost impracticable operation which it is very often represented to be. In the first place, it does not always imply the actual removal of capital already embarked in an employment. In a rapidly progressive state of capital, the adjustment often takes place by means of the new accumulations of each year, which direct themselves in preference towards the more thriving trades. Even when a real transfer of capital is necessary, it is by no means implied that any of those who are engaged in the unprofitable employment, relinquish business and break up their establishments. The numerous and multifarious channels of credit, through which, in commercial nations, unemployed capital diffuses itself over the field of employment, flowing over in greater abundance to the lower levels, are the means by which the equalization is accomplished. The process consists in a limitation by one class of dealers or producers, and an extension by the other, of that portion of their business which is carried on with borrowed capital. There is scarcely any dealer or producer on a considerable scale, who confines his business to what can be carried on by his own funds. When trade is good, he not only uses to the utmost his own capital, but employs, in addition, much of the credit which that capital [h]obtains for[h] him. When, either from over-supply or from some slackening in the demand for his commodity, he finds that it sells more slowly or [i]obtains[i] a lower price, he contracts his operations, and does not apply to bankers or other money dealers for a renewal of their advances to the same extent as before. A business which is increasing holds out, on the contrary, a prospect of profitable employment for a larger amount of this floating capital than previously, and those engaged in it become applicants to the money dealers for [j]larger[j] advances, which, from their improving circumstances, they have no difficulty in obtaining. A different distribution of floating capital between two employments has as much effect in restoring their profits to an equilibrium, as if the owners of an equal amount of capital were to abandon the one trade and carry their capital into the other. This easy, and as it were spontaneous, method of accommodating production to demand, is quite sufficient to correct any inequalities arising from the fluctuations of trade, or [k] other causes of ordinary occurrence. In the case of an altogether

[h-h]MS gives
[i-i]MS, 48 at
[j-j]57 large [*printer's error?*]
[k]MS any

declining trade, in which it is necessary that the production should be, not occasionally varied, but greatly and permanently diminished, or perhaps stopped altogether, the process of extricating the capital is, no doubt, tardy and difficult, and almost always attended with considerable loss; much of the capital fixed in machinery, buildings, permanent works, &c. being either not applicable to any other purpose, or only applicable after expensive alterations; and time being seldom given for effecting the change in the mode in which it would be effected with least loss, [l]namely,[l] by not replacing the fixed capital as it wears out. There is besides, in totally changing the destination of a capital, so great a sacrifice of established connexion, and of acquired skill and experience, that people are always very slow in resolving upon it, and hardly ever do so [m]until long after a change of fortune has become[m] hopeless. These, however, are distinctly exceptional cases, and even in these the equalization is at last effected. It may also happen that the return to equilibrium is considerably protracted, when, before one inequality has been corrected, another cause of inequality arises; which is said to have been continually the case during a long series of years, with the production of cotton in the Southern States of North America; the commodity having been upheld at what was virtually a monopoly price, because the increase of demand, from successive improvements in the manufacture, went on with a rapidity so much beyond expectation that for many years the supply never completely overtook it. But it is not often that a succession of disturbing causes, all acting in the same direction, are known to follow one another with hardly any interval. Where there is no monopoly, the profits of a trade are likely to range sometimes above and sometimes below the general level, but tending always to return to it; like the oscillations of the pendulum.

In general, then, although profits are very different to different individuals, and to the same individual in different years, there cannot be much diversity at the same time and place in the average profits of different employments, (other than the standing differences necessary to compensate for [n] difference of [o]attractiveness[o],) except for short periods, or when some great permanent revulsion has overtaken a particular trade. If any popular impression exists that some trades are more profitable than others, independently of monopoly, or of such rare accidents as have been noticed in regard to the cotton trade, the impression [p]is in all probability[p] fallacious, since if it were shared by those who have greatest means of knowledge and motives to accurate examination, there would take place such an influx of

[l-l]+48, 49, 52, 57, 62, 65, 71
[m-m]MS, 48, 52, 57 unless a change of fortune has become quite
[n]MS their
[o-o]MS *attractiveness*
[p-p]MS, 48, 49, 52, 57 must in all probability be

capital as would soon lower the profits to the common level. It is true that, to persons with the same amount of original means, there is more chance of making a large fortune in some employments than in others. But it would be found that in those same employments, bankruptcies also are more frequent, and that the chance of greater success is balanced by a greater probability of complete failure. Very often it is more than balanced: for, as was remarked in another case, the chance of great prizes operates with a greater degree of strength than arithmetic will warrant, in attracting competitors; and I doubt not that the average gains, in a trade in which large fortunes may be made, are lower than in those in which gains are slow, though comparatively sure, and in which nothing is to be ultimately hoped for beyond a competency. The timber trade of Canada is one example of an employment of capital partaking [q]so[q] much of the nature of a lottery, as to make it an accredited opinion that, taking the adventurers in the aggregate, there is more money lost by the trade than gained by it; in other words, that the average rate of profit is less than nothing. In such points as this, much depends on the characters of nations, according as they partake more or less of the adventurous, or, as it is called when the intention is to blame it, the gambling spirit. This spirit is much stronger in the United States than in Great Britain; and in Great Britain than in any country of the Continent. In some Continental countries the tendency is so much the reverse, that [r]safe and quiet employments probably yield a[r] less average profit to the capital engaged in them, than those which [s]offer greater gains at the price of greater hazards[s].

It must not however be forgotten, that even in the countries of most active competition, custom also has a considerable share in determining the profits of trade. There is sometimes an idea afloat as to what the profit of an employment should be, which though not adhered to by all the dealers, nor perhaps rigidly by any, still exercises a certain influence over their operations. There [t]has been[t] in England a kind of notion, how widely prevailing I know not, that fifty per cent is a proper and suitable rate of profit in retail transactions: understand, not fifty per cent on the whole capital, but an advance of fifty per cent on the wholesale prices; from which have to be defrayed bad debts, shop rent, the pay of clerks, shopmen, and agents of all descriptions, in short all the expenses of the retail business. If this custom were universal, and strictly adhered to, competition indeed would still operate, but the consumer would not derive any benefit from [u]it, at least as to price;[u] the way in which it would diminish the advantages

[q-q]48 of [*printer's error?*]

[r-r]MS I should not be surprised if safe & quiet employments yielded a considerably

[s-s]MS, 48, 49 , at the price of greater hazards, offer greater gains

[t-t]MS, 48, 49, 52, 57, 62 is

[u-u]MS it, as] 48, 49, 52, 57 it;

of those engaged in [v]the[v] retail trade, would be by a greater subdivision of the business. [w]In some parts of the Continent the standard is as high as a hundred per cent.[w] The [x]increase of competition however[x], in England at least, is [y]rapidly[y] tending to break down [z] customs of this description. In [a]the majority of[a] trades ([b]at least[b] in the great emporia of trade), there are now numerous dealers whose motto is, "small gains and frequent"—a great business at low prices, rather than high prices and few transactions; and by turning over their capital more rapidly, and adding to it by borrowed capital when needed, [c]the[c] dealers often obtain individually higher profits; though they necessarily lower the profits of those among their competitors, who do not adopt the same principle. [d]Nevertheless, competition, as remarked* in a previous chapter, has, as yet, but a limited dominion over retail prices; and consequently the share of the whole produce of land and labour which is absorbed in the remuneration of mere distributors, continues exorbitant; and there is no function in the economy of society which supports a number of persons so disproportioned to the amount of work to be performed.[d]

§ 5. [a][*Profits do not depend on prices, nor on purchase and sale*][a] The preceding remarks have, I hope, sufficiently elucidated what is meant by the common phrase, "the ordinary rate of profit;" and the sense in which, and the limitations under which, this ordinary rate has a real existence. It now remains to consider, what causes determine its amount.

[b]To popular apprehension it seems as if the profits of business depended upon prices. A producer or dealer seems to obtain his profits by selling his commodity for more than it cost him. Profit altogether, people are apt to think, is a consequence of purchase and sale. It is only (they suppose) because there are purchasers for a commodity, that the producer of it is able to make any profit. Demand—customers—a market for the commodity, are the cause of the gains of capitalists. It is by the sale of their goods, that they replace their capital, and add to its amount.

This, however, is looking only at the outside surface of the economical machinery of society. In no case, we find, is the mere money which passes from one person to another, the fundamental matter in any economical phenomenon. If we look more narrowly into the operations of the producer,

*[52] Vide supra, book ii. ch. iv. § 3 [pp. 242–4].

[v-v]+65, 71
[w-w]+65, 71
[x-x]MS, 48, 49 intensity, however, of modern competition
[y-y]+52, 57, 62, 65, 71
[z]MS, 48, 49 all
[a-a]MS, 48, 49 almost all
[b-b]+48, 49, 52, 57, 62, 65, 71
[c-c]MS, 48 these
[d-d]+52, 57, 62, 65, 71

[a-a]+57, 62, 65, 71 [MS, 48, 49, 52 *as title of* § 6 *below; cf.* p. 411[a-a]]
[b-b411]+57, 62, 65, 71

we shall perceive that the money he obtains for his commodity is not the cause of his having a profit, but only the mode in which his profit is paid to him.

The cause of profit is, that labour produces more than is required for its support. The reason why agricultural capital yields a profit, is because human beings can grow more food, than is necessary to feed them while it is being grown, including the time occupied in constructing the tools, and making all other needful preparations: from which it is a consequence, that if a capitalist undertakes to feed the labourers on condition of receiving the produce, he has some of it remaining for himself after replacing his advances. To vary the form of the theorem: the reason why capital yields a profit, is because food, clothing, materials, and tools, last longer than the time which was required to produce them; so that if a capitalist supplies a party of labourers with these things, on condition of receiving all they produce, they will, in addition to reproducing their own necessaries and instruments, have a portion of their time remaining, to work for the capitalist. We thus see that profit arises, not from the incident of exchange, but from the productive power of labour; and the general profit of the country is always what the productive power of labour makes it, whether any exchange takes place or not. If there were no division of employments, there would be no buying or selling, but there would still be profit. If the labourers of the country collectively produce twenty per cent more than their wages, profits will be twenty per cent, whatever prices may or may not be. The accidents of price may for a time make one set of producers get more than the twenty per cent, and another less, the one commodity being rated above its natural value in relation to other commodities, and the other below, until prices have again adjusted themselves; but there will always be just twenty per cent divided among them all.

I proceed, in expansion of the considerations thus briefly indicated, to exhibit more minutely the mode in which the rate of profit is determined.[b]

[a]§ 6. [*The advances of the capitalist consist ultimately in wages of labour*][a] I assume, throughout, the state of things, which, where the labourers and capitalists are separate classes, prevails, with few exceptions, universally; namely, that the capitalist advances the whole expenses, including the entire remuneration of the labourer. That he should do so, is not a matter of inherent necessity; the labourer might wait until the production is complete, for all that part of his wages which exceeds mere necessaries; and even for the whole, if he has funds in hand, sufficient for his temporary support. But in the latter case, the labourer is to that extent really a capitalist, investing capital in the concern, by supplying a portion of the

[a-a]MS, 48, 49, 52 [*paragraph, but no section division here; § 5 has this title. Cf.* p. 410[a-a]]

funds necessary for carrying it on; and even in the former case he may be looked upon in the same light, since, contributing his labour at less than the market price, he may be regarded as lending the difference to his employer, and receiving it back with interest (on whatever principle computed) from the proceeds of the enterprise.

The capitalist, then, may be assumed to make all the advances, and receive all the produce. His profit consists of the excess of the produce above the advances; his *rate* of profit is the ratio which that excess bears to the amount advanced. But what do the advances consist of?

It is, for the present, necessary to suppose, that the capitalist does not pay any rent; has not to purchase the use of any appropriated natural agent. This indeed is scarcely ever the exact truth. The agricultural capitalist, except when he is the owner of the soil he cultivates, always, or almost always, pays rent: and even in manufactures, (not to mention ground-rent,) the materials of the manufacture have generally paid rent, in some stage of their production. The nature of rent, however, we have not yet taken into consideration; and it will hereafter appear, that no practical error, on the question we are now examining, is produced by disregarding it.

If, then, leaving rent out of the question, we inquire in what it is that the advances of the capitalist, for purposes of production, consist, we shall find that they consist of wages of labour.

A large portion of the expenditure of every capitalist consists in the direct payment of wages. What does not consist of this, is composed of materials and implements, including buildings. But materials and implements are produced by labour; and as our [b]supposed[b] capitalist is not meant to represent a single employment, but to be a type of the productive industry of the whole country, we may suppose that he makes his own tools, and raises his own materials. He does this by means of previous advances, which, again, consist wholly of wages. If we suppose him to buy the materials and tools instead of producing them, the case is not altered: he then repays to a previous producer the wages which that previous producer has paid. It is true, he repays it to him with a profit; and if he had produced the things himself, he himself must have had that profit, on this part of his outlay, as well as on every other part. The fact, however, remains, that in the whole process of production, beginning with the materials and tools, and ending with the finished product, all the advances have consisted of nothing but wages; except that certain of the capitalists concerned have, for the sake of general convenience, had their share of profit paid to them before the operation was completed. Whatever, of the ultimate product, is not profit, is repayment of wages.

[b-b]+48, 49, 52, 57, 62, 65, 71

[a]§ 7.[a] [*The rate of profit depends on the Cost of Labour*] It thus appears that the two elements on which, and which alone, the gains of the capitalists depend, are, first, the magnitude of the produce, in other words, the productive power of labour; and secondly, the proportion of that produce obtained by the labourers themselves; the ratio, which the remuneration of the labourers bears to the amount they produce. These two things form the data for determining the gross amount divided as profit among all the capitalists of the country; but the *rate* of profit, the percentage on the capital, depends only on the second of the two elements, the [b]labourer's[b] proportional share, and not on the amount to be shared. If the produce of labour were doubled, and the labourers obtained the same proportional share as before, that is, if their remuneration was also doubled, the capitalists, it is true, would gain twice as much; but as they would also have had to advance twice as much, the rate of their profit would be only the same as before.

We thus arrive at the conclusion of Ricardo and others, that the rate of profits depends on wages; rising as wages fall, and falling as wages rise. In adopting, however, this doctrine, I must insist upon making a most necessary alteration in its wording. Instead of saying that profits depend on wages, let us say (what Ricardo really meant) that they depend on the *cost of labour*.

Wages, and the cost of labour; what labour brings in to the labourer, and what it costs to the capitalist; are ideas quite distinct, and which it is of the utmost importance to keep so. For this purpose it is essential not to designate them, as is almost always done, by the same name. [c]Wages, in public discussions, both oral and printed, being looked upon from the point of view of the payers, much oftener than from that of the receivers, nothing[c] is more common than to say that wages are high or low, meaning only that the cost of labour is high or low. The reverse of this would be oftener the truth: the cost of labour is frequently at its highest where wages are lowest. This may arise from two causes. In the first place, the labour, though cheap, may be inefficient. In no European country are wages so low as [d]they are (or at least were)[d] in Ireland: the remuneration of an agricultural labourer in the west of Ireland [e]not being[e] more than half the wages of even the lowest-paid Englishman, the Dorsetshire labourer. But if, from inferior skill and industry, two days' labour of an Irishman [f]accomplished[f] no more work than an English labourer [g]performed[g] in one, the Irishman's labour [h]cost[h] as much as the Englishman's, though it [i]brought[i] in so much

[a-a]MS, 48, 49, 52 §6.
[b-b]MS, 48 labourers'
[c-c]MS, 48 Nothing
[d-d]+57, 62, 65, 71
[e-e]MS, 48 is not
[f-f]MS, 48, 49, 52, 57 accomplish
[g-g]MS, 48, 49, 52, 57 performs
[h-h]MS, 48, 49, 52, 57 costs
[i-i]MS, 48, 49, 52, 57 brings

less to himself. The capitalist's profit is determined by the former of these two things, not [j]by[j] the latter. That a difference to this extent really [k]existed[k] in the efficiency of the labour, is proved not only by abundant testimony, but by the fact, that notwithstanding the lowness of wages, profits of capital [l]are not understood to have been[l] higher in Ireland than in England.

The other cause which renders wages, and the cost of labour, no real criteria of one another, is the varying costliness of the articles which the [m]labourer[m] consumes. If these are cheap, wages, in the sense which is of importance to the labourer, may be high, and yet the cost of labour may be low; if dear, the labourer may be wretchedly off, though his labour may cost much to the capitalist. This last is the condition of a country over-peopled in relation to its land; in which, food being dear, the poorness of the labourer's real reward does not prevent labour from costing much to the purchaser, and low wages and low profits co-exist. The opposite case is exemplified in the United States of America. The labourer there enjoys a greater abundance of comforts than in any other country [n]of[n] the world, except some of [o]the[o] newest colonies; but owing to the cheap price at which these comforts can be obtained (combined with the great efficiency of the labour), the cost of labour to the capitalist is [p]at least not higher, nor the rate of profit lower,[p] than in Europe. [q]

The cost of labour, then, is, in the language of mathematics, a function of three variables: the efficiency of labour; the wages of labour (meaning thereby the real reward of the labourer); and the greater or less cost at which the articles composing that real reward can be produced or [r]procured[r]. It is plain that the cost of labour to the capitalist must be influenced by each of these three circumstances, and [s]by no[s] others. These, therefore, are also the circumstances which determine the rate of profit; and it cannot be in any way affected except through one or other of them. If labour generally became more efficient, without being more highly rewarded; if, without its becoming less efficient, its remuneration fell, no increase taking place in the cost of the articles composing that remunera-

[j-j]+62, 65, 71
[k-k]MS, 48, 49, 52, 57 exists
[l-l]MS, 48, 49, 52 are not] 57, 62 have never been
[m-m]48 labour [*printer's error?*]
[n-n]MS, 48 in
[o-o]MS, 48, 49 our
[p-p]MS, 48, 49, 52, 57, 62 considerably lower
[q]MS, 48, 49, 52, 57, 62 It must be so, since the rate of profit is higher; as indicated by the rate of interest, which is six per cent at New York when it is three, or three and a quarter per cent in London.
[r-r]MS, 48, 49, 52, 57, 62 purchased
[s-s]MS, 48, 49 cannot be affected by any

tion; or if those articles became less costly, without the labourer's obtaining more of them; in any one of these three cases, profits would rise. If, on the contrary, labour became less efficient (as it might do from diminished bodily vigour in the people, [t]destruction of fixed capital, or[t] deteriorated education); or if the labourer obtained a higher remuneration, without any increased cheapness in the things composing it; or if, without his obtaining more, that which he did obtain became more costly; profits, in all these cases, would suffer a diminution. And there is no other combination of circumstances, in which the general rate of profit of a country, in all employments indifferently, can either fall or rise.

The evidence of these propositions can only be stated generally, though, it is hoped, conclusively, in this stage of our subject. It will come [u]out[u] in greater fulness and force when, having taken into consideration the theory of Value and Price, we shall be enabled to exhibit the law of profits in the concrete—in the complex entanglement of circumstances in which it actually works. This can only be done in the ensuing Book. One topic still remains to be discussed in the present one, so far as it admits of being treated independently of considerations of Value; the subject of Rent; to which we now proceed.

[t–t]MS, 48, 49, 52, 57 or from
[u–u]MS, 48 forth

CHAPTER XVI

Of Rent

§ 1. [*Rent is the effect of a natural monopoly*] The requisites of production being labour, capital, and natural agents; the only person, besides the labourer and the capitalist, whose consent is necessary to production, and who can claim a share of the produce as the price of that consent, is the person who, by the arrangements of society, possesses exclusive power over some natural agent. The land is the principal of the natural agents which are capable of being appropriated, and the consideration paid for its use is called rent. Landed proprietors are the only class, of any numbers or importance, who have a claim to a share in the distribution of the produce, through their ownership of something which neither they nor any one else have produced. If there be any other cases of a similar nature, they will be easily understood, when the nature and laws of rent are comprehended.

It is at once evident, that rent is the effect of a monopoly; though the monopoly is a natural one, which may be regulated, which may even be held as a trust for the community generally, but which cannot be prevented from existing. The reason why landowners are able to require rent for their land, is that it is a commodity which many want, and which no one can obtain but from them. If all the land of the country belonged to one person, he could fix the rent at his pleasure. The whole people would be dependent on his will for the necessaries of life, and he might make what conditions he chose. This is the actual state of things in those Oriental kingdoms in which the land is considered the property of the state. Rent is then confounded with taxation, and the despot may exact the utmost which the unfortunate cultivators have to give. Indeed, the exclusive possessor of the land of a country could not well be other than despot of it. The effect would be much the same if the land belonged to so few people, that they could, and did, [a]act[a] together as one man, and fix the rent by agreement among themselves. This case, however, is nowhere known to exist: and the only remaining supposition is that of free competition; the landowners being supposed to be, as in fact they are, too numerous to combine.

[a–a]MS, 48, 49 concert

§ 2. [*No land can pay rent except land of such quality or situation, as exists in less quantity than the demand*] A thing which is limited in quantity, even though its possessors do not act in concert, is still a monopolized article. But even when monopolized, a thing which is the gift of nature, and requires no labour or outlay as the condition of its existence, will, if there be competition among the holders of it, command a price, only if it exists in less quantity than the demand. If the whole land of a country were required for cultivation, all of it might yield a rent. But in no country of any extent do the wants of the population require that all the land, which is capable of cultivation, should be cultivated. The food and other agricultural produce which the people need, and which they are willing and able to pay for at a price which remunerates the grower, may always be obtained without cultivating all the land; sometimes without cultivating more than a small part of it; the [a]lands most easily cultivated being preferred in a very early stage of society; the most fertile, or those in the most convenient situations, in a more advanced state[a]. There is always, therefore, some land which cannot, in existing circumstances, pay any rent; and no land ever pays rent, unless, in point of fertility or situation, it belongs to those superior kinds which exist in less quantity than the demand—which cannot be made to yield all the produce required for the community, unless on terms still less advantageous than the resort to less favoured soils.

There is land, such as the deserts of Arabia, which will yield nothing to any amount of labour; and there is land, like some of our hard sandy heaths, which would produce something, but, in the present state of the soil, not enough to defray the expenses of production. [b]Such lands, unless by some application of chemistry to agriculture still remaining to be invented,[b] cannot be cultivated for profit, unless some one actually creates a soil, by spreading new ingredients over the surface, or mixing them with the existing materials. If ingredients fitted for this purpose exist in the subsoil, or close at hand, the improvement even of the most unpromising spots may answer as a speculation: but if those ingredients are costly, and must be brought from a distance, it will seldom answer to do this for the sake of profit, though the "magic of property" will sometimes effect it. Land which cannot possibly yield a profit, is sometimes cultivated at a loss, the cultivators having their wants partially supplied from other sources; as in the case of paupers, and some monasteries or charitable institutions, among which may be reckoned the Poor Colonies

[a–a]MS, 48, 49, 52, 57, 62 more fertile lands, or those in the more convenient situations, being of course preferred

[b–b]MS Unless by some application of chemistry to agriculture still remaining to be invented, such lands

of Belgium. The worst land which can be cultivated as a means of subsistence, is that which will just replace the seed, and the food of the labourers employed on it, together with what Dr. Chalmers calls their secondaries; that is, the labourers [c]required for supplying[c] them with tools, and with the remaining necessaries of life. Whether any given land is capable of doing more than this, is not a question of political economy, but of physical fact. The supposition leaves nothing for profits, nor anything for the labourers except necessaries: the land, therefore, can only be cultivated by the labourers themselves, or else at a pecuniary loss: and *à fortiori*, cannot in any contingency afford a rent. The worst land which can be cultivated as an investment for capital, is that which, after replacing the seed, not only feeds the agricultural labourers and their secondaries, but affords them the current rate of wages, which may extend to much more than mere necessaries; and leaves for those who have advanced the wages of these two classes of labourers, a surplus equal to the profit they could have expected from any other employment of their capital. Whether any given land can do more than this, is not merely a physical question, but depends partly on the market value of agricultural produce. What the land can do for the labourers and for the capitalist, beyond feeding all whom it directly or indirectly employs, of course depends upon what the remainder of the produce can be sold for. The higher the market value of produce, the lower are the soils to which cultivation can descend, consistently with affording to the capital employed, the ordinary rate of profit.

As, however, differences of fertility slide into one another by insensible gradations; and differences of accessibility, that is, of distance from markets, [d] do the same; and since there is land so barren that it could not pay for its cultivation at any price; it is evident that, whatever the price may be, there must in any extensive region be some land which at that price will just pay the wages of the cultivators, and yield to the capital employed the ordinary profit, and no more. Until, therefore, the price rises higher, or until some improvement raises that particular land to a higher place in the scale of fertility, it cannot pay any rent. It is evident, however, that the community [e]needs[e] the produce of this quality of land; since if the lands more fertile or better situated than it, could have sufficed to supply the wants of society, the price would not have risen so high as to render its cultivation profitable. This land, therefore, will be cultivated; and we may lay it down as a principle, that so long as any of the land of a country which is fit for cultivation[f], and not withheld from it by legal or

[c–c]MS, 48 who supply
[d]MS, 48, 49, 52, 57 obviously
[e–e]MS wants
[f–f]+52, 57, 62, 65, 71

other factitious obstacles,[f] is not cultivated, the worst land in actual cultivation (in point of fertility and situation together) pays no rent. [g]

§ 3. [*The rent of land consists of the excess of its return above the return to the worst land in cultivation*] If, then, of the land in cultivation, the part which yields least return to the labour and capital employed on it gives only the ordinary profit of capital, without leaving anything for rent; a standard is afforded for estimating the amount of rent which will be yielded by all other land. Any land yields just as much more than the ordinary profits of stock, as it yields more than what is returned by the worst land in cultivation. The surplus is what the farmer can afford to pay as rent to the landlord; and since, if he did not so pay it, he would receive more than the ordinary rate of profit, the competition of other capitalists, that competition which equalizes the profits of different capitals, will enable the landlord to appropriate it. The rent, therefore, which any land will yield, is the excess of its produce, beyond what would be returned to the same capital if employed on the worst land in cultivation. This is not, and never was pretended to be, the limit of metayer rents, or of cottier rents; but it is the limit of [a]farmers'[a] rents. No land rented to a capitalist farmer will permanently yield more than this; and [b]when it[b] yields less, it [c]is[c] because the landlord foregoes a part of what, if he chose, he could obtain.

This is the theory of rent, first propounded at the end of the last century by Dr. Anderson, and which, neglected at the time, was almost simultaneously rediscovered, twenty years [d]later[d], by Sir Edward West, Mr. Malthus, and Mr. Ricardo. It is one of the cardinal doctrines of political economy; and until it was understood, no consistent explanation could be given of many of the more complicated industrial phenomena. The evidence of its truth will be manifested with a great increase of clearness, when we come to trace the laws of the phenomena of Value and Price. Until that is done, it is not possible to free the doctrine from every difficulty which may present itself, nor perhaps to convey, to those previously unacquainted with the subject, more than a general apprehension of the reasoning by which the theorem is arrived at. Some, however, of

[g]MS [*no indication as to placing; cf.* II, xiii, 2[l–l], p. 372] to avoid misunderstanding I think it right to remark that although the nature & purpose of the present chapter compel me here to treat the question of population as a labourers' question, I do not consider it to be pecul[iar to them. *?* MS *overbound*] The principle for which I contend reaches far beyond what are commonly called the labouring classes. It includes all persons whatever except the few who being able to give to their offspring the means of independent support during the whole of life, do not leave them to swell the competition for employment

[a–a]48 farmer's [*printer's error?*] [b–b]MS, 48, 49 if it ever

[c–c]MS, 48, 49 must be [d–d]MS, 48, 49, 52 after

the objections commonly made to it, admit of a complete answer even in the present [e]stage[e] of our inquiries.

It has been denied that there can be any land in cultivation which pays no rent; because landlords (it is contended) would not allow their land to be occupied without payment. Those who lay any stress on this as an objection, must think that land of the quality which can but just pay for its cultivation, lies together in large masses, detached from any land of better quality. If an estate consisted wholly of this land, or of this and still worse, it is likely enough that the owner would not give the use of it for nothing; he would probably (if a rich man) prefer keeping it for other purposes, as for exercise, or ornament, or perhaps as a game preserve. No farmer could afford to offer him anything for it, for purposes of culture; though something would probably be obtained for the use of its natural pasture, or other spontaneous produce. Even such land, however, would not necessarily remain uncultivated. It might be farmed by the proprietor; no unfrequent case even in England. Portions of it might be granted as temporary allotments to labouring families, either from philanthropic motives, or to save the poor-rate; or occupation might be allowed to squatters, free of rent, in the hope that their labour might give it value at some future period. Both these cases are of quite ordinary occurrence. So that even if an estate were wholly composed of the worst land capable of profitable cultivation, it would not necessarily lie uncultivated because it could pay no rent. Inferior land, however, does not usually occupy, without interruption, many square miles of ground; it is dispersed here and there, with patches of better land intermixed, and the same person who rents the better land, obtains along with it inferior soils which alternate with it. He pays a rent, nominally for the whole farm, but calculated on the produce of these parts alone (however small a portion of the whole) which are capable of returning more than the common rate of profit. It is thus scientifically true, that the remaining parts pay no rent.

§ 4. [*The rent of land consists of the excess of its return above the return to the worst land in cultivation or to the capital employed in the least advantageous circumstances*] Let us, however, suppose that there [a]were[a] a validity in this objection, which can by no means be conceded to it; that when the demand of the community had forced up food to such a price as would remunerate the expense of producing it from a certain [b]quantity[b] of soil, it happened nevertheless that all the soil of that quality was withheld from cultivation, by the obstinacy of the owners in demanding a rent for it, [c] not nominal, nor trifling, but sufficiently onerous

[e–e]52 state
[b–b]MS, 48, 49, 52, 57, 62 quality
[a–a]MS was
[c]MS & this rent

to [d]be a material item in the calculations of a farmer[d]. What would then happen? Merely that the increase of produce, which the wants of society required, would for the time be obtained wholly (as it always is partially), not by an extension of cultivation, but by an increased application of labour and capital to land already cultivated.

Now we have already seen that this increased application of capital, other things being unaltered, is always attended with a smaller proportional return. We are not to suppose some new agricultural invention made precisely at this juncture; nor a sudden extension of agricultural skill and knowledge, bringing into more general practice, just then, inventions already in partial use. We are to suppose no change, except a demand for more corn, and a consequent rise of its price. The rise of price enables measures to be taken for increasing the produce, which could not have been taken with profit at the previous price. The farmer uses more expensive manures; or manures land which he formerly left to nature; or procures lime or marl from a distance, as a dressing for the soil; or pulverizes or weeds it more thoroughly; or drains, irrigates, or subsoils portions of it, which at former prices would not have paid the cost of the operation; and so forth. These things, or some of them, are done, when, more food [e]being wanted,[e] cultivation has no means of expanding itself upon new lands[f]. And[f] when the impulse is given to extract an increased amount of produce from the soil, the farmer or improver will only consider whether the outlay he makes for the purpose will be returned to him with the ordinary profit, and not whether any surplus will remain for rent. Even, therefore, if it were the fact, that there is never any *land* taken into cultivation, for which rent, and that too of an amount worth taking into consideration, was not paid; it would be true, nevertheless, that there is always some *agricultural capital* which pays no rent, because it returns nothing beyond the ordinary rate of profit: this capital being the portion of capital last applied—that to which the last addition to the produce was due: or (to express the essentials of the case in one phrase), that which is applied in the least favourable circumstances. But the same amount of demand, and the same price, which enable this least productive portion of capital barely to replace itself with the ordinary profit, enable every other portion to yield a surplus proportioned to the advantage it possesses. And this surplus [g]it is, which[g] competition enables the landlord to appropriate. The rent of all land is measured by the excess of the return to the whole capital employed on it, above what is necessary to replace the capital with the ordinary rate of profit, or in other words, above what the same capital would yield if it were all employed in as disadvantageous

[d-d]MS deter from its cultivation
[e-e]MS is wanted, &
[f-f]MS ; &
[g-g]MS , is what

circumstances as the least productive portion of it; whether that least productive portion of capital is rendered so by being employed on the worst soil, or by being expended in extorting more produce from land which already yielded as much as it could be made to part with on [h]easier[h] terms.

It is not pretended that the facts of any concrete case conform with absolute precision to this or any other scientific principle. We must never forget that the truths of political economy are truths only in the rough[i]: they have the certainty, but not the precision, of exact science[i]. It is not, for example, strictly true that a farmer will cultivate no land, and apply no capital, which returns less than the ordinary [j]profit[j]. He will expect the ordinary [k]profit[k] on the bulk of his capital. But when he has cast in his lot with his farm, and bartered his skill and exertions, once for all, against what the farm will yield to him, he will probably be willing to expend capital on it (for an immediate return) in any manner which will afford him a surplus profit, however small, beyond the value of the risk, and the interest which he must pay for the capital if borrowed, or can get for it elsewhere if it is his own. But a new farmer, entering on the land, would make his calculations differently, and would not commence unless he could expect the full rate of ordinary profit on all the capital which he intended embarking in the enterprise. Again, prices may range higher or lower during the currency of a lease, than was expected when the contract was made, and the land, therefore, may be over or under-rented: and even when the lease expires, the landlord may be unwilling to grant a necessary diminution of rent, and the farmer, rather than relinquish his occupation, or seek a farm elsewhere when all are occupied, may consent to go on paying too high a rent. Irregularities like these we must always expect; it is impossible in political economy to obtain general theorems embracing the complications of circumstances which may affect the result in an individual case. [l]When, too, the farmer class, having but little capital, cultivate for subsistence rather than for profit, and do not think of quitting their farm while they are able to live by it, their rents approximate to the character of cottier rents, and may be forced up by competition (if the number of competitors exceeds the number of farms) beyond the amount which will leave to the farmer the ordinary rate of profit.[l] The laws which we are enabled to lay down respecting rents, profits, wages, prices, are only true in so far as the persons concerned are free from the influence of any other motives than those arising from the general circumstances of the case, and are guided, as to those, by the ordinary mercantile estimate of profit and loss. Applying this twofold supposition to the case

h-hMS, 48, 49, 52, 57 easy
i-i+65, 71
j-jMS, 48, 49 profits
k-kMS, 48, 49 profits
l-l+52, 57, 62, 65, 71

of farmers and landlords, it will be true that the farmer requires the ordinary rate of profit on the whole of his capital; that whatever it returns to him beyond this he is obliged to pay to the landlord, but will not consent to pay more; that there is a portion of capital applied to agriculture in such circumstances of productiveness as to yield only the ordinary profits; and that the difference between the produce of this, and any other capital of similar amount, is the measure of the tribute which that other capital can and will pay, under the name of rent, to the landlord. This constitutes a law of rent, as near the truth as such a law can possibly be: though of course modified or disturbed in individual cases, by pending contracts, individual miscalculations, the influence of habit, and even the particular feelings and dispositions of the persons concerned.

§ 5. [*Is payment for capital sunk in the soil, rent, or profit?*] A remark is often made, which must not here be omitted, though, I think, more importance has been attached to it than it merits. Under the name of rent, many payments are commonly included, which are not a remuneration for the original powers of the land itself, but for capital expended on it. The additional rent which land yields in consequence of this outlay of capital, should, in the opinion of some writers, be regarded as profit, not rent. But before this can be admitted, a distinction must be made. The annual payment by a tenant almost always includes a consideration for the use of the buildings on the farm; not only barns, stables, and other outhouses, but a house to live in, not to speak of fences and the like. The landlord will ask, and the tenant give, for these, whatever is considered sufficient to yield the ordinary profit, or rather (risk and trouble being here out of the question) the ordinary interest, on the value of the buildings: that is, [a]not[a] on what it has cost to erect them, [b]but[b] on what it would now cost to erect others as good: the tenant being bound, in addition, to leave them in as good repair as he found them, for otherwise a much larger payment than simple interest would of course be required from him. These buildings are as distinct a thing from the farm as the stock or the timber on it; and what is paid for them can no more be called rent of land, than a payment for cattle would be, if it were the custom that the landlord should stock the farm for the tenant. The buildings, like the cattle, are not land, but capital, regularly consumed and reproduced; and all payments made in consideration for them are properly interest.

But with regard to capital actually sunk in improvements, and not requiring periodical renewal, but spent once for all in giving the land a permanent increase of productiveness, it appears to me that the return made to such capital loses altogether the character of profits, and is

[a-a]+65, 71 [b-b]MS, 48, 49, 52, 57, 62 or rather,

governed by the principles of rent. It is true that a landlord will not expend capital in improving his estate, unless he expects from the improvement an increase of income surpassing the interest of his outlay. Prospectively, this increase of income may be regarded as profit; but when the expense has been incurred, and the improvement made, the rent of the improved land is governed by the same rules as that of the unimproved. Equally fertile land commands an equal rent, whether its fertility is natural or acquired; and I cannot think that the incomes of those who own the Bedford Level or the Lincolnshire Wolds ought to be called profit and not rent because those lands would have been worth next to nothing unless capital had been expended on them. The owners are not capitalists, but landlords; they have parted with their capital; it is consumed, destroyed; and neither is, nor is to be, returned to them, like the capital of a farmer or manufacturer, from what it produces. In lieu of it they now have land of a certain richness, which yields the same rent, and by the operation of the same causes, as if it had possessed from the beginning the degree of fertility which has been artificially given to it.

[c]Some writers, in particular Mr. H. C. Carey, take away[c], still more completely than I have attempted to do, the distinction between these two sources of rent, by rejecting one of them altogether[d], and considering[d] all rent as the effect of capital expended. In proof of this, [e]Mr. Carey[e] contends that the whole pecuniary value of all the land in any country, in England for instance, or in the United States, does not amount to anything approaching to the sum which has been laid out, or which it would even now be necessary to lay out, in order to bring the country to its present condition from a state of primæval forest. [f]This startling statement has been seized on by M. Bastiat and others, as a means of making out a stronger case than could otherwise be made in defence of property in land. Mr. Carey's proposition, in its most obvious meaning, is equivalent to saying,

[c–c]MS An American political economist of merit, Mr. H. C. Carey,* breaks down [*footnote:*] **Principles of Political Economy*. Part the First, "Of the Laws of the Production and Distribution of Wealth." [Philadelphia: Carey, Lea and Blanchard, 1837.]] 48, 49 *as* MS . . . Carey,* takes away . . . *as* MS] 52, 57 *as* MS . . . economist, Mr. . . . *as* 48] 62 *as* MS . . . economist of reputation, Mr. . . . *as* 48

[d–d]MS, 48, 49, 52, 57, 62 : he considers [e–e]MS, 48, 49, 52, 57, 62 he

[f–f426]MS, 48, 49 This assertion at first sight presents itself as a most startling paradox, seeming to imply, that the lands of all countries, taken on the average, are not worth what has been laid out in improving them; and that, to the proprietors, the improvement of land has on the whole been a miscalculation. But on examining Mr. Carey's data, it appears that he by no means asserts this. In his estimate of the capital sunk in the land, he includes all which has been laid out in making roads and canals; that is, not in adding to the value of land already occupied, but in rendering other and rival lands accessible. Making up the account on this principle, the result brought out by Mr. Carey is perhaps correct, and if it is not, easily might be so. [*cf.* p. 425[f–f] *below*]

that if there were suddenly added to the lands of England an unreclaimed territory of equal natural fertility, it would not be worth the while of the inhabitants of England to reclaim it: because the profits of the operation would not be equal to the ordinary interest on the capital expended. To which assertion if any answer could be supposed to be required, it would suffice to remark, that land not of equal but of greatly inferior quality to that previously cultivated, is continually reclaimed in England, at an expense which the subsequently accruing rent is sufficient to replace completely in a small number of years. [g]The doctrine, moreover, is totally opposed to Mr. Carey's own economical opinions. No one maintains more strenuously than Mr. Carey the undoubted truth, that as society advances in population, wealth, and combination of labour, land constantly rises in value and price. This, however, could not possibly be true, if the present value of land were less than the expense of clearing it and making it fit for cultivation; for it must have been worth this immediately after it was cleared; and according to Mr. Carey it has been rising in value ever since.

When, however, Mr. Carey asserts that the whole land of any country is not now worth the capital which has been expended on it, he does not mean that each particular estate is worth less than what has been laid out in improving it[g], and that, to the proprietors, the improvement of [h]the[h] land has been[i], in the final result,[i] a miscalculation. [j]He means, not that the land of Great Britain would not now sell for what has been laid out upon it, but that it would not sell for that amount plus the expense of making all the roads, canals, and railways. This is probably true, but is no more to the purpose, and no more important in political economy, than if the statement had been, that it would not sell for the sums laid out on it plus the national debt, or plus the cost of the French Revolutionary war, or any other expense incurred for a real or imaginary public advantage. The roads, railways, and canals were not constructed to give value to land: on the contrary, their natural effect was to lower its value, by rendering other and rival lands accessible: and the landholders of the southern counties actually petitioned Parliament against the turnpike roads on this very account.[j]

[g-g]52, 57, 62 [*paragraph*] Mr. Carey, however, does not mean exactly what his assertion, without his explanations, might seem to imply. He does not assert that the lands of all countries, taken on the average, are not worth what has been laid out in improving them

[h-h]+65, 71

[i-i]52, 57, 62 on the whole

[j-j]52, 57, 62 In his estimate of the capital sunk in the land, he includes all which has been laid out in making roads and canals; that is, not in adding to the value of land already occupied, but in rendering other and rival lands accessible. Even with this correction, the proposition, in the only sense in which it supports his conclusions, is but a few degrees less unreasonable than the other. In the case supposed,

The tendency of improved communications is to lower existing rents, by [k]trenching[k] on the monopoly of the [l]land[l] nearest to the places where large numbers of consumers are assembled.[f] Roads and canals are not [m]intended[m] to raise the value of the land which already supplies the markets, but (among other purposes) to cheapen the supply, by letting in the produce of other and more distant lands; and the more effectually this purpose is attained, the lower rent will be. If we could imagine that the railways and canals of the United States, instead of only cheapening communication, did their business so effectually as to annihilate cost of carriage altogether, and enable the produce of Michigan to reach the market of New York as quickly and [n]as[n] cheaply as the produce of Long Island—the whole value of all the land of the United States (except such as lies convenient for building) would be annihilated; or rather, the best would only sell for the expense of clearing, and the government tax of a dollar and a quarter per acre; since land in Michigan, equal to the best in the United States, may be had in unlimited abundance by that amount of outlay. But it is strange that Mr. Carey should think this fact inconsistent with the Ricardo theory of rent. Admitting all that he asserts, it is still true that as long as there is land which yields no rent, the land which does yield rent, does so in consequence of some advantage which it enjoys, in fertility or vicinity to markets, over the other; and the measure of its advantage is also the measure of its rent. And the cause of its yielding rent, is that it possesses a natural monopoly; the quantity of land, as favourably circumstanced as itself, not being sufficient to supply the market. These propositions constitute the theory of rent, laid down by Ricardo; and if they are true, I cannot see that it signifies much whether the rent which the land yields at the present time, is greater or less than the interest of the capital which has been laid out to raise its value, together with the interest of the capital which has been laid out to lower its [o]value.[o]

---

of a second England, of equal natural fertility, added to the first, can any one doubt that those who were allowed to appropriate the new land, would, in proportion as it was reclaimed and brought under culture, find it answer in a pecuniary sense to make the roads requisite for bringing the produce to market? Mr. Carey would probably reply that by making these roads they might raise their own rents, but would certainly lower those of the old territory of England. This is perfectly correct, and shows the fallacy of the test assumed by Mr. Carey. It is perhaps true that the whole land of the world would not sell for the expense of bringing it into its present state, plus the expense of making all the existing communications. [*no paragraph*] [*cf.* p. 424[f–f] *above*]

[k–k]52 intrenching

[l–l]52 lands

[m–m]MS, 48, 49, 52, 57, 62 constructed

[n–n]+62, 65, 71

[o–o]MS, 48 value. This seems to me an altogether unimportant question.] 49 *as* MS . . . question.* [*footnote:*] *In a more recent work, entitled "The Past, the

Mr. Carey's objection, however, has [p]somewhat more of ingenuity than[p] the arguments commonly met with against the theory of rent; a theorem which may be called the *pons asinorum* of political economy, for there are, I am inclined to think, few persons who have refused their assent to it except from not having thoroughly understood it. The loose and inaccurate way in which it is often apprehended by those who affect to refute it, is very remarkable. Many, for instance, have imputed absurdity to Mr. Ricardo's

Present, and the Future," [London: Longman, Brown, Green, and Longmans, 1848, pp. 24–5,] Mr. Carey takes another ground of objection to the Ricardo theory of rent, namely, that in point of historical fact, the lands first brought under cultivation are not the most fertile, but the barren lands. "We find the settler invariably occupying the high and thin lands requiring little clearing and no drainage; those which can yield but a small return to labour; and as invariably travelling down the hills, and clearing and draining the lower and richer lands as population and wealth increase. . . . . When population is small, and land consequently abundant, the work of cultivation is, and always must be, commenced upon the poorer soils. With the growth of population and wealth, other soils yielding a larger return to labour are always brought into activity, with a constantly increasing return to the labour expended upon them."

It is true that the lands which require the greatest amount of clearing and draining are seldom the first cultivated: it is probably the fact, that in new countries cultivation usually begins on the hills, and descends from these to the valleys; and for this reason it may not unfrequently happen (though certainly not by any invariable law) that the richest lands remain longer unoccupied than others which are less naturally productive, even in proportion to the smaller amount of labour and outlay which their cultivation requires. Mr. Carey, however, will hardly pretend that in any old country the uncultivated lands are generally those which would pay best for cultivation. But let us even concede the point, and suppose with Mr. Carey that the progress of cultivation is upwards, from the barren to the fertile lands, not downwards, from the fertile to the barren; and that the wastes (for example) of England, Scotland, and Ireland are precisely the portions of those countries which are destined hereafter to become the most largely remunerative of the labour employed on them. This, it will be admitted, is no trifling concession; but even this would form no objection to the law of rent as laid down in the present chapter. If Dartmoor or Shap Fells are really the most fertile land in England, when they come to be cultivated they will yield the highest rent, and the lands which at that time will pay no rent will probably be the Essex Levels and the Carse of Gowrie. In whatever order the lands come into cultivation, those which when cultivated yield the least return, in proportion to the labour required for their culture, will always regulate the price of agricultural produce; and all other lands will pay a rent simply equivalent to the excess of their produce over this minimum. Whatever unguarded expressions may have been occasionally used in describing the law of rent, these two propositions are all that were ever intended by it.

If indeed Mr. Carey could show that the return to labour from the land, agricultural skill and science being supposed the same, is not a diminishing return, he would overthrow a principle much more fundamental than any law of rent. But in this he has wholly failed. It is not pretended that this natural law applies to a very early stage in the clearing and settlement of a country; and in this stage only have Mr. Carey's objections any shadow of foundation in the real order of the facts.] 52, 57, 62 value.* [*footnote:*] *as* 49 . . . Dartmoor and Shap . . . that was ever intended . . . *as* 49

[p-p]MS, 48, 49 at least thought and originality, and in that respect differs from

theory, because it is absurd to say that the *cultivation* of inferior land is the cause of rent on the superior. Mr. Ricardo does not say that it is the cultivation of inferior land, but the *necessity of cultivating* it, from the insufficiency of the superior land to feed a growing population: between which and the proposition imputed to him there is no less a difference than that between demand and supply. Others again allege as an objection against Ricardo, that if all land were of equal fertility, it might still yield a rent. But Ricardo says precisely the same. He says that if all lands were equally fertile, those which are nearer to their market than others, and are therefore less burthened with cost of carriage, would yield a rent equivalent to [q]the[q] advantage; and that the land yielding no rent would then be, not the least fertile, but the least advantageously situated, which the wants of the community required to be brought into cultivation. It is also distinctly a portion of Ricardo's doctrine, that even apart from differences of situation, the land of a country supposed to be of uniform fertility would, all of it, on a certain supposition, pay rent: namely, if the demand of the community required that it should all be cultivated, and cultivated beyond the point at which a further application of capital begins to be attended with a smaller proportional return. It would be [r]impossible[r] to show that[s], except by forcible exaction,[s] the whole land of a country can yield a rent on any other supposition.

§ 6. [*Rent does not enter into the cost of production of agricultural produce*] After this view of the nature and causes of rent, let us turn back to the subject of profits, and bring up for reconsideration one of the propositions laid down in the last chapter. We there stated, that the advances of the capitalist, or in other words, the expenses of production, consist solely in wages of labour; that whatever portion of the outlay is not wages, is [a]previous[a] profit, and whatever is not [b]previous[b] profit, is wages. Rent, however, being an element which it is impossible to resolve into either profits or wages, we were obliged, for the moment, to assume that the capitalist is not required to pay rent—to give an equivalent for the use of an appropriated natural agent: and I undertook to show in the proper place, that this is an allowable supposition, and that rent does not really form any part of the expenses of production, or of the advances of the capitalist. The grounds on which this assertion was made are now apparent. It is true that all tenant farmers, and many other classes of producers, pay rent. But we have now seen, that whoever cultivates land, paying a rent for it, gets in return for his rent an instrument of superior power to

[q-q]MS, 48, 49, 52, 57 this
[r-r]MS, 48, 49, 52, 57 difficult
[s-s]+62, 65, 71
[a-a]+49, 52, 57, 62, 65, 71
[b-b]+49, 52, 57, 62, 65, 71

other instruments of the same kind for which no rent is paid. The superiority of the instrument is in exact proportion to the rent paid for it. If a few persons had steam-engines of superior power to all others in existence, but limited by physical laws to a number short of the demand, the rent which a manufacturer would be willing to pay for one of these steam-engines could not be looked upon as an addition to his outlay, because by the use of it he would save in his other expenses the equivalent of what it cost him: without it he could not do the same quantity of work, unless at an additional expense equal to the rent. The same thing is true of land. The real expenses of production are those incurred on the worst land, or by the capital employed in the least favourable circumstances. This land or capital pays, as we have seen, no rent[c]; but the expenses to which it is subject, cause all other land or agricultural capital to be subjected to an equivalent expense in the form of rent[c]. Whoever does pay rent gets back its full value in extra advantages, and the rent which he pays does not place him in a worse position than, but only in the same position as, his fellow-producer who pays no rent, but whose instrument is one of inferior efficiency.

We have now completed the exposition of the laws which regulate the distribution of the produce of land, labour, and capital, as far as it is possible to discuss those laws independently of the instrumentality by which in a civilized society the distribution is effected; the machinery of Exchange and Price. The more complete elucidation and final confirmation of the laws which we have laid down, and the deduction of their most important consequences, must be preceded by an explanation of the nature and working of that machinery—a subject so extensive and complicated as to require a separate Book.

[c-c]+52, 57, 62, 65, 71

APPENDIX

[TO BOOK II]

Appendix[*]

IN 1846 THERE APPEARED an elaborate treatise,* by two authors, MM. Mounier and Rubichon, the latter of whom was by his own statement a public functionary for ten years preceding the French Revolution, and both appear to take their ideas of a wholesome state of society from the institutions and practices of the Middle Ages. In this book it is maintained, that while French writers and administrators are in a conspiracy to represent their country as making rapid strides in prosperity, the progress of the *morcellement* is in fact reducing it to beggary. An imposing array of official details, adduced in apparent support of this assertion, gave a degree of weight to it which it could not claim from any correctness of information or capacity of judgment shown by its authors. Their work was cried up as a book of authority by the *Quarterly Review*,† in an article which excited some notice by proclaiming, on the evidence produced by these writers, that "in a few years the Code Napoleon will be employed in dividing fractions of square inches of land, and deciding by logarithms infinitesimal inheritances." As such representations ought not to be without a permanent answer, I think it worth while to subjoin the substance of three articles in the *Morning Chronicle*, containing as complete a refutation of these writers and of their reviewer, partly from their own materials, as appears to be either merited or required.

[**This Appendix appears at the end of* Vol. I (*i.e., after* Bk. III, Chap. vi) *in all Library editions. For a note on its* MS, *see* Appendix I, *under* Mill, Unheaded leading articles, *Morning Chronicle.*]

*De l'Agriculture en France, d'après les Documents officiels. Par M. L. Mounier, avec des Remarques par M. Rubichon. [2 vols.] Paris [: Guillaumin], 1846.

†For December 1846. ["Agriculture in France," *Quarterly Review*, LXXIX (Dec., 1846), 202–38. *The quotation is from* p. 217.]

Substance (with omissions and corrections) of three articles in the *Morning Chronicle* of 11th, 13th, and 16th January, 1847, in reply to MM. Mounier and Rubichon and to the *Quarterly Review*, on the Subdivision of Landed Property in France

I

The reviewer makes an extraordinary slip at the threshold of his subject, in estimating the extent to which the *morcellement* has actually proceeded. He finds it stated, that among nearly five millions and a half of landed proprietors, there are 2,600,000 the revenue of whose land, as rated to the land-tax, does not exceed forty shillings, which sum he very candidly says, should rather be sixty, as the rated value is very much lower than the real value. On this he exclaims, "There already exist in France millions of examples that a *propriétaire* may be poorer than a peasant. . . . 2,600,000 families, comprising 13,000,000 persons, of each of which families the rated income does not exceed forty shillings, but say sixty shillings sterling, for the maintenance of five persons—and these are proprietors! The poorest day labourer would earn four times as much." He seems actually to suppose that these small proprietors, like great landlords, live only upon the *rent* of their land, forgetting that they have its *whole produce.* He might have known from the very documents he has quoted, and might have guessed if he had not known, that the forty shillings at which the land is rated in the collectors' books are not the gross produce of the little estate, but its *net* produce; the surplus beyond the expenses of cultivation: which expenses include the subsistence of the cultivators, together with interest on the capital. The reviewer himself shows that the rated *revenue* of all the landed property of France is about 4 per cent of its rated *value*, and does not therefore much exceed a reasonable rent. A writer who can mistake this for the whole income of a peasant cultivating his own land, gives the measure of his competency for the subject, and of the degree of attention he has paid to it.

We will now attempt to discover, from the reviewer's data and those of his authors, what may really be the condition of these 2,600,000 proprietors. As the French Government estimates the land-tax at one-tenth of the revenue of the land, [a]proprietors[a] rated at £2 (or 50 francs) pay, it is to be presumed, five francs. The average of the *contribution foncière* for all France is 2½ francs per hectare, and in the southern half of the kingdom,

[a–a]Source (MS), 48, 49 families [*for explanation of* Source (MS) *see* Appendix I, *under* Mill, Unheaded leading articles, *Morning Chronicle*]

which is the most divided, two francs. A hectare being about 2½ English acres, this gives from five to between six and seven acres as the portion of land which falls to the lot of each of the reviewer's forty-shilling or sixty-shilling freeholders. But, it may be said, this is not the *average* but the *maximum* of their possessions. We will therefore take another estimate grounded on official documents, from the reviewer's authorities, MM. Mounier and Rubichon. "It is hardly credible," they say, "that there are in France more than four millions of proprietors so poor, that they pay no more than 5f. 95c." (say 6f.) "to the *contribution foncière*." In this case the 5f. 95c. are certainly the average. Six francs of land-tax corresponds to six acres per family on the average of all France, and to seven and a half on that of the southern division, which contains the greatest proportion of small proprietors. A still more favourable result is given by the calculations of M. Lullin de Châteauvieux, a much better authority than these authors, who estimates the average holdings of the 3,900,000 poorest proprietors at eight acres and a half. Now, take any one of these computations in a fertile country like France, suppose as bad an agriculture as exists anywhere in Western Europe, and then judge whether a single family, industrious and economical as the French of the poorer classes are, and enjoying the entire produce of from five to eight and a half acres, subject to a payment of only tenpence an acre to the Government, can be otherwise than in a very desirable condition? We do not forget that the land is sometimes mortgaged for part of the purchase money, and the reviewer makes a great cry about the tremendous encumbrances by which the land of France is weighed down; not amounting, however, on his own showing, to forty per cent on the rental, which we should think [b] as favourable a return as could be made by any landed aristocracy in Europe. The interest on the mortgages of all France is estimated at twenty-four millions sterling for one hundred and fourteen millions of acres—less than five shillings per acre[c]. The[c] owner of from five to eight acres could afford to pay double this amount, and be very well off.

We are aware that this is an average, and that four millions of properties, averaging, according to M. de Châteauvieux, eight acres and a half, imply a great number of proprietors who have less. But there must be a proportional (though not an equal) number who have more; and it must not be supposed that this statement includes the large properties, one of which would be enough to keep up the average against a hundred extremely small ones. No properties are included which pay so much as twenty francs land-tax, corresponding on the average of France to twenty [d]acres—on that[d] of the south to twenty-five. When it is considered that of the whole

[b]Source (MS), 48, 49, 52, 57, 62, 65 is   [c-c]Source (MS) : the
[d-d]Source (MS) acres,

soil of France [e]only a third*[e] is in the hands of peasant proprietors, and that this [f]third[f] is not more subdivided than we now see, it will probably be thought that hitherto at least, the mischiefs of subdivision have not reached a very formidable height.

[g][Facts of a less conjectural character than the above have been afforded by the researches of M. de Lavergne. Of five millions of small rural proprietors, three millions at least, according to that high authority, pay less than ten francs of taxes, and possess, on an average, only one hectare (2½ acres). Two millions pay from ten to fifty francs, and possess, on an average, six hectares, or fifteen acres. These last, says M. de Lavergne, "enjoy sometimes a real affluence. Their properties are divided by inheritance; but many of them are continually making new acquisitions by purchase, and on the whole their tendency is more to rise than to descend in the scale of wealth." Respecting the amount of debts with which the peasant proprietors are encumbered, the facts are highly and unexpectedly favourable. By the latest authentic returns, the average indebtedness of the entire landed property of France, does not, according to M. de Lavergne, exceed one-tenth of the value; and in the case of rural property, it is only half that average, or one-twentieth. The burthen of interest he estimates, not at 40 per cent on the rental, but at 10 per cent only; and even this, he thinks, would now be an overstatement, "car les dernières crises ont amené une tendance générale vers une liquidation."†][g]

But it is not what France now is, so much as what she is becoming, that is the material point. Is the *morcellement* increasing, or likely to increase? The apologists of the French system have never denied that the land in many parts of France is too minutely divided. What they deny is, that [h]this[h] is a growing evil. They assert that the subdivision has reached its height, and that the reunions, by purchase, marriage, and inheritance, now balance the subdivisions. How stands the fact in this respect? Are the small properties tending to become still smaller, or not? The reader will be surprised when he finds that, with all their straining, M. Rubichon and his reviewer have failed of proving that the *morcellement*, in this sense of the term, is making any progress at all.

The reviewer has a curious theory on the subject. He thinks that "on the calculated average of three children to each inheritance,"[*] the piece of land now held by one proprietor must *necessarily* be divided among three in the next generation, and among nine in that which follows. Under what

*[62] Lavergne, *Economie Rurale de la France*, pp. 23 and 51.
†[62] Pp. 451–454.
[*Quarterly Review*, LXXIX, p. 212.]

[e-e]Source (MS), 48, 49, 52, 57 much less than half
[f-f]Source (MS), 48, 49, 52, 57 half
[g-g]+62, 65, 71 [*JSM's square brackets*] [h-h]Source (MS), 48, 49, 52, 57 it

system of landed property could a population increase at this rate, and not be reduced to starvation? But is it a fact that population is *anywhere* trebled in the space of a generation? We have here blunder within blunder of a very complicated description. In the first place, he should not have said three children to *one* inheritance, but to *two* inheritances; for as the French law in questions of property observes that impartial justice between the two sexes in which other laws are so often deficient, the mother's patrimony is on an average equal to that of the father. In the next place, could not the reviewer have taken the trouble to ascertain at what rate the French population is *actually* increasing? If he had, he would have found that in the 27 years from 1815 to 1842 it only increased 18 per cent, and during that period with progressively increasing slowness, namely, in the first eleven years 9 per cent, in the next nine years less than 6 per cent, and in the seven years from 1835 to 1842, 3$\frac{1}{10}$ per cent only.* This retardation we must take the liberty of attributing mainly to the prudence and forethought generated in the poorest class by this very subdivision of property.

Instead, therefore, of trebling in a generation, the population [i]increased[i] in that period about 20 per cent; [j] and if the growth of towns, and of employments not agricultural, in the same space of time, is sufficient to absorb this increase, there needs not be, and will not be, even if the law does its worst, any increase of subdivision. Now, the towns of France have increased, and are increasing, at a rate far exceeding the general increase of the population. We read only the other day in the *Siècle*,[*] as the result of the census just concluded, that Paris, which in 1832 had only 930,000

*These facts are taken from M. Passy. We may now add, in the *ten* years from 1847 to 1856 not quite 1⅝ per cent. Between 1851 and 1856 the increase in all France was not equal to that of Paris. Nearly all the poorer departments had diminished in population. See [Guilhaud de Lavergne, L., "Dénombrement de la Population de 1856,"] the *Journal des Economistes* for February 1857 [pp. 225–33]. [48, 49, 52 Passy. In page 289 of the present work, from a more complete comparison, which includes the results of the last census [52 result of the census of 1846], the increase of population has been shown to be even slower than is here represented.]

[**Siècle*, 29 Dec., 1846, p. 2.]

[i-i]Source (MS), 48, 49 increases

[j]MS, 48, 49 [*footnote:*] *Even this is a considerable overstatement. The census of 1806 showed a population of 29,107,425. In 1846, according to the census of that year, it had only increased to 35,409,486, being an increase of little more than 21⅝ per cent in forty years. The longest term ever assigned to a generation is thirty years.] 52 *as* MS . . . 35,409,480 . . . years. [*paragraph*] (The census of 1851, received while this volume was passing through the press, shows a population of 35,781,628, being an increase of only 1.08 per cent in the last five years, or 0.21 per cent per annum. This result the French minister ascribes partly to cholera and emigration, but partly also to the diminution of marriages.—See the *Moniteur* of May 14, 1852.) [De Persigny, F. "Rapport au Prince Président de la République Française," *Le Moniteur Universel*, CLV, 14 May, 1852, p. 731.]

inhabitants, [k]had in 1846[k] more than 1,350,000, an increase of nearly fifty per cent in fourteen years.* There is every reason, then, to infer, from these general data, that the *morcellement* is making no progress.

What facts have M. Rubichon and the Quarterly reviewer to oppose to these? One fact; which at first sight appears a very strong one. Between 1826 and 1835, the number of properties rated to the land-tax exhibited an increase of more than 600,000; being about six per cent in ten years. Let us first remark, that 600,000 separate assessments are equivalent only to about 300,000 proprietors; it being the common estimate of French writers, that on the average about two *côtes foncières*, or separate accounts with the land-tax, correspond only to a single proprietor. But if the reviewer had consulted his author just ten pages further on,† he would have found a cause sufficient to account for a considerable portion of this increase. There were sold between 1826 and 1835 domains of the State, to the value of nearly 134 millions of francs, or five and a half millions sterling. The very nature of such a sale implies division. And we are the more inclined to ascribe much of the apparent increase of division to this circumstance, because in the ten years preceding those in question, the *côtes foncières* increased in number by little more than 200,000; an alarming proof, according to the reviewer, of the progressive advance of the evil; but, as we suspect, arising partly from the fact, that during the earlier decennial period a smaller, though still a considerable, amount of public domains were alienated.

In addition to the State lands, a great extent of Communal lands were likewise alienated during the same period: and it is further necessary to subtract all the additions made to the number of *côtes foncières* by the extension of building, and [l]by[l] the natural subdivision of town property, during ten years. All these items must be accurately estimated and deducted, before it can be affirmed with certainty that in the rural districts there was during those years any increased division of landed property at all. And even if there was, increased *division* does not necessarily imply increased *subdivision*. Large estates may have been, and we believe were in many instances, divided, but the division may have stopped there. We know of no reason for supposing that small properties were divided into others still smaller, or that the average size of the possessions of peasant families was at all diminished.

It so happens that facts exist, more specific and more expressly to the

*[57] In 1856 the department of the Seine, which consists almost entirely of Paris, had risen to 1,727,000 inhabitants; while Lyons, Marseilles, St. Etienne, Bordeaux and Nantes (or at least the departments containing them) had largely increased in population.

†Mounier and Rubichon, vol. i. p. 110.

[k–k]Source (MS), 48, 49 has now [l–l]+48, 49, 52, 57, 62, 65, 71

point than any of M. Rubichon's. A new *cadastre*, or survey and valuation of lands, has been in progress for some years past. In thirty-seven cantons, taken indiscriminately through France, the operation has been completed; in twenty-one it is nearly complete. In the thirty-seven, the *côtes foncières*, which were 154,266 at the last *cadastre* (in 1809 and 1810), have only increased by 9011, being less than 18 per cent in considerably more than thirty years, while in many of the cantons they have considerably diminished. From this increase is to be subtracted all which is due to the progress of building during the period, as well as to the sale of public and communal lands. In the other twenty-one cantons the number of *côtes foncières* is not yet published, but the number of *parcelles*, or separate bits of land, has *diminished* in the same period; and among [m]those[m] districts is included the greater part of the *banlieue* of Paris, one of the most minutely divided districts in France, in which the *morcellement* has actually diminished by no less than 16 per cent. The details may be found in M. Passy's little work, "Des Systèmes de Culture." So much for the terrible progress of subdivision.

We cannot leave this part of the subject without noticing one of the most signal instances which the reviewer has exhibited of his incompetency for the subject he treats of. He laments over the extraordinary number of sales of landed property which he says the law of inheritance constantly occasions; and indeed the sales of land are shown to have amounted in ten years to no less than one-fourth part of the whole territorial property of France. Now, whatever else this extraordinary amount of sale and purchase may prove, the whole of it is one gigantic argument [n]against[n] the reviewer's case; for every sale of land which is caused by the law of inheritance must be a sale for the express purpose of preventing subdivision. If land, sold in consequence of an inheritance, is nevertheless subdivided, this cannot be an effect of the law of inheritance; it would only prove that land sells for a higher price when sold in small portions: that is, in other words, that the poor, and even, as the reviewer would have us believe, the very poor, are able to outbid the rich in the land market. This certainly does [o]not[o] prove that the very poor of France are *so* very poor as these writers try to make out, while it [p]does[p] prove that, if so, they must be by far the most industrious and economical people on the face of the earth, for which some credit ought surely to be given to the system of peasant properties.

II

We have shown that the four millions of landowners in France who can be reckoned among peasant proprietors, those whose holdings fall short of

[m-m]Source (MS), 48 these
[n-n]Source (MS), 48, 49 *against*
[o-o]Source (MS) *not*
[p-p]Source (MS) *does*

twenty acres, are computed by one of the best [q] authorities to possess on the average eight and a half English acres each, and [r] from no authentic documents can the average be brought much below that amount; a fact wholly incompatible with their being in the state approaching to starvation in which M. Rubichon and his reviewer [s]represent them to be[s]. It is equally certain that if there is bad agriculture on these small estates, it is from some other cause than their smallness. Farms of this size are consistent with agriculture equal to any on the face of the earth.

We shall now, however, touch upon another kind of *morcellement*, which does amount to a serious inconvenience, and wherever it exists must have a strong tendency to keep agriculture in a low state. This is the subdivision, not of the land of the country among many proprietors, but of the land of each proprietor into many detached pieces, or *parcelles*, as they are technically designated. This inconvenience has been experienced in other countries besides France, as in the canton of Zurich, in the Palatinate, and (as respects holdings, though not properties) in Ireland. In France it is carried to so great an excess, that the number of *parcelles* is ten times the number of *côtes foncières*; and as there are supposed to be twice as many *côtes foncières* as proprietors, the curious fact is disclosed, that on the average of France the estate of every landowner consists of twenty fragments in twenty different places. The consequences are a subject of general and increasing complaint. Great loss of time and labour; waste of cultivable soil in boundaries and paths; the inaccessibility of many *parcelles* without trespassing on other properties; endless disputes and frequent litigation—are enumerated among the evils: and it is evident what obstacles the small size and dispersed position of the *parcelles*, and their intermixture with those of other proprietors, must oppose to many kinds of agricultural improvement.

For a considerable portion of this evil the French law of inheritance may fairly be held responsible. A certain amount of it is inevitable wherever landed properties are undergoing a double process of division and recomposition: marriages, for example, must in general bring together portions of land not adjacent. But if parents had the power of bequest, the owner of twenty *parcelles*, even if he adhered to the spirit of the law of equal division, would give some of the portions entire to one child, and others to another. The law, on the contrary, must divide with *exact* equality; and as it is generally impossible to adjust the value of patches of unequal fertility, vineyards, meadows, arable, &c., so as to satisfy everybody, it continually happens, especially in the more backward parts of France, that when the settlement is made by division instead of sale, each co-heir insists on taking a share of every *parcelle* instead of the whole of some *parcelles*; from

[q]Source (MS), 48, 49 living [r]Source (MS), 48, 49 that
[s-s]Source (MS), 48, 49 would represent them

whence, no doubt, the amazing multiplication of these little patches in many parts of France. [t]

That French agriculture, and the condition of the peasant population, are injuriously affected by this sort of *morcellement*, is so far true, that it must considerably retard the improvement which might otherwise be expected, and which, in spite of all hindrances, does even now, to a great extent, take place. More than this we cannot admit. There are conclusive proofs of great and rapid improvement in some parts of France, and M. Rubichon and his reviewer have no evidence whatever of retrogression in any.

They produce tables of the average amount of different kinds of food consumed by the population; also tables of the number of cattle, the amount of produce per hectare of the different kinds of cultivation, &c., calculated from the official documents. These estimates, assuming their correctness (which, so far as that quality is attainable, we generally see no reason to discredit) are indicative, doubtless, of a low and backward state. But statistics are only evidence of the present. Where are the statistics of the past? That the agriculture of a great part of France is rude and imperfect is known to all Europe; but that it ever was better, is an assertion opposed to all evidence, and we shall not take M. Rubichon's word for it, no more than for the notion that the [u] general condition of the mass of the people has been deteriorating from the time of Louis XIV.* if not earlier. At this

*It did deteriorate in the early part of the reign of Louis XIV, not because the peasants *bought* land, but because they were compelled to *sell* it. "Au moment," says Michelet (*Le Peuple*, ch. 1 [pp. 7–8]), "où nos ministres Italiens, un Mazarin, un Emeri, doublaient les taxes, les nobles qui remplissaient la cour obtinrent aisément d'être exemptés, de sorte que le fardeau double tomba d'aplomb sur les épaules des faibles et des pauvres, qui furent bien obligés de vendre ou donner cette terre à peine acquise, et de redevenir des mercenaires, fermiers, métayers, journaliers. . . . Je prie et je supplie ceux qui nous font des lois ou les appliquent, de lire le détail de la funeste réaction de

[t]Source (MS), 48, 49 [*paragraph*] This evil, while it would not exist to any very material extent except under the peculiar French law of inheritance, is not inevitable even under that law. The enormous extent of sales of land, amounting in ten years to a fourth part of the landed property of France, are a clear proof that in general the adjustment of inheritances is not effected by a subdivision of the land, but by sale; which, it needs scarcely be remarked, does not necessarily imply parting with the land, there being nothing to hinder the heirs themselves from becoming the purchasers. We have no doubt it would be found that this rational mode of executing the law is tending more and more to become universal. To hasten the undoing of the mischief which has been already done, the Government has been often urged (in some instances by Councils-General of Departments) to propose a law authorizing the consolidation of landed properties by a general valuation and exchange of allotments, in every commune in which the majority of the proprietors may apply for it; and unless the evil is seen to be correcting itself by a spontaneous process, nothing, we should think, can long prevent the adoption of so salutary an expedient.

[u]Source (MS), 48, 49 food and

last proposition we cannot repress our wonder. In the reign of Louis XIV., Marshal Vauban, a great authority with all who are themselves authorities, and even with M. Rubichon, estimated that one-tenth of the population of France were beggars, and five of the remaining nine-tenths little above beggary. In the same reign, Labruyère claimed credit for apprising the *salons* of Paris that a strange nondescript sort of animals, who might be seen in the fields, and were much addicted to grubbing in the earth, were, though nobody would suppose it, a kind of men. Some readers may remember the picture drawn by the old Marquis Mirabeau of the rural population in the middle of the eighteenth century; nor was Arthur Young's, at the opening of the Revolution, much more favourable. Compare this with any authentic account, or with the testimony of any observant resident or traveller, respecting their condition now. M. Rubichon's statistics comprise no returns of the rate of wages. We are quite willing that our case should rest upon the result of an inquiry into that one point.

As for agriculture, when it is recollected that, at the beginning of this century, in the greater part of France the culture of artificial grasses might be said to be unknown, and that the course of cultivation consisted solely of grain crops and fallows, it will be difficult to make us believe that, even in the most backward parts of the country, there has not been a considerable improvement from so miserable a level.

[v][Look now at the facts collected by M. de Lavergne. Fallows have been reduced, since 1789, from ten to five millions of hectares. The number of hectares under wheat has risen from four to six millions, while the inferior grain, rye, has fallen off; that under artificial grasses, from one to three millions; under roots, from 100,000 to two millions; under the more peculiar and expensive crops, from 400,000 to one million. "Thanks to this better distribution of the soil, which allows six millions more of hectares to be devoted to the feeding of animals, and consequently to the production of manure; thanks to marling, to irrigation, to draining, to more efficient tillage, the yield of all crops has increased; wheat, which gave at an average only eight hectolitres per hectare (seed deducted) now gives twelve, and as the breadth sown has also increased, the total produce has more than doubled. The same thing has taken place with cattle, which, receiving twice as much sustenance, have increased, both in numbers and quality, so as to double their produce. The crops for manufacturing use have extended themselves; silk and colza have quintupled; home-grown sugar is an entirely

---

Mazarin et de Louis XIV. dans les pages pleines d'indignation et de douleur où l'a consignée un grand citoyen, Pesant de Boisguillebert, réimprimé recemment dans la Collection des Economistes. Puisse cette histoire les avertir dans un moment où diverses influences travaillent à l'envi pour arrêter l'œuvre capitale de la France, l'acquisition de la terre par le travailleur."

[v–v443]+62, 65, 71 [*JSM's square brackets*]

new product; the produce of the vintage has doubled. Even wood, being better defended from the ravages of animals, and better managed in consequence of an increased market, has obtained an increase of annual profits, though too often at the expense of the capital." *][v]

The blind zeal with which M. Rubichon presses everything into the service of his theory, in which he is faithfully echoed by his reviewer, makes them lay great stress upon the increase of roots, and other inferior kinds of culture, as a proof that the population is sinking to an inferior kind of nutriment; as if the same thing was not happening in England; as if it was not a necessary condition of an improved rotation of crops, that other cultures should increase in a greater proportion than grain culture, and even at the expense, in some degree, of the inferior kinds of grain.

We have admitted, and again admit, the unsatisfactory state of cultivation on a very great portion of the soil of France; but would it be any better if the estates were large? Is it any better now on the large estates? When M. Rubichon and his reviewer talk of the small properties as "creating a new Ireland in France," his own pages make it known that the large properties, in the backward parts of France, are already an Ireland, in the very worst feature of Irish landed mismanagement, the system of middlemen. It is a general practice, according to M. de Châteauvieux, with the great proprietors of the central departments, to let their land *en bloc*, to a middleman, usually an attorney or a notary, who sublets it in small portions on the *métayer* system, and is not only, as in Ireland, the hardest and most grasping of landlords, but having only a temporary tenure, and being no agriculturist, of course expends nothing in improvements. Of fifty-seven millions of acres cultivated by tenants, twenty-one millions [w]are held [w] by farmers at fixed rents, and thirty-six millions on the *métayer* tenure; which in France implies all the defects, with very few of the advantages, of proprietary cultivation; the only exceptions being La Vendée and a few of the adjoining departments, where the large proprietors are resident, a primitive relationship subsists between them and their tenants, and the *métayers* have in general, as in Tuscany, a virtual fixity of tenure. We do not believe it will be found in any part of France that the small properties are under a bad agriculture, and the large properties under a good one. They are both bad, or both good. Where large farms exist and are well cultivated, the small properties also are well managed and prosperous.

And this brings us to the principal cause, both now and formerly, of the unimproved agriculture and scanty application of capital to the soil of France. This is, the exclusive taste of the wealthy and middle classes for town life and town pursuits, combined with the general want of enterprise of the French nation with respect to industrial improvements. It is truly,

*[62] *Economie Rurale de la France*, pp. 52, 53.

[w-w]Source (MS), 48, 49, 52, 57, 62 only are held

though epigrammatically, said [x] by M. Rubichon, that the Frenchman, generally, knows but one way of getting rich; namely, thrift. He does not understand sowing money freely to reap it largely. This is the true cause why, when large properties are sold, they bring the greatest price by being much subdivided. The peasants, thanks to the Revolution, to the small properties, and to their own unparalleled [y]frugality[y], are able to purchase land, and their savings[z], together with the money which they imprudently borrow for the same purpose,[z] are the only part of the wealth of the country which takes that direction. We are often told, that it does not answer to capitalists to buy land at the extravagant price which the passion of the peasantry for land induces *them* to give, amounting often to forty years' purchase. It does not answer to pay that price in order to live idly on the rent in Paris, or the large provincial towns. But if there was one particle of the spirit of agricultural improvement in the owners of the monied wealth which is so largely increasing in the manufacturing and commercial districts, few speculations would be more profitable than to buy land in many fertile and ill-cultivated parts of France, at even more than forty years' purchase of its wretchedly low rental, which would soon be doubled or trebled by the application of capital, with ordinary agricultural knowledge and enterprise. If the *petite culture* is half as wasteful and unprofitable as is pretended, the profit would be proportional of substituting [a]the[a] *grande culture* for it. [b] But with a people who dislike rural pursuits, and in the pursuit of money-getting prefer the beaten ways, there can be [c]little[c] other farming than peasant farming.

III

The *cheval de bataille* of M. Rubichon and his English followers against the *petite propriété*, is the cattle question; not without cause, since on this subject they have an indisputable basis of fact, however inadequate to sustain the superstructure they have raised upon it. The supply of butcher's meat to some of the principal towns, especially Paris, is less copious than formerly. It has increased greatly, but in a less ratio than the population. Of the fact there is no doubt, since on this point there are trustworthy statistics of the past as well as of the present. In 1789 the consumption of meat in Paris averaged 68 kilogrammes (150 lbs.) for each person; in

[x]Source (MS) somewhere in these volumes,

[y-y]Source (MS), 48, 49 prudence

[z-z]+52, 57, 62, 65, 71

[a-a]Source (MS), 48, 49, 52, 57, 62 *la*

[b]Source (MS) The thing would be soon done if the love of industrial progress should ever supplant in the French mind the love of national glory, or if the desire of national glorification should take that direction.] 48 *as* MS . . . would soon be . . . *as* MS] 49 *as* 48 . . . should supplant . . . *as* MS

[c-c]Source (MS), 48, 49, 52, 57 no

1841 it was but 55 (121 lbs.), and there are also complaints of a falling off in the quality.

The Quarterly reviewer treats very cavalierly the explanation given of this fact by M. Cunin-Gridaine, Minister of Commerce and Agriculture. "This is to be accounted for by the revolution which has taken place in the working classes; Paris having become the *most manufacturing town* in Europe." *Industrielle* is not exactly synonymous with manufacturing, but let that pass. On this the reviewer:—"This seems a strange explanation. The new population of Paris is to starve on an ounce" (five ounces) "of meat per diem. How is that? Pooh! says the Liberal Minister, they are only manufacturers. This solution will not be very agreeable to those theorists amongst us who confound the extension of manufactures with the welfare and comfort of the working people. The more candid Minister of Louis-Philippe *assumes* that a manufacturing population must of necessity be worse fed than other classes." The reviewer is evidently no Œdipus. But he might have found in another page of M. Rubichon's treatise, what the Minister meant. In a town such as Paris before the Revolution, in which there was, comparatively speaking, no production at all, but only distribution—the population consisting of the great landlords, the Court and higher functionaries paid by the State, the bankers, financiers, government contractors, and other monied classes, with the great and small dealers and tradesmen needful for supplying these opulent consumers, and few labourers beyond those who cannot be wanting in so large a town—all will see that the richer must bear an unusually high numerical proportion to the poorer consumers in such a city. Suppose now that a Manchester or a Glasgow grows up in the place. It is pretty evident that while this would add a little to the richer class, it would add twenty times as much to the poorer. Considering now that the upper and middle classes in France are great consumers of animal food, while the poor consume very little [d]of it, the portion[d] of each poor person might in these circumstances increase very much, while yet the average consumption per head of the whole city, owing to the diminished proportional numbers of the richer class, might be considerably diminished. We have little doubt that this is the fact, and that the great increase in the inferior kinds of animal food introduced into Paris would prove to be for the use, not of those who formerly used the superior kinds, but in a great measure for those who seldom obtained animal food at all.

This, however, does not explain the whole of the change which has taken place; for the *price* of butchers' meat has also risen in the Paris markets so materially as to be a source of great privation and complaint. The rise may be ascribed to various causes. In the first place, "France has till lately always been a large importer of cattle; and down to 1814

[d-d]Source (MS), 48, 49 , the ration] 52, 57 , the portion

they were exempted from all duty. In that year, however, a duty of three francs was laid on each head of cattle imported;" and in 1822 the duty "was suddenly raised to 55 francs, an increase which has well nigh put a stop to the importation."* Secondly, the *octroi*, or town custom duty, now so burthensome, did not exist at all in 1789, and has been largely increased at various periods, both in Paris and most other towns, since its first establishment. [e]A third cause is that the trade of butcher in Paris is a monopoly, the number of butchers being limited, and to so small a number, that the privilege bears a high pecuniary value.† This we believe to be the principal cause of the high price and diminished consumption of meat in Paris. Two circumstances are almost decisive in proof of his opinion. One is that while the consumption per head of butcher's meat has diminished, that of almost every other article of food has largely increased. The other is, that in the *banlieue* of Paris, which differs from Paris itself in no material circumstance but that of being beyond the *octroi*, and exempt from the butchers' monopoly, the consumption per head of meat, instead of diminishing, has augmented in a remarkable degree; as it is affirmed to have also done in all the great towns of France, Paris excepted.‡[e]

*[Source (MS) *in text*] M'Culloch's Geographical Dictionary, art. France [Vol. I, pp. 855–6].

†[62] Now [1862] no longer true, the occupation having been thrown open.

‡[52] On the first point: "La consommation du beurre, qui était représentée en 1812 par une valeur de 6,935,929 francs, s'élevait en 1847 à 13,303,435 fr.; celle de la marée, qui était en 1812 de 4,183,532 fr. atteignait en 1847 la valeur de 6,908,423 fr.; celle des œufs, de 3,857,150 fr. en 1823, s'élevait à 6,727,867 fr. en 1847. En 1833, la valeur de la volaille consommée s'élevait à presque 7,000,000 fr.; en 1842, c'était 10,000,000 fr.; et dans les années qui ont suivi, cette valeur s'est élevée à plus de 9,000,000 fr. C'est-à-dire que la consommation des principales denrées, beurre, œufs, volaille et marée, s'augmentait pendant une période de trente-cinq années dans des proportions supérieures à l'accroissement de la population, tandis que la consommation de la viande de boucherie diminuait de 10 kilogrammes par individu, ou de 20 pour cent."

On the second point: "En 1812, la population de la banlieue de Paris était de 91,000 habitans en nombres ronds. Cette population consommait alors 8930 bœufs, 528 vaches, 6844 veaux et 27,558 moutons, donnant un poids total de viande de 3,500,000 kilog. en nombres ronds, soit 38 kilog. et demi, à peu près, par individu et par an. Depuis 1812, la consommation en viande et la population n'ont pas cessé de s'accroître dans la banlieue; mais l'accroissement n'a pas suivi les mêmes proportions. En 1821, la consommation était de 5,400,000 kilog. et s'est augmentée constamment depuis; enfin, en 1835, c'était 8,500,000 kilog. En cette même année, la population de la banlieue était de 170,000 habitans, dont la consommation individuelle était de 50 kilog. par an, soit 11 kilog. et

[e–e]Source (MS), 48, 49 These causes are enough of themselves to account for a considerable part of the enhancement complained of.

But if there were not these causes, there is cause almost sufficient in the very fact of an increased and rapidly increasing population. Paris has added, in fourteen years, between four and five hundred thousand to its inhabitants, an increase of nearly one-half. The agriculture of a country must be rapidly improving indeed, if an increase like this can take place in a single market without compelling it to draw its supplies from a larger surface and a greater distance, and therefore at an increased expense. Where would London have been by this time, for the supply of its markets, [f]were it not[f] for our great coasting trade, and the invention of steam [g]communication[g], which conveys not only cattle but carcases from the extremity of Scotland as cheaply as they [h]could formerly[h] be brought from Buckinghamshire? The cattle for the supply of Paris must travel by land, from distances varying from 50 to 150 leagues (this rests on the authority of a Committee of the Municipal Council of Paris in 1841), and after so long a journey have either to be brought to market out of condition, or to be fattened in the immediate neighbourhood. Can any one, then, be surprised that a [i]double[i] population cannot be so [j] cheaply supplied as one of half the number?

To these [k] causes of the diminished supply of butcher's meat in the towns, we are not afraid to add [l]another[l], which, though resting mainly on general considerations, we should not be wholly unable to support by positive evidence. This is, the increased consumption by the country people. They have less animal food, in proportion, to spare for the towns, because they retain more of it for their own use.

On what evidence is it asserted that small properties imply deficiency of cattle, and consequent deficiency of manure? That they are not favourable to sheep farming seems to be admitted; [m]yet in France, as well as in the United Kingdom, the number of sheep has doubled in the course of a

---

demi d'augmentation de 1812 à 1835. . . Nous devons faire remarquer que dans ces chiffres de la consommation de la banlieue, nous ne comprenons que la viande achetée sur les marchés à bestiaux de Paris: le chiffre du bétail acheté par les bouchers extra-muros, dans les foires, dans les fermes et sur les marchés des départemens, n'étant pas et ne pouvant pas être constaté. Nous n'avons pas les chiffres de la consommation de la banlieue de Paris depuis 1835. . . L'accroissement prodigieux de la consommation dans la banlieue de Paris, correspond à une augmentation du même genre dans toutes les grandes villes de France, Paris excepté."

These details are extracted from an article ["La liberté et le monopole,"] by M. Charles Béranger, in the journal *La République* of January 1, 1851 [p. 2].

[f-f]Source (MS) but
[g-g]Source (MS), 48, 49 navigation
[h-h]Source (MS), 48, 49 can
[i-i]Source (MS), 48, 49, 52 doubled
[j]Source (MS), 48, 49 well or so
[k]Source (MS), 48, 49 three
[l-l]Source (MS), 48, 49 a fourth
[m-m448]Source (MS), 48, 49, 52, 57 but

century.* It is true that in quality, instead of the extraordinary improvement which has taken place in England, they have remained almost stationary. But[m] the breeding and fattening of horned cattle [n]is[n] so perfectly compatible with small capital, that in the opinion of many Continental authorities, small farms have the advantage in this respect, and so great an advantage as to be more than a compensation for their inferiority in sheep.† It is argued that the *petite propriété* must diminish [o]the number of[o] cattle, because it leads to the breaking up of natural pasture. But when natural pasture is fit for the plough, a greater number of cattle than were supported on the whole, may be supported on a part, by laying it out in roots and artificial grasses; and it is well known that on the stall-feeding system there is much greater preservation of manure. The question of *petite culture*, in relation to cattle, is, in fact, one and the same with the question of stall-feeding. The two things must stand or fall together. Stall-feeding produces, *cæteris paribus,* a greater quantity of provisions, but in the opinion of most judges a lower quality. Experience must decide.

This brings us back to the causes assigned by the committee of the Paris town-council, for the falling off in the quality of the beef consumed at Paris. One is, the extraordinary increase in the consumption of dairy produce. Milk is now brought from distances of thirty leagues, and within six or eight leagues of Paris no calves are now bred up, all being sold at the earliest moment possible. In consequence, a great part of the beef sold at Paris is the flesh of cows too old to be fit for producing milk. A second cause assigned is, the increase of stall-feeding. But the committee make an instructive distinction. In Normandy, which affords the greatest portion of the supply, the quality, they say, has deteriorated; but in La Vendée, and the central provinces, the Limousin, Nivernais, Bourbonnais, and La Marche, "there is improvement in weight, in fatness, and from some districts in number," though these countries have also adopted stall-feeding; and in this, say the committee, there is no contradiction, since "what is a deterioration in the rich pasturages of Calvados, is improvement in the *petites herbes* of the Allier and the Nièvre."

It may now be left to the reader to judge if the case of our adversaries has not broken down as completely on this, their strongest point, as it has done on every other point of any importance.‡

*[62] Lavergne, *Essai sur l'Economie Rurale de l'Angleterre, de l'Ecosse, et de l'Irlande,* 3me éd. p. 16.

†See this question discussed in Book I. ch. ix. of the present work, pp. 144–7.

‡[57] The consumption of butcher's meat at Paris would seem to have considerably increased since the first publication of this discussion. The following table is extracted by M. Michel Chevalier (in the *Journal des Economistes* for

[n–n]48 seems to be
[o–o]+48, 49, 52, 57, 62, 65, 71

We cannot close this long controversy without producing evidence of the extraordinary improvement, extraordinary both in amount and in rapidity, which is taking place in the productiveness of the agriculture of some parts of France. We quote from another work by an authority already cited, M. Hippolite Passy, several times a minister of Louis-Philippe, and well known as one of the [p]most influential[p] politicians and publicists of France. This tract, published in 1841, is an examination of "the changes in the agricultural condition of the Department of the Eure since 1800." The Eure is one of the five departments of Normandy, and belongs to the region of which M. Rubichon admits the agriculture to be the best in France; but only (as he contends) because the *morcellement* has not had time to produce its effects, having commenced in that region only from the Revolution, and he assigns to it accordingly no privilege but that of Outis in the Odyssey, to be devoured the last. Let us now see the facts. This department fortunately possesses an accurate agricultural *statistique* for the year 1800, drawn up by a *préfet* who took great pains to be correct in his information. M. Passy's pamphlet is a comparison of these returns with those collected by the [q] French Government in 1837.

In this interval of thirty-seven years, scarcely any new land [r]was[r] taken into cultivation, nearly all fit for culture [s]having been[s] already occupied. But fallows [t]had[t] diminished from 172,000 hectares to a little more than 80,000. The cultures which supply cattle [u]had[u] increased in a much greater proportion than any others: instead of 17 per cent of the cultivated area they [v]occupied[v] 37 per cent. Horses [w]had[w] multiplied from 29,500 to 51,000, horned cattle from 51,000 to 106,000, sheep from 205,000 to 511,000, and as their food [x]has[x] increased in a still greater ratio, and there [y]was[y] importation besides, all kinds of live stock [z]were[z] better fed, and [a]had[a] gained in size, weight, and value. The produce per

---

July, 1856) [XI (2e Série), 124], from the elaborate work of M. Husson, entitled "Les Consommations de Paris:"

Average annual consumption per head of animal food:

Viande de boucherie	62 kilog.	586 grammes
Porc et charcuterie	10 kilog.	267 grammes
Volaille et gibier	9 kilog.	841 grammes
Poisson	12 kilog.	767 grammes
Total	95 kilog.	461 grammes

or about 210 English pounds.

[p-p]Source (MS), 48 first
[q]Source (MS), 48 present
[r-r]Source (MS) has been
[s-s]Source (MS) being
[t-t]Source (MS), 48 have
[u-u]Source (MS), 48 have
[v-v]Source (MS), 48 now occupy
[w-w]Source (MS), 48 have
[x-x]49, 52, 57, 62 had
[y-y]Source (MS), 48 is
[z-z]Source (MS), 48 are
[a-a]Source (MS), 48 have

hectare of all kinds of grain, and of most other kinds of produce, [b]had[b] considerably increased, of some kinds nearly doubled. These changes [c]had[c] chiefly been effected during the second half of the period, so that the improvement [d]was[d] as progressive as on M. Rubichon's theory should have been the deterioration. There [e]had[e] been no perceptible variation in the proportion between the *grande* and the *petite culture*; nor [f]had[f] the division of properties at all promoted the division of farms. On the soils where small farms are most profitable, large properties are rented to small tenants; where the reverse is the case, a single farmer often rents the lands of several proprietors, and this arrangement extends itself more [g] as the subdivision of property advances. The consumption of food per head of the population [h]had[h] largely increased—in the ratio, according to M. Passy, of about 37 per cent; and while the agricultural wealth of the department [i]had[i] increased, according to his estimate, by 54 per cent, the population [j]had[j] only increased 5 per cent.*

Though the Eure belongs to the most productive and thriving region of France, it is not the most productive or the most thriving department. The Nord, which comprises the greater part of French Flanders, and is a country of small farms, maintains, according to M. Passy, proportionally to its extent, a third more cattle than the Eure; and the average produce of wheat per hectare, instead of seventeen, is twenty hectolitres, about twenty-two English bushels per acre.

Results almost as satisfactory may be deduced from a statistical account of a much less improved district than the Eure, the most eastern district of Brittany, the arrondissement of Fougères, published in [k]1845[k], by the *sous-préfet*, M. Bertin. "It is only since the peace," says this intelligent functionary, "that the agriculture of the arrondissement has made much progress; but from 1815 it has improved with increasing rapidity. If from 1815 to 1825 the improvement was as one, it was as three between 1825 and 1835; and as six since that period."[*] At the beginning of the century little wheat was cultivated, and that little so ill, that in 1809 the produce

*During the last two [57, 62, 65 two last] quinquennial periods [48, 49, 52 last quinquennial period], the population of this department, on the showing both of the census and of the register of births and deaths, has [52 had] actually diminished.

[**Translated from* Bertin, Amédée, and Maupillé, Léon. *Notice Historique et Statistique sur la Baronie, la Ville et l'Arrondissement de Fougères.* Rennes: Marteuille & Lefas, 1846, p. 352.]

[b-b]Source (MS), 48 has
[c-c]Source (MS), 48 have
[d-d]Source (MS), 48 is
[e-e]Source (MS), 48 has
[f-f]Source (MS), 48 has
[g]Source (MS) and more
[h-h]Source (MS), 48 has
[i-i]Source (MS), 48 has
[j-j]Source (MS), 48 has
[k-k]Source (MS), 48, 49 1846

per hectare was estimated only at 9 hectolitres[l]; rather more than 10 bushels per acre[l]. [m]In 1845,[m] M. Bertin estimates it at 16[n], or upwards of 18 bushels per acre[n]. The cattle, being better fed, and crossed with more vigorous breeds, have increased in size and strength; while in number, horned cattle, between 1813 and 1844, multiplied from 33,000 to 52,000, sheep from 6300 to 11,000, swine from 9300 to 26,100, and horses from 7400 to 11,600. New and valuable manures have been introduced, and have come largely into use. The extent of meadow land has increased and is increasing, and great attention has of late been paid to its improvement. This testimony comes from an enemy of the *morcellement*, who, however, states that it is advancing very slowly, and is not likely to advance much further, the co-heirs not dividing each *parcelle*, but either distributing the *parcelles* among them, or disposing of them by private or public sale. Some farmers, he says, who are also proprietors, have the good sense to sell the few fields which belong to them, in order to increase their farming capital. M. Bertin is an enemy to stall-feeding, which, he says, is not practised in his arrondissement. The increase of live stock is [o]therefore[o] the more remarkable. It may not be useless to mention an assertion of this writer, that the official publication from which M. Rubichon's data are taken greatly understates the number of horned cattle in France, by the accidental omission of a column in summing up, by which the number is brought below ten millions, when it ought, according to M. Bertin, to be thirteen.

Of the food of the inhabitants he says, that not long ago it was composed almost exclusively of milk, buckwheat cakes, and rye bread, but has greatly improved in quantity, quality, and variety, especially in the last ten years and now consists of wheaten bread, or bread of two-thirds wheat and one-third rye; with butter, vegetables, and [p]in "[p]good farms" about a kilogramme (or 2¼ lbs.) of pork per week for each person. There is also some consumption of other flesh-meats among the labouring people, and the arrondissement contains 63 butchers' shops, where fifteen years ago there were not 30; the increase not being in the towns (or rather town), but in the villages. The clothing of the rural population is substantial, "and different for every season, which is always a sign of general comfort," and "persons in rags are very rare in the arrondissement."

We cannot further extend this long discussion; but enough has been said, to enable our readers adequately to appreciate the terrible predictions of alarmist writers respecting the consequences of the Division of Landed Property in France.

[l-l]+65, 71
[m-m]Source (MS), 48, 49, 52, 57 At present
[n-n]+65, 71
[o-o]Source (MS) all
[p-p]Source (MS), 48, 49, 52, 57, 62 "in

For Product Safety Concerns and Information please contact our EU representative GPSR@taylorandfrancis.com
Taylor & Francis Verlag GmbH, Kaufingerstraße 24, 80331 München, Germany

www.ingramcontent.com/pod-product-compliance
Ingram Content Group UK Ltd.
Pitfield, Milton Keynes, MK11 3LW, UK
UKHW020025200926
475702UK00014B/2061
* 9 7 8 0 4 1 5 4 8 7 4 9 8 *